conclusion   178

A MANAGERIAL ODYSSEY

Problems in Business and Its Environment

SECOND EDITION

A
MANAGERIAL
ODYSSEY

*Problems in
Business and Its
Environment*

SECOND EDITION

ARTHUR ELKINS
University of Massachusetts, Amherst

DENNIS W. CALLAGHAN
University of Rhode Island

ADDISON-WESLEY PUBLISHING COMPANY

Reading, Massachusetts • Menlo Park, California
London • Amsterdam • Don Mills, Ontario • Sydney

PREFACE

Since the publication of our first edition, the area of Business and its Environment—or Business and Society—has progressed in at least three directions. First, the course and the area are becoming more solidly accepted as a part—indeed a necessary part—of business-school curricula. Second, topical material is making steadily increasing inroads into the professional journals, bringing to bear higher degrees of research and scholarship—as opposed to dogmatism—in the field. Indeed, the increasing number of professors and students doing solid research in the area is heartening. Lastly, the area seems to be going along a close parallel to the areas of business policy and strategic planning. This latter development reinforces our own belief expressed earlier, that training in the area of business and its environment must be of a managerial, as opposed to a sociological, and sometimes adversary, nature.

This edition has several significant changes from the first, although the general format and pedagogical objectives remain unchanged. Reaction from users indicates that the general breakdown of concept, problems, and measurement is highly functional to the development of various combinations of specific course material.

In this edition, the introductory text fronting each of the sections—or chapters, as they are now called—is significantly broadened and expanded, bringing into the discussion more issues and greater depth. Thus the student is presented with additional material for digestion in a context that is not as limiting as an individual article with a single topical approach.

We have added chapters on Consumerism and Ethical Issues to the "Problems" part of the book. The Consumerism chapter responds to consistent requests of users and reviewers, and fills a gap representing an important issue. The chapter on Ethical Issues reflects the growing concern within society for the highest standards of conduct in the behavior of private managers as well as of public officials.

In Part III, we have added a chapter on Social Decision-Making and Policy, and the entire part has been retitled, "Social Decision-Making and Measurement." While all of the problem sections of the book are designed to force the student to think in managerial terms, the concern with "social policy" on the part of business firms necessitates, in our judgment, some independent treatment.

In terms of the readings, twenty-three of the articles throughout the book are new. One critical objective we have pursued is to select material that does not grow obsolete within a short time after publication date. Indeed, given long production processes in publishing a book, some material could be out of date before publication if careful attention is not paid to the problem. We are, however, concerned and cognizant of the rapidly changing developments in the field and the swift changes taking place in society. In selecting material, therefore, we tried to make the material long lasting enough so that the book could be used for a number of years, while not, however, avoiding any really crucial issues.

The bibliographies following each chapter have been expanded significantly. This reflects not only our belief that students should read more in the field, but the increasing amounts of available literature as well.

Finally, we have added "Questions for Discussion" to each of the chapters. These could aid instructors in leading and focusing class discussions, but are primarily added to assist students in relating to the various concepts and arguments and directing their study efforts.

Acknowledgments for Second Edition

We wish to thank the authors and publishers who allowed us to reprint not only the newly added readings, but those continued over from the first edition. Also our thanks to the companies who furnished us data for the cases. Tim L. Bornstein, Robert Comerford, Leslie Ball, Nicholas Speranzo, Gordon K. C. Chen, Barbara Brittingham, Albert Della Bitta, and David Loudon researched and contributed cases or assisted in case development. Tim Bornstein, Professor of Law and Industrial Relations at the University of Massachusetts, also read, critically evaluated and, through his comments, significantly improved portions of the introductory text material.

A number of colleagues at other institutions gave us critical and helpful comments in reacting to the first edition and to our outline for the second. Professors Rogene A. Buchholz (Washington University, St. Louis, Mo.), Winston Hill and Michael D. Mitchell (California State University at Chico), Walter Klein (Boston College), William Naumes (Clark University), Frank Norwood (Texas Wesleyan University) and Vincent Szymborski (Wayne State University) evaluated our outline for the second edition and spent time with us on the telephone, carefully and helpfully responding to our questions. We are grateful to them for their time and their willingness to comment.

Michael Merenda, now at the University of New Hampshire, Agnes Missirian, on leave from Babson College, and Thomas McAuley certainly were not reticent about commenting on the first edition while teaching sections of the course at the University of Massachusetts.

Thanks goes to the Research Center at the University of Rhode Island for providing support time for graduate student assistants. Tom Sanderson and Linda Kruhmin, undergraduate assistants at the University of Massachusetts, assisted with bibliographies, proofreading, duplicating, and other generally unheralded "gopher" activities that book authors always find necessary. Judy Rose so effectively relieved one of the authors of a number of the chores entailed in chairing a department that he was better able to devote uninterrupted periods of time to the book's development. Every administrator should be blessed with such an effective, efficient, and good-natured assistant.

Our association with Addison-Wesley Publishing Company has always been an extraordinarily pleasant one. The major share of credit for that goes to Keith Nave, Senior Editor, who was totally supportive and helpful not only during the revision, but in the development of the project which resulted in the first edition as well. Mary Cafarella of Addison-Wesley, a copy editor *par excellence*, offered considerable assistance in easing the design and production process.

Finally, we owe the greatest debt to the hundreds of students who were patient and helpful while we attempted to develop, refine, and revise what we hope continues to be a meaningful and useful educational experience. We trust that we have, in some small way, contributed to their effectiveness as they start on their own managerial Odysseys.

Amherst, Massachusetts   A.E.
Kingston, Rhode Island   D.W.C.
January, 1978

CONTENTS

FOUNDATIONS
AND A FRAME
OF REFERENCE

The *Odyssey,* as you may recall, was the title of Homer's epic travelogue of Odysseus' perilous journey back to Ithaca after the conquest of Troy. In his travels, Odysseus faced a series of strange, complex and difficult, and often unknown challenges before returning safely home.

We have chosen the title *Odyssey* for this book because the area of Business and its Environment deals with a series of complex and difficult problems being newly thrust upon the manager. Business and its Environment, or Business and Society is the study of the relationship of the firm and managers to social problems and issues. These issues, albeit old in the context of human history, are relatively new in the context of managerial decision frameworks. It is only within the last twenty or so years that managers have been constrained to give social problems more than minimal consideration (and business-school curricula usually reflected that minimum consideration). Questions of race and ethnicity, pollution and environment, peace and war, conservation, energy, politics, government relations, international relations, ethics, and the like are now particularly important factors in management decision-making. These topics are the stuff of "Business and its Environment." In our opinion, they constitute a real Managerial Odyssey.

The newly challenging problems are not necessarily isolated in their contexts, either. Older, traditional business decisions are taking on new dimensions. For example, a plant-location decision traditionally involved consideration of transportation costs, labor costs, access to markets, fuel and energy availability, and other similar factors — in a few words, the typical business parameters. Now, for the same decision, a manager must consider environmental spoilage, affirmative-action hiring in terms of minorities, dealings with local agencies (planning boards, zoning boards, citizens' action groups), the impact of the plant on local schools, sewerage systems, roads and community facilities, and a host of other "social" factors along with the more traditional economic business considerations.

THE MODERN MANAGER: TARGET FOR CRITICS

Managers today face new challenges of several sorts. In the most extreme forms, these challenges are directed at their very existence as decision-makers, or at the form of business organization currently sustaining them. That is, critics in this

1

furthest mode would like to replace the corporate or private form of business operation with some other forms, be they government-owned or -controlled enterprises, cooperatives, or some other supposedly more responsive type of organizational control mechanisms. Despite the sometimes vociferous nature of these critics, however, their numbers are small and their position is often not taken very seriously.

But other critics are taken seriously. These include the generalists who condemn the roles and behaviors of modern managers, as well as the particularists singling out for correction specific attributes of the corporation or business. In many cases, no mutual exclusivity separates these critics — a Ralph Nader, for example, brackets both categories.

The general critic questions the profit motive — that is, whether business should pursue profit as its primary objective or whether managers should de-emphasize profit and guide the corporation toward objectives encompassing social welfare. The term *social responsibility* is generally applied to corporate behavior prescribed under this critique.

Critics of specific acts of business and managers focus on such particular problems as pollution, minority or female hiring, occupational safety and health, defense contracting, and the like.

Whatever the content, today's critics put the business person or the manager in a new role. The traditional cost-and-profit calculus is now altered to include value formulations and responses that may consume organizational resources for no apparent benefit to the firm or at least none that is apparent to the traditional beneficiaries of business efficiency, the shareholders. Indeed, demands promulgated by the various interest groups now surfacing about the business firm may put managers into severe value-conflict situations. Such demands may be inconsistent within and between groups, may require drastic and sometimes impossible reallocations of the firm's resources, and may challenge a manager's personal mores or creeds, perhaps even forcing managers to reexamine their adherence to some of the established norms of the American enterprise system.

A STRATEGY FOR STUDYING BUSINESS AND ITS ENVIRONMENT

Our objectives in this book are to acquaint you with the challenges presently facing managers and to make you aware of the managerial roles (and role conflicts) in responding to them. We hope to move beyond the level of abstract generalizing to that of operational problems. Many managers operate at levels and positions in direct contact with the firm's publics. It does them little good to vaguely pontificate about social problems or social responsibilities. It does them more good to be aware that they might meet a real, perhaps explosive, problem and will need to be prepared to tackle it in a decisive manner.

The general format for each section of the book, and hence for each problem area to be covered, is an introduction, a series of readings, and a case or two. The introductions are designed to frame the issues you will be facing and articulate various positions on those issues and problems.

In terms of the background readings, we have tried to be scrupulously fair in selecting them, exposing you to as many sides of an issue as possible. The issues are complex and each has many sides. Social problems involve values, and various interest groups may have conflicting values. The manager who is meeting social issues must try to understand the values, views, and tactics of all the participant interest groups. The manager may not come to agree with all or any of them; and his or her decision may not reflect any values but personal ones.

THE PLAN OF THE BOOK

Generally the book follows a concept, problem, decision and measurement scheme. Major parts deal with concepts and theories, specific operational problems, social policymaking and social measurement or accounting, in that order.

Concepts and theories

The first major part is divided into two sections. Chapter 1 deals with prescriptions of business-firm behavior—that is, what scholars, practitioners, and laymen think corporations and businesses *should* be, whom business *should* serve, and what groups *should* reap benefits from the firm. The discussion in this part is normative, and obviously the articles reflect the value system of the respective writers.

Juxtaposed against the prescriptions of corporate and managerial standards presented in Chapter 1 are the theoretical descriptions of actual corporate and managerial behavior presented in Chapter 2. The student is alerted to compare the prescribed or normative patterns of Chapter 1 with the patterns scholars describe as a firm's real behavior in Chapter 2.

Although the theme of the book centers about operational problems and operational managerial responses, we include this general overview to give the student a framework of value systems that might condition behavior in specific situations. For example, the behavior of a firm that is guided by a profit-maximization creed might be quite different, in a pollution controversy, from the behavior of a firm that professes a "social responsibility" philosophy.

Problems

The second major part of the book moves us into several specific strategic and operational problem situations. Obviously, more problems exist than we have room to include, but we think the issues we have included are representative of those which the operating manager or the staff person on the firing line might face. First, in Chapter 3, we cover the business firm as it relates to problems in the workplace, changing attitudes toward work, and the younger generation's approach to work. In recent years we have seen profound changes in outlook toward some of the traditional institutions and practices of our society. Religion, the family, government, sexual conduct, and education are being increasingly confronted by new values and new practices. A cornerstone traditional value, commonly called the *work ethic,* also has shown signs of crumbling, and this challenge has profound implications for business decision-making.

Closely related to changing views of work and their effect on the corporation are the relatively new problems for the firm in the area of equal opportunity. A women and minority-group members demand places in the social and economic hierarchies of society, the business firm must face the complex problem of applying equal-opportunity legislation and affirmative-action guidelines, as well as emerging social standards in hiring, promotion, pay and assignment decisions. At the same time, managers must be careful to avoid discriminating against white males (reverse discrimination), an issue that is receiving more attention as the civil rights drive reaches a stage of maturity. Chapter 4 addresses these issues.

Chapter 5 involves the business firm and the physical environment. Environmental protection is probably the most basic topic in the whole panorama of business–society issues. It certainly has received a lion's share of attention in the media. But the pollution problem is also one where the local manager is apt to be in the spotlight. The chairman of the board often is not the person under fire to clean up; usually the division manager, who may be five or six levels down in the hierarchy, bears the brunt of local crusades against pollution. The local manager represents the corporation to the local community and must respond to the petitions of local officials.

Closely related to environmental issues are those involving the energy crisis (Chapter 6). Although this is a relatively recent problem, no one issue has come onto the scene with more resounding force. At least three business positions in the energy area are relevant to students of business and its environment. The first involves those firms engaged in the supply of energy. In this case, decisions ranging from power-plant siting, nuclear energy, and new or untapped sources of energy, to those involving the rationing of oil, gasoline, and electricity among customers, are all relevant. The second involves businesses that are trying to sustain the necessary energy supply to keep operating. In this case, managers must apply efforts to switch fuels or conserve in other ways, and sometimes these efforts cycle right back to the pollution issue. The final position concerns those firms that manufacture energy-consuming devices and the effects that society's new energy consciousness has on them.

Chapter 7 focuses on the business firm and consumerism. Our society is now in its third round of consumer activism, all related to times of increasing price levels. Most observers, however, believe that this round will be more pervasive and have longer lasting effects that will stay with business firms. The reasons for the increase in staying power of this movement over the previous ones are increasing educational levels and the higher level of sophistication present in larger numbers of consumers.

In Chapter 8, we focus on an international problem as it affects the American business firm. That problem is *apartheid* in South Africa and the turmoil in southern Africa in general. Our objective in this section is not so much to study apartheid, but primarily to focus on another country's problems and the effects of American business presence. Apartheid is a significant problem for illustration, but similar problems in Latin America, other parts of Africa, or the Middle East, and their relations to American business can be similarly instructive. A second objective in the section on apartheid is to study its effect on the operations and relationships of the American firm back in the United States. How does the firm respond to local protest groups, American blacks, and others who see a connection between the corporation's presence in South Africa and its operations in the United States? For example, how does a corporation respond to boycotts called against it as a U.S. parent, to protest actions of a South African subsidiary?

Chapter 9 of Part II deals with business and government. Governmental relationships are complex; and the subject, which includes topics such as antitrust laws and various other types of regulation, consumes whole courses, let alone sections of a single book. But in an age when government is becoming more involved in business affairs and when the protests in other areas—pollution, affirmative action, energy policy, and the like—manifest themselves in government action, the relationships of managers and governmental agencies become even more crucial. Nor should business people confine themselves to thinking in terms of the federal government; relationships with state and local officials, particularly for the small-business owner or the manager of the local plant, are equally as important in such areas as licensing, regulation, zoning, and certification.

In Chapter 10, we explore the topic of business ethics. Throughout the past few years, many corporations have been accused of obtaining business through payoffs to middlemen and government officials, particularly in transactions involving foreign governments. In addition, there has been a renewed interest in the ethics of interpersonal relationships, personal conduct, and personal advancement.

Finally, Chapter 11 discusses business and its critics. While this topic cuts across the lines of the substantive issues previously covered, it is important that business persons be familiar not only with the problems raised by critics and activists, but with the strategies and tactics they employ as well.

Social decision-making and measurement

The last major part of this book focuses on the making of policy for social issues and the measurement of the effectiveness of social efforts. Chapter 12 will cover decision-making and policy-making in the social-issue area. This is a relatively uncharted wilderness for managers. We shall, in our introduction, offer some guidelines to considering social factors, and then, in the readings, cover some proposed policy-making processes.

Chapter 13 will conclude the book with coverage of measurement or *social accounting*. Social accounting is a new and emerging tool designed for measuring the degree and impact of business actions in socially important areas. At the present stage of development, social accounting is imprecise and not widely adopted. But we believe that exposure to social accounting is necessary if one is to even start applying efficiency and effectiveness criteria to the firm's social activity.

SOME THOUGHTS ON BUSINESS EDUCATION

One last word about our intent in this book. In recent years, the process of education in business administration has come to stress less the inculcation of specific bits of information and more the grounding in broader concepts and tools — in short, a managerial approach. In line with such a focus, we hope the student will find that our topic and case selection will aid in developing a process of critical thinking, an appreciation of the issues and types of problems that might arise beyond those of a traditionally business nature, and an ability to act in complex situations, where no formulas are available for quick and ready answers. We trust that students will look on the problem situations and other material presented as conditioners of critical thinking in some rather complex areas, rather than as a catalogue of specific situations they are being trained to handle mechanically.

A NOTE ON CASES

Some of the same caveats expressed in the last paragraph apply to the cases. These are not designed as preparation for a specific incident one may meet in his or her business career. Cases are, quite simply, vehicles to force the practice of systematic analysis and decision-making. Also, cases rarely have school or "textbook" solutions. Solutions can and do differ among students (and even among professors); the student's task is to analyze the data, logically derive a decision solution, and then prepare for the implementation of that decision.

Cases can be handled in many ways. A student may take the role of a consultant or staff analyst, in which he will prepare a logical, written recommendation of policy or action. Typically, the sequence of attacking a case in that mode includes fact analysis, problem formulation, tentative solutions, selection of the course of action, and development of a plan for implementation. Another use of the case is role-playing, in which the parts illustrated in the case are assigned to various actors (students) and the roles played out. Several of our cases lend themselves well to role-playing techniques.

The cases in this book are designed to be used with the readings. Typically, cases require the use of assumptions, and they almost invariably require more information than is included. The readings should help in this respect, although unrealistic and unwarranted assumptions should always be avoided.

USE OF OTHER SOURCES

Bibliographies have been included after each section. The student is encouraged to read further in the field. Since the area of business and environment is so new — less than the 20 or so years practitioners have been facing the problems — there is little in the way of standard literature. Indeed, the literatures of economics, sociology, and political science, as well as business, are relevant to the field. The eclecticism of the discipline not only adds to the challenge — it enhances the perspectives one may need to operate in the field. It also adds to the fun of the course.

PART 1
CONCEPTS AND
THEORIES

1. *Conceptual and Ideological Prescriptions for Business Behavior*

Increasingly within the past twenty or so years, managers have been facing a complex of problems relating to social issues. These problems often result from a growing awareness by various groups of the social ramifications of business decisions. For example, sellers of produce and wine have been asked to remove non-union products from their shelves and have been picketed when they refused to do so. Nuclear power-plant sites have been picketed and occupied by protesters. Shareholder meetings are disrupted or increasingly used by groups protesting such diverse issues as investment in South Africa, insufficient minority hiring, compliance with the Arab boycott of Israel, trade with communist countries, pollution of streams and rivers, and product safety, among many others.

Just imagine yourself a manager facing one of those problems. Suppose, for example, that you are a project manager of a nuclear-power station under construction, and a local committee of social activists comes to you and at the very least asks that you publicly debate the issue of nuclear power with an opponent of nuclear use, and at the most wants you to cease construction, under threat of possible violence. How would you respond? How would you sift through your mind the many factors impinging upon such requests and such a problem? Could you say that nuclear power will be the most efficient energy source? Could you say that the slim probability of accidents, or the problems of ecology brought about by the cooling process, are none of your concern? Could you say that power-company customers want, and are entitled to, the lowest-cost power? Or could you offer a rejoinder that one self-appointed social action group has no right telling others what to do, or how to live, or restricting their options?

And then how would you react to a picket line thrown up in front of your site by such a committee or, even more serious, to a physical occupation of the construction site?

This is just one of an increasing complex of new problems faced by business people and managers. These problems aren't easily solved by resort to the profit calculus—indeed use of the word "profit" may often exacerbate an already violatile situation—or by simple formulas. But, increasingly, those problems require response.

Again, these problems and managerial responses to them are the topics of this book. What questions—in a social context and with social (as well as profit) ramifications—does the manager or the entrepreneur deal with? And how does the manager deal with them?

In this section, we introduce general, normative (prescriptive) models and doctrines of corporate and managerial roles. In the context of corporate response to social issues, these are designed to provide theoretical frameworks for analysis—theoretical guidelines, albeit general, for business behavior. Scholars and observers pose the question: What *should* the role of business and the business firm in American society be? And if business should move to adopt new and more involved stances relative to social problems, are there any costs, problems, vicissitudes, or pitfalls in such movement?

THE TRADITIONAL MODEL OF THE FIRM

Models or theories are abstractions. They do not encompass every element present in a real-world situation; they cannot. Models must be general enough to reasonably describe a range of situations. Overspecificity will preclude the use of a model for such general purposes. Thus, much of the complexity of the real world is omitted in favor of extreme simplification. While oversimplification often opens the door to criticism that a model is useless, that criticism usually emanates from people who misunderstand the model, are unfamiliar with its uses, or seek to use it for unintended purposes.

Such simplification (and such criticism) is the case with the traditional model of the business firm. Developed in economics, the imaginary *simple* firm that one finds is nothing more than a segment in a much larger, more important, and greater encompassing body of theory. The traditional assumptions of complete rationality in decision-making, profit maximization as the firm's primary and singular objective, and the single mind of the firm and the entrepreneur, are looked upon in economic theory not as precise definitions of reality, but as good enough generalizations (descriptions of reality) to allow the economist to generate reasonably accurate predictions of resource allocation and income distribution—the ultimate objectives of the microeconomics exercise.

Despite the caveats regarding the limited objectives of the model of the firm in economic theory, that imaginary and generalized firm *does* closely approximate the *prescribed* firm of traditional Western political and economic dogma. Under the free-enterprise system, business firms are expected to seek profits; that is, all relationships should be treated in a revenue–cost–profit context. Resources are to be purchased (cost), goods produced for sale to customers (revenue), and residual resources (profit) distributed to owners. Business decisions are to have extremely simple parameters; the entrepreneur or manager simply arranges the lowest-cost resources in the most efficient configuration, sells to customers willing to pay the highest prices, and derives the maximum possible profit from the situation.

As we noted, the real world is different from that of the simple model; and it is more complex than the world of dogma as well. The real-world business person is not as bright or mentally powerful as the one in the mythical world, and the real world is a more difficult place in which to operate. Many problems cannot be solved swiftly or easily through resort to the profit calculus. Nonpecuniary *values* play a major role, in that the most profitable way may not be the "right" way according to the manager's scale of ethical values. What introduces this complexity and what brings questions of values into managerial decision-making?

First, we must consider *market structure*. Few instances of pure or perfect competition exist, and there are few examples of totally powerless firms. Almost every firm has some sort of market power, be it the local drugstore with its several-city-block monopoly, the firm that operates as a small town's only employer, or the only steel company in a country. Hence, free choice, the important element in economic doctrine, may be seriously constrained. This constraint may be even more evident when one is considering the concentration of sellers or buyers on the larger national or international level—four automobile companies, three aluminum companies, or seven major oil companies, for examples. Under such circumstances of monopoly, monopsony, high concentration, or limited product or employment choice for individuals, the job applicant who suffers discrimination, for instance, may not have the option of applying to another, nondiscriminating employer. The customer who doesn't like a corporate or business policy (or even a product) doesn't always have the alternative of buying from another seller.

Second, the *conceptual structure* of the firm, either as an entrepreneurship or as a corporation operated by managers in a fidiciary arrangement strictly for the benefit of the owners or shareholders, also does not correspond to reality. The major portion of economic activity is carried on by large corporations, and large corporations are controlled by management, not by their owners. Shareholders generally have little power to dictate corporate direction, objectives, or strategy; and, typically, the proxy machinery for elections to boards of directors is firmly in the hands of management. This means that values other than those prescribed in traditional economic doctrine—profit maximizing—may be brought to bear on the decision-making within the firm. These values could be toward management's own self-interest, but also toward objectives that dissipate rather than accumulate wealth for the owners of the firm—the shareholders.

Third, the assumptions in economic doctrine of *free and readily available information* and *maximum individual knowledge* are tenuous indeed. Not all information is available, and individuals are sometimes incapable of making even simple decisions. For example, the smaller investor rarely possesses information (or the expertise to interpret the information that he does have) compared to that available to the large investment houses or funds. On a more mundane level for most people, try dividing 49¢ by 6.8 ounces in your head at a supermarket counter.

In essence, the imperfections in the marketplace (and the structure of the firm internally) mean that firms are not automatically driven—by the invisible hand—to behave in such a way that social problems or excessive use of power are minimized. Firms and managers and entrepreneurs have discretion; and business behavior guided by managerial discretion does not result in market conditions that represent or reflect the optimal social results described or prescribed by the models. Thus, social issues assume greater importance.

Approached from another way, the firm engaging in competitive struggle has its price driven down and its profits squeezed (to the point of opportunity costs, according to economic theory). The (purely or perfectly) competitive firm would have little time, energy, or resources to devote to social issues. Without discretion and without profits, social issues would be irrelevant to the firm. In such a condition, it would also not be in the best interests of the firm to act antisocially in its own affairs; employees would be hired according to skills, information would be made understandable and easily accessible, products would be produced under the demands of a severe and controlling market discipline.

THE SOCIAL-RESPONSIBILITY DOCTRINE

Recognizing the complex nature of the real world and the interdependence of its components, and the power inherent in its various institutions, a number of scholars and business practitioners have proposed that business firms should become more socially responsible. That is, business firms should use the discretion and power they possess in a socially acceptable manner.

The general social-responsibility doctrine holds that firms are surrounded by various constituent or interest groups, each having some call on the firm's resources and energies. Shareholders hold no special status in this doctrine, sharing importance with labor, government at all levels, customers, neighbors, suppliers, minority groups, other financial factors, and others. Management, acting as a hub activity, is entrusted with distributing its effort and its corporate rewards or resources equitably among these groups. Figure 1 illustrates this conceptual notion. Thus, the doctrine calls for the firm to simultaneously strive for lowest prices, well-built products, fair wages, attractive and clean plant sites, voluntary pollution-control efforts, contributions to charity, training programs for the disadvantaged, and other social and economic actions, while maintaining fair dividends for its shareholders. Note that the social-responsibility doctrine is designed to recognize the supposedly imperfect market structures; managerial judgment, therefore, is called for as a substitute to market mechanisms in many of the relationships between the firm and its surrounding interest groups.

Some very attractive philosophical rationales are offered to substantiate the call for social responsibility. In 1971, the Committee for Economic Development,

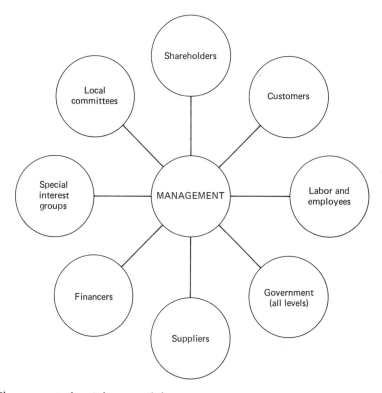

Fig. 1   The concept of social responsibility.

an organization of some 200 business people and educators involved in research and study of political, social, and economic issues, produced a statement entitled *The Social Responsibility of Business Corporations.** Two basic reasons were advanced as favoring the adoption of social responsibility — the *changing social contract* with business and *enlightened self-interest.*

The notion of a social contract is not new. Ralph Currier Davis, for example, in the mid-1930's articulated a similar concept with his tripartite breakdown of business objectives into service, collateral, and secondary.† Basically, the social contract idea is that "Business functions by public consent, and its basic purpose is to serve constructively the needs of society — to the satisfaction of society." Implicit in all of that is the possibility that, should business fail to discharge its service role, society would seek some type of institutional arrangement other than private ownership to serve its ends.

---

*Committee for Economic Development. *Social Responsibilities of Business Corporations.* (New York: CED, 1971.)

† Ralph C. Davis, *Industrial Organization and Management.* (New York: Harper and Row, 1951.)

Historically, this service role was discharged and effected by the efficient production of goods and services. But according to the CED, the expectations have broadened. They describe business responsibilities in terms of three concentric circles. "The *inner circle* includes the clearcut basic responsibilities for the efficient execution of the economic function—products, jobs, and economic growth." This is quite close to the traditional product-and-service expectations as articulated by Davis.

"The *intermediate circle* encompasses responsibility to exercise this economic function with a sensitive awareness of changing social values and priorities: for example, respect to environmental conversation; hiring and relations with employees; and more rigorous expectation of customers for information, fair treatment, and protection from injury." This circle seems to correspond to the increasing categories of costs being imposed upon business by society's agent, government.

Finally, "the *outer circle* outlines newly emerging and still amorphous responsibilities that business *should* assume to become more broadly involved in actively improving the social environment." According to the CED, "Society is beginning to turn to corporations for help with major social problems such as poverty and urban plight," even though business may not have had a direct hand in creating the problems.

The concept of social contract is not without its critics. If the basis of the American society is the individual, and the individual is endowed with certain inalienable rights of life, liberty, and the pursuit of happiness, then the whole concept of a social need taking precedence over or forming a contract that conditions those individual rights becomes subject to question. In this sense, business owes nothing other than what it wants to give or needs to give in order to induce people to deal with it. It has the right to survive or fail as it sees fit.

A more solid base might rest with the second rationale offered by the CED, *enlightened self-interest*. Under this concept, "there is broad recognition . . . that corporate self-interest is inexorably involved in the well-being of the society of which business is an integral part, and from which it draws the basic requirements needed for it to function at all—capital, labor, customers." Additionally, according to the CED, the "doctrine of enlightened self-interest is also based on the proposition that, if business does not accept a fair measure of responsibility for social improvement, the interests of the corporation may actually be jeopardized." Thus, either government action, consumer boycotts, picket lines, negative publicity, or other types of activity may have deleterious long-range as well as short-range effects on the corporation.

CRITIQUE OF THE SOCIAL-RESPONSIBILITY DOCTRINE

Despite its attractiveness, the increasingly articulated social-responsibility view has some serious operational and philosophical problems that managers must be aware of.

First, no simple rules for decision-making exist for the manager. With a profit-maximization philosophy, the manager at least has a single operational objective at which to aim. All other considerations become either constraints on a manager's action, or costs. But the socially responsible manager is reminded of multiple objectives or of fulfilling obligations to all or a great number of the firm's constituent groups. About the only operational decision rule that exists is a *sequencing* of decisions—take care of one group first, then the other, and so on. But this decision rule may create more problems than it solves, as the manager is left with a whole host of equity appeals and decisions.

Other, more serious problems of a philosophical nature exist, however. Several critics have pointed out that the business person's role is economic. Managers can act privately in the economic role because they are expected to do so, but they are not empowered to (nor are they especially fitted to) act in social areas. These are the areas of decision usually reserved for elected representatives.

That distinction becomes more important when one links the concept of social responsibility to the question of power. It has been argued that the socially responsible manager can be socially responsible only because that manager has the power to gain excess resources through some exclusive market position. That is, the firm's powerful position allows the manager to price goods in such a way as to secure what economists have called "pure" profit—or a privately raised tax that enables the manager to be socially responsible and to distribute corporate rewards according to personal or some perceived societal value systems. Thus, the question becomes, "Who elected the business person to tax and then distribute rewards according to his/her own values?"

The problem, then, is also to decide whose values are appropriate. The socially responsive manager's behavior in Birmingham, Alabama, for example, may not coincide with the socially responsive behavior of a manager in Boston, Massachusetts; yet both may be responding to social values of their particular areas. Whose values are "correct"? What if the operations of the firm transcend geocultural boundaries?

Social values are by no means universally accepted; there are very few that are part of the national fabric of a society so that one manager's behavior would always be judged socially responsive by all groups. Given this essential fact, those who would criticize the business person for using power to exploit a community resource for the firm's own interest should be equally critical of the business person who uses power to exploit a community resource for some *other* group's interest, even though, in the latter case, the values behind the business person's decision happen to coincide with those of the critic. The process of exploitation is still present, but the ox is being gored for a different purpose.

And finally, the social-responsibility doctrine vests power with the business person without providing a mechanism (other than a moral trust) which would prevent the manager or business person from turning and using that power in another way. In many ways, the doctrine resembles a call for a benevolent dictatorship, but gives no indication of what happens when the benevolent dictator leaves the scene. It also implicitly requires that all business people assume the same posture, but offers no mechanism for assuring that that will happen.

Perhaps the major, all-encompassing criticism of the doctrine is that there is *no common definition* of social responsibility for the manager to adhere to. The term is really a tough one to deal with, for managers and academicians alike. Dow Votaw calls the term "a brilliant one; it means something, but not always the same to everybody."*

Votaw, two paragraphs later, however, goes on to write, "the primary goals are to determine, with as much accuracy as possible, the real nature of the forces with which we are concerned and to consider a few of the often overlooked implications of the phenomenon of social responsibility."

The contradictions in those two quotes should be easily evident. Since social responsibility is a term loaded with imprecision and multiple definitions, one would be hard-pressed to call the many things that such a term represents a *phenomenon*, let alone have the preordained confidence that we possess the capacity for determining the forces and implications of such an all-inclusive notion.

In fact, each manager exists in a unique firm and, more importantly, is confronted with masses of social problems and issues that emanate from a surrounding, pluralistic social system. Any attempt to reduce those problems to simple and general sets of "responsible" behaviors may be wishful thinking.

The problems involve conflicting subsets of society, alternative value systems, contradictory claims, diverse cultures and norms, and swiftly changing attitudes, beliefs, and outlooks. The claim that the issues for a manager, entrepreneur, or business person will encapsulate themselves into a simple set of socially responsible behavior patterns with simple parameters—in the face of the conflicts in the buzzing mass we call society—is a gross oversimplification. The involvement of a firm in social issues is a terribly complex situation.

AN EXAMPLE

Let us briefly trace out a possible incident to illustrate a socially responsible manager's practical problems. Suppose a management group responded to a local activist group and instituted a training and placement program for hardcore unemployed persons. What pressures might arise among other interest groups?

It shouldn't be too difficult to conceive of reactions. Older employees might gripe "It took me three years to apprentice to this job and now they're getting it handed to them on a silver platter." Customers might be affected by higher prices, poor quality, or late deliveries. Shareholders might express concerns over higher costs and lower profits—if they are in a position to make such a complaint. Government might pressure the firm into moving faster, particularly if the firm has a government contract and is therefore pledged to an affirmative-action program. If a union were involved, it might complain about violations of established apprenticeship or training programs. Foremen may complain about becoming trainers and policemen for new employees whose work habits are not regular or customary.

---

*Dow Votaw and S. Prakash Sethi, *The Corporate Dilemma: Traditional Values versus Contemporary Problems.* (Englewood Cliffs: Prentice-Hall, Inc., 1973.)

In essence, the problem becomes much more complex than just providing jobs or doing a "socially responsible" thing. It also raises the question of values. Whose values is the manager or the management responding to? What makes the manager socially responsible in this case? Aren't the complainers' values of equal importance?

THE MANAGERIAL QUANDARY: NO MODEL FILLS THE BILL

Neither the normative economic model nor the social-responsibility model make it easy for the manager. The economic doctrine suffers from being descriptive and prescriptive for structural conditions within markets and firms that don't exist; and the social-responsibility model, in its present state of development, is vague and poses serious philosophical questions.

Yet the real world goes on and the manager must live in it and move with it. Problems will continue to arise and decisions will continue to be required. No two managers may choose identical paths, and there is little in all the management literature that will standardize value-laden decision-making. And social problem-solving may force the manager into a political role rather than the economic one that entrepreneurs and managers have traditionally been assigned.

The essence of our conclusion in this section, then, is that management is caught in a thicket. There are no PERT diagrams, no capital budgeting formulae, no inventory-control models with which to handle the social problems now facing managers and business people. Managers are now navigating uncharted waters.

THE READINGS

Our first selection, "The Corporation in Crisis," by John C. Perham, is a review of some of the dangers facing the corporation as an institution and some of the possible corporate responses to those dangers.

The title of Keith Davis' article explains well the thrust of it. In "Social Responsibility is Inevitable," Davis discusses the changing needs of people, the changing role of management, the changing business and economic system, and the changing society, and concludes that "The social-responsibility model provides an overlay on the traditional economic mission of business. The traditional business role of economic entrepreneurship is amended to include that of social trusteeship."

The next selection by Milton Friedman, well-known University of Chicago economist and Nobel laureate, is essentially a restatement of classical economic and political doctrine. Viewing social responsibility as basically a subversive doctrine, Friedman is incisive in cutting through to some of the political, economic, and philosophical weaknesses of the thesis.

Our final selection is an essay on profits, reprinted from TIME. While many in our society applaud the notion of profits, at the same time they are suspicious. "It is an historic irony that in the U.S., the stronghold of world capitalism, so few citizens understand that profits provide the basis for the prosperity on which rests the well-being of both individuals and the nation."

The Corporation in Crisis

John C. Perham

Can the corporation survive? That may seem like a foolish question about an institution that has provided so much of this nation's wealth and power, but even business' most ardent champions admit that it is a legitimate one. The corporation, and the system it represents, is being attacked as never before. It is under assault from the government, charged with everything from bribery to price-fixing, from polluting the air and water to turning out unsafe products in unsafe working conditions. Dissident stockholders echo those charges and further contend that companies are neither living up to their social responsibilities nor giving their owners enough information about corporate activities. Most vociferous of all are the economic doomsayers, who predict that the corporation will indeed be toppled from its leading as the main driving force in the U.S. economy.

Business leaders generally are confident that the business form defined by Chief Justice John Marshall more than 150 years ago will prevail. But they acknowledge that they face a tough fight against many strong forces. Strongest of all, of course, is the federal government which over the years has wielded ever-increasing power over business through a growing maze of laws and regulations.

Currently, moreover, business is confronted by perhaps the most antibusiness Congress since the New Deal. According to the U.S. Chamber of Commerce, there are some fifty-six major issues before Congress that are of direct concern to business—from national health insurance to federal economic planning. Among the major bills now in the Senate hopper are two aimed at the oil industry, another that would require every major corporation to have two independent members on its board of directors to watch out for bribes and payoffs, and Ralph Nader's proposal to make all large companies federally chartered.

To critics who find many aspects of modern America abhorrent, the corporation, which seems so impersonal and inhuman, makes an inviting target. It is especially inviting to the doomsayers, who believe that the prevailing market system, in which millions of individual buying and selling decisions determine the direction in which the economy moves, must be replaced by some kind of socialist setup in which government makes the big decisions. Well-known economist J. Kenneth Galbraith, for one, has written thousands of words arguing that what he calls America's private affluence and public squalor can only be relieved by putting corporations under much tighter government controls. Liberal idea man Richard Goodwin, who was a speech writer for Presidents John F. Kennedy and Lyndon B. Johnson, is convinced that the major corporations will inevitably be absorbed by the state, with government bureaucracy taking over the planning role. And Socialist Michael Harrington, in his latest book, *The Twilight of Capitalism,* argues that today's businessmen, and the economists who advise them, are so self-serving that they themselves are the greatest threat to free enterprise.

Perhaps the most widely circulated of the recent doomsday books is *Business Civilization in Decline* by veteran economist-writer Robert L. Heilbroner. According to Heilbroner, capitalism will probably disappear within a century. Our natural resources are becoming exhausted, he says, and therefore neither national nor industrial growth can continue at their historic rates. "The end of corporate growth," Heilbroner writes, "will bring the progressive elimination of the profits that have been both the means and the end of the accumulation of private property." He foresees a vast increase in national economic planning, in which the corporation's role will grow continually smaller, that of government correspondingly larger. What will eventually emerge is a static but tightly controlled society where, he says, "the traditional pillars of capitalism—private property and the market—have been amended beyond recognition."

In response, business can argue that the United States must have growth, even if not at the hectic pace of fifty or one hundred years ago. Only by increasing production, and therefore jobs, can the nation generate the tax dollars to pay for all the demands of its citizens, whether it be better health care, cleaning up the environment or reversing urban decay. As for natural resources, experts now believe that the world's resources are much more adequate than they predicted three years ago. And while some domestic resources, like oil, are being rapidly depleted, the U.S. coal supply is centuries away from exhaustion. But the technology to find new and better uses for coal and other resources will also cost a great deal of money.

Unfortunately, corporate leaders have always been notoriously unsuccessful in taking their case to the public, and pervasive myths about business—and the profit motive—still persist. In several recent public polls, for instance, most respondents estimated that the average manufacturer's after-tax profit was 25 percent and even 30 percent. The actual figure is about 5 percent.

Clearly, business must improve its communications with the outside world. Above all, corporate leaders must explain more effectively the efforts they are making to help solve the problems of society—and the tremendous costs of those efforts. For example, while no corporation today can afford to be indifferent to the job of protecting the environment, it has to somehow reconcile its responsibility to control pollution with the hard necessity of continuing to make a profit.

U.S. corporations will spend $9.5 billion on pollution control this year, according to a recent McGraw-Hill survey. These outlays yield no direct return on the bottom line. Nor is it true, as some people argue, that spending on pollution-control equipment creates just as many jobs as any other kind of capital investment. According to a U.S. Steel study, an investment in new steel capacity, like the $75 million pipe mill announced by Big Steel in May, creates thirty times as many jobs as the same amount put into pollution-control equipment because of its multiplier effect on the economy.

With the government calling the tune on not only pollution control but energy, occupational safety, equal opportunity, and many other vital issues, the biggest problem for most corporations is to achieve a better working relationship with the Washington bureaucracy that administers the laws. Corporations are going to have to live with government agencies, like it or not. What is needed is a better dialogue and a more reasonable division of responsibility.

To deal with proliferating government rules and regulatory bodies, companies have had to create a kind of bureaucracy of their own by adding layers of high-priced talent—lawyers, government relations and personnel experts, and the like—and to spend many corporate man-hours in costly and essentially unproductive paperwork. They also have to do business with government agencies that are mostly run by lawyers and technicians who have little understanding of the realities of the business world. Boris Yavitz, dean of the Columbia Graduate School of Business, observes that many government agencies seem to feel that if they could only get their regulations written tightly enough, the economy would hum along smoothly and productively. "They seem to have no appreciation that it is business that must do the basic job of production and distribution," Yavitz says. "All government can do is provide constraints and incentives; it can define the playing field. But only business can play the game."

Even some longtime corporate critics are questioning the wisdom of current regulatory policy, among them Christopher Stone, professor of law at the University of Southern California and author of *Where the Law Ends: The Social Control of Corporate Behavior*. Stone says: "I used to criticize the old-line agencies like the Interstate Commerce Commission and the Civil Aeronautics Board because they were too closely wedded to the industries they are supposed to regulate. But those older agencies now look good in comparison to some newer ones, such as the Occupational Safety and Health Agency, which are totally insensitive to corporate costs."

No responsible business leader denies that corporations must change in order to meet new needs. But many people, both inside business and out, question whether really meaningful change can come about through government edict. Business, they say, must do the job itself. Even critics admit that corporations, many of which have survived any number of new challenges, have shown remarkable flexibility over the years.

Nor do they deny that the corporate form of business, as developed to the fullest extent in the U.S., has proven the greatest engine of production ever created. The mass output it has made possible is the bedrock on which America's rising prosperity over many decades has been based. Stone, who has long argued that the corporation should be more closely controlled by society, nevertheless believes that it is still the only workable system. "There is nothing to put in its place except government," he says. "And government is far less responsible than the typical corporation—which, after all, has an ultimate accountability in the income statement, the balance sheet, and the annual report."

Corporations today are also accountable to society as a whole. And the recent revelations of wide-scale bribes and payoffs have further alienated an already skeptical public. But the subject of corporate ethics is a mass of conflicting moral and practical considerations, and there are no simple answers. The Congress and regulatory agencies are looking for solutions. So, significantly, are a number of corporate leaders, who are trying to figure out ways for business to police itself.

The first step, many executives feel, is to draw up a code of conduct for companies to follow. Such a code could not be enforced legally, but it would be subject to the weight of public opinion backed by the full disclosure of any corporate violations. The twenty-four-nation Organization for Economic Cooperation and Development finished setting up such a code of conduct for multinational companies in May. Some companies have also written or are writing their own codes, among them BankAmerica, IBM, Celanese, and Caterpillar Tractor.

Once the guidelines are laid down, most authorities agree, overseeing enforcement is primarily a job for each company's board of directors. But if boards are going to play a truly responsible role in keeping their companies out of trouble, they must include more outsiders than in the past—such as representatives of the foundations, leaders in the academic world, retired executives and retired government officials. It is felt that outside directors, while also concerned with a company's profits, have a more detached view than insiders about the firm's overall responsibilities.

Some corporate leaders are also beginning to realize that they cannot get business' message across simply by reacting to outside pressure. Chairman Reginald Jones of General Electric Co. argues that business must develop its own constituency—the middle class that not only invests in, but works for and buys from the corporation. All these people have a direct economic and political stake in the corporation's success, Jones points out. "We'll have to win our constituency issue by issue like any successful politician," he says, "demonstrating how specific proposals will affect the lives and pocketbooks of the people whose support we need."

One way to gain that constituency, some observers think, is to give employees a larger voice in decision making. The idea of giving workers seats on company boards is just now being raised in this country, but there are other ways of extending workers' participation. One is to get more shares of company stock into their hands—through profit sharing, pension or thrift plans, which are all based in whole or part on company contributions, or through such newer incentives as the Employee Stock Ownership Plan (ESOP), which allows employees to earn shares without paying for them.

Management consultant Robert Sibson believes that workers are beginning to realize that their own prosperity ultimately rises or falls with that of the company that employs them. "We are seeing the first faint beginnings of a curious new alliance between worker and employer," he says. "Both are becoming increasingly concerned, for example, about the economic burdens they bear on behalf of the unemployed and other nonworkers."

A new cooperation also seems to be developing between those recent enemies: dissident stockholders and top management. There are still many points at issue between the dissidents and management, as recent annual meetings have dramatically illustrated. But responsible groups of shareowners, such as the church-sponsored organizations, are now conducting a year-round dialogue with representatives of the many major corporations, often at the very highest level. That dialogue, both sides admit, is bearing fruit in improved mutual respect and understanding, ranging over the whole spectrum of social issues. "The door of confidentiality has been pushed open several degrees," agrees Tim Smith, who is project director for the Interfaith Center on Corporate Responsibility.

Then, too, the growing willingness of a handful of corporate manage-ments — among them Mobil Oil, Citicorp, U.S. Steel, BankAmerica, General Elec-tric, and General Motors — to speak out on issues of the day is very slowly educat-ing the public about some of the problems that corporations, and all Americans, face. But nearly everyone agrees that business generally must do a more sus-tained job. Herbert Schmertz, Mobil's vice president of public affairs, says: "Cor-porations can't jump into the fight and out again. They have to stay in it for the long haul. And they have to be just as dedicated as their critics."

Social Responsibility Is Inevitable

Keith Davis

Is social responsibility a mere fad, a trend of the moment, or is it a fundamental and lasting change in the direction of business? It can be argued that business already has enough responsibility trying to achieve economic effectiveness in an uncertain world. Its economic burden is heavy and its responsibilities are many, so why saddle business with new obligations that may overburden it and weaken its economic effectiveness? Especially in these troubled economic times should not business strictly follow its traditional economic mission? Yet society is dynamic; change is everywhere. So the old economic mission that business per-formed so well may be changing also. The following discussion proposes that substantial social involvement by business is inevitable. It is a fundamental development that is a long-run secular trend *regardless of temporary cyclical swings*. It is not a fad of the moment.

When the term *social responsibility* is used, many images are created in executives' minds. Related terms, such as *social concern, social conscience, social involvement,* and *social response* have similar effects. I have selected the term social responsibility because it appears to have the most widespread use when a person is referring to the need for business to be concerned about the social effects of its actions.

The philosophy is that social outputs of business are a significant variable in the quality of life; therefore, business can no longer think almost exclusively of economic outputs. Social considerations should carry major weight in all business decisions and actions. This general concern about the social outputs of business will be called the *social responsibility model.*

The idea of social responsibility implies that business decision makers recognize some obligation to protect and improve the welfare of society as a whole along with their own interests. The net effect is to enhance quality of life in the broadest possible way, however the quality of life is defined by society. In this way harmony is achieved between business actions and society's wants. The businessman becomes concerned with the total effect of his economic and institutional actions on society. This is clearly a *system* way of thinking. It accepts the fact that business is attached to an extended social system on which it is partly dependent; consequently, certain obligations or social responsibilities arise from this attachment.

NEW CONDITIONS REQUIRE NEW MODELS OF THOUGHT

The traditional economic model of business operations has served business well. Business needs to make no apology for its profound role in bringing economic plenty to many parts of the world. The job that business has done ranks high among civilization's all-time achievements. If conditions have changed, however, then the old model may not apply precisely the way it applied in the past. In a dynamic world businessmen are not going to solve tomorrow's problems with yesterday's theories.

Both business and society have changed from what they were several decades ago. The changes in both have increased the gap between business's economic way of life and society's social needs, creating an incongruence between the lifestyles of business and the society in which it operates. As shown in Figure 1, business has built more social concern into its lifestyle in recent decades, but society's expectations have increased even faster. What once was a small gap in lifestyles permitting modest accommodation between two social forces is now a wide gap making accommodation more difficult. The result has been a heightened state of tension between business and society. The gap between the two is so large that some persons on each side do not understand or sympathize with needs of the other. They are prone to go their own way, repeating their own rhetoric and grumbling that the other party ignores their needs.

The existing lifestyle gap and the resultant tension are not necessarily a result of unreasonable attitudes by either party. Rather, the changing times have pulled lifestyles further apart, so the old way of doing business no longer fits the new conditions. The old way was appropriate and successful in its day, but today it is an anachronism out of joint with the times, particularly in an advanced and affluent nation such as the United States. Some old characteristics that no longer fit are unrestricted release of pollutants into air and water, discriminatory hiring and promotion, various forms of "let the buyer beware," and disregard of a firm's community impact.

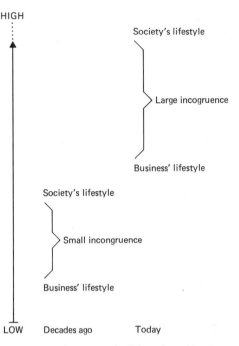

HIGH

Society's lifestyle

Large incogruence

Business' lifestyle

Society's lifestyle

Small incongruence

Business' lifestyle

LOW   Decades ago   Today

Fig. 1   A developing incongruence between the lifestyles of business and society.

The incongruence between business's lifestyle and society's lifestyle requires intelligent, creative actions to dispel differences and reduce tensions. From a practical point of view it may be assumed that the social environment is the independent variable and business is the dependent variable. The major burden for adaptation, therefore, is upon business. Eventually it must change to meet society's expectations, not the other way around. There may be minor adaptations by society as it comes to understand business better, but the major changes surely will be required of business.

The principal adaptation that business can make to resolve business–society incongruence in lifestyles is for business to be more socially responsible. As will be explained throughout this discussion, social responsibility is the only evident system that can deal effectively with the new conditions found in society. It is a functional necessity in an interdependent society having complex social relationships. Economic activities in the social system are so related to everything else in the system that business must operate with social responsibility toward all those that it affects. Business cannot compartmentalize itself into just one specialty, such as economic outputs, because its activities are too intermingled with all of society. In short, social responsibility for business is inevitable.

The incorporation of social responsibility into the new business model will not destroy the basic economic mission of business. That mission is needed. All societies require a business function, and they need business institutions. What the new model will do is provide social responsibility as an overlay on the traditional economic mission of business. The mission will be reinterpreted and amended, but its basic nature will remain. If the amendment can be achieved effectively, business eventually will find that its vigor and viability are increased rather than depleted. The amendments to the model should be favorable for business because they will bring the business lifestyle more nearly into congruence with society's lifestyle, thereby dispelling tensions and increasing cooperation. Society also should benefit, so both business and society will be better off with incorporation of the social responsibility model.

In order to understand in more detail why social responsibility is inevitable it is appropriate to examine four long-run changes that have established a new environment for business. These changes are: the needs of people; the role of management; the business and economic system; and the society in general. We will focus on certain key items in each of these areas.

THE CHANGING NEEDS OF PEOPLE

A profound cause at the root of the social responsibility issue is the changed needs of people. Formerly the quest for economic income and security dominated the American lifestyle. Since business was an economic institution providing economic benefits, it was congruent with human wants and was reasonably well accepted in spite of cyclical rises and declines in public favor. Today the American lifestyle has shifted more to social desires, so business's economic mission is no longer congruent with society. The trend can be explained in terms of the familiar Maslow need hierarchy that is used in understanding motivation.*

Maslow proposed that human needs exist in some order of priority so that as basic needs are relatively well satisfied, other needs arise to dominate human expectations. In the Maslow hierarchy basic physical and security needs have been followed by social needs. If we accept the idea that physical and security needs have been relatively satisfied in advanced nations, and there is ample evidence to support this conclusion, then it follows that social needs will tend gradually to dominate public expectations. This reasoning suggests that the changes in public expectations are fundamental, far-reaching, and significant. They are likely to last until they are reasonably satisfied, allowing people to move to new priorities according to their hierarchy of needs.

All people do not move uniformly along a hierarchy of needs, and people have different ways of expressing their needs, so there will always be differences among people. All that the Maslow hierarchy explains is the basic direction of public expectations. If this line of reasoning is accepted, then ecological issues, racial unrest, and similar social issues are not *causes* of the social responsibility trend. Rather, they are *effects* of a much more fundamental causal factor, the far-reaching change in expectations of people. Since human expectations are changing, it follows that business activities need to move toward more social concern for business to remain viable. The more business can contribute to the satisfaction of social expectations, the more it will tend to prosper.

---

*A. H. Maslow, "A theory of human motivation," *Psychological Review* (1943), pp. 370–396.

The foregoing discussion suggests that production of goods is no longer the central focus of the social system. Since human expectations are changing, production goals now must share the spotlight with the elusive goal of quality of life. New relationships between business and society need to be defined that will bring business activities closer to quality-of-life desires. These relationships are represented by the social responsibility model.

THE CHANGING ROLE OF MANAGEMENT

A crucial development in mangement has been the separation of ownership and management roles. Historically the owner of a business was also its active manager, and his management approach developed directly from his ownership. Under these conditions management and ownership interests were the same. Today many small businesses still operate this way, but the business world is dominated by large firms in which ownership and management are two separate groups with different interests. The ownership role has changed to an investor role as ownership has been dispersed through stock markets to millions of persons who lack personal knowledge of the business and the proprietary interest of traditional owners. Of equal importance is the fact that direct business invest-ment has shifted from individuals to institutions. Individuals place their money in mutual funds, insurance plans, pension funds, and trust funds, whose managers then invest the funds as representatives of small investors.

As a result of the shift from ownership to an investment role, management has become more of a differentiated and independent role. It is increasingly semiprofessional, with accession to its position by competence rather than by ownership. In this environment there is an increasing tendency for managers to view their responsibilities as primarily to the firm, rather than to the owners. They perceive themselves as balancing demands of many groups in such a way that reasonable payouts are provided so that the firm can continue to operate effec-tively. Rather than maximizing profits in the traditional way, the new viewpoint tends to seek optimum or satisfactory profits within constraints imposed by many power groups in society. The result is that social claims increasingly are being incorporated into the decision models of management. In effect, this is a trend toward the social responsibility model.

Essentially the managerial role is changing from that of ownership to *trustee-ship* for a wide range of claimants that relate to business. The reasoning that sup-ports this shift in role is that society commits to management social and econo-mic resources with the expectation that management will employ them wisely to provide just payouts to all related groups, *including ownership*. As with legal trustees, management is expected not to dissipate the resources under its care and to enhance them if at all possible, producing more outputs than inputs. But these outputs are for all of society rather than solely for the owners. Although in the short run management may hold social resources by means of legal forms such as incorporation of the business, in the long run management legitimizes its custody of these social resources by being an effective trustee. The Committee for Economic Development describes the trusteeship role as follows:

The modern professional manager also regards himself, not as an owner disposing of personal property as he sees fit, but as a trustee balancing the interests of many diverse participants and constituents in the enterprise, whose interests sometimes conflict with those of others. The chief executive of a large corporation has the problem of reconciling the demands of [many groups]—all within a framework that will be constructive and acceptable to society.

THE CHANGING BUSINESS AND ECONOMIC SYSTEM

Changes in the business and economic system further contribute to the need for a social responsibility model. One key change is the shift from small proprietorships as the primary form of organization to giant corporate forms of business. Another is the change from nearly pure competition to an economy dominated by monopolistic competition.

The trend toward corporate forms of organization has been strong and continuous for the last century. It has significantly altered the flow of responsibility for business actions. The proprietor has unlimited responsibility for his actions, and his responsibility is rather easy to establish since it derives directly from his decisions as owner. On the other hand, the owners of corporations have limited liability and are rarely responsible for decisions made by the firm, even though these decisions have vast social impact. In corporate organization the corporation is responsible for its decisions, but it is an invisible being and lines of responsibility are difficult to establish. Corporations act on the basis of policy and group decisions, and they develop vast bureaucracies that are difficult to understand and penetrate. When a decision is made to move an existing plant or to manufacture a product that has certain user risks, just who is responsible and how does an affected outsider penetrate the bureaucracy and get his viewpoint heard? The ecology and consumerism movements are two strong confirmations that many unsolved issues of corporate responsibility remain.

The corporate form of organization has made possible giant business institutions extending their influence throughout a nation or to many nations. Large size was needed to serve mass markets as population expanded, to provide complex technology, and to secure capital, but size creates new problems of its own. Economic and social power derive both directly and indirectly from size. Some firms dominate a town; others dominate a technology; and others dominate an industry. Some multinational businesses are so large that their sales exceed the gross national product of some nations. In their economic and social influence they have become an economic nation-state, competing for resources and influence with political nation-states. In this new environment it is only natural that questions of social responsibility should arise, because responsibility accompanies power in the organizational model that most people hold.†

---

†For an expansion of power–responsibility relationships see Keith Davis and Robert L. Blomstrom, *Business and Society: Environment and Responsibility,* third edition (New York: McGraw-Hill, 1975), Chapter 3.

A key economic change has been the shift from almost pure competition to an economy dominated by oligopolistic competition in which a limited number of businesses exert influence on each product market. In the classical model of pure competition proposed by Adam Smith in 1776, atomistic businessmen were so controlled by the forces of the market that they had negligible power. Having no social power, they could hardly be said to have social responsibility. Smith's classical model rather accurately represented the real marketplace of that time. In Smith's day there was little product differentiation, but today it is substantial. Many more differences could be mentioned, but it all boils down to the fact that modern business has social power over such matters as consumer needs, product safety, and employee development. Social responsibility issues derive from this evident social power.

THE CHANGING SOCIETY

Several broad changes affecting society in general are causing the social responsibility model to be inevitable. One is that modern society is immensely more complex and interdependent than it once was. Business plays a key role in many parts of this web. Jobs depend upon successful business activity, and the work itself plays a role in a person's life satisfaction and fulfillment. A nation's level of affluence depends on business productivity, and business research plays the dominant role in advancement of applied technology. What has happened is that business now occupies many strategic positions along the complex chain that brings products and services to people. This puts business in a position to affect lifestyle, thereby raising issues of responsibility for that power.

Another influence is the increasing load on our natural environment. It is well documented that business is a substantial contributor to that load. The environment has been a *free good* that business could use as it wished. This reasoning especially applies to air and water, which were considered part of a *public common* available to all. This made them an economic externality that business did not need to figure into its cost system, so relatively minor attention was given to them. A steel firm could use the air or the river as a common dumping ground for its wastes without paying for this service. In this manner both business and its customers avoided paying costs for the degradation of the common resources, and these costs were transferred to society as social costs. The problem was minor as long as the load on the common was light, but when it became heavy, then society found itself with burdensome costs that it did not wish to bear. The result has been increasing attention to the social responsibility model.

Another factor is the gradual growth of pluralism in the American society. Pluralism is a social system in which a substantial number of diverse groups maintain autonomous participation and influence in the system. Many more traditional societies are dominated by only a few powerful institutions and offer few options for the common man to express his desires. The American system is much more fractionated, having many organizations through which people can express their wants. They range from the Sierra Club to the Urban League, but the important point is that they represent many centers of power in the system. So many are pressing upon business with their individual interests that business has no opportunity to strike a detente with them in order to free itself from social tension so that it can pursue economic matters singlemindedly. Pluralistic groups insist on being heard because business actions impinge on their interests, and many of the issues that they raise are essentially issues of social responsibility.

OPTIONS AVAILABLE TO BUSINESS

The foregoing developments present a powerful argument for significant business concern about its social outputs. The social responsibility model appears to be an inevitable part of business's future. The only choice business has is how to go about responding to social responsibility expectations. The following options are available, ranging from those that are less desirable to those more desirable.

One option is *withdrawal,* by which business recedes into its shell, reducing its interface with society and trying to mind its own business. It mumbles its traditional rhetoric and accepts social obligations only when they are forced upon it. This approach is similar to an individual who withdraws from society. It generally reflects some type of alienation from the system and tends to reduce the withdrawing party's influence in the system.

Another option is the *legal approach.* Business depends on the law to protect it from change, because it knows that laws are amended very slowly in a large social system. When the law finally is changed, business delays change through long and expensive court battles. Business may finally be changed toward more socially responsive decision making, but it will fight and kick and drag its feet all the way. Both society and business may be losers in this battle because needed social progress is delayed or prevented. Some legal battles may be necessary to define properly the role of business in society, but excessive delaying tactics probably weaken both business and society.

An additional option is *bargaining,* by which business negotiates with pressure groups that make claims upon it. In this manner it attempts to resolve disputes with negotiated settlements that often produce some change. As business has learned in the past, settlements can be elusive because the interests of pressure groups change rather rapidly. Furthermore, a settlement with one group may not be satisfactory to other groups, so business needs always to keep complete system relationships in view as it bargains. Bargaining is not a desirable total solution, because in the long run it leads to a situation in which the strongest party wins regardless of the rightness of its cause; however, bargaining is a necessary short-run tactic for operating activities.

A final option is *problem solving.* In this approach business makes a genuine study of society's and business's values and needs, and it attempts to reconcile them in constructive ways. Effort is directed toward finding optimum ways for social progress, considering the interests of all parties in the situation. Business recognizes the full system impact of its decisions on an interdependent global community, and it acts with this global view in mind. In this manner business itself becomes more viable because it is an instrument of social progress rather than an opponent or a passive receptor.

Even in the problem-solving mode there are poorer and better ways to respond. A minimum type of problem solving is to seek solutions only in areas of high public pressure and expectation. A more advanced response is to anticipate public pressures and expectations, responding to them in a preventive way before they become major irritants. A more mature approach, although few firms may be able to go this far, is to determine which social problems are affected by business power and as an obligation of power to move forthrightly to solve them.

An individual business will probably use several of the options mentioned, but problem solving is the option with the most promise. Business can lead in achieving social advancement the same way it has led toward economic and technological advancement, provided its objective is social problem solving.

CONCLUSIONS

Social responsibility refers to the need for business to be concerned about the social effects of its actions. Substantial social responsibility is inevitable because of a multitude of changes in the business environment. These changes are so significant that they have created a major incongruence between the traditional economic lifestyle of business and society's desired lifestyle. Social responsibility of business is a functional necessity in the modern business world. Business's only option is whether to move forthrightly into the social arena or to be forced into it fighting and kicking all the way. Obviously the former option presents a more viable social role for business in the future.

Finally, the social responsibility model is not a new business mission. All societies need a business function to provide economic outputs. The social responsibility model merely provides an overlay on the traditional economic mission of business. The traditional business role of economic entrepreneurship is amended to include that of social trusteeship. What is needed is economic outputs *and* social outputs, not one instead of the other. If business effectively integrates these two outputs, its future should be more promising than its past.

The Social Responsibility of Business Is to Increase Its Profits

Milton Friedman

When I hear businessmen speak eloquently about the "social responsibilities of business in a free-enterprise system," I am reminded of the wonderful line about

The New York Times Magazine, September 13, 1970, pp. 33, 122–126.© 1970 by The New York Times Company. Reprinted by permission.

the Frenchman who discovered at the age of 70 that he had been speaking prose all his life. The businessmen believe that they are defending free enterprise when they declaim that business is not concerned "merely" with profit but also with promoting desirable "social" ends; that business has a "social conscience" and takes seriously its responsibilities for providing employment, eliminating discrimination, avoiding pollution, and whatever else may be the catch-words of the contemporary crop of reformers. In fact they are—or would be if they or anyone else took them seriously—preaching pure and unadulterated socialism. Businessmen who talk this way are unwitting puppets of the intellectual forces that have been undermining the basis of a free society these past decades.

The discussions of the "social responsibilities of business" are notable for their analytical looseness and lack of rigor. What does it mean to say that "business" has responsibilities? Only people can have responsibilities. A corporation is an artificial person and in this sense may have artificial responsibilities, but "business" as a whole cannot be said to have responsibilities, even in this vague sense. The first step toward clarity in examining the doctrine of the social responsibility of business is to ask precisely what it implies for whom.

Presumably, the individuals who are to be responsible are businessmen, which means individual proprietors or corporate executives. Most of the discussion of social responsibility is directed at corporations, so in what follows I shall mostly neglect the individual proprietor and speak of corporate executives.

In a free-enterprise, private-property system, a corporate executive is an employee of the owners of the business. He has direct responsibility to his employers. That responsibility is to conduct the business in accordance with their desires, which generally will be to make as much money as possible while conforming to the basic rules of the society, both those embodied in law and those embodied in ethical custom. Of course, in some cases his employers may have a different objective. A group of persons might establish a corporation for an eleemosynary purpose—for example, a hospital or a school. The manager of such a corporation will not have money profit as his objective but the rendering of certain services.

In either case, the key point is that, in his capacity as a corporate executive, the manager is the agent of the individuals who own the corporation or establish the eleemosynary institution, and his primary responsibility is to them.

Needless to say, this does not mean that it is easy to judge how well he is performing his task. But at least the criterion of performance is straightforward, and the persons among whom a voluntary contractual arrangement exists are clearly defined.

Of course, the corporate executive is also a person in his own right. As a person, he may have many other responsibilities that he recognizes or assumes voluntarily—to his family, his conscience, his feelings of charity, his church, his clubs, his city, his country. He may feel impelled by these responsibilities to devote part of his income to causes he regards as worthy, to refuse to work for particular corporations, even to leave his job, for example, to join his country's armed forces. If we wish, we may refer to some of these responsibilities as "social responsibilities." But in these respects he is acting as a principal, not an agent; he is spending his own money or time or energy, not the money of his employers or the time or energy he has contracted to devote to their purposes. If these are "social responsibilities," they are the social responsibilities of individuals, not of business.

What does it mean to say that the corporate executive has a "social responsibility" in his capacity as businessman? If this statement is not pure rhetoric, it must mean that he is to act in some way that is not in the interest of his employers. For example, that he is to refrain from increasing the price of the product in order to contribute to the social objective of preventing inflation, even though a price increase would be in the best interests of the corporation. Or that he is to make expenditures on reducing pollution beyond the amount that is in the best interests of the corporation or that is required by law in order to contribute to the social objective of improving the environment. Or that, at the expense of corporate profits, he is to hire "hard-core" unemployed instead of better-qualified available workmen to contribute to the social objective of reducing poverty.

In each of these cases, the corporate executive would be spending someone else's money for a general social interest. Insofar as his actions in accord with his "social responsibility" reduce returns to stockholders, he is spending their money. Insofar as his actions raise the price to customers, he is spending the customers' money. Insofar as his actions lower the wages of some employes, he is spending their money.

The stockholders or the customers or the employes could separately spend their own money on the particular action if they wished to do so. The executive is exercising a distinct "social responsibility," rather than serving as an agent of the stockholders or the customers or the employes, only if he spends the money in a different way than they would have spent it.

But if he does this, he is in effect imposing taxes, on the one hand, and deciding how the tax proceeds shall be spent, on the other.

This process raises political questions on two levels: principle and consequences. On the level of political principle, the imposition of taxes and the expenditure of tax proceeds are governmental functions. We have established elaborate constitutional, parliamentary, and judicial provisions to control these functions, to assure that taxes are imposed so far as possible in accordance with the preferences and desires of the public — after all, "taxation without representation" was one of the battle cries of the American Revolution. We have a system of checks and balances to separate the legislative function of imposing taxes and enacting expenditures from the executive function of collecting taxes and administering expenditure programs and from the judicial function of mediating disputes and interpreting the law.

Here the businessman — self-selected or appointed directly or indirectly by stockholders — is to be simultaneously legislator, executive, and jurist. He is to decide whom to tax by how much and for what purpose, and he is to spend the proceeds — all this guided only by general exhortations from on high to restrain inflation, improve the environment, fight poverty, and so on and on.

The whole justification for permitting the corporate executive to be selected by the stockholders is that the executive is an agent serving the interests of his principal. This justification disappears when the corporate executive imposes taxes and spends the proceeds for "social" purposes. He becomes in effect a public employe, a civil servant, even though he remains in name an employe of a private enterprise. On grounds of political principle, it is intolerable that such civil servants—insofar as their actions in the name of social responsibility are real and not just window-dressing—should be selected as they are now. If they are to be civil servants, then they must be selected through a political process. If they are to impose taxes and make expenditures to foster "social" objectives, then political machinery must be set up to guide the assessment of taxes and to determine through a political process the objectives to be served.

This is the basic reason why the doctrine of "social responsibility" involves the acceptance of the socialist view that political mechanisms, not market mechanisms, are the appropriate way to determine the allocation of scarce resources to alternative uses.

On the grounds of consequences, can the corporate executive in fact discharge his alleged "social responsibilities"? On the one hand, suppose he could get away with spending the stockholders' or customers' or employes' money. How is he to know how to spend it? He is told that he must contribute to fighting inflation. How is he to know what action of his will contribute to that end? He is presumably an expert in running his company—in producing a product or selling it or financing it. But nothing about his selection makes him an expert on inflation. Will his holding down the price of his product reduce inflationary pressure? Or, by leaving more spending power in the hands of his customers, simply divert it elsewhere? Or, by forcing him to produce less because of the lower price, will it simply contribute to shortages? Even if he could answer these questions, how much cost is he justified in imposing on his stockholders, customers, and employes for this social purpose? What is his appropriate share and what is the appropriate share of others?

And, whether he wants to or not, can he get away with spending his stockholders', customers', or employes' money? Will not the stockholders fire him? (Either the present ones or those who take over when his actions in the name of social responsibility have reduced the corporation's profits and the price of its stock.) His customers and his employes can desert him for other producers and employers less scrupulous in exercising their social responsibilities.

This facet of "social responsibility" doctrine is brought into sharp relief when the doctrine is used to justify wage restraint by trade unions. The conflict of interest is naked and clear when union officials are asked to subordinate the interest of their members to some more general social purpose. If the union officials try to enforce wage restraint, the consequence is likely to be wildcat strikes, rank-and-file revolts and the emergence of strong competitors for their jobs. We thus have the ironic phenomenon that union leaders—at least in the U.S.—have objected to Government interference with the market far more consistently and courageously than have business leaders.

The difficulty of exercising "social responsibility" illustrates, of course, the great virtue of private competitive enterprise—it forces people to be responsible for their own actions and makes it difficult for them to "exploit" other people for either selfish or unselfish purposes. They can do good—but only at their own expense.

Many a reader who has followed the argument this far may be tempted to remonstrate that it is all well and good to speak of government's having the responsibility to impose taxes and determine expenditures for such "social" purposes as controlling pollution or training the hard-core unemployed, but that the problems are too urgent to wait on the slow course of political processes, that the exercise of social responsibility by businessmen is a quicker and surer way to solve pressing current problems.

Aside from the question of fact—I share Adam Smith's skepticism about the benefits that can be expected from "those who affected to trade for the public good"—this argument must be rejected on grounds of principle. What it amounts to is an assertion that those who favor the taxes and expenditures in question have failed to persuade a majority of their fellow citizens to be of like mind and that they are seeking to attain by undemocratic procedures what they cannot attain by democratic procedures. In a free society, it is hard for "good" people to do "good," but that is a small price to pay for making it hard for "evil" people to do "evil," especially since one man's good is another's evil.

I have, for simplicity, concentrated on the special case of the corporate executive, except only for the brief digression on trade unions. But precisely the same argument applies to the newer phenomenon of calling upon stockholders to require corporations to exercise social responsibility (the recent G.M. crusade, for example). In most of these cases, what is in effect involved is some stockholders trying to get other stockholders (or customers or employes) to contribute against their will to "social" causes favored by the activists. Insofar as they succeed, they are again imposing taxes and spending the proceeds.

The situation of the individual proprietor is somewhat different. If he acts to reduce the returns of his enterprise in order to exercise his "social responsibility," he is spending his own money, not someone else's. If he wishes to spend his money on such purposes, that is his right, and I cannot see that there is any objection to his doing so. In the process, he, too, may impose costs on employes and customers. However, because he is far less likely than a large corporation or union to have monopolistic power, any such side effects will tend to be minor.

Of course, in practice the doctrine of social responsibility is frequently a cloak for actions that are justified on other grounds rather than a reason for those actions.

To illustrate, it may well be in the long-run interest of a corporation that is a major employer in a small community to devote resources to providing amenities to that community or to improving its government. That may make it easier to attract desirable employes, it may reduce the wage bill or lessen losses from pilferage and sabotage, or have other worthwhile effects. Or it may be that, given the laws about the deductibility of corporate charitable contributions, the stockholders can contribute more to charities they favor by having the corporation make the gift than by doing it themselves, since they can in that way contribute an amount that would otherwise have been paid as corporate taxes.

In each of these—and many similar—cases, there is a strong temptation to rationalize these actions as an exercise of "social responsibility." In the present climate of opinion, with its widespread aversion to "capitalism," "profits," the "soulless corporation" and so on, this is one way for a corporation to generate good will as a by-product of expenditures that are entirely justified in its own self-interest.

It would be inconsistent of me to call on corporate executives to refrain from this hypocritical window-dressing because it harms the foundations of a free society. That would be to call on them to exercise a "social responsibility"! If our institutions, and the attitudes of the public make it in their self-interest to cloak their actions in this way, I cannot summon much indignation to denounce them. At the same time, I can express admiration for those individual proprietors or owners of closely held corporations or stockholders of more broadly held corporations who disdain such tactics as approaching fraud.

Whether blameworthy or not, the use of the cloak of social responsibility, and the nonsense spoken in its name by influential and prestigious businessmen, does clearly harm the foundations of a free society. I have been impressed time and again by the schizophrenic character of many businessmen. They are capable of being extremely far-sighted and clear-headed in matters that are internal to their businesses. They are incredibly short-sighted and muddled-headed in matters that are outside their businesses but affect the possible survival of business in general. This short-sightedness is strikingly exemplified in the calls from many businessmen for wage and price guidelines or controls or income policies. There is nothing that could do more in a brief period to destroy a market system and replace it by a centrally controlled system than effective governmental control of prices and wages.

The short-sightedness is also exemplified in speeches by businessmen on social responsibility. This may gain them kudos in the short run. But it helps to strengthen the already too prevalent view that the pursuit of profits is wicked and immoral and must be curbed and controlled by external forces. Once this view is adopted, the external forces that curb the market will not be the social consciences, however highly developed, of the pontificating executives; it will be the iron fist of government bureaucrats. Here, as with price and wage controls, businessmen seem to me to reveal a suicidal impulse.

The political principle that underlies the market mechanism is unanimity. In an ideal free market resting on private property, no individual can coerce any other, all cooperation is voluntary, all parties to such cooperation benefit or they need not participate. There are no "social" values, no "social" responsibilities in any sense other than the shared values and responsibilities of individuals. Society is a collection of individuals and of the various groups they voluntarily form.

The political principle that underlies the political mechanism is conformity. The individual must serve a more general social interest—whether that be determined by a church or a dictator or a majority. The individual may have a vote and a say in what is to be done, but if he is overruled, he must conform. It is appropriate for some to require others to contribute to a general social purpose whether they wish to or not.

Unfortunately, unanimity is not always feasible. There are some respects in which conformity appears unavoidable, so I do not see how one can avoid the use of the political mechanism altogether.

But the doctrine of "social responsibility" taken seriously would extend the scope of the political mechanism to every human activity. It does not differ in philosophy from the most explicitly collectivist doctrine. It differs only by professing to believe that collectivist ends can be attained without collectivist means. That is why, in my book *Capitalism and Freedom*, I have called it a "fundamentally subversive doctrine" in a free society, and have said that in such a society, "there is one and only one social responsibility of business — to use its resources and engage in activities designed to increase its profits so long as it stays within the rules of the game, which is to say, engages in open and free competition without deception or fraud."

Profits: How Much Is Too Little?

David B. Tinnin

Profit is today a fighting word. Profits are the lifeblood of the economic system, the magic elixir upon which progress and all good things ultimately depend. But one man's lifeblood is another man's cancer.
— *Economist Paul A. Samuelson*

And so it is. Profits are called by many names these days, many of them bad. *Obscene, exorbitant, excessive* are the leading pejoratives. By contrast, *nonprofit* has gained an altruistic, almost hallowed connotation. Psychologically, that prejudice may be understandable, but economically it makes no sense. Profits can, of course, be immoral — if they are exploitative, for example, or result from price-fixing schemes or monopolies. But most profits are not so earned. Instead, they are an essential and beneficial ingredient in the workings of a free-market economy.

Nobel Laureate Samuelson addressed his pugnacious remarks to a forum of European and U.S. business leaders and economists at Harvard earlier this year. At the invitation of Management Expert John Diebold, the leaders had gathered to discuss new challenges to the role of profits in Western economies. Almost without exception, the speakers testified to the pressures and pinches now afflict-

ing the profit system. In some instances, most notably Sweden, Socialist governments are levying confiscatory taxes on corporate profits and insisting upon huge
contributions to pension funds, which in turn are being used to buy up the companies; "fund Socialism" was the term Swedish Economist Erik Lundberg
employed to describe the process. In Britain, the Labor Party's left wing continues to demand the nationalization of shipbuilding, aircraft production and
banking—in disregard of the fact that most of Britain's already nationalized
industries are chronic money losers whose inefficiences are a major cause of the
country's dismal economic plight. In West Germany, the unions still support the
profit motive but are demanding a more decisive voice in how earnings are allocated between workers and shareholders.

In the U.S., attacks on profits are more rhetorical than real. No excess-profits
tax has been levied on U.S. corporations since the Korean War. In fact, the regular federal tax on corporate profits has been lowered over the past three years
from 52% to 48%. Hardly anyone questions the basic right of business to make
some profit. The question has been, how much?

With the resurgence of corporate profits, that question is likely to be posed
more often and more insistently. Opinion polls suggest that a majority of the
public believes that corporations earn much more than they actually do, and
favor higher taxes on profits. Hence, it would behoove Americans, too, to rid their
minds of what Samuelson characterizes as the suspicion that profits are "an
exploitative surplus which fat men with an unfair penchant for arithmetic skim
from the gross national product."

Dark suspicion of profit is an ancient turn of mind. Within Western culture
there are deeply ingrained philosophical and religious misgivings about the
morality of profits—most simply put, that to earn from the labors of another is an
intrinsically evil form of extortion. Michel de Montaigne, the 16th century French
thinker, entitled one of his essays "The Profit of One Man Is the Damage of
Another." His thesis: "Man should condemn all manner of gain."

However, as the era of capitalism dawned two centuries ago, the profit motive found an able defender. In *The Wealth of Nations,* Adam Smith argued that
profits are the legitimate return for risk and effort and that the "Invisible Hand"
of market forces would convert private greed into public benefits. A century
later, Karl Marx was not so sure. Arguing the opposite view, he asserted that
labor, not capital, was the essential ingredient that added value to goods or raw
materials in the manufacturing process. Thus, in his view, profit was the "surplus
value" that the capitalist unjustifiably tacked on to the real worth of the product.
In the early part of the century, Bernard Shaw and his fellow Fabians contended
that profits should be taxed into oblivion in order to create a new, socialist order.
They believed that the profitless economy would function more effectively—and
they were wrong. Since the onset of the Industrial Age 100 years ago, profits have
proved to be indispensable to a prosperous economy.

In a capitalist economy, profit is, above all, the motivator. Without a hope
of reasonable profit, no one would start a business, introduce a new product or
service, or even continue producing an old one. And without the reality of profit,
no business in the long run can keep itself alive—except by government subsidy,

which has to be paid partly out of taxes levied on the profits of other businesses. Says Democratic Senator William Proxmire of Wisconsin, often a critic of U.S. business: "Profits are what drive this great economy."

There are, of course, other ways of organizing production. Communist nations manage to achieve growth by following detailed output and investment plans drawn up and enforced by a state central planning agency. But the state-owned economies in Communist countries are almost always disjointed by bureaucratic stupidity. The most frequently cited example is agriculture. It is true that the Soviet Union suffers from natural handicaps, including bad weather and arid soil. Even so, the basic problem is its communal farming system, which fails to provide the farmers with sufficient motivation. The dismal results are well known; Moscow must buy huge tonnages of grain from the profit-seeking farmers of the U.S.

Profit is also important as a measure of efficiency in industrial enterprises — a way of keeping economic score. Whether a business is well or badly run, whether investments are productive or misguided, whether the products are competitive and appealing — judging performance without reference to profits is like watching a baseball game where nobody bothers to count runs. Again, the Soviet experience has demonstrated the efficacy of profits. For years a Soviet factory manager fulfilled his quota under the central plan by turning out a certain amount of goods regardless of expense or popular demand. But now, in order to improve quality and control costs, most Soviet-bloc countries have set up managerial systems that rely heavily on profits — though they are called, of course, by other names.

Whatever their role in the Soviet-bloc economies, profits are essential to the smooth functioning of American society. Government services, from the federal to local level, rely crucially on corporate income and property taxes. U.S. corporations paid $40.6 billion in federal income taxes last year and an estimated $6.6 billion to state and local governments. For Washington, a decline in corporate profits would immediately cause a larger budget deficit. For state and local administrations, money-losing companies can mean reductions of public services, ranging from dirty streets due to a lack of funds for sanitation men to layoffs of teachers.

The profits that are left after taxes are either paid out as dividends to stockholders ($32.1 billion in 1975) or reinvested in the business ($33.2 billion). Most of those profits that are turned into dividend checks are then taxed a second time, as income, when they reach the shareholders' mailboxes — an excess that Democratic Presidential Candidate Jimmy Carter says he disapproves of.

There is an old myth, which should have been laid to rest decades ago, that dividends flow mainly into the pockets of wealthy individuals. Actually, there has been a historic if little heralded shift in the pattern of share ownership. In terms of dollar value, nearly half of all corporate shares these days are owned by institutions such as pension funds, insurance companies, college endowments, even churches. Without even realizing it, millions of Americans rely on corporate strength for their own future security. The assurance of a retirement income, the soundness of an insurance policy, the availability of a college scholarship—all may well depend heavily on the continued profitability of U.S. corporations.

As for retained earnings, they are a prime source of the investments in new plant and machinery that increase production, improve product quality and create jobs. Aggressive and innovative companies often retain high percentages of their profits for expansion. One example: Levi Strauss & Co., whose jeans clothe the world. The company, a large share of whose stock is owned by the Haas family, generally retains nearly 90% of its profits for reinvestment, like the recent opening of a new factory in the little town of Roswell, N. Mex. The plant created 350 new jobs, each at a cost to the company of $17,000.

Other companies may choose to borrow the money for expansion. But even then the investment depends on profit, since lenders will not advance expansion funds to a company that has little prospect of earning money. In the long run, an absence of profit means that a company cannot buy the plant and equipment it needs to remain competitive. The ultimate losers are the workers. Or, in the words of an unexpected defender of the profit system, British Labor Party Prime Minister James Callaghan: "If there are no profits, there will be no jobs."

Why, then, the widespread suspicion of profits? In the U.S., the biggest reason is probably a wild misunderstanding of just how much profit corporations actually make. In one poll conducted by the Opinion Research Corp. of Princeton, N.J., a majority of those questioned thought that companies averaged 33¢ profit on each dollar of sales. A sampling of college students by Standard & Poor's yielded an even higher estimate: 45¢. The actual figure is below 5¢—and the overall trend has been downward. According to a FORTUNE survey, the 1975 median profit margin of the nation's 500 largest industrial corporations shrank to 3.9% of sales. That was the thinnest margin in 17 years.

In 1976, it is true, profits are climbing back. But over the long run, an ever increasing percentage of national income has been shifting away from profits toward wages and salaries. In 1950, 64.1% of corporations' domestic income was used to pay wages, salaries and fringe benefits, while profits comprised 15.6%; by 1975 the share of wages and salaries had risen to 76%, while profits had fallen to only 8.3%.

Today profits, far from being too high, are still too low to ensure the nation's continued economic health. Among the top 20 industrialized countries, the U.S. in recent years has fared badly in terms of new industrial investment per capita; only Luxembourg and Britain rank lower. As a result, the U.S. may already, in fact, have become enmeshed in an intolerable economic dilemma in which the nation's private employers no longer create enough new jobs to absorb young workers coming into the labor force. Otto Eckstein, a member of TIME Board of Economists, warns that the production capabilities of a number of important basic industries, including chemicals and paper, are so limited that they could create bottlenecks that would impede the U.S. from cutting its unemployment rate much below 6% in the immediate future. Such a high jobless level means increasing welfare rolls and social unrest.

The forecasts of capital requirements for the next decade, however, are stated in figures that are almost incomprehensibly huge; the estimates range up to $4 trillion for the new plants that will be needed to bring the U.S. nearer to becoming a fully employed society. But investment capital on that scale will certainly not be available unless there is a strong and sustained rise in profits that carries well beyond 1976.

Despite general agreement about the need for tremendous amounts of new capital, there is no consensus about how the money should be raised. Liberal economists generally favor more generous individual tax cuts and an ever growing money supply to stimulate consumer buying, which in turn creates heightened economic activity. Conservative economists, on the other hand, argue that there has been too much emphasis on consumption and not enough on accumulation. They would prefer federal policies that would enable companies to keep more of their earnings either through higher depreciation allowances for the purchase of new equipment or a further lowering of the corporate tax rate. Ideally, there should be a mix of both approaches so that the consumer, as well as the investment sectors of the economy, would remain healthy.

Given the confusion over profits, it is questionable whether the U.S. can actually arrive at such a solution. While there is a need for greater understanding about the beneficial role of profits, there is also a need for clearer reporting of corporate income. As Management Expert Peter Drucker has pointed out, the three main measures used by corporations today—gross and net income plus earnings per share—are far too superficial. A much more analytical system is required that would relate the firm's performance to more telling indicators, such as the return on invested capital, competitive strength, the company's historical earnings trend, and relation of research expenditures to the development of new products.

Equally bad, under the present system, earnings are compared only with the preceding quarter—or year. This leads to wild gyrations in the loss and gain columns. The profit may be up 75% from a year ago, but then, a year ago may have been miserable. These swings are, humanly enough, magnified by corporate officers, who pooh-pooh losses while boasting about profit increases in hyperbolic press releases. The press then magnifies the problem by often reporting profits in language more appropriate to space shots or sporting events: profits leap, soar, skyrocket—or plunge, plummet, nosedive.

It is time for a more sober analysis of profits and their importance as the engine of economic growth. It is a historic irony that in the U.S., the stronghold of world capitalism, so few citizens understand that profits provide the basis for the prosperity on which rests the well-being of both individuals and the nation.

QUESTIONS FOR DISCUSSION

1. Keith Davis pronounces that "social responsibility is inevitable." He bases this assertion on the changing needs of people, the changing role of management, the changing business and economic system, and the changing society. Explain Davis' thinking with respect to those changing elements and the impact of the change on the social and economic role of business.

2. What does Milton Friedman mean when he terms "Social Responsibility" a fundamentally subversive doctrine? Discuss.

3. Explain and critique the concept of "social contract."

4. Explain and critique the concept of "enlightened self-interest."

5. John Perham opens his article, "The Corporation in Crisis," with a question: "Can the corporation survive?" What reasons does he cite for even posing such an important question?

6. Economist Henry Wallich proposes "that corporations can perform some social activities better than government, and in undertaking to do more than the law requires, they are shifting activities from the public to the private sector." Compare this stance with Friedman's assertion that social responsibility is "pure and unadulterated socialism."

7. Suppose you are a small shareholder in a corporation practicing "increased social responsibility." Your company's annual reports have recently been glorifying the organization's activities in jobs for the hard-core unemployed, plant beautification, and charitable contributions. How would you reconcile your personal interests with those activities of the corporation?

SELECTED READINGS

Anshen, M., *Managing the Socially Responsible Corporation*. (New York: Free Press, 1974.)

Chamberlain, N., *The Limits of Corporate Responsibility*. (New York: Basic Books, 1973.)

Chamberlain, N., *The Place of Business in America's Future: A Study in Social Values*. (New York: Basic Books, 1973.)

Committee for Economic Development, *Social Responsibilities of Business Corporations*. (New York: CED, 1971.)

Commoner, B. *The Poverty of Power*. (New York: Knopf, 1976.)

The Corporation and Social Responsibility, Proceedings of a Symposium, University of Illinois, 1967.

Corson, J. J., *Business in the Humane Society*. (New York: McGraw-Hill, 1971.)

Drotning, P. T., "Why nobody takes corporate social responsibility seriously," *Business and Society Review*, Winter, 1972–73.

Eells, R., *The Meaning of Modern Business*. (New York: Columbia University Press, 1960.)

Fremont-Smith, M. R., *Philanthropy and the Business Corporation*. (New York: Russell Sage Foundation, 1972.)

Friedman, M., *Capitalism and Freedom*. (Chicago: University of Chicago Press, 1962.)

Heyne, P. T., *Private Keepers of the Public Interest*. (New York: McGraw-Hill, 1968.)

Jacoby, N. H., *Corporate Power and Social Responsibility*. (New York: Macmillan Publishing Co., Inc., 1973.)

Manne, H. G., and H. C. Wallich, *The Modern Corporation and Social Responsibility*. (Washington D.C.: American Enterprise Institute, 1972.)

McKie, J. W., ed., *Social Responsibility and the Business Predicament*. (Washington, D.C.: The Brookings Institution, 1974.)

Monsen, R. J., *Business and the Changing Environment*. (New York: McGraw-Hill, 1973.)

Paluszek, J. L., *Will the Corporation Survive?* (Reston, Virginia: Reston Publishing, 1977.)

Silk, L., and D. Vogel, "A question of legitimacy," *Across the Board*, October, 1976.

Votaw, D., and S. P. Sethi, *The Corporate Dilemma: Traditional Values versus Contemporary Problems*. (Englewood Cliffs, N.J.: Prentice-Hall, Inc., 1973.)

Walton, C. C., *Ethos and the Executive*. (Englewood Cliffs, N.J.: Prentice-Hall, Inc., 1969.)

2. Positive Theories of the Modern Manager and Corporate Behavior

In contrast to normative prescriptions of business behavior—statements of what managers *ought* to do—this chapter will present positive or *descriptive* studies of *actual* managerial behavior and corporate roles. Included is a sampling of the many theories and empirical studies of how firms and managers behave and the motivations behind that behavior.

In this introduction, we shall briefly discuss some selected models of the firm and of managers. The readings will expand on the models and introduce some additional ones as well.

As students digest the models in this introduction, they should try to compare the managerial types described with those prescribed in Chapter 1. Are the managers as seen in actual roles (both theoretically and empirically) so vastly different from the types that social critics would like to see? Are there any descriptive models that will allow us to understand the ease (or difficulty) a firm or manager may experience in trying to respond to environmental or societal pressures? We shall have more to say on this at the close of this introduction.

Most positive or descriptive theories focus on a particular structural level for study; that is, some focus on the firm as an entity, others on managers, and still others on markets and industries. In models of the firm, the thesis is that the firm as an entity has a life of its own—the firm acts, the firm behaves, the firm has objectives, etc. In effect, it is *persona ficta,* a fictitious person. Although the firm, in reality, is a conglomeration of managers (and workers and technicians), the connecting link between the behavior and motivations of individual managers and those of the firm is not always clear. That is, does the behavior of a firm result from the sum total of managerial behavior or from something apart from the personal motivations of managers? Do curious cross-cancellations of opposing personal behaviors govern the firm's position?

Max Weber (like most classical organization theorists) describes the manager or the bureaucrat as leaving personal feelings outside the organization and adopting the corporate or organizational point of view when on the job. Most recent work and the observations of managerial lifestyles, of course, reveal the unreality of that description. But we are still nowhere near a definitive explanation of why a firm behaves as it does. We still have much to learn about how individual managers acculturate the corporation and vice versa.

THE THEORY OF THE FIRM IN TRADITIONAL ECONOMICS

In the introduction to the previous chapter, we briefly examined the traditional economic theory of the firm. Since the theory of the firm is essentially a positive model and since it is possibly the most misunderstood and most maligned abstraction of all, we should like to expand upon it in this section. Quite simply stated, the firm *in economic theory* is a magnificently powerful computer; it functions as an entity—objectives and actions are those of the entrepreneur—and the (possibly dysfunctional) actions of individual members of a bureaucratic structure are not part of the analysis. The external environment (product and resource markets) creates the need for action, and the entrepreneur (or firm) chooses rationally, from *all* possible alternatives, the means or course of action that will maximize the profits of the firm. Rationality, in the theory, means that the decision-maker seeks out (and can identify) all available alternatives and is able to choose the one(s) which will maximize returns. The key assumptions in the theory of the firm are profit maximization, rationality, and the single-mindedness of the organization.

Most observers, however, agree that when we move into the real world, particularly in dealing with oligopoly, monopoly, or otherwise imperfect market structures, and consider the real-life frailties and abilities of managers as well as the complexity of organizations, the key assumptions of the theory of the firm become questionable. The real-life oligopolist or monopolist (or oligopsonist or monopsonist) is under no compulsion to maximize; as a matter of fact, the entrepreneur in less than perfectly competitive market structures may be under compulsion from several quarters to *limit* profits. Some firms are satisfied with "adequate profits" and most managers do not know how to maximize, or indeed cannot determine whether (or when) they have in fact maximized.

Why, then, do economists defend with so much apparent vigor a model so obviously divorced from reality? Economists will argue that they are not really interested in actual firm behavior or objectives *per se*, but only in what occurs in the market in terms of resource allocation. Theorists must simplify in their abstractions, and economists pick out the assumptions of profit maximization, rationality, and simple-minded action not because they form a precisely accurate picture of firm behavior, but because they are good enough mechanisms to lead analysts to what they are really interested in: reasonably accurate predictions of market behavior and resource allocation.* In a very real sense, what is called the theory of the firm is in fact a theory of industries or markets, not firms.

Even though some recent work does focus on the firm, it must be recognized that the economist's analysis simply doesn't include the firm as its primary frame of reference. And even though the traditional model of the firm fails to provide a basis for a sound theory of markets in oligopoly situations (a topic we cannot

---

*The essence of this rationale can be found in Milton Friedman, *Essays in Positive Economics*. (Chicago: University of Chicago Press, 1953); or Sherman Krupp, *Patterns in Organization Analysis*. (Philadelphia: Chilton Company, 1962); pp. 6-10.

cover here), nevertheless the criticism leveled by scholars in other disciplines—whose primary interest or focus *is the firm*—is unwarranted.

MODIFIED ECONOMIC MODELS OF THE FIRM

A number of economists, focusing on the firm as the firm, have offered an interesting variety of positive models, particularly of oligopolistic enterprises (those with some degree of market interdependence with other firms, yet also with a considerable amount of discretion). While we shall not explore these frameworks in great detail, we should like to sample a few simply to point out the variety of objectives attributed to the firm and motivations attached to managers and enterpreneurs.

William Baumol pictures sales maximization as the firm's goal, as opposed to profit maximization in the traditional model. Subject to a minimum profit constraint (adequate profits?), the firm will seek to maximize *total revenue*. The basic premise behind this theory is that business prestige rides heavier on sales than profits, and that business people—particularly oligopolists—are more prone to nonprice competition (advertising, model changes, variety in models, etc.) than to price competition.*

In another theory, developed by Melvin Reder, the primary objective is the entrepreneur's need to retain control of the firm. The entrepreneur allows the firm to grow and make a profit provided that growth does not cause the portion of assets owned personally by the entrepreneur to fall below a required minimum. Until that point, the entrepreneur behaves like the profit maximizer of traditional theory.†

In a third approach, postulated by Kenneth Boulding, the firm is pictured as a homeostatic mechanism (homeostasis is a tendency to return to an original state); in this model the firm seeks to maintain a desired balance-sheet structure; and variance from that structure will cause management to take action to *restore* the structure to its original state.‡

Other models have been developed, but the previous ones are included simply to illustrate the richness in revised positive approaches in terms of alternatives in objectives and managerial motivations ascribed to the firm. The alternative objectives seem to correspond more closely to both observed behavior and the utterances of business executives than does the objective of profit maximization.

---

*W. J. Baumol, "On the theory of oligopoly," *Economica* New Series XXV (August, 1958), pp. 187–89. See also Baumol, *Business Behavior, Value, and Growth*, Rev. Ed. (New York: Harcourt, Brace & World, 1967); Chapter 6.

†M. W. Reder, "A reconsideration of the marginal productivity theory," *The Journal of Political Economy*, LV (October, 1947); pp. 450–8.

‡K. E. Boulding, *A Reconstruction of Economics*. (New York: John Wiley and Sons, Inc., 1950).

MODELS OF MANAGEMENT AND THE MANAGER

A number of scholars choose to center on the manager or management, rather than on the firm as an entity. While we might bring in the whole field of organizational behavior and its related disciplines, we shall restrict our outline to a few descriptions relating most closely to the role of managers in determining the objectives of the firm and in guiding the organization toward those objectives. In essence, we will confine ourselves to those models that modify the traditionally assumed objectives of business behavior — profit and growth.

Thus, for example, Herbert Simon's "Administrative Man" seems to reflect the frailties of real-life managers more than does the powerful, completely rational economic man of classical (or indeed modified) economic theory.* Whereas the imaginary "man" of economic theory is rational, always knows how to act, and can survey all the alternatives confronting him in order to maximize or achieve the established goal, administrative man has *bounded rationality*. With bounded rationality, the manager is seen as having internal and external limits to the exercise of rationality. These limits include "skills, habits, and reflexes which are no longer in the realm of the conscious, . . . his values and those conceptions of purpose which influence him in making decisions, (and) the extent of his knowledge of things relevant to his job." These limitations increase as one progresses up the organizational hierarchy and deals with grosser and more extensive organizational problems. Thus, as Simon points out, he is interested in the "behavior of human beings who *satisfice* because they have not the wits to *maximize*."†

Satisficers select alternatives that may not necessarily maximize, but "are good enough." Administrative Man, then, is the one who is familiar with such terms as share of market, adequate profits, and fair price. He is a nonmaximizer simply because he cannot maximize or figures that maximizing is not worth the effort.

Following along the path of the Simon work is the *Behavioral Theory of the Firm*, by Cyert and March.‡ While the whole theory is much too involved to cover in detail here, in brief it interrelates subtheories of organizational goals, organizational expectations, and organizational choice. The firm is depicted as a coalition of interest groups, and the goals of the total organization become defined and clarified in the process of "side payments" made in response to the various demands of the members of the coalition. Thus, the firm has a high potential for conflict; the model includes mechanisms the firm uses for resolving conflict.

Cyert and March's firm avoids uncertainty through the use of standard plans and procedures when possible and the avoidance of planning when uncertainty

---

*H. A. Simon, *Administrative Behavior*, 2nd ed. (New York: Macmillan Co., 1957.)

†*Ibid.*, pp. 40–41 and xxiv.

‡R. M. Cyert and J. G. March, *A Behavioral Theory of the Firm*. (Englewood Cliffs, N.J.: Prentice-Hall, Inc., 1963).

prevails. The organization will gradually shift goals on the basis of learned experience, will learn to attend to some standards of performance and ignore others, will "learn to pay attention to some parts of (its) comparative environment and ignore others," and will learn to adopt as standard, search patterns for problems which have been successful for solving those problems in the past.

In essence, the firm of Cyert and March is basically a safety-seeking, slowly adapting organization, which changes behavior only if some given arrangement is altered or if some familiar behavior pattern does not succeed.

Another interesting view of the firm and managers, by Monsen and Downs, hypothesizes that "owners desire steady dividend income and gradual stock appreciation, while managers act to maximize their own lifetime earnings." Coupling these motives with a bureaucratic structure, the authors believe, "management will deviate systematically from achieving ownership objectives." The theory then goes on to explain the strategies of managers at various levels of management—top, middle, and lower—in meeting their objectives. In sum, the model assigns the roles of maximizers to managers—only in terms of their own personal incomes—and satisficers to owners—since they are so remote from the firm that it is impossible for them to press for maximization.*

One last description of managers is that of John Kenneth Galbraith, in his book *The New Industrial State*.† Galbraith's thesis is that the modern corporation, because of the imperatives of large-scale production, heavy capital commitments, and sophisticated technology, must plan far into the future. In order to ensure success for the plans, the consumer must be managed so that his behavior will correspond to the needs of the corporation; and the state must be an active participant, moderating economic fluctuations and providing certainty in the economic environment. The key group in the corporation engaging in all this planning and managing, Galbraith calls the *technostructure*, the highly trained and closely knit group that guides the corporation and its environment to the primary end of survival of the firm or the technostructure—in essence, the preservation of management.

AN ORGANIZATIONAL MODEL OF OLIGOPOLY

With the exception of Galbraith's attempt to link a model of management with market activity, very few of the models available form effective links between the various levels of analysis. The following model is one attempt. It builds on the contributions of others and attempts to explain the behavior of firms in oligopoly situations—that is, where there are few enough firms so that the behavior of each firm is interdependent with the reactions and behavior of the others.

In the model, the firm is viewed as a coalition of several elements—very much like the firm in the Cyert and March model. Each of the elements exerts its

---

*J. Monsen and A. Downs, "A theory of large managerial firms," *Journal of Political Economy*, LXXII (June, 1965); pp. 221–236.

†J. K. Galbraith, *The New Industrial State*. (Boston: Houghton Mifflin Company, 1967.)

own demands on the coalition's resources. These elements of the coalition or sources of demands are shareholders, suppliers, customers, labor, management, etc. Focusing on management as a subcoalition in the firm, *management's environment* is viewed as the other coalitional elements.

Management's objective as a subcoalition is to secure and increase its proportion of the firm's resources and payments. In addition, management is viewed as having limited problem-solving capacity and seeks to devote the primary utilization of that capacity to allocating the payments gained in the coalition among members of its own managerial subcoalition. *Management views the allocation of resources amongst its members as its primary problem.*

To accomplish these objectives, management must gain power over its environment—the other elements of the coalition. Briefly, a power position is defined as one in which the opponent's alternatives are closed off and one's own alternatives are maintained.* Power positions for management in relation to other coalitional elements will normally increase payments, increase certainty, reduce problems, and allow management to devote its problem-solving capacity to problems within its own subcoalition. (These managerial subcoalition problems are also viewed in terms of power.)

In terms of the customer element of the coalition (or the firm), management may gain the power it needs by securing a monopoly, but as long as the customer has alternatives (other firms to "join"), management has little power over the customer. One way management can gain power over customers is to seek "agreement" or similar patterns of behavior with other managements facing similar problems. This agreement need not be formal, but could be tacit or what has been called "conscious parallel action"; on the other hand, formal conspiracies are not ruled out either. This "agreement" forms another coalition which we term the "industry organization."

The motives of the member managements to "form" the industry organization are to gain dominance over common environmental elements (in the case being discussed, this means customers), reduce uncertainty in the relations with these elements in order to relieve themselves of some problems, guarantee at least a minimum level of payments to each of the managements, and codify and make consistent rules of competition.

The industry organization will stay in operation and accomplish its purposes as long as it is able to solve its problems, keep communications among its members established and functioning, stave off external threats (i.e., substitute products, foreign products, government action, or coalitions among customers), and keep its individual managements satisfied with their memberships. When the industry organization disintegrates because it can no longer handle its problems or communicate among its members, the oligopoly ceases to exist and the structure of the market becomes basically competitive.

This type of application of concepts from organization theory to the problem of oligopoly is recent and falls into line with the increasing application of

---

*Richard Emerson, "Power dependence relations," *American Sociological Review*, XXVII (February, 1962); pp. 31–32.

organizational, psychological, and sociological concepts to what had effectively been the domain of economic theory. The beauty of much of the work is that it not only gives observers a more realistic description of each of the levels of analysis (in this case, the manager, the firm, and the industry), but provides linkages between the levels of analysis to give the observer accurate descriptions of the whole structural and behavioral processes.

SOME THOUGHTS ON NORMATIVE DOCTRINES AND POSITIVE MODELS

Few of the descriptions examined in this introduction present the manager as a selfless server of humanity. The manager is pictured as either a profitseeker, sales maximizer, self-aggrandizer, survival-seeker, a satisficer, or pain minimizer. Yet certain of these models might accommodate the inclusion of environmental pressures as costs or constraints resulting from power phenomena; and that may be the only link between normative social responsibility doctrine and the real motivations and behavior of management.

By relying on terms of reference such as "Thou shalt because I think it is right," social-responsibility proponents have neglected to build into the system the fact that others with power to act may simply not care or agree that "It is right." Rhetoric aside, there is no solid theoretical or empirical evidence to show that managers engage in social responsibility because it is the "right" thing to do, because some social critic calls for "multiple objectives," or because some reformer says that "a social goal is as important as your private goal." Rather, it is more likely that managers and firms engage in socially responsible activity because it is the advantageous thing to do in terms of the firm's or the managers' welfare. The firm either has something to gain or acts to avoid losing something it already possesses. And if socially responsible activity is not advantageous in those self-interest terms, it simply is not, in most cases, undertaken.

In those terms, the behavior which advocates might label socially responsible is explainable in terms of costs or constraints on the doing of business, much as is Social Security, workmen's compensation, overtime, or fire insurance. With such an outlook, socially responsible actions would be perfectly compatible with the self-interest behavior and motivation described in many of the positive models.

THE READINGS

Our first selection, by Monsen, Saxberg, and Sutermeister, separates the motives of managers from those of the firm. The authors explain several sources of pressure on managers, as well as the nature of these pressures in terms of specific motivational processes and goals. They conclude that "The modern manager desires to maximize his self-interest in terms of lifetime income—but the maximization of lifetime income implies far more than money alone to the manager in contemporary Western society. It often includes other goals and reflects various motivational pressures."

The second article, "Toward a Positive Theory of Corporate Social Involvement," by Arthur Elkins, is an effort to start building theory around corporate social involvement. Elkins writes, "Corporate social expenditure is a positive phenomenon despite the criticism by traditionalists that corporations should stay out of the social area. Whether right or wrong, corporations are engaging in 'social-responsibility' activities." Elkins then attempts to construct five motivational bases to explain why managers move their firms into social involvement; one of those bases is managerial ego satisfaction.

The Modern Manager: What Makes Him RUN?

R. J. Monsen,
B. O. Saxberg, and
R. A. Sutermeister

The development of a cadre of professional managers for publicly owned corporations has brought into focus the divergence between the self-interests of the manager and the interests of the business firm and its owners. This article attempts to integrate organizational behavior theory with recent developments in the economic theory of the firm. The thesis is that the owner-manager of the traditional firm in economic theory has been transformed into the modern professional- and bureaucratic-oriented manager who works to achieve personal goals that may not be the same as the goals of the business.

THE MODERN MANAGER

The motivation of the entrepreneur, in traditional economic theory, has generally been assumed to be that of profit maximization. While other motives (such as the perpetuation of the family firm and the attainment of power and prestige) have been mentioned, traditional economic theory even today relies upon a model in which the firm aims at maximization of profits.* This monistic theory of motivation can be defended where one individual both owns and manages the firm; in this case, his self-interest is congruent with profit maximization. The development of the giant corporation, however, has produced the professional manager, described by one author as follows:

> The primary responsibility for business leadership in the large corporation has devolved upon a group of men who are professional managers. Their position

*For a more extensive treatment of the motivation of the classical entrepreneur, see R. J. Monsen, B. O. Saxberg, and R. A. Sutermeister, "La Motivation Sociologique de L'entrepreneur," *Economie Appliquée,* XVII (December, 1964).

is not achieved through ownership. They are salaried experts, trained by education and experience in the field of management. Though only salaried managers, they find themselves responsible for making the decisions which affect not merely the dividends their stockholders receive but also the price consumers pay, the wages their workers earn, and the level of output and employment in their own firms and in the economy as a whole.*

In the modern giant corporation, ownership is usually diffused among shareholders who are divorced from the management of their corporations; in fact, most managers no longer have large ownership in the corporations they manage. Therefore, changes in the private assets of the managers are not tied directly to changes in the assets of the corporation, and they need not identify with the profit-maximizing goals of the owners. Only if corporate profit or performance falls badly, particularly compared to the performance of the industry as a whole, will the scattered and generally anomalous owners vote management out of office.

What then are the manager goals? The basic desire of the professional manager is to maximize his self-interest or lifetime income in monetary and non-monetary terms.† He may not even attempt to maximize the firm's profits, for such attempts might involve risks endangering his own interests—success in increasing profits may bring a bonus, but losses may mean loss of position and lifetime income.

Public opinion has imposed additional restraints upon pure profit-maximizing behavior. Since the turn of the century, the self-interest of owner-managers has not been accepted as the only legitimate objective of a business firm. Any organizational unit functioning as a social system, such as a firm, exists as a subsystem in society, which ultimately legitimizes the continued existence of its subsystems. Such legislative measures as the Interstate Commerce Act, the Sherman Antitrust Act, the Clayton Act, and the Wagner Act have established the framework within which society permits business to operate.

The transformation of the owner-manager of the traditional firm to the professional manager of the modern firm is reflected in various motivational pressures.

SOURCES OF PRESSURES

Personality

Some of the motivational pressures on the modern manager arise out of his own personality, influenced by family background, education, and the culture of his society. For example, an individual may have an authoritarian personality, reflected, as discussed later, in a pressure for power. Another individual may have a high level of need for achievement.

---

*Robert Aaron Gordon, *Business Leadership in the Large Corporation* (Washington: The Brookings Institution, 1945), p. 318.

†For a complete development of this thesis, see R. Joseph Monsen, Jr., and Anthony Downs, "A Theory of the Large Managerial Firms," *Journal of Political Economy,* LXXIII (June, 1965), pp. 221–36.

The achievement motive in personality

The works of Darwin and Marx lead one to believe that man is mainly adaptive to conditions in the environment. The research carried out by McClelland and his coauthors establishes an interesting case that man is creative in response to consciously or unconsciously internalized motives.* Their investigations have concentrated on the thesis that some people have a greater need for achievement than others. Achievement is not equated with success in financial or material terms, or any other tangible or intangible results; rather, achievement *per se* is the motive, the need, and the goal. The achievement drive in the personality results in needs for such things as money, power, status, and so forth. Economic development depends upon the presence in society of a sufficient number of high achievers; the modal personality of one society may show a higher level of need for achievement than might be found in another.

Though the empirical investigations have not clearly delineated distinctions between entrepreneurs and managers, the results appear to suggest that a preponderance of men in business-leadership positions show high achievement personalities. In this context we are attracted by the finding reported by McClelland that the entrepreneurial manager evidently is not a gambler or habitual risk-taker. Confronted with a choice of potentially high profits in a situation of chance uncertainty, or moderate profits but a strong possibility that he can affect the outcome (a calculable risk), he will choose the latter.

McClelland regards the need for achievement as the crucial component in the personality of the entrepreneur-manager. In a cultural environment where the values of the Protestant ethic form a core, a child internalizes a need for achievement in greater measure than where they are absent. Moreover, the need for achievement is greater in families where children are encouraged to develop early self-mastery and independence; it is also affected by the family's social status. Thus we find that high need for achievement is associated with a middle-class family background in which the father is either a member of a white-collar or professional occupational group, or in business. This also suggests a better-than-average family educational background where education is regarded as an important avenue in improving one's position in life.

The societal culture, as well as the experiences of socialization during childhood, will govern the level of aspirations and establish attitudes toward success and failure. For example, a strong motivating force in the manager's life may be fear of failure *per se*. Our professional managers are interested in maximizing

---

*This work is reported mainly in David C. McClelland, John W. Atkinson, Russell A. Clark, and Edgar L. Lowell, *The Achievement Motive* (New York: Appleton-Century-Crofts, Inc., 1953); David C. McClelland, A. L. Baldwin, U. Bronfenbrenner, and F. L. Strodtbeck, *Talent and Society* (Princeton, N.J.: D. Van Nostrand Co., Inc., 1958); David C. McClelland, *The Achieving Society* (Princeton, N.J.: D. Van Nostrand Co., Inc., 1961). See also the critical evaluation of *The Achieving Society* in Fritz Redlich, "Economic Development, . Entrepreneurship, and Psychologism: A Social Scientist's Critique of McClelland's Achieving Society," *Explorations in Entrepreneurial History* (2d series; Fall, 1963), pp. 10–35.

their lifetime incomes, yet, regardless of monetary rewards, they are likely to be high achievers by the nature of their personality makeup.

If we accept Maslow's need hierarchy as relevant, a man is characterized beyond the needs for security, safety, and love by still higher-level needs, those of esteem and self-actualization. Profits, material wealth, and other tangible aspects of success can serve as a feedback for the entrepreneurial manager, indicating that he is still innovating, still creating. After all, the values, choices, and behavior of other individuals indicate that they compete for a common set of resources. He is therefore conditioned by them to see economic reality in terms of the choices they make. Wood has expressed this as follows: ". . . profits, in a competitive enterprise economy, are an objective test of the social value of ideas and innovations — and the ultimate test of business performance.*

Environmental pressures

Small groups. The executive of the corporation, together with members of top management, establishes the values that will permeate the behavior of the firm as a social system with a culture of its own. The personal value hierarchy of the executive serves to routinize some of the demands of the position, which otherwise might involve him in conflict situations rampant with psychological pressure. It enables him to make social decisions with some confidence. Employees will accept the values of the management and the firm for which they work, just as the executives and the firm itself must function within the value system of society as a whole. But it should also be acknowledged that there are, within the business enterprise, a number of collectives or groups based on hierarchical level, occupation, or some other unifying base, and characterized by value systems of their own. The values within these social systems may conflict or even be mutually exclusive — they remain ideals or standards whereby judgments and evaluations are made. Each member will therefore choose a value hierarchy that will provide for him a set of personal operative values.

Throughout his lifetime the manager will belong to numerous membership groups, such as social or business clubs, the values of which he will not necessarily embrace. It is significant that as long as such an organizational group functions only as a membership group the executive personality shows little effect from this membership. Many groups, however, go beyond this function and are, in fact, reference groups; their values are internalized in the member, forcing a commitment from him. Even though a reference group may later be reduced to the status of a membership group only, it is unlikely that the member will totally eradicate the influence of its values. In addition, there are groups to which he aspires that also serve as reference groups. In each case, through anticipatory socialization, his behavior reflects an approach to and adoption of the values he has imputed to the group. Thus, within the context of the business organization, the executive is subject to considerable pressure as he constantly tries to decide with which group's values his behavior should conform.

---

*Laurence I. Wood, "The Corporation and Society," Conference on Education for Business (Crotonville, N.Y.: Aug. 2, 1963), p. 5. (Speech by vice-president and general counsel of General Electric.)

The immediate social environment of the manager contains a number of other small groups that exert pressure on his motivation. The most important groups within the firm are those of other managers and employees. Outside the firm are groups of peers, that is, managers of other businesses who meet for lunch, at clubs, or in community organizations. Competitors also affect the entrepreneur's motivations. Thus, it can be said that "modern management — especially in the large corporation — operates in a group setting, with group decisions — and group attitudes, constraints, and aspirations — although individual roles may be sharply differentiated."*

The relationships between the small groups inside and outside the firm and the various motivations of the entrepreneur are numerous and complex. If the entrepreneur is facing difficult competition in his industry, he may be motivated primarily to protect his own security by increasing his competence, and quite secondarily to increase his power, build up his status, and earn prestige from competitors. A manager who is seeking satisfactory relationships and interactions with his fellow managers strives for recognition, status, and prestige through their approval of his actions. Therefore, the manager's peers have a major effect upon the direction of his motivation. A manager interested in gaining approval from his subordinates may be more concerned with his actions, interactions, and the prestige enjoyed with this group than with competence and power. Likewise, if he is interested in his employees as individuals, he may be motivated by a desire to help them develop their own abilities.

Large external groups. The executive of the firm is under further motivational pressure from a number of large societal groups that form the external environment for the firm in modern industrial society. The major ones — unions, government competitors, church, and educational institutions — play varying roles of importance in a manager's life. As restraints or incentives they affect his motivation — to action or inaction.

In recent times, behavior toward *unions* by professional managers in corporations with broadly diffused ownership has been strikingly different from that characterized by the typical two-person zero-sum game imagined in classical economic theory.† The modern manager's motivation stems from the fact that promotion within many large companies depends upon having, among other qua-

---

*C. Addison Hickman, "Managerial Motivations and the Theory of the Firm," *The American Economic Review,* XLV (May, 1955), p. 550.

†The main effect of the trade union upon the motivation of the traditional entrepreneur is essentially that of an opponent in a game in which the less the entrepreneur concedes to the union the greater the return to him will be, as in the typical case of the two-person zero sum game. Likewise, the position of the union is essentially that of an opponent whose aim is to increase his share of the company income as much as possible. Traditionally the entrepreneur, therefore, is expected to be motivated by both fear of the union as an adversary and by the desire to enhance his own position and firm profit as much as possible by opposing the union's demands. This can be described as the classical type of impact of the union upon the entrepreneur.

lifications, a good "record with labor." As he becomes viewed as more of a conciliator between opposing groups—stockholders, unions, government, and consumers—the manager who is the most amiable and conciliatory, and whose decisions are less often attacked, often makes the most rapid rise in the modern corporate hierarchy.

In the modern large-scale enterprise, we question whether the two-person zero-sum game in the classical firm, with the manager on one side and the union on the other, applies; it is often management's own gain to solve speedily any labor crisis, even if the solution might be adverse in the long run to the company. The explanation for this may be that the manager has more to gain in income, status, and career opportunities by being conciliatory toward labor and unions than he has by driving a hard bargain to increase profits for the stockholders and the company in which he may own no or very few shares.

The *government* affects the motivations of the entrepreneur largely through taxation and regulation. In the classical firm the entrepreneur is thought of as resisting all government intervention in his decision-making and, in particular, increased tax burdens upon the firm because they lessen his own personal profit and income. This strong classical ideology is still quite common among management men and members of various industry associations.

However, in the large firm with diffused ownership, the ideology held by management is usually more liberal, and allows for a governmental role that is still commonly rejected by owner-managers of small businesses. The attitude prevailing in modern professional management is frequently referred to as the "managerial ideology," in contrast to the classical ideology of business. In the managerial ideology, management may resent government regulations, particularly as they impinge on their own sphere of decision-making. However, they are largely resigned to the influence of government; in fact, their business often depends upon government as a major purchaser. In addition, they are usually consulted in governmental decision-making more than management in middle-size and small business. Therefore, they actually have fewer feelings of alienation. Moreover, government taxation policies have less impact upon professional management because their income stems mainly from fixed salary, stock options, and company expense accounts, which are less directly related to company profits than the income of the owner-entrepreneur. Professional managers, then, generally think of the government as a cooperating partner. It is not possible to make blanket statements about the impact of government upon managerial behavior. It is more feasible to consider managers as representatives of distinct, though frequently overlapping, interest groups, holding ideologies that reflect their socioeconomic position and background. This also explains why business groups frequently exhibit very different patterns and degrees of frustration and antagonism toward governmental policies.

Various industry and business associations reinforce particular ideologies of management. Generally, such associations are based more upon industry aims and economic interests. They tend to call pragmatically upon government for whatever may be to their advantage.

The *competition* of other businesses obviously has a strong effect upon the motivation of professional managers. In the modern firm where the mores and rules of playing the game may be different from those in the classical firm, the competitor's image of himself as a professional manager is also likely to affect his behavior. To some degree, all managers think of themselves as members of a professional fraternity with certain horizontal mobility. As long as a manager's image as "a good manager" remains intact, his opportunity to move out and up in other firms is good. Thus, the modern manager plays to an audience (if indeed the managers of competing firms can be thought of as an audience).

In large oligopolistic industries (with firms involved in price-fixing or combined in cartels), one firm often considers other firms less as competitors than as cooperators with whom the market is shared, and with whom policies are compared and standardized, as among members of a professional management fraternity. How oligopolistic or monopolistic an industry may be, or how competitive it may be, therefore, will affect management motivation and behavior.

The impact of *religious affiliation* upon the motivation of entrepreneurs is difficult to determine in contemporary society. Certainly in the industrial revolution in England, various Protestant sects, such as the Quakers, originally played an influential part. It has become increasingly difficult to say that the Protestants in modern America have shown a greater entrepreneurial spirit than any other group. It is often argued that churches, although memberships are soaring, are having less effect upon the behavior of their members than they had upon earlier, more inner-directed generations. There is some evidence that today's other-directed individual, in Riesman's terms, responds much more readily to peer groups or economic interest groups than to religious organizations.* If this is so, business behavior might more easily be explained in contemporary society by psychological and sociological variables than by the religious or philosophical differences that Weber originally found in an earlier and perhaps more inner-directed society of previous generations.

The prestige of our *educational institutions* has increased tremendously. Today, more than ever before, schools and universities are the major institutions that transmit cultural values and norms in our society. At the primary levels particularly, they may affect the personality of the individual through cultural conditioning. In this process seldom can one escape the pervasive impact of our educational institutions on his way of thinking or acting.

At the college level, programs are increasingly oriented toward professionalization. The graduate school of business itself is rapidly attempting to make management a profession, and the modern professional manager is accredited by his M.B.A. In addition, education often affects his motivation by raising his level of aspiration and achievement needs.

Bureaucracy. Concern has been expressed by Riesman that the inner-directed man of the Protestant ethic is being replaced by an other-directed man in res-

---

*For additional information on the "other-directed" man, see David Riesman, *The Lonely Crowd* (New Haven, Conn.: Yale University Press, 1950).

ponse to the demands of bureaucratically organized work and life conditions. Instead of having a man equipped with a gyroscope that sets the course, we have developed a radar-equipped man constantly tuning in for course and direction from those surrounding him—mass society *par preference*. Whyte acknowledges this development in his description of "the organization man," who is geared to become a member of any group that he judges will further him in the business organization, and who regards success in terms of teamwork and group membership rather than individual performance and achievement.* Dale sharpens this question:

> ... shortcomings of the new managers seems to be distrust of innovation in procedures and practices. 'What are other companies doing?' is the question most commonly asked management associations. . . . The manager thinks of himself as a problem solver rather than as an innovator, and as such he seeks a ready-made solution rather than striking out on his own in a search for something better than anyone has yet tried.†

In Whyte's terms, the Protestant ethic has been replaced by a social ethic where "belonging" occupies a preferred position. Fromm has commented on the prevalence of the market-oriented personality—a man is worth something only in terms of the package of salable goods he represents and the demand that exists for it. Finally, Presthus speaks of the pressures of bureaucratically run organizations whose employees are characterized by addiction to routine and mediocrity, with deference to superiors and willingness to conform to the organizational requirements. The modal personality, developed in such a bureaucratic context and characterized by these qualities of conformity, is represented by the upward mobiles who know how to use the bureaucratic apparatus to their advantage as they make their way in the organization. They are likely to become the business leaders of the future. They leave behind them the great mass of indifferent employees who never cared to identify with the objectives and goals of the organization in the first place or became frustrated in the process, and the ambivalent who are imaginative and creative nonconformists frustrated by the bureaucracy in achieving the success they deem they have merited.

In designing the elements of his bureaucratic theory, Weber took into account only the structural parts of the organization and the anticipated consequences from this theoretical scheme.‡ In reality, as complex organizations have approached the conditions of bureaucracy outlined by Weber, unanticipated consequences have appeared in the satisfying of personal objectives by the organizations' personnel, including managers.

---

*References in this paragraph to William H. Whyte, Jr., *The Organization Man* (Garden City, N.Y.: Doubleday & Company, Inc., 1957).

†Ernest Dale, "Executives Who Can't Manage," *The Atlantic,* CCIX (July, 1962), p. 61.

‡Max Weber, *The Theory of Social and Economic Organizations* (New York: Oxford University Press, 1947).

Social responsibilities. The firm is usually assumed to have four broad areas of social responsibility: the stockholders, the employees, the customers, and the government. Many stockholders claim that they are "the forgotten men." Generally, they are not given a great deal of information about the running of the company, and management usually feels that it fulfills its responsibility by maintaining the traditional dividend and seeing that the price of the stock follows the market relatively closely, at least on the upside. Recent court cases, however, have held that management owes to the stockholder wise and prudent decisions and a separation between the interests of the company and management's own financial interests.

The employees of the firm represent another area of obligation. The long-run trend has been for firms to assume increasing responsibility for the employment, health, and retirement of its employees. Part of this obligation, of course, has been assumed by government. Such concerns as safety regulations on the job have been pursued by both government and unions. Generally, the larger the company the more security it offers its workers in the form of sickness and retirement benefits. Unions have attempted to provide workers with bargaining power and have thus enabled them to exact various fringe benefits.

In this century, government regulations and agencies such as the Pure Food and Drug Administration, as well as consumer cooperatives and consumer testing groups, have provided increasing protection for the consumer. Firms today, then, do have some checks upon them beyond the power of the consumer to withdraw patronage; in the last analysis, however, the customer's main protection is to deal with firms of established reputation. The market mechanism still ultimately rewards the firms that can produce most efficiently. There exists, therefore, a premise that firms need to maintain a satisfactory image with their customers.

The firm's responsibility to the government can be separated into three areas: payment of taxes and conformance with regulations, adherence to specifications on products sold to the government, and compliance with verbal inducements by the government in the interest of avoiding price increases and other forms of economic and social unrest. Growth in the direct and indirect power of the government has brought about a change in the government's relations with business. The reluctance of U.S. Steel to avert a price increase until President Kennedy resorted to threats, or the exposure of illegal price-fixing by General Electric, Westinghouse, and other electrical goods manufacturers, indicates that a business philosophy of social obligation has not yet been fully accepted.

The concept of social responsibility of business and of stockholders, consumers, labor, and government has, in the course of recent history, become increasingly emphasized. The business firm has little choice but to be aware of the social responsibility attributed to it by the public.

Thus the pressures on the manager stem from a number of sources. The accompanying figure is a representation of these pressures and the sources from which they derive.

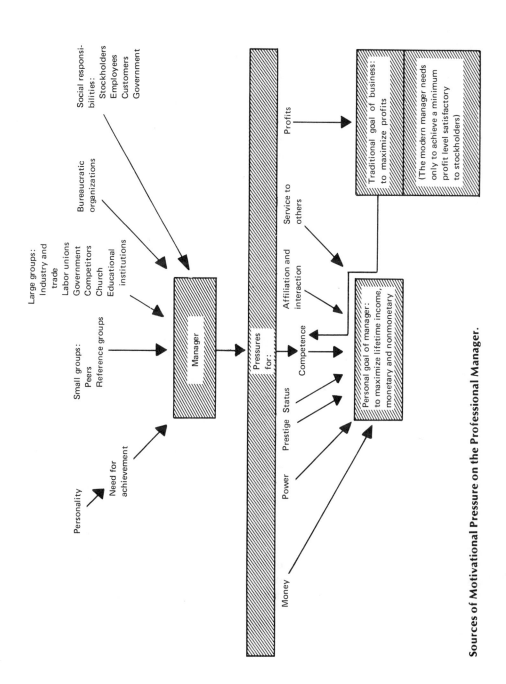

Sources of Motivational Pressure on the Professional Manager.

NATURE OF PRESSURES

The sources of motivational pressures on the professional manager have been discussed. The manager responds to these pressures by striving for specific intermediate goals in order to attain his personal goal of maximizing his lifetime income in both monetary and nonmonetary terms.

Money

The need for money derives from strong sociological as well as financial motives. Money serves in our society as a general symbol of success and thus becomes an indication in the marketplace of power, status, prestige, and competence.

Power

Managers frequently are possessed by an urge for personal power—control of resources, and freedom to manipulate persons and events both inside and outside the firm. In our society the enhancement of personal power is suspect; yet, in recognition of the concrete existence of personal power as a managerial motive, the prevalence of authoritarian personalities in executive positions is widely accepted. Hagen, for example, speaks of the authoritarian personality as one in which ". . . satisfaction in yielding to the judgment and wishes of superiors and satisfaction in dominating inferiors are interwoven." He further states:

> An individual who thus perceives each contact with other persons as involving a danger of conflict and a threat of pain may conceive of dominating others rather than merely attacking them as a solution to the threat and an outlet for the rage which is within him. This need will express itself as a need to obtain performance from others by command, to influence or direct the behavior of others, to affect others so as to obtain desired performance from them.‡

There are, in practice, various ways in which power is reflected. The manager may be characterized by an authoritarian personality indifferent to the attitudes and needs of subordinate executives and employees; at the other extreme, he may be quite solicitous of and responsive to the ideas and feelings of his subordinates and go out of his way to gain acceptance of his authority. Tannenbaum and Schmidt view the various styles of leadership, ranging from autocratic to democratic, as points along a continuum; as one moves from the extreme autocratic to the extreme democratic style of leadership, unilateral decision-making through the use of authority by the manager decreases, and the area of freedom in decision-making by his subordinates increases.* The style of leadership chosen by a manager, then, partially reflects the motivations of his personality structure.

---

‡Everett Hagen, *On the Theory of Social Change* (Homewood, Ill.: The Dorsey Press, 1962), pp. 73, 108.

*Robert Tannenbaum and Warren H. Schmidt, "How to Choose a Leadership Pattern," *Harvard Business Review,* XXXVI (March-April, 1958), pp. 95–101.

Status and prestige

Status refers to the position a person occupies in an organizational hierarchy or social system. Prestige, on the other hand, refers to his personal qualities in commanding the respect and admiration of others. Parsons points out several standards by which status can be measured: birth—membership in a particular family (which may include a company presidency), social class, race, or sex; personal qualities—age, strength, intelligence, and personality; achievements—results of personal efforts and the success that has thereby accrued to the company; possessions—especially such belongings as cars, houses, clothes, jewels, and art; and authority—the right to command action, frequently legitimized by being tied directly to a defined hierarchical position.*

The manager automatically achieves considerable status when he becomes his firm's top executive, and may move quickly to acquire the proper status symbols. These include money, usually considered an economic incentive only, titles, an elaborately decorated office, membership in elite clubs, and a home in the "right" neighborhood. These symbols are extremely important in the United States with its "success" culture and its high degree of spatial and social mobility.†

Prestige is generally considered to be conferred by others and may involve fellow employees, colleagues in other businesses, stockholders, the public, and customers.‡

Maslow's hierarchy of needs emphasizes esteem as one of the high-level needs, including self-esteem based on respect and esteem from others.§ Thus, peer groups and other reference groups may often activate the latent desire of the entrepeneur for status, prestige, recognition, and importance.

---

*Based upon Talcott Parsons, *Essays in Sociological Theory Pure and Applied* (New York: Free Press of Glencoe, Inc., 1949), pp. 171–72. Parson's sixth standard of power, which he defines as status achieved by illegitimate means, has been omitted from this list.

†The reports about the increasing voluntary and involuntary professional mobility of corporation executives bear out the loss of the traditionally assumed close identification between the objectives of the company and those of its management. Managers today exhibit a marked change from a firm- or job-oriented view to a management profession-oriented view. See Seymour Freegood, "The Churning Market for Executives," *Fortune,* LXXII (September, 1965), pp. 152–54 ff.

‡Based upon William G. Scott, "Executive Incentives and Constraints in the Corporate Setting," *Human Relations in Management* (Homewood, Ill.: Richard D. Irwin, Inc., 1962), p. 361 ff.

§A. H. Maslow, "A Theory of Human Motivation," *Psychological Review,* L (July, 1943), pp. 370–96.

Competence

There is little doubt that a strong motivating pressure on managers is the desire to do [their] work efficiently. At its simplest, this striving for competence can be attributed to fear of failure and a desire for security. At higher levels it is more likely to be a striving for excellence, a desire to be creative, or a desire to fulfill a need for self-actualization. As well as seeking intrinsic satisfaction, the manager may also cherish the recognition and prestige that will be conferred on him by competitors, fellow executives, and employees.

Many entrepreneurs are perhaps unconsciously motivated by a need to understand and manipulate their physical environment. In the broadest sense, they like to make things happen, to create events rather than merely await them passively.* For them the prosperity and growth of the firm become the outward manifestations of competence. Even if higher profits are not forthcoming, they may still be motivated by this strong desire for excellence—to do the job well for its own sake.

Affiliation and interaction

Although some entrepreneurs are probably satisfied with a pure power relationship over subordinates, others may desire to develop affective relationships and interactions with them. Some managers work hard to establish a personal bond with associates and subordinates to earn respect not only as competent managers but as individual human beings. Such a manager may, as Likert says, ". . . adapt his behavior to take into account the expectations, values, and interpersonal skills of those with whom he is interacting." He may choose to focus his attention on the personal worth of the subordinate and subscribe to Likert's principle of supportive relationships:

> The leadership and other processes of the organization must be such as to ensure a maximum probability that in all interactions and all relationships with the organization each member will, in the light of his background, values, and expectations, view the experience as supportive and one which builds and maintains his sense of personal worth and importance.†

Other managers may view successful personal interaction with others as a means of increasing the level of performance of the firm. Instead of emphasizing the formal organization as the instrument for achieving the firm's objectives, they stress the informal relations that cut across the formal organization structure ". . . when its own chain of command or decision or communication is tied

---

*See Robert W. White, "Motivation Reconsidered: The Concept of Competence," *Psychological Review,* LXVI (September, 1959), pp. 297–333. White treats the competence motive as one felt by most people, not just by entrepreneurs.

†Rensis Likert, *New Patterns of Management* (New York: McGraw-Hill Book Co., Inc., 1961), p. 95. Quote in preceding paragraph, p. 103.

into the informal network of groups within the organization, so that the network can be used to support the organization's goals.*

Service to others

Although it is not always readily recognized, there are managers who are motivated to subordinate self-interests and devote their efforts exclusively to serving the firm or the public, employees, and customers. Thus a manager's personal ambitions may change into a powerful desire to serve the business enterprise itself as an independent and living entity. Others may be concerned with the needs and development of subordinates:

> I believe it is practical and relevant to attempt a conceptual framework from which to derive practical applications in daily management and I believe that it is pertinent and sound for us, as managers, to concern ourselves with man's eternal struggle within himself to be free and yet to be ordered. I believe it is of special importance for us in management to attempt to rescue talented individuals from the lowered aspirations, the boredom, and the habits of mediocrity so often induced by life in an organization. I believe we should become painfully aware that we have established organizational settings in which order, harmony, and predictability have been given more emphasis than individual achievement and excellence. I believe that business management must continue to try to develop a process of life that strives for meaning and purpose, having as our goal the climate which permits every person to serve the values that have nurtured him, with the freedom of the mature and the responsible.†

Though behavior thus labeled as service to others can be altruistic, it is more likely to be related to the entrepreneur's personal motives to achieve prestige and rewarding personal relationships through interaction with the social environment.

Most entrepreneurs are probably motivated by a combination of psychological and sociological factors including desires for sufficient competence and power to ensure the perpetuation of the business and their own security, a position of status in the organization, in the industry, and in the community, and prestige or respect from all those with whom they associate.

This discussion of the interrelationships of economic self-interest theory and organizational behavior theory reveals the behavior of the modern professional manager to be necessarily at odds with the postulates of traditional economic theory. His interests are not identical to those of the owners of the firm. The modern manager desires to maximize his self-interest in terms of lifetime in-

---

*Bernard Berelson and Gary A. Steiner, *Human Behavior* (New York: Harcourt, Brace and World, Inc., 1964), p. 370.

†James E. Richard, "A President's Experience with Democratic Management," in Paul R. Lawrence and others, *Organizational Behavior and Administration* (Homewood, Ill.: The Dorsey Press and Richard D. Irwin, Inc., 1961), p. 896.

come—but the maximization of lifetime income implies far more than money alone to the manager in contemporary Western society. It often involves other goals and reflects various motivational pressures.

Many times these pressures are conflicting in nature and place the manager under considerable strain. The strain increases when there is a conflict between achieving his own personal objectives and working toward maximum profits for the firm. It is our contention that the manager will most frequently resolve the conflict by emphasizing his own personal goals.

Toward a Positive Theory of Corporate Social Involvement

Arthur Elkins

Within the past two decades of active corporate involvement in social problems and issues, hundreds of books and articles have been published on the pros and cons of the doctrine of corporate social responsibility (e.g., 11, 19, 21, 29).* Although few observers—including scholars and practitioners—can agree on a universal definition of social responsibility, the doctrine is the topic of conferences, seminars and training programs. The literature contains a host of prescriptions for corporate action, ranging from a "middle" approach advocated by the Committee for Economic Development (7) and the proposals of Preston and Post (25), to the reformist ideas of Linowes (19), Sethi and Votaw (29), to the critical and traditional opposition of Friedman (13), Manne (20) and Heyne (16). Indeed, *Business and Society Review* is almost totally devoted to social responsibility issues, and its ideological commitment to a reform posture is quite clear.

But most of the writing in the "field" seems to be normative or prescriptive. Aside from a limited number of surveys of corporate response to social issues (4, 6, 8, 21), or corporate commitment to pollution abatement (18), and citations of individual programs, little positive literature is available on the firm and its social activities. Few writers, for example, study the reasons "why" corporations engage in what they call socially responsible behavior.

Many management writers glibly accept prescriptive reasons for corporate social activity, assuming that managers and corporations engage in social activity primarily because of ethical, moral, or societal reasons. While these may be reasons cited in corporate public relations releases, there is no a priori reason to suspect that they are the real motivations.

Reprinted by permission from *Academy of Management Review* (January, 1977), pp. 128–133.

*Numbers refer to reference list at end of articles.

This article attempts to open up a discussion and perhaps will spur further theory building and empirical research on the real motivating forces for socially related activities by corporations and managers. Corporate social expenditure is a positive phenomenon despite the critiques of traditionalists that corporations should stay out of the social area. Whether right or wrong, corporations are engaging in "social responsibility" activities.

For example, insurance funds and companies pledged $2 billion to the development of inner city cores (2). Paper and chemical companies have voluntarily cleaned up pollution. Levi Strauss hired and trained unskilled minorities. Polaroid was involved in affirmative action before the concept became fashionable or even compulsory. Both Polaroid and a major New York bank started programs for the rehabilitation of released convicts (17). Several hundred corporations were involved in the JOBS program. Social responsibility also includes the more traditional corporate monetary contributions that now total some $950 million and have varied in ten years from .75 to 1.25 percent of taxable corporate profits (9).

Although sympathetic observers may *think* or wish that executives are engaging in an ethically based campaign, neither they nor the cynics, who may believe that executives are simply pulling the wool over the public's eyes, can explain corporate motivations for social expenditure with anything near certainty.

It is time to challenge the rhetoric which ascribes all corporate social activity to morally "correct" motives, and indicts other less active firms as morally bankrupt. Management scholars should try to understand what really motivates managers and executives to take on activities in the social sphere.

This article constructs five motivational bases—four briefly and one in some detail—in an effort to explain "why". No claim to constructing the definitive theory of corporate social involvement is made. The purpose simply is to initiate research into this relatively new phenomenon.

"CORPORATE MORALITY"

Some corporate executives obviously do treat social activity as an ethical imperative; they feel that they are responding to "higher" moral principles and exhibit a missionary zeal in directing corporate activities to socially oriented ends. Perhaps Edwin Land at Polaroid and the late Eli Goldston of Eastern Gas and Fuel Associates can be named as individual executives who genuinely believe in the social mission of business and who try to implement decisions based on perceived moral, ethical, or societal values. Such executives are not concerned with whether complete closure is attained in defining social responsibility or in categorizing activities to be included. The important point is that corporations "get involved in good actions".

While more than a few executives would want the public to ascribe their behavior to the "nobler" motives, one can assume that as a real motivating force behind corporate social activity, the ethical imperative is rare. Much of the proffered moral concern rationalizing corporate social activity may be only a subterfuge for more traditional business values.

PROTECTIVE STRATEGY

For many firms, corporate social responsibility is extremely inexpensive insurance. They engage in social responsibility for fear of physical loss if they do not, or to try to placate aroused, militant communities. Social responsibility rhetoric and socially responsive activities surged following riots in Watts, Detroit, and Newark. In periods of social quiet, both rhetoric and activity often seem to subside.

One can pass normative judgments on the propriety of paying to keep the firm secure, but in positive terms, this "defense posture" is a legitimate explanation for social involvement.

PUBLIC RELATIONS AND ADVERTISING

Some corporations undertake social activity because of the public relations or advertising value. Given the high cost of product advertising and the immense amount of "free" news-type public relations releases that media will carry, corporations may find it less expensive to spend money on social activities and receive the free public relations exposure, than to spend large sums on paid product advertising. One commentator attributes much of Levi Strauss' activities to their product market of socially active young (5).

Conversely, the purpose of social activities may be to overcome the negative effects of other corporate product or employment activity. For example, some corporations involved in defense business during the Vietnam War, particularly with such products as napalm and anti-personnel mines and bombs, are now heavily into social involvement. Having suffered public relations setbacks because of the manufacture of lethal weapons, they are now trying to generate a better public image by job training, Native American reservation projects, and self-initiated pollution control projects. More importantly, managers are trying to inform the public about these actions.

PROFIT SEEKING LABELED SOCIAL RESPONSIBILITY

For some corporations and managers, social responsibility is just traditional profit-seeking clad in another garb. The Committee for Economic Development actually prescribed this motive under the rubric of self-interest (7), but it is a primary motive in the positive sense as well. Companies which sell street lighting to cities should be willing to undertake street-lighting surveys for inner cities, not necessarily in the interests of reducing crime as is often stated, but to sell more street lights. Firms that offer grants for research into the effects of multi-media instruction would be acting in their own self-interest if they were sellers of audio-visual equipment. Computer manufacturers have done complete work flow surveys for cities and states in order to sell the computer installation and the various software packages, although the efficient operation of state and local governments may be advertised as the goal of the effort.

THE MANAGERIAL EGO SATISFACTION MODEL

How can one understand the college support, community fund support, and myriad other activities that seem unrelated to corporate protection, corporate profit, or corporate products? Another possible explanation is offered where none of the above would relate. With the primary purpose of leading to further research, this positive model approach uses fairly elementary, but well-documented theoretical and empirical behavioral and economic constructs, and centers not on corporate or organization behavior, but on the desires and needs of managers. Many commentators have hypothesized that managerial motivation may not be consonant with stated corporate goals or that corporate direction may really be dictated by the goals of controlling managers, despite formal organizational goal statements to the contrary (23). This is the basis of the proposed "Managerial Ego Satisfaction Model".

The model uses four interrelated parts: corporate concentration and power; pure profit, organizational slack or discretionary resources; separation of ownership and management; and hierarchy of needs governing individual behavior.

Corporate concentration and power. Few observers of business would deny that most business firms have some degree of power (3, 26). Indeed, an initial slogan of social responsibility proponents was the admonition to business firms to "use your power responsibly".

Empirically, one need only scan the data on concentration ratios to realize that most major industries—four-digit Standard Industrial Classifications—are securely controlled by the top 20 companies and in most instances by the top eight or even four (3, 26, 28). But even low concentration ratios may be deceiving. If concentration ratios for drugstores were available, they would undoubtedly show low sales concentration. But the corner drugstore may still be blessed snuggly with a three or four block monopoly, and even if such businesses do not possess these unique little monopolies, they often have a professional association where activities are geared to mitigate the effects of competition. Bar associations, medical associations and licensing arrangements among trades and professions also mitigate the rigors of competition and simulate the results of monopoly control.

So the first construct is that business firms generally have power in the marketplace, resulting from either market structural imperfections or cooperative efforts on the part of business firms to mitigate against the rigors of competition.

Discretionary Resources. Corporations in industries that exhibit high conentration ratios and businesses that are less than competitive possibly have some degree of what economists call pure profit and organization theorists label organizational slack (10). One cannot go overboard with this generalization, because some corporations, even pure monopolies, fail and some may be so badly managed or marginal that even a monopoly position in a necessary product market would not help. Or they may have a monopoly in a non-existent market—e.g., buggy whips—or a market where the product loses out to a new technological development—vacuum tubes to transistors, for example.

Pure profits and organizational slack do not relate to the accounting concept of profits. Accounting is simply a recording of what management or some regulating agency determines to be revenues and costs; discretionary resources must include not only the profit pile left over after all accounting costs are recorded, but also those costs which add to managerial well-being, are not necessary for the generation of the achieved level of sales, and are under the control of management for expenditure. For example, the plush carpeting or designer furniture in the president's office or the extra laboratory technicians in the R&D department may be a cost (capitalized or expensed) to the corporation, reflected that way on the corporate books. But another way of looking at those expenditures is as allocations of a discretionary resource under the control of management, since the expenditures may have little if any effect on the generated level of sales. If these costs were not incurred, they would be reflected as the profits that they truly are.

Thus the second construct of this model is that firms generally have discretionary resources available for disposition.

Separation of ownership and management. Studies from Berle and Means (1) to Schumpeter (27), Monsen and Downs (23), and Galbraith (14), show that managers hold a firm lock on real decision centers and that stockholders are relatively powerless (although this lack of power may be changing with the growth of pension and investment funds).

Shareholders, supposedly the recipients of corporate profit and the dictators of corporate direction and objectives, are relatively passive and powerless figures in almost all cases. No more than a handful of proxy challenges to incumbent managements have been successful. It is a rare day when management backed proposals are defeated at an annual meeting or when a shareholder proposal that management does not support is passed. Even Campaign GM, a project backed by the material and prestige resources of the Nader groups, achieved only a two percent vote at the GM shareholders meeting (12, p. 452). Thus, top managers retain almost absolute autonomy in decision-making on corporate direction (3).

In summary, the model has managers generally operating (a) under conditions of market power, (b) usually with discretionary resources, and (c) with general decision autonomy. What makes those managers operate? What motivates powerful top executives to continued activity? Although executives in high positions could appropriate additional resources to personal use, that may not be the answer. Top level executives are already very well paid, with stock option plans, sheltered income plans, pension systems, and other income devices. They generally have other perquisites of high managerial position, such as automobiles, carpets, personal secretaries, and first class travel. More personal income or material benefits are not necessary.

Individual needs. Management literature is replete with models of motivation drawn chiefly from psychology (e.g., 15, 22). Despite problems in applying the formulae, and failure to verify some specific models, there is general agreement that needs may vary according to the levels of resources available to the individual. Economists have long used the concept of diminishing marginal utility and the psychological theories of Maslow and Herzberg are quite consistent with this economic idea.

Using "higher level" needs of the various psychological and managerial approaches, in this model, managers might be motivated to use their decision autonomy to allocate some available discretionary resources, gained through their corporation's market power, to take on activities *from which they personally derive psychic satisfaction or credit.* In other words, they might commit the organization to projects under the rubric of "social responsibility" when in fact they are fulfilling their own ego needs.

For example, colleges need funds and in exchange may offer honorary degrees, building names, or distinguished lectureships. Honorary chairmanships of many campaigns are exchangeable for corporate resources and for the time that the corporation executive makes available; the charity gains prestige from having the corporate officer from a large organization (not to mention the large contribution) and the corporate officer gains prestige from being asked and recognized.

Publicity, recognition, fame, respectability, and the like may be goals for the corporate executive who has plenty of personal resources. Corporate officers who have a great deal of organizational resources at their disposal, have decision power, and are well satisfied personally with material possessions will strive to move the corporation (and use its resources) in directions that result in the executive gaining ego satisfaction and recognition.

SUMMARY AND CONCLUSION

The purpose of this article is to initiate work, both theoretical and empirical, toward understanding the real reasons why corporations engage in social responsibility. Four rather simple models have been presented, and some elementary constructs have been interrelated to build a model based on managerial self-interest.

Corporate social activity is a positive phenomenon. It is time to move from the relatively soft normative — almost sermonizing — approach to the generation of positive knowledge of the real motivating factors involved in that ongoing phenomenon.

REFERENCES

1. Berle, Adolph A., and Gardiner C. Means. *The Modern Corporation and Private Property* (New York: Macmillan, 1932).

2. "Billion Dollar Programs Reviewed," *Response,* No. 8 (July 1973).

3. Blumberg, Phillip I. *The Megacorporation in American Society* (Englewood Cliffs, N.J.: Prentice-Hall, 1976).

4. Brown, James K., and Seymour Lusterman. *Business and the Development of Ghetto Enterprise* (New York: The Conference Board, 1971).

5. Burck, Gilbert. "The Hazards of Corporate Responsibility," *Fortune,* June 1973).

6. Cohn, Jules. "Is Business Meeting the Challenge of Urban Affairs?" *Harvard Business Review,* Vol. 48 (March-April 1970).

7. Committee for Economic Development. *Social Responsibilities of Corporations* (New York: CED, 1971).

8. Corson, John J., and George A. Steiner. *Measuring Business's Social Performance: The Corporate Social Audit* (New York: Committee for Economic Development, 1974).

9. Council for Financial Aid to Education, Inc. *Corporation Support for Higher Education* (New York: CFAE, 1972).

10. Cyert, Richard M., and James G. March. *A Behavioral Theory of the Firm* (Englewood Cliffs, N.J.: Prentice-Hall, 1963).

11. Eells, Richard. *The Meaning of Modern Business* (New York: Columbia University Press, 1960).

12. Elkins, Arthur, and Dennis W. Callaghan. *A Managerial Odyssey: Problems in Business and Its Environment* (Reading, Mass.: Addison-Wesley, 1975).

13. Friedman, Milton. "The Social Responsibility of Business is to Increase Its Profits," *New York Times Magazine,* September 13, 1970, pp. 33, 122–26.

14. Galbraith, John Kenneth. *The New Industrial State* (Boston: Houghton Mifflin, 1967).

15. Herzberg, Frederick. *Work and the Nature of Man* (Cleveland: World Publishing Co., 1966).

16. Heyne, Paul T. *Private Keepers of the Public Interest* (New York: McGraw-Hill, 1968).

17. "How Social Responsibility Became Institutionalized," *Business Week*, June 30, 1973.

18. Laury, James R., Michael Gennett, and Richard J. Olsen. "Pollution Control in the 500 Largest United States Industrial Corporations," *Report #6*, Bureau of Business Research, Ball State University, February 1975.

19. Linowes, David. *The Corporate Conscience* (New York: Hawthorn Books, 1975).

20. Manne, Henry G., and Henry C. Wallich. *The Modern Corporation and Social Responsibility* (Washington, D.C.: American Enterprise Institute, 1972).

21. McKie, James W. *Social Responsibility and the Business Predicament* (Washington: Brookings, 1975).

22. Maslow, A. H. *Motivation and Personality.* (New York: Harper, 1954).

23. Monsen, R. J., and A. Downs. "A Theory of Large Managerial Firms," *Journal of Political Economy*, Vol. 72 (June 1965), 221–36.

24. Monsen, R. J., B. O. Saxberg, and R. A. Sutermeister. "The Modern Manager: What Makes Him Run?" *Business Horizons,* Fall 1966.

25. Preston, Lee E., and James E. Post. *Private Management and Public Policy* (Englewood Cliffs, N.J.: Prentice-Hall, 1975).

26. Reid, Samuel Richardson. *The New Industrial Order* (New York: McGraw-Hill, 1976).

27. Schumpeter, Joseph. *Capitalism, Socialism, and Democracy* (New York: Harper, 1942).

28. Subcommittee on Antitrust and Monopoly. *Concentration Ratios in Manufacturing Industry,* 1963. Subcommittee on Antitrust and Monopoly, U.S. Senate, 90th Congress, 1st session.

29. Votaw, Dow, and S. Prakash Sethi. *The Corporate Dilemma: Traditional Values Versus Contemporary Problems* (Englewood Cliffs, N.J.: Prentice-Hall, 1973).

QUESTIONS FOR DISCUSSION

1. How does Simon's "Administrative Man" differ from the more traditional "Economic Man"?

2. With respect to positive economic models of the firm, a number of theorists have proposed alternatives to the profit-maximization assumption. Explain and comment on some of these alternatives.

3. A manager, as an *individual* and as a member of a management team, is faced with a number of (often conflicting) pressures and demands that influence his/her behavior. What are the sources of these demands and pressures? Give examples, if necessary.

4. In the text, we introduce the rudiments of an organization-theory-based model of oligopoly industries. Explain the basis of the model and discuss the interrelationships of the managerial, firm, and industry levels. Discuss the concept of power as it relates to the coalitions in the model.

5. In his article "Toward a Positive Theory of Corporate Social Involvement," Elkins offers five motivational bases for corporate social involvement, including one based on the satisfaction of managerial ego needs. Explain the development of the ego-need model.

6. Can positive models of the firm be used to reconcile the discrepancies between proponents of the firm being an economic instrument only, and the social-responsibility advocates. How? Elaborate.

SELECTED READINGS

Alchian, A. A., "The basis of some recent advances in the theory of management of the firm," *Journal of Industrial Economics,* November, 1965.

Barber, J., *The American Corporation: Its Power, Its Money, Its Politics.* (New York: Dutton, 1970.)

Bell, D., *The Coming of Post-Industrial Society: A Venture in Social Forecasting.* (New York: Basic Books, 1973.)

Berle, A. A., Jr., and G. C. Means, *The Modern Corporation and Private Property.* (New York: Macmillan, 1932); (Rev. ed., New York: Harcourt, Brace and World, 1968.)

Cyert, R. M., and J. G. March, *A Behavioral Theory of the Firm.* (Englewood Cliffs, N.J.: Prentice-Hall, 1963.)

Galbraith, J. K., *The New Industrial State,* Rev. ed. (Boston: Houghton Mifflin, 1972.)

Galbraith, J. K., *Economics and the Public Purpose.* (Boston: Houghton Mifflin, 1973.)

Kelso, L. and P. Hetter, *Two Factor Theory: The Economics of Reality.* (New York: Random House, 1968.)

Marris, R., *The Economic Theory of "Managerial" Capitalism.* (Glencoe: The Free Press, 1964.)

McGuire, J. W., *Theories of Business Behavior.* (Englewood Cliffs, N.J.: Prentice-Hall, Inc., 1964.)

McGuire, J. W., "Perfecting capitalism—An economic dilemma," *Business Horizons,* February, 1976.

Mintzberg, H., *The Nature of Managerial Work.* (New York: Harper and Row, 1973.)

Monsen, R. J., Jr., and A. Downs, "A theory of large managerial firms," *Journal of Political Economy, 73* (June, 1965); pp. 221–236.

Nader, R., and M. Green, *Corporate Power in America.* (New York: Grossman Publishers, 1973.)

Reid, S. R., *Mergers, Managers, and the Economy.* (New York: McGraw-Hill, 1968.)

Trebing, H. M., *The Corporation in the American Economy.* (Chicago: Quadrangle Books, 1970.)

Wasson, C., Sturdivant, F. D. and D. H. McConaughy. *Competition and Human Behavior.* (New York: Appleton-Century-Crofts, 1968.)

PART 2
PROBLEMS

3. *Business as a Place of Work*

The changing character of work and employees' reactions to work are two topics currently in vogue. The literature of management, organization behavior, labor relations and economics, and the popular business press are very much concerned with employee attitudes toward work, assembly lines, or corporate life in general. More and more, despite high unemployment rates, one hears of young operative workers rebelling against the pace, monotony, and powerlessness involved in repetitive work, or of the young executive opting out of the corporate "rat race."

Nor is the subject of work of interest only from the psychological and sociological points of view. The physical safety and health of employees is also becoming an area of concern. The federal government has passed the Occupational Safety and Health Act, and the subsequent discoveries that workers were being exposed to toxic chemicals, dangerous fibers and minerals, and other harmful working conditions have focused attention not only on the problems of industrial health and safety, but on the methods and agencies of law enforcement in the area as well.

In this introduction, we shall examine some of the traditional theories of work and its effects, along with some of the contemporary countertheory and ideology. Then we shall look at some of the evidence on outlooks toward work. We shall rely heavily on a study published in 1972 entitled *Work in America* assembled by a distinguished group of scholars under the auspices of the United States Department of Health, Education, and Welfare. Also, from the *Work in America* study, we shall offer some comments on the younger worker. Is he or she a rebel and are there generational differences between today's young workers and those of earlier years?

Then we shall look at attempts to adapt the workplace to the changing outlooks on work. Techniques such as job enrichment, job enlargement, and the Volvo and Saab experiments in Sweden are attracting increasing amounts of attention among managers and in the literature.

CLASSICAL MANAGEMENT THEORIES OF WORK

Much of the classical literature on management is based on one very simple assumption, which is very much akin to the hedonistic assumption of economic theory: Man works for money. Man was assumed to be extraordinarily malleable if only further injections of pecuniary incentive were applied. Hence, the first systematic management theory, Scientific Management, came to personify piece-rate systems, rigidly defined job specifications, procedures and methods determined through meticulous physiological study.

Also implicit in the earliest classical management theory is the assumption that knowledge flows from the top of the organization downward, and the higher in the organization one moves, the more intelligent and knowledgeable one is assumed to be. Frederick Taylor, who is called the father of Scientific Management, illustrated that assumption in his classical confrontation with a manual laborer pseudonymed "Schmidt."* In his work, Schmidt was to follow Taylor's directions to the letter in order to be a "first class man." Following Taylor's instructions, Schmidt's productivity (and pay) increased dramatically, although the pace and style of Schmidt's labor would today be considered peonage by many. But his behavior fell completely within the assumptions of the Scientific Management school and its outlook toward man and work.

Formal organization theory was based on similar assumptions early in its development, stressing higher-level jobs rather than those on the factory floor. Early formal organization theory, including bureaucracy theory, stressed the organization chart and the job description, hierarchical control, and downward flowing authority and knowledge. Early theory operated on the assumption that as long as an individual was sufficiently paid, he would fill a given organizational position, perform according to the job description, and leave all personal feelings outside of the workplace.

Many of today's organizations are still designed on the basis of the simple assumptions of scientific management and the early approaches to formal organization theory. In the early days, those assumptions might have had fairly wide validity. After all, labor pools were drawn from the immigrant masses; if one set of workers didn't conform to company rules (often arbitrarily applied), other workers could be drawn out of the large, generally poor population. Work was hard and physically taxing, but money was the first thing most of the common laborers needed, so it did provide the incentive for conformance.

COLLECTIVE BARGAINING APPROACHES TO WORK

The 1930's were the turning point for union activity. While the Clayton Act and the Norris–LaGuardia Act provided some impetus for unionization among the major industries, it was the National Labor Relations Act (popularly known as the Wagner Act) that gave the real impetus to unions by declaring collective bargaining or union representation of workers to be in the public interest. One might

---

*Frederick W. Taylor, *Principles of Scientific Management.* (New York: Harper and Bros., 1911.)

have expected that unions would have been concerned with the increasing regimentation of the workplace. But union organization and negotiation throughout the 1930's, late 1940's, and through the 1960's, emphasized wages, job security, pensions, supplemental unemployment benefits, seniority, and other tangible benefits. In essence, the collective bargaining relationship often stressed all the things that reinforced the basic assumptions of classical management theory: people work for money or material benefits.

MODERN CRITIQUES OF FORMAL
AND CLASSICAL MANAGEMENT THEORY

More recent management theory recognizes that man is motivated by a complex web of factors, rather than simply by money in isolation. Furthermore, when a person enters an organization, personal needs, desires, attributes, and even idiosyncrasies are not left behind. In other words, the whole person enters the organization, not part of the person, who will automatically accept the organization's prescriptions for activity.

The original of the modern behavioral models is that put forth by Abraham Maslow.* Maslow's thesis is that individuals have levels of needs starting with the most basic physiological ones and moving to higher-level ones as the more basic ones—food, water, etc.—are satisfied. The five levels of needs in the Maslow thesis are physiological, safety and security, companionship and affection, self-esteem, and self actualization. The crux of Maslow's thesis is that a satisfied need is not a motivating need; hence progressively larger doses of money may not succeed in motivating proportionately if the recipient is fairly well endowed with the material benefits that money can supply. Note that the basic thesis here is completely opposite to the underlying assumptions of scientific management—that man is malleable and is motivated by material reward alone.

Other theorists in the Maslow mode include Chris Argyris, Douglas MacGregor, and Frederick Herzberg. Argyris developed a theory that the modern organization demands control, but that the maturing individual demands autonomy. When the maturing individual demanding autonomy encounters the demanding organization, the individual becomes frustrated and regresses—returns to a state of childlike dependency. This regression reinforces the organizational assumption that man needs direction and control, and the cycle starts all over again.†

Douglas McGregor posed a similar dichotomy; "Theory X" type managers, according to McGregor, assume that people need to be directed and controlled, that they find no intrinsic values in work, and that they find work inherently distasteful. The "Theory Y" manager, on the other hand, assumes that work is a natural activity for individuals, that individuals will commit themselves to work

---

*Abraham H. Maslow, *Motivation and Personality*. (New York: Harper and Row, 1954.)

†Chris Argyris, *Personality and Organization*. (New York: Harper and Row, 1957.)

objectives, that the degree of commitment is a function of the rewards, that the average person seeks responsibility and does not shun it, and that such capacity for psychological growth is widely rather than narrowly distributed within the population.*

Obviously, the manager ascribing to Theory X assumptions will adopt a different superior-subordinate posture than the one who ascribes to those in Theory Y. The Theory X manager will tend to be very autocratic and production-centered, whereas the Theory Y manager will act with more "people-centered" approaches—he will be democratic and supportive of the growth needs of subordinates.

Finally, in this group, the newest approach is that of Frederick Herzberg and his two-factor theory of motivation.† The basis of the Herzberg approach is that individuals basically have two needs—the need to grow psychologically and achieve, and the need to avoid pain from the environment. The growth need motivates and the pain avoidance need, while not motivating, will result in increased unhappiness if satisfaction is decreased.

Psychological growth or achievement needs are stimulated by organizational mechanisms that induce psychological growth, and these are basically found in the content of the job. Hence, according to Herzberg, the growth or motivating factors are internal to the job. These factors are perceived as opportunity for advancement, recognition for achievement, interesting or important work, responsibility, and growth or advancement.

The "hygiene factors," or those stimulating pain avoidance, are in the job environment, and hence they are extrinsic to the job. These are company policy and supervision, interpersonal relationships, working conditions, salary, status, and security. These hygiene factors increase unhappiness if they are negatively applied, but neither the negative nor increasing positive application of hygiene factors will increase individual motivation. Only the positive application or presence of the growth or motivating factors will do that.

All of these approaches have been subjected to criticism. One critic, responding to Argyris, Maslow, and McGregor's emphasis on mental growth, scolded university professors for being so concerned with self-actualizing behavior when in fact most people in production jobs still seek primarily pecuniary rewards. And, he continued, even if the production workers cared, the costs of altering production lines to accommodate catering to higher-level need satisfaction might just be too great.‡ Other critics have questioned the rigor of the methodology employed in developing some of these models.

---

*Douglas McGregor, *The Human Side of Enterprise.* (New York: McGraw-Hill, 1960.)

†Frederick Herzberg, *Work and the Nature of Man.* (New York: World Publishers, 1966.)

‡George Strauss, in Leonard Sayles, *Individualism and Big Business.* (New York: McGraw-Hill, 1963), pp. 67–80.

THE WORKER

The first question we might ask in trying to determine whether our places of work cause dissatisfaction would be to try to find some statistical evidence that workers are not happy with their jobs. One question which the *Work in America* study posed to shed some light on that question was the following: "What type of work would you try to get into if you could start all over?" Forty-three percent of the white-collar workers (including managerial) answered "same." Only 24 percent of the blue-collar workers answered "same." These data correlate positively with earlier studies, particularly in the automobile industry. Responses in that industry often related to not wanting to have one's offspring working on the assembly line or in manual tasks.

Sources of job dissatisfaction

Among the sources of dissatisfaction cited in the *Work in America* study were (1) what they called the *anachronism of Taylorism*, (2) diminishing opportunities to be one's own boss, and (3) bigness. Under the first category, the study cited complaints of the push for quantity, not quality, rigidity of rules and regulations, and the breakdown of work into the smallest possible tasks.

In categories two and three, the data amply illustrate the problem. In the year 1850, only fifty percent of the nation's work force were wage and salary workers. By 1970, that percentage reached ninety. In 1950, eighteen percent of the labor force were self-employed; by 1970 that percentage halved to nine percent. These data show the relatively decreasing opportunity to be one's own boss. Coupled with that is the fact that, out of over 3.5 million industrial units, twenty percent accounted for over fifty percent of the industrial employment and .3 percent for over twenty-seven percent of employment.

In general, surveys have found four ingredients in the alienation of workers from their work; a sense of powerlessness, a meaningless character of work, isolation, and self-estrangement (or depersonalization). In essence, a disconnection from the creative, meaningful character of work. If all these data are correct, then the theories stressing the propensity of the human being to develop and the organization to constrain and prevent that development, may have some reinforcement.

MANAGERIAL JOB DISSATISFACTION

One of the surprising findings of many recent surveys is that job dissatisfaction is occurring in managerial ranks as well as with operative workers. The *Work in America* survey reported that one out of three middle managers is now willing to join a union, and a similar study by the American Management Association found half of the middle managers surveyed favoring a change in the law (National Labor Relations Act) to allow collective bargaining between middle and top managements. Large numbers of middle managers were of the opinion that they would be unionized in the near future. These are significant findings when stacked up against the ideological commitment to management prerogatives and the supposed anti-union stance that managers are presumed to maintain.

Generally, middle managers have several substantive complaints. One is concerned with the lack of influence that middle managers have throughout the organization and on the organization's goals, policies, and mode of operation. In another study, some managers were cited as concerned with the lack of their organization's commitments to socially responsible corporate activities.

Managers were outspoken about the need to compete to gain attention and resources, and complained about the tension, frustration, and infighting that this intra-organizational competition led to. And some middle-management executives felt like parts of a machine, which could be replaced when a technologically superior part is available. Indeed, in a rapidly advancing technological age, many executives feel obsolescent.

In a DUN'S REVIEW article,* many middle-management executives complained that their firms exhibited little reverse loyalty during a recession period. Executives were expected to show complete loyalty and work hard for the corporation, they protested, but when the slightest shrinkage in bottom-line profits appeared, the corporation showed no hesitancy to "take the meat cleaver" to its staff.

GENERATIONAL CHANGES

Another key question in examining today's work force is to consider the differences that separate today's generation from earlier ones. Most assuredly, today's younger people generally are better educated and more affluent than any previous generation. As a result, they have had exposure to fewer basic deprivations and fewer constraints on their thoughts. They have been exposed to more basic ideas and concepts and their aspirations for using their creative faculties are higher. Their education has given them higher expectations and their affluence makes them much less tolerant of psychically unrewarding activity. Indeed, the powerlessness to be creative and the inability to be one's own master, coupled with the sheer size, complexity, and power of organizations with which younger people come in contact, fuel many of the frustrations of younger, aspiring men and women.

Allied to affluence and education is the fact that traditional patterns of authority in society are being challenged. If, on the outside, people are successful in using the courts, are challenging elected officials, and critically examining the dogmas of religion, are violating the taboos of society, and, in the case of students, are confronting and receiving concessions from college administrators, then it is foolhardy to assume that such challenges cannot penetrate the corporate structure.

Changing attitudes toward work

All of the above data seems to indicate that a change in the outlook toward work has taken place, particularly among the young. The so-called *work ethic* was a

---

*George J. Berkwitt, "Management, sitting on a time bomb?", *DUN'S,* July, 1972.

key governing value in our society. Briefly, the work ethic stressed the value of work for its own sake—as something necessary for every person—as well as the belief that hard work pays off in the end. In a romantic, Horatio Alger sense, Americans generally believed that the pot of gold lay at the end of the rainbow and that hard work would get you there.

The work-ethic view is now being challenged and tested severely. In a series of surveys of college students, conducted by Daniel Yankelovich, the drop in percentages of respondents believing that "hard work will pay off" was astounding. In 1968, 69 percent agreed with the idea that work pays off, while in 1971, the number dropped to 39 percent. Obviously events since then may change the data—many observers now see students "going straight" again—but the astonishing drop in just three years must surely be recognized as significant in demonstrating the fragility of a long-cherished and widely held societal value.

The real test of change in the work ethic, however, comes not from surveys, but in the workplace—the changes that take place in the actual behavior and attitudes of people on their jobs. The evidence seems to be bearing out the thesis that outlooks toward jobs and work are changing markedly. Operative workers rebel at the dirty, boring tasks that their fathers and grandfathers grudgingly accepted and that generations of management consultants extolled as "efficient." Loyalty to one's employer may be an anachronism; loyalty to one's peer group may be more important. Turnover rates in many plants and industries are increasing rapidly. Personal needs take precedence over organizational plans and schedules; for example, absenteeism is becoming epidemic for many firms, and employees feel no qualms in routinely taking days off.

All of this poses extremely difficult decision-making situations for management. Recruiting is becoming extremely difficult; one employer recently hired 20 young people through a special section of his state's employment service. The new employees were trained for routine jobs that required little skill. Inside of four days, not one of these new employees remained with the company. They simply rebelled at the routine work.

Work design is no longer a simple, readily accepted, engineering process. The most celebrated case, of course, involves the General Motors Corporation Vega plant at Lordstown, Ohio. Considered one of the most advanced plants in the world, the Lordstown installation used the latest in autobuilding technology including the use of robots—called Unimates—for welding car bodies. Eventually, GM engineered the plant to produce one hundred cars an hour. But the workers, mostly young, rebelled at the pace demanded by the line. A twenty-two day strike idled some 10,000 employees. Speedup, job monotony, and the inability of workers to gain some voice in decisions affecting their assembly lines were all cited as factors. Discontent is still reported to exist at Lordstown and protests erupt periodically.

Even more significant than one strike, however, is the fact that unions are raising the issue of "humanization of the workplace" in collective-bargaining negotiations. Traditionally and through the 1960's, as we noted, unions emphasized wages, job security, unemployment benefits, overtime, and other such items. In essence, union demands reinforced the assumptions of classical management theory that sufficient extrinsic rewards could motivate someone to occupy almost any job at the workplace. That picture is now changing as unions raise the issues of job design, the pace of the line, decision-making on the job, and other conditions formerly considered prerogatives of management.

The changes in lifestyles and the resultant modification of the work ethic are just as pronounced at the management level as they are at the operative level. Only a few years ago, the man in the gray flannel suit was the accepted stereotype of a successful business executive. Two or three hours of commuting on a dirty, hot, and crowded milk-run train were accepted as the standard pain of success. Today, as we noted, we hear of executives suffering the same boredom and role conflict that operatives do; and the drop out rate among managers is becoming sufficiently high as to cause concern in executive suites.

CORPORATE RESPONSES TO THE NEW WORK ETHIC

How do corporations respond to the new environment from which they draw their most important resources—employees and executives? Some do nothing, of course, on the assumption that enough people imbued with the work ethic will still be looking for jobs, or that new lifestyles are just a passing fancy. A survey of one group of top executives who were queried about the new ethic among younger middle managers, produced some interesting results. Some top managers seemed sympathetic with the aspirations of frustrated middle managers, and called for carefully thought-out programs in which top management would communicate with and nurture aspiring young middle managers. Others were less sympathetic. Some blamed business schools for raising aspiration levels much too high. Still others contended that only the misfits leave industry, while innovative managers stay on.* Companies that take the do-nothing approach with their employees might be right, but they must be prepared to suffer the possible increased absenteeism and turnover accompanying their wait-and-see strategy.

On the other hand, many organizations are engaging in job enlargement, job enrichment, team production, flexible hours and flexible day scheduling, and similar techniques designed to reduce monotony and boredom and increase workers' participation in the planning for their own jobs. Job enlargement is a technique that might work on assembly-line jobs; it simply means adding to the variety of tasks a worker is given to do. Job enrichment adds some of the planning, design, and scheduling to the operative worker's tasks. Perhaps the most novel experiments in job enrichment and job enlargement are being performed in Sweden, where whole plants are being built to operate under these systems. However, the Swedish approach may not be to the liking of American workers. A small group of auto workers was sent to Sweden to observe and work under "progressive" conditions, and the consensus of the workers was that the system could

---

*Robert Levy, "Top management—and turned-off executives," DUN'S, August, 1972.

not work in U.S. plants on the scale that it is being treated in Sweden.* On the other hand, a number of work-design experiments have been tried in the United States, but the plant sizes are much smaller than the huge plants of most major industries. Some of these experiments have been scrapped, and some have come under criticism for taking the credit for increased motivation, when, in fact, some additional, more traditional incentives were also added at the same time.†

On the managerial level, some corporations are dropping dress codes and status differentials, and are enlarging the scope of work as well. Experiments with flexible arrivals and departures are also being conducted. McDonald's, the nationwide hamburger chain, undertook an interesting course when it built its new corporate headquarters; work areas were designed with no fixed walls and a waterbed room is available for personnel to relax and unwind.

This is not a book on organization design, but we mention these techniques briefly since the changes they respond to emanate primarily from the organization's environment. Alert organizations and managements are the ones that can forecast these changes, understand them, and deal with them effectively.

THE READINGS

"Who Will Do the Dirty Work Tomorrow?" by Edmund Faltermayer (from *Fortune*) is an interesting piece on the limits to filling the so-called menial tasks that have little possibility of being mechanized. Faltermayer describes some of the mechanisms that firms and organizations might have to use to induce people to take on the "dirty work." He also finds some surprising groups of people cleaning, hauling, washing dishes, and waiting on tables. Yet admittedly, the costs are high—turnover and absenteeism among the most serious ones.

The second reading, David Kramarsky's "The Blue-Collar View of Management," details the views the workers have of their immediate supervisors and of higher managers. The article offers some interesting insights on employees' needs and concerns, and some suggestions for improving the climate between manager and worker.

Finally, we are including an article relating to *physical* safety in the workplace, Joseph Mason's, "OSHA: Problems and Prospects." In 1970, Congress passed the Occupational Safety and Health Act in response to the rapidly increasing number of deaths and accidents in the workplace. As important as our knowledge of the workplace in terms of the impact on the employees' psychological health is our concern with the employees' physical safety. Hence our inclusion of this important article. The Mason article "reviews the key provisions of the . . . Act, presents an overview of the emerging problems and controversies since the passage of OSHA, and offers guidelines in addressing the problem of job-related safety."

---

*"Doubting Sweden's way: American workers view team-assembly methods at Saab engine plant." *Time,* March 10, 1975.

†E. Lauck Parke and Curt Tausky, "The mythodology of job enrichment: Self-actualization revisited," *Personnel,* LII,5 (September–October, 1975), pp. 12–21.

Who Will Do the Dirty Work Tomorrow?

Edmund Faltermayer

In the computer age, millions of men and women still earn wages by carrying food trays, pushing brooms, shoveling dirt, and performing countless other menial tasks in ways that haven't changed much in centuries. Traditionally, these jobs have been taken by people with no choice: high-school dropouts, immigrants with language difficulties, members of racial minorities, women, and young people (as well as unemployed family heads in desperate straits and disproportionate numbers of ex-convicts, alcoholics, the mentally retarded, and people with personality disorders). But various currents of change—including egalitarianism, rising expectations, and ever-more-generous government programs of support for nonworkers—are tending to make it harder to fill such jobs as time goes by. Some observers, indeed, foresee an eventual drying up of the pool of labor available to do menial work.

Yet many of these "jobs of last resort," as they have been called, involve essential tasks that it would be difficult to dispense with or to mechanize. Under the pressure of rising wages, the U.S. has traveled far down the road of reducing menial labor, which currently engages somewhere between 10 and 15 percent of the working population. But we are approaching the limits of how far we can go, or wish to go.

NO REPLACEMENT FOR ELBOW GREASE

On farms, for example, machines have replaced most manual toil. But a visit to California's Imperial Valley, one of the most efficient agricultural regions in the U.S., reveals that a surprising amount of "stoop" labor still survives. At construction sites, machines now do most of the heavy digging, but men with shovels still must work behind them. Much of the restaurant industry has shifted to self-service and throwaways, but growing numbers of Americans want to dine out in conventional fashion, with the food served on china plates.

In an effort to simplify cleaning, developers have modified the design of new office buildings, stores, and hotels, and industry now supplies improved chemicals and equipment. But Daniel Fraad Jr., chairman of Allied Maintenance Corp., which cleans offices, factories, and passenger terminals across the U.S., sees few remaining breakthroughs in productivity. Years ago, he says, his company abandoned a mechanical wall-washing device after it was found to be less efficient than a man with a sponge. Says Fraad, himself a former window washer: "In the final analysis, cleaning is elbow grease."

All this helps explain why the century-long process in which Americans have been moving out of low-status jobs is decelerating and may even be reversing. Productivity in the remaining menial occupations is growing more slowly than in most other fields, and shorter working hours often necessitate larger working staffs even where the amount of work remains the same. According to the Department of Labor, the percentage of Americans who were either "nonfarm laborers" or "service workers" was higher in 1972 than in 1960.

Declines in some menial jobs, most notably maids and housekeepers, have been more than offset by increases in other occupations. The 1970 census showed 1,250,000 "janitors" at work in the U.S., up from 750,000 a decade earlier. In the same period the ranks of unskilled hospital workers, i.e., "nursing aides, orderlies and attendants," rose by nearly 80 percent to 720,000, and the number of "garbage collectors" doubled. Between now and 1985, the Bureau of Labor Statistics has predicted, openings in many low-status jobs will increase faster than total employment.

DESPERATION IN DALLAS

But who, in this era when the Army feels compelled to abolish K.P., will want to wait on tables, empty bedpans or, for that matter, bury the dead? In some cities it's already hard to keep menial jobs filled. In the booming Dallas region, with its unemployment rate of only 2.1 percent, jobs for waitresses, private guards, trash collectors, and busboys were recently going begging.

One restaurant owner who is short of "bus help" revealed that his current roster consists of an illiterate black man in his fifties, a white girl who is somewhat retarded, a divorced white man in his sixties with personality problems, and an unattached white man in his forties "who goes out and gets drunk each day after he finishes his shift."

In slack labor markets such as Boston, where the unemployment rate has been running above the recent national figure of 4.7 percent, employers are experiencing troubles of a different sort. There seem to be enough people to fill most menial jobs, but they just don't stay around.

At the popular Sheraton-Boston Hotel, the turnover among chambermaids is about 150 percent a year. On pleasant weekends, when absenteeism runs high, the hotel hurriedly telephones local college students on a standby list. Down in the kitchens, turnover among dishwashers on the night shift exceeds a phenomenal 400 percent a year. Sometimes, the hotel has to ask the local U.S.O. to send over Navy men on shore leave who want to earn some extra money by helping out in the kitchens.

THE INCENTIVES NOT TO WORK

In Boston, as in many other cities outside the South, liberal welfare benefits make it possible for a great many people to stay out of the labor market if they don't like the work and wages available. Stricter administration of welfare, currently being attempted in a number of states, may remove some cheaters and induce some other recipients to work. Under a 1971 provision of federal law, welfare mothers with no preschool children are required to register for work. But it would be unrealistic to expect a tightening effective enough to make any large number of welfare recipients take menial jobs.

A number of factors besides generous welfare have been eroding the supply of people available for menial work. Perhaps the leading expert on this subject is economist Harold Wool of the National Planning Association. Wool points out that during the Sixties society's efforts to keep young people in school reduced the number of dropouts entering the labor force. At the same time, he says, the U.S. drew down much of its remaining "reserve" of rural labor migrating to cities.

Most important of all, minority groups, especially blacks, began pushing in earnest toward equality in employment. According to Wool's reckoning, black young men with at least one year of college (but not teen-agers or young women) have actually achieved occupational parity with their white counterparts. This remarkable social achievement has been too little noticed.

Today a great many young black people refuse to take jobs they consider demeaning. Wool observes that while a decade ago 20 percent of the black young women who had graduated from high school worked as domestics, only 3 percent were settling for that kind of work in 1970. "The service-type job," he says, "has become anathema to many blacks, even on a temporary basis." This helps explain why some service jobs are hard to fill even in cities where unemployment among young black people runs at dismayingly high rates.

It seems clear, then, that in years ahead the traditional supply of menial workers will not meet the demand. Some work will go undone. Many prosperous families whose counterparts even a decade ago would have employed household help now get along without any. Corners are clipped in services. Some restaurants, for example, have reduced the number of items on their menus, which among other things trims the customer's decision-making time and enables the waitress to move along faster.

THE $12,886-A-YEAR TRASHMEN

But a lot of menial work will have to be done, one way or another. Society will have to respond to the tightening of the labor supply by improving pay and working conditions. Right now there are many places where the federal minimum wage of $1.60 an hour cannot buy work. In northern cities, even members of the so-called "secondary labor force"—women and young people whose pay supplements a family's principal source of income—are usually not willing to work for $1.60. For those groups, $2 to 2.50 is the real market "minimum" needed to balance supply and demand.

It may be a portent of things to come that New York City now pays its unionized sanitation men $12,886 a year (plus an ultraliberal pension). Hardly anybody ever quits, and thousands of men are on a waiting list for future job openings. At Chrysler Corp., unskilled "material handlers," whose job includes pushing carts around the plant floor by hand, get $4.90 an hour, which draws plenty of young married men, both white and black.

At Boston's Massachusetts General Hospital, the minimum starting pay for "dietary service aides" and "building service aids" is $2.78, more than local hotels pay busboys and chambermaids. But even so, few native Bostonians, black or white, are entering such jobs these days. Most of the hospital's recent hires for entry-level jobs are immigrants from Jamaica and other Caribbean islands, or recent black arrivals from the rural South.

HIGH STANDARDS FOR SWABBING DOWN

Higher pay, if high enough, clearly helps improve the status of menial work. Another way to improve its status is to raise the quality and complexity of the work itself. Some of the credit for a fairly low turnover rate at Massachusetts General Hospital goes to a training program begun in 1968 for those "building service aides," who previously had gone by the relatively servile titles of "maid" and "houseman."

The one-month program, which involves eighty hours in a classroom and a loose-leaf manual resembling one used by higher-skilled workers at the hospital, is not mere industrial-relations gimmickry. "Janitorial work in a hospital is different than in an office building," says Ruth MacRobert, the hospital's personnel director. "Here they need to learn aseptic techniques, and the fact that they can't use slippery compounds that might cause a patient to trip and fall. If there's a spill, they can't leave broken glass lying around. It's a lot different than swabbing down a deserted office. Who cares if the John Hancock Building is wet and slippery after hours?"

A pleasanter work climate can also help make low-status work less lowly. Lack of amenity on the job is particularly noticeable in the clangorous kitchens where some of the country's 2,860,000 food service workers earn their living. Jan Lovell, president of the Dallas Restaurant Association, believes his industry is improving the work atmosphere but will have to do more in order to survive. In the most menial jobs, he says, "we used to have a tradition of taking the dregs of society off the street and working them twelve hours a day." This, he says, was bad for management as well as the worker.

"A few days ago it wasn't unusual for a restaurant to buy a $12,000 dishwashing machine and hire two drunks or wetbacks at $75 a week who might forget to turn the water on. Today you pay one guy $150 a week who does the work of two. But maybe we also need to put in a radio and a rug on the floor. The restaurant business has been hot, dirty, and sweaty. Who needs it?"

TO REPLACE A "VANISHING BREED"

Still another strategy is to make menial jobs a stepping-stone to something better. Texas Instruments, for example, offers a prospect of advancement to anyone who signs on to push a broom. Six years ago, in an effort to get better-quality work (and save money too), T.I. terminated contracts with outside cleaning firms and created a staff of its own to clean its factories and offices in the Dallas area. As in so many menial occupations, the staff has a nucleus of mature people who never aimed much higher in life, a majority of them black men in their fifties and sixties who in one supervisor's words are "a vanishing breed."

To lure younger replacements, the company offers a starting wage of $2.43 an hour, exactly the same as in production, and allows anyone to seek a transfer after six months. And like other T.I. employees, the sweepers are entitled to an exceptional fringe benefit: 90 percent of the cost of part-time education.

In a way, though, "promotability" makes it even harder to maintain a staff. Over the course of a year about 40 percent of T.I.'s "cleaning service attendants" move on to other jobs within the company, in addition to the 36 percent who quit or retire. One recently arrived janitor who is already looking around is Willie Gibson, a soft-spoken, twenty-year-old high-school graduate. Willie has been talking to "the head man in the machine shop" about the possibilities of a transfer. "There ain't nothing wrong with cleaning," he says, "It's got to be done. But me, I feel I can do bettter."

Texas Instruments is forced to search ceaselessly for replacements, who these days include Mexican-Americans and a few whites as well as blacks. Recruiting methods have included the announcement of janitorial vacancies from the pulpit of a black church.

A MAGNET FOR ILLEGALS

Until the early 1920's, immigration provided an abundant supply of menial workers. And recent years have seen something of a resurgence. Legal immigration has grown to 400,000 a year and now accounts for a fifth of the country's population growth. While many of the newcomers are professionals from the Philippines and India, the ranks also include a great many unskilled men and women from Mexico, the West Indies, and South America.

In addition, it is estimated that between one million and two million illegal aliens are at large in the U.S., mostly employed in low-status jobs. And the number of illegal aliens, whatever it may be, is undoubtedly growing. "Suddenly, in the last few months, there have been more of the illegals," says an official of the Texas Employment Commission in Dallas. The hiring of illegal immigrants is against the law in Texas, and the federal Immigration and Naturalization Service periodically rounds some of them up and deports them. But the very low employment rate in Dallas, the official says, acts as a magnet pulling in the illegals, who work mainly in small enterprises that are not scrupulous about observing the law.

In northern cities, illegal immigration began to increase during the late 1960's. New York City alone may have as many as 250,000 illegals, including Chinese and Greeks as well as Haitians, Dominicans, and other Latin Americans. Such people can be an employer's dream. Often they have no welfare or unemployment compensation to fall back on, since applying for such assistance could reveal their existence to the authorities. In an era of liberal income-maintenance programs for the native population, says New York State Industrial Commissioner Louis Levine, such people "have a total incentive to work."

TOWARD SELF-SUFFICIENCY IN DIRTY WORK

To rely on increasing of immigrants to perform menial jobs, however, is to put off true long-range solutions to the problem. Sooner or later, every mature nation intent upon keeping its cultural identity will have to figure out a way to get most of the work done with its own native-born.

The U.S. cannot, and should not, close the door to all immigration, but a crackdown on illegal immigrants seems overdue. In addition to penalties against employers who hire illegal immigrants, an effective crackdown might require some device such as identity cards for all citizens. While repugnant to many Americans, such controls have long been a fact of life in France.

The U.S. is in a better position than most countries to move toward a state of "self-sufficiency in dirty work." Americans are generally free of Europe's in-grained class consciousness, and under certain conditions are rather flexible about the jobs they will take. And in recent years, in fact, white Americans have been moving into low-status jobs as black Americans move out. Most of these native-born recruits to menial work are women or young people.

In view of all the attention given to the women's liberation movement in recent years, it may seem paradoxical that many women have been moving into the lower end of the occupation scale. But there is not really any paradox. The desire of *some* women to pursue careers in managerial and professional fields should certainly not preclude employment of a different kind of women in a different kind of situation—the woman who is not a breadwinner and does not want a career, but who does want the freedom to divide her life between housekeeping and periods of work that entail no encumbering commitments between employer and employee.

A lot of these women are in jobs that are fairly pleasant, and whose "menial-ness" has more to do with society's prevailing view than the nature of the work itself. Some restaurant work falls into this category. That is the opinion, for example, of Peggy Easter, a middle-aged white woman who waits on tables at Jan's Restaurant, a moderate-priced but clean and well-run establishment in a Dallas suburb. "Some people look down on this kind of work," she says. "But there's an art to this, and I like the hectic, fast pace because I have lots of nervous energy."

Like many waiters and waitresses, Mrs. Easter works only part time, coming in for three and a half hours each day during lunchtime. Her only child is married and her husband works full time as a diesel mechanic. With growing numbers of married women wanting to get out of the house, it is reasonable to expect that more Peggy Easters will turn up in the years ahead.

A BULGE FROM THE BABY BOOM

Young white people have moved into low-status jobs in even greater numbers than women. In 1960, according to census data, only 8 percent of the country's janitors were young whites under twenty-five. By 1970 that figure had jumped to 22 percent. Some of the movement of white young men *down* the occupational status scale (which partly accounts for that "parity" between blacks and whites who went to college) is a result of the postwar baby boom. Many of the young janitors, kitchen workers, and construction laborers are part-time workers from the ballooning population of high-school and college students. Others are full-time employees who, meeting heavy competition for jobs from their numerous contemporaries, have taken menial jobs until they can find something better. Another factor here is that many young whites live in the suburbs, where fast-food and other service jobs have grown more rapidly than in the cities.

Because the baby boom began waning in the late 1950's, the bulge in the number of employable young people will begin to recede during the middle and late 1970's. During the current decade as a whole, the sixteen to twenty-four age group will increase by 16 percent—somewhat less than the entire labor force, and far less than the phenomenal 48 percent growth during the Sixties.

To some extent, however, this demographic slowdown could be offset by a reduction in school hours, particularly in the high-school years. A growing number of educators and sociologists favor more part-time exposure of teenagers to the working world, where they can benefit by rubbing shoulders with adults. One principal at a high school in the Northeast confided not long ago that all the basic material in his three-year curriculum, including the course necessary for entering college, could be given in half the time. Not many principals, perhaps, would go that far, but certainly high-school education is now a very inefficient process. Any reduction in classroom time, of course, would make more teenagers available for work, and much of that would be work generally considered menial.

AGAINST THE GRAIN

In any event, it seems reasonable to expect that young people will be taking on more of those dirty jobs. According to a well-entrenched American tradition, almost unthinkable in much of Europe, it is healthy for sons and daughters of the middle class to wait on tables, scrub pots, and even clean toilets as part of their "rites of initiation" into the world of work. Late in the nineteenth century, the American author Edward Bellamy, in the Utopian novel *Looking Backward,* foresaw a day when all the onerous tasks of of society would be performed by young people during a three-year period of obligatory service.

A formal period of "national youth service," a proposal that has been revived in recent years, runs against the American grain. But less extreme policies to encourage the employment of more young people would be a step in the right direction. Lots of young people might welcome earlier introduction to the world of work, especially high-school students, who these days seem increasingly inclined to work anyway.

"DIRTY WORK CAN BE FUN"

Charles Muer, who operates a chain of restaurants headquartered in Detroit, employs young part-time workers extensively and considers it entirely feasible that they could take over most of the kitchen work. "You might have to pay them more," he says, "but productivity would be high. Kids are strong and enthusiastic, and dirty work can be fun, especially if you enjoy your co-workers and the management is nice."

Others are skeptical. "You've got to screen young people," says a hospital administrator, "and you can't leave them off by themselves where they'll goof off." Some tasks cannot and should not be performed by the young, particularly those involving nighttime shifts or long commuting distances. And some parents, of course, would object to their children's taking jobs they consider demeaning.

John R. Coleman, the president of Haverford College whose experiences last year as an incognito ditchdigger and trash collector are described in his book *Time Out*, advises many of his students to get a taste of menial work. The parents most likely to be upset by such an idea, Coleman says, are "people unsure of their own status."

There's another and perhaps more formidable impediment. Until now the large number of young people bumping from one job to another as they slowly settle into careers has provided much of the labor pool for temporary dead-end work. (See "A Better Way to Deal with Unemployment," FORTUNE, June, 1973.) But some of the desirable education reforms now being tested are designed to enable high-school graduates to jump right into jobs with career ladders. If "career education" or something like it becomes widespread, it may become necessary to get that menial work out of students *before* they graduate. That would entail new social arrangements of some kind.

In an ideal world, all menial work would be a passing thing, whether for adults seeking a temporary change from their normal routine or for young people who can count on better jobs later on. It won't turn out quite that way, of course. Some people because of limited ability or sheer inclination, will mop floors or wait on tables throughout their working lives. If recent trends continue, however, their pay will rise and with it their self-esteem — and, of course, the costs of their labor, at a time when lots of other things are also getting costlier.

THE AIRLINE ROUTE

An indication of the direction things will move in can be seen in the way some airlines get their planes cleaned up between runs. The American Airlines system, for example, embodies nearly all of the features that society will probably have to incorporate into its low-status jobs. At New York's LaGuardia Airport a force of 185 "cabin service clerks" (an old designation rather than a recent euphemism) cleans floors, scrubs lavatories, and empties the ashtrays into which airline passengers grind their cigarettes. The men go about their work briskly, with no indication that they consider it demeaning. Two-thirds of them are white, the rest black and Puerto Rican. Their pay starts at $4.57 an hour, with a maximum of $5.15.

The job is not a dead end. Some recent hires are college graduates who, in the words of H. Lee Nichols, the staff's black manager, "get a foot in the door with an airline by taking a job like this." Most of these workers move on, replaced by a steady supply of new men attracted by the pay and the prospects for advancement. After all, Nichols says, "five years of cleaning ashtrays, if you have any drive, can get to you."

The Blue Collar View of Management
Today's laborers are very different from those of a generation ago, and their view of the people they work for demands a reassessment of practices.

David Kramarsky

A steelworker, quoted in the first chapter of *Working* by Studs Terkel, talks about his view of management. The head of his company, like the head of his union, is "living it up," he says.

This is not an isolated case. The antagonism between the blue collar worker and the white collar manager has been perpetuated by unions and the media, and not least of all by workers and managers themselves, who in many cases see themselves cast in an adversary relationship. And while it is true that the goals of top management differ from the goals of blue collar employees, this is not necessarily so when one compares the goals of line managers to those of laborers.

The line manager, like the worker, is concerned with wages. Both are concerned with job fulfillment, communication, and maximization of their potential, though they may express it as an escape from boredom. Productivity, for both the manager and the laborer, is often a factor of continued employment and advancement and, in fact, has little to do with an abiding concern for the profits of the company.

One could well ask: If their interests are so close, why the antagonism?

WITH A CAPITAL M

Historical stereotypes are a key factor in understanding the conflict between labor and management. To many workers, a manager is synonymous with Management, always spelled with a capital M, representing the policy-making people in the company for which they work. In contrast to the line manager, the goals of Management are always corporate, never personal, because in a corporate structure the purpose of the leading executives is tied directly to profits. In this light, the title of manager is prejudicial to blue collar workers, who carry stereotypes born in the history of the labor movement and fueled by labor activists. The direct antagonism between laborer and manager does not involve the administrative manager directly, but as we see it, there is a certain discomfort, as well as a certain displeasure that workers have in their dealings with any manager, not just top management. There is also a surprising aspect to the relationship between the blue collar worker and the line manager: a certain sympathy exists for middle management's position.

Reprinted with permission from *Administrative Management* (March, 1977), 38-3, 26-9, 104-105, copyright 1977 by Geyer-McAllister Publications, Inc., New York.

For managers, the world of work has been a relatively stable environment. Managers, at least in this country, have always been individuals who can demand and receive a certain amount of respect on the job. Historically, the managers were never lower-class individuals, but rather offspring of the industrial revolution, like the middle class to which they commonly belong.

Contrast this historical perspective with the blue collar worker. In manufactoring, maintenance, construction, and other labor-intensive industries, the laborer, even the skilled laborer, has been at the bottom. Work conditions and salaries were serious concerns for laboring people into the 19th century, and questions of prestige, meaning, and security on the job were hardly main issues in the minds of blue collar workers during the long uphill climb. In the workers' struggle against the bosses, if they are left with a stereotype of management as a force that attempts to squeeze out the greatest effort for the least possible remuneration, it is not without supporting historical fact.

Throughout the struggle of the working class, executives have been portrayed as "living it up." Workers who never get outside their own home towns hear about executives vacationing in the sun. And laborers eating from brown bags with one eye on the clock see executives hailing cabs on their way to two-martini, two-hour lunches. Executives' offices oftentimes are larger than the homes of blue collar employees, and executives rarely notice the laborer, who in turn, is emphatically aware of the differences between them.

The stereotypes are, of course, exaggerated to emphasize a partial truth. It is the partial truth that keeps the image alive in the minds of workers, who see it directly, and in the eyes of managers, who assume that workers think of them according to the prescribed definition. The image tends to perpetuate itself because of the communication gulf between workers and managers.

THE OFFICIAL VIEW

"The collective bargaining process is the key communication between worker and employer," says Al Zack, director of public relations for the AFL-CIO. This automatically creates a tension, because the procedures of collective bargaining presuppose an adversary relationship. Though collective bargaining works best when the two sides are close to agreement, even in those rare situations it serves the interest of both sides to assume some sort of hostile pose, demanding more consideration, fair treatment, and good faith than they are receiving.

However, even though the sides assume a *pro forma* hostility, Zack contends that an observer can get "an accurate reflection of what a labor union member thinks and does through union actions." While unions and management meet in an adversary relationship, union actions can indicate particular displeasure with the actions of management in any number of ways. But observers find that unions very seldom indicate any cessation of hostilities with management, aside from accepting contract terms and saying they are "satisfied."

Jerry Borstel, director of communications for the International Union of Electrical, Radio, and Machine Workers (IUE), suggests that there are areas where labor and management approach common ground: "We generally agree on the need for prosperity, good business, and a healthy economy," he says. But he adds, "Our objectives are fundamentally in conflict, and it's good to recognize that. One of the appeals of the labor movement is that it's not hyprocritical about its hostility."

According to Borstel, unions and management represent opposing forces in a system that has been worked out to provide workers with the voice they need. While the unions are in conflict with management's means they are not opposed to the ends, specifically because the unions are designed to protect the jobs of members, which includes preservation of the companies for which union members work.

In this light, it is easier to understand the headlines that appeared in newspapers across the country during the 1975 recession, stating that labor and management were working in a new spirit of cooperation. Hostilities ceased because both parties recognized that the very playing field was threatened, and without the field there could be no clash of opposing forces — or no forces at all.

Observers note that the adversary relationship between labor and management is not the same kind of situation that exists in a courtroom, for example. [We] found that on the local level, most union representation, even full-time representation, comes from the rank and file. One maintenance worker, who requested anonymity, said that the entire collective bargaining process would work better if union leadership, from top to bottom, were people who had worked in the same kinds of jobs as the people they represent.

But this kind of representation could possibly intensify the bitterness of difficult struggles between labor and management. Borstel notes that, "union members would not necessarily agree that negotiations resolve the conflicts between labor and management. Negotiators with that background often have a more hostile attitude toward management, because they contend with the problems every day."

BLUE COLLAR BLUES

The problems that workers have to contend with have been described above in a brief discussion of stereotypes. A much broader description of the "blue collar blues" is offered in *Work In America*, the report of a task force commissioned by Elliot Richardson in 1971, when he was secretary of health, education, and welfare under President Nixon.

Key problems cited by the report stem from the increased level of education among today's laborers, the denigration of workers by the media that results in low self-esteem, white collar privileges on the job, white collar abuse of power, and the failure of white collar bosses to listen to suggestions from the rank and file.

The Work In America study states that in 1960, 26 percent of all white workers and 14 percent of all black workers had completed high school. By 1969, those figures had changed to 41 and 29 percent respectively, a factor which the report says accounts for worker complaints of increased monotony and little chance to exercise individual judgment. The jobs are the same, but the people in them are different. A well-educated blue collar worker may also view a management-level employee as an intellectual equal, or even inferior, a factor that can damage boss/worker relations.

This finding is borne out by the comments of Ben Blau, vice-president for technical assistance at the Work In America Institute, a group established by HEW after completion of the namesake study. "There is less distance in attitudes between manager and laborer today than a generation ago," he says. The factors that account for the change, according to Blau, are education, the media, broadened worker interests, and the increased role the worker plays in the community.

"The changes are not uniform," Blau added. "Worker interests are still narrow, but more and more, they are being assimilated into those of the middle class intellectual."

The Work In America study also found that blue collar workers are pointedly aware of white collar privilege: no time clocks to punch, paid vacation, paid sick leave, and a private pension. In contrast, the report found that 27 percent of all blue collars do not have paid vacations, 40 percent have no paid sick leave, and as many as 70 percent will never draw a company pension, though their companies have pension plans.

However, communication was the central issue in the report: "The most consistent complaint . . . has been the failure of bosses to listen to workers who wish to propose better ways of doing their jobs. Workers feel that bosses demonstrate little respect for their intelligence."

"A STONE WALL"

Talking to a manager, according to Tom Powers, a lathe operator at an upstate New York manufacturing plant, "is like talking to a stone wall. You can tell him what you want to, but it doesn't go anywhere." To Powers, such a reaction indicates that, "I am so low on the totem pole that it doesn't matter what I think. If I were a manager, my most important consideration would be the people under me, because they are the ones who will make me look good or bad."

Fred Hicks is a Manpower employee in Pittsburgh. Despite two years of college, he chooses to do blue collar work as a temporary employee because he likes his freedom. At the same time, he is very aware of the problems that hourly workers face. "Managers don't seem to be aware of the problems of blue collar workers, or they don't care." He says managers hold themselves aloof, and perpetuate cultural and social divisions. "It would be nice," he says, "if they had their divisions and smaller salaries and they came to work without neckties." Hicks would like to see the ties go because it would encourage managers to do the same things as the people that work for them. "A good manager would not ask you to do anything he wouldn't do," he says.

Reactions such as these are widespread. In fact, [we] found that interviews and statistics support the view that blue collar morale is on the decline. This drop can be tied directly to management's ability—or inability—to communicate.

For example, statistics provided by Opinion Research Corp., Princeton, N.J., show a consistent growth in the number of hourly employees who are dissatisfied with the human relations qualities of the companies for which they work.

The Opinion Research data base is drawn from questionnaires returned in studies of industrial relations at 350 major manufacturing plants. Each question has at least 50,000 respondents, and some have up to 100,000. While this data base shows that workers in the 1970s are happier with their level of compensation and their type of work, a number of areas show the same seven to 12 percent decline in satisfaction from the 1960s to the 1970s. Among these concerns are:

- Job security, called by ORC the single most important concern of *all* workers.
- The stature of the company compared with other companies.
- The stature of the company compared with its own past.
- The ability of top management to do its job.
- The quality of products turned out by the company.
- Management fairness in dealing with problems and promotions.
- The ability of workers and management to work together.
- Relations between employees and managers.
- Management friendliness.
- The worker's ability to see an immediate boss with a problem or complaint.
- Management action on a problem or complaint.
- Management supportiveness.

The figures from ORC point to complex problems between labor and management, and these figures will be available to the public later in the year, as the research firm presents them at seminars on industrial relations in St. Louis and New York. But what emerges most clearly from these figures is that the hourly worker today is less able to accept the idea of management infallibility and is, therefore, more watchful and more demanding.

"Today workers are preoccupied with management adequacy," says Dr. Arthur Shostak, professor of sociology at Drexel University in Philadelphia. "They want to know if the guys running the company are competent to run it."

MANAGEMENT ABILITY

According to Shostak, in the past workers never doubted management's ability to run the show, but today, in light of the scandals that have shaken business and government, the opinion of the worker and the public in general has taken a general downward reckoning. "There is new uncertainty," says Shostak, and as a result, workers are more susceptible to rumor and misunderstanding. Thus, while workers are more concerned about how management is running the company, they are still uninformed about procedures and changes. Management, by providing more information about company procedures, could boost morale, says Shostak.

On the other hand, workers have different ideas about why morale is down in the industrial operations in the country. "Morale is down because we're a bunch of numbers, not names anymore," says Walt Tuckey, a skilled worker. Thirty-five years with the same company, Tuckey remembers when the CEO came out into the shop and tried to know the names of the people there. "He shook hands, he mingled. He wanted to know what problems there were," he says. Since then, the policy has changed, and Tuckey states that productivity has dropped since the end of the "friendly" policy five-and-one-half years ago.

Fran Spina, an industrial trouble-shooter in the same plant, suggests that better communication could solve the morale problem and the productivity problem at the same time. "I know that the company has doubled in size, but that shouldn't change things," she says. "We're all one company, but in one plant they have one policy and here we have another. Across the street they have still another. It's like three different companies, but we're all under one roof." A concern such as this one could be resolved by better communication, either by management explaining why different policies are necessary or by trying to effect consistent policies throughout a large company.

The same is true for many other specific worker concerns, which, of course, differ from company to company. For example, in the widely publicized wildcat strike at General Motors' plant in Lordstown, Ohio, exactly four years ago this month, workers objected to a management policy forbidding "doubling up" even though the practice improved product quality and offset assembly-line boredom and many foremen approved it. At Eastman Kodak's plant in Rochester, N.Y., the workers are concerned with "frequencies," a system that penalizes them for each absence, regardless of its duration. For example, a worker at Kodak Park who is late five times is in greater danger of being skipped over for a promotion than a worker who is out for two weeks at one time.

A LITTLE RESPECT

Suggestions for improving industrial relations come from many sources, and the scholarly sources debate questions of employee needs, the hierarchy of their desires, and so forth. But much of this kind of academic debate is as useless to managers as it is to blue collar workers, who want to feel that their company at least has some concern for their interests.

Perhaps the best suggestion [we] heard came from Dr. Shostak, who said, "The worker likes to be taken seriously, and responds to a little respect." Mike Cooper, who works for ORC and is an industrial relations specialist in his own right, says that "management would be better off not to ask workers what they think if they do not plan to follow up a study with action." What both men are saying is that management cautiously must open a line of communication in order for relations to improve, but that opening communications is not enough.

The first step in an industrial relations program must be to find out what the worker thinks. This may be done in any number of ways, from mingling with them, to developing a formal study of worker reactions, such as the ones ORC does for its clients. Of course, any research will probably turn up a complex of problems, ranging from simple to insoluble. Management must then address the problems and the workers at the same time.

One way of doing this, according to Cooper, is to allow workers to see the results of the research and propose their own solutions to the problems that they have raised. Another possible approach is to take swift action to remedy some of the more easily handled complaints, thereby defusing what Cooper calls the "latent distrust" of the blue collar worker. At the same time, management will have to show that some of the longer-term problems are being tackled in the new atmosphere of open and accurate communication.

A CERTAIN SYMPATHY

It is uncommon, [we] found, that a worker will be actually angry at management. Instead, while workers are frustrated, they are also sympathetic to the plight of management. "Managers are caught in the middle of a political hassle," said one junior staff member. "You get up the ladder," he said, "and then they yank it out from under you."

The manager, according to Fran Spina, is "like a shepherd in the field, trying to keep all of his sheep together. I feel sorry for him in a sense. The pressure's on him from above and below, and pretty soon it's one big pressure party—you don't even know if you can talk to your foreman."

The worker, then, is sometimes hostile, often disenfranchised, and in many instances prepared to recommend ways of improving the overall management outlook of the company. When [we] caught up with representative workers outside the working environment, such as in stereotypical blue collar bars or in their homes, and evoked their reactions, the results were often surprising, as we have noted.

At the same time, many workers are unconcerned about management, which is perhaps one reason why they have chosen their lifestyle. "Management?" asked one worker. "I think they should get rid of the whole damn thing." He laughed and bought another beer.

OSHA: Problems and Prospects

Joseph Barry Mason

The Williams and Steiger Occupational Safety and Health Act (OSHA) became law in 1970. The act now covers some 60 million workers and 5 million work places.[1] As such, it probably has more impact on the American worker than any legislation since the Wagner Act of 1935.

The need for such legislation was clear. Between 1969 and 1973 more persons were killed at work than in the Viet Nam war. Further, 2.2 million persons are disabled on the job each year, with a resulting loss of 240 million man days of work, a loss much greater than that caused by strike.[2] The National Safety Council has estimated that the cost of wage losses, insurance costs, medical expenses, and related costs such as time spent investigating and reporting accidents exceed $3.9 billion annually.[3] Cost to employers for workmen's compensation coverage as a part of the insurance cost is more than $4.8 billion.[4]

Even ignoring human pain and suffering, the economic costs of job-related accidents are astounding. Equally disturbing is the fact that from 1958 to 1970 the accident frequency rate increased more than 33 percent.[5] It was against this background of tragedy and economic loss that the Occupational Safety and Health Act was passed.

Currently, inspections are increasing in all types of businesses. For example, it was recently stated that "retail inspections, like OSHA inspections in general, are on the upswing ... there were 2,228 July–November last year [1974] versus 1,209 in the same 1973 period."[6] January 1975 inspection data for retailing showed that 875 inspections were made in establishments employing over 42,000 persons. Only 12 percent of the firms inspected were found in compliance with safety regulations; more than 3,400 violations were found.[7]

This article reviews the key provisions of the Occupational Safety and Health Act, presents an overview of the emerging problems and controversies since the passage of OSHA, and offers guidelines in addressing the problem of job-related safety.

AN OVERVIEW OF THE OCCUPATIONAL SAFETY AND HEALTH ACT[8]

Employee coverage. OSHA covers all employers whose business affects interstate commerce.[9] The only employees exempted are those employed by federal, state, and local governments, and special provisions also have been made for them. The size of the business is irrelevant. For example, OSHA officials have said of the small business proprietor, "we appreciate it is more difficult for him to comply, but if we find violations, he will be cited. Ignorance, as in common law, is no defense with OSHA."[10] Employers who are already subject to the standards established by another federal agency are not covered by the act if the other agency continues its duty of enforcement.

OSHA standards. The act provides for four kinds of standards. These are: (1) interim standards, put into effect as soon as it is practical and based on already existing federal guidelines; (2) consensus standards, which are developed after obtaining the views of interested parties and which are typically those established by various trade associations;[11] (3) permanent standards that would replace or supplement interim standards if the interim standards are determined not to be in the best interest of employees' safety; and (4) temporary emergency standards, which can be issued quickly when a finding suggests that employees are exposed to a serious hazard.

In response to its congressional mandate, OSHA has established five priority areas for inspection.[12] The first priority is situations that pose an immediate danger to the health or safety of workers. The second priority is where a fatality has occurred. The third priority is an inspection based upon a valid employee complaint. The fourth priority consists of target industry and target health hazards. The last category is a general inspection of all industries.

New agencies created. OSHA was responsible for the creation of three new federal agencies: the Occupational Safety and Health Administration within the U.S. Department of Labor; the National Institute of Occupational Safety and Health in the Department of Health, Education and Welfare; and the Occupational Safety and Health Review Commission, an independent agency of the Executive Branch.[13]

The Occupational Safety and Health Administration is given the authority to develop standards, conduct inspections, determine compliance with the standards, and initiate enforcement actions against employers who they believe are not in compliance. The National Institute of Occupational Safety and Health (NIOSH) performs research, training, and educational programs in occupational safety and health. Its most important contribution is the recommendation of new standards. The Occupational Safety and Health Review Commission adjudicates enforcement actions of the Department of Labor when they are contested by employers, employees, or unions. The Occupational Safety and Health Administration only proposes penalties. The Review Commission has the sole authority for assessing penalties.

Employer penalties. The responsibility of the OSHA inspector is to determine that an establishment is in compliance with the appropriate standards. If a violation is noted, it is reported to the OSHA area director, who then proposes a violation and informs the employer of the proposed penalty. If the employer disagrees with the citation or the proposed penalty he may contest it by advising the Labor Department within fifteen working days of the citation. When notification is received that an action is being contested, the Review Commission is notified and the adjudicatory process begins. The commission assigns the hearing to an administrative law judge. The hearing typically occurs in the community where the alleged violation took place or as close to the community as possible. It is the responsibility of OSHA to prove that the violation has occurred. Following the hearing, the judge may issue an order to affirm, modify, or vacate the citation or proposed penalty. The order is final after thirty days unless the commission reviews the decision. If an employer decides not to contest the citation he must correct the situation that is in violation of the standards. If he cannot do so within the proposed abatement period, he can seek an extension.

Penalties provided by the act include fines up to:

> • $10,000 for each violation by any employer who willfully or repeatedly violates the obligations of the act, or regulations, standard, rule, or order issued in connection with it.

- $1,000 upon employers receiving a citation for a violation, serious or otherwise.

- $1,000 a day upon an employer who fails to correct, within the time permitted for correction (or after review proceedings for a contested order), a violation for which a citation has been issued.

- $10,000, or imprisonment for not more than six months ($20,000 and one year for a second offense), upon an employer who willfully violates any standard, rule, or order, or regulations prescribed, if such violation causes death to any employee.

- $1,000 or up to six months imprisonment for any person giving advance notice of any inspection.

- $10,000 or up to six months imprisonment, or both, for knowingly making a false statement, representation, or certification.

- $1,000 for each violation upon an employer who violates any of the posting requirements.[14]

Types of regulations. There are two basic types of OSHA regulations: horizontal regulations, which apply to all industries and relate to such features as fire extinguishers, electrical groundings, and machine guards; and vertical provisions, which apply to particular industry groups such as construction.[15]

The various OSHA regulations typically call for minimum safety and health precautions. Ordinarily these are consensus standards that have been derived from previous legislation developed by such organizations as the National Fire Protection Association or the American National Standards Institute. Consensus standards traditionally have been benchmarks against which an employer could measure his company's performance. None of the consensus standards was initially designed with the idea that they would become legislative minimums to which an employer must conform. One writer said "business took the position that we already live by consensus standards so let's write them into the act. But the fact is that they have never read them nor has anyone else who was involved in this legislative process."[16]

Employer responsibility. Responsibilities for OSHA violations reside almost entirely with the employer. As has been stated, "Congress has required the employer to be responsible for every unsafe working condition. For example, the employee can perform an unsafe act, against the direct order of the employer, and the employer will be liable under workman's compensation laws in some states, as well as under OSHA. . . . An employee deliberately could create an unsafe or hazardous condition, report it, and the employer specifically is barred from discriminating against the employee under the act."[17] Thus, no incentive exists for employees to follow OSHA's standards except for their innate concern for their own safety. Significantly, the National Safety Council estimates that 75 to 85 percent of industrial accidents are caused by persons who lack "safety consciousness."[18]

Requirements for record keeping. Three forms of records are required: a log of occupational injuries and illnesses, a supplemental record, and a summary record. These records remain at the place of business and must be made available for examination by federal or state inspectors. An occupational injury or illness must be logged within six working days after the notification, and any lost work days should be recorded. With appropriate summaries, the logs will indicate what occupations or departments are incurring injuries or illnesses and show the areas to be checked during safety inspections.

The act also requires that the records be located at the lowest possible organizational level. This is necessary to provide records for safety inspectors as close as possible to the point of operations. This also prevents pooling of information so that high-frequency injuries are not averaged with statistics from other areas where safety problems are minimal.[19] The only instances in which records are not needed are minor injuries requiring only first aid treatment. OSHA defines first aid as "one-time treatment and subsequent observation of minor scratches, cuts, burns, splinters, and so forth which do not normally require medical care."

For firms with branches, it is a sound idea to keep separate records for each of the various branches. This enables inspection to occur at the lowest possible level and as near as possible to the site of the occurrence.

IMPACTS ON OVERALL CORPORATE STRATEGY

Impact on purchasing. One writer has stated that "the purchasing triangle of quality, delivery and price may well be enlarged to a rectangle of quality, delivery, price and safety."[20] The purchasing agent as the company's primary interface with suppliers must be familiar with the provisions of the act and with its still-evolving standards so that he can insure that products purchased meet the requirements of OSHA.

The act clearly makes each employer responsible for the safety and welfare of his employees. However, less clarity exists as to how the actions of suppliers, customers, and independent contractors affect his duty as an employer. Emerging areas of concern include "a buyer's responsibility to insure supplier compliance with the act, legal exposure to a buyer in the event a supplier fails to comply, a buyer's legal recourse against a supplier who fails to comply, and a buyer's responsibility when suppliers, customers and independent contractors come on the buyer's premises."[21] A buyer is not prohibited from dealing with a supplier who violates the act, nor is he required to obtain assurances from a supplier that he is complying with all appropriate provisions of the act. Thus, as a buyer he is not legally required to refer to or incorporate the act as part of his purchase order.

For a variety of reasons, however, it is desirable for a buyer to refer to the act in contracts with suppliers.[22] For example, a buyer may wish to protect himself against a situation where a supplier is temporarily prohibited by a court order from continuing production of an item until the safety hazard is corrected. Thus, the purchasing agent would find it desirable to structure a contract so that the supplier assumes the risk for a work stoppage and delay in delivery which results from his violation of OSHA regulations.

Buyers also find it to their advantage to insist that goods purchased comply with OSHA standards and regulations. Many suppliers, however, are reluctant to guarantee in broad terms that their products meet OSHA standards. Consequently, some buyers are solving this problem by knowing the OSHA requirements and including these requirements as part of the specifications for purchase. A failure to meet the requirements would be a breach of contract.

Another area of concern is the responsibility of a subcontractor or subsupplier when on the premises of the buyer. An employer may incur liability under OSHA if he allows employees to be exposed to any hazardous conditions which may be created by a subcontractor. A buyer thus would want to have a written statement that whenever a subcontractor is on the premises all activities conducted by him are in accordance with OSHA.

The final area in which a buyer may have additional responsibility is in the leasing of equipment. Appropriate language probably should be included in a lease agreement to insure that equipment and machinery are properly "guarded," as specified in OSHA standards. Overall, buyers increasingly are seeking the broadest possible contractual coverage regarding possible OSHA requirements when dealing with suppliers.

It appears that the risks involved will be passed on by most firms in the form of negotiated express warranties or insurance against the risk of OSHA enforcement. As has been stated, "in both situations the cost eventually will be borne by the consumer, who ultimately must pay for the safe environment of production as an added cost of consumer goods."[23]

Financial impact on small businesses. Various legislative amendments have been offered to exempt small businesses from OSHA requirements. This probably is not in the public interest, however. Approximately 30 percent of the nation's work force is in businesses with fewer than twenty-five employees, and these small businesses have the highest injury rates.[24] Also, if small businesses such as subcontractors were exempted from the act, unsafe practices by their employees could cause unnecessary risks for workers on larger jobs. Finally, it is possible that if the small business proprietor were excluded from the act, large businesses might be placed at a competitive disadvantage because compliance with OSHA is expensive.[25]

Small businesses have a particularly difficult time complying with the standards because the cost for improvements in working conditions is often prohibitive and the owner of a small business may have difficulty understanding the standards and how they relate to him. A special feature of the legislation amended the Small Business Act to provide loans to businesses for meeting health requirements. Any small business is eligible for such loan "if it is likely to suffer substantial economic injury" without such assistance. Businesses must, however, meet normal SBA standards as to employment and size in terms of sales volume.

The major areas likely to require corrective expenditures by virtually all businesses have been stated as follows:

   • Companies will have to take a stronger position on enforcing existing internal rules and regulations concerning maintenance and housekeeping. This could mean that additional maintenance personnel must be hired.

• Internal safety programs may have to be beefed up, primarily to insure that employees are informed of their responsibilities under the act and are complying with requirements.

• Purchases of personal protective equipment will continue to increase for such items as safety shoes and glasses.

• General in-plant utility equipment might have to be purchased or installed, including such items as ladders, scaffolding, railings, fire extinguishers, and first-aid kits.

• The area that may require the greatest single expenditure is in major machinery and equipment purchases and plant modifications to meet OSHA standards; this includes ventilating equipment, noise- and vibration-control equipment, roll bars and backup alarms on materials-handling equipment, machine guards, fire doors, new walls and flooring, and so on.[26]

OSHA generally is not welcomed by small businesses. As was recently stated, "OSHA will probably destroy more businesses than lack of financing will. . . . When OSHA regulations slipped through Congress there was not a coherent body that scrutinized what the effects would be. OSHA is the glaring example of how uncoordinated our government activity can be and how punitive they can be on small business in a very unintentional manner."[27]

Labor-management relations. The act may have a major impact on contract negotiation and administration as e ployees become familiar with their rights under the act. Unions are likely to become increasingly concerned with upgrading working conditions in addition to establishing special benefits for affected workers. Thus, employers are going to have to engage in more safety training for their supervisors and employees. They must also become more diligent in disciplining employees for not complying with safety work rules. This action may lead to more grievance procedures by the union. Therefore, OSHA may have major negative impacts on management-labor relations.

Public relations programs. When a firm is issued a citation, the notice must be posted until the violation is corrected or for three working days, whichever is longer. Thus, even if a violation can be corrected in ten minutes, the citation must remain visible for three days. Serious violations can bring major adverse publicity. Also, as has been stated, "the citation, particularly if it is upheld, may provide a third-party accident victim or his family with an excellent basis to sue directly the corporation, its officers, plant manager, etc., while at the same time collecting workmen's compensation from his own employer."[28]

Increasing attention must be given to the public relations function in explaining management's side to the community, to employees, to stockholders, and to the news media when violations are noted. Proper coordination of the public relations function can minimize problems with employees. OSHA can have a negative impact on management-labor relations if the situation is not handled properly and may seriously damage the employer's reputation with his various publics.

The specific impacts of OSHA vary by type of business, and it is not possible to highlight all of them. However, a brief focus on retailing as one type of business may serve as an example of the type of general problems that may be encountered by virtually all businesses.

OSHA AND RETAILING

John H. Stender, Assistant Secretary of Labor for Occupational Safety and Health, points out that OSHA standards are records of historical problems in that "most violations are the obvious, such as improper wiring, electrical equipment not grounded, unsafe stairs or ladders, obstructions, inadequate or unmarked egress, or no fire extinguishers."[29] Apparently OSHA inspection data are reflective of this view. In fiscal 1974 for supermarkets, variety stores, and department stores, the standards violated most often "pertained to the electrical code, portable fire extinguishers, means of egress, guarding floor and wall openings and holes, power transmission apparatus, handling materials, and personal protective equipment."[30]

George Groves, Safety Director for Food Fair, points out that "80 percent of wholesale and retail-related accidents are due to unsafe *acts* by employees versus only about 20 percent due to unsafe *physical* conditions." He goes on to state that "many OSHA inspections have little or nothing to do with job safety or health."[31]

The costs of necessitated changes in retail structures are likely to be quite high because of necessary changes in old buildings and providing for the new requirements in new buildings. Old buildings, for example, may not meet such standards as the electrical code and are likely to require ripping out of old wiring and installation of new equipment. One supermarket executive who asked not to be identified recently indicated that changes in one ten-year-old, 12,000-square-foot store would approximate $3,000. He went on to say that if all of these changes had to be made immediately, it would come close to bankrupting the company because of the hundreds of stores it operates.[32]

Mack Wilhite, head of the 1,900-store Flemming Company, indicates that "OSHA regulations combined with more stringent Department of Agriculture and state laws will make sanitation considerations extremely important and add to costs. It is not unreasonable to expect that they will add $1.00 to $1.50 per square foot to the cost of constructing new stores."[33]

The consensus among various design experts and manufacturers reveals that the following changes probably will be necessary in new and remodeled stores:

• More use of expensive flooring—quarry tile with nonslip sealed grout for preparation areas.

• Sealed walls and overhead tiles capable of being washed down with germicidal cleaning agents.

- Shielding on slim lines and other lights over preparation areas.

- Grounded three-pronged outlets throughout the store. Waterproof outlets in areas to be sanitized.

- All preparation equipment designed for easy cleaning and sanitizing. This means waterproofing of electrical components and more expensive finishing on machines.

- Separate work areas, saws, sinks, and coolers will be needed for red meats, poultry, and fresh fish.

- Sinks and other fixtures should meet national sanitation standards. Woods and other natural products will have to be replaced by more expensive materials in most cases. Stainless steel of higher quality will have to be used.

- Separate sinks will have to be provided in each perishable prep area; they must be equipped with dispensers of germicidal solutions.

- Sprinkler systems will be required almost without exception.[34]

Many people are beginning to believe that a meaningful program of self-inspection is the key to being in compliance with OSHA. Self-inspection and training programs as well as assignment of more enforcement activities to the states seems to be the direction OSHA is heading. For example, twenty-six states now have OSHA-approved programs.[35]

Organizational responsiveness is necessary for a meaningful self-inspection program. Top management should also give consideration to safety and health records in supervisory evaluations. Likewise, increased employee and supervisory training programs are desirable.

Compliance can be obtained from OSHA by calling an OSHA regional office and asking questions. Another possibility for assistance is the workman's compensation insurance carrier for a firm. Insurance companies have a major incentive in offering advice and counsel because it gives them a differential advantage over competition. Insurance companies may, however, carry out inspections using their own standards. Thus, an insurer's requirements may not cover all areas specified by OSHA.

DISCUSSION

An enlarged sense of social responsibility and increasing numbers of accidents led to passage of the Occupational Health and Safety Act. The federal government now has adopted as national domestic policy that the cost of safety can no longer be balanced against the cost of accidents. Similarly, John J. Sheehan, Legislative Director of the United Steel Workers of America, has stated: "The safety of workers should not be traded off in terms of wage costs. Safety is an *issue of public policy* and the cost of doing business, and *not the cost of dealing with the unions*. While collective bargaining can and does supplement public sector regulation, it cannot substitute for it."[36]

Preventive safety and health can be made to work for retailers and other businesses. Such an approach may help to reduce workman's compensation costs, hospitalization costs, and perhaps lost time from accidents. One corporate officer of a large corporation has stated, for example, "We have cut out lost-time per million man-hours by almost 50 percent," while the manager of another smaller company has pointed out that it has "reduced its workman's compensation costs by 25 percent in a one-year period."[37]

OSHA is not without its problems, however. Employees talk about vagueness in the standards and complain that different OSHA inspectors are likely to provide different answers to the same question.

Another area of uncertainty relates to the assessment of penalties for violations. It has been pointed out that many people believe that the fining process is criminal in nature, which assures an accused firm of all of the constitutional guarantees of a criminal proceeding.[38] However, the federal government apparently feels that fines and penalties are regulatory and that traditional constitutional safeguards, which abound in criminal cases, are not applicable in administrative matters.

In a similar vein, it has been stated that the "Act presumes that the employer is responsible for every injury even if an employee caused the harm when acting against a direct order of the employer. . . . There is no incentive for employees to follow OSHA standards other than innate concern for their own safety, a reality that predated OSHA."[39] He further states that "Congress has placed in the hands of the Secretary of Labor a grant of power unprecedented in the history of the United States. Although the problem must have a high priority in America, it can never be so compelling as to require an approach that subverts the Constitution."[40]

Regardless of the various controversies surrounding the implementation of OSHA, it is a reality that will continue to become even more of a factor in business. As was recently stated, "so to that list carrying the inevitable entries, death and taxes . . . now add OSHA compliance."[41] Much pressure for legislative relief is being exerted, however. Thus, it behooves management to stay alert to possible changes in the legislation that could affect their business. For example, a U.S. District Court has held that OSHA inspectors cannot enter a business for an inspection without a search warrant. The decision is being appealed to the U.S. Supreme Court because a judge will not issue a warrant without justification. Such justification is often difficult to show prior to inspection. If the decision of the District Court is upheld, effective enforcement of the law would be very difficult.[42]

REFERENCES

1. Lawrence P. Ettkin and J. Brad Chapman, "Is OSHA Effective in Reducing Industrial Injuries?" Labor Law Journal (April 1975), p. 236.

2. House Committee on Education and Labor, Occupational Safety and Health Act, RH #91–1291, 91st Congress, Second Session, 1970.

3. U.S. Department of Labor, Job Safety and Health, Number 1 (Washington: Government Printing Office, November-December), p. 32.

4. U.S. Department of Labor, The President's Report on Occupational Safety and Health (Washington: Government Printing Office, May 1972), p. 1.

5. Don Cordtz, "Safety on the Job Becomes a Major Job for Management," *Fortune* (November 1972), p. 113.

6. "OSHA Chief Doesn't See it the Way Chains Do," *Chain Store Age Executive* (April 1975), p. 17.

7. *Ibid.*

8. For more detailed information, see Marjorie Gross, "The Occupational Safety and Health Act: Much Ado about Something," *Loyola of Chicago Law Journal* (1972), p. 247; Horneberger, "Occupational Safety and Health Act," *Cleveland State Law Journal* (1972).

9. Stephen R. Kirklin, "OSHA: Employer Beware," *Houston Law Review* (November 1973), p. 429.

10. "The Book on OSHA Rules: Do It Anyway," *Iron Age* (19 October 1972), p. 17.

11. "OSHA: A Worthwhile Law with Several Uncorrected Faults," *Industry Week* (14 October 1974), p. 21.

12. William A. Steiger, "OSHA: Four Years Later," *Labor Law Journal* (December 1974), p. 726.

13. Robert D. Moran, "How to Obtain Job Safety Justice," *Labor Law Journal* (July 1973), pp. 387-388.

14. Edward J. Kehoe, "The Federal Occupational Safety and Health Act: Its Impact on Management, Safety, and Public Relations," *Public Relations Journal* (August 1972), p. 25.

15. Fred K. Foulkes, "Learning to Live with OSHA," *Harvard Business Review* (November-December 1973), p. 60.

16. "OSHA: A Worthwhile Law with Several Uncorrected Faults," *Industry Week* (14 October 1974), p. 21.

17. Ronald L. Tatham and James H. Coogan, "OSHA: Anticipating Problems Between Purchasing Manager and Supplier," *Journal of Purchasing* (November 1973), p. 63.

18. Foulkes, op. cit., p. 62.

19. "How the Safety Act Affects Banks," *Banking* (May 1972), p. 61.

20. "Purchasing—OSHA's Man in the Middle," *Purchasing* (6 February 1973), p. 37.

21. John D. Jackson, "Let the Standards Do the Talking," *Purchasing* (6 February 1973), p. 47.

22. *Ibid.*

23. Tatham and Coogan, op. cit., p. 67.

24. Foulkes, op. cit., p. 63.

25. See Jack R. Nicholas, Jr., "OSHA, Big Government and Small Business," *MSU Business Topics* (Winter 1973), pp. 57-64.

26. J. Daniel Coogan, Jr., "Financing Compliance with OSHA," *Industrial Development* (May-June 1973), p. 11.

27. "Small Business: The Maddening Struggle to Survive," *Business Week* (30 June 1975), p. 98.

28. Kehoe, op. cit., p. 26.

29. "OSHA Chief Does Not See It the Way Chains Do," *Chain Store Age Executive* (April 1975), p. 17.

30. *Ibid.*

31. "The OSHA Tangle," *Chain Store Age Executive* (April 1975), p. 15.

32. "Chain's Plan Takes the Sting out of OSHA," *Chain-Store Age* (August 1973), p. E-27.

33. "The OSHA Man is Coming and He's Changing *Your* Buying Habits," *Progressive Grocer* (December 1972), p. 35. For further information on sanitation requirements, see Joseph Barry Mason and Morris L. Mayer, "Regulation of Sanitary Practices in the Food Industry: New and Emerging Guidelines," *MSU Business Topics* (Summer 1975).

34. *Ibid.,* p. 15.

35. "OSHA Chief Does Not See It the Way Chains Do," p. 17.

36. John J. Sheehan, "OSHA and Job Safety Plans," *Monthly Labor Review* (April 1974), p. 44.

37. Foulkes, op. cit., p. 88.

38. Tatham and Coogan, op. cit., p. 64.

39. Kirklin, op. cit., p. 446.

40. *Ibid.,* p. 449.

41. "OSHA and the Metal Working Industry," *Iron Age* (21 June 1973), p. 38.

42. "A Hobbled OSHA Seeks Relief," *Business Week* (12 April 1976), p. 95.

QUESTIONS FOR DISCUSSION

1. Suppose you have been hired as a consultant to a plant operating with an assembly line. Management is experiencing significant worker discontent and they can't understand why. Pay is above average and fringe benefits are excellent. Make a list of questions you might need to ask in order to tackle and advise on the problem.

2. In his article, "The Blue Collar View of Management," David Kramarsky states, "The first step in an industrial-relations program must be to find out what the worker thinks." On what bases and for what reasons does Kramarsky make that statement? Do you agree?

3. Discuss the impacts the OSHA is having on company strategy, policy, and programs.

4. "Society's menial tasks are increasing as the demand for social and public service increases. Many of these jobs are being filled, but the costs in terms of turnover and absenteeism are great—even in high-unemployment areas." Suppose you are a manager of a chain of fast-food restaurants. How would you cope with your increased need for help when there seems to be increased resistance by individuals to holding a menial task for long periods of time?

5. Contrast early classical theories of work and their underlying assumptions

with the more recent behaviorally based aproaches. Explain some of the critiques of the behavioral approaches, also.

6. Delineate and discuss the sources of job dissatisfaction as put forth in the *Work in America* study. What is the state of job satisfaction among middle managers? How is this state caused, according to observers? What can be done to alleviate managerial job dissatisfaction?

7. Discuss some of the responses that organizations may adopt in trying to cope with changing work ethics and the new attitudes of both operative and managerial employees.

SELECTED READINGS

Abbott, W., "Work in 2001, "*Worklife,* October, 1976.

Argyris, Chris, *Integrating the Individual and the Organization.* (New York: John Wiley, 1964.)

"The Blue-Collar Blues, " *Newsweek,* May 17, 1971.

"Boredom on the Assembly Line," *Life,* September 1, 1972.

Bowers, D. G., and J. L. Franklin, "American work values and preferences," *Michigan Business Review,* March, 1977.

Gyllenhammar, P. G., "How Volvo adapts work to people," *Harvard Business Review,* July–August, 1977.

Herzberg, Frederick, *Work and the Nature of Man.* (New York: World Publishers, 1966.)

Lawrence, F. G., "Middle managers voice their discontent," *Industry Week,* September 6, 1975.

Maslow, Abraham, *Motivation and Personality.* (New York: Harper and Row, 1954.)

McGregor, D., *The Human Side of Enterprise.* (New York: McGraw-Hill, 1960).

Oates, D., "How far will worker power go?", *International Management,* February, 1977.

O'Toole, J., "Lordstown: Three years later," *Business and Society Review,* Spring, 1975.

Reck, R., "Can the production line be humanized?", *MSU Business Topics,* Autumn, 1974.

Scobel, D. N., "Doing away with the factory blues," *Harvard Business Review,* November–December, 1975.

Sheppard, H. L., and N. Herrick, *Where Have All the Robots Gone?* (New York: The Free Press, 1972.)

Taylor, R. N., and N. Thompson, "Work-value systems of young workers," *Academy of Management Journal,* December, 1976.

Terkel, S., *Working.* (New York: Pantheon, 1974.)

Townsend, R., *Up the Organization.* (New York: Alfred A. Knopf, Inc., 1970.)

"Why nobody wants to listen to OSHA," *Business Week,* June 14, 1976.

Wiggins, R. L., and R. D. Steade, "Job satisfaction as a social concern," *Academy of Management Review,* October, 1976.

Work in America, Report of a Special Task Force to the Secretary of Health, Education and Welfare. (Cambridge: M.I.T. Press, 1972.)

Case

KINGSFORD MOTOR SALES, INC.

Kingsford Motor Sales, Inc., is a dealer for three lines of new cars—two domestic and one foreign—located in Kingsford, New Hampshire, a community about twelve miles above the Massachusetts border. Kingsford Motors is one of New England's highest-volume auto dealerships outside of the Boston area. Aggressive price cutting and a reputation for good service have attracted customers from an area radiating up to about 75 miles from the company's facility. On an average day, Kingsford sales personnel would move six to eight new cars and perhaps another six used vehicles. Sometimes sales reached 20 new cars a day. During the 1974 energy crisis, KMS was fortunate. While they did have over 120 large cars on hand, and these did not move well despite price cutting to below cost, they also had over 200 compact and foreign cars to sell; salesmen had little difficulty moving the smaller cars for full sticker prices.

Kingsford, the Community

The city of Kingsford is a community of some 68,000 people. It is primarily an industrial city, but its periphery and the surrounding towns are agricultural. Kingsford is an old community, founded in 1670 and incorporated as a city in 1864. The city's industrial plants are old and relatively inefficient, and have suffered the vicissitudes of business cycles, changing markets, import competition, and physical depreciation. Recently, two new plants were built on the outskirts of the city, the first new construction since the Second World War. Populationwise, the city has a mix typical of many New England industrial centers: old-line families descended from early settlers and factory owners, descendants from the immigrations of the late 1800's, and the "new" immigrants—unskilled blacks and Puerto Ricans—who have moved into some of the older homes in the city's core. Currently the community is experiencing the serious emigration of its younger citizens.

Kingsford's youth have not been isolated from the events and trends generally affecting youth throughout the country. Long hair and sloppy clothing are the vogue, along with the speech patterns common to the young. Some drugs have been reported in the high school. Students at the high school have won concessions such as the elimination of lunchroom attendance, restroom passes, and compulsory study hall, and the student newspaper was recently the object of a state legislative investigation because of an article studded with four-letter words. The city's newspaper periodically runs editorials denouncing the new lifestyles and the general "lack of discipline" among Kingsford young people.

Kingsford Motor Sales, the Organization and History

KMS was founded in 1929 by John Tilden to sell and service one prestige line of cars. Until 1950, John Tilden kept the agency relatively small, selling about one car a week and knowing all of his customers. Service was a byword with the agency, and the company was known as a place where "you paid the price but were assured of being well taken care of." John Tilden was a conservative man and his dealership reflected that philosophy. Convertibles and station wagons were not stocked; of the ten or so cars kept on hand, all were sedans, and rarely was there a two-toned car on the lot. Tilden prided himself on the highest ethical conduct. In 1946, one local resident offered Tilden $400 extra to put his name higher on the waiting list for the first postwar automobiles. Tilden not only turned down the sum, but refused to sell the man a car at all.

John Tilden died in 1952 and his two sons, Jim and Steve, took over the business. In 1954, the Tilden brothers purchased 14 acres of land on the outskirts of town and built a new showroom and service center. They dropped the prestige car agency and took on one of the low-priced three. In 1959, they accepted the agency for a medium-priced, high-fashion line, and in 1965, added a foreign-car line as well. Soon after the new agency opened, the Tildens started advertising in the Boston papers and on TV stations around New Hampshire, Massachusetts, and Maine. Price cutting became standard (advertising stressed the low overhead of the New Hampshire location), and the agency used appeals with the newest style of vehicles and flashy accessories. In essence, the younger Tildens aimed at a mass selling dealership and keyed in on what they were convinced buyers were looking for — lowest price combined with high-style, high-performance automobiles. KMS salesmen felt no reluctance in pushing accessories, particularly those of a style appealing to the younger auto buyer. One of the city's sage older citizens, when passing the Tilden operation, was heard to comment, "If old John could see what those two kids did to his business, he'd turn over in his grave."

NEW CAR PREPARATION

When a car was sold, the salesman would fill out the sales papers, arrange for financing and prepare a work order to service the car for delivery. KMS guaranteed 24-hour delivery of a new vehicle picked off the lot; and if the customer insisted, the car could be ready by the close of business on the day it was purchased.

Since cars were sold so rapidly, a special service area and crew were employed, separate from the repair service unit. The new-car preparation team consisted of two mechanics, an undercoating specialist, a body man, and a wash man. One of the mechanics, Sam Forbes, acted as foreman of the crew, but generally the salesmen went directly to whoever was working on "his car" to rush the work along. KMS had a 12-step standard new-car preparation procedure (called the "dirty dozen" by salesmen). These steps were:

1. Check lubrication and oil levels (sometimes cars were found to come from the plant unlubricated or with less oil than specified).
2. Winterize to 40 degrees below zero.
3. Check timing and ignition; adjust if necessary.
4. Align and balance wheels; check tire pressure.
5. Check and adjust brakes.
6. Check and adjust transmission.
7. Undercoat (if ordered by customer).
8. Install radio and other dealer-installed accessories.
9. Check and adjust door, hood, and trunk alignments.
10. Touch up scratches.
11. Test-ride.
12. Wash, clean, and vacuum.

THE WASH RACK

Of all the jobs, the wash rack required the least skill, but was the dirtiest. After a car had gone through all the mechanical and body checks, it was delivered to the rack where it was washed and vacuumed, the stickers peeled off the windows, and the floor mats installed. This was the last station of the dirty dozen, and the one where salesmen waited impatiently to get the car for delivery. Sometimes a salesman directed his customer to the wash area to wait for the car. The wash-rack attendant was thus under pressure to get the car out. And if any scratch or imperfection, such as leaks, showed up, he was usually the first to hear about it in no kindly manner. Even though the wash-rack attendant had no role to play in the car's manufacture or preparation, he bore the brunt of a buyer's dissatisfaction. He was often asked such questions as "Can I trust that salesman?" or "Did he give me the best deal?" or "Is this car really gone over like they say it is?" Occasionally he was asked, "How do you disconnect the air-pollution device on this car?"

Tim Wallace

Tim Wallace was the fourth wash-rack attendant KMS employed in the last two years. He was 20 years old, having quit Kingsford High School at age 16 to work in a paper plant. He lasted at the paper plant three months, walking off the job complaining that the chemical smells made him nauseous. Tim then pumped gas on the 11:00 P.M. to 6:00

A.M. shift at the independent gas dealership on Main Street for about four months (one night, he just didn't show up). The next morning, he enlisted in the Army. After basic training, Tim was sent to infantry school and then to Vietnam for a year; he was wounded slightly and spent the final year of his service at Fort Dix, New Jersey in a training company. Tim reached the rank of corporal before his discharge.

The Army and his war experience added little to Tim's skills for civilian life, but they did have an effect on his lifestyle. He grew a beard, wore long hair with a headband, and moved in with a radical commune in Desmond, Massachusetts. Tim experimented briefly with drugs, but stopped abruptly; he left the commune when that style of life started becoming unpopular and returned with his girl friend, Lucille, to Kingsford, where they took up residence in an old farmhouse north of town. Tim had a motorcycle for transport. Some of the older residents had unkind things to say about Tim and Lucille, but generally they were not harassed.

When he applied for the wash-rack job at KMS, Steve Tilden at first was reluctant to even interview him. Tilden was hoping to get someone who was "straight," who could be relied on, and who would work hard, be punctual, and appreciate the fact that he had a job to do. After all, even though the wash-rack required little skill, it was still an important phase in new-car delivery, particularly for a high-volume dealer such as KMS. But when no one else applied for the job, Tilden hired Wallace.

Tim Wallace on the Job

For about four months, Wallace performed well; he showed up on time and his production rate, as well as the quality of his work, was quite satisfactory. One day, a customer complained about paper shavings in the back seat; the salesman brushed them out and said nothing, thinking the event a minor annoyance. But salesmen started receiving complaints about unwashed windows, cleaning compound left unwiped, water on the floors, etc. Steve Tilden talked to Wallace, who shrugged and said, "I'm doing my best. What do you have to do to please all those rich fat cats?"

Tilden also noted that Wallace started arriving five to ten minutes later and leaving five to ten minutes earlier each day. One day Tim called in sick (on sick days, a grease-and-oil man from the regular maintenance shop was called into service on the new-car wash rack). When asked the next day what was wrong, Tim just said, "Nothing much; just a 24-hour bug." Tilden could see no aftereffects of illness.

About a month later, Wallace called in sick again. At about 2:00 P.M. Sam Forbes, the foreman, called Wallace's house to find out how long he was going to be out. No one answered the phone. The next morning, Wallace replied to Tilden's questioning by saying that he was over at the drug store buying some aspirin. He seemed upset at having his whereabouts checked on.

Wallace called in sick again a week later. About 10:00 A.M., Forbes called Wallace's home and got no answer. At about the same time, a salesman told Tilden that he thought he saw Wallace and "some hippy girl" motorcycling down the interstate highway toward Boston.

Forbes burst into Tilden's office. "That damn Wallace is out again and I can't reach him. God, I know that they've got the same problems in the maintenance shop with the guys on the grease and wash racks, but the wash-rack on our end is too important. We've got to get those cars to customers. What the hell is this younger generation coming to?"

4. *Business and Equal Opportunity*

In the last quarter-century, most businesses at one time or another have faced the issue of discrimination. With the rapid development of the civil rights movement in the 1950's and the passage of the Civil Rights Act of 1964 (particularly Title VII, covering employment), the elimination of overt discriminatory practices and the re-evaluation of procedures in recruitment and selection to eliminate any implicit discrimination became important challenges for management. Certainly, personnel departments must now be increasingly professional and analytical in scrutinizing practices of recruitment, testing, screening, wage and salary administration, promotion, and evaluation.

Issues of employment discrimination and the growing aspirations of members of minority groups and women are, however, extremely complex ones. We introduce the topics by first dissussing some basic data on the underutilization of women and minority group members. Then we follow with a brief review of the laws, some indication of the problems in the enforcement of the laws, and finally some notes on managerial responses, problems, and opportunities resulting from the campaign against discrimination.

SOME DATA ON MINORITIES AND WOMEN

The civil rights struggle for blacks is the oldest of the contemporary campaigns and the earliest in terms of major impacts. While much of the early publicity focused on sit-ins and boycotts instituted to secure such basic rights as desegregation in public facilities, restaurants, transit vehicles, and swimming pools, as well as on voting rights and school integration, considerable attention was, and continues to be, directed at employment practices and manpower utilization.

In 1960, blacks constituted about 9.5% of the civilian labor force, but the percentage of blacks in various categories of employment varied markedly from the percentage breakdown of the total labor force. For example, whereas 43.3% of the total labor force was employed in white-collar jobs, only about 16% of the black labor force was so employed (and, of these, almost half were clerical workers as opposed to one-third clerical in the white-collar category for the total labor force). Further, while only 12.2% of the labor force was employed in service work, fully 31% of the blacks were so employed.

By 1975, the picture had improved somewhat. Almost 30% of the blacks were now in white-collar jobs (although half of these were still in clerical work) as opposed to 48.6% white-collar in the total labor force. The percentage of blacks in service work declined to 26 percent, but this figure was still more than twice that for the general labor force. The greatest change came in farm workers. While in 1960, 12 percent of the black labor force was in farm work, by 1975, the figure had dropped to 2.8 percent.*

The data also show that black employment is still heavily concentrated in low-wage sectors and industries, and that blacks generally are more adversely affected by recessions than are whites. Black unemployment rates are consistently almost double those of whites and the median income of black families hovers about 60 percent of the median income for white families, although this is an increase from the 55-percent figure of 1960.

A more recent civil-rights movement involves the aspirations and rights of women and the placement of women in job categories where traditionally they were not found. In 1960, women comprised 30 percent of the civilian labor force. By 1974, that figure had increased to 39 percent. But as with blacks, the breakdown of women in specific job categories is heavily skewed toward relatively unprestigious work. Women are found primarily in clerical, operative, and service-worker roles. They are vastly underrepresented in craft, supervisory, and professional management roles.

Similar problems of underrepresentation can be found with other minorities — Hispanic-Americans, American Indians, and Asian-Americans. While one may doubt that proportional representation of blacks, women, Hispanics, or Indians in each of the specific occupational categories will ever be attained (whether it is wise social policy to attempt to engineer such proportions is an issue that continues to be hotly debated), nevertheless, a legacy of discrimination clearly shows in the data. Minority-group members and women often lack marketable skills and have historically been prevented from entry into many better-paying and prestigious positions.

THE LAW AND SOME CASES

Since 1964, the federal government and many of the states have enacted legislation aimed at preventing discrimination in employment. In the major federal law, the Civil Rights Act of 1964 (as amended in 1968 and 1972), Title VII covers employers with "fifteen or more employees for each working day in each of twenty or more calendar weeks in the current or preceding calendar year. . .", as well as labor unions and employment agencies. The Act prohibits discrimination on the basis of race, color, religion, sex, or national origin in hiring, firing, compensation, and/or any other condition of employment. The law also prohibits the segregation or classification of employees in any way that adversely affects an employee's status because of race, color, religion, or national origin. Finally, the Act normally bars the publication of job openings or notices specifying race, sex, color, religion, or national origin as job requirements.

There are very few exemptions to the Act. Religious institutions are exempt for the activities of the particular religion at hand. On the other hand, religious

---

*Manpower Report of the President, 1975 (Washington, D.C.: U. S. Government Printing Office, 1975).

institutions cannot discriminate on the basis of sex, color, or national origin — only religion. In general, the law also exempts jobs where employment of a particular sex is for *bona fide* business reasons.

Sex discrimination is also the subject of an earlier law. One year prior to the passage of the Civil Rights Act, Congress passed the Equal Pay Act, which barred pay and fringe-benefit differentials based on sex. All major businesses and institutions are covered by the Act.

Another discriminatory pattern, and one that should receive much more attention, is that involving age. The Age Discrimination in Employment Act of 1967 was passed to protect individuals between the ages of 40 and 65 from being discriminated against in employment and job conditions. The Act, enforced by the Secretary of Labor, also forbids employers to exclude newly hired individuals, age 40 to 65, from participation in pension plans if that age group among existing employees is already included.

Enforcement of Title VII rests with the Equal Employment Opportunity Commission. The EEOC, created by the 1964 Act, originally was empowered only to attempt rectification by conciliatory methods, with the complainant taking the case to court in the event EEOC intervention failed. With the 1972 amendment, however, the Commission or the United States Attorney General was empowered to file suit in federal courts.

The court may issue injunctions against unlawful discrimination and order affirmative action in terms of quotas for future employment in an organization as a remedy if past patterns of discrimination have been found to exist. More often the awards concern "making the individual whole again." This means that if a person has suffered discrimination, as defined by the Act, the employer may be ordered to hire or promote that person; in addition, the worker may be awarded back pay, or given other benefits.

The EEOC has been winning its cases, and its ability to go to the courts has given it some clout to negotiate some substantial out-of-court settlements. American Telephone and Telegraph Company paid, in an out-of-court settlement, over $45 million in back pay to women and minority-group employees who had been discriminated against in terms of pay and job advancement. Nine major steel producers agreed to a back-pay, interest, and future-pay settlement that could run as high as $80 million the first year.

Much of the case law and guideline regulation relates to the finer points of what are considered the routine processes of personnel selection. Open, explicit discrimination or bigotry is practiced by very few managers these days (though, unfortunately, this was not always the case), but many of the so-called standard tools of personnel selection have been held suspect or implicitly discriminatory; and it is in these areas that the EEOC and the courts have made significant impacts. Some of these areas will be covered as we explore the following situations.

1. Testing   3. Hiring minorities
2. Hiring women   4. Hiring single female parents

5. Using arrest records and credit ratings

6. Recognizing religious practices

7. Hiring males for previously female jobs

1. Tests. Personnel tests—aptitude, intelligence, ability, and psychological—have had ups and downs in terms of their use as aids in the employee selection process. At times, the use of tests is extremely popular; at other times test utilization reflects a faddishness. In recent years, the controversy has been on the possible cultural biases involved in tests. That is, some have charged that most of the commonly used tests are designed for a white, middle-class world and that blacks and other minority groups are at a disadvantage if their environments do not correspond to the implicit world of the test.

The challenge to tests in general came on the issue of their job-relatedness. In a landmark case, *Griggs vs. Duke Power Co.*, the use of certain tests (and the requirement of a high-school diploma) was challenged on the grounds that they were unrelated to performance on the job. Hence, if they purported to measure intelligence or achievement or ability, and these factors *could not be related to job performance in any precise manner*, and if certain groups would normally score lower on these tests (in the Griggs case, specifically blacks) because of lower educational levels, then the tests were discriminatory and their use was condemned by the Act. The key burden of proof is job-relatedness—not the fact that the tests were applied equally to all applicants.*

The Civil Rights Act does not prohibit the use of tests if such tests are directly related to job performance. Thus, a typing test for a typist would be perfectly appropriate, but an educational achievement test might not be appropriate. And, in a recent case, verbal ability tests were ruled appropriate if discriminatory *intent* was not present in the situation.† But this case should not necessarily be thought of as overruling *Griggs*. The employer, the Washington, D.C., Police Department, had an active program of soliciting minority applicants and was hiring a large number of nonwhites. More blacks were failing the test because more were being recruited.

2. Hiring females. Several principles (mostly myths) formerly dominated management thinking on the hiring of women. Women were thought to be early quitters in order to get married, to follow their husbands to better paying jobs, or to bear children, and generally inclined to be absent more often than males. Further, managers were often concerned about how women would blend in with an all-male work force or with customers who were primarily male. Such considerations are now illegal.

In hiring, management can make no assumptions about the marital intentions of a female applicant, her family plans, or her ability to perform because of family situations. Nor is the compatibility of a woman with other employees to

---

Griggs v. Duke Power Company, 401 U.S. 424 (1917).

†*Washington v. Davis*, 426 U.S. 229 (1976).

be a factor. As with religion, sex can be a factor in hiring only when such a factor is a *"bona fide* occupational qualification." And such cases are extremely rare. Indeed, pregnancy at the time of hiring is no bar to hiring and leaves of absence for maternity must also be granted. However, in the very controversial *General Electric v. Gilbert* Case, the Supreme Court ruled that the company is not obligated to include pregnancy within the coverage of health insurance plans.*

3. Hiring minorities. Similar strictures against discriminating against blacks, Hispanic-Americans, and other minorities are provided for in the law, subsequent court cases, and interpretive regulations. Compatibility with employees' or customers' wishes may not be a factor in employment; neither are language or speech patterns if they are not a factor related to success on the job at issue. But in *Espinosa v. Farah Manufacturing Co.*, the Supreme Court ruled that the Civil Rights Act's prohibition of discrimination based on nationality does not protect noncitizens of the United States against an employment policy of hiring only citizens.†

4. Hiring female single parents. Organizations often take a paternalistic view toward the families of employees and have often refused an individual, particularly a woman, if the manager feels that the children of the applicant could not be cared for adequately while she worked. Obviously, such a concern was not altogether altruistic; the organization was concerned about the possible absenteeism of the mother in order to care for the children.

In one court case, however, this "concern" was ruled illegal and the woman involved was ordered hired. The court ruled that the company could not presuppose that the existence of the children would affect the work or the reliability of the parent on the job.‡ Obviously, if the employee proved unreliable as an individual in the future, then the company could take action for cause, but again, they could not *presuppose* that child-care activities would interfere with work performance.

5. Using arrest records and credit ratings. Again, job relatedness is the criterion in this area. It was a common practice to check out arrest records and credit ratings, and adverse reports in these areas were often causes for not hiring. But there are several problems in using this data. Often it is inaccurate, particularly the credit ratings. Secondly, arrests are not convictions and certain groups may be shown to have higher per capita arrest records than others simply because of residence in an area populated by minority groups who are subject to "sweep" arrests.

In one case, a black applicant was denied a job because he had a large number of arrest citations on his record. The company argued that such a long

---

General Electric v. Gilbert, 13 FEP Cases 1 (1976).

†*Espinosa v. Farah Manufacturing Company,* 414 U.S. 86 (1973).

‡*Phillips v. Martin Marietta Corp.,* 400 U.S. 542 (1971).

arrest record indicated a degree of instability that they were unwilling to accommodate. The court ruled, however, that blacks would tend to have a higher number of arrests than whites since ghettos were subject to frequent sweep arrests and hence to use the arrest record—not a conviction record—against a black applicant constituted discrimination.*

6. Religious practices. The EEOC regulations contain stipulations requiring the employer to reasonably accommodate employees whose religious practices require a schedule differing from the normal work week. Thus, Jews and Seventh Day Adventists, whose Sabbath is Saturday (beginning at sundown on Friday), or Moslems, whose Sabbath is on Friday, must be accommodated if the company *can reasonably do so.*

In many cases, employers were ordered by lower and state courts to reinstate employees who were fired because they could not work on Friday evening and Saturday. Often, the employer also operated on Sunday and could have easily rescheduled the employee for Sunday work hours and an evening at another time. In *TWA v. Hardison,* however, the Supreme Court held that an employer's duty to accommodate an employee's religious beliefs does not require violation of the seniority rights of other employees or require the employer to incur additional costs.†

7. Hiring males for previously female jobs. The opening of male-dominated jobs to females is not the only result of the changing social mores and the passage of the Civil Rights Act of 1964. Female-oriented jobs are now open to males as well, and it is against the law to deny a male a job simply because of sex. Thus, such positions as airline cabin attendant, nurse, and secretary are now increasingly being opened to males.

SENIORITY AND THE CIVIL RIGHTS ACT

Bona-fide seniority systems are sustained under the Civil Rights Act of 1964. In terms of remedies under Section 7, however, the courts have generally ruled that applicants and employees who were discriminated against and denied jobs on the basis of race should later not only be hired with appropriate back pay, but were entitled to accumulate seniority that would have accrued had they been hired or promoted at the time they originally applied. No claims are made for seniority denied before the law was passed in 1964 and the decisions also do not go so far as to substitute preferential seniority for minorities and women who could not claim actual discrimination in hiring. Relative to the latter situation, critics claim that seniority systems were established at a time when, in general, women and minorities were excluded from hiring, and hence the seniority system in force in many of the nation's workplaces is implicitly discriminatory and should be put aside. This issue usually arises when layoffs occur and the last

---

*Gregory v. Litton Systems, Inc., 472 F. 2d 631 (9th Cir. 1972).

†TWA v. Hardison, 14 FEP Cases 1697 (1977).

hired are the first fired. In many cases, the last hired are minority group members and women.

Another recent case, however, reinforced the law's protection of *bona-fide* seniority provisions. The court reaffirmed that seniority systems that are without discriminatory intent are lawful even if the effect is to discriminate.* Many observers view this decision (along with several others in the Civil Rights area) as moving from a test of *effect* to one of *intent* in the determination of the legality of a particular practice. Much of the law and most of the regulations—from *Griggs* forward—had been built on the test of effect despite the absence of any evil intent. The newer decisions seem to be moving back to the standard of intent.

AFFIRMATIVE ACTION

Another stage in the government's campaign against discrimination is Affirmative Action. Under Executive Order 11246 (amended by E.O. 11375) promulgated by President Lyndon B. Johnson, all businesses and institutions holding federal contracts (or subcontracting for a federal contract) of $50,000 or more, and having 50 or more employees, are often required to develop numerical goals, plans, and timetables for implementation to increase the numbers of females and minority group employees in all categories within their firms.

Compliance with the Executive Order is guided by the Office of Federal Contract Compliance of the Department of Labor. OFCC may designate the contracting agency as the compliance office for a particular contract or area; the Department of Health, Education and Welfare, for example, monitors the affirmative-action activities of universities.

Affirmative Action goes beyond the Civil Rights Act of 1964 in that employers not only are required to practice nondiscrimination, but are required to take steps to *actively search* for qualified minorities and women to fill positions and to upgrade the skills and utilization of women and minorities within the firm. (Department of Labor Orders were issued in 1975 requiring similar affirmative action for handicapped persons and Vietnam Veterans.) In one very real sense, Affirmative Action is requiring the government contractor to do what sound personnel management might prescribe also; that is to make as wide a search as possible for qualified applicants.

Affirmative Action requires the government contractor to:

1. Take a racial and sexual census of employees. No employee can be forced to participate in such a census; hence, it can be gathered visually for women, blacks, and Asian Americans, and by names on the payroll records for Spanish-surnamed Americans.

2. Determine the proportion of women and minority members in the labor market from which the organization draws. (In terms of universities and many managerial positions in industry, such a market may be a national one. For operative employees, the labor market may be very local one.)

Teamsters v. United States, 14 FEP Cases 1514 (1977).

3. Determine in which of the areas (in terms of job classifications) the company is deficient in its utilization of minority-group members and women, relative to the determined proportions of those groups in the general workforce or labor market.

4. Establish goals, timetables, and plans for action for increasing the utilization of minority-group members and women in the deficient areas.

5. Apply good-faith efforts to meet the goals.

6. Periodically report on the actions taken and the progress toward meeting the established goals.

Government officials repeatedly stress that Affirmative Action does not require an organization to follow a quota system; nor does it require the organization to hire nonqualified personnel. The contracting organization can fail to meet its goals, so long as it shows good-faith efforts in the attempt to meet them.

But that raises several problems for the organization in effecting affirmative action. First, the burden of proof in terms of "good faith" is on the contractor, and some overzealous government bureaucrats may subject an organization to a real quota system by rejecting the organization's attempts at good faith. Second, a manager, in attempting to keep the government away from the organization, may simply "fill the quota" without regard to the superior qualifications of rejected candidates.

Some legal experts have charged that there is a contradiction between the Civil Rights Acts and Affirmative Action, in that rejected white males' civil rights may be violated if individuals with inferior qualifications are hired on the basis of race and sex. In one case, involving university admissions, a University of Washington Law School applicant sued the University for violating his civil rights when minority students with qualifications inferior to his were admitted and his application was denied. A lower court ruled for the applicant and he was admitted to the law school, and remained enrolled even though a higher court reversed the decision. The student continued the case. When the case finally reached the U.S. Supreme Court, the student was ready to graduate, so the Court ruled the issue moot.

Another very similar case, however, is currently being heard by the Supreme Court. A student was denied admission to the University of California at Davis Medical School; the California Supreme Court ruled in his favor, but the university regents have opted to carry the case to the U.S. Supreme Court. Some other cases are now before the lower courts in this area, some involving employment in major corporations. In terms of the contradiction, however, the Civil Rights Act does provide for the court's ordering Affirmative Action—including explicit quotas—to remedy *specific patterns of discrimination* (real or implicit) *found to exist*.

Finally, in terms of problems, Affirmative Action has the possibility of attaching a stigma to individuals hired under the program even when the stigma is undeserved. Thus, a reputation that one was hired only because of race or sex may be difficult to live with in terms of relationships with fellow employees, customers, and even one's friends.

Penalties under Affirmative Action are strictly economic. The only penalty is loss of contract. No civil or criminal penalties are possible (except in court-ordered cases under Title VII); but loss of contracts can be a serious penalty for a business firm, particularly if key components of the organization's resources are tied to government work.

MANAGERIAL RESPONSES, PROBLEMS AND OPPORTUNITIES

The new laws, regulations, and court interpretations of them impose several obligations on management. First, traditional sources of recruitment may no longer be adequate. Management must expand its practices to include not only offering equal opportunity in the selection process, but also assuring that potential applicants have equal access to notices of job openings. Second, traditional selection devices such as tests, profiles, and employment reviews must be re-evaluated for validity, reliability, cultural bias, and necessity. The Griggs test of job relatedness is still the one for management to follow.

Companies must also re-evaluate their concepts of sex requirements for jobs, and discard many of the prevailing myths about the performance of women and minority-group members. All of this, of course, increases the need for competent professionalization of the personnel department. In fact, many observers credit the new regulations with pulling the personnel department (of which staffing is a part) out of the dustbin of management. The personnel function is now an important and critical area for the well-being of the organization.

Lastly, some critics argue, companies and society should realize that having an essentially black or minority work force with a white supervisory staff might entail costs in terms of lost productivity, job disruption, poor communication, and frustration. In essence, by actively promoting minority-group members to supervisory positions and managerial ranks, companies develop productive links with operative employees that they might not be able to develop with white-only supervision.

THE READINGS

The first two articles focus on the status of women and blacks in U.S. society. Shirley H. Rhine (in the *Conference Board Record*) traces changes in the status of blacks (using the 1970 census data) in terms of income, employment, entrepreneurship, education, and geographical location. Leonard A. Lecht (also in the *Conference Board Record*) details the problems of women in the workplace in terms of gaining salary and entrance into the higher-paying and prestige jobs. According to Lecht, the progress is slow, and the possibility of the gap widening between the career aspirations of women and the reality of the labor markets is very real.

As we mentioned earlier, Affirmative Action is now required for government contractors with respect to handicapped workers. The article by Decker and Peed entitled "Affirmative Action for the Handicapped" details how the requirements are to be met and what a company can do to ensure that it is fulfilling its obligation.

Finally, we have included Daniel Seligman's *Fortune* article, entitled "How 'Equal Opportunity' Turned into Employment Quotas." Seligman examines the vague circumstances for applying numerical remedies by the courts, as well as the associated problems of Affirmative Action programs. Seligman's stance is quite clear; he questions the possible inconsistency between equal opportunity and affirmative action. He writes, "For a democratic society to systematically discriminate against 'the majority' seems quite without precedent. To do so in the name of nondiscrimination seems mind-boggling."

The Economic Status of Black Americans

Change has already lessened some of the historical differences

Shirley H. Rhine

Concern about the depressed condition of the majority of black Americans has undoubtedly broadened and deepened in recent years. It was fostered by a combination of events culminating in the civil disorders and race riots of the 1960's. Heightened pressure by blacks and other disadvantaged groups, as well as by many segments of the more affluent white population, certainly hastened the passage of the Civil Rights Act and the Economic Opportunity Act, in 1964.

The former prohibits discrimination in employment, education, public facilities, voting rights in Federal elections and primaries, and in programs receiving Federal assistance. The principal objective of the Economic Opportunity Act is the extirpation of poverty through a variety of programs for improving the education, training, work experience, and health of the disadvantaged so they may upgrade their earning ability.

Although less than a decade has elapsed since the passage of these basic legislative acts, they have apparently already had a significant impact. This article attempts to depict how much progress blacks have made in recent years, and how well off they are today compared with the white population.

From *The Conference Board Record,* August, 1972. Reprinted by special permission of The Conference Board.

The median income of black families* in 1970 was $6,279, or 61% of the $10,236 figure for white families.† While the gap remains substantial, it has shrunk markedly since 1965 when the average income of black families was only 54% that of the whites. However, black families are somewhat less well off vis-à-vis whites than is indicated by a comparison of median family income of the two groups, since black families are inclined to be larger. In March 1971 the average number of persons per black family was 4.26 compared with 3.52 per white family.

The narrowing of the discrepancy between incomes of blacks and whites since the mid-1960's undoubtedly reflects the influence of the Civil Rights Act. The relatively high rate of growth of the economy as a whole during the latter half of the 1960's probably also played a part in the reduction of the black-white income spread. Periods of rapid economic expansion, when demand for manpower is great, tend to be particularly favorable to the disadvantaged groups in the labor force. The competitive disadvantage of minority groups in finding employment and obtaining promotions tends to diminish in periods of rapidly growing manpower needs.

In recent decades the most dramatic annual rise in the ratio of incomes of blacks to whites occurred in 1966 when it rose to 58% from 54% in 1965. It is relevant to note that 1966 was the first full year in operation of the Equal [Employment] Opportunity Commission, which went into effect in July 1965. Moreover, from 1950 to 1965 there was no notable reduction in income differentials between whites and blacks.

From 1965 to 1970 the gap between average family income of blacks and whites narrowed proportionately more in the South than in the rest of the nation. Nonetheless, family income of blacks in the South in 1970 was still only 57% that of whites, markedly below the other three regions (Chart 1). The differential between incomes in the South and the rest of the country is considerably more pronounced for blacks than for whites.

Female heads of families are far more common among blacks than among whites. In 1971 some 29% of black families were headed by women as against only 9% of white families. This contributes significantly to the black-white family income gap since the median income of female-headed families is considerably lower than that of males — 54% lower for black families in 1970 and 46% lower

---

*Statistical series from the Bureau of the Census and the Bureau of Labor Statistics do not always break out blacks separately. Some of the series apply to nonwhites, which include American Indians, Japanese, Chinese, Filipinos, Asian Indians, Koreans, Polynesians, Indonesians, Hawaiians. Aleuts, and Eskimos, in addition to blacks. (Persons with Spanish surnames, such as Puerto Ricans, are classified according to color, i.e., white or black.) Since blacks account for 90% of the nonwhite population, trends in the latter are virtually identical with trends in the former. For this reason, the designation "blacks" is used throughout.

†Here and below, "income of families" applies exclusively to families and does not include unrelated individuals.

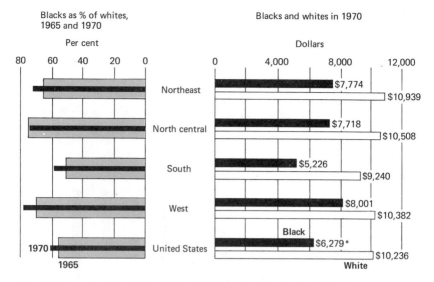

Blacks as % of whites, 1965 and 1970

Blacks and whites in 1970

Per cent

Dollars

80	60	40	20	0		

0	4,000	8,000	12,000

Northeast — $7,774 / $10,939

North central — $7,718 / $10,508

South — $5,226 / $9,240

West — $8,001 / $10,382

United States — Black $6,279* / White $10,236

1970 / 1965

* Since slightly more than half of the black families in 1970 lived in the South and only 8% lived in the West (region where incomes of black families were highest), the median income of black families for the United States as a whole is closer to that of blacks in the South than in the rest of the country.

Chart 1 Median family income. *(Source:* Bureau of Census.)

for white. Hence, among families headed by men, the median income of blacks in 1970 was 73% that of whites.

Blacks are far less likely than whites to have income from interest, dividends, rent, estates, trusts, or royalties. Only 11% of the black families had income from one or more of these sources in 1970, compared with 45% of white families. However, blacks are more likely to receive public assistance and welfare payments. Some 22% of the black families received income from these sources in 1970 as against only 4% of white families.

During the past two decades the number of black families with annual income of $10,000 or more has been increasing at a considerably faster rate than the number of white families in that income range, particularly between 1965 and 1970. During the five-year interval the number of black families in the $10,000-and-over bracket (in constant 1970 dollars) doubled, while the number of white families in that category increased by one-third. Even so, only 28% of the black families had income of $10,000 or over in 1970, compared with 52% for whites (Chart 2).

INCIDENCE OF POVERTY

In 1970 there were still 1.4 million black families and 3.7 million white families below the official low-income level* despite substantial progress during the past

---

*The concept of poverty, or low income, as used here was developed by the Social Security Administration in 1964 and revised by a Federal Interagency Committee in 1969. Poverty thresholds vary by family size, sex and age of the family head, number of children, and farm-nonfarm residence. They are updated annually to reflect changes in the Consumer Price Index. The poverty line for a nonfarm family of four was $2,973 in 1959, $3,743 in 1969 and $3,968 in 1970. In 1970 it ranged from $2,500 for a two-person family to $6,400 for a family of seven or more persons.

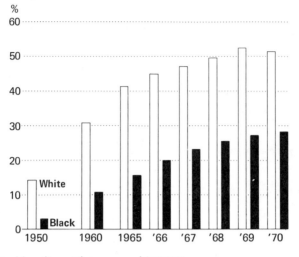

Chart 2 Percent of families with income of $10,000 or more. (*Source:* Bureau of the Census.)

decade in reducing poverty. From 1959 to 1970 the proportion of families below the poverty threshold fell from 48% to 29% among blacks and from 15% to 8% among whites. Virtually all of this gain was achieved between 1959 and 1968, with no marked change in 1969 and 1970, the latest year for which data are available.

Unlike white families, black families below the low-income level are predominantly headed by women. In 1970 some 43% of the black families below the poverty line had a male head compared with 70% of the white families.

Among both blacks and whites, families with a female head are more prone to be below the poverty line than those with a male head. Among blacks, 54% of the families headed by women were below the poverty threshold in 1970 as against 18% of those headed by men. Among whites, the respective ratios were 25% and 6%. Moreover, the proportion of families in poverty headed by men has declined far more precipitously in the past decade than those headed by women (Chart 3).

Explanations for the high incidence of poverty among families headed by women are quite obvious. First, a substantial portion of these women have young children. Consequently, many of them are unable to leave the home to take jobs or are able to work only a limited number of hours a week. As a result they tend to have no earnings or very small earnings, and often have to rely either wholly or partially on public assistance. Also, women on the average have smaller incomes than men. In addition, a woman head is less likely to have another adult in the family to contribute earnings, whereas a man may have a wife who can also work.

One reason why black families with a female head have proportionately larger numbers in poverty than their white counterparts is that black women tend to have lower-paying jobs and more dependents than white women. Secondly, it is more common for black women who are widowed to be less adequately

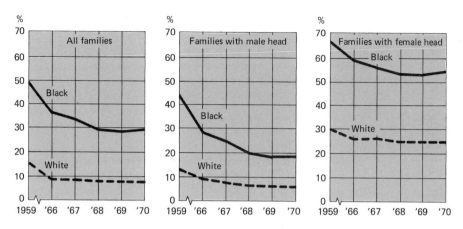

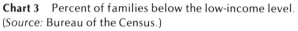

Chart 3   Percent of families below the low-income level.
(*Source:* Bureau of the Census.)

provided for by life insurance and/or savings. Black women who are divorced or separated from their husbands are less likely to receive support payments from their erstwhile or estranged spouses, and when such support is received it is more likely to be smaller than for whites.

Some 45% of the black families and 21% of the white families below the poverty threshold received public assistance or welfare payments in 1969 (the latest year for which data are available). Among the reasons for the higher proportion of black families in poverty that receive public assistance are:

> • On the average, far wider presence of female heads among black families below the low-income level than among white. A substantially smaller proportion of women than men who head such families are employed. Among families in poverty, slightly less than 30% of the female heads were employed in 1970 compared with 58% of the male heads among blacks and 50% of the male heads among whites.

> • In families below the poverty line where the head is employed, earnings of the heads in black families are, on the average, lower than in white ones.

> • Whites are more likely to have assets, such as savings, which would disqualify them for public relief.

FAMILIES WITH TWO INCOMES

Husband–wife families in 1970 represented 89% of total white families* and 70% of total black families.† Wives in black families are more likely to be gain-

---

*The other 11% are families with a female head (9%) and families, other than husband-wife families, with a male head (2%).

†The other 30% are families with a female head (27%) and families, other than husband-wife families, with a male head (3%).

fully employed and to contribute a larger share to the family coffer. Among husband–wife families, 54% of the wives in black families were working in 1970 compared with 38% of white wives. For families where both husband and wife worked, wives on the average contributed 31% of the family income among blacks and 26% among whites.

Median income for families with both spouses working shows a considerably smaller gap between blacks and whites than for other types of families. In 1970 the median income of black husband–wife families where both worked was 79% of their white equivalents.

The income differential between black and white families in this category tends to be correlated with the age of the family head, i.e., the differential is smaller for families where the husband is young than where he is older. For example, in 1970 among families where both spouses worked and the husband was under 35 years old, the median income of black families was 89% that of white, compared with 66% for those families with a head aged 55–64.

In the North and West, among families with both spouses working, blacks seem to be well on their way toward achieving income parity with whites. (In the South, not only is the average income of white families below the rest of the country but the ratio of black to white is also lower.) Among families where both husband and wife worked, the median income of black families was 92% of whites. Also in the North and West, in 1970, the ratio of the median income of black families with both husband and wife working to their white counterparts graduated from 81%, where the head was between 55 and 64 years old, to 104%, with a head under 35 years old.

The achievement of parity with whites, or even slightly more, in the North and West for the latter group of black families can be attributed to the greater annual earnings of black wives compared with white. For families where the head was under 35 years old, the mean earnings of wives in black families was 130% that of white wives, while for husbands in black families it was 90% that of the white husbands. Higher earnings of black wives reflects more work time during the year. In 1970 in the North and West 52% of the wives in black families, where the husband was under 35 years, worked 50 to 52 weeks, compared with 36% of their white counterparts. Whether, among black families, working wives with husbands under 35 also worked more hours per week than their white counterparts cannot be determined since the relevant data are not available.

BLACKS IN THE LABOR FORCE

The percentage of the noninstitutional population 16 years and over that is in the labor force is, in the aggregate, virtually the same for blacks and whites—60.9% and 60.1%, respectively, in 1971. However, when viewed by age and sex, labor force participation rates between blacks and whites show marked differences.

Black men have lower participation rates than white men in all age groups, particularly among teen-agers. However, black women have a higher participation rate than white at all ages, except for the 16–19 group where it is substantially lower and the 20–24 category where it is only nominally lower (Table 1).

TABLE 1.   Civilian labor force participation rates,* by age, sex, and race

Age	Men		Women	
	Black	White	Black	White
Total, 16 years & over..........	74.9	79.6	49.2	42.6
16 and 17 years.................	32.4	49.2	21.9	36.4
18 and 19 years.................	58.9	67.8	41.4	55.0
20 to 24 years..................	81.5	83.2	56.0	57.9
25 to 34 years..................	92.9	96.3	59.2	43.6
35 to 44 years..................	92.0	97.0	61.0	50.2
45 to 54 years..................	86.9	94.7	59.4	53.7
55 to 64 years..................	77.8	82.6	47.1	42.5
65 years and over...............	24.5	25.6	11.5	9.3

(1971 averages)

*Percent civilian noninstitutional population in the labor force.

Source: Bureau of Labor Statistics

On the whole, black women of necessity carry a larger share of the family financial burden than white women. First, a far larger share of black families have female heads—29% in 1971, compared with only 9% of the white families. Second, since black husbands on the average earn less than their white counterparts and tend to have somewhat larger families to support, black wives are more strongly motivated to contribute to the family income.

Only 36% of the total black population was in the labor force in 1971 as against 41% of the white. It is quite evident that a significantly larger share of the black population is economically dependent, which is traced to the higher proportion of black children under 16 years old than white.

BLACK UNEMPLOYMENT

Unemployment rates historically have been considerably higher for blacks than for whites. This phenomenon stems from a variety of sources:

> • Largely as a consequence of a relatively greater number of school dropouts among blacks in the labor force than among whites, blacks are more heavily concentrated in low-skill jobs whose holders are generally more vulnerable to both cyclical and secular unemployment.

> • Since blacks on the average have fewer years of schooling, often of a lower quality than whites, they are frequently at a competitive disadvantage in the market for middle-range and upper-range jobs.

> • Racial discrimination, while receding, has also been a deterrent in the hiring of blacks.

During the entire decade of the 1960's the jobless rate among blacks was at least twice as high as among whites, but in the past two years it was running about 80% higher. In 1971 the unemployment rate averaged 9.9% for blacks and 5.4% for whites.

In contrast to most previous periods of rising unemployment when blacks tended to suffer sharper increases than whites, the unemployment rate for blacks rose by 55% from 1969 to 1971 compared with 74% for the whites. The Bureau of Labor Statistics attributes the narrowing differential between the unemployment rate of blacks and whites to combination of factors: (a) rising educational level of blacks has permitted them greater access to occupations that are less vulnerable to employment cutbacks during cyclical declines; (b) paucity of blacks in those industries which experienced the sharpest declines in employment such as defense and aerospace industries; (c) industries where relatively large numbers of blacks are employed, such as service industries and government, did not undergo severe reductions in employment; (d) relatively large enrollment of blacks in manpower programs; (e) decline in discriminatory practices among employers in laying off of black workers during a period of employment cutbacks.

MOVING UP THE LADDER

Upward mobility in the occupational scale during the 1960's was far more dramatic for blacks than for whites. From 1960 to 1971 the number of professional and technical workers among blacks rose 128% and the number of managers, proprietors and officials rose 92%, compared with 45% and 21%, respectively, for whites. Conversely, the number of blacks in those occupations which tend to be least remunerative—private household workers, farmers and farm workers, and nonfarm laborers—registered steeper declines in the past decade than the number of whites in these jobs (Chart 4).

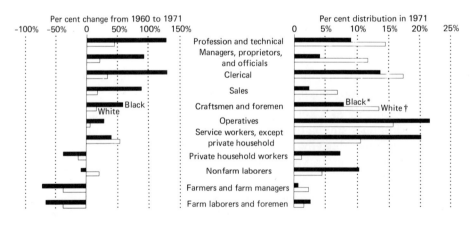

*Percent of total black employment
†Percent of total white employment

Chart 4   Employment by occupation.
(*Source:* Bureau of the Census.)

The marked improvement in the occupation profile of blacks in the past decade has accrued from a variety of sources:

- Heightened demand during the 1960's for professional and technical workers, particularly for teachers, engineers, and technicians. Opportunities for jobs are naturally more numerous in those occupations where demand is expanding and applicants become increasingly scarce.

- Decline of racial bias in employment, undoubtedly partly attributable to the Civil Rights Act of 1964.

- The level of education attainment of blacks in the labor force has been rising at a faster rate than for whites.

- The mushrooming of programs, sponsored both by government and private groups, for training the unskilled and upgrading those with low-level skills has enabled many blacks and other disadvantaged to obtain better jobs.

Despite the impressive growth in the number of blacks in the more coveted occupational groups and declines in the least desirable ones, their number is still disproportionately small in the former and large in the latter (Chart 4). Moreover, even within each occupational group, earnings for full-time male workers are consistently lower for blacks than whites. However, for women, earnings of blacks more closely approach those of whites for each of the occupational classifications, and for private household workers even exceed whites by 10% (Chart 5).

The black-white earnings differential has shrunk substantially more for women than for men in the past decade. Part of the explanation for this is that there was an especially sharp increase in demand in those occupations which attract mainly women—clerical workers, teachers, and nurses. Hence, opportunities for moving up into better-paying jobs were probably greater for black women than for black men. In addition, black women have, on the average, higher levels of educational attainment than black men—55% of the black women in the labor force in 1971 had at least a high school education compared with 45% of the black men. Consequently, black women were better able to take advantage of the greater availability of higher-paying jobs.

Another reason why black women have made greater gains than black men in reducing the lag between their earnings and those of their white counterparts is that wages and salaries of white women have risen proportionately less than the earnings of white men during the past decade. Sex discrimination may have restrained gains in earnings of white women.

The gap between earnings of blacks and whites for all full-time workers, both men and women, is greater than within individual occupational groups since there are proportionately far more blacks than whites in the lower-paid occupational groups and proportionately fewer in the higher paid ones.

Per cent

Note: Earnings data were not published for any group which had fewer than 75,000 persons:
*Fewer than 75,000 black females
†Fewer than 75,000 black or white males

Chart 5   Median earnings of year-round full-time workers in 1970, blacks as percent of whites, by sex.
(*Source:* Bureau of the Census.)

To what can the earnings differentials between whites and blacks within each occupational group be attributed? A combination of factors probably contribute to this reality:

> • There is a broad range of jobs within each occupational group with an equally broad range of wage levels, and blacks and other minority groups tend to be somewhat more heavily concentrated in the lower tiers of the occupational scale within each broad category.

> • Particularly in the better-paying jobs, blacks tend to be younger than whites. Consequently, on the average they earn less than whites in specific job classifications, reflecting less experience and seniority. Also, at entrance levels, blacks often are less qualified owing to inferior educational opportunities at segregated schools.

> • A disproportionately large number of blacks live in the South where earnings are significantly lower than in the rest of the country.

> • Discrimination, while declining, doubtless still exists and operates as an earnings depressant; e.g., opportunities for promotions and advancement may still be more limited for blacks than for whites.

The disproportionality in occupational distribution between whites and blacks, it should be noted, is considerably less pronounced among younger workers than among older ones, particularly at the middle-and lower-pay levels. In 1970 the proportion of persons aged 24 through 34 who were in occupations at the middle-pay level was 55% for both blacks and whites, while 35% of the blacks between the ages of 55 and 65 were in the middle-range occupations compared with 52% of the whites. Conversely, some 29% of the blacks in the 24–34 age group were in lower paid jobs compared with 13% for whites. But for those aged 55 through 65, fully 55% of the blacks were in the lower-level occupations as against only 21% of the whites (Chart 6).

BLACK BUSINESSES

Blacks are particularly underrepresented as entrepreneurs. According to a recent study of the U.S. Bureau of the Census,* in 1969 blacks owned 163,000 firms, or only 2.2% of the total 7.5 million firms in the United States. An even more dramatic indicator of the relative paucity of black-owned businesses is their share of all minority-owned firms. While blacks accounted for about three-fourths of the minority population,† they possessed only one-half of all minority-owned businesses.

The share of business activity accounted for by minority firms is especially tiny. Gross receipts of black-owned businesses represented only 0.3% of gross receipts of all firms, and other minorities had 0.4%.

Minority-owned businesses are far more likely than the rest of the business population to be small, one-person or family-run operations. Over three-fourths of the black-owned and two-thirds of other minority-owned firms had no paid employees; in 1969 they had average gross receipts of $7,000 and $8,000, respectively. For firms with one or more paid employees, those owned by blacks averaged four employees and gross receipts of $95,000; similarly, those owned by other minority groups also averaged four employees and gross receipts of $102,000. A mere 2% of the firms owned by blacks, as well as by other minorities, has gross receipts of $200,000 or more in 1969.

Minority-owned businesses are overwhelmingly sole proprietorships, constituting 91% of black-owned firms and 84% of other minority-owned firms. Con-

---

*U.S. Bureau of the Census, *Minority-Owned Business; 1969.* The study embraces all private industries with the exception of agriculture, railroad transportation, offices of physicians and dentists, legal services, and nonprofit organizations. Most of the data have not been compiled for earlier years so no information on the time trends is available. However, the Bureau of the Census plans to prepare a similar set of tabulations for 1972, scheduled for 1974 publication. It would be interesting to see whether, in the three-year period from 1969 to 1972, blacks and other minority groups have made significant gains as owners of business enterprises.

†"Minority population" as used in this context includes blacks, Spanish-speaking groups (of Mexican American, Puerto Rican, Cuban, and Latin American ancestry) plus Orientals and American Indians.

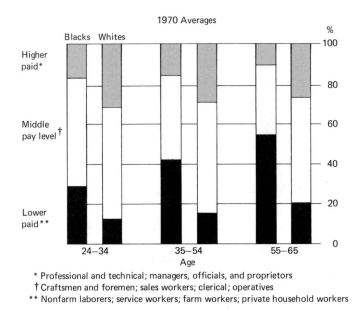

* Professional and technical; managers, officials, and proprietors
† Craftsmen and foremen; sales workers; clerical; operatives
** Nonfarm laborers; service workers; farm workers; private household workers

Chart 6   Distribution of employment by occupational levels for selected age groups.
(*Source:* Bureau of the Census.)

versely, the corporate form of business, which accounts for some 19% of U.S. business firms, is relatively rare among minority-owned firms; only 2% are corporations (Chart 7).

In view of the rarity of the corporate form, which is designed to enlist comparatively large investments through the participation of many persons, it is not surprising that black-owned firms are substantially underrepresented in industries which tend to require relatively large amounts of capital and/or relatively high levels of managerial skill. These industries are manufacturing, wholesale trade, finance, insurance, and real estate. (Table 2).

The kinds of business where black ownership is relatively large are selected services (dominated by beauty shops, barber shops, laundry and dry cleaning plants, building maintenance services, and auto repair services and garages), retail trade (nearly three-fifths of the firms are eating and drinking places or food stores), and transportation and other public utilities (four-fifths of the firms in this group are in taxicab service or trucking and warehousing).

The geographic distribution of minority-owned firms, as would be expected, conforms rather closely with the geographic scatter of the minority populations. Hence, the black-owned firms are heavily concentrated in the South, while the majority of other minority businesses are located in the West (including Hawaii and Alaska) where the bulk of Mexican-Americans, Japanese, Chinese, Filipinos, and Hawaiians reside (Table 3).

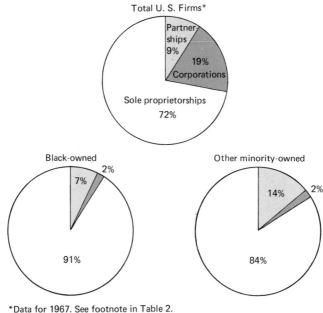

*Data for 1967. See footnote in Table 2.
Note: Note to Table 2 also applies to data in this chart.

Chart 7   Distribution of firms by legal form of organization, 1969.
(*Source:* Bureau of the Census.)

EDUCATIONAL ATTAINMENT

The gradual shrinkage of the wide gap in education attainment that has traditionally existed between whites and blacks has contributed toward the economic
gains of blacks. In 1959 the median years of school completed by persons in the
civilian labor force 18 years and over was 8.7 years for blacks and 12.1 for whites.
By 1971 the figure of 11.9 years for blacks was only a half-year less than the 12.5
years for whites. While the number of school years completed by white workers
has been virtually the same for men and women since the late 1950's, black
women have been averaging one more year of schooling than black men.

The relative change between 1959 and 1971 in the proportion of persons in
the labor force 18 years old and over that had not completed high school was
virtually identical for blacks and whites. For blacks it fell from 73% in 1959 to
50% in 1971; for whites it dropped from 47% to 31%. However, the relative gain
in the percentage of blacks in the labor force who are college graduates was
much larger than for whites. For blacks it rose from 4% in 1959 to 7% in 1971,
and for whites it rose from 10% to 14%. The share of the black labor force that
had at least graduated from high school but had not graduated from college grew
from 20% in 1959 to 42% in 1971, a relatively greater increase than for whites,
which expanded from 42% to 55% over that 12-year interval.

TABLE 2. Number of firms in 1969

Industry Division	All Firms*		Black-Owned Firms		Other Minority-Owned Firms	
	Number (000's)	Percent of Total	Number (000's)	Percent of Total	Number (000's)	Percent of Total
All Industries, Total	**7,489**	**100.0**	**163**	**99.9**	**159**	**99.9**
Contract Construction	856	11.4	16	9.8	14	8.8
Manufactures	401	5.4	3	1.8	5	3.1
Transportation and other public utilities	359	4.8	17	10.4	7	4.4
Wholesale trade	434	5.8	1	.6	4	2.5
Retail trade	2,046	27.3	45	27.6	52	32.7
Finance, insurance and real estate	1,223	16.3	8	4.9	14	8.8
Selected services	1,803	24.1	56	34.4	45	28.3
Other industries and not classified	367	4.9	17	10.4	18	11.3

*From the Internal Revenue Service, "Statistics of Income, 1967," latest year for which complete data are available. The Bureau of the Census study notes that the 1969 data for all firms are expected to show approximately the same relationship between minority-owned firms and total firms as is shown by using 1969 data for the former and 1967 data for the latter.
Note: These data exclude the following businesses: agriculture, railroad transportation, offices of physicians and dentists, legal services, and nonprofit organizations.
Source: Bureau of the Census

TABLE 3.   Regional distribution of minority-owned firms in 1969

	Number of Firms	Gross Receipts (Millions)	Percent of Total	
			Number of Firms	Gross Receipts
Black-Owned Firms				
Northeast	24,392	$ 675.1	15.1	15.4
North Central	36,635	1,188.3	22.6	27.0
South	83,262	2,054.5	51.4	46.8
West	17,761	476.1	10.9	10.8
United States[a]	162,050	4,394.0	100.0	100.0
Other Minority-Owned Firms				
Northeast	18,891	$ 614.2	11.9	10.0
North Central	12,330	418.4	7.7	6.8
South	41,873	1,491.0	26.4	24.3
West	85,374	3,606.2	53.9	58.8
United States[b]	158,468	6,129.3	99.9	99.9

[a]Excludes 1,023 firms, with gross receipts of $80.3 million, not specified by region.
[b]Excludes 417 firms, with gross receipts of $35.3 million, not specified by region.
Note: Note to Table 2 also applies to this table.
Source: Bureau of the Census

While younger persons in the workforce are on the average better educated than older members among both blacks and whites, the educational gap between younger and older workers is considerably more pronounced for blacks. Moreover, among young adults, the educational differential between whites and blacks seems to be disappearing.

In 1971, for persons between the ages of 20 and 34, including those who were not in the labor force as well as those who were, the median years of school completed was 12.3 years for blacks, closely approaching the 12.7 years for whites. For persons 35 years old and over, blacks averaged 9.1 years of schooling compared with 11.3 years for whites.

While there is concrete statistical evidence that impressive strides have been made toward closing the educational gap between blacks and whites in terms of quantity, particularly among young adults, changes in quality are more difficult to ascertain. However, it is probable that the quality lag has also begun to shorten. This assumption is based on the large-scale shifts of the black population from the rural South to the metropolitan North and West where standards of education are higher; the greater proportion of blacks being educated in desegregated institutions at all levels—elementary, secondary, and universities and colleges; and efforts to improve instruction in ghetto schools.

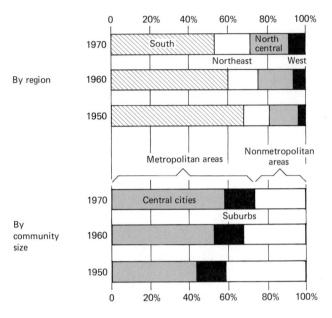

Chart 8   Geographic distribution of black population.
(Source: Bureau of the Census.)

BLACK MIGRATION

Another trend of recent decades which probably has had a salutary effect on the income of blacks is their large-scale exodus from the South, together with their passage from rural areas to central cities; i.e., the migration from lower-earnings areas to those of higher earnings. While part of the farm-to-city migration of blacks was intraregional, most of it was from the rural South to the urban North and West.

As a result of these geographic shifts, the proportion of the black population living in the South dropped from over three-fourths in 1940 to two-thirds in 1950, and then to slightly over one-half in 1970; the proportion living in central cities climbed from 44% in 1950 to 58% in 1970, while those residing outside metropolitan areas declined during the past two decades from 41% to 26% (Chart 8). The chief impetus for these shifts has been the shrinkage of employment opportunities in rural places, particularly in the South, as agriculture has become increasingly mechanized since the 1930's. Many submarginal farms have been withdrawn from cultivation and the land allocated to nonfarm uses, while industrial expansion has taken place in the metropolitan areas.

The migration pattern of the whites in recent decades has differed markedly from that of the blacks. While larger numbers of whites have also left rural areas for reasons similar to the blacks, the dominant trend for the whites has been away from metropolitan centers to suburban communities. By 1970 only 28% of the whites lived in central cities compared with 35% in 1950; the proportion living in suburban rings of metropolitan areas rose from 28% in 1950 to 40% in 1970.

As family needs and preferences are not uniform, so the impetus for the flight of whites from inner cities to the suburbs is not traceable to a single cause. Undoubtedly, some white families were motivated, at least in part, by the heavy influx of blacks. Others may find suburban residence more gratifying than urban for any number of reasons: greater safety in the streets, less noise, cleaner air, better schools, more play area for children, more spacious accommodations in a suburban house than a city apartment, and the appeal of home ownership and the building up of equity in a house.

It should be noted that many blacks, primarily those in the middle class, have also fled the city for surburbia in the past two decades. However, this trend has been minimal compared to the rather massive exodus of blacks from farms and other rural areas to the city.

REDUCING THE GAP

The ineluctable conclusion that emerges from a comparison of the economic status of blacks and whites is the vastness of the chasm that has historically existed between the two. However, available evidence unequivocally demonstrates that there have been significant advances in reducing that breach, particularly in the past five or six years.

The gains have not been uniform for all blacks, of course. The younger generation of black workers, those under 35 years old, have benefited more than older workers from the improvement of the economic climate for minorities during the 1960's. This is only to be expected. Expanding educational opportunities, together with expanding opportunities for better-paying, higher-prestige jobs, apply mainly to the young, rather than to middle-aged or older persons who, for the most part, are unable to avail themselves of these additional options for upward mobility.

Also, the black–white lag in earnings has been diminishing faster for women than for men. While there has been a substantial reduction in the number of black families below the poverty threshold, some 29% of black families were still below the low income level in 1970 as against 8% of the white families. Despite the South's having made proportionately greater gains than the rest of the country in reducing the black–white income discrepancy during recent years, the black–white ratio of median family income is still lowest in the South.

Women at Work

The numbers improve, but
the problem remains the same

Leonard A. Lecht

Our society has become committed to expanding employment opportunities for women, and the past 10 years have witnessed many instances of break-throughs by women into new fields. However, the changes to date have generally been modest. Should this slow pace of change continue for another decade, it will generate a continuing gap between women's career aspirations and reality in the labor markets.

The drive for equal employment opportunity for women reflects underlying demographic, economic, educational and social changes. Declining birthrates, rising divorce rates, "later" marriages, women's lib, and more widespread educational opportunity have all contributed to changes in social attitudes encouraging greater female participation in the labor force. For instance, by 1973, over half of all women in the 20-to-44 year age group were either working or looking for a job. Mothers with school-age children were as likely to be in the labor force as were unmarried young women in the 1950s.*

Because of the rapid increase in female labor force participation, women have made up a more-than-proportionate share of the recent labor force growth. Between 1964 and 1974, women constituted three-fifths of the work force increase; further, it is expected that women (like nonwhites) will make up a larger share of the labor force in 1985 than in 1975 or 1970. Thus, in the coming decade, measures which expand the opportunities open to women will affect more people, and a larger segment of the work force, than would have been the case a decade or two earlier. Similarly, the economic, political and social consequences of discriminatory barriers will become more important because their impacts will be more widespread.

If the developments of the past 10 or 15 years continue, women will be better represented in higher-paying fields in the 1980s. A larger proportion of bank officials, designers and mechanical engineering technicians would be women. Offsetting these changes, most of the employment increases for women would take place in occupations in which women have traditionally predomi-

From *The Conference Board Record*, September, 1976. Reprinted by special permission of The Conference Board.

*Manpower Report of the President, 1975, p. 57.

nated. Thus the largest increase in employment for women between 1970 and 1985 would occur in clerical occupations.*

The consequences of limited access to job opportunities for women are evident in three areas. One is the concentration of women in a small number of traditionally "female" occupations; another is their heavy representation in low-paying jobs, and lesser representation in the better-paying fields. Thirdly, in occupations in which women predominate, greater-than-average educational attainment is not accompanied by greater-than-average earnings.

The "female" occupations include nursing and health service jobs, most clerical fields, retail salesclerks, many operatives jobs—i.e., dressmakers or solderers—and service jobs concerned with child care, personal care or food service. Barriers to entry in many other fields, together with the presistence of stereotypes defining what are appropriate "men's jobs" and "women's jobs," limit most women to seek employment in a relatively narrow range of occupations. A steady supply of women focusing their job searches in the fields which have traditionally employed them assures the availability of large numbers of job applicants and encourages low earnings.

PROSPECTS FOR THE COMING DECADE

Women will increase their representation in most fields in the next 10 years both because of equal employment measures and because they will make up a larger proportion of the labor force. More women will be employed in professional, managerial and technical fields, and more breakthroughs can be anticipated in crafts such as electrical work and auto mechanics. However, over two-fifths of the total increase in employment for women is projected to take place in the clerical and service fields. While there will be many individual instances of women embarking on careers as auto mechanics or TV repairmen, the skilled crafts are expected to account for only slightly more than 3% of the employment growth. The distribution of the changes in employment suggests that women will continue to be marginally represented in laboring and farm occupations—two slowly growing or declining fields (Table 1).

Concentration on broad occupational groups obscures significant changes in a number of occupations within the larger groups. Women are expected to increase their representation in technical fields, including drafting and medical

---

*The findings reported in this article are based on a study of changes in occupational characteristics undertaken by The Conference Board for the U.S. Office of Education, "The Implications of Changes in Occupational Characteristics in the Next Decade for Planning in Vocational Education" (OEG-0-74-1678, 1976). The study focuses on 123 occupations involving some degree of skill but which usually do not require a college degree. The occupations considered are expected to account for the employment of nearly three-fifths of all gainfully employed women in 1985. The study omits two groups of occupations, professional fields requiring a college degree and private household work. The opinions expressed in the article do not necessarily reflect the position or policy of the U.S. Office of Education.

TABLE 1.   Distribution of changes in employment
for women, 1970 to 1985

Employment increase (in millions)	**7.6**
Percent Distribution of Increase:	
Professional and technical workers	8.2%
Managers and administrators, except farm	3.6
Salesworkers	10.1
Clerical workers	44.4
Craftsmen and foremen	3.4
Operatives	7.4
Service workers	23.9
Laborers, except farm	0.1
Farm occupations	1.1
Total	100.0

Sources:. U.S. Department of Commerce. Bureau of the Census.
Occupational Characteristics, 1970; U.S. Department of Labor.
Bureau of Labor Statistics, *Occupation-by-Industry Matrix Projec-
tions* (unpublished), 1974.

and scientific-engineering technical specialties. Many more women will be
employed as bus drivers, especially in driving school buses. Within the clerical
field, the representation of women is expected to increase in the few occupations
which had predominantly employed males in the past. Shipping and receiving
clerks and stock clerks are examples.

The occupations which have a preponderance of women in their work force
are characterized by low earnings. In 1970, for example, over three-fourths of the
women in the occupations included in the Office of Education study were at
work in fields which paid under $8,000 a year. This was approximately $2,000 or
more below the $9,945 median for all workers in 1970. The concentration of
female employment in lower-paid jobs is illustrated by the representation of
women in the 10 highest-paying and the 10 lowest-paying occupations among the
123 considered. Their representation in 1970 and the projected representation in
1985 are described in Table 2.

As the projections indicate, women are expected to increase their representation in a majority of the better-paid occupations. However, the proportion
of women in all of the high-paying fields would be less than their overall percentage in all the study occupations in the mid-1980s or in total employment. In nine
of the 10 low-paying fields women would make up a larger share of the work
force than the comparable percentage for all the occupations considered in the
study. They would constitute nine-tenths or more of the work force in five of the

TABLE 2.
Representation of women in ten highest-paid and ten lowest-paid occupations

Occupation	1970	1985*
Ten Highest Paid:		
Stock and bond sales agents	8.6%	12.5%
Managers and administrators, n.e.c.	11.6	11.0
Bank officials and financial managers	17.4	23.5
Sales representatives, manufacturing	8.5	5.7
Real estate appraisers	4.1	8.7
Designers	23.5	30.3
Personnel and labor relations workers	31.2	28.7
Sales representatives, wholesale	6.4	9.9
Computer programmers	22.7	18.7
Mechanical engineering technicians	2.9	7.3
Ten Lowest Paid:		
Practical nurses	96.3	97.8
Hairdressers and cosmetologists	90.4	92.4
Cooks, except private household	62.8	60.4
Health aides, except nursing	83.9	79.2
Nurses aides	84.6	88.9
Sewers and stitchers	93.8	93.5
Farm laborers	13.2	17.4
Dressmakers and seamstresses	95.7	94.2
School monitors	91.2	95.8
Child-care workers, except private household	93.2	88.4
All study occupations	35.9	40.5
All occupations	37.7	39.0

*Projected
Sources: See Table 1

low-paid occupations listed in the table. (If more detailed breakdowns were available, it is likely that they would show the least-favored group to be made up of individuals with a double labor market disadvantage—nonwhite women.)

The economic return on greater educational attainment is typically low in the occupations employing large numbers of women. The preponderantly female occupations characterized by above-average educational achievement usually pay less than predominantly male fields with similar or lesser educational credentials. The average number of years of schooling completed for both men and women in the employed civilian labor force in 1970 amounted to 12.4 years.* But the economic return associated with greater educational attainment was considerably less for women than for men (Table 3).

*Manpower Report of the President, 1975.

TABLE 3.   Educational attainment and earnings, predominantly male and predominantly female occupations

Occupation	Median Years of Schooling Completed in 1970	Median Earnings of Full-Year Workers*		Percent Change, 1970– 1985
		1970	Projected 1985	
Occupations Employing Largest Number of Males:				
Auto mechanics	10.5	$ 9,070	$13,270	46%
Carpenters	9.7	9,720	14,390	48
Deliverymen	11.7	9,060	12,720	40
Farm owners and tenants	10.5	7,780	15,910	104
Foremen	12.7	12,320	19,160	56
Heavy equipment mechanics	11.1	10,300	15,070	46
Managers and administrators, n.e.c.	13.8	16,770	26,040	55
Salesclerks, retail trade**	12.7	6,470	9,480	47
Sales representatives, wholesale	13.8	13,690	21,030	54
Truck drivers	9.0	9,640	16,160	68
Occupations Employing Largest Number of Females:				
Bookkeepers	13.7	6,530	9,600	47
Cooks	9.1	5,470	8,570	57
Hairdressers and cosmetologists	13.0	5,770	8,650	50
Nurses aides	11.8	4,890	6,940	42
Practical nurses	13.2	5,870	8,910	52
Salesclerks, retail trade**	12.7	6,470	9,480	47
Secretaries	13.9	6,860	10,100	47
Sewers and stitchers	8.5	4,880	6,970	43
Registered nurses	14.2	8,090	11,970	48
Typists	13.7	6,070	8,890	46
All U.S. Occupations	12.4	9,945	15,260	53

*In 1973 dollars.

**This occupation is listed in both groups since it provides employment to large numbers of both men and women.

Sources: See Table 1

As the table illustrates, the earnings projections for 1985 imply that if the relationships between changes in earnings and in productivity characterizing the recent past continue through the coming decade, the differentials in earnings between men and women will remain and in some instances widen.

Most of the significant developments in the affirmative action programs affecting women have taken place since 1970 and, therefore, have had only a limited effect on the projections. The 1972 Equal Employment Opportunity Amendments, or the EEOC guidelines on discrimination because of sex under

Title VII of the Civil Rights Act are examples. The precedent-making consent decree agreed to by the American Telephone and Telegraph Company, a major indicator of progress toward greater equality of opportunity, was entered into as recently as 1973. However, there has been little evidence up to now that these developments have been substantially reflected in the changes in occupational distribution for women. (For example, in 1974, 98% of all secretaries were women, a proportion almost identical with 1970 and the one projected for 1985.)

WHY SUCH SLOW PROGRESS?

The projections imply a continuing labor market disadvantage for women in the coming decade. But what do these or similar projections mean, and what significance should be attached to them? Essentially the projections represent points on a scale illustrating "What would happen if" the experience of the past 10 or 15 years were to continue through the mid-1980s. A movement away from the traditional counseling and occupational education in the schools, changes in the career aspirations of women, and more general acceptance of equal employment measures would bring about a greater-than-anticipated change in the occupational distribution for women. These developments would outmode projections based on the experience of the recent past.

The extent to which the employment of women is concentrated in a limited number of less well-paid occupations indicates that many underlying factors probably contribute to maintaining the present arrangements. The persistence of the stereotypes of "men's jobs" and "women's jobs," the influence of the schools, and the propensity for younger women to continue entering the traditional female fields reinforce the effects of discriminatory barriers in hiring and in promotions which channel most women into less skilled and less responsible positions. High replacement rates in predominantly female occupations signify that lack of seniority and experience frequently restrict opportunities for women to advance. Withdrawal from the labor force is often followed several years later by reentry in a beginning-level position.

Part of the explanation for the slow shifts in the occupational distribution for women is that younger women, the newer entrants into the labor force, tend to enter the fields that already employ large numbers of women. By continuing in the steps of their predecessors, the younger women help to perpetuate low earnings by assuring a steady stream of new additions to the supply of labor in the preponderantly female occupations.

This tendency is illustrated by 10 selected occupations—registered nurses; secretaries; calculating machine operators; stenographers; typists; dressmakers and seamstresses; sewers and stitchers; child-care workers; hairdressers and cosmetologists; and practical nurses. Women made up 90% or more of the employed work force in all of these occupations in 1970. In all but one (calculating machine operators), nine-tenths of the under-35 work force were female. These data imply that the social and psychological factors and the educational experiences that affect career aspirations have generally maintained existing employment patterns for women rather than changing them. As the younger entrants largely continue to find employment in the "female" fields, they increase the likelihood that similar concentrations of employment for women will characterize the next decade.

For most women, other than those in the professions, high school and community college mark the time that formal career planing takes place. These plans, and the related occupational preparation, have typically been oriented toward preparing women for a short period of employment in anticipation of an extended or permanent withdrawal from the labor force shortly after marriage. The Federally supported vocational educational system is the largest of the channels through which training is acquired by young people for the occupations which do not usually require a four-year college degree. The distribution of enrollments for women within the major vocational program areas shows that the vocational programs primarily direct young women toward the fields in which they have traditionally been employed. The data on enrollments are summarized in Table 4.

As the table indicates, the preponderant concentration for women has been in programs preparing them for employment in clerical jobs. The information in the table also implies that planning in vocational education will be concerned with increasing the occupational choices open to women in the next five or 10 years. For instance, more women will be participating in trades and industry programs in 1977 than in 1970. However, a majority of the women enrolled in voca-

TABLE 4.   Enrollment of women in major
vocational program areas

	Percent Distribution of Female Enrollments	
Program	1970	1977*
Agriculture	0.8%	1.9%
Distributive education	12.1	11.5
Health occupations	7.8	12.7
Office occupations	68.8	59.1
Technical occupations	1.3	1.2
Trades and industry	9.2	13.6
Total	100.0	100.0

*Projected

Note: Home economics (gainful) has been omitted from this list because of the unavailability of detailed projections of enrollment by sex in 1977. In 1970 an estimated 5.9% of the female vocational enrollments were in gainful home economics programs related to the occupations considered in the study.

Sources: U.S. Office of Education. *Trends in Vocational Education, Fiscal Year 1972, Vocational Education Information,* No. II, 1973, and unpublished U.S. Office of Education data on enrollments by sex.

tional programs intended as preparation for gainful employment in 1977 would still be enrolled in the office occupations area.

Encouraging women to prepare for employment in fields historically regarded as "women's jobs" eases the problem of placement after they have left school. The importance attached to training leading to placement in clerical jobs is consistent with the expectation that women's participation in the labor market is short term and in anticipation of an extended withdrawal from the labor force.

It remains true that women, as a group, are more likely to withdraw from the labor force than men. Their replacement rates, accordingly, are considerably higher than those for men. The differences are illustrated in Table 5.

TABLE 5.   Projected percentage of job openings arising from replacement needs

(Selected occupations)

Occupation	Percentage of Job Openings Arising from Replacement Needs, 1970 to 1985
Occupations Employing Largest Number of Men:	
Auto mechanics	51.0%
Carpenters	64.0
Deliverymen	53.0
Foremen	61.5
Heavy equipment mechanics	47.0
Managers and administrators, n.e.c.	58.5
Sales representatives, wholesale	56.5
Truck drivers	56.5
Occupations Employing Largest Number of Women:	
Bookkeepers	79.5
Cooks	77.0
Hairdressers, cosmetologists	75.5
Nurses aides	64.0
Practical nurses	55.5
Secretaries	69.0
Sewers and stitchers	87.5
Registered nurses	69.5
Typists	74.5
All Occupations	69.0

Note: Excludes farm occupations because of limited number of job openings, and salesclerks, retail trade because this occupation provides employment to large numbers of both men and women.

Sources: Derived from U.S. Department of Labor, Bureau of Labor Statistics. *Tomorrow's Manpower Needs,* Supplement No. 4. *Estimating Occupational Separations from the Labor Force for States,* and *Occupation-by-Industry Matrix* (unpublished), 1974.

It is evident that replacement demand is a more important source of job openings for women than for men. Job openings due to replacement needs are expected to exceed the national average in six of the nine occupations listed as employers of women. Replacement demand is less than the national average for all of the occupations included in the table as employing large numbers of men. The differences, to a considerable extent, reflect institutional arrangements which often make it difficult for women with family responsibilities to work. So, the greater availability of child-care facilities to working women, or the more widespread adoption of flexible work hours would make it feasible for many women to exercise the option of remaining in the labor force or returning to it soon after they have left.

The potential growth of interest in exercising this option is underscored by the increase in the proportion of women in the 20-to-34 year age group in the labor force. Between 1960 and 1973, for example, the percentage of women in the 20-to-24 year age group in the labor force rose from 46% to 61%, while the corresponding increase in the 25-to-34-year group went from 36% to 50%.*

CORRECTING MYOPIC PLANNING

The problem with short-term career planing and the occupational preparation geared to it, is that it overlooks the far-reaching changes that are taking place in female participation in the labor force. Many women who leave the labor force because of child-rearing responsibilities seek to return soon after their children are born, or after they are off to kindergarten or nursery school. Reentry into jobs held before is often impossible and, where possible, it usually offers few long-term career prospects. For women who do not withdraw from the labor force because of child-rearing responsibilities, jobs entered into on the basis of short-term planning horizons frequently lead to dead ends.

"Women's need for a wider range of occupational choices remains acute," according to the 1975 *Manpower Report of the President*. The transition from school to work has dominated much of the planning in career education and manpower programs, and in planning company recruitment programs for entry-level workers. Allowing for the importance of this transition, it is only one significant turning point in the labor market experience for women.

Reversing this process, which freezes the traditional stereotypes in the occupational distribution for women, involves creating new types of institutions and programs adapted to the needs of adult women in the labor force. Considerably greater emphasis would be placed on "lifetime learning," on counseling for second careers, and on company and publicly supported training and upgrading programs for adults who are locked into a narrow range of job skills and options. However, the prospects for more desirable job opportunities for women in new fields will, in the end, be bounded by the willingness of employers to hire females for positions related to their training.

Ibid.

Affirmative Action for the Handicapped

The Labor Department has simplified its rules for hiring disabled and handicapped workers. The objective is to open up new jobs without strapping employers in the red tape of compliance.

Louis R. Decker and Daniel A. Peed

The federal government acted last month to spur employment of handicapped workers through affirmative action. New regulations adopted by the Labor Department reinforce previously established official policy by redefining affirmative action requirements for companies obligated to hire and promote the handicapped under Section 503 of the Vocational Rehabilitation Act of 1973.

The Act requires all employers with federal contracts over $2,500 to take affirmative action to recruit, hire, and promote handicapped persons who meet "reasonable" qualifications for jobs. Under the new rules, however, nonexempt firms holding federal contracts of $50,000 or more and having 50 or more employees must prepare and have available for inspection upon request a written affirmative action plan. The new rules also provide for a job-related standard in hiring; every physical and mental qualification must be justified for the particular job for which a handicapped person is applying.

The new regulations represent refinements of proposed enforcement and other clarifying requirements originally submitted last August. They were designed to reflect 1974 amendments to the original legislation and help improve overall administration and enforcement of the law. For example, they clarify the definition of a "handicapped" individual and related aspects of contractor obligations. Labor Department officials describe the revised rules as greatly "simplified" and designed to make compliance easier by eliminating much previously required "red tape."

Since hire-the-handicapped legislation was enacted nearly three years ago, Labor Department compliance officers have processed some 700 complaints as of March 1976. All were resolved without litigation, however, with the exception of only three or four "difficult" cases, which federal officials then described as "approaching" court action (although there was still hope of peaceful settlements).

The Labor Department's Employment Standards Administration (ESA) contends that it is "complaint-oriented" rather than compliance-oriented. Emphasis on "screening in" applicants, not "screening out," thus becomes the key to success in a hire-the-handicapped effort, according to a department spokesman.

Reprinted by permission of the publisher from *Personnel,* Vol. 53, No. 3, May–June, 1976. © by the American Management Association, Inc.

HOW SECTION 503 OPERATES

The most significant aspect of the Act's regulations, therefore, is the basic provision that enables handicapped persons who believe an employer has unfairly discriminated against them to file a complaint with ESA. What kind of complaints, then, should employers expect?

Rejection because of physical handicaps. Most of the complaints received by the ESA have been from persons who claimed they were excluded from jobs or were passed over for promotion solely because of their physical limitations. Complaints range from individuals with a "bad knee" to amputees, diabetics, epileptics, the partially or totally deaf and blind, and those suffering from cancer or some other debilitating or terminal illness.

Employers may be understandably reluctant to hire epileptics for driving trucks or cars. But does epilepsy necessarily bar an applicant from all production line or related plant jobs?

Can a blind person perform satisfactorily in a data processing department? How about an applicant suffering from cancer?

Frequent complaints have come from people with back trouble who have been barred from jobs requiring lifting and loading. To what extent are they handicapped?

Contractors are required to hire only "qualified handicapped" individuals, a definition that means a handicapped person who is "capable of performing a particular job, with reasonable accommodation to his handicap, at the minimum level of productivity applicable to a nonhandicapped incumbent employee." To date, ESA's Handicapped Workers Task Force has tried to settle each case "on its merits." As a result, jobs have been found for certain epileptics, persons with cancer, blind workers, and many others with the above disabilities.

With the new regulations, handicapped persons now will probably apply for jobs previously thought to be beyond their physical or mental capabilities. Thus employers will have to show hard evidence that a particular handicap definitely prevents a person from handling certain jobs.

Rejection because of physical appearance. Handicapped persons may complain that they have been barred from jobs requiring close or extensive contact with the public because of personal characteristics such as ugly scars, bent or deformed posture or gait, or speech defects. Employers should clearly specify job requirements and validate them against physical characteristics, that is, appearance or impression required for successful performance.

Tests and selection procedures. Mentally retarded or psychologically handicapped persons may be expected to complain about intelligence and psychological tests on grounds they are discriminatory. (Many such cases have come before the Equal Employment Opportunity Commission, charging that tests are slanted against the disadvantaged—minorities, the poor, the undereducated.) Employment standards officials call this category a "can of worms," and it may well be that employers will have to furnish convincing data that certain IQ levels, psychological traits, or specialized skills are really necessary for various jobs. A few cases involving dexterity tests and the mentally retarded already have been processed. But representatives of such persons (rehabilitation counselors, psychologists, legal advisers) may be expected to bring test cases in the future.

Lack of physical accommodations. Ramps and special walkways at private and public institutions have become fairly common in recent years though many older plants and office buildings still lack such facilities. ESA officials expect few complaints about inadequate accommodations, but to avoid them, employers will probably have to install special facilities for the handicapped, such as wheelchair ramps at stairways, special doors, special washroom fixtures, and special parking areas.

WHAT CONSTITUTES AFFIRMATIVE ACTION

What kind of affirmative action policy does the federal government want? Reacting to the legislation's requirements, many businessmen may say, "So what? We've been hiring handicapped workers for 20 years. It's good business to hire the handicapped; everybody knows that. Why all the fuss over new rules and regulations?"

In enacting the 1973 Act, Congress opted for affirmative action for the handicapped because statistics show that a large proportion of the nation's 12 million employable handicapped persons simply are not getting jobs. The Labor Department thus has spelled out the following types of activities that should be included in an affirmative action program:

1. Outreach and positive recruitment.
2. Internal communication of the obligation to employ and advance the handicapped. Such communication should foster acceptance and understanding of the handicapped among other employees and management.
3. Development of internal procedures ensuring fair treatment of the handicapped.
4. Use of all available recruiting sources — state employment and vocational rehabilitation agencies, workshops, and other institutions that train the handicapped.
5. Reviewing employment records to determine availability of promotable handicapped persons.
6. Accommodation of physical and mental limitations of qualified handicapped employees.

Department of Labor spokesmen have stressed that affirmative action for the handicapped is based on "reasonable accommodation," not goals or timetables. This means that when qualified handicapped persons apply for and/or hold jobs with them, employers should take their handicaps into account, facilitate their entry and exit from the place of work, and make necessary adjustments enabling them to work as effectively as their nonhandicapped fellow workers.

FULFILLING THE OBLIGATION

Employers are bound to ask, "How can I upgrade our organization's employment practices to meet affirmative action requirements for the handicapped?"

- A good first step would be to review present employment records and try to determine who in the company is handicapped, where they are assigned, and how long they've been working. Supervisors and foreman will know whether such handicaps are related to the capabilities they possess. A crosscheck with personnel could identify available openings for recruitment, promotion, transfer, or extra training for qualified handicapped persons.

- Check out what improvements in plant and office facilities are needed to upgrade physical accommodation of handicapped workers.

- This initial review of employment practices and conditions could serve as a platform on which to build an effective affirmative action program. But remember that a good plan should go beyond basics such as advancement and better accommodation of handicapped employees already on the roster. Meaningful recruitment efforts should be demonstrated.

Suppose, for example, a department or division has a backlog of unfinished statistical work or an extra heavy mailing. A call to the local state vocational rehabilitation office could identify names of handicapped individuals who have registered as capable of doing clerical of statistical work. Those found qualified after interviewing and screening by the personnel department could prove to be valuable additions to the workforce.

Alternatively, some work might be contracted out to a sheltered workshop that handles assignments sourced from private firms. State vocational rehabilitation offices can arrange contacts with such workshops. When a contract assignment is completed, it may be possible to hire some of the clerks or other workers off the workshop's roster for full-time assignments.

Better recruiting thus becomes the key to good affirmative action. Keep in contact with state employment agencies and rehabilitation departments, educational institutions training the handicapped, and employment agencies; each will aid you in the expansion of a pool of handicapped persons available for interviews and selection. When this effort is accompanied by a thorough knowledge of handicapping conditions in relation to job performance, a company is well on the way to a successful affirmative action plan.

How "Equal Opportunity" Turned into Employment Quotas
Some strange things have been happening, in government and industry, in the name of "nondiscrimination."

Daniel Seligman

Soon after it came into office, the Nixon administration proposed that critics "watch what we do instead of listening to what we say." By this eminently reasonable standard, the administration today might be judged to favor quotas in employment. The President has repeatedly assailed them; in fact, the elimination of quotas was identified in a major campaign statement as one of ten great goals for the nation in his second term. Yet during his years in office, and with some powerful encouragement from the executive branch of the U.S. Government, quotas have taken hold in several areas of American life. The controversies about them have centered on their appearance in the construction industry and on university campuses. Oddly enough, very little attention has been paid to employment quotas in large corporations.

The omission is very odd indeed, for it is in corporate employment that quotas are having their major impact on the American labor force and on relations between the races and sexes. Nowadays there are scarcely any companies among, say, the FORTUNE 500, that are not under pressure from the government to hire and promote more women and minority-group members; and many of these companies have responded to the pressure by installing what are, in effect, quota systems.

In most of the controversy over quotas, there is no real disagreement about ultimate objectives. Most educated Americans today would agree that several minorities, and women, suffer from discrimination in employment, that the discrimination is destructive and irrational, and that working to end it is a proper activity for government. Unfortunately, it is not clear what government should do—and all too clear that wise policies do not flow naturally from good intentions.

In discussions of this issue, people who don't define their terms can dither on for quite a while without getting anywhere. Let us begin, accordingly, with some definitions and distinctions. Among companies that have no intention of discriminating against women or minorities, four different postures may be discerned:

1. Passive nondiscrimination involves a willingness, in all decisions about hiring, promotion, and pay, to treat the races and sexes alike. However, this posture may involve a failure to recognize that past discrimination leaves many prospective employees unaware of present opportunities.

2. Pure affirmative action involves a concerted effort to expand the pool of applicants so that no one is excluded because of past or present discrimination. At the point of decision, however, the company hires (or promotes) whoever seems most qualified, without regard to race or sex.

3. Affirmative action with preferential hiring. In this posture, the company not only ensures that it has a larger labor pool to draw from but systematically favors women and minority groups in the actual decisions about hiring. This might be thought of as a "soft" quota system, i.e., instead of establishing targets that absolutely must be met, the top officers of the company beef up employment of women and minority-group members to some unspecified extent by indicating that they want those groups given a break.

4. Hard quotas. No two ways about it—specific numbers or proportions of minority-group members must be hired.

Much of the current confusion about quotas—and the controversy about whether the government is imposing them—derives from a failure to differentiate among several of these postures. The officials who are administering the principal federal programs tend, of course, to bristle at any suggestion that they are imposing quotas; they have been bristling with special vigor ever since the President's campaign statements on the subject. Their formulations tend to be somewhat selfserving, however. The officials turn out, when pressed, to be denying that the government is pushing employers into posture No. 4. The real issue is No. 3, preferential hiring, which many government agencies are indeed promoting. Meanwhile, the President and a few other administration officials concerned with equal-employment opportunity sound as though the objective of the program is to promote pure affirmative action—posture No. 2.

THE CONCILIATORS HAVE MUSCLES

The U.S. government's efforts to end discrimination in employment are carried out through two major programs. One was set in motion by Title VII of the Civil Rights Act of 1964, which forbids discrimination based on race, color, religion, sex, or national origin. The act established an Equal Employment Opportunity Commission, which now has two main functions. The first is enforcement: the commission may sue in a U.S. district court, on its own behalf or for other claimants, when it believes that discrimination has taken place. The EEOC has had the power to sue only since March, 1972—previously it was limited to conciliation efforts—and has filed only about twenty-five suits in that time. Chairman William H. Brown III believes that when the commission gets warmed up it might be filing an average of five suits a week.

In practice, Brown suspects, not many of these are apt to be litigated; the right to go into court is useful to the EEOC mainly for the muscle it provides in conciliation efforts. If the EEOC did get into court, it would have to prove outright discrimination; in principle, that is, an employer might comply with Title VII simply by practicing passive nondiscrimination—posture No. 1. However, the conciliation agreements extracted from those accused of discrimination typically call for more than that. Most of the agreements negotiated thus far involve preferential hiring.

The commission's other main function is information gathering. Every enterprise with 100 or more employees must file annually with EEOC a form detailing the number of women and members of four different minority groups employed in each of nine different job categories, from laborers to "managers and officials." The minority groups are Negroes; Americans of Mexican, Puerto Rican, Cuban, or Spanish origin; Orientals; and American Indians (who in Alaska are deemed to include Eskimos and Aleuts). With some 260,000 forms a year to process, the EEOC is having some difficulty in staying on top of the data it is collecting. "Obviously, we can't look critically at all the reports," Brown concedes. Eventually, however, he hopes to develop some computerized procedures for finding patterns of discrimination, i.e., procedures somewhat analogous to those employed by the Internal Revenue Service in deciding which tax returns to audit.

Meanwhile, the EEOC is getting a fair amount of help from people who believe they are being discriminated against. When any complaint is received at the commission, even one with no visible substance to it, an EEOC staff member pulls the file on the company in question and looks for patterns of discrimination. In fiscal 1972 more than 30,000 charges were filed.

SPECIAL RULES FOR CONTRACTORS

The other major federal program is based on the special obligations incurred by government contractors. This program may be traced all the way back to 1941, when President Franklin D. Roosevelt issued an executive order outlawing racial discrimination by defense contractors. Every President since Roosevelt has issued one or more orders extending the reach of the ban. It applies now to subcontractors as well as primes, to civilian as well as military purchases, and to services as well as goods. It affects every division and every subsidiary of any company with a contract worth $10,000 or more. It covers women as well as racial, religious, and ethnic minorities. And it has entailed increasingly expansive definitions of "nondiscrimination." Right now, about a quarter of a million companies, employing about a third of the U.S. labor force, are covered by the executive orders.

At the time President Nixon took office, most government contractors were operating under Executive Order 11246, which had been issued by President Johnson in September, 1965. The order as later amended by Johnson, required "affirmative action" by employers—but did not specify what this meant in practice. The Office of Federal Contract Compliance had never developed guidelines for determining whether contractors were in compliance. It was left to the Nixon administration to make the program operational.

The administration's first major decision about the program was to make it, in the marvelous label applied by the Labor Department, "result-oriented." Affirmative action could have been defined so that it required companies to incorporate certain procedures into their personnel policies—but did not require that any particular results follow from the procedures. The difficulty with this approach was that companies determined to discriminate might simply go through the motions while continuing to exclude women and minority-group members. "It just would have been too easy for them to make patsies of us," said Laurence Silberman, who was solicitor of the Labor Department at the time, and who participated in the formulation of the program. An alternative approach, which was the one essentially adopted, would require each company to set goals and timetables for hiring specified numbers of women and minority-group members; would allow the government to review the goals to ensure that they were sufficiently ambitious; and, if they were not met, would require the company to prove that it had at least made a "good-faith effort" to meet them.

This approach was certainly calculated to produce results. The difficulty was that it also seemed likely to produce *reverse* discrimination by companies fearful of losing their contracts. The administration recognized this problem from the beginning, and agonized over it quite a lot. "No program has given me greater problems of conscience than this one," said Silberman recently, just before leaving the Labor Department to go into private law practice in the capital. In the end, however, the administration always came back to the view that a program that didn't achieve results would be a charade—and that the only way to ensure results was to require goals and timetables.

The rules of the new game were first set forth in January, 1970, in the Labor Department's Order No. 4, signed by then-Secretary George P. Shultz. At the time, it seems clear, businessmen did not pay a great deal of attention to Order No. 4. It is perhaps worth noting that the momentous changes signaled by the order had never been debated in Congress, not even during the great outpouring of civil-rights legislation in the 1960's. Anyone looking for examples of the growing autonomy of the executive branch of the federal government could do worse than focus on this quite unheralded administrative regulation.

TRYING TO BE REASONABLE

Specifically, Order No. 4 requires that every contractor have a written affirmative-action program for every one of his establishments. Every program must include a detailed report on the company's utilization of each of the four basic minorities in each of its own job categories. (A "Revised Order No. 4," issued by Secretary of Labor J.D. Hodgson in December, 1971, called for reports on women, too.) Whenever there are job categories with fewer women or minority-group members "than would reasonably be expected by their availability," the contractor must establish goals for increasing their utilization.

Well, how does one determine the appropriate utilization rates? The order makes a great show of being helpful in this regard, listing eight criteria that contractors should consider in trying to answer the question. The first is "the minority population of the labor area surrounding the facility"; others include "the availability of minorities having requisite skills in an area in which the contractor can reasonably recruit," and "the degree of training which the contractor is reasonably able to undertake as a means of making all job classes available to minorities." The criteria certainly give contractors a lot to think about, but they do not, in the end, make clear what would be a reasonable utilization rate for, say, black mechanics. A contractor focusing on this matter might find himself utterly confused about the number of blacks in town who were already trained as mechanics, the number who were "trainable," the amount he was expected to spend on training, the distance he was expected to travel to recruit, etc.

In practice, contractors are encouraged to assume that they are underutilizing women and minorities and, accordingly, they have goals and timetables just about everywhere. For example, International Business Machines Corp., which has long been a model employer so far as fair-employment practices are concerned, has goals and timetables today at every one of its 400-odd establishments in the U.S.

Because the criteria are so vague, the goal-setting procedure often becomes an exercise in collective bargaining, with the outcome dependent on the respective will and resourcefulness of the company's top executives and the government's compliance officers. The government is ordinarily represented in these matters by whichever of its departments is contracting for the company's services; the OFCC does some, but not much, coordinating. On the whole, the enforcement varies considerably in both fairness and effectiveness from one company to another. Furthermore, some companies deal with several different departments; Union Carbide, for example, is monitored by the Atomic Energy Commission and the Departments of Defense, Transportation, Labor, Interior, and Agriculture.

The compliance officers themselves are career civil servants, and they seem to come in all varieties. Two quite different criticisms of them are often heard. One is that they are apt to be knee-jerk liberals, persuaded in advance that the big corporation is guilty. The other is that they have often lazily adopted the position that anything the company proposes is fine with them. Herbert Hill, the labor specialist of the National Association for the Advancement of Colored People, is prepared to regale anyone who wants to listen with tales of compliance officers who have been co-opted by corporate personnel departments. One senior official of the Labor Department who has been in a good position to observe the contract-compliance program was asked recently what he thought of these two criticisms. "They're both true," he answered, adding, after a moment's reflection, that the compliance officers also included many thoughtful and conscientious public servants.

WHAT'S HAPPENED TO MERIT?

There is no doubt that, between them, the EEOC and the contract-compliance program have transformed the way big business in the U.S. hires people. Even allowing for those co-opted compliance officers, the government has gone a long way toward wiping out old-fashioned discrimination in the corporate universe. But it is increasingly evident that, in doing so, the government programs have undermined some other old-fashioned notions about hiring on the basis of merit.

The undermining process can be discerned in the campaigns, waged successfully by EEOC and OFCC, against certain kinds of employment standards. Employers who demand certain skills, education levels, or test-score results are presumed to be discriminating if their standards have the effect of excluding women or minority-group members. To counter this presumption, the employer must demonstrate conclusively that the skills are in fact needed for the job. If

---

A.T.&T. Gets the Message

The American Telephone & Telegraph Co., which had been spending a lot of time with the equal-employment opportunity forces of the U.S. government, made a remarkable settlement with them in January. Back in 1970, A.T.&T. had a request for rate increases pending before the Federal Communications Commission. The Equal Employment Opportunity Commission asked the FCC to deny the request on the ground that the company pursued discriminatory hiring and promotion practices and was, in fact, "the largest oppressor of women workers in the U.S." The petition clearly reflected an effort by the EEOC, which then had no enforcement powers, to use the muscle that comes naturally with the FCC's power over rates.

The FCC inquired, naturally, what discrimination had to do with rates. The EEOC responded that if the company did not discriminate against women, its costs would be lower: discrimination resulted in high turnover rates, the commission argued, and these saddled the company with heavy training costs. Early in 1971 the FCC began hearings on discrimination in the company.

Meanwhile, as a leading federal contractor, A.T.&T. was negotiating with the General Services Administration on goals and timetables for greater utilization of women and minorities. In September, 1972, GSA and the company reached an agreement under which 50,000 women and 6,600 minority-group members were to get better jobs over a fifteen-month period. The agreement was immediately questioned by two other agencies, the Office of Federal Contract Compliance and the EEOC, both of which undertook to renegotiate it.

The terms accepted by those agencies in January called for lump-sum payments of some $15 million to 13,000 women and 2,000 male minority-group members, who had been discriminated against in the past. It also called for immediate raises, aggregating $23 million, for some 36,000 workers who had been discriminated against. Finally, it roughly doubled the company's "ultimate goals" for hiring male operators and clerical workers and females employed in craft jobs. Ordinarily, goals are supposed to be set in detailed "utilization analyses" at each of the company's establishments (A.T.&T. has about 700). But in this case no one was pretending that the goals had any scientific basis.

test-score results are involved, he must also demonstrate that the tests reliably predict the skills in question and, finally, that "alternative suitable . . . procedures are unavailable for his use." One argument the employer *cannot* make is that he had no discriminatory intent in establishing the requirements. Under Title VII, as administered by the FEOC, the intent is irrelevant: it is only the effect that matters — which represents a major alteration in the law of discrimination.

The altered concept became the law of the land in March, 1971, when the U.S. Supreme Court upheld the EEOC's view, and overruled a court of appeals, in *Griggs v. Duke Power.* The company had required applicants for certain jobs to have a high-school diploma and also to score at certain levels in aptitude tests. There was no contention that Duke Power intended these standards to have a discriminatory effect, and it was agreed that they were applied impartially to blacks and whites alike. It was also agreed that the standards resulted in very few blacks being hired. The company argued that it wanted to use the standards to improve the over-all quality of its labor force; but it could not demonstrate that the standards had a direct relationship to the jobs being performed. In ruling that the standards had to be dropped, Chief Justice Warren E. Burger, who wrote the Court's opinion, upheld the EEOC's contention that Title VII "has placed on the employer the burden of showing that any given requirement must have a manifest relationship to the employment in question."

Anyone pondering the particulars of the Duke Power case would have to feel sympathy for the black workers involved. Growing up in a society that had denied them a decent education, they were unfit for many skilled jobs. When they applied to do some relatively unskilled work that they could perform, they were excluded by educational standards — which, the facts suggest, really were extraneous to the company's needs. Unfortunately, the logic of the Duke Power decision suggests that some perfectly reasonable standards are now in trouble, too. Companies that have high standards and want to defend them will immediately perceive that the ground rules, which not only place the burden of proof on the employer but require coping with some formidable-looking validation procedures, are not inviting. Many will obviously conclude that it is simpler to abolish their standards than to try justifying them.

The new law presents special management problems to the numerous companies that have traditionally hired overqualified people at entry-level jobs, expecting them to compete for the better jobs. Dr. Lloyd Cooke, who monitors Union Carbide's equal-employment-opportunity program, suggested recently that most big companies like his own could no longer assume there were a lot of highly qualified people searching out their own paths to the top. "Now we must develop upward mobility models that include training along the way."

In addition to all their problems with tests and formal standards, federal contractors often face a new kind of pressure on the informal standards they may have in mind when they hire and promote people. Revised Order No. 4 specifies: "Neither minority nor female employees should be required to possess higher qualifications than those of the lowest-qualified incumbent." The logic of this rule is inexorable, and it too implies lower standards. In any organization that has a number of people working at different levels of skill and competence—a corporate engineering staff, say, or a university economics department—whoever does the hiring would ordinarily be trying to raise the average level of performance, i.e., to bring in more people at the high end of the range. If the organization must take on applicants who are at the low end or face charges of discrimination, it can only end up lowering the average.

Professor Sidney Hook, the philosopher, has assailed the possibilities of this "fantastic" requirement in universities. "It opens the door," he has written, "to hiring persons who cannot meet *current standards of qualification* because, forsooth, a poorly qualified incumbent was hired by some fluke or perhaps ages ago when the department was struggling for recognition."

WHAT CONGRESS HAS PROSCRIBED

For reasons that are certainly understandable, neither the EEOC nor the OFCC has ever said in writing that it believed the law to require some hiring of less-qualified people. To do so would apparently conflict with some of President Nixon's animadversions against quotas. In addition, it would seem to go against the plain language of the laws in question. It is, after all, logically impossible to discriminate in favor of blacks without discriminating against some whites; thus anyone espousing preferential hiring of blacks would be bucking Section 703(a) of Title VII, in which it is deemed unlawful for an employer "to . . . classify his employees in any way which would deprive or tend to deprive any individual of employment opportunities . . because of such individual's race, color, religion, sex, or national origin." In *Griggs,* Chief Justice Burger reaffirmed the intent of the law in plain terms: "Discriminatory preference for any group, minority or majority, is precisely and only what Congress has proscribed."

In pushing preferences for women and minorities, the government's lawyers and compliance officers repeatedly offer the assurance that "you never have to hire an unqualified person." Since unqualified persons are by definition unable to do the job, the assurance is perhaps less meaningful than it sounds. The real question is whether employers should have to hire women or minority-group members who are less qualified than other available workers.

The answer one gets in conversation with EEOC officials is clear enough. If hiring someone who is less qualified will help an employer to utilize women or minorities at proper levels, then he should do so. Chairman Brown was asked recently what an employer should do if he was presumed to be underutilizing women and there were two applicants for a job: a fairly well qualified woman and a man who was somewhat better qualified. "If it's just a question of 'somewhat better,' you should probably hire the woman," he replied.

THE LAWYER'S PREDICAMENT

How can the lawyers who run the federal programs justify preferences that seem to violate the intent of the basic statutes? Not all the lawyers would respond in the same way, but most of them would point to some court decisions at the appellate level that call for preferential hiring and even hard quotas. They would also note that the Supreme Court has declined to review these decisions. In one important case, for example, the Alabama state troopers were ordered by a federal judge to hire one black trooper for every white man hired until the overall ratio was up to 25 percent black. Most of the lawyers would also agree with the formulation by William J. Kilberg, the Labor Department's associate solicitor for labor relations and civil rights: "In situations where there has been a finding of discrimination, and where no other remedy is available, temporary preferential hiring is legal and appropriate."

Kilberg himself believes strongly that preferences should be limited to these special circumstances — in which it is indeed hard to argue against them. But other government lawyers view them as natural and desirable in a wide range of circumstances. They argue, for example, that it is unnecessary to require a finding of discrimination; they contend that companies underutilizing women or minority-group members are, per se, guilty of discrimination and that it is appropriate, in reviewing their goals and timetables, to push for some preference. Furthermore, the EEOC tends to the view that any past discrimination justifies preferences, i.e., it often fails to consider whether other remedies are available.

Last fall H.E.W.'s Office of Civil Rights made a major, but only partially successful, effort to clarify the ground rules of the contract-compliance program. J. Stanley Pottinger, who has headed the office for most of the past three years (he recently moved over to the Justice Department), put together a volume spelling out some guidelines. At the same time, somewhat confusingly, he issued a covering statement that went beyond anything in the volume. It said, "Nothing in the affirmative-action concept requires a university to employ or promote any faculty member who is less qualified than other applicants competing for that position." That statement was, and indeed still is, the only formal declaration ever issued by any contract-compliance official ruling out a requirement for hiring less-qualified job applicants.

Many contractors who read the statement took it for granted that the same rule would apply to corporate employment. Unfortunately, anyone talking about this matter to officials of the Labor Department soon discovers that they regard university hiring problems as somewhat special. There is a view that faculties have a unique need for "excellence," but that in the business world, and especially at the blue-collar level, most jobs are such that employers suffer no real hardship when "less-qualified" people are hired.

A MESSAGE TO JACK ANDERSON

Meanwhile, corporate executives tend to take it for granted that, in practice, reverse discrimination is what affirmative action is all about. Whoever it is at International Telephone & Telegraph Corp. that leaks internal memorandums to columnist Jack Anderson recently sent along one on this subject. In the passage that Anderson published, Senior Vice President John Hanway was proposing to another executive that thirty-four rather high-ranking jobs "lend themselves readily to being filled by affirmative-action candidates," i.e., they should be filled by women or minority-group members.

Companies' public declarations about affirmative action do not ordinarily propose so blatantly to prefer these groups, but the dynamics of the program more or less guarantee that there will be preferences. Revised Order No. 4 says, "Supervisors should be made to understand that their work performance is being evaluated on the basis of their equal employment opportunity efforts and results, as well as other criteria."

Supervisors are indeed getting the message. At I.B.M., for example, *every manager* is told that his annual performance evaluation—on which the prospects for promotions, raises, and bonuses critically depend—includes a report on his success in meeting affirmative-action goals. A memo last July 5, from Chairman C. Peter McColough to all Xerox managers in the U.S. (it was later published by the company), warned that "a key element in each manager's overall performance appraisal will be his progress in this important area. No manager should expect a satisfactory appraisal if he meets other objectives, but fails here." At Xerox, furthermore, the goals are very ambitious these days. Something like 40 percent of all net additions to the corporate payroll last year were minority-group members.

In principle, of course, a line manager who is not meeting his targets is allowed to argue that he had made a "good-faith effort" to do so. But the burden of proof will be on the manager, who knows perfectly well that the only surefire way to prove good faith is to meet the targets. If he succeeds, no questions will be asked about reverse discrimination; if he fails, he will automatically stir up questions about the adequacy of his efforts and perhaps about his racial tolerance too (not to mention his bonus). Obviously, then, a manager whose goals call for hiring six black salesmen during the year, and who has hired only one by Labor Day, is feeling a lot of pressure to discriminate against white applicants in the fall. "In this company," said the president of one billion-dollar enterprise recently, "a black has a better chance of being hired than a white, frankly. When he's hired, he has a better chance of being promoted. That's the only way it can be."

SOME KIND WORDS FOR ABILITY

The future of the "quotas issue" is hard to predict, for several reasons. One is the continuing blurriness of the Nixon Administration's intentions. For a while, last summer, these appeared to have been clarified. In August, Philip Hoffman, president of the American Jewish Committee, sent identical letters to Nixon and McGovern expressing concern about the spread of quota systems in American education and employment. Both candidates replied with letters assailing quotas. The President wrote to Hoffman: "I share your support of affirmative efforts to ensure that all Americans have an equal chance to compete for employment opportunities, and to do so on the basis of individual ability . . . With respect to these affirmative-action programs, . . . numerical goals . . . must not be allowed to be applied in such a fashion as to, in fact, result in the imposition of quotas."

This declaration was followed by a number of newspaper articles suggesting that the administration was preparing to gut the affirmative-action program. The articles were wrong, however. Before the reply to Hoffman had been drafted, a number of administration officials—they included White House special consultant (on minorities) Leonard Garment, Silberman, and Pottinger—met to discuss the program and to consider whether the time had come to change it. Specifically, they considered whether to drop the requirement for goals and timetables. And they decided, as they had in earlier reviews, to resolve their doubts in favor of standing pat.

It seems clear that the Nixon letter to Hoffman temporarily shook up some members of the equal-opportunity bureaucracy, but it doesn't seem to have led to any major changes in the way the federal program is implemented. Many executives, including some who are vigorous supporters of the program, confess to being baffled by the contrast between the President's words and the bureaucracy's actions. General Electric's man in charge of equal-employment-opportunity programs, whose name happens to be Jim Nixon, remarked recently that he kept reading in the papers that "the other Nixon" was cutting back on affirmative action, but "around here, all we see is a continuing tightening of the noose."

Perhaps the simplest explanation of that contrast between words and actions lies in the very nature of the program. It is logically possible to have goals and timetables that don't involve preferential hiring—and that happy arrangement is what the Administration keeps saying we have now. But there are built-in pressures that keep leading back to preference: the implicit presumption that employers are "underutilizing" women and minority-group members; the further presumption that this underutilization is essentially the result of discrimination; the extraordinary requirement, quite alien to our usual notions about due process, that unmet goals call for the employer to demonstrate good faith (i.e., instead of calling for the government to prove bad faith). It seems reasonable to speculate that at some point the administration will abandon goals and timetables, conceding that they lead in practice to preferential hiring and even quotas. Indeed, some of the program's senior officials regard the present format as temporary. Pottinger, who has spent a lot of time in recent years arguing that goals don't mean quotas, nevertheless says, "I sure hope they're not permanent."

In any case, one would have to be skeptical of the long-term future of any program with so many anomalies built into it. For a democratic society to systematically discriminate against "the majority" seems quite without precedent. To do so in the name of nondiscrimination seems mind-boggling. For humane and liberal-minded members of the society to espouse racial discrimination at all seems most remarkable.

THE CRUELTIES OF REVERSE DISCRIMINATION

One immediate threat to the program may be discerned, meanwhile, in a number of suits against corporations and universities, alleging some form of reverse discrimination. H.E.W. now has an "ombudsman" working full-time on such complaints. It seems likely that companies engaged in preferential hiring will be hit by more such suits as the realities of their programs sink in on employees and job applicants.

But even aside from all the large litigious possibilities, there are surely going to be serious problems about morale in these companies. It is very difficult for a large corporation to discriminate in favor of any group without, to some extent, stigmatizing all members of the group who work for it. G.E.'s Nixon, who is himself black, says that talk about hiring less-qualified minority-group members makes him uneasy—that "it puts the 'less-qualified' stamp on the minorities you do hire." In companies where reverse discrimination is the rule, there will be a nagging question about the real capabilities of any black man who gets a good job or promotion. The question will occur to the white applicants who didn't get the job; it will occur to customers who deal with the black man; and, of course, it will occur to the black himself. Perhaps the cruelest aspect of reverse discrimination is that it ultimately denies minority-group members who have made it on their own the satisfaction of knowing that.

In short, businessmen who are opting for preferential hiring, or who are being pushed to it by government pressure, may be deluding themselves if they think they're taking the easy way. It seems safe to say that at some point, even if the government does not abandon its pressures for preference, more business-men will begin resisting them. It should go without saying that the resistance will be easier, and will come with better grace, if those businessmen have otherwise made clear their opposition to any form of discrimination.

QUESTIONS FOR DISCUSSION

1. Discuss the progress made by women in breaking down the barriers to higher-level jobs and comment on the prognosis for the future. If you were a consultant to the Department of Labor, what recommendations would you make for closing the gap that Lecht speaks of in his article, "Women at Work"?

2. Detail and discuss as specifically as possible the differences in the economic status between blacks and whites in the United States.

3. What is the state of the law relative to the use of arrest records in employment recruitment and selection? Why may the use of arrest records be discriminatory?

4. What is the state of the law relative to the use of tests in employment recruitment and selection? Cite and explain the cases that established the current state.

5. Discuss the basic laws relating to equal opportunity in terms of race, religion, national origin, sex, and age.

6. Differentiate between equal opportunity as defined by the Civil Rights Act of 1964 and Affirmative Action as considered under Executive Order 11246. Discuss the possible inconsistencies cited by authors such as Seligman.

7. What problems does Affirmative Action pose and cause for managers? How would you as a manager deal with those problems?

8. The newest Affirmative Action program is for the handicapped. Discuss the challenges and problems of the new Affirmative Action requirements under Section 503 of the Vocational Rehabilitation Act of 1973.

SELECTED READINGS

Baron, A.S. and E.T. Reeves, "How effective has Affirmative Action legislation been?", *Personnel Administration,* January, 1977.

Brown, G.D., "How type of employment affects earnings differences by sex," *Monthly Labor Review,* July, 1976.

Bunzel, J.H., *"Bakke vs. University of California,"* Commentary, March, 1977.

Burton, G.E., et al., "Recruiting, testing, selecting: Delicate EEO areas," *Management World,* October, 1976.

Churchill, N.C., and J. K. Shank, "Affirmative Action and guilt-edge goals," *Harvard Business Review,* March–April, 1976.

Cohen, S. J., "Basis of sex bias in the job-recruitment situation," *Human Resources Management,* Fall, 1976.

Cross, T.L., *Black Capitalism.* (New York: Atheneum Publishers, 1969.)

Domm, D.R., and J. E. Stafford, "Assimilating blacks into the organization," *California Management Review,* Fall, 1972.

"Evaluating the impact of Affirmative Action: A look at the Federal contract compliance program" (A symposium of articles and comments), *Industrial and Labor Relations Review,* July, 1976.

The General Electric Company, *Women and Business: Agenda for the Seventies;* (New York: General Electric, 1972.)

Gery, G.J., "Equal opportunity —Planning and Managing the process of change," *Personnel Journal,* April, 1977.

Ginsberg, E., and A.M. Yohalem, eds., *Woman's Challenge to Management.* (New York: Praeger, 1974.)

Glazer, N., *Affirmative Descrimination: Ethnic Inequality and Public Policy.* (New York: Basic Books, 1976.)

Gross, B.R., (editor), *Reverse Discrimination.* (Buffalo, N.Y.: Prometheus Books, 1977.)

Kreps, J., *Sex in the Marketplace: American Women at Work.* (Baltimore: Johns Hopkins Press, 1971.)

McKay, A.V., "Americans of Spanish origin in the labor force: An update," *Monthly Labor Review,* September, 1976.)

Neill, S. B., "Accentuating the Affirmative," *Worklife,* October, 1976.

O'Connell, J.H., Jr., "Black capitalism," *Review of Black Political Economy,* Fall, 1976.

Pettigrew, L.E., "Reverse discrimination—Fact or fantasy?" *Integrated Education,* November–December, 1976.

Purcell, T.V., and G.F. Cavanaugh, *Blacks in the Industrial World.* (New York: The Free Press, 1972.)

Rabinowitz, D., "The bias in the government's anti-bias agency," *Fortune*, December, 1976.

Rhine, S. "The senior worker—Employed and unemployed," *The Conference Board Record*, May, 1976.

Richbell, S., "*De Facto* discrimination and how to kick the habit," *Personnel Management*, November, 1976.

Robertson, D.E., "Update on testing and equal opportunity," *Personnel Journal*, March, 1977.

Russell, J.J., "Institutionalizing Affirmative Action," *The Journal of Afro-American Issues*, Winter, 1977.

Sibal, A.,"The E.E.O.'s Dilemma," *Business and Society Review*, Winter, 1976–77.

Van Den Haag, E., "Reverse Discrimination: A brief against it," *National Review*, April, 29, 1977.

Case 1

DUTCHLAND POWER IN DUTCH*

Background of the Case

Following a particularly severe winter and as a result of the recent energy crisis, the Dutchland Power and Light Company, New City, Pennsylvania applied for and received a one-year grant from the federal government to provide home-based educational services to its residential consumers in methods of energy conservation. One component of the project involved advertising for and hiring ten educational specialists knowledgeable in the area of home management and energy requirements to work with homemakers in their geographic area on the ways they could conserve energy in their homes and thereby reduce their energy consumption. Following a one-week orientation session, the specialists were to work through community agencies and groups to establish a series of home contacts; the primary activity of the specialists was to work with families, especially low-income families, in their homes, studying family patterns and suggesting ways to reduce energy usage.

One of the terms of the grant award was that the Dutchland Power and Light Company, in hiring and employing the educational specialists, would follow an aggressive affirmative-action program in seeking the consultants. Partially as a result of a governor's Upward Mobility program three years ago, the Company had hired a personnel officer with strong commitments to hiring and upgrading women and minor-

---

*This case was prepared by Barbara Brittingham and Dennis Callaghan, University of Rhode Island. All rights reserved.

ities. In the proposal for the federal grant, the Company acknowledged the importance of hiring specialists from the geographic area they would be serving. Management felt that local people, familiar with the special characteristics of neighborhoods and towns, would be most knowledgeable about living patterns in the area and particular needs or attitudes of the local clientele.

The following advertisement was placed in local papers:

WANTED: EDUCATIONAL SPECIALISTS

We are seeking an educational specialist with knowledge of home management practices and energy utilization to work with families in the _____ area helping them to reduce energy consumption and lower their energy bills. Successful applicants should have a background in home management, experience working with homemakers in their own settings, and be familiar with the community and its special needs. This job requires the use of a car. Time of employment: October 1, 1976 to September 30, 1977.

Apply by August 30 to:

Frederick Edwards, Personnel Officer
Dutchland Power and Light Company
110 Madison Street
New City, Pennsylvania
       An Equal opportunity/affirmative action employer.

Edwards received the applications and reviewed them. He and Georgia Winters, Training Coordinator, interviewed all of the applicants for the position. Each applicant was rated on the following characteristics:

1. Background in home management
2. Experience working with homemakers in their own settings
3. Familiarity with the community
4. Access to a car

The top three candidates for each geographic region were re-interviewed before the final selection. For all ten positions, the applicant pool was as follows:

17 white males
94 white females
6 minority males
21 minority females

Dutchland Power hired the following:

1 white male
7 white females
0 minority males
2 minority females

The Affirmative Action Complaint. On October 15, 1976, Frederick Edwards was notified by Susan Shoppe, the State Affirmative Action Officer, that George Anderson, a white male, had filed a discrimination complaint against Dutchland Power for their failure to hire him as an educational specialist. Mr. Anderson charged "reverse discrimination," stating that he believed that Dutchland Power had not hired him because he was a white male.

On October 20, Susan Shoppe, Frederick Edwards, and Georgia Winters met to discuss the Anderson complaint. Edwards and Winters assured Shoppe that, although Dutchland Power actively recruited women and minorities for the position, they did not feel they had in any way discriminated against white males in the hiring. A review of the specifics in the case indicated that, for the geographic area in question, Dutchland Power had hired Mrs. Phyllis League. Specific qualifications of Mrs. League and Mr. Anderson were as follows:

Mrs. Phyllis League

Three years of college education with specialization in home-economics education with coursework in Home Management.

One year experience as a cooperative extension agent with Larson County, working with homemakers in the area of food purchasing and meal planning and nutrition.

Had lived in the geographic area of the position for five years. Was active in school and community organizations.

Had access to a car.

Mr. George Anderson

Four years of college education in the areas of small business administration and sociology. Bachelor of Arts degree.

Two years of managing a small grocery store.

Did not and had not lived in the geographic area in question.

Resided in a neighboring community. Had helped to coordinate a community action program for employment of women and minorities.

Had access to a car.

After spending an hour and a half with Edwards and Winters, Shoppe informed them she would return to her office and review the facts in the case. She informed them that, as is the customary practice of the State Affirmative Action office, she had co-filed Anderson's complaint with the regional office of the Equal Employment Opportunities Commission. She informed them that they would receive a written copy of her findings and recommendations within three weeks.

On November 7, 1976, Edwards received the following letter from Shoppe.

Re: Complaint of discrimination filed by Mr. George Anderson

Dear Mr. Edwards:

I have reviewed the facts in the case of Mr. George Anderson who applied to Dutchland Power and Light Company for the position of educational specialist. Based on the material you submitted to me and the information received from Mr. Anderson, I do not find probable cause that Mr. Anderson was treated in a discriminatory fashion by Dutchland Power. As I mentioned to you earlier, the complaint has been co-filed with the regional office of the Equal Employment Opportunities Commission. I will forward my findings to them and to Mr. Anderson. Though EEOC may choose to take action on Mr. Anderson's behalf, the State Affirmative Action Office has concluded its investigation of the complaint.

We thank you for your cooperation in this matter. The assurance of affirmative action and equal opportunity is the responsibility and opportunity of all citizens.

Sincerely,

Susan Shoppe
Senior Complaint Investigator

Further Developments in the Case

On December 1, 1976, Frederick Edwards received communication from the regional EEOC office saying they wished to meet with him to discuss George Anderson's complaint. They explained that they had received Susan Shoppe's letter reporting her findings but wished to pursue the complaint to their own satisfaction. A meeting was arranged for December 15 with Edwards, Winters, Shoppe, and Georgette Manchester from EEOC.

After a meeting to review the facts and documents in the case, EEOC requested copies of the applications for all candidates for the ten positions. On January 15, 1977, Edwards received a communication from EEOC stating that they did not find probable cause for discrimination in the case of George Anderson, but that they were pursuing the matter on a class action basis on the behalf of a Mr. Jerome Phillips, a white male with a degree in Family Ecology and prior consumer work in the area of family budgeting with a social action agency. Mr. Phillips was an unsuccessful applicant in another regional area and had applied for a position for which a minority female had been hired. Mr. Phillips had not yet filed a complaint of discrimination, but EEOC explained that they would be in contact with him to ask him if he were interested in doing so. They asked to arrange a conciliation meeting with Dutchland Power to discuss future hiring practices, with particular emphasis on increasing the number of males for such positions.

In the conciliation meeting, on January 23, 1977, EEOC asked that Dutchland Power agree to the following terms:

1. Establish affirmative action goals of hiring 60 percent men for all further home-related positions (the 60 percent estimate was based on the percent of men in the workforce in the nearest standard metropolitan statistical area).

2. Pay Jerome Phillips $3,436 in back pay for not being hired as an educational specialist.

3. Offer Mr. Phillips a position at comparable pay to the educational specialists within Dutchland Power.

Manchester from EEOC explained that contact with Jerome Phillips indicated that, for personal reasons, he did not wish to file a complaint of discrimination, but that he would be interested in future employment with Dutchland Power.

After meeting with other management officials of the Power company, Edwards wrote to EEOC telling them that:

1. While they were interested in hiring without regard to sex stereotypes, they believed that the 60 percent figure for home-related positions was an unrealistic figure. Information obtained from other agencies indicated that, of the workforce in the area who were qualified for home-related positions, approximately one-fourth were male. Edwards proposed that their affirmative action figure for positions in this area be set at 25% male.

2. Dutchland Power did not feel it had discriminated against Jerome Phillips for the position for which he had applied. They explained that at the time of the interview, Mr. Phillips had expressed doubts as to his own interest in the position. Edwards and Winters also felt that the personal skills in relating to homemakers were much higher on the part of the minority candidate who was hired. Dutchland Power did not therefore feel that it owed Phillips back pay.

3. Edwards also explained that Dutchland Power could not at this time offer Mr. Phillips a position with the company. He proposed however, that Mr. Phillips be notified of and interviewed for all future positions at the company for which he was interested.

In a subsequent communication, EEOC said that the Power Company response was interpreted as a failure on the part of the Company to agree to conciliation. They turned the case over to the Justice Department.

In two meetings, officials from the Justice Department met with Edwards and Winters of the Power Company and reviewed the facts in the case and the proposed conciliation agreement. Dutchland Power would not agree to the 60 percent goal which they felt was unrealistic; nor would they agree to paying Phillips back pay or offering him a position immediately.

An impasse had apparently been reached and the parties were preparing to go to court.

The Press Takes Notice

In the meantime, word of the recent events at Dutchland had reached the city desk of the *New City Register*. On February 22, a brief half-column news release appeared on page one of the evening paper. While the story was accurate for the most part, bar its brevity, it carried the headline, "Reverse Discrimination at Dutchland Power."

Within five minutes of reading the article, Dutchland's President and Chairman, Bud Downey, was on the phone to Frederick Edwards. After being assured by Edwards that the Anderson case was legally settled and that the Phillips case was still pending, Downey immediately called the Editor of the *Register* at his home. The Editor admitted that the headline was a journalistic error and promised to run a clarification in the morning paper. The clarification was to simply state that the headline should have read, "Reverse Discrimination Alleged at Dutchland Power." It would appear on page 10. Further, the Editor offered three full columns of space in the "Letters to the Editor" section for a more complete rejoinder if Downey wished to take advantage of it. Not wishing to overdramatize the company's concern, Downey declined the offer for the time being.

Within two weeks of the original news release, Dutchland Power received over 200 letters sympathetic to the EEOC position and the cause of both Anderson and Phillips. These came even after the *Register's* correction appeared in the morning paper. Seven of the letters had been "copied to" the Energy Research and Development Administration, the sponsor of the grant Dutchland received. Only two letters had been received in support of the Dutchland position.

Upon learning of the volume and tone of the mail the company had received, Mr. Downey concluded that the *Register's* editorial correction was far from effective. He then rethought the Editor's offer of a Dutchland prepared rejoinder, and decided that it was now absolutely essential that the company prepare one. He also felt strongly that the published letter should include not just a statement of the company's indignation over the original error, but should also inform readers of the severe legal and philosophical dilemma that the company had faced and would likely continue to face.

Mr. Downey turned the letter writing job over to Mr. Edwards, though the letter would ultimately be signed by Downey.

After working on a draft of the letter for four hours, Edwards had only a single line to show.

To the Editor of the *New City Register:*

Case 2

CALVIN COOLIDGE CHAIR CO.

Article 16 of the collective bargaining agreement provides as follows:

ARTICLE 16. PROMOTION AND BIDDING

When a vacancy occurs in an existing job classification or when a new job classification is created, the Employer will promptly post a notice of such vacancy on each bulletin board for a period of not less than five (5) days.

A notice of vacancy will state that interested employees shall have ten (10) working days after the first day of posting within which to bid for the vacancy by filing a written bid with the Personnel Office.

If two or more employees shall bid for the vacancy, seniority shall govern between employees whose ability to perform the job is relatively equal.

If, in the opinion of management, employees who bid for the vacancy lack sufficient qualifications, the employer may hire qualified persons from the outside.

On May 14 the Employer posted the following notice on each employee bulletin board:

NOTICE OF JOB VACANCY

Forklift Operator, Shipping & Receiving Dept.

Rate — 3.90 per hour

Qualifications — Prior experience preferred, not required.

Closing Date — May 28.

E. Dubinsky,
Personnel Manager

On May 29, Personnel Manager Dubinsky called for the bids for the forklift operator's vacancy. To his surprise there were only three bidders. From a brief study of their job bids and a look at their personnel files, Dubinsky put together these brief profiles:

John C. Bach — age 19.

Present job: mail clerk.
Present rate of pay: $2.15.
Education: High school graduate.
Family: Unmarried.
Physical: Height — 5'6"; weight — 145.
Attendance: Excellent.
Prior experience with forklift: None.
Seniority: 10 months.

Gloria C. Vivaldi — age 28.

Present job: Packer.
Present rate of pay: $2.33.
Education: High school graduate and AA degree in business from King Tut Community College.
Family: Married; no children.
Physical: Height — 5'6"; weight — 120.
Attendance: Good.
Prior experience with forklift: None.
Seniority: 8 years, 3 months.

Mario Delmonica — age 63.

Present job: Janitor.
Present rate of pay: $2.28.
Education: 8th grade.
Family: Married; grown children.
Physical: Height — 5'11"; weight — 225.
Attendance: Average.
Prior experience with forklift: 6 weeks' experience approximately 10 years ago when employed by another firm.
Seniority: 29 months.

Dubinsky reviewed these profiles with a sense of disappointment. He regarded Delmonico as the best qualified because of his prior experience and because he seemed psychologically best suited to getting along with the tough, all-male crew that works on the shipping and receiving dock. On the other hand, Dubinsky had doubts about Delmonico's age. (Dubinsky knew, but neither the Union nor employees knew, that the Employer was contemplating implementation of a mandatory retirement policy for employees upon reaching age 65.) Dubinsky had different kinds of reservations about John Bach, who had effeminate mannerisms and about whom employees circulated nasty little rumors. Although Bach's overall employment record was quite satisfactory, Dubinsky wondered whether the young man's personality was unsuited to operating heavy equipment and to the social environment of the shipping and receiving dock. In Bach's favor were his youth and his good record for attendance and punctuality.

Dubinsky regarded Gloria Vivaldi's bid as something of a joke—but not entirely. She had a reputation as a practical joker. She was attractive and well liked by her co-workers and supervisors. In her present job classification, she was required occasionally to lift heavy boxes which she did with apparent ease. She had talked about running for the presidency of the Union, and a number of female employees seemed eager to support her candidacy. In recent weeks it was suspected, but not proven, that she and friends had pasted little stickers around the plant which said: "OFF the MCP's."*

If her bid were rejected, would she file a grievance under the contract? Would she go to the Equal Employment Opportunity Commission? Or what else?

The following day, after a long discussion of the matter with Mrs. Nickelmoose, Dubinsky notified each of the three bidders that, in the opinion of management, he or she lacked "sufficient qualifications" to perform the forklift operator's job and that management intended to advertise the job outside the plant. Simultaneously he sent the following notice to the Modigliani office of the U.S. Employment Service:

> The Calvin Coolidge Chair Co. has an opening for an experienced forklift operator. $3.90 per hour. Contact E. Dubinsky, Personnel Mgr.

The next afternoon Dubinsky interviewed and hired an applicant referred by the U.S. Employment Service, E.V. Debs. Debs, a white male, age 34, had had five years' experience as a forklift operator.

Through the plant's grapevine, Bach and Vivaldi heard about Debs's employment. Each of them, without the knowledge of the other, called the chairman of the Union's grievance committee and demanded that the Union file a grievance on his or her behalf.

---

*Male chauvinist pigs.

congregate—and supply it with sufficient affluence and product—and the environmental problems surface very rapidly. Air becomes polluted, garbage mounts up, and waste multiplies.

In this sense, then, a 10-percent increment in population in New York City is much more environmentally disastrous than that same number of people spread out over, say, 1000 smaller towns. Perhaps, then, part of the solution to pollution implies population dispersion (as well as a decrease in the rate of population growth) and methods to encourage such dispersion. More on this in later sections.*

ISOLATING THE CULPRIT

To what extent is each of these factors—population, affluence, and technological change—responsible for today's level of pollution? Barry Commoner attempted to measure the effect of the three factors, utilizing the following formula, and applying it to several products and product categories:

$$\frac{\text{Pollution}}{\text{emitted}} = (\text{Population}) \times \left(\frac{\text{Economic good}}{\text{per capita}}\right) \times \left(\frac{\text{Pollutant output per unit}}{\text{of economic good produced}}\right)$$

Commoner defines the *economic good per capita* as affluence, and *pollution output per unit of economic good produced* he views as attributable to technical change. He found for the relevant products and categories that the *increase in population* accounted for from 12 to 20 percent of the various increases in total pollutant output since 1946, whereas the *affluence factor* accounted for from one to five percent. "The technology factor—that is, the increased output of pollutants per unit of production resulting from the introduction of new productive technologies since 1946—accounts for about 95 percent of the total output of pollutants, except in the case of passenger travel, where it accounts for about 40 percent of the total."[†]

Commoner's formula seems lacking, however, in several respects. Economic good per capita is, of course, related to technological change and also to population. It cannot be labeled as simply affluence. Increasing pollutant output per unit of economic good produced can just as easily result from constant technology as from an increasing "introduction of new productive technologies." Old-fashioned plants pushed beyond scale, old-style equipment, and less control can all contribute to an increased pollutant output *per unit of good produced* as total production is increased. Nevertheless, Commoner's reasoning on the determinants of pollution goes to the root causes: population, affluence, and technological change.

It is easy to see why economic growth becomes the whipping boy of some environmentalists. Its roots and those of pollution are quite similar: increasing

---

*For a discussion of the urban and population problem, see Jacoby, *op. cit.*

†Commoner, *op. cit.*, pp. 175–177.

productivity, population growth, and technological change. Does that mean that the two are mutually inclusive? Let us examine briefly a school of thought that does hold that view.

THE ZERO GROWTH APPROACH

Zero economic growth has been offered as a solution to the pollution problem. Since it is growing production and growing consumption that lie at the base of society's ills, this school of thought would have society stop growth and fix some balance between man, production, and nature.

Kenneth Boulding seems clearly in this camp. Describing the growth-oriented economy as a "Cowboy Economy," Boulding then compares that to what he calls the "Spaceman Economy."

> In the spaceman economy, what we are primarily concerned with is stock maintenance, and any technological change which results in the maintenance of a given total stock with a lessened throughput (that is, less production and consumption) is clearly a gain. This idea that both production and consumption are bad things rather than good things is very strange to economists. . . .*

Jacoby points out three faults in the Zero Growth argument. First, Zero Growth does not consider the *pattern* of growth. Were current patterns of production and consumption merely maintained, we would simply stabilize at current levels of pollution. Second, since growth is a function of investment and technology as well as of population, this would imply *stopping all three.* Population growth is extremely difficult to stop in a short period of time, saving rates show little inclination to decline, and a paralysis in technological change is virtually inconceivable so long as man remains a thinking animal.

Finally, Jacoby argues that Zero Economic Growth is undesirable. "A rising GNP will enable the nation to easily bear the costs of eliminating pollution." What is needed is a *redirection of the growth* that will inevitably take place.†

In addition, Edwin Dale points out that the American labor force for the next twenty years is already born. "It is hard . . . to imagine a deliberate policy to keep a large portion of it unemployed." The only way to reduce growth of output might be to cut hours of work, but even then, Dale forsees a growth rate of 2 percent rather than 4 percent. He simply writes off the hope for zero growth.‡

Our next step is to investigate methods of curbing pollution within the context of economic growth. Few economists would argue that we could shut off growth even if we wanted to, but many do offer programs for making pollution control compatible with economic growth. After a brief digression to cover the concepts of costs involved, we move into some of those methods.

---

*From Kenneth E. Boulding, "The Economics of the Coming Spaceship Earth" reprinted in Sheldon W. Stahl, "Social Cost—The Due Bill for Progress," *Monthly Review, Federal Reserve Bank of Kansas City,* (April, 1972), p. 16.

†Jacoby, *op. cit.,* pp. 189–190.

‡Edwin L. Dale, Jr. "The Economics of Pollution," *The MBA,* (January, 1971), pp. 9–10.

THE COSTS OF PRODUCTION

Before moving into methods for curbing pollution, perhaps we should investigate briefly the area of costs, since it is in this area, most economists believe, that our most powerful weapons for curbing industrial pollution lie.

Production of goods and services involves several types of costs. Most of our economic thinking considers only the private internal costs of producing: What does it cost a company to make a particular product and get it out on the market? This means that our calculations include as costs labor, materials, marketing costs, interest on borrowed money, etc. In pure economic theory, costs also include a return to capital invested and a return to entrepreneurship. Most analyses of production costs do not include anything the company does not have to pay for, or the costs that the company, through its actions, imposes upon its neighbors.

But another type of cost—external costs—is now beginning to show up in the calculus; and it is through working on these that most economists seem to find the means of controlling pollution. Externalities are those hazards or inconveniences inflicted upon another person or community of persons for which the originating party does not pay. Smoke, soot, dirt, water pollutants, etc., are viewed as reducing the well-being of the other person or persons, yet the original producer is not required to pay compensation for this reduction of well-being or pay to *prevent* the polluting output in the first place. As long, however, as the inflicted party had no demand on the resources polluted or had so much of the resources he couldn't be bothered in caring about them, external costs were nothing to be considered.

The concept of omitting external costs from the total cost, then, rested on two assumptions: that there was an absence of objective criteria for evaluating social dangers; and that externalities were of little import in the overall determination of costs. Hence, the fascination with the concept of "free goods."*

With the increase in awareness by many elements of society, it is now clearly evident that total (social) costs of production involve both the previously contained internal costs and the now relatively important external costs. Can external costs, however, be allocated by the market mechanism inherent in the free enterprise system? The answer is no, unless the external costs are imposed upon the polluter.

Wenders cites the following hypothetical paper-producing problem to illustrate the weakness of the market mechanism relative to external costs.

> Suppose there are two methods available for the production of paper at the rate of 100,000 tons per year. Method A has no external costs (i.e., there is no pollution resulting from its production) and thus has private costs equal to (total) social costs. Method B, even though having less private costs to the firm, has very high external costs in the form of pollution, so its (total) social costs are much higher.

---

*Stahl, *op. cit.,* p. 14.

Hypothetical Costs for Producing 100,000 tons of Paper Annually

	Private costs	External costs	Total costs
Method A	$20,000,000	0	$20,000,000
Method B	$10,000,000	$50,000,000	$60,000,000

Obviously, the rational cost-minimizing firm will choose method B, and it would have little choice if it is in competition with other paper mills facing the same situation. Barring some legal compulsion, there is nothing in the market system to compel or even induce the producer to choose any system whose costs are over the minimum internal costs of production.*

Another example relates to consumers. In 1970, General Motors Corporation tried to sell a pollution-reduction kit for $26. During the first month only a relative handful of kits were sold in a market with several hundred thousand buyers. This lack of interest takes little explanation; "an automobile owner would not install the device, because other people would reap the benefits of the cleaner air made possible by the expenditure."†

In sum, the market is incapable of handling or assigning external costs without the intervention of the governing power. "When large external costs or benefits are involved, there is conflict between the decision that serves the self-interest of the individual and that which serves the collective welfare of society."‡ The market mechanism is capable only of enforcing private economic efficiency.§

A DIGRESSION: SHOULD WE CHANGE THE SYSTEM?

One might be tempted to ask, given the inability of the market system to independently internalize or allocate external costs, whether the system itself ought to be changed. There are many variations on this theme, of course, ranging from complete socialism to private ownership with *complete* state regulation. Let us briefly examine two variations.

First, socialization of industry and business. This ultimate step would transform the multitude of free market decisions now being made privately to a central planning apparatus and state ownership. But there is nothing automatic in this step toward the solution of pollution problems. The Soviet Union, the world's most notable example of a centralized industrial society, would have seen no

---

*John T. Wenders, "An Economist's Approach to Pollution Control," *Arizona Review,* XIX (November, 1970), pp. 1–5.

†Jacoby, *op. cit.,* p. 192.

‡*Ibid.*

§"Economic efficiency requires that rates of return should be equalized among different uses, but the market mechanism is only capable of equalizing the *private* rates of return, thus the total of social rates of return will differ whenever external costs are present." Wenders, *op. cit.,* p. 3.

need to sign an environmental treaty with the United States if it were not suffering similar environmental problems. In fact, pollution problems in the Soviet Union are now being seen as quite immense. And as Jacoby points out, "Managers of socialist enterprises are judged by the central planners on the efficiency of their operations, and are under as much pressure to minimize internal costs and throw as much external cost as possible on the public as are the managers of private firms in market economies who seek to maximize stockholder profits."*

Moreover, he adds, a state combination of political and economic function dilutes one of the checks on economic processes present in the market system.† Under our present system, separation of the social-political functions from the economic is an advantage, since the sociopolitical system can intercede with the economic to correct social imbalances. For example, antitrust laws have as much a political and social rationale as an economic one. Without the check of the political system, the economic system's dysfunctional qualities could not be mitigated easily.

A second approach stresses what are called "misplaced priorities." The proponents here would argue that private spending encourages multitudes of polluting products and hence results in a lack of resources available for public necessities such as schools, hospitals, public transportation, etc. The solution would be to tax away larger proportions of disposable income, dampen consumption, and devote more of the nation's product to public need. This concept is quite similar to that of John Kenneth Galbraith's approach in one of his earlier works, *The Affluent Society*.‡ But while Galbraith's approach was aimed at solving pressing social needs, others have decried "a pursuit of consumer gadgetry with all its senseless by-products of waste and pollution."§

At an initial glance, this seems like an attractive proposition. But looking deeper, one finds that almost one-third of our total product is now publicly generated, and the prospect for increasing this proportion would run into formidable opposition.

Practical politics is not alone, however, in militating against the misplaced priorities approach. Edwin Dale points out another obvious flaw in the argument. Simply shifting spending from private to public needs does not reduce total spending, and there is no immutable law which states that publicly initiated projects use less resources or generate less external costs than does private spending. Public employees consume, just as do private employees; schools require steel, lumber, tile, brick, and carpeting just as private homes and offices do; public employees (presumably government spending will add to the army of

---

*Jacoby, *op. cit.*, p. 189.

†*Ibid.*

‡John Kenneth Galbraith, *The Affluent Society*, (Boston: Houghton Mifflin Co.).

§Dale, *op. cit.*, p. 12.

these) spend their paychecks just as private employees do; and even a sewage treatment plant requires steel and electricity. In short, the same criticisms leveled at private spending can be leveled at public spending; nothing is inherent in the system of public spending that will guarantee us any less pollution than we have now.*

BUSINESS VOLUNTARISM

Many commentators have suggested that business firms might voluntarily absorb the costs of pollution control. Voluntary absorption falls under the rubric of the social responsibility approach,† a doctrine that has become a favorite topic of business meetings, courses in business schools, and interestingly enough has provided something of a confluence of evolving business ideology and the social idealism of the young. In essence, business is being asked to act not like the rational economic man shown in our previous examples, but like something akin to an eleemosynary institution voluntarily absorbing the added costs.

The doctrine of social responsibility includes pollution control under the umbrella of a whole host of social issues that proponents insist the corporation should be involved with: urban renewal, minority employment, better government, consumerism, and the like. Under the doctrine, management becomes an arbiter of sorts, parceling out corporate resources to competing claims on the corporation. The stockholders, who might demand maximum profits, are considered only one of the claimants. The community upon whom the corporation heaps external costs becomes another.

Jacoby abruptly dismisses the expectation that social responsibility will result in corporations absorbing the external costs voluntarily. The competitive market puts each firm under pressure to minimize costs, and few firms—particularly if they lack some degree of monopoly power, where the increased costs can simply be passed on—will voluntarily put themselves at a cost disadvantage relative to other firms.‡

Milton Friedman rejects social responsibility on philosophical grounds as well. He terms it a "fundamentally subversive doctrine." "There is only one social responsibility of business—to use its resources and engage in activities designed to increase its profits so long as it stays within the rules of the game . . ."§

---

*Ibid.

†Many sources provide some background to the social responsibility doctrine. One of the earliest, and still one of the best, is Richard Eells, *The Meaning of Modern Business* (New York: Columbia University Press, 1960). See also, *Social Responsibilities of Business Corporations* (New York: Committee for Economic Development, 1971).

‡Jacoby, *op. cit.,* pp. 192-3.

§Milton Friedman, *Capitalism and Freedom* (Chicago: University of Chicago Press, 1962), pp. 133-6.

Paul Heyne voices a similar objection on the grounds that the businessmen are "placed in positions where they must make decisions that they are not competent to make." He goes on to say:

A decision against stream or air pollution must be a collective decision, because it requires simultaneous action on the part of many people. It is therefore properly a political decision. It is up to the legislature or some other appropriate body to determine the public interest and establish the appropriate sanctions. When we cast this burden upon the businessman's conscience, we are being just neither to the public nor to the businessman.*

What is being said here on several grounds is that the rules of the game must be changed. One cannot expect—indeed *should not* expect—businessmen to voluntarily do things if the evaluation of their performance is to be based on profit. Nor is voluntarism fair; there will always be those businessmen who will reject social responsibility, leaving those who voluntarily undertake it at a severe disadvantage. We simply have here a case of idealism smacking into practical reality.

Now that we have established the problem in terms of the market's inability to assign external costs; seen, however, that another system might not necessarily be any better; found faults with alternative systems; and pointed out reasons why any expectation of business voluntarism is impractical, let us examine the possibility of changing the rules of the game.

Basically, the issue centers on the relation of the political system to the economic system. The problem resolves itself down to the necessity for government intervention in the productive system to restore the equity between pollution producers and those affected, indirectly using as tools of enforcement the price mechanism and self-interest.

Of course, ample precedent exists for government's role here; all sorts of social problems, ranging from child labor, social security, and labor legislation, on the one hand, to antitrust on the other, have been handled through government intervention into the economic system. Indeed, one school of thought suggests that businessmen welcome this sort of intervention, since it relieves them of decision-making and establishes firm, consistent, and in many cases, self-serving standards.†

Before proceeding, however, let us remind ourselves of the basic problem of economic growth versus environmental pollution. None of the mechanisms to be described in the next few pages are designed to slow growth *per se*. What might result from some of the methods described below is a change in the composition of the national product and/or some redistribution of income. The systems are de-

---

*Paul T. Heyne, *Private Keepers of the Public Interest,* (New York: McGraw-Hill Book Co., 1968), p. 92–4.

†See, for example, George T. Stigler, "The Theory of Economic Regulation." *The Bell Journal of Economics and Management Science,* II (Spring, 1971), pp. 3–21.

signed to charge polluting firms (or consumers) the full (or at least partial) costs of their actions.

CARROT APPROACHES

The carrot approach involves basically the paying of part or all of the costs of pollution by the public. Its mechanisms are tax credits or, in some cases, subsidies granted to the polluter in an effort to impel him to clean up. Businessmen, naturally, favor this approach. In a 1966 survey by the National Industrial Conference Board, the vast majority of the 441 companies surveyed seemed to prefer these types of incentives over programs involving penalties.*

At present, most of these programs involve the states rather than the Federal government. The federal government does offer some tax advantages, most notably the allowing of accelerated depreciation of pollution-abatement equipment. Seven states also allow such accelerated depreciation.

Exemption from the property tax on pollution-control facilities is allowed in 24 states, but some states disallow the exemption if the facility produces a marketable by-product. Twelve states exempt such equipment from sales and use taxes, while six states allow a direct income-tax credit. New York allows the option of "taking either the usual one-percent tax credit allowed for new equipment of any kind, or deducting the entire cost of the pollution control equipment from taxable income.†

Some basic problems are involved with the incentive approach. First, opponents argue that society's concerns with pollution stem from a basic inequity in the system, with society on the short end. Why pay polluters—even a part of the costs—for the loss of a right (to freely pollute) when that right is inequitably held?‡

Secondly, with external costs absorbed by the public, the wealthier, who may pollute relatively more, pay proportionately less of the cost. From this point of view, the distribution of the external costs continues to be inequitable and the sources of pollution don't pay their full share.§

A third criticism goes right to the heart of the matter, the incentive. Without some concurrent regulation, polluters have no incentive to use pollution control unless the subsidy or tax credit were 100 percent or more. Why should a firm add costs voluntarily even if the government ends up paying 90 percent?# Further-

---

*National Industrial Conference Board, "Pollution Abatement in Industry: Policies and Practices," Reprinted in *Issues in Business and Society*, ed. William T. Greenwood (Boston: Houghton Mifflin Co., 1970), pp. 475–81.

†*Pollution Control: Perspectives on the Government Role,* (New York: Tax Foundation, Inc., 1971), pp. 21–22.

‡Jacoby, *op. cit.,* p. 194.

§*Ibid.*

#Wenders, *op. cit.,* p. 3.

more, tax credits or exemptions have no effect on the marginal firm, since it probably pays no tax anyway; marginal firms many times are the foremost polluters.* To some extent, this argument repeats the social responsibility problem all over again, and some would argue that, since the firm must be regulated anyway, then the total cost ought to be placed where it belongs, on the polluter and his product.

Another disadvantage of tax incentives is that they create preferences for equipment rather than changes in the productive process. It may be that some simple reworking of production methods or research into changing the process may be more useful and efficient, but the tax-credit incentive pushes the firm toward a solution of pollution-control equipment rather than to the only partially recoverable costs of research or managerial effort involved in production-process redesign.†

Related to the preceding criticism is the argument that aid is given to polluters and that incentives may conceivably distort production patterns by rewarding the dirty producers, but giving no rewards to the clean ones.‡

Finally, our history of paying people *not* to do things has not been all that successful. Farm subsidies, for example, have a notorious history of favoritism, overpayment, and bureaucratic inefficiency; many would argue that the benefits do not seem appropriate to the costs.§

It is too easy, however, to write off the tax incentive and subsidy approach, however. Despite the arguments to the contrary, a certain amount of equity rights are acquired by the polluting firm if only because society, by doing nothing in the past, has allowed a firm to lock itself into a mode of business operation. To that extent, and to the extent that other methods of control may create problems of unemployment and community readjustment, some temporary subsidy or tax incentive (or some relaxation of other regulation methods and standards) to allow the firm to unlock itself, might well be in order.#

STICK APPROACHES

The most equitable approaches and the methods calculated to yield the most efficient allocation of resources may be those forcing the *internalization of external costs* or the absorbing by the firm (or polluting consumers) of the total cost of production (or consumption).

Many methods have been proposed to force such internalization: taxation, regulation, amenity rights, and product taxes, to name a few.

---

*Tax Foundation, *op. cit.,* p. 32.

†*Ibid.*

‡*Ibid.,* pp. 32–3.

§Wenders, *op. cit.*

#Jacoby, *op. cit.,* p. 194.

Direct regulation

Direct regulation of polluters involves government action in setting the standards of environmental quality and prescribing the mechanisms to achieve the reduction in pollution. All polluters would then be required, under some penalty, to reach the prescribed level of pollution abatement.

But straight regulation has some serious disadvantages. It may not allow polluters to choose a least-cost method of pollution abatement. Standards and procedures set at some central level may not be flexible enough to allow producers to make a choice of equipment, process change, or product change.*

In addition, there may be situations where the cost of the prescribed abatement procedures may be so high for an individual producer that he would be driven out of business, whereas the cost of collectively handling the wastes of several similar-size polluters may inflict relatively less of a burden. Thus, one could conceive of a situation where the minimum costs for installation of pollution-control equipment would drive an individual mill out of business, whereas a *public processing plant* to handle wastes generated by several such smaller mills would be economically financed through a less onerous taxing scheme. Direct regulation, with no thought to flexible programming, would thus drive out those mills whose scale of operation was too small to support the installation of relatively expensive equipment.

Operationally, our history of regulation is even bleaker than the history of subsidies. Regulatory commissions come under all sorts of political pressures, and hence become the vehicle for disastrous compromise. Indeed, many commentators have noted that regulatory commissions go through a life cycle, with the last stage of that cycle being one where the commissions become captives of the regulated.†

Scarce resource rights

One novel solution, possibly less popular because it grants a "right" to pollute, views air, water, and land as scarce resources whose use for waste disposal may be paid for by effluent producers.

> Generally, the mechanism would operate as follows: First, a technical survey would determine approximately how much waste matter the air and water in a given region could accommodate without deleterious effects. Certificates entitling the holder to utilize the purifying capacities of the river for a specified number of units of waste material would be issued and sold, up to a total fully utilizing the natural resource. Only holders of certificates would be entitled to discharge waste; all others would be required to process wastes to render them harmless, meeting standards to be established by the certificate-issuing board before releasing them.‡

---

*Wenders, *op. cit.,* p. 4.

†For example, Marver H. Bernstein, *Regulating Business by Independent Commission* (Princeton: Princeton University Press, 1955).

‡Tax Foundation, Inc., *op. cit.,* pp. 36–7.

Several unique points ought to be recognized in this proposal before it is unceremoniously brushed off. First, the rights themselves would be marketable, and hence, the cost of the rights should be pushed very close to the costs of installing in-plant pollution control equipment.

Second, maximum efficiency in the use of the natural resource would result, but since the certificates would be scarce (and become scarcer as time goes on), there is an incentive to develop more efficient in-plant pollution-control measures.

Finally, groups that want a cleaner environment and would want standards higher than the minimums calculated would be able to take some direct action, where their attempts at political action are too slow or unsuccessful. They could buy up blocks of certificates and thus withhold further effluent while concurrently forcing further and speedier development of pollution-control equipment, as the available resources for dumping are taken off the market and become scarcer.*

Amenity rights

An interesting approach to internalizing the external costs involves the guarantee of amenity rights to abutting property owners. Jacoby proposes a constitutional amendment to guarantee those rights. Owners of abutting property would then be entitled to sue for redress in the event of noise, soot, and water damage. In theory, at least, producers of pollution would internalize the costs of paying the legal bills and damages, or by installing the control devices necessary to save the costs of litigation and legal liabilities.†

On the other hand, this proposal puts forth a costly and time-consuming process for the plaintiff as well as the defendant and, given the state of undercapacity in today's judicial processes, other mechanisms of internalizing the costs might be preferable.

The pollution tax

A final method of pollution abatement that we might discuss is the pollution tax. Under this scheme, the polluter would pay a tax on his pollution output. The tax would be so calculated as to force the polluter to pay the total costs (internal as well as external) of production.‡

Presumably the effluent of an industrial establishment would be metered (just as water is now metered) and the tax per unit calculated from comparing the total outflow with the costs of reducing the pollution by the desired percentage.

Now the firm would be confronted with several alternatives. It could cease polluting, with a key advantage to the firm under the tax scheme being that it would be free to choose whatever method might accomplish that goal most effi-

---

Ibid.

†Jacoby, *op. cit.*

‡Wenders, *op. cit.*

ciently.* Or the firm could continue to pollute, but would have the costs of the tax added to its total costs of producing. Both of these alternative courses of action internalize the total costs of production.

Critics might argue, however, that the second alternative still leaves the firm polluting, and undeniably this may be true. But several points of rebuttal may be made. Most important, it is the aggregate level of pollution that must be reduced, not that of each individual firm. Some firms may find it relatively cheap and easy to avoid the tax and may have a scale of operation big enough to sustain the costs of a pollution-control system efficiently. Other firms may have a degree of monopoly power in the marketplace and be able to pass on the increases in costs. Other firms, however, may be too small to need a system and these would prefer to pay the tax. So long as the *total industry pollution output* was reduced, the problem of the single firm polluting should not be troublesome. And as a further safeguard, the tax could be adjusted to make the number of firms willing to install pollution-control equipment sufficient to decrease the level of pollution to its desired state. One would have to argue for zero pollution to complain about a single firm's impact, and to my knowledge, few proponents of environmental quality support that view.

The tax system also sets the stage for community or concerned action. Communities could build regional systems—at least for water pollution and solid waste disposal. Firms that are too small to support internal pollution-control systems or systems that require large capacities to be economically viable, could be included in pollution-abatement programs through the use of the tax system. This would mean that a community could build a treatment plant; the polluters would pay the costs; marginal firms would pay only their share; large firms could process part of their effluent internally and be taxed on the other part while filtering it through the community system; and a genuine community or regional solution would decrease the pollution to a level desired.†

A tax system has some added quality even if only from the point of view of efficiency of enforcement. Somehow, the United States has had a history of success with its various taxes that it hasn't had with other forms of regulation. Taxes seem to be paid with a lesser amount of litigation. Finally, the mechanism for collection already exists and has shown some degree of efficiency.

THE POLLUTING CONSUMER

Up to now, we have dealt principally with the polluting producer and have covered schemes designed to assign or internalize the costs generated by the production processes. But many products generate costs during and after

---

*Ibid., p. 4.

†Allen Kneese and Blair Bower, *Managing Water Quality: Economics, Technology, and Institutions* (Baltimore: Johns Hopkins Press: 1968) cited in Stephen W. Campbell, *A Survey of Industrial Water Pollution in the Pulp and Paper Industry of the United States*, unpublished thesis, University of Massachusetts, 1972.

consumption, the primary examples being exhausts from automobiles during use, and the disposal of packages and solids after use. Quite obviously, if the producer must internalize his costs, a complete system should require the consumer to do so also.

Most of the methods described for the producer can easily be applied to the consumer, where the act of consuming can be individually and easily isolated. Thus, taxing polluting exhausts, or adding a tax to products requiring solid waste disposal have been proposed. With automobiles, the United States has adopted the regulatory approach; simply requiring each vehicle produced to come equipped with emission-control equipment. But the obvious fault with this system is already apparent; some consumers have simply disconnected the systems; others do not maintain them.

For solid waste, a unique proposal is to add the cost of disposal to the unit when sold, with a refund granted upon proper disposal. Thus a sum (say $35 for an automobile, one cent for a beer bottle) would be added to the purchase price (somewhat like the way an excise tax is added), and when the consumer brought the used product to a disposal station, he would receive a credit. While this would not resolve and apportion the costs of solid-waste disposal, the tax would still provide the incentive for proper disposal. Since solid-waste disposal is a generally accepted municipal or regional function, assuring its use and discouraging litter and abandonment may be all that is necessary in the regulation of consumer habits.

With air pollution, the tax system seems useful. Controllers could meter the air pollutants from consumer heating systems, car exhausts, etc., and set the tax appropriately. Some consumers would then be induced to install the necessary equipment or maintain that already installed at peak efficiency.

EFFECTS OF INTERNALIZING TOTAL COSTS

Whichever method is adopted of forcing producers (and consumers) to internalize the external costs of production, there will be an effect on the relative price structure of various products. Products which are polluting in production or in end-use would now become relatively more expensive than those which do not pollute. Electric power would be charged at its full cost; so would automobiles, paper, and the myriad of other products used. Thus, the search for cleaner alternative ways to produce and consume would also be enhanced; for example, hydro-electric plants might become more useful (less costly) than steam generating or atomic plants.*

Another result of forcing the internalization would be the development of uses for presently polluting by-products. Conceivably, methods would be introduced for allowing recovery of valuable materials that now go up in smoke or down the drain. Some critics might ask why this is not being done now, if the recovery is a profitable operation. But most firms rank projects on a rate-of-return basis. If a productive project is ranked against a recovery project and the

---

*Wenders, op. cit., p. 4.

latter yields a lower rate of return, management effort will be devoted to the former and the effluent will continue to flow. But if the firm is forced to absorb the costs anyway (that is, undertake the project previously rejected), then what was previously an unsatisfactory project on a ranking basis becomes relatively attractive.

Finally, the internalization of total costs could have an effect on the distribution of income. Costs now incurred for health, property maintenance, recreation, and travel would be reduced. This reduction would aid low-income people. People who buy or use discretionary products would now find their costs increased. In effect, the subsidies now granted to those who consume more would be eliminated; automobiles would cost more, as would other polluting products; the means of producing and consuming polluting products would cost more. This would mean that resources now flowing freely to the affluent, with the tacit subsidy granted by society at large, would be paid for by the consumer with some benefits concurrently flowing to the less affluent.*

A PROBLEM IN ABSORBING EXTERNAL COSTS

Before one gets too caught up with plans for internalizing the external costs of production and consumption, he ought to be aware that there are problems in installing the system as well. While it is easy to armchair formulate a system for internalizing costs, it is much less easy to implement it. One author comments:

> Setting these prices on a comprehensive scale just once, not to mention changing them as conditions alter, would be an operational nightmare. Aside from the complexities of the administrative task, there would be widespread inducements to fraud, which probably would not be completely resisted. Furthermore, much pollution is the result of joint activities of industry and others, which raises questions of joint costs and their allocation.†

THE QUESTION OF STANDARDS

Most observers agree that any standards set must be national in origin and in scope.‡ Allowing states and political subdivisions to devise and enforce standards might mean a repeat of the dangerous game played in the 1950's with industrial development. Some states would develop low standards or no costs in an effort to achieve more industrial development, just as they granted tax holidays and free plants to induce firms to move. On the other hand, the setting of standards on the national level does not preclude their being set at some minimally acceptable national level with the states and political subdivisions free to develop more stringent ones. Nor does it mean that there will not be any differential in costs among various areas of the country.

---

*Jacoby, *op. cit.,* p. 194.

†Steiner, *Business and Society, op. cit.,* p. 175.

‡Wenders, *op. cit.,* p. 5.

Suppose national standards are set for pollution control and we taxed so much per unit of effluent, with the total tax to equal or exceed the costs of clean-up necessary to reach the standards. It would seem that less congested places and more rural areas would have no costs (or lower total costs) than places such as New York City or Los Angeles. This would mean—at least up to the situation where a high minimum fixed cost is necessary regardless of the effluent flow—that the tax per unit would be lower for the firm in rural, less populated, less industrialized areas, than it would be for the one in the urban concentrated area.

Theoretically, then, a natural inducement is created. Firms and people should be induced to move to a less polluted area (even when the standards are similar) to avoid paying the higher tax. This will reduce the level of pollution, and hence the tax, in the urban areas and increase both in the rural areas. Theoretically, at some point, equilibrium will be reached.

The level of pollution need not be allowed to exceed standards in any of these areas. The tax can be varied according to the increasing and decreasing costs of abatement to standards, and the total tax bill will guide the firm in appropriately making the decision to install control equipment. But population and industrial dispersion should lessen the demand for public amenities in cities and be beneficial in bringing the actual level of pollution to the desired standards.

How high should standards be set? Generally speaking, the higher the standards, the higher the cost. "The optimum level of pollution is [reached] when any further reduction of pollution is not worth the cost." But how do we measure some of these costs and benefits? What is the value of a natural vista unaffected by smoke and soot? These are decisions we have just begun to contemplate and these are areas where environmental specialists can make their greatest contributions. The question becomes one of trade-off, and only society can make these decisions through the political process.*

But critics should recognize some of the side-effects of higher than necessary standards. We have already noted the fact that internalization of costs will raise the prices of "dirty" products relative to those of "clean" products. Clearly some products will cost less—chiefly services such as recreation, health, etc. Some will cost more. But nobody has yet pointed out the effect that these increased product costs (inflation) will have on international trade and our already adverse balance of payments.† Obviously, the effect will be substantial and will entail large amounts of planning and indeed compromise.

OTHER NECESSARY PROGRAMS

The transfer of costs to identifiable polluting parties is an equitable solution, but a program consisting of only that step is clearly inadequate. Much pollution results from the little polluters, individuals and small businesses, as well as from governmental units (and one must appreciate that government accounts for

---

*Ibid.

†Steiner, op. cit., p. 174.

almost one-third of Gross National Product), and other public institutions such as hospitals, universities, etc. It has generally been accepted that society will provide services where the cost would be intolerable for the individual citizen, where some wide-spread public need is demonstrated over a large portion of the population, where the scope of the action is too great for one person or small group of persons to handle the problem individually, where the solution of one problem would lead to others unless that solution was handled centrally, or where the public health and safety were at stake due to an unattended need. So governments have often provided, for example, solid-waste disposal, sewerage, and water supplies.

However, government does not always do a total or efficient job, and that which it does do, ofttimes has harmful side effects. Thus, a town may have a sewerage system, but the effluent may also flow untreated into the nearest stream.

While it is not within the bounds of this paper to analyze public needs, most observers agree that sewerage treatment, waterway management, rapid transit, and other public systems are clearly inadequate. Some call for massive programs shared by all levels of society to remedy the deficiencies, in addition to the control and taxes where individual polluters can be isolated and controlled.* Whether society is prepared or amenable to making the sacrifices, however, is another question.

POLITICAL AND VALUE PROBLEMS IN POLLUTION CONTROL

Technical and allocational problems are not the only constraints on strategies for improving the environment. Our very political heritage and governmental structure also offer problems and militate against fast and revolutionary change. Against that background, the change accruing over the past ten years has been phenomenally rapid and profound.

The Tennessee Valley Authority to the contrary notwithstanding, in general, public control and ownership is anathema to most Americans. While increasing erosion of this anathema is evident, the fact remains that it is present, and any control over private affairs must be applied gradually in small increments.

Another problem, however, is even more profound. Our political and governmental division of powers is not geared to tackling a problem such as pollution. The Federal system creates boundaries where natural boundaries don't necessarily exist, and pollution does not follow political boundaries. Pollution problems often call for regional compacts and districts, whose formation is often accompanied by calls for local autonomy and compromise.

Additionally, any environmental planning and control must take place within the context of planning for other needs. One of the key constraints on environmental control, for example, has always been the concept of "Environmental unemployment," most typically associated with the smaller marginal firm or the older mill town. With increasing unemployment from decreases in defense expen-

---

*Jacoby, op. cit., pp. 195–6.

ditures, for example, it is fairly difficult to add unemployment resulting from environmental control.

A final constraint concerns the organization of various governmental bodies. Typically, governments are organized around defined constituencies; farmers, veterans, labor, business, etc. But environment is a much broader concern cross-cutting many of the traditional government agencies.* So far, governments have not been prone to handle well the pervasive and boundary-spanning problems such as pollution control.

With these problems in mind, let us now look at some of the additional pressures present at various levels of government.

Local

Some of the most effective work on environmental protection should probably take place at the local level. Pressure can probably be most easily applied on local officials and the results are most visible and easily measured against grass-roots desires and values. But local pollution-control measures and participation have definite limits. First, resources are probably most limited at the local level; the tax base in most local communities is already severely strained. Second, as already mentioned, pollution does not stop at political boundaries. But the key constraint to local action is the fact that the pressure that can be brought to bear by citizens' groups can be just as effectively counterbalanced by industrialists, particularly when jobs are at stake. This leads to the possibility that local communities will engage in competition to assure minimal pollution standards rather than maximal ones.

State and regional levels

Here the citizen is less a part of the "system" and compromise more a part of the process. But where air travels and rivers flow through political boundaries, efforts must be either state- or region-wide.

Clearly, centralizing decision-making to a higher level—state and regional—must have a rationale and criteria for application. For examples, several local areas must use the same medium, standards by necessity have to be identical or compatible among local units, and communities must be incapable of mustering the technical skills or resources necessary to adequately handle the problem.

Increasingly, these criteria have been recognized as regional compacts and multi-community or multi-state consortiums have come into being. But the trade-off between local autonomy and centralized control is always present.†

---

*See Lynton K. Caldwell. "Environmental Quality as an Administrative Problem," *The Annals of the American Academy of Political and Social Science,* CD (March, 1972) pp. 108–15.

†See "U.S. Steel Forced into Vast Antipollution Program," *New York Times,* (August 27, 1972), p. F–3 for a demonstration of local and regional "power" versus a major corporation.

National level

Clearly, it is at the national level that most effective action can take place. The federal government possesses the resources and the power to effectively set and enforce standards to get the job done. But there are several constraints on action at the Federal level, just as there are at the local and state levels. National standards must allow variance to account for local needs and values and by their very nature may be diluted because of the necessary consideration given to varying needs.

Highly organized pressure groups have more visibility at the national level in comparison to the grassroots action by common citizens. Only recently have public-oriented citizens' groups started to effectively organize; and there is a serious question as to whether they will represent substantial numbers of people or just determined small groups. In any event, at the present, paid lobbyists, industrial representatives, and commercial groups may be more active at the Federal level.*

Finally, the federal government is not monolithic in nature. Often, the action by one office is negated or offset by an opposite action of another. The celebrated case of the Surgeon General's warning against smoking, concurrently with the Agiculture Department's campaign to increase smoking in Thailand is illustrative of the problem.

International level

While no government body exists on the international level, the effect of the environment movement upon international relations can be seen in the recent international conference on the environment held under United Nations auspices in Stockholm, and the treaty on the environment signed by the United States and the Soviet Union.

But, given the present state of international relations and the nonexistence of international government, the question of effective pollution control imposed by some international organization or even by treaty seems remote. Controls may indirectly as well as directly affect many other kinds of activity; and while industrially advanced nations may be able to absorb the costs of pollution control, many of the less developed nations, already at a disadvantage relative to the more advanced countries, are not willing to have the control imposed upon them while they are attempting to develop and industrialize.

While international relations remains a game of competing nationalism, it seems that little beyond the conference stage can be expected at that level.

It seems, then, that any political action must be predicated upon several relatively strong traditions and certain political realities. First, time-honored values do not change overnight. Such institutions as private property, economic freedom, etc., must be considered as relatively inflexible constraints in the control process.

---

*See R. Joseph Monsen and Mark W. Cannon, *The Makers of Public Policy*, (New York: McGraw-Hill Book Co., 1965).

Second, we must consider pollution abatement a relatively long-term project. Education becomes the primary vehicle for sustaining the commitment to concern with the environment.

In addition, anyone who proposes to work in the pollution field must realize that, whereas standards of environmental purity are technically objective, they are politically subjective. Thus, compromise, almost by definition, is built into the process.

Finally, in the United Sates, at least, pollution control must work within a Federal system, with its various levels of power, and its emphasis on as much local autonomy as possible. In addition, it must work within a governmental organization structure which is constituent-oriented rather than problem-oriented.

SUMMARY AND CONCLUSIONS

In this paper, we have discussed the concepts of economic growth and its basic determinants, defined pollution and its basic sources, and indicated the magnitude of the costs. We have investigated what might be called grand schemes such as zero growth, a change in the system of production, and a change in the priorities of society. We have discussed the concept of production costs, and catalogued the various approaches within the free market system designed to allocate and perhaps internalize external costs and curb pollution. Finally, we pointed out some of the political and value problems involved in any pollution-abatement program.

If anything is made clear by this paper, it is that the problems are easy to talk about and write about and the solutions can glibly flow, but the ramifications are indeed immense. Instituting that grand strategy may not be impossible, but it is a great deal harder than it looks at first glance.

The Challenge of the Environment:
A primer on EPA's statutory authority

AIR

The alarming deterioration of the quality of the air we breathe has forced us to take a hard new look at air pollution, its causes, its results, and the means we have at our disposal for stopping it. While it is difficult to measure with any precision the costs Americans are paying for polluted air, we know the dollar total is enormous. Our most careful estimate is that about $6 billion each year is lost because of pollution-rated sickness and premature death. If we add an estimated $10 billion in property losses each year, we come up with a total of $16

Excerpt from "The Challenge of the Environment: A Primer on EPA's Statutory Authority," U.S. Environmental Protection Agency, December, 1972.

billion a year for polluted air—a pollution bill of about $80 per American per year.

EPA estimates that it will cost $15 billion spread over the next five years to control air pollution from existing sources. Simply letting pollution continue will be far more expensive than spending what it takes to curb it.

Statistics do not tell the entire story. The abatement of air pollution* in many cases will force industry to reduce obsolescence and inefficiency in its operations. For in many industries, the older and less efficient plant is also the biggest polluter. Forced to clean up, many plants will be compelled to be more efficient. Moreover, the recaptured by-products of industrial activity may provide usable, marketable products. Taking all of these factors into account, it makes good practical sense to end air pollution in America.

Legislative background

The Federal government's concern with air pollution officially began with the Air Pollution Act of 1955, authorizing the first Federally-funded air pollution research. Passage of the Motor Vehicle Pollution Control Act of 1965 expanded Federal activity to include setting emission† standards for automobiles.

Current Federal activity in air pollution abatement and research stems from the Air Quality Act of 1967 and the Clean Air Act of 1970. This undertaking is perhaps EPA's most controversial and comprehensive program and is certainly the most sweeping Federal pollution control scheme. The Clean Air Act set up a new system of national air quality standards and called for a roll-back of auto pollution levels.

Research

Specifically, the Clean Air Act, as amended, directs EPA to conduct research on the causes, effects, extent and ways to control air pollution. The agency is charged with the duty of providing technical and financial assistance to State and local air pollution control agencies and special investigations by EPA may be instituted at the request of State governments. Federal interagency cooperation is encouraged and EPA's own research is directed into specific areas, including health problems, fuel combustion, aircraft emissions, cost-benefit studies, and control technology.

Ambient air quality

The 1970 Act was the first law to call for national, uniform air quality standards based on geographic regions. Ambient air quality‡ is regulated by two sets of

---

Pollution Abatement—ending pollution. Distinguished from pollution control (which may only reduce pollution) and penalties (which principally punish violations).

†*Emissions*—what is discharged into the air by a pollution source. Distinguished from "effluents" which are discharged into water.

‡*Ambient Air Quality*—the average atmospheric purity as distinguished from discharge measurements taken at the source of pollution. The general amount of pollution present in a broad area.

standards, both determined by EPA. Primary standards concern the minimum level of air quality that is necessary to keep people from becoming ill. These levels are based on the proven harmful effects of individual pollutants. Secondary standards are aimed at the promotion of public welfare, and the prevention of damage to animals, plant life and property generally. EPA has now set primary and secondary national standards for six pollutants: sulfur oxide, particulate matter, carbon monoxide, hydrocarbons, photochemicals, and nitrogen oxide. Standards for these pollutants establish the maximum amount of each pollutant that will be permitted in the atmosphere consistent with public health and welfare.

Interstate regions

Since pollution does not follow State boundaries, the Administrator was given expanded power to establish interstate air quality regions;* each State however, retains authority for implementing national standards within its portion of an interstate region.

Implementation plans

State governments within each air quality region determine how national air pollution objectives are to be reached, subject to a three-year deadline for primary standards and a more flexible timetable for secondary standards. The States have submitted implementation plans showing in detail how and when they will achieve these standards within their own territory.

Federal standards apply to a list of identified pollutants that constitute the chief health problems associated with air pollution. The States have the broad responsibility of deciding which activities to regulate or prohibit in order to achieve the national standard. The Administrator will then review the individual implementation plan under prescribed criteria set out in the act itself: whether it expeditiously meets primary standards within the three-year timetable; whether it includes appropriate emission limitations, schedules, and timetables for compliance; whether it provides for sufficient monitoring capabilities; whether it provides for review of new sources of pollution; whether it is sufficient from the point of view of intergovernmental cooperation within the air quality region; and whether it provides for sufficient personnel, money, review, and inspection. The Administrator must substitute a plan of his own if the State fails to submit one, or if the State fails to revise its plan to meet the objections he has raised.

Although States are required to meet the national primary standards by 1975, the Clean Air Act provides for waiver of that deadline for up to an additional two years if compliance is technologically impossible and reasonable alternatives are inadequate.

WATER

Three out of every four people in the United States get their drinking water from public supply systems. In 1969, a Federal study found half of these systems sub-

---

*Air Quality Control Regions — the law requires the country to be divided into geographical units, reflecting common air pollution problems, for purposes of reaching national standards.

standard. Health specialists are increasingly concerned about neutralizing toxic substances and viruses when natural water purification fails. We are finally realizing that there are limits to natural purification — that our nation's waters cannot indefinitely absorb an endless avalanche of waste.

Legislative background

Federal water legislation dates back to the nineteenth century, when Congress enacted the River and Harbor Act of 1886, recodified in the Rivers and Harbors Act of 1899. It is only within the last seven years, however, that major water pollution legislation has been passed.

Recognizing the threat that dirty water posed to the public health and welfare, Congress enacted the Federal Water Pollution Control Act (FWPCA), in order to "enhance the quality and value of our water resources and to establish a national policy for the prevention, control and abatement of water pollution." FWPCA and its several amendments set out the basic legal authority for Federal regulation of water quality.

The original Act was passed in 1948. Its amendments broadened the Federal government's authority in water pollution control. The Water Pollution Control Act Amendments of 1956 strengthened enforcement provisions by providing for an abatement suit at the request of a State pollution control agency; where health was being endangered, the Federal government no longer had to receive the consent of all States involved. The Federal role was further expanded under the Water Quality Act of 1965. That act provided for the setting of water quality standards which are State and Federally enforceable; it became the basis for interstate water quality standards. The Clean Water Restoration Act of 1966 imposed a $100 per day fine on a polluter who failed to submit a required report. The Water Quality Improvement Act of 1970 again expanded Federal authority, and established a State certification procedure to prevent degradation of water below applicable standards.

Despite the improvements achieved by each amendment to the original Act, the result of this sporadic legislation was a hodgepodge of law. Eleven reorganizations and restructurings of Federal agency responsibility compounded the difficulty of effectively implementing the law. To solve these problems, the 1972 amendments to the FWPCA restructured the authority of water pollution control and consolidated authority in the Administrator of the Environmental Protection Agency.

Goals and policy

The objective of the Act is to restore and maintain the chemical, physical, and biological integrity of the nation's waters. In order to achieve this objective, the Act sets two goals. The first national goal is the elimination of the discharge of all pollutants into the navigable waters of the United States by 1985. The second national goal is an interim level of water quality that provides fo the protection of fish, shellfish, and wildlife and recreation by July 1, 1983. In this framework, Congress gave the Administrator the legal tools necessary to make inroads into the problems of water pollution control, while continuing to recognize the primary rights and responsibilities of the States to prevent, reduce, and eliminate pollution.

SOLID WASTE

America's high level of technological developments combined with our standard of living has produced a staggering accumulation of waste and refuse. Our appetite for resources promises to continue to swell, but our methods of dealing with the waste products of our way of life remain rather primitive. This nation generates 360 million tons of solid waste each year—garbage, trash and other solid materials, exclusive of sewage and dissolved material. That 360 million tons may double within ten years. In 1970, each American consumed 578 pounds of packaging material alone. While the levels of solid waste continue to grow, the most common method of disposing of the by-products of America's comsumption is the same as it was a century ago: open dumping.

We have historically operated on the assumption that the earth, water and air around us will absorb all of our waste products indefinitely. We now are beginning to realize that the earth, the oceans, and the atmosphere are finite, and that nature's capacity to assimilate more waste is coming to an end.

Legislative background

In 1965, Congress enacted the Solid Waste Disposal Act, the first Federal legislation to attempt to deal with the effects of solid waste disposal on the environment. Up to that time, only five States had made any kind of organized effort to address the problem. The Federal program under 1965 Act was largely a system of grants which stressed State and local responsibility.

By 1970, the more far-reaching implications of disposing of used resources and waste products were widely recognized. Congress amended the 1965 Act with the Resource Recovery Act of 1970, which officially recognized the potential economic benefits of recovering a portion of the "trash" we were casually discarding. That legislation also directed new grant programs to urban areas, where solid waste problems were getting out of hand.

Nature of federal role

Although the primary responsibility for the management of solid waste materials clearly resides with State and local officials, Federal activity was directed by Congress into several areas:

1. construction, demonstration, and application of waste management and resource recovery systems for the preservation of air, water, and land resources;

2. technical and financial assistance to agencies in planning and developing resource recovery and waste disposal programs;

3. national research and development programs to develop and test methods of dealing with collection, separation, recovery, recycling, and safe disposal of non-recoverable waste;

4. guidelines for the collection, transportation, separation, and recovery and disposal of solid waste.

5. training grants in occupations involving design, operation, and maintenance of solid waste disposal systems.

NOISE

Our experts define noise as "unwanted sound." The national recognition of noise as a pollutant is relatively recent, probably because it is generally confined to a specific geographic locality and temporal period, and because its deleterious effects are less patent than those of other forms of pollutants. Each of us has noticed such "garden-variety" pollutants as waste in rivers, or auto emissions in the air. We may shrink back from a river because of its peculiar color or odor, or be offended by noxious fumes from the antique buses that still service many cities, but noise, being less tangible and enduring, tends to be less sensually and aesthetically offensive.

Legislative background

The Airport and Airway Development Act of 1970 and the Federal Aid Highway Act identify noise as one factor among others to be considered in the planning, development, and construction of airports and highways. EPA is required to evaluate environmental factors involved in such projects and to report its findings to the Secretary of Transportation. He, in turn, must take them into consideration before making a final decision on the feasibility of a given project.

The Noise Pollution and Abatement Act of 1970, directed that substantial research be undertaken to study a wide range of problems concerning harmful effects of noise. In 1971, EPA set up its own Office of Noise Abatement and Control to study the effect of noise on public health and welfare.

With enactment of the Noise Control Act of 1972 came the first major piece of Congressional legislation in this area. The stated purpose of the Act is to establish a vehicle for the effective coordination of Federal research and activities in noise control, to authorize the establishment of Federal noise emission standards for products distributed in interstate commerce, and to provide information to the public respecting the noise emission and noise reduction characteristics of such products.

In addition, the Act amends the Federal Aviation Act of 1958 to provide for interdepartmental action between FAA and EPA in the prescription of standards and regulations relating to the control and abatement of aircraft noise and sonic boom. It further provides for similar cooperation between the Department of Transportation and EPA in the promulgation of standards and regulations relating to the noise emission of interstate railroad and motor carriers.

Noise emission standards

Under the Noise Control Act, the Administrator is given the authority to prescribe regulations for products designated as major noise sources, where noise emission standards are feasible and where the product falls into one of the following categories: construction equipment, transportation equipment, any motor or engine, electrical or electronic equipment. Each regulation must include a noise emission standard which sets the limits on emissions from a given product, and which, based on published criteria, is a requisite for the protection of the public health and welfare. Factors for consideration are the magnitude and conditions for use, the degree of noise reduction achievable through the application of the best available technology, and the cost of compliance. The Administrator is also authorized to devise regulations for other noise sources where standards are feasible and when it is determined that the source poses a threat to the public health and welfare. The Administrator must give labeling instructions for designated products, which will put the prospective user on notice of either the product's exceptionally high noise emission level or its effectiveness in reducing noise.

Enforcement

Under the Noise Control Act, the Administrator may issue an order, after notice and a hearing, specifying such relief as he deems necessary to protect the public health and welfare, and may request judicial action to restrain violations of the Act. There are criminal penalties for the following willful and knowing acts: the distribution in commerce of any new product not conforming to the emission standards specified or the designated labeling requirements; the noncompliance with an order of the Administrator; or the failure to maintain certain records, make certain reports and tests, or provide certain information. Private citizens also can bring civil actions for violations of the Act.

It's Time for New Approaches to Pollution Control

If we persist on the present regulatory paths, costs will outweigh benefits and, oddly enough, the environment may get dirtier.

Tom Alexander

Sometime late in the Sixties, pollution ceased to be a morally neutral problem subject to rational analysis and balanced solutions; it acquired, instead, the status of sin. Congress wrote tough legislation—the Clean Air Act amendments of 1970 and the Water Pollution Control Act amendments of 1972—to stamp it out. What the amendments added up to were decisions by the U.S. Congress not only to rearrange a considerable number of American habits and institutions, but also to repeal some laws of economics, physics, and logic.

By any standards other than their own moral absolutism, to be sure, the clean air and water acts hardly stack up as failures—as anyone can see whose memory spans more than a decade. The airline traveler descending from the sub-stratospheric blue and black discerns along the horizon fewer of of those brown, city-capping photochemical domes and almost none of the miles-long, trailing smoke plumes that used to serve as checkpoints and wind socks for pilots. In mid-day city canyons, the fumes don't churn so visibly anymore. In Cleveland, they're building boutiques along the Cuyahoga River, which used to cause periodic excitement downtown by catching fire. From the Appalachians to the Cascades, shy mountain streams that used to make their escape from paper-mill towns rafted with foam and stinking black with sulfite liquor now manage to sparkle a bit in the sunlight. Crab traps once more dangle from hardware-store ceilings of little towns up the Hudson, even in the face of all the warnings about PCB's and such.

THE EASY CONQUESTS ARE OVER

The cruder but more authoritative perceptions of scientific instruments confirm that the tonnage of floating and flying contaminants is much less than it was (see charts, page 218). And huge capital outlays already committed will result in considerable further improvements in the near future.

But now the easy conquests are over and the battles between the law and reality have begun. A good many chastened legislators would admit that, in the familiar pattern of the recent past, the government overestimated the potency of statutory wand waving and underestimated the ability of complex systems to convert good intentions into perverse outcomes. It appears that if the laws were actually to be enforced as they are written or as courts have interpreted them, the end result might be a no-growth economy, if not a bankrupt nation.

WATCHBIRDS AGAINST LENIENCY

In their fervor of environmental puritanism in the early Seventies, the lawmakers assigned environmental goals a top national priority, before which other goals and preferences would have to yield. They set air-quality standards to be met by 1975, with provisions for a two-year extension. If modifications to automobiles, factories, and power plants proved insufficient, then states and cities were to impose controls on traffic and land use. The water legislation required all industries and municipalities to install by 1977 what was airily called the "best practicable technology" for treating their wastes. This was to be followed in 1983 by the more stringent "best available technology."

To the overworked Environmental Protection Agency, Congress gave the tasks of setting the specific standards and giving precise meaning to such terms as "best practicable" and "best available" technology—as well as responsibility for enforcing the laws. The agency could delegate some of the planning and enforcement burden to the states, but only so long as the states performed according to federal expectations. Lest EPA follow the normal tendency of regulatory agencies to compromise and be reasonable, Congress severely limited its authority to exercise discretion. As watchbirds against leniency, private citizens were granted standing in court to sue the agency for failure to comply with the letter and the spirit of the law. Since then, much of the EPA's over-strained manpower resources have gone into defending the agency against more than a thousand suits, brought both by environmentalists seeking sterner enforcement and by companies seeking relief from what they regard as arbitrary and ruinous interpretations of the statutes.

The most momentous of the citizen suits revolved around a passage in the clean-air amendments indicating that the legislative purpose was to "protect and enhance" the quality of the nation's air. Courts have interpreted "protect and enhance" to mean that no significant deterioration should be permitted anywhere. This could be taken to imply that nowhere in the country could much in the way of industrial growth be permitted. In the water-pollution legislation, the environmental puritanism was explicit. Congress stated that the ultimate goal—to be reached in 1985—was nothing less than the "elimination of discharge" of all pollutants into the nation's rivers, streams, and lakes.

SOME CITIES MAY NEVER MAKE IT

Far from attaining such a state of ultimate grace, however, society is having trouble even achieving the short-range goals established by existing laws. At least half the nation's designated air-quality regions are violating the minimum standards they were to have met in 1975, and it now appears that some major cities may *never* be in compliance. Probably fewer than half the nation's municipalities will meet the 1977 water-pollution regulations either, and for some, compliance is well over a decade away. Many cities and states are flatly refusing to implement the elaborate traffic-control and land-use plans that were supposed to go into effect when less drastic measures failed to bring air quality to mandated levels. And as for the harassed Environmental Protection Agency that is supposed to be enforcing the law, there's little it can do about many of these violations except to pretend they're not happening.

EPA does have more clout with industry. So far the agency has devoted most of its attention to the major polluters, mainly in basic industries—nonferrous metals, pulp and paper, iron and steel, petroleum refining, chemicals, and electric utilities. Around 80 percent of the plants in these industries are in compliance or on schedule (many of the rest are seeking relief in the courts). But the costs have been substantial. George Weyerhaeuser, president of Weyerhaeuser Co., attributes a good part of 1974's doubling of pulp prices to pollution-abatement expenditures and plant closings. And last year, David Anderson, manager of environmental quality control for Bethlehem Steel, told a startled Senate committee that without some softening of the stringent rulings on air quality, it was possible that no new steelmaking capacity would be built in the U.S.

So far, according to EPA surveys, eighty-one industrial plants employing 18,000 people have been forced to close, partly or entirely because of emission standards—plants that could neither meet the standards with existing equipment nor afford to buy new equipment. Most of the plants, to be sure, were old and already marginal. On the other hand, the surveys covered only plants with twenty-five or more employees, and it is generally accepted that far greater numbers of small operations have been forced out of business or soon will be.

Conflicts between environmental puritanism and economic and political realism have forced the government into a variety of ad hoc legislative repairs, regulatory compromises, and legally questionable evasions. Last March, the EPA exempted eight major steel mills along Ohio's Mahoning River from compliance with the water-emission standards, though the Mahoning may well qualify as America's dirtiest river. EPA granted the relief because of the impact that closing the mills would have on the area's economy.

More and more, EPA is granting exemptions, variances, and "extensions" or simply overlooking violations. Adminstrator Russell Train rationalizes the situation this way: "We don't have enough manpower to enforce all the statutes everywhere, so we tend to pick out those situations where our actions will have the most beneficial effect." Whatever the justification, the effect of selective enforcement is to undermine the credibility and purpose of federal statutes, to generate uncertainty and to delay decision-making by planners and investors, to reward those who choose to lobby or to fight the issues in the courts, and to penalize their competitors who have made good-faith efforts to comply.

The health-at-any price view

In sum, then, the realities are demanding that we regard environmental cleanliness not as a categorical imperative but as one more good that can be purchased only at a cost in other things of value. Many people insist, to be sure, that the need to protect the public health is a nonnegotiable justification for whatever price society must pay for the cleanup. In the case of water pollution, however, public health practically ceased to be an issue earlier in this century with the general introduction of chlorination in drinking-water supplies. The real purposes of the clean-water amendments, as their language makes clear enough, are mainly aesthetic and recreational — "the protection and propagation of fish, shellfish and wildlife and to provide for recreation in and on the water."

As for air pollution, what is remarkable is that after more than twenty years of research, very little more can be said about its actual threat to health than that it isn't good for you. Last year the National Academy of Sciences made a frank assessment that comes close to wrecking the basis for the present standards on particular pollutants: "The specific chemical species responsible for toxicity have not been identified, and the levels of pollutants necessary to cause toxic effects have not been determined."

Whatever the damage from pollution, it is irrational to try to eliminate it without regard for costs. As a practical matter, societies are generally unwilling to pay the extremely high costs of virtually eliminating all danger. A case in point is auto safety. The National Academy of Sciences estimates that automotive accidents cause somewhere between twelve and 100 times as many fatalities as automotive air pollution. Yet no one seriously proposes nationwide 35-mph speed limits or even stoplights and pedestrian tunnels at every intersection. Along the same lines, there can be no escape from the necessity of viewing such questions as the appropriate level of environmental cleanliness in terms of cost-benefit trade-offs.

INTO THE HUNDREDS OF BILLIONS

To the extent that the government has considered the costs of the environmental cleanup at all, it has tended to underestimate them. In its 1973 annual report, for example, the federal Council on Environmental Quality projected that total private and public investment in air and water pollution equipment to meet federal standards would amount to about $65 billion for the ten-year span 1972–81. Somewhat less than half of that, $31.4 billion, would go for water pollution. The CEQ's latest projection, for the period 1975–84, comes to $127 billion, with water pollution accounting for $65 billion. But a very different picture recently emerged in a staff report by the National Commission on Water Quality, a panel of Congressmen and private experts, chaired by Vice President Nelson Rockefeller.

The commission spent two and a half years and $17 million analyzing the impact of the 1972 water-pollution-control legislation, and concluded that the required public and private capital expenditures would lie somewhere between $160 billion and $670 billion. The major point of uncertainty here is whether the law actually requires that rainwater runoff from city streets be collected and treated before discharge into streams. In any event, these figures, huge as they are, do not include operating and maintenance costs, which would push the totals quite a bit higher.

So far there has been no comparable examination of the costs and benefits of air-pollution control. Various pieces of evidence, however, indicate that the government may be underestimating these costs too. The Council on Environmental Quality, for example, projects that the capital investment for controlling air pollution from electric utilities will amount to $13.4 billion between 1974 and 1983. But in a study done for the utility industry, National Economics Research Associates came up with a figure over twice as big, $28 billion. If the costs of conforming to the air-pollution regulations have been understated to the same extent as water-pollution-control costs appear to have been, the cumulative costs of pollution abatement could lie in the trillion-dollar range by the middle of the Eighties—comparable to the outlays for defense or education.

Hardly anyone in government really believes that such sums will be spent. In writing its regulations, the EPA now pays far more attention to costs of various kinds than it did a year or two ago. The agency is currently sponsoring intensive analyses of the six basic industries most affected, with a view to their economic health. Congress itself has granted the Council on Wage and Price Stability authority to intervene in EPA's rule making when it seems likely that environmental regulations would have an inflationary impact out of proportion to the benefits.

AN EXTRA 1.7 PERCENT COSTS A LOT

The council is particularly concerned about the way pollution-abatement costs rise disproportionately as the standards grow tougher. Observes William Lilley

III, acting director of the council: "When the iron and steel industry eventually meets the 1977 water-discharge standards, their pollutants will be down 97.3 percent from the no-control level. Meeting the 1983 standards will result in a 99 percent reduction. Yet the cost to the industry of going from the 1977 standards to the 1983 standards will be two-thirds the cost of meeting the 1977 standards. Is it going to be worth it?"

That same question was raised in a much broader context by the National Commission on Water Quality in its report to Congress this spring. Viewing with horror some of its own cost projections, the commission expressed doubt about the advisability of proceeding beyond the 1977 effluent standards, except as required to control the most toxic wastes. For one thing, the commission pointed out, runoff waters from agricultural lands, streets, etc., carry so large a load of pollutants that many streams and rivers in the U.S. would remain polluted even if all point-source discharges were eliminated.

The inescapable tendency of costs to increase disproportionately as standards become more stringent is only one of serveral fundamental constraints that environmental puritanism has been bumping into. Another important constraint is that pollution abatement consumes energy. Stack-gas scrubbers required by EPA can absorb as much as 10 percent of a power plant's energy output. Mandated emissions standards for automobiles threaten to increase their gasoline consumption considerably. At the time the existing federal clean-air and clean-water legislation was-drafted, hardly anyone worried about the impact on energy supplies and costs, but the great surge in energy prices and the nation's troubling dependence on imported oil have made the energy penalties of pollution control a matter of serious concern.

Yet another constraint is that basic law of nature, the conservation of matter. The authors of environmental legislation often seem to assume that air or water, as the case may be, is isolated from other components of the environment. They appear to take it for granted that once a substance is removed from either air or water, it ceases to exist. Everything, however, must go somewhere, and what usually happens is that a substance kept out of the waterways, for example, winds up in the atmosphere, in the sea, or on land.

An unpleasant consequence is that efforts to cope with one kind of pollution tend to impede and complicate efforts to deal with other kinds of pollution. Consider, for example, the problem of what to do with solid wastes. Well before the air and water acts were even in existence, mayors and city managers across the U.S. were commiserating with one another about that besetting challenge. Most are running out of acreage for dumps and landfills. But air standards often bar incineration, and ocean dumping is increasingly proscribed. What's more, the efficient new sewage-treatment plants mandated by the Water Pollution Control Act produce roughly twice as much sludge as the old plants did.

In other words, the very process of pollution control produces pollution. The chemicals that are added in advanced water treatment are often troublesome, even toxic, pollutants. (Ordinary chlorine, for example, is now known to combine with certain organic materials to form chloroform, a known carcinogen.) The residues from many industrial treatment processes are huge quantities of brines, nearly impossible to reuse or store. And those new stack-gas scrubbers for coal-burning power plants will produce an immense outpouring of calcium sulfate in the form of a soupy slurry.

Many of these pollutants are far from innocuous. There's increasing evidence that one of the severest environmental health problems of all may be the washing or leaching of toxic salts, heavy metals, and organic carcinogens into groundwater aquifers. Once there, some of these substances pose a more intractable menace than the much-discussed radioactive wastes.

LESSONS FROM LAKE TAHOE

The tendencies of pollution-abatement programs to show exponentially rising costs, to drive up national energy consumption, and to produce pollution of their own culminate in the disturbing prospect that our present style of pollution abatement—trying to push too fast along narrowly conceived paths—may be making the environment dirtier. Some trailbreaking analysis along this line of thought has been carried out by Frank Schaumburg, head of the civil-engineering department at Oregon State University. A couple of years ago, for instance, Schaumburg and research colleague David Antonucci undertook an investigation of the environmental impact of a highly advanced new sewage-treatment plant at South Lake Tahoe, California, and they came to some troubling conclusions.

The treatment facility constructed at South Lake Tahoe to protect the lake's famous purity is frequently regarded as one model for the "best available technology" that existing legislation mandates for 1983. It puts sewage through the conventional primary and secondary treatment and then through a tertiary process that includes half a dozen additional stages of filtration, chemical extraction, and disinfection. All this not only takes money, energy, and other resources, but also generates a lot of pollution. Nitrogen, for example, is extracted from the water in the form of ammonia, which wafts into the atmosphere. The chemical-rich sludges are incinerated (the ashes are used for landfill). The carbon filters are cleaned by heating, which disperses their contaminants as gases.

For each million gallons of water treated, the third stage removes, on average, 230 pounds of organic matter, fifty-eight pounds of phosphorus, and twenty-seven pounds of nitrogen. In the course of doing so, the process consumes 1,600 pounds of lime, 340 pounds of alum, and 31 pounds of activated carbon, and uses 65 million BTU's of energy, equivalent to eleven barrels of oil or three tons of coal. Two-thirds of this energy is expended at Tahoe; the rest is used elsewhere, mostly in the production of treatment chemicals. (This analysis does not count *all* the energy used—i.e., in transporting things to the treatment plant or in constructing the plant itself.)

It's hard to escape the conclusion that there's got to be a better way. Schaumburg argues that, for one thing, we ought to make more use of nature's immense capacity to cleanse the environment through a variety of chemical, physical, and biological processes—a renewable and non-polluting resource.

Nature, that great recycler, suggests an additional way of coping with the troublesome tendency of waste treatment to create pollution: produce less waste in the first place. If we put more reliance on conserving, reusing, and recycling resources, in other words, we could reduce our reliance on energy-consuming, pollution-producing methods of pollution control.

Some technically advanced companies have already begun to adopt conservation-oriented processes. For example, 3M has found savings of more than $10 million in raw-material and waste-disposal costs through changes in fifteen processes. The cost of the program to date has been less than $1 million. Similar successes are reported by Dow Chemical and Union Camp, among others.

PROPELLING THE BOAT TOO FAST

On the whole, it is not likely that much progress toward cleaner and less wasteful technologies will be made without continuing governmental pressure. Such pressure, however, must be applied with knowledge, prudence, and patience, lest it wind up merely spreading pollution around and making it worse, all at great cost. Industries, technologies, and even cities have their own natural time scales for change, the pace being determined by the workings of such sequences as the depreciation and retirement of capital equipment and the research, development, test, scale-up, and production cycle. Attempting to force change too rapidly—as the present environmental protection laws have tried to do—is like trying to propel a boat beyond its own inherent hull speed, as established by the laws of hydrodynamics. The result is scant additional progress, lots of waves, noise, and wasted energy—and in the extreme, destruction of the boat.

Congress is now studying various proposals for rewriting the legislation to incorporate more recognition of obstacles and conflicting considerations. What the proposed amendments usually entail, however, is a return to something like the style of pre-1970 regulation, characterized by more flexibility and more case-by-case evaluation—a style that didn't work very well. The lawmakers, it seems, continue to hope that with sufficient persistence, the already intricate regulations can be tinkered into something that will fly.

But if government can't do well in administering rules that are comparatively uniform, inflexible, and simple, what chance does it have trying to shape laws to fit each industry and each plant within that industry, each region, each technological promise, each conflict of values and change of circumstance? The information, if it could be gathered at all, would swamp the bureaucracy—in fact, it's already swamped.

Society long ago devised institutions for dividing up this kind of information overload—institutions called "markets." Many economists have been proposing that we harness market forces to serve environmental ends. They contend that results could be achieved far more efficiently and with far less damage from side effects.

The economists' approach would recognize water courses and air as publicly owned resources. Traditionally, polluters have had free use of these resources and thus no incentive to be economical in using them. In the process, their actions may have benefited society as a whole and certain consumers in particular, but they have also shoved costs off onto other people in the form of dirt, eyesores, and damage to health. So, say the economists, let's charge the users and force them to incorporate that cost into planning, production, and pricing. One would expect that producers would try to pass the cost along, but also that forces of competition would impel them to try to reduce the cost. Otherwise, producers would probably have to reduce output. In any case, a cleaner environment would be achieved.

The generally favored approach would be to impose a tax or "effluent charge" on every polluter according to the amount and relative harmfulness of the discharges. These prices could be shaped to the special problems of given regions and could vary over time, like any price. To be sure, standards of some kind or even flat prohibitions might be necessary for the most dangerous pollutants.

With the present arrangements, one effect of the tight and uniform requirements has usually been to force the adoption of near-term "end-of-pipe" technology, generally add-on devices to remove pollutants. The more flexible effluent-charge approach would foster the use of a variety of methods to reduce pollution—recycling, changes in processes, shifts to less polluting materials—as well as development of more efficient pollution-removal technology. What's more, the regulatory approach provides no incentive to reduce pollution beyond the mandated standards. In theory at least, effluent charges would provide incentive all the way to zero.

CONCENTRATING EFFORT WHERE THE PAYOFF IS HIGH

Another virtue of the effluent-charge approach is that it would permit each company to work out its own least-cost mix of process changes, pollution controls, and effluent charges. Some companies and industries can reduce their pollution loads much more cheaply than others. Cost-benefit considerations suggest that pollution-abatement efforts should be concentrated where payoff is relatively high. One study the National Academy of Sciences did for the Rockefeller Commission estimated that simply concentrating abatement effort where it cost the least—rather than uniformly everywhere—would save 40 percent of the capital costs of achieving water quality equivalent to that implied by the 1977 standards.

Until recently, effluent-charge proposals have met with little favor among legislators, environmentalists, and regulators—and least of all, oddly, among businessmen. Effluent charges have been called a "license to pollute" and impossible to enforce. The first objection has about the same rigor as calling a regulatory fine a "license to break rules." As for the second, the effluent-charge system would be basically self-enforcing, like the income tax. Taxing sulfur dioxide emissions, for example, would be a matter of measuring the sulfur content of the coal burned and the removal efficiency of cleaning devices.

The most telling objection to effluent charges is that it might be hard to set tax levels that would be effective in reducing pollution without doing as much damage as the regulatory approach. Indeed, the information required to set the charges at optimum levels does not now exist, and would have to be acquired through experimentation. But one virtue of the effluent-charge approach is that it would permit the administering agencies to experiment without crippling the economic system or eroding the credibility of the legal system.

THE NEGLECTED HAZARDS

Even with all the shortcomings, the environmental legislation now on the books has brought a considerable cleanup, and it can be argued that, despite all the special-case hardships, the benefits have exceeded the costs. But by the time the air and water standards now mandated for 1977 are finally met in most parts of the country, the cleanup will have proceeded about as far as our present knowledge can justify in the light of escalating costs. Efforts to push much further in the same directions by the same methods will entail huge waste and possibly severe damage to the economy.

There's good reason to suspect that even now we may be spending too much money and manpower on pollutants that are no longer much of a problem, while neglecting pollutants that are genuine hazards. In particular, very little is known about thousands of new substances that, like the PCBs, have been finding their

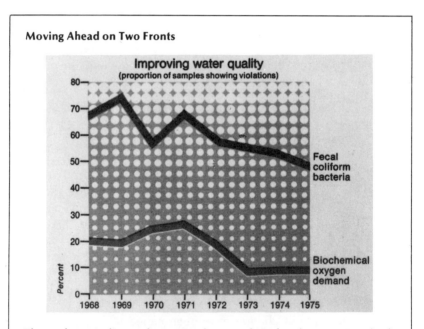

Moving Ahead on Two Fronts

These charts indicate that we've been making headway against both water and air pollution. The chart above shows two separate measures of water quality in some American rivers. Biochemical oxygen demand is associated with the decomposition of organic matter; bacteria involved in the processes of decomposition consume dissolved oxygen, which is then unavailable for fish and other aquatic life. The lines on the other chart show, for the U.S. as a whole, EPA estimates of the tonnages of various pollutants discharged into the atmosphere. The trend has been unmistakably downward. The increase in oxides of nitrogen in the early 1970's reflects growth in the number of sources, plus the technical difficulty of controlling those oxides.

way into water and air. Most of these are present in low levels, but many are known to be toxic or carcinogenic, and only a few are now controlled.

For the late 1970's and the 1980's, clearly, the nation will need new approaches to the maintenance of environmental quality. What seems most promising in the light of what we have learned so far is a flexible mix of approaches, with more reliance on natural processes, more emphasis on conservation and recycling, more awareness of the connectedness of things, and probably extensive use of effluent charges as an alternative to rigid regulation. But whatever the exact lineaments of the optimal program, the time to begin the process of rethinking and reshaping is now. In the time scales of long-range planning, 1983 is almost upon us. Before long, businesses will have to start planning for new facilities for the 1980's. As months go by, the stringent standards that existing law mandates for 1983 and beyond will become more and more burdensome. If those standards are ultimately to be judged ruinous—and such a verdict seems inevitable—that judgment had best be rendered soon.

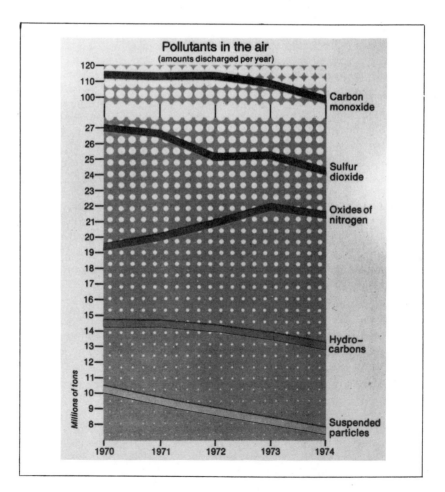

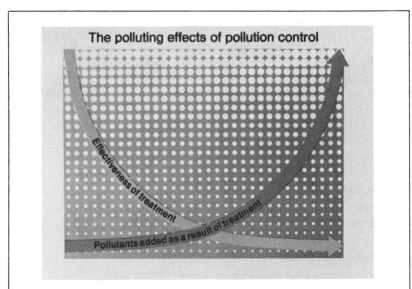

It's a losing game to push waste treatment too far, argues engineer Frank Schaumburg of Oregon State University. He illustrates the concept schematically with two idealized curves. The curve descending from the left represents the effectiveness of pollution abatement in terms of, say, pounds of contaminants removed per unit volume of air or water. The rising curve represents the contaminants produced as a result of the cleanup process itself (see text). Beyond the point at which the two curves intersect, Schaumburg suggests, waste treatment tends to do the environment as a whole more harm than good.

QUESTIONS FOR DISCUSSION

1. Define "externalities" and "external costs" and differentiate the latter from business production costs.

2. Develop the arguments on both sides and discuss the problems of environmental protection and energy provision, ends standards versus process standards, and environmental enhancement versus employment.

3. Many methods have been proposed to force the internalization of "external costs" by the polluting firm. Among these are (a) direct regulation, (b) scarce resource rights, (c) amenity rights, and (d) the pollution tax. Evaluate and discuss the specific pros and cons of each method.

4. "When large external costs or benefits are involved, there is conflict between the decision that serves the self-interest of the individual and that which serves the collective welfare of society." Comment, explain, and evaluate that statement.

5. Tom Alexander, in his article "It's Time for New Approaches to Pollution Control," concludes that "For the late 1970's and the 1980's, clearly, the nation will need new approaches to the maintenance of environmental quality." Discuss the "new approaches" recommended by Alexander and others. What problems and disadvantages can you conceive of with some of the suggested approaches?

6. Suppose you are a staff member of an industry research and lobbying organization, and were asked to prepare a response to the zero-growth approach to pollution control. What factors would you include in your analysis?

SELECTED READINGS

Clean Air and Water News, Commerce Clearing House, N.Y. (Weekly).

Cohn, H. B., "Environmentalism—Costs and benefits," *Public Utilities Fortnightly,* July 31, 1975.

Commoner, B., *The Closing Circle.* (New York: Alfred Knopf, 1971.)

The Conference Board, *Corporate Organization for Pollution Control.* (New York: The Conference Board, Inc., 1970.)

Edmunds, S., "Trade-offs in assessing environmental impacts," *California Management Review,* **XIX,** No. 1, 1976.

Edmunds, S., and John Letey, *Environmental Administration.* (New York: McGraw-Hill Book Company, 1973). Note particularly Section 1 and Chapters 12, 16, 17, 22 and 23.

Environment Reporter, Bureau of National Affairs, Inc. A Weekly Review of Pollution Control and Related Environmental Management Problems.

"E.P.A.: The tricks of the trade-off," *Business Week,* April 4, 1977.

Fir, R. W., "Facing up to pollution controls," *Harvard Business Review,* March–April, 1974.

Goldstein, J., *How to Manage Your Company Ecologically.* (New York: Rodale Press, 1971.)

Lund, L., "Industrial pollution-control costs," *The Conference Board Record,* April, 1976.

Mills, E. S., and F. M. Peterson, "Environmental quality: The first five years," *American Economic Review,* June, 1975.

Quarles, J. R., Jr., "Pollution control—Not by law alone," *The Conference Board Record,* April, 1976.

Ross, S. S., "By and large, the environmental cleanup is progressing quite nicely, thank you," *MBA,* February, 1973.

"Technology isn't the villain—after all," *Business Week,* February 3, 1973.

Wernette, J. P., "Perspective on environmental problems," *University of Michigan Business Review,* July, 1975.

Case

R. B. BRISTOL, INC.*

On July 28, 1972, R. B. Bristol, Inc., an Uxbridge, Massachusetts textile manufacturing firm, filed with the Department of Public Health a request for variance from the "Regulations for the Control of Air Pollution in the Central Massachusetts Air Pollution Control District." Specifically, the request was for variance from Regulation 5.1.2. which prohibited the firm from burning fuel oil with a sulfur content in excess of 1 percent. R. B. Bristol, Inc., was requesting permission to burn 2.2-percent sulfur-content fuel oil. The firm subsequently submitted testimony on its behalf at a public hearing conducted on August 15, 1972. After a review of the evidence, the Department of Public Health at its meeting of February 22, 1973, voted to deny the requested variance.

Company background

R. B. Bristol, Inc., founded in 1813, is a manufacturer of fine woolen fabrics and materials. The firm's textile products include a wide variety of finished and unfinished apparel fabrics, both woven and knitted, for men's, women's and children's wear. A smaller portion of their output includes unwoven textured and spun yarns. All of their products are of the highest grade and are used by some of the most exclusive garment designers and manufacturers in the U.S. Additionally, Bristol holds a contract from the U.S. Government to supply fine woolen materials for selected military apparel and equipment.

Bristol's main office and four of its plants are located in the town of Uxbridge, Massachusetts. Uxbridge is a relatively small town with a population of 8,300. Bristol serves as the largest industrial operation and dominant employer in the town, employing 823 from a work force of approximately 3,000. Three other smaller textile mills are also in operation in Uxbridge. Bristol's fifth plant is located ten miles away in Worcester, a city with a population in excess of 180,000.

There are 23 stockholders of R. B. Bristol, Inc., and all are individuals or trusts domiciled in Worcester County. The majority of the stock is held by individual stockholders who live in Uxbridge and are active full time in the management of the business. The President and Chairman of the Board is R. H. Bristol, a fourth generation direct descendant of the founder, R. B. Bristol. The First Vice President is the

*While this case was based on a true corporate situation, names, dates, places, and selected fact and figures have been changed in order to maintain anonymity of the firm actually involved. © Copyright 1974 Dennis Callaghan and Arthur Elkins.

sister of R. H., Mary Lou Bristol Adams. The Second Vice President is a cousin of R. H., Baker C. Bristol.

For many years, R. B. Bristol, Inc., has been a healthy company operating in the black as a national leader in its field. The firm has continually invested substantial amounts in the modernization and updating of plant and equipment in Uxbridge and Worcester. This had aided in keeping the company healthy, profitable, and competitive. In 1970 through 1972, the total expenditures averaged 1.8 times the company's net profit after taxes. The Company anticipated further major capital-expenditure projects in Uxbridge and Worcester which are expected to continue at least at the 1970–1972 levels for the foreseeable future. The expenditures will finance replacement, expansion, and modernization of the textile manufacturing equipment, and the company's share of the Town of Uxbridge's contribution to expansion of the local joint town sewage-treatment plant. Capital expenditures for plant, machinery, and equipment for the 10-year period ending December 31, 1972 totaled $14,500,000. Substantially all of this was for facilities directly related to production and manufacturing operations, for stream improvement, and for research and development facilities. (See Exhibit I for financial data.)

Since 1961 the firm has had a profit-sharing plan which distributes a percentage of net profit (before income taxes) to all employees relative to their individual base earnings. Distribution is made to a deferred fund or partly in cash, as elected by the employee. Further, since 1953, the firm has had a funded pension plan. Pension liability for all employees is now fully funded.

R. B. Bristol, Inc., for many years has been actively contributing to local charitable and community service organizations. (See Exhibit II for total annual expenditures which flow into the local community.) Most recently, the firm has contributed properties for use as recreational areas, including Granite Lake to the Town of Linwood, Bolton Lake to the Massachusetts Department of Natural Resources, and land in the Woodbury Park area of Uxbridge to the Town for playground purposes. In process now is a contribution of property to the Town of Uxbridge for sanitary landfill purposes. It is anticipated that company policy will include further contributions providing the firm is economically able to do so.

Owners and management of the firm encourage employees to actively participate in community affairs. Areas in which employees have served and are serving in responsible capacities are:

Uxbridge Town Government and School Committee
Uxbridge Community Chest
Worcester Medical Center
Central Massachusetts Health Planning Council
Uxbridge Community Recreation Association (YMCA)

EXHIBIT I

R. B. BRISTOL, INC.
CONSOLIDATED INCOME ACCOUNTS
Years Ended January 31,

	1972			1971	
Net Sales			$32,930,016		$27,407,093
Cost of sales		$24,409,104		$21,102,420	
Selling and other expense		3,264,640	27,673,744	2,475,729	24,078,149
Operating Profit			$5,256,272		$3,828,944
Interest expense		$ 474,729		$ 571,104	
Income taxes		2,401,054	2,875,783	1,693,365	2,264,469
Net Income			$2,380,489		$1,564,475
Previously retained earnings	$588,297			$402,214	
Less: Distribution	−72,000			−265,000	
Credit		−516,297	1,949,538	−137,214	901,360
Retained Earnings			$4,330,027		$2,465,835
Earnings per common share			$1.35		$0.98
Average number of common shares			1,762,151		1,600,000

EXHIBIT I (continued)

R. B. BRISTOL, INC.
CONSOLIDATED BALANCE SHEET
January 31, 1972

Assets

Cash	$ 837,803	
Receivables, net	3,650,680	
Inventories	5,227,930	
Prepayments	183,152	
Total Current Assets		$ 9,899,565
Property, etc., net	$6,283,798	
Other assets	517,577	6,801,375
Total Assets		$16,700,940
Net Current Assets		$ 4,631,310
Depreciation		3,397,432

Liabilities

Notes payable	$ 787,375	
Accounts, etc., payable	4,279,998	
Income taxes	200,882	
Total Current Liabilities		$ 5,268,255
Long-term debt	$2,483,115	
Common stock ($1)	1,840,000	
Capital surplus	2,779,543	
Retained earnings	4,330,027	11,432,685
		$16,700,940

EXHIBIT II

Total Annual Expenditures from R. B. Bristol, Inc., which flow into the local community:

Property taxes to Uxbridge (20% of total tax revenue comes from Bristol) and Worcester..	$ 393,000
Added payments to Uxbridge and Worcester for sewer and water services...	57,000
Payroll including profit-sharing distribution, and payments to pensioners..	8,454,000
Payments to local suppliers and contractors.........................	2,576,000
Charitable contributions, principally to local charitable and community service organizations..................................	63,000
Total to local community.....................................	*$11,543,000*
Income and machinery taxes to *Commonwealth of Massachusetts*	$ 264,000

Worcester County Natural Resources Council, Inc.
Association of Business and Commerce, South Central
Massachusetts
Salvation Army
Goodwill Industries
Worcester Boys' Club
Boy Scouts, Campfire, Girl Scouts
Uxbridge Rotary and Lions service clubs
Local churches

In addition to contributions of time, personnel, funds, and properties to the local community, Bristol management believes that it has consistently maintained a keen awareness of the general environment in which it operates. Among the areas in which Bristol owners and managers claim the firm has been far ahead of others in forecasting and meeting social demands are fair-labor practices, union recognition, equal employment opportunity, and, most recently, pollution control.

INVESTMENT IN POLLUTION CONTROL

The operations involved in textile manufacture were (and are) inherently "dirty." The first two stages of operation include fiber preparation, yarn spinning, and weaving, knitting, and/or braiding of yarns into gray or unfinished fabric. These processes result in a great deal of solid waste. The final stage of finishing the fabric requires bleaching, dyeing, printing, waterproofing, coating, and/or other treatments. In this stage the waste is primarily in liquid form, consisting of heavy concentrations of raw chemicals diluted in water or other liquid agents. Traditionally, Bristol, like other textile firms, dumped all of the liquid and a substantial portion of the solid waste into a nearby river. On occasion, Bristol would add additional bleaching agents to the waste emitted in order to remove the color from what often became unsightly slicks around the discharge port.

In 1958, Bristol undertook a voluntary program to substantially reduce the effluents emitted by its plants into the Blackstone River, along which the four Uxbridge plants are located. In years past, the firm had concentrated on minimizing solid discharges, but in 1958 it began to concentrate on liquid wastes. Adapting existing technology to its requirements, Bristol installed a $250,000 treatment plant which far surpassed the effectiveness (and cost) of any others employed by firms of comparable size in the textile industry. The equipment and treatment processes were far more sophisticated than would have been needed to meet the Federal Water Pollution Control Act of 1948, as amended in 1956, had Bristol been dumping *four times* its volume of effluent. (Bristol had been complying with Federal and State standards prior to installation of the treatment plant.) Since 1958, the firm has spent over $1,250,000, in combating the effluent problem (including funds spent at the Worcester plant). Continuing operation of the waste-treatment plant costs in excess of $120,000 per year. Its efforts have been recognized through awards presented by the Sierra Club (1969) and the Audubon Society (1970). The Blackstone River leaving the Bristol mill sites in Uxbridge far surpasses the standards established by the Massachusetts Department of Water Pollution Control. By 1971, fish had begun to return to the river, after an absence of over 100 years. The firm has, throughout recent years, kept well ahead of Federal and State regulations regarding water-pollution control.

Although Bristol's primary voluntary interest in pollution control centered on stream pollution, the firm has, in past years given some voluntary attention to air-pollution abatement. Owners and management have become actively concerned on those few occasions when area residents have complained of "heavy" concentrations of malodorous smoke in the air. Recognizing that on these occasions the wind was out of the north, the explanation normally given was that industrial emissions from Worcester were being blown southward over Uxbridge and that the Bristol plants on the north side of town were, if anything, adding just slightly to the problem. In any case, Bristol management was concerned and in 1968 offered to install pollution-abatement equipment at its main steam-boiler facility as soon as the "appropriate technology" was available. Since that time management has kept abreast of recent developments in air-pollution control equipment with the intention of installing such equipment when proven effective for the kind of abatement needed in their plants.

Bristol's main air polluter is its steam generating plant which is located centrally to the four mills in Uxbridge. Steam is an essential element for the company, being used in heating, drying operations and pressure-operated equipment. Additionally, Bristol uses excess steam for the generation of electricity in its steam turbines. The firm produces only a small portion of electricity in this manner, purchasing the bulk of its requirements from the Massachusetts Electric Company. On occasion, however, the firm has produced enough electricity so that it was able to sell back to the utility company a portion of its output.

In order to produce the necessary steam, Bristol uses fuel-oil fired boilers, a most efficient means of steam generation. With recent technological innovations and proper operating procedures, Bristol has managed to operate the plant at 80 percent efficiency which is about as good as possible. Excess heat and smoke is exhausted through two 110-foot stacks. The stack emission is nearly invisible except when the "tubes are blown" for about 1 ½ minutes per day. On a Bailey Meter Smoke Density Recorder installed by the firm, normal emissions are at a level below 1 on the Ringleman chart of 0 to 5, except when "blowing tubes." During these short periods a dense pitch-black smoke is emitted, which normally dissipates within minutes. On certain days, when a temperature inversion occurs, the blown smoke has lingered for hours. A few complaints have been registered by area residents during these periods, but mention of the influence of the weather has relieved the tensions. After two particularly bad days of smoke retention, the firm ran small commercial advertisements in the local newspaper explaining the temporary effect of the weather on dissipation and also mentioning that Bristol was not emitting any more smoke than usual.

BRISTOL'S AIR POLLUTION AND THE LAW

The Federal Clean Air Act of 1963 had little impact on the operators of the Bristol mills. Being limited to interstate air pollution, the law had little applicability to Bristol except when winds were out of the north creating the possibility that emissions could be blown seven miles south into Rhode Island. Although the possibility existed, the Act was never applied in legal suit or used as an order of compliance in any cases involving Uxbridge area firms.

The 1967 Air Quality Act (actually an amendment to the 1963 Act) had, and still is having an indirect effect on Bristol operations. This law set the ground rules for Federal-State standard-setting for air quality-control regions. A direct result of this law was the division of Massachusetts into eight air-pollution control districts. The Massachusetts regulations, administered by the Department of Public Health, established a number of limitations and requirements for each of the districts. Regulations were established for the Central Massachusetts Air Pollution Control District in 1970 and included the Uxbridge area in the jurisdiction.

The new State regulations of 1970 were drafted by the Division of Environmental Health of the Department of Public Health and were approved by the National Air Pollution Control Agency.* The rules and regulations for the Central Massachusetts District were such that many firms in the district would have to make significant adjustments in operations in order to comply with them. R. B. Bristol, Inc., was among those firms affected.

The most significant portions of the regulations included first, the establishment of an acceptable level of particulate emissions. For a fossil fuel plant the size of Bristol's, the limit was set at 0.12 pounds per million BTU output. Secondly, any facility burning residual fuel would be required to use fuel oil with a sulfur content of one percent or less by weight. Most plants, including Bristol's, had been burning 2.2 percent sulfur content fuel. These new regulations included a one-year "grace period" such that affected firms would be required to be in compliance by November 1971.

IMPACT OF THE REGULATIONS

By October, 1971, the Bristol steam generating plant was operating on one-percent sulfur content #6 fuel. The immediate impact of the use of one-percent fuel was an increase in cost of 2¢ per gallon. Also, the one-percent fuel was 2 percent less efficient than the 2.2-percent sulfur fuel used previously. The 2.2-percent oil gave an average of 110 pounds of steam per gallon, while the one-percent oil gave only 107 pounds of steam per gallon. This efficiency differential resulted in the use of approximately 300 gallons more per day at the preexisting annual usage of 5,800,000 gallons. This loss of efficiency plus the substantial difference in cost per gallon means an added cost to the company of $116,000 per year.

Fuel oil is the third largest cost item to Bristol. Raw materials are first, payroll second, fuel oil third, and electricity fourth. In this fourth largest cost item, electricity, Bristol also felt the effects of the pollution regulations. Massachusetts Electric Company was also within the governance of the regulations and it, too, found increased costs through losses in efficiency and higher costs per gallon when it had to switch to lower sulfur-content fuel. These costs were passed on, at least in part, through increasing electric power prices. Between 1969 and 1972, the power costs incurred by Bristol increased $120,000 per

---

*In July, 1976, shortly before the effective date of the State regulations, the Environmental Protection Agency was established according to reorganization plans initiated at the White House. Henceforth, the EPA would have jurisdiction over coordination, and approval of state-drafted regulations.

EXHIBIT III

Increases in Major Elements of Expense

	1969	1972	4-year percent increase
Freight	$248,542	$ 283,024	14%
Avg. straight-time hourly rate	2.60	3.50	35%
Fringe benefits	987,190	1,198,625	21%*
Electricity	462,761	582,333	26%
Fuel oil	312,199	625,586	100%
Local real estate taxes	224,342	348,693	55%

*A further increase in Blue Cross–Blue Shield is expected to substantially increase this figure for future periods.

year, at least a portion of which was a direct result of the State regulations. (Reference Exhibit III for Increases in Major Elements of Expense, 1969–1972.)

Technical problems were also incurred as a result of the use of the lower sulfur-content fuel. Bristol, like most other #6 fuel-oil users, had purchased relatively low-cost Arabian oil prior to the State Regulations. Arabian oil, a high sulfur-content, asphalt-based fuel, had presented few technical difficulties in transfer from storage tanks through a preheating injection system, into the burners of the steam generating system. In order to supply a low sulfur-content fuel, however, refiners and suppliers often distribute Venezuelan oil, which is a lower-viscosity, higher-pour oil and has a naturally lower sulfur content. The Venezuelan oil is paraffin-based; this results in the possibility of separation of the paraffin during preheating. If the paraffin were to separate, it could solidify and "gum up" the injectors, resulting in a shutdown of all operations for a lack of steam. In order to prepare for this possibility, Bristol contracted with Roger Dentley, Inc., a large reliable engineering firm, to study the problem. The engineers recommended changes to existing Bristol equipment in the amount of $48,570, not including engineering contingencies or the overhead and profit for the engineering firm. As of May, 1973, Bristol had not made the recommended changes, but it had not experienced any particular difficulties with the paraffin-based fuel.

Bristol continued the use of one-percent sulfur-content fuel until June, 1972. At that time, a temporary four-month variance went into effect, allowing all plants in the Central Massachusetts Pollution Control District to return to the use of 2.2-percent fuel. This decision had been made earlier in the year by the Division of Environmental Health upon the urging of many firms in the District. It was felt that the threat of sulfur-dioxide pollution would be reduced during the warmer months because of the likelihood of fewer severe temperature inversions and greater dissipation of all gaseous emissions. Nearly all firms in the District, including Bristol, returned to the use of 2.2-percent fuel oil. During the summer of 1972, the Massachusetts Department of Public Health conducted periodic tests for sulfur-dioxide concentrations in the district and found that all were below the Federal and State primary and secondary standards.

Aware of the impending lapse of the four-month variance, Bristol management and the firm's attorney prepared an application for a 1-year variance from the State regulations so that it could continue to burn the 2.2-percent fuel. Application for variance was the accepted procedure provided for in the regulations themselves. Associated with the request for variance was the requirement to submit formal written testimony on behalf of the firm. Bristol submitted its application on July 28, and presented its formal testimony at a scheduled public hearing before a Hearing Examination Board of the Department of Public Health on August 15, 1972.

THE HEARING AND TESTIMONY

The hearing was held in an open chamber room in the County Office Building in Worcester. In attendance were three Department of Public Health officers serving as the Examination Board, a number of Bristol management people including R. H. and Baker C. Bristol, Bristol's attorney, Weston Miles, a number of witnesses testifying in behalf of the firm, and two "regulars" at pollution-control hearings who attended in order to testify against award of the variance. There were no unattached spectators.

Weston Miles opened the testimony on behalf of R. B. Bristol, Inc. In his prepared presentation he emphasized the "unfavorable economic conditions" affecting the firm and the "relatively stagnant Uxbridge economy." He mentioned the recent erosion of Bristol's competitive advantage by disproportionate increases in taxes, wages, and benefits, raw materials costs, and particularly fuel costs, noting the 100-percent increase in the prior three years. He further mentioned Bristol's contributions to the local community and the possibility that future contributions may be affected by these increasing costs in manufacturing.

On the matter of proving economic hardship, which is normally a means by which a firm can earn a variance award, Miles said, "In our opinion it should not be just the marginal companies who are helped by variances. The healthy companies are the ones who provide steady jobs without layoffs, provide support to the communities, and are able to keep their pollution-control equipment operating effectively. They should be regarded as assets to the community and State with all reasonable cooperation given to them to keep them healthy."

The attorney continued the detailed testimony mentioning most of the facts favorable to the firm's position covered earlier in this case. He mentioned the Department of Health report indicating that the sulfur-dioxide concentrations in the County were well below the Federal and State primary and secondary standards during the past two months when 2.2-percent fuel was burned. He also related the technical problems and associated expenses involved in handling the 1-percent fuel.

At the conclusion of his first round of verbal testimony, the attorney turned the floor over to State Representative William Ryan. In a brief statement, the Representative emphasized the importance of Bristol to the economic life of Uxbridge, noting the value of Bristol's equipment, payroll, taxes, and contributions to community activities. He urged that the variance be granted since the one-percent sulfur-content fuel requirement did appear to be having an adverse financial effect on the firm's well-being.

The next witness was Mayor Daniel Lanham of Woonsocket, Rhode Island. Woonsocket is a city of 50,000 located seven miles downriver from Uxbridge. The Mayor, in a very brief statement, noted the company's well-recognized efforts in the area of water pollution. As on other occasions, the Mayor publicly praised the work of Bristol management in bringing the Blackstone, "one step closer to its natural state."

Following the Mayor was Lewis L. Robertson, Deputy Commissioner of the Department of Community Affairs. Mr. Robertson reiterated many of the arguments presented by Attorney Miles. In each of his references to the town in which the Bristol plants are located, however, he mentioned the Town of Oxford, a small town eight miles west of Uxbridge. His closing remarks included, "The community looks to Bristol for employment, tax payments, and civic leadership. To weaken this connection by reducing the competitive advantage of Bristol through a variance denial would inevitably harm the community of Oxford both economically and socially . . . For this reason, and because of the excellent ambient air quality existing in the southern portion of Worcester County, the Department of Community Affairs recommends favorable action on this request."

Alan C. Blake, Executive Director of the Worcester County Development Commission spoke next. He noted Bristol's increasing employment levels, which were particularly profound in light of a decline in the number of residents employed by textile manufacturers in the county from 3170 (1970) to 2828 (1972). He further pointed to the "economic as well as physical aspects of the 'quality of life' in Worcester County." Mr. Blake additionally stated that "economic hardship would see a multiplier effect on the town of Uxbridge." He closed with

"The Commission respectfully submits that the possible decrease in air pollution is not worth, at this time, the economic hardship and the serious consequences that may be presented by failure to grant the variance."

Next, John J. McKie, Chairman of the Uxbridge Board of Selectmen, spoke on behalf of the firm. He pointed to the philanthropy of the Bristol family, stating that the family, "has been in effect, one of the outstanding pillars of strength to the community for years long past." He further mentioned that Philip Bristol, former President of the firm, was for many years Chairman of the Southern Worcester County Stream Pollution Committee. "His efforts resulted in the construction of the Blackstone Interceptor Sewer in conjunction with local towns. This project was, in a sense, a pioneering effort in the field of pollution control."

Ralph L. Wilanski, Executive Director of the Central Massachusetts Natural Resources Council, Vice President of the Massachusetts Association of Conservation Commissions, and presently a member of the Governor's Committee on the Environment, served as the last witness for Bristol. "We are concerned that the overall State standards take into consideration regional differences and that we do not lose sight of the fact that the achievement of environmental quality is interdependent upon sustaining a healthy economic climate for Worcester County . . . Therefore, we respectfully request that the Public Health Council grant this variance with consideration for overall investment planning to achieve a better environment."

In closing the testimony on Bristol's behalf, Attorney Miles pointed to two alternatives to the use of one-percent fuel on a continuous basis. His first suggestion to the Hearing Board was the use of "fuel switching." "At Bristol we have the capability for immediate fuel switching. The engineer on duty has authority to carry out this procedure. We have one tank which could be filled with one-percent sulfur #6 oil for use during an air-pollution episode. Some minor piping installation will be necessary before this can be used, but if our variance is dependent upon having the ability to fuel-switch, we will set up the system in this manner. The tank capacity is 20,000 gallons, a one-day supply. We could easily switch over to the lower sulfur oil on five minutes' notice. Our fuel oil suppliers have assured us that they could keep this tank filled with one-percent sulfur oil, if necessary, for extended pollution episodes."

As a second alternative, Miles mentioned the future possibility of using "stack scrubbers," which would require a major investment on the part of the firm in order to adapt and improve existing technology to meet the needs of the textile industry. As a compromise, Miles indicated that Bristol would prefer to invest the differential fuel cost of

$116,000 per year in the research and development of such a system rather than "pouring funds into the use of one-percent sulfur-content fuel which has highly questionable results."

Miles formally closed the testimony on behalf of R. B. Bristol, Inc., with, "We respectfully, but urgently request that this petition of a variance to permit us to burn 2.2-percent sulfur oil be granted at the earliest possible moment, for one year from the date of allowance of this request."

Speaking against the request for variance were the two "regulars" of pollution-control hearings. The first was a representative of the Audubon Society and the second a representative of the Tuberculosis Association.* Both had attended many hearings on issues similar to Bristol's, delivering much the same testimony at each of them. Without referring to specific details surrounding the Bristol case, each delivered long and impressive presentations on the perils of air pollution in the Commonwealth. Citing specific cases of the results of uncontrolled air pollution, each speaker effectively portrayed the need for strongest application of pollution-control laws in the maintenance of public health. Both speakers mentioned the effectiveness of the enforcement of existing regulations in stabilizing the pollution levels in the State. Although appearing not to listen attentively, each member of the Board was well aware of the positions taken by the "regulars" in opposition to the variance request.

At the conclusion of testimony the Chairman of the Hearing Board, as per standard procedure, indicated that the proceedings of the hearing would be brought before the Board of the Department of Public Health at a future meeting. There a decision would be made as to disposition of the variance request. The Board meeting was to be public, but no preannounced date could be set for consideration of the case.

THE DECISION

Although no Bristol representative attended the Department of Public Health Board meeting, Bristol obtained word of the decision shortly after the February 22, 1973 meeting at which the case was considered. Late in March, 1973, the firm received the only official response to its application from the Department of Public Health. The entire text of the body of the letter follows:

The Department of Public Health, in response to your letter of July 28, 1972 for a variance in the application of Regulation 5.1.2. of the "Regulations for the Control of Air Pollution in the Central Massachusetts Air Pollution Control District" to permit the use of 2.2-

---

*In 1970 the wife of a financial officer at Bristol had been asked by the Tuberculosis Association to serve in the post of representative at air-pollution hearings. As a member of the Association, she considered, but declined the offer.

percent sulfur-content residual fuel oil at your plants in Uxbridge, Massachusetts, conducted a public hearing on August 15, 1972.

After review of the evidence, the Department, at its meeting of February 22, 1973, voted to deny the variance.

Signed,

The Commissioner of the
Department of Public Health

OTHER DEVELOPMENTS

During the months between the hearing and the decision, Bristol management had met with representatives of Smith Electric, a large manufacturing firm in Worcester, with the hope of developing an acceptable alternative to the use of one-percent sulfur fuel. Together the two firms hired Dr. James N. Voelexen, Associate Director of the Atmospheric Sciences Research Center in Boston. Dr. Voelexen outlined a plan which he stated would be the most sophisticated in the U.S. It involved the installation of sensors in the Worcester area and as far away as 30 miles, to measure pollution levels of both the background and stack plume. There would also be a meteorological tower in Worcester to collect local data on wind direction and velocity, temperature, etc., from ground level to 1000 feet above ground level. All of the information collected would be transmitted by telephone lines to a real-time computer in Worcester. The computer would continuously work with a model to predict the air-pollution levels 24 hours in advance. As soon as high levels were predicted, participating firms would be notified and would switch to low-sulfur oil.

On April 15, 1973, Smith Electric applied for variance, based on "economic hardship and public good," as did Bristol. In testimony Smith Electric outlined its fuel-switching proposal. In July, 1973, Smith received denial of its application.

In April 1973, Bristol was asked, "off the record," if it would install sulfur-dioxide monitoring devices at its own expense if it were allowed to return to 2.2-percent fuel for the coming summer months. If it would not agree, the State indicated that it was not likely that the EPA would approve the State's request for a temporary variance for the Central Massachusetts District for the June-through-September period. Also mentioned was the fact that only a few of the larger firms in different sections of the District had been asked to install such equipment, although all firms would reap the benefits. Bristol and four other firms in the District agreed; the temporary variance was granted.

In the summer of 1973, Bristol management learned that the (U.S.) Energy Policy Office had proposed a federal regulation which, if it became effective, might prohibit Bristol from burning low sulfur-content fuel for a period of 12 months from its effective date.* The proposed regulation was introduced in light of an expected heating-oil crisis in the winter of 1973–74. Although the regulation had not been acted upon by late August, Bristol's attorney had suggested that the firm alert their fuel suppliers to the need for high, rather than low, sulfur fuel for the winter. There was no assurance that the regulation would become effective in the near future.

---

*EPO REG 2 (Proposed) "Priorities for Use of Certain Low-Sulfur Petroleum Products," *Federal Register,* Vol. 38, No. 167, Wednesday, Aug. 29, 1973, Regulation pursuant to Section 203(a) of the *Economic Stabilization Act of 1970* as amended.

6. *Business and the Energy Issue*

Enough has been written about the energy crisis to fill volumes. Apart from Watergate and the Vietnam War, the energy crisis is the topic of the 1970's. While the most severe energy deprivations occurred after the Arab nations put a boycott into effect in October, 1973, the current energy problem involves much more basic political, environmental, economic and social factors.

ENERGY SUPPLY—A COMPLEX WEB

The basic problem with energy seems to be that energy provision and use is a complex web, in which shortages and blockages in one sector set off repercussions throughout the entire system. In the short run, at least, the supply is relatively finite, given the configurations of use and supply channels of distribution. And in the past few years, users have been pressing the ability of domestic sources to supply energy in the forms in which it is being used.

The breakdown in such a delicate chain can start quite simply. One example will serve to illustrate. In 1954, the Supreme Court, in a case involving the State of Wisconsin and the Phillips Petroleum Company, ordered the Federal Power Commission to regulate the prices of natural gas. When, in 1954, gas was plentiful and alternative sources of energy were cheap, the low price posed little problem. But by 1970, the price of natural gas, kept low through regulation, was less than one-third that of refined petroleum. As a result, utilities turned to gas to fuel generators for electric power because it was so cheap. But the low price also took the incentive out of exploration for new sources. The inevitable happened in 1971. Natural-gas deliveries were cut and utilities started converting to oil. Oil refineries were hard pressed to supply heating oil and therefore curtailed the refining of gasoline. And so the problem broadened. All of this happened before the Arab states even thought of embargoing oil shipments to the United States.

Compounding the energy crisis for the United States is the fact that most of the *readily available* oil sources are outside of the United States. Foreign sources of oil met about 26 percent of United States needs in 1973; roughly 42 percent of the need is now met by foreign sources. One estimate is that the United States would have an outflow of $30 billion in payments by 1985 at 1973 prices; with the increase in oil prices since that year, $70 to $90 billion in outflow might be a reasonable figure to expect.

Yet basic sources of energy within the United States seem to be plentiful. It has been estimated that the United States possesses, in known and proven reserves, a 65-year supply of oil, a 50-year supply of natural gas, a 300-year supply of coal, a 35-year supply of uranium, and a 35-year supply of recoverable shale oil. While these projections are, of course, calculated at present rates of consumption, they do not account for new resource discoveries or changes in technology (breeder reactors and nuclear fusion, coal gasification and liquefaction, geothermal, wind, and solar energy) or conservation measures that will reduce reliance on traditional fuels and methods.

But the problem persists, in the short run, of providing fuel and energy from existing sources and channels. Technology is a longer-run source of relief, since the capital equipment required to supply energy does not appear overnight. One estimate is that capital costs to supply additional energy and open up new sources will by 1985 total over $500 billion. Money is not the only problem, however; time is a factor as well. It takes several years to find and tap a new oil field and develop the systems to get the oil out to market. It takes over ten years to build a nuclear power plant.

THE GEOPOLITICS OF OIL

Oil still appears to be the kingpin in the energy crisis, and most analysts foresee oil remaining the primary fuel at least until the turn of the century. And any discussion of oil means bringing in the Organization of Petroleum Exporting Countries, commonly known as OPEC.

OPEC is, quite frankly, a cartel of oil-producing countries, chiefly Middle Eastern, African and Latin American. The cartel meets periodically to set prices on oil and allocate market shares. Members of the cartel range from the producer with the largest known reserves, Saudi Arabia, to smaller members such as Gabon; and obviously, the power of the larger members to influence the market has an effect on the behavior of the smaller members.

The key to a cartel staying in existence is its ability to keep all of its members satisfied with its operation, particularly those members who, if they cheat on the rest, will have an effect on the market. Thus, if one of the smaller members either exceeds the assigned quota or sells oil at a lower-than-posted price, there is not too much concern among the larger members. But if one of the *larger* members should buck the tide, then that would have a significant effect on the viability of the cartel. This power was demonstrated recently when Saudi Arabia did indeed block a large price increase in oil by simply refusing to go along. The result was a short-lived, two-tiered pricing system for oil, but that broke down very quickly as customers rushed to Saudi Arabia.

Most observers predicted the quick demise of OPEC, but others are surprised by the resiliency the organization has shown. Cracks have shown up in OPEC's armor, however. As the world demand for oil began to fall, due to the worldwide economic recession of 1974–76 (in part caused by the dramatic increases in the price of oil promulgated by OPEC), the revenues of the member nations began to fall. Just when many people in the Western world were fearing that the oil countries were going to invest their revenues and take over the industries of the West, some of the oil-producing countries started borrowing themselves. What had happened was that the revenues had fallen so much that the countries could not meet the payments for projects (including large orders of military hardware) that were committed for long ago.

Another way that OPEC would possibly dissolve is if alternative sources of energy are developed. To the extent that the Western world (including Japan) discovers new sources of oil or develops alternative energy sources, then the reliance on OPEC oil decreases and OPEC's dominance is diminished. Again, however, most observers do not see oil's predominant position being eroded in the near future.

STRATEGIES FOR INDUSTRIALIZED COUNTRIES

The industrialized countries, particularly the United States, seem to be engaging in two strategies to cope with the need to sustain the high volume of energy. In the short run, the aim is toward conservation, either voluntary or compulsory. In the longer run, reliance is on newer technology and alternative energy systems.

Short-run alternatives include the following:

1. Voluntary conservation
2. Taxation of energy
3. Taxation of energy-using systems
4. Rationing

Voluntary conservation efforts worked extremely well during the 1973 boycott crisis, but the effects were amazingly short-run in nature. Besides the fact that gasoline and other forms of energy are being shown to be quite price-inelastic, the public soon forgets that a crisis occurred and slackens off the voluntary conservation efforts.

Taxation of energy primarily means putting a stiff tax on gasoline and fuel for cars and trucks. Twenty-five percent of the energy consumed in this country goes into transportation, and of that over ninety-five percent is oil-based. If a tax is put on gasoline, the hope is that consumption will be sufficiently decreased and that a large portion of oil imports will be cut. Two problems immediately arise with the tax proposal. First, gasoline prices have nearly doubled since 1973 and the consumption of fuel has not decreased significantly. If gasoline is so price-inelastic, then the tax would have to be extremely high in order to induce people to cut consumption. Five to six cents a gallon may not do the job. Secondly, a gasoline tax would fall disproportionately upon the poor; the rich would not feel the extra tax burden as much as would the poor. This means that there would be clarion calls for exemptions and the intent of the tax would be diluted. Some have suggested that the poor be given an income-tax credit for their gasoline purchases, but since many pay no taxes anyway, that may have no mitigating effect on their plight. Many people who have considered the tax scheme reject the poverty problem as a consideration, and keep the focus on energy conservation.

Taxation of energy-using systems means primarily a tax on automobiles. There are two ways of doing this. First, a tax might be imposed on the automobile at the time of purchase, depending on the gasoline efficiency of the particular automobile. The advantage of this is that, if cars are price-sensitive, then buyers will forsake the gas guzzlers for the more economical, and hence less costly, cars. But a one-time tax has the effect of sunk costs; consumers have shown no reticence in buying the more expensive top-of-the-line cars now being offered by automobile companies. Once the tax is paid, there is no further incentive to induce the consumer to conserve. Another method might be to place a yearly excise tax on automobiles according to their gas-consumption ratings. That way, the consumer has a yearly added burden to pay and might react differently than he would with a one-shot payment. Of course, the question remains as to why automobiles must be singled out in the first place. Other energy uses may be as (or more) inefficient, but the tax ideas are usually confined to automobiles. The answer to that, of course, is that the automobile is the largest consumer of oil and the easiest to get at for a conversation program.

Rationing is the final type of short-run undertaking to conserve energy. Under a system devised during the Nixon Administration, each car or each licensed driver within a family was to be issued coupons entitling him/her to so many gallons of gasoline. Both the payment for the gasoline and the coupon were to be presented, in order for gasoline to be purchased. Unlike past rationing systems, the coupons under this new system could be bought and sold, so a secondary market is possible. Rationing distributes a commodity according to numbers (although the system in force during World War II did account for varying need by occupation); the system attempts to overcome the alleged deficiency in rationing by price or taxation increases—i.e., that the poor would be squeezed out of the market. On the other hand, rationing does away with the market system's chief strength—sending the most product to where it is most highly valued by the price system.

All of the short-run strategies are designed to coincide with longer-run strategies whose purpose is to lessen dependency both on fossil fuels and on foreign sources of fuel or energy. Thus, research into the more esoteric types of energy provision such as solar, wind, geothermal, shale, coal derivatives, and nuclear, where the lead time between laboratory experimentation and economically feasible energy systems is long, is undertaken while the short-run conservation efforts are going on simultaneously. Some of the problems, however, do not revolve about economic feasibility. Nuclear energy, as we pointed out earlier, is economically feasible and the technology is already available. But the political processes have expanded the number of agencies whose approval is necessary to site a nuclear plant; and court challenges by activist groups can multiply to hold up the process for ten to fifteen years. Similar conditions face the expansion of the reserves of other fossil fuels, such as coal, oil, and natural gas. These may be the most difficult of the obstacles to overcome and may constitute the heaviest challenge to long-run energy independence for the industrialized societies.

THE ENERGY CRISIS AND BUSINESS FIRMS

Basically, we can isolate three relationships of the energy crisis and business firms. First, some firms are in the energy-provision business. Their problem is essentially a production and marketing one; they must provide energy sources while at the same time dealing with the increasing constraints imposed by political and environmental-protection forces. Secondly, all firms are energy users to some extent, and face the problems of switching sources, converting to other fuels, or conserving energy. In the face of mounting costs across the board and environmental constraints, as well as competition in markets for their products, these firms face some difficult decision-making. Finally, many firms produce energy-consuming devices such as automobiles, air conditioners, toasters, and electric toothbrushes. These firms are under increasing pressure to build energy efficiency into their products.

THE ENERGY PROVISION PROCESS

The energy-provision process is a quite complicated chain of events and interrelationships. Even without political and governmental regulations or environmental constraints, the provision of energy is a complex, costly system. The figure below illustrates some of these interconnections in very simple form.

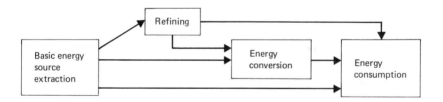

All energy starts as a basic material, such as coal, oil, uranium, gas, or solar light. About half (in present forms of use) is ready for immediate consumption—principally coal and gas. But other forms of basic energy—oil, uranium, increasingly large volumes of coal—require some refining before being usable. From basic extraction and refining, energy moves to consumption and to conversion—to electricity—which is also consumed. Great efficiency is lost in the conversion process as well as in the consumption process—about two-thirds in electricity generation and 30 percent in gas heating, for examples.

The various problems all along the chain are immense. Basic production is expensive, is subject to high risk of failure, and is often environmentally hazardous. Coal mines underground are often dangerous and dirty places to work, with miners subjected to various hazards including black lung disease. Strip mining, where large shovels take carloads of coal out of a surface cut, is more efficient than underground mining, but is environmentally destructive. Oil reserves are found increasingly offshore; aside from being expensive to tap and long-run propositions in terms of the exploration-to-production cycle, the chance of environmental damage to beaches and marine life is always present. Refineries take three to five years to construct, must operate near capacity to be efficient, and pose a variety of environmental hazards. Conversion units (power plants) are increasingly difficult to site. Nuclear plants are involved in the controversy over radiation leakage and safeguards against catastrophe; it takes as much as 10 to 15 years to plan a nuclear plant, get it approved, and build it. Both steam-generating and nuclear plants use large volumes of water, which, when returned to its source, often is warmed enough to cause thermal pollution. Coal, the most abundant energy source, is a prime polluter, and cleansing methods to eliminate stack gases are still not well developed. Finally, increased capital for utilities, coupled with the increasingly militant approaches of the state regulatory agencies, pose problems in building any generating capacity.

Between the links in the chain are pipelines, ships, and other methods of transportation. Pipelines can no longer be built routinely. Operation of the Alaskan pipeline from the North Slope, where reserves, at the 1972 consumption rate, were estimated to be capable of supplying 40 percent of total U.S. oil demand for 25 years, started in mid-1977, after being delayed several years in process because of its alleged potential for environment spoilage. Tankers of increasing size also pose increasing risks from ruptures and oil spills. Dangerous nuclear wastes must be transported and disposed of safely.

Energy provision has its competitive aspects, too. Gas and electricity fight fiercely for the home heating market, and both compete against oil. With increased technology in the coal industry, that energy source might return as a viable heating fuel. Nuclear plants compete with coal- and oil-fired power plants. While many of the major oil companies have vast coal reserves and are in the nuclear fuel business as well, the energy industry is still highly populated. *Business Week* aptly summed up the competition in a quote from Walter Meade, an energy economist at the University of California: "The energy business is like a big tent that covers everyone in the business. When they all step into that tent, I think they're going to kill each other."

BUSINESS AS ENERGY CONSUMER

Manufacturing consumes about 27.5 percent of the energy used in the United States and transportation another 25 percent. This consumption is exclusive of energy being used as feedstocks for manufacturing processes (in plastics, for example). Energy shortages, then, pose several hard decisions for fuel-consuming firms. First, regularly used fuels may no longer be in ready supply, nor may they still be the cheapest, so managers are faced with evaluating alternative fuels. Second, conservation and efficiency may be the order of the day. Certain inefficient uses of energy will be eliminated or changed simply because the increased price no longer keeps them tolerable. For example, office buildings might be redesigned, no longer being sealed compartments but structures using more of the natural heat and cooling. Freight could be shipped by rail instead of trucks. Manpower utilization may increase as capital-intensive processes are no longer competitive with labor-intensive ones. On the other hand, a continual rise in the minimum wage may militate against such a switch, as will sheer inertia on the part of the managers.

Although most observers, as we mentioned earlier, trace the energy crisis much farther back than 1973, it was the Arab oil embargo that brought the results of the crisis down to the level where it affected most individuals. That embargo probably caused more managers to change and adapt than any single event barring all-out world war. One survey found that managers raised prices, substituted raw materials, changed production processes or techniques, invested in energy-saving equipment, simplified product lines, rationed customers, and sometimes closed their facilities.

In many ways, the price system (or market) should spur conservation simply by raising prices; in other ways, regulation might be necessary. For example, using scrap in many industries consumes much less energy than processing newly mined ore. Yet recycling may not be undertaken despite the savings in fuel costs, particularly if the firms in the industry have sufficient market power to pass on increased costs to their customers. Some regulation may then be required to *force* recycling.

In any event, the era of inexpensive, abundant energy seems to be over, and energy is becoming a more important parameter in managerial decisions. It would seem, however, that, barring unforeseen complications or some nonefficacious government regulation, business persons and managers might be able to react chiefly to market forces in their decisions, although the decision-making will be increasingly difficult.

BUSINESS AS A PRODUCER OF ENERGY-CONSUMING DEVICES

Like business, the consumer is faced with some difficult energy-conservation choices. Gasoline prices have nearly doubled since 1973, and electric rates are up by more than one hundred percent in some parts of the country; as a result, many consumers are becoming extremely energy-conscious. This means that energy-consuming products will be increasingly examined for their energy-use efficiency, as well as for other attributes.

If business is not aware of energy inefficiency, the government may well be. Already legislation is on the books requiring certain gasoline mileage performance for automobiles by 1985. And air conditioners, housing (through the use of more and better insulation), washers, dryers, and a whole host of consumer products using electricity or other forms of energy can be made more efficient. For example, according to the Environmental Protection Agency, reducing the average car's weight from 3500 pounds to 2500 pounds would save an estimated 2.1 million barrels of crude oil a day, or one-seventh of the daily usage in the United States at 1970 rates. The process of "down sizing" is already taking place; General Motors started it in 1977, with Ford and Chrysler following in 1978. The

American public still has not lost its appetite for bigger cars, however. The year's best sellers in 1977 were the larger cars—those which had already been cut down in size as well as those which had not been.

Nevertheless, business should find whole new groups of energy-conscious customers to serve. Solar-heated houses are already being built, and it is quite possible that solar energy could find additional consumer uses. Some people have suggested windmill power and geothermal power, opening up whole hosts of exciting possibilities.

Thus energy producers, energy users, and producers of energy-using products all face challenges as a result of the energy crisis. Technology may provide many of the long-run solutions, but in the short run, at least, managers will face not only technical problems, but social, political, economic, and environmental ones as well.

THE READINGS

The first article is a compilation of data relative to energy supplies, uses, sources and costs. That data is followed by Chauncey Starr's article entitled "How Well Will We Meet Our Energy Needs in the Year 2000?" According to Starr, "The answer to this question will be determined largely by decisions made in three critical areas: goal targeting, resource management, and timing." He concludes, "Hopefully, today's energy supply problem will one day be as obsolete as the threatened food crisis of 1922. Something to bear in mind, though, is that the food crisis was resolved in large part by foresight, technological drive, and a national recognition of the need to act. Everyone understood the need for food. But how many now understand the need for energy?"

Much has been written on the need for alternative energy sources as the industrialized societies face the longer-run problems of energy supply. Philip W. Quigg, in our last selection, examines the possibilities of alternative sources, along with their prospects and environmental impacts.

The Scorecard on Energy

The debate over President Carter's program to conserve the dwindling supply of easily extracted energy is likely to rage in Congress and elsewhere for months to come. As it does, here is a ready guide to who has the energy, who uses it and what the prospects are for alternative sources.

THE APPETITES GET BIGGER

In 1974, the world used 212.6 quadrillion British Thermal Units—or quads—of energy. By 1985, that demand is expected to grow by 58% to 334.8 quads. For comparison, a gallon of gasoline produces 125,000 BTU's.

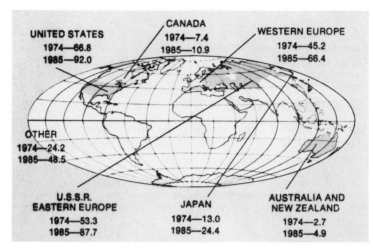

THERE IS PLENTY OF ENERGY, BUT . . .

The world has more than 20,000 quads of proven reserves, enough to last about 100 years at the 1974 consumption rate, but only sixty years at the rate projected for 1985 (distribution of reserves by %).

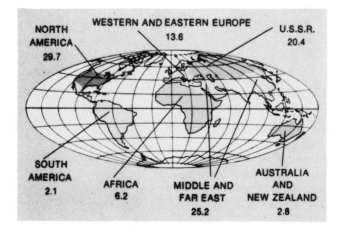

THE 'GAS GUZZLING' WEST

With energy-eating industries, such as Luxembourg's huge steel mills, the Western nations use up to 500 times as much fuel per person as do some of the less developed nations.

Per capita energy use in millions of Btu's

Luxembourg	542.8	Soviet Union	146.2
United States	319.0	France	120.6
Canada	272.7	Japan	109.4
Belgium	186.4	Switzerland	100.4
Sweden	161.2	Italy	89.6
West Germany	158.3	India	5.6
East Germany	155.5	Ethiopia	.9
United Kingdom	151.8		

WHERE THE POWER IS

With its huge coal supplies, North America has more proven recoverable reserves of energy — even excluding oil shale and tar sands, in which the continent is rich — than the Middle and Far East combined.

Distribution of reserves by %

	Coal 14,458 Quads	Crude Oil 3,741 Quads	Natural Gas 1,832 Quads	Uranium 781 Quads
Africa	2.5	14.0	11.0	25.3
Middle and Far East	18.0	58.9	23.6	0.4
Western and Eastern Europe	17.8	1.5	8.4	5.9
U.S.S.R.	23.0	8.9	31.6	
North America	35.2	8.0	20.7	54.2
South America	0.3	8.4	3.3	1.5
Australia/ New Zealand	3.2	0.3	1.4	12.7

The U.S.

The biggest consumer of energy by far, the U.S. burns the equivalent of 35 million barrels of oil a day, about 30% of total world use. In the past, oil and natural gas were so cheap there was little incentive to develop America's huge coal reserves or to make machinery more efficient.

CARTER'S PROPOSED DIET

The President says that even with his plan, energy consumption will grow 25% by 1985; but without it, by 30%.

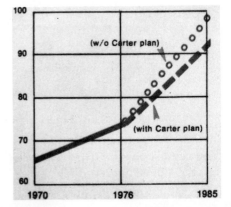

(w/o Carter plan)

(with Carter plan)

AN EVER-INCREASING DEPENDENCE ON IMPORTED OIL

Before the Arab embargo, the U.S. imported 26% of its oil. The figure is now 42% and is headed towards 51% by 1985. President Carter would like to lower imports to 38%.

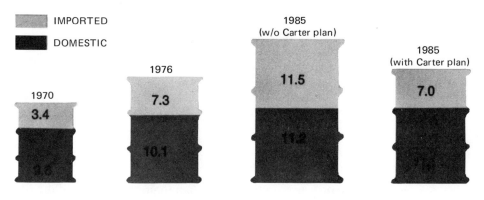

HOW AMERICA USES ITS FUEL

Each year, the U.S. consumes an amount of oil equal to 20% of its proven reserves and an amount of natural gas equal to 9% of its known supply. But uranium and coal resources are barely used.

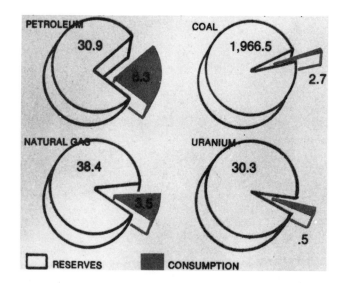

SECTOR BY SECTOR, IT ADDS UP TO A VAST WASTELAND

Historically, fuel has been so cheap in the U.S. that there has been little incentive to develop energy-efficient machinery or construct well-insulated buildings. Almost two-thirds of the fuel consumed does no work.

RESIDENTIAL	4.4	1.8	TOTAL CONSUMPTION	
COMMERCIAL	2.5	1.2	WASTE	
INDUSTRIAL	8.7		4.3	
AUTOMOBILES	4.8		4.2	
OTHER TRANSPORTATION	4.5		4.0	
UTILITIES	10.0		6.8	

GETTING MORE TO THE GALLON

Today's new cars go farther on a gallon of gas than their counterparts did a decade ago. By 1985 the average car produced by each manufacturer must be able to get 27.5 miles to the gallon.

Miles per gallon figures for 1977 models

	Best Mileage	Poorest Mileage	Average Mileage
General Motors	Chevette 36 mpg.	Cadillac 14 mpg.	18.4 mpg.
Ford	Bobcat/Pinto 30 mpg.	Ford/Mercury 13 mpg.	17.1 mpg.
Chrysler	Dodge Colt 35 mpg.	Dodge Royal Monaco/ Plymouth Gran Fury 11 mpg.	16.6 mpg.
American Motors	Gremlin 25 mpg.	Matador 14 mpg.	19.2 mpg.

The Economics

As energy prices have soared, the impact has been staggering; surpluses pile up in OPEC while other nations struggle to adjust to higher costs. President Carter's proposed cure could add substantially to energy inflation.

MIDDLE EAST BUILDUP

With soaring oil prices, the rush of dollars to OPEC swelled to a flood, subsiding somewhat as the recession reduced energy demands, and as OPEC nations have invested their huge earnings in Western technology.

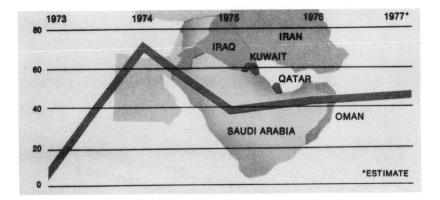

STILL A CHEAPER RIDE . . .

In the U.S., where the federal tax is only 4 cents a gallon and local taxes an average of 8 cents, the goverment's share of what consumers pay at the pump is relatively small.

. . . BUT THE COST COULD RISE RAPIDLY

If the federal tax is raised 5 cents a year — as the Carter plan allows — and OPEC prices continue to rise, gasoline prices at the pump could double by 1985.

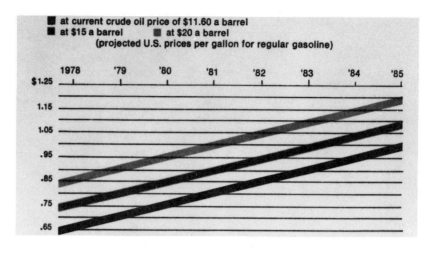

■ at current crude oil price of $11.60 a barrel
■ at $15 a barrel   ■ at $20 a barrel
(projected U.S. prices per gallon for regular gasoline)

A BIGGER BITE

In 1972, the cost of energy was only 3.6% of GNP in the U.S. By 1976, it was 8%.

A BETTER BUY

Fuel oil is expensive, yielding only 26% as much energy per dollar as coal. On average in the U.S., a consumer can buy for $100 . . .

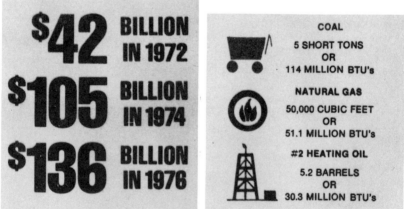

$42 BILLION IN 1972

$105 BILLION IN 1974

$136 BILLION IN 1976

COAL
5 SHORT TONS
OR
114 MILLION BTU's

NATURAL GAS
50,000 CUBIC FEET
OR
51.1 MILLION BTU's

#2 HEATING OIL
5.2 BARRELS
OR
30.3 MILLION BTU's

SOURCES: UNITED STATES ENERGY DATA: Federal Energy Administration; Department of the Interior; Environmental Protection Agency; Brookhaven National Laboratory. WORLD ENERGY DATA: World Energy Conference, "Survey of Energy Resources"; The Organisation for Economic Co-operation and Development; Department of the Interior. ECONOMIC DATA: Department of the Treasury; Federal Energy Administration; National Coal Association; American Gas Association.

How Well Will We Meet Our Energy Needs in Year 2000?

Over half a century ago prominent food and agricultural authorities sounded an alarm because food production was when falling behind population growth, and predicted inevitable shortages unless certain trends were reversed. In this article, an acknowledged expert in energy matters sounds a similar warning about the possibility of serious energy shortages in the future and urges timely — but considered — action for their avoidance. In addition, various options available to American society in growth rates in energy consumption are described and their implications evaluated.

Chauncey Starr

The 1920's witnessed a crash program of agricultural expansion, aided by new technology on farms and in factories, that multiplied food production and averted what had been thought to be a threatening crisis. So successful was the effort that the U.S. came to export food to much of the rest of the world, in addition to feeding its own 215 million people. The parallel is encouraging, but the question remains: Will the U.S. be similarly successful in mustering resources to feed the nation's large and growing needs for energy? The answer to this question will be determined largely by decisions made in three critical areas: goal targeting, resource management, and timing.

What follows is an attempt to outline some alternative approaches and to suggest a mixture most likely to yield success.

FIXING THE TARGET

How much energy will we need in the year 2000? Two indicators give us a good idea: our anticipated standard of living and the size of our future labor force.

Historically, energy consumption and prosperity rise and fall together. A strong appetite for energy marks those periods when employment is healthy and the economy is growing. Energy consumption falls with waning employment and a sagging national economy.

The gross national product, because it measures the vast array of goods and services that are turned out by the U.S. economy in any given year, mirrors living standards. The links that exist between energy, employment, and GNP provide a method for predicting future energy needs. If we know roughly the number of people working at some future date and the quantity of goods and services they need to produce, we can make a reasonable estimate of the energy supplies required to support production.

Reprinted from the September 23, 1976, issue of *Public Utilities Fortnightly*.

Fixing an energy target by this method inevitably touches on certain issues of broad economic and social policy. Most conspicuous is the growth issue. Are we ready to settle back and accept a no-growth economy, or do we want to push for the steadily increasing levels of goods and services that will be necessary to lift millions of Americans to a standard of living many consider minimally desirable? A no-growth economy—with a drastic change in mass social aspirations—should not be allowed to occur as an unconscious and unintended byproduct of energy shortages.

This targeting analysis focuses on two possibilities: no growth and the alternative of continuing growth at an appropriate rate.

QUANTIFYING PROSPERITY

The historical growth rate of the U.S. economy over the period 1955–75 averaged 3.5 per cent per year in constant dollars. Accompanying this expansion was a swelling work force. The Bureau of Labor Statistics predicts a civilian work force of 113 million by the year 2000, up from about 85 million today. Almost all this labor force is born by now, so future birthrates can have very little effect on its size. Based on experience, how much energy will it take to support the output of a work force this size?

The answer—taking into account potential changes in energy availability, technology, environmental costs, *and conservation*—comes to about 150 quads (1 quad = 1 quadrillion Btu), with an uncertainty of ± 10 per cent. Historical growth would project 170 quads, conservation might save about 20 per cent, and environmental costs may add about 10 per cent—leading to probable 150 quads. (Figure 1, opposite) This figure, which is twice our present national energy consumption, is the estimated amount of energy we will need in the year 2000 if the economy continues to grow as it has and many think it must for the benefit of all segments of our population.

NO GROWTH?

A no-growth situation would freeze the ratio of employment to energy use at its present level; that is, keep fixed the energy consumed per employed worker and fix the mix of industrial, commercial, domestic, recreational, and other energy-related activities. Freezing this employment-energy ratio would be tantamount to maintaining all major social and economic patterns, only replicating this mix in the future to accommodate an increased labor force.

What this no-growth option would really mean becomes clearer if we compare the nation's actual experience in the year 1970 with what 1970 would have been like had our technology and economic productivity been frozen shortly after World War II—say, in 1948.

The no-growth scenario would replicate the 1948 economy in an expanded form for a population that had grown from 147 to 205 million. In this hypothetical situation, the social structure and economic mix for 1970 would have been the same as those that existed in 1948. These have been described in the U.S. Department of Commerce's monumental study, "Social Indicators 1973." Thus, the

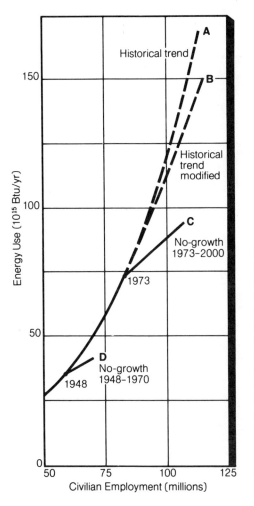

Fig. 1 Growth in energy use. Continuing the nation's historical growth trend will require far more energy than the no-growth option, which would freeze socioeconomic progress at roughly current levels (represented here by 1973 data). **A** pinpoints an energy demand of 170 quads for the year 2000, based on historical growth. **B** indicates a downward modification to allow for conservation savings of 20% and environmental costs of 10%. **C**, falling well below **A** and **B**, shows what the projected level of energy demand would be in the year 2000 if the no-growth option is chosen. **D** indicates what the no-growth option would have resulted in had it been followed from 1948 until 1970.

actual changes that did occur between 1948 and 1970 can be considered a measure of the effect of increased productivity per worker, associated with increased energy input into the economy. (It is important to recognize that increased productivity per worker is the result of technological development of energy-converting machinery that can produce more goods and services, so that increased productivity generally brings with it increased energy need per unit of output.)

Actual energy use in 1970 totaled 68 quads, compared with what might have been a 1970 level of only 41 quads under such no-growth conditions; that is, the 1970 work force could have been supported with an energy input 60 per cent as large as was actually used if the nation had been willing to live in 1970 as it did in 1948. What, then, did the nation get in return for this actual 1.66 multiplication of energy consumption per employed worker between 1948 and 1970?

A glance at Figure 2 shows that the consumer's paycheck actually bought much more in 1970 than it did in 1948, reflecting a substantial rise in the U.S. stan-

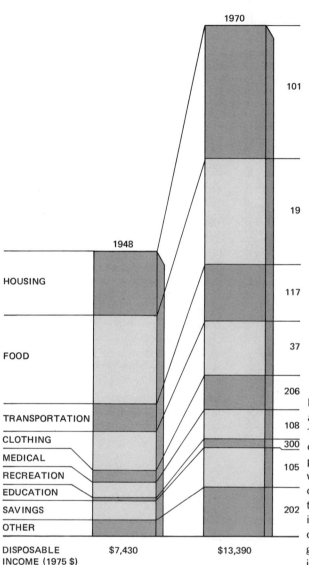

% INCREASE

Fig. 2 Family income, 1948 and 1970. Between 1948 and 1970, disposable family income nearly doubled in real purchasing power. Consumers were able to buy more—especially in areas such as recreation and education—and still increase their savings. Americans thus enjoyed substantial growth in economic well-being during this period.

dard of living. A 66 per cent increase in energy consumption per employed worker supported a 90 per cent increase in real family income. The percentage of personal income required to furnish necessities such as food and clothing declined, whereas purchases in discretionary areas such as medical care, education, and recreation increased substantially. The rise in mean family income moved a fifth of the population out of the poverty bracket to a level above the threshold of acceptable nutrition and housing.

These economic changes triggered a profound social impact as well. One example was the massive entry of women into the work force. This entry was no doubt hastened by new labor-saving devices for the home and the increased use of office and factory machinery that could be operated by brains rather than brawn. Had the percentage of women in the work force been frozen at the 1948 level (28 per cent, compared to the 1970 actual of 38 per cent), 7.8 million fewer women would have held paying jobs in 1970.

The year 1970, then, would have looked quite different had we opted for a no-growth economy in 1948. But does the same logic apply to a growth versus no-growth decision in 1976? What about the contention that today, in contrast to 1948, we have all the labor savers we can possibly use?

Granted that most of us are capable of brushing our teeth, opening a can of soup, or carving a turkey without the aid of energy-consuming devices; it is quite another matter to reject historical and more substantial benefits of increased use of capital- and energy-intensive machine production per U.S. worker: more employment, less poverty, better health, more education, better housing, and more recreation. These benefits are by no means trivial, and an aware public is not likely to accept less if it does not have to—especially while the lowest income fifth of our population remains below the acceptable level of housing, nutrition, and personal welfare.

For the foreseeable future, then, it is likely that we will keep shooting for the historical increase in national prosperity, with an energy target in the year 2000 that is large enough to accommodate this goal. Any smaller target would necessarily place stunting restraints on our options for social progress.

SWITCHING FUELS

The second major area of choice in fixing our energy capabilities for the year 2000 involves management of fuel resources. How can we reduce our dependence on foreign oil? Should a greater percentage of our national resources be converted to electricity? What are the best choices for fuel conservation? Can new power sources help? All these questions will have a bearing on our ability to meet our energy needs by the century's end.

To see what a staggering increase the target figure represents, consider the nation's level of energy consumption in 1973. Total fuel consumption in that year was 75 quads, just about half of what will be required in the year 2000. Of those 75 quads, there were 35 quads of oil, 23 quads of natural gas, 13 quads of coal, three quads equivalent of hydro, and one quad equivalent of nuclear. The picture, then, in 1973—and one that still applies today—is of an economy heavily dependent on oil and gxs to meet its fuel needs.

This picture is destined to change. Availability and cost problems with foreign oil and gas dictate that the increase in energy consumption be fueled by other sources. Alternatively, our national vulnerability to foreign intervention in U.S. policies will increase if we become more dependent on foreign oil. The most feasible indigenous alternatives for such large-scale increase over the next quarter century are coal and uranium, both of which are available domestically.

Even if oil and gas supplies can be maintained at present levels (at best a gamble) and hydro also increased slightly, coal and nuclear capabilities must grow from a combined total of 14 quads to 85 quads by the year 2000. This represents an increase of about six times today's level for this pair.

The focus on coal and uranium as our major fuels has definite consequences for the form in which most energy will be delivered. Specifically, the increased use of coal and uranium points to increased electrification.

Electric power plants will be the only substantial means for converting coal into usable energy by the year 2000. The manufacture of synthetic oil and gas from coal, potentially a very important development, will not yet have had the opportunity to make a sizable commercial impact. Even if such conversion processes become commercial in the 1980's, they can meet only a small fraction of national needs by the year 2000 because of construction lead time. And nuclear energy from uranium can be utilized only when converted to electricity.

In 1973, the fraction of the nation's primary energy that was converted to electricity was 26.4 per cent. For some time that fraction had been growing steadily. During the years 1950–70, the electric fraction of primary energy use grew at a compound annual rate of 2.63 per cent. Extended to the year 2000, this rate of fractional increase yields a primary fuel fraction of 53 per cent. This means, if present trends continue, by the century's end about 53 per cent of all our primary energy resources will be converted to the form of electricity.

Many uncertainties affect this figure. It would be best for planning purposes to sketch a range of possible outcomes — say 10 per cent, give or take, in either direction. Figure 3 shows how the resultant alternatives (a range of 43 per cent to 63 per cent) would impact the various energy-using sectors of the national economy.

The first alternative (43 per cent electrification) assumes only modest growth in the electricity-using fraction: Space heating, water heating, and cooking would still be handled mostly by oil and natural gas, but an increasing array of labor-saving devices and appliances for the home would run on electricity. More urban mass transit systems would switch to electricity, but the use of electric cars in the year 2000 would still be quite limited. The second alternative — and the one most likely to occur — assumes greater technological change and consequent increases in the use of electricity. The third alternative assumes an accelerated conversion to electricity stimulated by severe shortages of oil and gas.

THE EFFICIENCY PUSH

The campaign to slash the nation's future energy consumption hinges on two strategies: decreasing use and increasing efficiency. Reducing end-use activities is basically a social option, implying a change in life-styles. Getting more end use out of available energy resources is a technical challenge, focused on ways energy might be better harnessed and stored to perform various tasks, such as driving machinery, generating heat, or providing light. The emphasis here will be on technical improvements as a means of yielding energy savings without sacrificing our end-use options. The goal is doing better — not doing without.

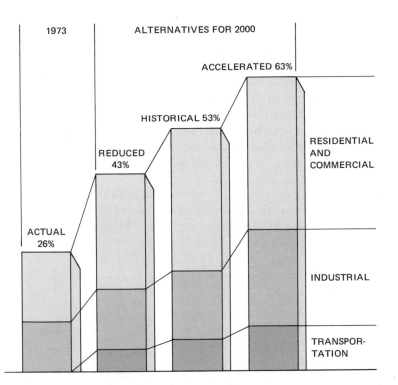

Fig. 3 Electric energy use. The industrial sector is the nation's main consumer of energy, followed closely by the residential and commercial sectors. Residences and commercial enterprises, however, are the main users of that percentage of total energy delivered in the form of electricity. Shown here are the percentage of total energy used by the electric fraction and three alternatives for the growth of that fraction.

The potential savings of both electric and nonelectric energy stemming from conservation efforts range from none to 40 per cent. As most conservation requires a capital investment in more efficient equipment, the extreme technical limits are unlikely to be achieved. The middle value (20 per cent) is thus more reasonable as a planning target. These estimates reflect the result of actions that can be taken now; e.g., better insulation of residences, installation of already developed energy-saving devices over the next five to ten years, and introduction of foreseeable new technology over the next twenty-five years.

The gradual savings accumulated in this manner should add up to an impressive 20 per cent or so by the year 2000. Actual savings will more likely occur sooner in the electric than in the nonelectric sector, despite the greater potential in the latter, because the technology of conservation is more easily applied to electric uses and because the conservation effort can be centralized in the technical aspects of large power systems and in the manufacturer's design of mass-produced equipment. In contrast, the insulation of homes, for example, involves many individual decisions.

SOLAR AND GEOTHERMAL

New energy sources that could conceivably help out by the year 2000 are but two: solar and geothermal. Except for dry steam geothermal (a very scarce resource), these are not yet at the stage commercially that would permit a meaningful estimate of their growth.

Solar's main contribution during the next quarter century will be in heating new homes and commercial buildings. Solar energy converted to electricity is not likely to be available at all on a commercial scale during this period. And the availability of geothermal electricity is a gamble because of engineering and hydrothermal resource issues.

Probable sources of electricity for the year 2000 are shown in Figure 4 (below). Included are the fairly optimistic estimates of solar and geothermal contributions projected by ERDA. Even with these hopeful estimates, coal and nuclear power must still provide about 80 per cent of the electricity generated. No foreseeable technology can substantially alter this outlook.

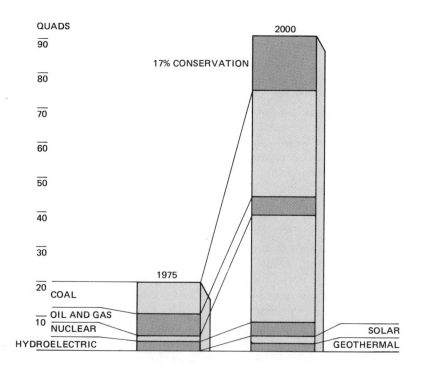

Fig. 4   Electricity output by fuel source. The swing to electricity between now and the year 2000 will result in a requirement for 90 quads of electric output if historical usage patterns hold. But 15 quads of that total can be eliminated by using the electricity more efficiently. That saving amounts to three-fourths of the electricity consumed in the U.S. in 1975. Still, a vastly expanded coal and nuclear power capacity will need to be in place to meet the almost quadrupled electricity requirement that will remain.

ENVIRONMENTAL COSTS

Protecting or improving the environment while meeting energy needs will generally mean additional energy costs. We must expect to pay such costs, and our estimates of future resource needs should take them into account.

Consider, for example, the decrease in conversion efficiency of conventional power stations caused by the switch from water-cooled to air-cooled condensers (a measure designed to reduce ecological effects on water resources). Owing to the higher temperature of the steam cycle condenser with air cooling, fuel consumption rises about 6 per cent to 10 per cent for fossil fuel-fired plants and 7 per cent to 13 per cent for nuclear plants. In addition, because the air-cooled system costs more to begin with, there is a 10 per cent to 15 per cent increase in capital investment per unit output.

More familiar is the case of car antipollution devices, which, as most motorists now know, can ruin even the most diligent efforts to save on gasoline mileage. Or again, placing electricity distribution apparatus underground can save the landscape, but it increases capital and material costs substantially. Conservation by increased efficiency may more than compensate for the costs of meeting environmental objectives, but the net savings may be only half what could be achieved by conservation alone.

NET CAPABILITY

Taking the fuel resource picture as a whole, then, it seems that the best avenues toward ensuring our national future supply are increased electrification and increased conservation through greater efficiency. Figure 5 (page 260) shows how these factors translate into a range of targets for future electricity production.

Each estimate of electricity demand, based on the total projected energy need for the year 2000, is a function of two factors: the fraction of total energy that is likely to be supplied in the form of electricity and the amount of energy saved through conservation efforts. Without conservation, total national need by the year 2000 is 170 quads. If 53 per cent of this energy is converted to electricity, 9,000 billion kilowatt-hours would be the result. If we assume 53 per cent and reasonable success in conservation—the combination of circumstances most likely to occur—then the target figure becomes roughly 7,500 billion kilowatt-hours for the year 2000, about 3.8 times present electricity production.

If a reasonable level of conservation is applied to all energy use, and environmental costs are added, we would expect a total energy consumption target of 150 quads. This is consistent with our electricity production target of 7,500 billion kilowatt-hours.

ACTING NOW

Timing is the third critical area of decision making that affects future energy supply.

Very long lead times are required to bring about a change in the national energy mix. Historically, it has taken from thirty to fifty years for new processes to make a substantial impact on energy supplies. As we have seen, it is already

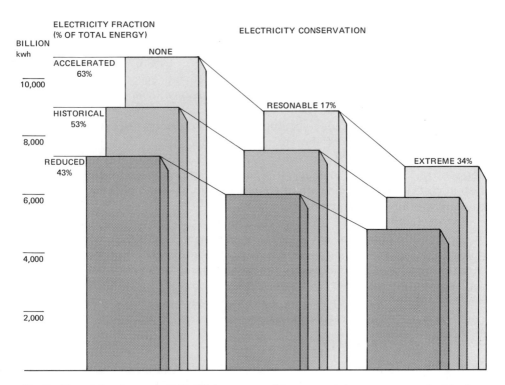

Fig. 5 Electricity demand, 2000. With a reasonable conservation program and with electricity supplying 53% of our total energy requirements, the U.S. will need nearly 7,500 billion kilowatt-hours for the year 2000 in order to sustain national growth at historical levels. If conservation efforts fail, the target will have to be adjusted upward to a figure closer to 10,000 billion kilowatt-hours.

too late for new power sources, such as solar and geothermal, to make more than very small and scattered inroads before the century's end.

Because electricity is the one energy source that is commercially viable today and is likely to have the fuel necessary for rapid growth over the next twenty-five years, electricity is the logical choice for action. Massive expansion of electric power capabilities cannot wait if the industry is to be responsible for providing at least 7,500 billion kilowatt-hours of usable energy by the year 2000. And this is only a minimum target. If conservation efforts fall short, we will need even more.

But what about overexpansion? How can we know that all this added capacity will really be needed? Perhaps relations with the oil-producing nations will change for the better. Perhaps unforeseen events will fatten our oil reserves. Perhaps vast new deposits of oil will be discovered. None of these possibilities alters the need to act now. Considering the time it takes to get new electric generating facilities on line, there will be plenty of opportunity to change course should the circumstances warrant.

The alternative to immediate action is to delay and risk energy starvation. If we expand too quickly today, we can slow down tomorrow. But if we delay now, we will have no recourse.

CAN WE MEET THE TEST?

Clearly, maintaining the level of economic growth that Americans have come to regard as natural will be no easy task over the next quarter century. Feeding the machinery of progress will require a steady diet of energy.

It is clear, too, that our fuel sources will have to change in order to meet that need. The prudent choice is to rely on native coal and uranium for conversion to electricity. Accompanying this fuel switch and the resultant growth of the electric fraction will be a vigorous campaign to boost efficiency in energy use. Such conservation technology is as important as supply technology.

Meeting a target of 7,500 billion kilowatt-hours in 2000 will require almost four times our present electricity supply, at a growth rate of about 5.7 per cent per year. And this target assumes reasonable conservation measures. If such measures fail, then we will need, as Figure 5 shows, a supply more in the neighborhood of 9,000 to 10,000 billion kilowatt-hours.

Hopefully, today's energy supply problem will one day be as obsolete as the threatened food crisis of 1922. Something to bear in mind, though, is that the food crisis was resolved in large part by foresight, technological drive, and a national recognition of the need to act. Everyone understood the need for food. But how many now understand the need for energy?

Alternative Energy Sources

Philip W. Quigg

The vast verbiage devoted to the energy crisis has dwelt largely on its immediate impact and on measures to cope with it. Less attention has been given to alternative sources of energy, because they cannot help us in our present predicament. Nor, in fact, can coal, oil, and gas in the very short term, for it will be some time before substantially larger quantities of those traditional fuels can be produced. The easy assumption that an abrupt switch to coal would save the situation has now been seen as an illusion; the coal industry can hardly meet its present commitments.

Nevertheless, it is indisputable that coal will recapture its former importance; no other source can make a major contribution to the energy supply over

Reprinted by permission from World Environment Newsletter (February 9 and 23, 1974), appearing as a regular feature in *Saturday Review/World.* © Philip W. Quigg.

the next two decades. Coal now provides only 17.2 percent of U.S. energy—considerably less than that of Europe, substantially more than that of Japan. The environmental consequences of increased reliance on coal will be profound, even if ways of purifying it are perfected.

The ready availability of coal in the United States must not be allowed to delay the search for alternative sources that are less detrimental to the environment. It is significant that Japan, which has no oil and limited coal, is planning to spend a far higher proportion of its GNP on research and development of non-fossil fuels than is the United State or Europe.

In examining the following analysis of so-called esoteric energy sources, one is struck by how long they have been around. Some, like coal gasification, geothermal, wind, and tides, have been in use for decades or centuries, while the theoretical potential of others has been known for at least a generation. With the sudden doubling and tripling in the costs of energy, every one of them appears to be economically competitive, if the technology can be developed or perfected.

For twenty-five years, cheap fuel and the promise of limitless nuclear energy have deterred any concentrated research into alternatives to oil and gas or the more efficient use of coal. In retrospect, our lack of foresight seems astounding. Yet more remarkable is the fact that even now in the United States, research into solar and geothermal energy, not to mention more remote technologies, is not being adequately funded. Of the projected $11 billion that the administration proposes to spend over the next five years on energy research and development, 96 percent is to be devoted to nuclear power (more than half) and fossil fuels, plus conservation. Even the $11 billion total is less than "the minimum viable effort" recommended by expert panels appointed by the administration.

The paucity of fundamental research and, even more, of pilot projects to test the feasibility of alternative energy sources enhances the difficulty of forecasting when and to what extent "new" sources will become significant. Billions of dollars have been spent so that we may learn how difficult it is to produce nuclear energy by means that are clean and safe. Having hardly begun to examine other alternatives to fossil fuels, we cannot know what technological pitfalls lie ahead.

But much more is involved than discovering new technologies. Most close observers of the energy problem agree with Chauncey Starr, who wears many energy hats, that "the most pressing energy need is for a coherent and long-range program to plan and manage our national and international energy systems. It takes ten to twenty years for a significant alteration in the trends of these huge systems. Waiting until the situation becomes intolerable must now be recognized as intentionally planned neglect—a societal irresponsibility difficult to condone."

Although there is enormous variation among estimates of how much energy may be derived from non-fossil fuels by the end of the century, a measure of consensus prevails on the following points: (1) none will be a significant factor for at least a decade, and (2) even by the end of the century, no new source of energy will have replaced fossil fuels. Most students of the energy problem (though not, apparently, governments) also agree that all potential sources should receive public financing—whether or not they have reached the pilot stage.

It can be argued, too, that the United States has special responsibilities to develop alternative sources. As consumer of 35 percent of the world's energy, as the largest producer of oil, and as the country with the largest reserves of coal, the United States not only is unusually blessed but also is in no small part responsible for the global energy shortage and soaring prices. What most countries of the world need is not merely the opportunity to buy fuels at now-inflated prices but also indigenous sources of energy. Some of the misnamed esoteric energy sources, notably the sun, are more promising prospects in the developing world of the tropic zone than in the industrialized nations. But it is the latter that must develop the technologies.

Concentration in this two-part series on new supplies of power neglects the importance of reducing the growth in demand through conservation and more efficient power generation. A leading example of the latter is the combined gas-steam turbine systems, in which propulsion technology developed by the aircraft industry is being applied to stationary power plants. The expectation is that present conversion efficiencies can be increased from a high of about 40 percent to 58 percent or even more in coal-fired systems that are virtually free of sulfur. Greater efficiency in power generation, mining and smelting, transportation, construction, and manufacturing, combined with a revised sense of values, may be the most promising alternative of all.

COAL GASIFICATION

The gaslight era was illuminated by coal. Since then research into ways to increase the heating value and lower the cost of coal gas has been occasionally energetic, more often fitful. Most of the research has been conducted in Western Europe, which had ample coal but no oil or natural gas until the recent discoveries in the North Sea. When pipeline technology made it possible to bring natural gas from the American Southwest to the East Coast, U.S. research on coal gasification withered. Now at least four different processes are being investigated.

To the layman, they all seem basically similar. The variants have to do with the size of the coal and how it is fed into the reactor, whether air or oxygen is used in combustion, whether the operation occurs under pressure, and whether the raw gas is methanated (by combining carbon monoxide and hydrogen). Some choices depend on whether the objective is to produce a gas high in Btu's, suitable as a substitute for natural gas and economically transportable by pipeline over long distances, or whether the aim is a so-called producer of gas of relatively low heating value but adequate for on-site electric generation. Each plant must be tailored to the characteristics of the coal used, which may vary enormously.

For humanitarian, environmental and economic reasons (a rare and happy combination), the most desirable possibility is that coal can be gasified right in the underground seams—an idea first explored in the Soviet Union in the early Thirties. Following World War II, *in situ* gasification attracted worldwide interest, but experiments thus far have had very limited success. The process has proved difficult to control and has produced a gas of low quality. But experiments go on. In a new variant, which the AEC's Lawrence Livermore Laboratory is now testing, explosives are detonated at the bottom of a seam, making the bed permeable. Then the coal is ignited from the top, a mixture of steam and oxygen is pumped down the shaft, and gas is recovered from the bottom of the hole.

Environmental impact

Successful underground gasification is a goal ardently to be wished for. It will reduce the need for strip-mining, avoid the hazards of deep mining, minimize pollution, and reduce costs. Other methods of gasification do not have all those advantages but will reduce air pollution from the direct burning of high-sulfur coal. (See also "Coal Liquefaction.")

Prospects

The first commercial conversion plants are not expected until 1980, but with increased funding that schedule may be shortened, at least for producer gas. The newer processes have not reached even the pilot stage, and much engineering work is required.

COAL LIQUEFACTION

The technology for obtaining oil from coal has not proceeded much beyond the achievements of the Germans during World War II, when price was no object. The two processes they developed then still appear to be the most promising. Both remain complicated and expensive, and both require gasification as the first step. The more efficient of the two requires extremely high temperatures and pressures, which make reduction in costs difficult.

A distinction needs to be made, however, between coal oil that can be refined into synthetic substitutes for various natural petroleum products, such as gasoline, and that which can be made into a low-sulfer fuel for industry and utilities. The former involves more expensive and complex processes, but a modified form of coal liquefaction, designed primarily to remove pollutants before or during combustion rather than afterward, may prove more practical and economical than expensive stack-gas scrubbers.

Under one system—*solvent refining*—coal at high temperature and under pressure is converted into a molten mass in a solvent containing a small amount of hydrogen. The undissolved sulfer is then filtered off, and the solvent is distilled away. The refined coal can be fed in its molten state directly into a furnace, or it can be allowed to cool into a shiny solid for transportation elsewhere. The by-products removed in the process offset some of the costs, and the refined coal is both low in impurities and exceptionally high in heating quality.

Another system is called *fluid-bed burning,* because the combustion process gives the appearance of a bubbling boil. Finely ground coal is sprayed into a chamber and mixed with chips of limestone, which react with oxides of sulfer to form calcium sulfate. This can then be extracted, separated, and the limestone recycled.

Environmental impact

The most detrimental aspects of coal conversion, whether to gas or oil, lie in the vast quantities of coal—much of it strip-mined—that will be needed. To produce 100,000 barrels of synthetic oil requires 35,000 tons of coal per day—more than twice the output of the largest mines now being worked. Similarly, there will be an astronomical demand for water, which may have to be brought from long distances. Whatever the price to the environment, it simply is not known whether sufficient water will be available for coal gasification and liquefaction on a significant, hence economical, scale. (A liquefaction plant may cost half a billion dollars.)

Moreover, liquefaction produces nitrogen oxides, which can be removed only at high cost and with the consumption of large amounts of hydrogen.

Prospects

Obtaining oil from coal is technically more difficult and more expensive than coal gasification; hence its commercial production is probably more remote. The great attraction of liquefied coal is that it could be fed directly into existing pipelines and ultimately could alleviate the petroleum shortage. The U.S. Department of the Interior has one liquefaction plant in operation and another under construction. The Navy has successfully tested a destroyer powered by oil produced from coal and hopes to start converting other ships within a few years. But unless there is a crash program, refined synthetics from coal oil are not likely to be widely available commercially until the next decade.

MHD

For the past ten years, studies have been conducted on the possibility of converting coal directly into electricity—an effort somewhat comparable to the alchemist's dream of turning lead into gold. MHD, or magnetohydrodynamics, involves burning coal or other fuels at high temperatures (4000° to 5000°F.) to produce a very hot ionized gas. The charged gas is passed through a strong magnetic field, and electrons are drawn off to form electric current. That is the theory; the problems have proved formidable and do not appear close to solution. Not the least of these is the formation of high concentrations of nitric oxide. MHD is still in the stage of fundamental research, although the Soviet Union is said to have two pilot plants in operation, and it appears to be further advanced with the technology than other nations are. Some scientists believe that other processes for achieving high thermodynamic efficiencies may completely overtake MHD, thereby making it redundant. Thermonuclear fusion would have the same effect.

OIL FROM SHALE AND TAR SANDS

In many countries shale oil was produced commercially before petroleum was discovered. In the intervening years, new processes for extracting oil from shale have continued to be tested, often in large pilot plants, but the estimated costs then seemed excessive. When the Department of the Interior offered leases on three tracts in 1968, no serious bidders could be found. But starting last month, six new tracts are being leased in Colorado, Utah, and Wyoming, which are thought to have 1.8 billion barrels of oil recoverable from shale. Each tract is 5000 acres in size but geologically different.

Oil shale is widely available, though its quality varies. The best yields thirty-five gallons or more per ton of shale. In the United States the oil potentially available in shale is believed to be forty times greater than proved oil reserves, including Alaska. Federal lands alone are believed capable of yielding 600 billion barrels of shale oil.

Vast quantities of oil or tar sand also exist; the largest and richest known are in Alberta. The Athabasca deposits are thought to contain 80 billion barrels of oil recoverable by methods now in use — and potentially much more. A sudsidiary of the Sun Oil Company has been operating there since 1967 at a loss of several million dollars a year. A large U.S.-controlled consortium, Syncrude, which hopes to be producing by 1978, is already spending $2 million a month on start-up costs.

Economics and technology

After oil sand has been mined, it is treated with a mixture of steam and hot water so that the oil can be extracted. Syncrude expects capital costs of $1 billion just to produce enough oil for a 100,000-barrel-a-day refinery.

Development of oil shale is likely to be more rapid, partly because scientists consider its chemical properties more promising. Even with high-grade shale, it takes 1.4 tons to produce a barrel of oil and leaves 1.2 tons of waste. The sheer volume of the raw material required virtually dictates that the oil be extracted where the shale is found. The shale may be mined first and then processed, or it may be liquefied *in situ*. The latter is accomplished by breaking up the shale to ensure permeability, then igniting the shale at the bottom of a hole drilled into the formation. At a temperature of 900°F, the hot gases created distill the hydrocarbons from the shale, and the oil is then drawn off into a second hole.

A variant of that method, now being tested, is to dig a cavern under the shale and set off an explosion. The fragmented shale collapses into the cavern and is thus made permeable in one stroke. It has not gone unnoticed that this process might be achieved even more simply and economically with nuclear explosives.

Environmental impact

It will be evident that obtaining oil from shale will impose heavy environmental costs in disruption of the land and in visual, air, and water pollution. A study by the Environmental Impact Assessment Project, sponsored by the Ford Foundation, asserts that in Colorado shale waste and water made saline in the mine operation will be dumped into the Colorado River. It also warns that toxic by-products released will include mercury, cadmium, lead, and fluorine.

Not only is the waste material enormous, but also by volume it will be considerably larger than the original shale, having been altered from finely stratified rock to rubble. A plant producing 50,000 barrels of oil daily will have to dispose of more than a ton of shale waste every second. The open firing of the shale will obviously cause air pollution; how much is a matter of dispute. Finally the process will require huge amounts of water; and in Colorado, where the highest grade of shale is found, water is already in short supply. Several environmental organizations are protesting the mining of oil shale, charging the Interior Department's final impact statement is inadequate.

Similarly, extracting oil from sand will require large amounts of water and leave vast quantities of waste. However, the Athabasca field is in a remote area several hundred miles north of Edmonton. Since the ground is spongy and sticky, alternative land uses are limited and sufficient water is available. Thus, the environmental impact should not be particularly adverse.

Prospects

The cost of producing shale oil commercially is believed to be in the neighborhood of five dollars per barrel, which would make it already competitive. But both the risks and the initial capital investment are high. Production in the United States is expected to start in 1978, and the Interior Department calculates that by 1985 approximately 1 million barrels per day may be produced. That is approximately 10 percent of the anticipated increase in demand for oil between now and then.

The Athabasca oil sands are now producing about 50,000 barrels a day. That figure may quadruple by 1980 and reach 1 million barrels by 1990 — equivalent to the daily amount that Canada exports to the United States today.

WASTE

The great attraction of using waste as an energy resource is that it is there; no exploration is required to find it. On the contrary, means must be found to get rid of it. The burning of municipal waste to generate electricity and to provide steam for home heating has been practiced in Europe for many years. Now at least twenty U.S. cities and several industrial plants are doing, or planning to do, likewise.

In Milan, Italy, streetcars and subways will soon run on electricity from generators fueled by waste. A Philadelphia company intends to convert 90 percent of that city's waste into a marketable fuel that will be sold either in a finely shredded form or as briquettes. General Motors is planning to burn 55,000 tons of refuse a year from its own plants in the Pontiac, Michigan, area to furnish much of the energy needed by its truck and coach division. Nashville, Tennessee, will soon be burning its solid waste to provide air conditioning as well as heating.

The technology for separating waste into its component parts (organic matter, glass, metals) is available and advancing rapidly. After it has been shredded and separated by air blowers and vibrating screens, the combustible material (about 80 percent) is normally mixed with coal or oil so that it will burn more efficiently. In the much-publicized St. Louis experiment, waste makes up only 10 percent of the fuel. In a few instances boilers are fired entirely by shredded refuse; the most notable example is a generating plant on the outskirts of Paris.

Gasification and liquefaction

In more sophisticated systems, the refuse may be converted to gas or oil in much the same way that is being tired with coal. Hydrogenation converts the carbon content of the trash to oil, using high temperatures and pressures. A ton of dry waste produces about two barrels of oil (before subtraction of the fuel used in the process).

A slightly less efficient method is pyrolysis, a distillation process that produces both oil and a low-energy gas. Though it, too, requires high temperatures, the process takes place at atmospheric pressure—a considerable economy. Both of those methods are still in the experimental stage, but encouraging progress is being made. The Coors Brewery, outside of Denver, which has the largest brewing plant in the world, is experimenting with a gasification project fueled entirely by municipal trash and garbage. If early successes continue, all of Denver's municipal waste will be used to provide all of the brewery's fuel requirements.

The principal drawbacks to using refuse as a fuel are that its Btu output is low; it may cause corrosion in boilers; the variations in the content of the material from season to season and from place to place complicate efforts to achieve uniform combustion; and because neither the supply of refuse nor the demand for energy is constant; garbage may accumulate at times when demand for power is low and be insufficient at times of peak load. Also, since refuse can be used efficiently only in large generating plants, the costs of collection over a wide area may be high. In most cases, however, those costs are borne by the municipality and do not add to the costs of the fuel.

Fermentation

Many of these drawbacks do not apply to anaerobic decomposition, a method of accelerating decay of organic matter to produce the odorless, colorless gas, methane. Small plants can be highly efficient. There are more than 2500 bio-gas installations in India alone, and throughout East Asia many are just large enough to provide for the needs of a family or farm. The notion of "an anaerobic digestor in every home" is not entirely fanciful. Since there is an upper limit to the size of a digestor (the fermentation vessel), an installation to serve a city would require many digestors. But a farm family could meet all its energy requirements with a single unit, and urban dwellers might reduce their external needs by half.

Unlike methods that use waste for combustion, fermentation needs moisture and benefits from a combination of solid waste and sewage; their chemical properties complement one another, and sewage can provide the water that is needed. Thus waste from animal feedlots, dairies, canneries, and other agricultural processing; municipal trash and garbage; sewage; and much more are grist for the fermentation mill. Each pound of organic matter can produce about ten cubic feet of methane, and the residue at the end of the four-to-seven-day process can be used as a clean, rich fertilizer, either sprayed onto fields in liquid form or dried for easier distribution. It may also be recycled as an animal feed.

Methane is inescapably produced in sewage plants. In many places in Europe and Asia, the gas is captured and piped to homes and factories. In the

United States it has generally been considered a nuisance; certainly no effort has been made to maximize its production. Elsewhere, too, fermentation has been used to reduce the bulk of waste or to produce nutrients rather than gas.

Environmental impact

The use of solid waste for power generation offers immense environmental benefits. It reduces the misuse of land for dumping refuse and lessens water and soil pollution. It also encourages the recycling of the glass and metals that must be removed.

To be sure, refuse is by no means a "clean" fuel when it is burned, and what goes into the garbage will affect what comes out as air pollutants. But as plants are converted to accept refuse, or new ones constructed, pollution controls can be built in.

Processes for producing gas and oil from waste are cleaner and in turn produce fuels that are low in pollutants. Fermentation takes place in a closed system, and in terms of the process and the product (methane), it deserves the highest environmental marks of all conversion systems in commercial use.

Prospects

Most estimates of the potential of waste as a fuel are still highly theoretical, partly because we do not know how much waste we can practically collect. One U.S. estimate (by the Bureau of Mines) is 15 percent, though the smaller countries of Europe should easily exceed that figure. The least efficient process is burning of solid waste for direct generation of electricity or space heating and cooling. That is unlikely to exceed 1 or 2 percent of energy consumption anytime in the future. The greatest potential is for the production of methane, because fermentation uses all forms of waste, wet and dry, and because it requires minimal fuel in the process of conversion. Here the constraints are largely structural and institutional and, therefore, most difficult to forecast. Nevertheless, the mounting prob-

---

Flywheels

Many means of storing energy are being explored. One of the most intriguing is flywheels. By virtue of stronger, lighter materials and more advanced design, engineers foresee giant flywheels operating in a partial vacuum at 3500 revolutions per minute and charged with 10,000 to 20,000 kilowatt-hours of energy for use in peak periods of demand for electricity. Smaller units with about 30 kilowatt-hours of stored energy would drive a small car for 200 miles at 60 miles an hour, and they could be recharged in five minutes. In terms of a barrel of crude oil, such a flywheel system would be five times more efficient than the internal-combustion engine and would be totally free of pollution in operation. Unused, the flywheel would keep its "charge" for at least six months.

Above all, perhaps, flywheels offer a means of storing the intermittent energy of sun, wind, and tides.

lems of waste disposal and the need to recycle metals, in combination with the energy shortage, should provide strong incentives to increase the use of waste as an energy source.

FLOWER POWER AND ALGAE

The farming of vegetable matter especially for burning (after sun drying and shredding) is most frequently proposed as a waste supplement to ensure a constant supply of fuel. Sunflowers and sugarcane are among the plants being tested, but the amount of farmland and water required to make a significant contribution to the fuel supply is staggering. Artificially stimulating algae growth may be more practical but the problems of harvesting and drying would be substantial. Others have suggested tree farms for fueling an on-site generator. One calculation has it that a tree plantation of 400 square miles could produce about 400 megawatts of electricity.

Although these fuels would be low in sulfur and their ashes could be returned to the soil, their use is otherwise unappealing. It would seem more logical to find ways to collect and utilize the lumbering and agricultural wastes that already exist. In terms of efficiency and land use, flower power (promoted as a form of solar energy) rates poorly and seems unlikely to come into commercial use.

THE NUCLEAR OPTION

The fission reactor

Of all non-conventional sources of energy, nuclear fission has received far and away the most development support. When the U.S. Atomic Energy Commission was founded in 1946, it expected that nuclear reactors generating electricity would become, without undue difficulty, our most important source of energy. It was anticipated that by about this time conventional fission reactors of the light-water or gas-cooled type would provide energy almost equal to that of the fossil fuels. The fission reactor's unique "clean air" characteristics appeared to make it a most desirable option. Nuclear fuels are a compact source of energy, and their use involves lower mining and transportation costs that coal requires: Water pollution, land disruption, and human injuries associated with mining are correspondingly reduced.

The rate at which nuclear power has entered into the production of electricity has been greatly disappointing to its supporters. In the United States there are some three dozen operating reactors, supplying about 5 percent of the nation's electrical capacity. Initial delays were largely related to the problem of establishing reliability and safety for commercial operation. More recently, fears have mounted concerning the environmental impact of large-scale use of nuclear fission. The optimistic period for fission technology ended around 1970.

Unforeseen natural disasters and human actions ranging from carelessness to deliberate sabotage are of critical concern. Of all sources of energy, nuclear fission is potentially the most hazardous to human health and to the environment.

The breeder

A further disadvantage of the conventional fission reactors in commercial operation today is that they utilize less than 1 percent of the energy in naturally occurring uranium. These reactors consume the fissionable uranium isotope U-235 (0.71 percent of natural uranium) and convert only small amounts of the dominant uranium isotope U-238 into fissionable plutonium. While experts differ as to the quantities of uranium that are economically recoverable, reliance on conventional fission reactors for a significant portion of our electrical energy demand would require the use of expensive, low-grade uranium ores. As a consequence, great emphasis has been placed on the development of the "breeder" reactor, which produces more fissionable material than it consumes and theoretically utilizes between 50 and 80 percent of the uranium.

However, breeders pack more energy into less space than the ordinary reactors do, making the possibility of a meltdown more frightening. Their radioactive wastes are much richer in highly toxic plutonium, the staff of which weapons are made.

In the United States, the AEC is predicting that by the year 2000 there will be 900 nuclear power plants in operation, and the Federal Power Commission is renewing the prediction of three decades ago: that nuclear plants will meet 50 percent of the nation's energy needs within twenty to thirty years. Japan and some European countries foresee even greater dependence on nuclear fission, but some are meeting stubborn resistance from significant sectors of the public.

Fusion

The possibility of obtaining power from a controlled thermonuclear reaction has steadily receded in time. Some believe that the process will never be perfected; others forcast that significant power from fusion is possible by the end of the century.

The fusion process involves the interaction of very light atomic nuclei, such as hydrogen, to create highly energetic new nuclei, particles, and radiation. Oversimplified, the problem is how to contain the reaction at astronomically high temperatures and pressures. The fusion processes being explored include the magnetic containment of the fusion plasma (ionized gas) and laser-induced fusion. In the first process, the plasma is surrounded by a neutron-moderating blanket and contained by very large superconducting magnets. The other process uses a giant laser pulse to impinge on a deuterium-tritium pellet.

The advantages of nuclear fusion are now legendary: for all practical purposes, an inexhaustible source of clean energy with minimal environmental impact, primarily thermal pollution. But control of the fusion process involves many scientific phenomena that are not yet adequately understood, and research has not yet reached the stage of engineering feasibility. Controlled nuclear fusion is conceptually attractive but has a highly uncertain outcome.

GEOTHERMAL

At least eighty nations have geological conditions indicating that the earth's heat is within potential reach as a source of energy. Today, usable geothermal energy is being produced only in the United States, the Soviet Union, Italy, Iceland, Japan, New Zealand, and Mexico. For the most part these developments are not recent but go back many decades — in the case of Italy, to 1904. The total electric power produced amounts to about 1100 megawatts, or the equivalent of a single large fossil-fueled power plant. Geothermal power is now being tapped in Kenya and Ethiopia, and serious exploration is proceeding in Turkey, Chile, El Salvador, Nicaragua, and Taiwan. It is in lands having a history — however ancient — of earthquakes and volcanoes that heat from the earth's molten interior can be expected to be within man's technological grasp.

Geothermal energy need not be converted to electricity to be useful. As in Reykjavik, Iceland, hot springs may be used for home and industrial heating, or they may be applied to desalinization and mineral separation. While some geothermal reservoirs have very hot water with temperatures as high as 550°F, others, such as those underlying Hungary and parts of the Soviet Union, are of relatively low temperatures (around 200°F) suitable for space heating and residential hot water.

A Hydrogen Energy Regime

A chemical fuel having attractive qualities for replacing oil and gas is hydrogen, which is non-polluting and virtually inexhaustible. Moreover, it is an ideal form in which to store and transport other forms of energy, especially from such intermittent sources as the sun, wind, and tides. The proponents of hydrogen have used the term "the hydrogen economy" to describe a regime in which it would be the predominant fuel. As a gas, it would be delivered by pipeline to homes or plants for use directly by burning or by conversion to electricity in on-site fuel cells. Hydrogen would be burned in engines, as gasoline and other petroleum products are. It is a clean and efficient fuel for internal-combustion engines and appears to have good promise for aircraft propulsion. The range of aircraft would be increased two to three times for the same weight of fuel. Liquid hydrogen does have the disadvantage that it must be kept at very low temperatures.

Hydrogen is not a "natural" fuel, but it can be synthesized readily from conventional fuels or it can be produced simply by splitting molecules of water — including ocean water — into hydrogen and oxygen. This electrolysis process requires an input of electrical energy derived from new or old energy sources. Hydrogen may also be produced by biological processes and photosynthesis. Any organic matter would serve, including waste. Of all these processes, electrolysis now seems the most practical for large-scale use.

Environmental Impact
Hydrogen is a clean, non-polluting fuel. It is, however, a hazardous material that must be handled with all due precautions. We have had extensive experience with pipelining hydrogen over short distances, using pipeline materials and pressures similar to those for natural gas.

The limited energy that has so far been tapped from the earth's interior has come entirely from sites of natural outcroppings of steam or hot water. These occur in only a few places in the world; the most notable example in the United States is the Geysers, ninety miles north of San Francisco, where efforts are being made to increase output from 237 to 1000 megawatts.

Any widespread use of geothermal energy requires exploratory drilling deep into the earth to reach either steam, hot water (also brine), superheated rock, or possibly magma (molten rock and gases).

The economics and technology

Geothermal steam is cooler than that normally used in power generation. This means lower efficiency and a higher capital investment per watt of output.

Hot water at high temperatures may be converted into steam for direct power generation. This is being done successfully, though with low efficiency, in New Zealand and at the relatively new plant at Cerro Prietto, Mexico. At lower temperatures the water must be used to heat a liquid that has a lower boiling

---

Liquid hydrogen is regularly shipped in railroad tank cars and truck trailers. Handled with proper practices and in equipment designed to ensure its safety, hydrogen could be used without undue risk.

The transmission of energy via hydrogen in underground pipelines avoids the visual population, loss of energy, and misuse of land characteristic of the transmission of electricity via high-voltage power lines. Electrolysis facilities can be placed in the optimum locations either for utilizing fuel sources or for dispersing polluting by-products of the power production.

Among the most important advantages of hydrogen is that it adds to the feasibility of other energy sources, which may be limitless but variable (sun, wind, etc.) and can be converted to hydrogen at peak periods.

Prospects

A hydrogen-energy regime is already technically feasible. The cost of hydrogen produced from electricity must always be higher than the cost of the electricity. But its storage advantages and the lower transmission and distribution costs, compared with electricity, make it attractive. It should already be possible to sell hydrogen energy to the average customer at a price lower than he now pays for electricity and lower than he soon will pay for natural gas.

Perhaps the principal obstacle to be overcome is public fear of the hazards of hydrogen, sometimes described as the "Hindenburg syndrome." In part because of this concern, some have suggested "the methanol economy" could be a transition route from an oil to a hydrogen economy. Methanol, a synthetic compound of hydrogen, has the advantages of being safer, possibly cheaper, and more easily adaptable to the automobile.

point, such as Freon or isobutane, which in turn drives the turbines. One such plant using this so-called binary system is in operation in the Soviet Union, and another is planned.

The geothermal fluid may in fact turn out to be brine—with up to 30 percent solids (salt, silica, carbonates)—and highly corrosive. In this case a binary system is essential in order to keep the brine isolated. Enough hot brine is believed to be under the Imperial Valley in California to produce 20,000 megawatts for a century.

The most widespread and possibly the richest source of geothermal energy is probably dry hot rock, which can be used to heat water fed from the surface. To permit the water to pass over multiple surfaces of the rock and absorb its heat, water is initially pumped down the bore hole under high pressure, thus hydraulically fracturing the rock. The heated water then rises by natural convection through a parallel bore hole, and after its heat has been trapped, it it returned by gravity to the underground rock in a continuous cycle.

So far this is theory, but it has been successfully tested to the extent that hydrofracturing (developed by the oil industry for reviving tired wells) can be achieved in granite and other crystalline rock formations at relatively modest pressures; and the cracks will not cause the water to leak away, as some feared. Thus the technology appears promising and will receive a full-scale test soon.

Scientists are now assessing a two-by-five-square-mile area near Marysville Montana, where hot rock lies only a mile below the surface at a temperature of at least 932°F (500°C). It is estimated that for a period of thirty years, this relatively small source could provide nearly 10 percent of all electricity now used in the United States. Experiments on removing this dry-rock heat will begin next summer, when an exploratory hole will have been completed.

Environmental impact

Geothermal energy is not so free of environmental consequences as some of its proponents suggest; its impact will vary widely with the quality of the steam and/or water that emerges and will be dependent on whether subterranean pressures prevent returning them to earth. If so, the problems of disposal may be formidable, though having adequate water for cooling is an asset, and relatively pure water may find agricultural and other uses. In the case of hot dry rock, substantial quantities of surface water will be required. In other respects, hot rock seems the most environmentally satisfactory source of geothermal energy. The fear that hydrofracturing, especially in earthquake-prone areas, may cause dangerous geological instabilities has been somewhat lessened.

In populated areas noise and odor pollution may be serious, though not insurmountable. Steam escaping under high pressure is ear-splitting, and the frequent presence of hydrogen sulfide, unless extracted, will fill the neighborhood with the odor of rotten eggs.

As with other forms of on-site power generation, which will be increasingly common, the electricity must be carried to where it is needed. This means an expansion of transmission lines with their attendant problems of land use, visual pollution, and energy loss.

Prospects

There is no question that geothermal energy offers a gigantic potential. For example, the Russians estimate that their geothermal potential is probably equal to their reserves of petroleum, coal, and lignite combined. Moreover, unlike many other so-called esoteric sources, the basic technology is at hand. The uncertainties lie largely in economics and geography. Little is known about costs of exploration and extraction. If geothermal energy is to be competitive in the near term, it will be only in those areas where the earth's heat is close to the surface. In the United States, that means in the West, where the energy shortage is less severe.

Development in the United States has been excruciatingly and inexcusably slow. The R&D budget for this fiscal year is a paltry $11 million—and scheduled to rise to $40 million next year. Only this year are the first leases being issued for exploratory drilling on federal land—where most of the best prospects exist. Nevertheless, a study by the National Science Foundation estimates that by 1985 the United States will generate, 132,000 megawatts of electricity from geothermal energy and that by the end of the century the output will reach 395,000 megawatts—or more than the total generating capacity of the United States today. From a different perspective, the Joint Atomic Energy Committee estimates that by the year 2000, geothermal will provide less than 5 percent of U.S. energy requirements.

SOLAR

The limitless potential of solar energy today captures some of the excitment generated by thermonuclear energy two decades ago, when its promise seemed imminent. The new interest in solar radiation is deserved, but again high expectations may be disappointed; years of neglect of this primordial source will not be overcome quickly.

By now every literate person has read something about solar energy; therefore we will encapsulate this section even further than others.

The possibilities

• *To supplement conventional methods of heating and cooling homes and commercial buildings* through the use of large panels that "collect" the sun's radiation and store it by transferring the heat to water, rocks, or (more recently) special salts. The technology is available, but each system and its components must be custom-designed. The usual objective in the north temperate zone is that solar energy should meet half the space-conditioning requirements of a given structure.

• In addition to heating, *to install solar cells that will convert the sun's heat directly into electricity* for household light and appliances. Excess power might be stored in conventional batteries, in flywheels, or chemically as hydrogen for use at peak periods of demand on public utilities. One experimental house combining space heating and photovoltaic conversion exists at the University of Delaware. Though the findings are not yet published, it is hoped that solar energy will provide 80 percent of the building's heating and electric needs at an added capital cost of 10 percent. With a fifteen-year amortization and abundant fuel savings, such a system would be highly competitive.

• *To capture the sun's thermal energy in a solar furnace by concentrating large amounts of solar radiation.* With parabolic mirrors or plastic lenses, automatically steered, the sun's rays would be focused on a large boiler, probably mounted on a tower. The heat would be converted to electricity initially by a steam turbine generator, with possibly more sophisticated methods to follow.

• *To generate massive quantities from solar heat captured in hundreds of miles of pipe containing a liquid with a low boiling point.* The pipe, laid out in deserts or raised above grazing land, would be coated with a material designed to allow solar radiation to penetrate but not to escape. In theory, the amount of electricity that could be generated is limited only by the high capital costs and amount of land that could be devoted to the purpose. Such a project would be practical only in areas of maximum sunshine. Much further research is required.

• *To put into synchronous orbit one or more giant satellites with solar cells spread out over several miles, which would transmit electric energy by microwave to earth stations.* Placed in pairs, so that one was always outside the earth's shadow, such satellite stations could provide an uninterrupted supply of energy. The financial and energy costs of placing the satellites in orbit would, however, be astronomical.

Of these possibilities, only space heating and cooling and small-scale conversion to electrical energy are in any sense imminent. Since the basic technology is available, the key question is how far and how rapidly mass production can reduce costs.

Environmental impact

Although solar energy may be the most non-polluting of all sources, it of course has environmental implications.

Solar ranching clearly has important consequences for land use. Hundreds of miles of heat-absorbing pipe extending over vast areas of desert may be viewed either as a productive use of waste land or as an insult to the natural environment and especially to its fauna. The same would be true of the huge antenna required to receive microwaves from space and convert them into electricity.

Extensive use of solar energy may cause one other form of pollution not often mentioned: visual pollution. The incorporation of solar collectors into structures of attractive and varied design will be a severe challenge to architects. Because these solar panels must be oversized in relation to the structure, because they must all face south (in the Northern Hemisphere) and at approximately the same angle, the appearance and orientation of houses may leave much to be desired.

In any case, the environmentally adverse aspects of solar energy are minor compared with its assets as a potentially unlimited source of clean energy that is available everywhere.

Prospects

It is possible that solar heating units will be commercially available in five years. Much testing remains to be done to determine which systems and their components are most reliable and economical. How rapidly solar heating is thereafter adopted will depend on many factors involving attitudes and incentives. The most important motivation will be the shortage of fuel oil and electricity as it is felt by the individual consumer at the end of the decade.

More ambitious schemes for converting solar radiation to electricity are fairly distant. Thus the use of the sun as an energy source will evolve slowly, in part because there are no economies of scale.

In the United States, the Joint Atomic Energy Committee anticipates that solar energy will constitute about 6 percent of the supply by the year 2000. Taking a longer look, a Solar Energy Panel formed by the National Science Foundation and NASA estimated that by the year 2020 solar energy "could" provide as much as 35 percent of the nation's space heating and cooling and 20 percent of its electricity.

Perhaps the brightest prospect for solar energy is in the developing world. If photovoltaic cells can be mass-produced at reasonable cost, there is the possibility that the most remote area can have enough electricity.

WIND

Windmills were first used to generate electricity in Denmark more than eighty years ago, and it is in that country that the most successful large wind turbine is found. Yet its output is only 200 kilowatts. The most ambitious experiments have been in the United States, the Soviet Union, Germany, and India; most were undertaken many years ago, then their lack of success did little to encourage further research and development.

Today, however, there is not only fresh motivation, but also new, lighter materials, improved understanding of aerodynamics, and more efficient means of storage. Whereas the most celebrated U.S. experiment (in the Forties in Vermont) used a two-bladed propeller 175 feet in diameter and weighing sixteen tons, today's experiments use lightweight propellers with a diameter of six to twenty-five feet and advanced aerodynamic design.

Since the energy available in a twenty-mile-an-hour wind is eight times that at ten miles an hour, there is obviously a premium on placing turbines where the wind is strong as well as steady. One suggestion is to put floating windmills off the Atlantic coast. Twenty to fifty thousand would provide the base load for a good part of the East Coast; when the wind fails, conventional power plants would meet power needs. Another plan is to place windmills atop existing transmission towers. One student calculates that there is enough wind over the western plains to supply half the electric-power requirements of the United States.

Almost the only objection that can be raised to wind power on environmental grounds is that it will cause visual pollution. Technologically advanced wind generators scattered by the tens of thousands over several states would lack the appeal of windmills of old.

A new age of sail?

One of the most fascinating possibilities is that square-rigged cargo ships, entirely automated and capable of speeds of twelve to sixteen knots or more, can be made as reliable as, and more economical than, freighters fueled by oil. As with windmills, the technology relies on new light materials and on advanced aerodynamic design. According to plans developed by German engineers, sails would be set, trimmed, and furled by push button from the bridge. The ships would have auxiliary power and would not be suitable for all runs. But in the heavily trafficked North Atlantic, for example, the wind is said to be reliable 85 percent of the time.

TIDES

Despite millennial interest in the power of tides, there are only two places on earth where it is being harnessed to generate electricity—one in the Soviet Union, which generates 400 kilowatts, and one in northern France, which generates 240,000 kilowatts. Though much more could be done to capture tidal energy, the opportunities will always be limited geographically: There are not many places where the difference in elevation between high and low tide—the head—is sufficient to make electricity generation practical.

Tidal installations of the future will almost certainly have special holding basins, pumped storage, flywheels, or hydrogen conversion to provide constant power from intermittent tides. The most likely site is Canada's Bay of Fundy, where the fifty-foot head is the highest in the world.

The required dams across bays or estuaries obviously will have an impact on the marine environment, which must be studied in each case.

OCEAN CURRENTS

The unimaginable energy in ocean currents may be tapped using "underwater windmills." The Florida Current, only one component of the Gulf Stream, is said to carry fifty times the flow of all the freshwater rivers of the world. Near the surface it moves at speeds that sometimes exceed 5.5 miles per hour. If the total flow between Miami and Bimini could be harnessed, it would amount to about 25,000 megawatts.

So far, an experimental turbine has not even been designed, and there is some doubt that the low RPMs could generate electricity economically. But the attractions are obvious: Usable currents are moderately widespread in the world; they are relatively constant; the energy would be pollution-free; and the environmental impact on the marine or coastal environments would be minimal.

THERMAL GRADIENTS

These same qualities apply to thermal gradients, a term that describes the fact that surface waters in the ocean may be as much as 45°F warmer than the water at 1000 feet or more. This difference can be a source of energy.

The warm water would flow through a heat exchanger, causing another fluid—probably ammonia—to boil. The vapor would drive a turbine to produce electricity, which might be carried to shore by cable or used *in situ* to extract hydrogen from seawater. Cold water from lower depths would then be used to cool the vapor back into a liquid, and the cycle would start over.

The potential of thermal gradients has been known for at least half a century. In 1929 a Frenchman produced 22 kilowatts of useful power, using a thermal gradient of less than 20°F. Until quite recently, almost all research in the field was conducted by France.

Although efficiency is low, many claim that the system can easily be made competitive. An added bonus is the fact that nutrients from deep-sea water can be used to great advantage in the cultivation of shellfish. From an environmental viewpoint, thermal gradients appear to be most desirable.

Its wide adoption may be slowed by the fact that extremes of water temperature are not found where energy demand is greatest. The principal potential is in tropical or sub-tropical waters. In the long run thermal gradients could become an important source of energy for many developing nations.

QUESTIONS FOR DISCUSSION

1. "... Energy provision and use is a complex web, in which shortages in one sector set off repercussions throughout the entire system. In the short run, at least, the supply is relatively finite, given the configurations of use and supply channels of distribution." Discuss the sensitivity of such a system to catastrophic events and other interferences. Illustrate with examples.

2. OPEC is a cartel-like structure to control the world's oil supply. Discuss the relationship of the consuming nations to the producing nations and the various possible scenarios that could develop in such a relationship. What do you see as the future of OPEC?

3. Evaluate the pros and cons of the various short-range strategies being contemplated within the Western industrialized world. Given the values of the American people, which do you see as most likely to succeed in achieving the objectives of conservation and consumption efficiency?

4. Evaluate the long-term prospects of some of the newer (and some say esoteric) energy sources—e.g., solar, wind, tides, geothermal, etc.

5. Chauncey Starr in his article "How Well Will We Meet Our Energy Needs in Year 2000?" examines three areas in which decisions must be made: goal targeting, resource management, and timing. He sees the major role for electricity. "Taking the fuel resource picture as a whole, then, it seems that the

best avenues toward ensuring our national future supply are increased elec-trification and increased conservation through greater efficiency," he writes. What are the bases for that conclusion by Starr?

6. Evaluate the role of the price system relative to the use of energy in the mix of productive inputs. Do you see any changes in the mix of capital and labor brought about by increased energy costs and decreased availability?

SELECTED READINGS

Alexander, T., "ERDA's job is to throw money at the energy crisis," *Fortune,* July, 1976.

Alexander, T., "Industry can save energy without stunting its growth," *Fortune,* May, 1977.

Appleby, A. J., "The high price of future energy," *Energy Policy,* June, 1976.

Cunningham, B., "Energy in a nuclear age," *American Federationist,* July, 1976.

"Energy: Where intervention is inevitable," *Business Week,* April 4, 1977.

The Energy Problem and the Middle East. (New York: American Academic Association for Peace in the Middle East, 1973.)

Freeman, S. D., *Energy: The New Era.* (New York: Walker and Company, 1974.)

"Marketplace can bring conservation," *Industry Week,* November 1, 1976.

Netschert, B. C., "Energy vs. environment," *Harvard Business Review,* January–February, 1973.

Robinson, C., "Energy markets and energy planning," *Long Range Planning,* December, 1976.

Safer, A. E., "Employment and energy independence," *Business Economist,* September, 1976.

"U.S. business and the energy crisis," *Energy Policy,* September, 1976.

Case

GROTON PRODUCTS, INC.

Mort Casper was just hired as the first general staff assistant to Alex Groton, President and principal owner of Groton Products, Inc. Casper just completed the MBA program at Rutgers during the evenings, and, previous to joining Groton, worked as a routing manager for a large paint and varnish company.

Groton is in the plastics business and manufactures household items such as wastebaskets, vegetable bins, small tubs, laundry bas-kets, and dinner sets. It also contracts with automobile companies for such items as dashboards, door panels, arm-rests, and other molded plastic parts. Alex Groton built the business up from less than a million dollars a year in 1959 to one now doing $40 million in business and employing over 200 people.

At the present time, the company operates in Newark, New Jersey, in a plant built in 1908. The plant is extremely expensive to operate, and Groton has been unable to secure any property insurance on it for the past seven years. The lighting and ventilating systems are archaic and the plant layout is extremely inefficient. The only virtue of the building was its low price; Groton picked the building up in 1958 for $24,000 and the seller was so anxious to unload that he was willing to take a second mortgage for the down payment.

Groton called Casper in one day and said "Mort, I don't know what the hell you're doing now, but whatever it is, I want you to drop it. We just can't stay in this ——— plant any longer. Find us another site—anywhere—and make sure the operating costs are as low as possible. I just tallied our last year's energy tab and it was 28 percent above the previous year's. You know our production volume was only up by nine percent. I'm through buying these bargain-basement buildings and then watching our earnings go flying out through the cracks in the walls."

Casper knew what he meant. Plastic processing is an energy-intensive process to start with and could even be more so if the company used the latest in automatic molding and stamping equipment. Not only is the basic stock derived from petroleum, but the process takes a great deal of energy for heating, cooling, mixing, heat-forming, reworking scrap, and, with this plant, for lighting, ventilating, and air conditioning. Alex had been complaining about the increasing oil, gas, and electricity bills since prices started rising in a spiral after the 1973 Arab oil embargo.

Casper returned to his office (such as it was—a cubicle carved out of the box-storage area) and thought that he really had to start from scratch on this one. He took a legal pad out of his desk, started writing and then stopped. He said to himself, "I don't really know a lot about this business, the first thing I better do is get some data, and determine the questions I want answered. Then I'll take a shot at the answers."

7. Business and Consumerism

One recent problem to face business—or at least one recently recognized as a serious concern—falls under a very general rubric of *consumerism*. The word has many varying definitions and encompasses many points of contention against the institution of business. Indeed, the movement really does not seem to have a central focus beyond the fact that it deals with the complete satisfaction of consumer wants, if such a potentially conflict-laden objective can ever be reached.

Observers have offered many definitions of consumerism. One of the simplest is that given by Virginia Knauer, who said that the slogan has changed from "Let the Buyer Beware" to "Let the Seller Beware".[1] Peter Drucker offers the following: "Consumerism means that the consumer looks upon the manufacturer as somebody who is interested, but who really does not know what consumers' realities are. He regards the manfacturer as somebody who has not made the effort to find out, who does not understand the world in which the consumer lives, and who expects the consumer to be able to make distinctions which the consumer is neither willing nor able to make."[2]

But the Drucker definition really does not give much credit to consumers in terms of rationality, intellectual power, or calculating ability. Indeed, it reinforces the Galbraith thesis (and the earlier one of Vance Packard) that consumers are indeed manipulated by sophisticated behavioral techniques in the hands of calculating marketers.

Perhaps to capture the essence of the rise of consumerism is to recognize the disparity in power between the individual consumer and the marketing firm, which is generally a large organization with great accumulations of resources. Perhaps, with that in mind, the best definition for our purposes is that of Philip Kotler, who defines consumerism as a "social movement seeking to augment the rights and powers of buyers in relation to sellers."[3] Rights, of course, are always present, but the individual may lack the willingness to pursue them and the re-

---

[1] Cited in Richard H. Buskirk and James T. Rothe, "Consumerism—An interpretation," *Journal of Marketing,* **34** (October, 1970), p. 55.

[2] *Ibid.*

[3] Cited in Folke Olander and Hakan Lindhoff, "Consumer action research: A review of the consumerism literature and suggestions for new directions in research," *Social Science Information,* 1975.

sources for meeting the expenses of pursuing them. Kotler's definition, then, does not define specific action; it simply raises the issues of *equalizing power.*

Consumerism develops, according to some observers, for several reasons. One of the most commonly mentioned is *increasing education and sophistication* on the part of consumers. Indeed, it has always been the middle and upper classes who have demonstrated the most sophistication in shopping and who participate in those groups in the forefront of the consumer movement. Secondly, *rising prices,* which mean a decline in the real income for a large part of the population, are cited. Other reasons include the promise of better conditions as a result of organization and the emergence of articulate leadership.[4] Given that most of these conditions are occurring, consumers could be expected to seek more satisfaction for their dollars and be less inclined to accept a *caveat emptor* (let the buyer beware) attitude on the part of vendors.

There have been consumer movements prior to our present one. Robert O. Hermann traced the consumer movements of the 1900's, the 1930's, and the 1960's. In all of these periods, price increases — after a period of relative price stability or even price decreases — seemed to be an important catalyst to consumer unrest. Hermann's analysis of other periods of price increases which did not lead to consumer unrest pointed out such mitigating factors as war conditions or patriotic fervor.[5]

Another important contributing factor to consumer activism is the change in the concept of product liability. Producers, not just sellers, now face a doctrine of strict liability and can be held liable for damages if a product placed on the market caused injury while the injured party was using the product for the purpose for which it was intended. Prior to the establishment of that concept of law, there had to be a direct buyer–seller relationship established.[6]

Under the current state of the law, a number of the suits involve old equipment because there is no statute of limitations, nor is the manufacturer absolved of liability if the equipment or product involved is modified or changes hands. These concepts have opened the way not only for individual suits, but for class action as well, where one person or group sues in the name of all persons affected.

Finally, the doctrine of *caveat emptor* is no longer accepted as readily by the courts, consumers, or even manufacturers and other business buyers. Disguised or hidden defects, a product that is less than what was advertised, unfilled or extra bulky packaging, sizes less than pictured, etc., now not only are potentially illegal, but are no longer passively accepted by consumers.

---

[4] R. O. Hermann, "Consumerism: Its goals, organizations, and future," *Journal of Marketing,* **34** (October, 1970), p. 56.

[5] *Ibid.,* pp. 56–58.

[6] "Product Liability — The search for solutions," *Nation's Business,* June, 1977, p. 26.

HOW DOES CONSUMERISM MANIFEST
ITSELF IN THE MARKETPLACE?

As we said, consumers are no longer accepting with passivity the advertising, the products, or the appeals of marketers. They are questioning the efficacy of products, ridiculing and protesting advertising, and suing for satisfaction.

Resort to the courts is an increasing phenomenon, particularly in the area of product safety. And there are costs to this rise in the number of suits. Insurance companies claim to have paid almost $9 billion on product liability claims during the years 1974 to 1976. Premium increases have averaged 150 to 200 percent for the same period; and in some industries, the increase is as high as 700 percent.[7]

In addition, the numbers of groups dealing with consumer issues is rising. One observer claims that, "because of the lack of an overall philosophy," there is no real unified consumerist movement. Rather, he claims, there are convenient coalitions consisting of labor unions, cooperatives, credit unions, product-testing organizations, and the like.[8] And they are sometimes in conflict. Labor unions representing utility workers would have nothing to do with protest groups demanding a rollback of utility rates.

Whether in concert or by themselves, however, these groups are being increasingly effective. A group called Action for Children's Television (ACT) has been very successful in reducing the alleged violence on children's television programming, chiefly on Saturday morning; and they are now working to reduce the hard-sell advertising aimed at young children. Consumers' Union, the oldest and best financed of the consumer groups, has had a long history of success in testing products and maintaining the integrity of their tests. That organization, however, has been labeled as a middle-class or rich man's organization giving information to individuals who least need it, and somehow missing the low-income people who need the assistance most. Finally, in several states, groups have intervened in utility-rate hearings to protest rate hikes, or have succeeded in changing the rules pertaining to the disconnecting of service to the poor, the sick, and the elderly. In some states, most notably California, consumers are being appointed to regulatory bodies with increasing regularity.

Consumer boycotts of products, which many people advocate as the ultimate consumer weapon, seem to have had limited success, and they seem to be less the result of organized activity than spontaneous reaction. For example, when sugar prices skyrocketed in 1976, many consumers simply stopped buying sugar. One cannot say that this was not partly a market reaction illustrating the well-known notion of elasticity of demand; but many consumers were convinced that some giant conspiracy existed among the sugar refiners and they were reacting to that as much as to the price. A similar boycott was started against coffee, which came into short supply because a frost destroyed a large part of the Brazilian coffee crop. But that boycott has not been too successful either. Generally,

---

[7] *Ibid.*

[8] Hermann, *op. cit.,* p. 58.

consumer boycotts unrelated to some other cause (such as farm workers, J. P. Stevens employees, etc.) are really not too effective.

THE ROLE OF GOVERNMENT

Like many of the other areas of government regulation of business, laws and regulations relating to consumers did not start with this latest round of consumerism. Pure Food and Drug legislation, for example, was originated in 1906 and changes were made in the law during the 1930's; the jurisdiction of the Food and Drug Administration was expanded during the thalidomide disaster; only recently has the FDA come under fire for its actions against saccharin and a drug called Laetrile, which its proponents hail as a cure for cancer.

Since the early 1960's, however, many additional pieces of consumer legislation have been passed by Congress and signed by successive presidents. Among these laws are the following:

The Fair Packaging and Labeling Act (1966) This law provides for the prevention of deceptive packaging and labeling of many consumer commodities. The law requires statements as to the type of product contained in the package, the name and location of the producer, the net quantity (in easily readable type), and the number and size of servings. The law enables the Federal Trade Commission to challenge the size of the package relative to the size or the capacity of the product contained therein.

Truth in Lending Act (1968) This act requires disclosure of credit terms, specifically the annual percentage rate, in order to allow consumers to easily compare the cost of credit (state laws, however, not federal laws, control the actual maximum rate to be charged).

Fair Credit Reporting Act (1970) This act requires that consumer reporting agencies exercise their responsibilities with fairness, impartiality, and with respect for a consumer's right to privacy. It is designed to ensure accuracy of information contained in credit dossiers, removal of obsolete information, limited use of information, notices to affected individuals, an individual's right to access to information, and an individual's right to contest information.

Consumer Products Safety Act (1972) This act created the Consumer Product Safety Commission to regulate the safety of most consumer products (excluding food, drugs, motor vehicles, boats, etc.) The Act is estimated to cover the safety of over 11,000 individual products. The Commission is empowered by the law to establish standards of consumer safety.

Magnuson-Moss Warranty Act (1975) This law established the requirements of minimum-disclosure standards and minimum-content standards for written warranties. Calls for warranties to be written in simple language. The Federal Trade Commission is empowered to prescribe the rules for warranties.

Government regulators are often convinced that the public needs the protection offered by such regulation. For example, S. John Byington, Chairman of the U.S. Consumer Product Safety Commission, states, "Personally, I believe that government has a definite role and a substantial responsibility to regulate—and to regulate vigorously—wherever and whenever the marketplace is not adequately protecting the interests of consumers. Consumer product safety is such an area".[9]

Other observers, however, are not convinced that the present mode of government regulation is the most effective and efficient. Mr. Byington's own agency has come under heavy fire for spending two whole years of effort developing standards on swimming-pool slides. It has also incurred the wrath of bicycle enthusiasts for setting excessive safety standards on ten-speed bikes, and has been charged with spending an inordinate amount of time challenging the sale of, and then finally destroying, a small quantity of mislabeled containers of windshield-washer solvent.

Murray Weidenbaum and others have attacked such government regulations—particularly consumer protection—on the grounds that it is not even cost-effective; that it is more costly to consumers. He estimated that, without the federally mandated safety and environmental requirements, a 1974 automobile would cost $320 less than it actually did cost. In general, Weidenbaum's point is made in the following statement. ". . . the public does not get a 'free lunch' by imposing public requirements on private industry. Although the costs of government regulation are not borne by the taxpayer directly, in large measure they show up in higher prices of the goods and services that consumers buy. These higher prices, we need to recognize, represent the 'hidden tax' which is shifted from the taxpayer to the consumer."[10]

Few people, including Weidenbaum, argue about the legitimate need for the government to equalize the power differential between individuals and organizations. The argument is that the cost may often exceed the benefit; and Weidenbaum and others argue that alternative methods to expensive government bureaucracies may be a better answer.

The ultimate in consumerism, some think, however, is the creation of a cabinet-level position of Secretary of Consumer Affairs. So far this has not occurred at the federal level, although a few states, such as Massachusetts, have established such a position. But legislation to create an Agency for Consumer Advocacy is in the Congress, where chances for eventual passage are fair. Such an agency would have "the authority to intervene on behalf of consumers before government regulatory agencies [and] . . . appeal to the federal courts if not satisfied with the outcome of those proceedings. [Also] the agency would serve as a clearinghouse for consumer complaints, maintaining a public record of individual allegations and individual responses to them."[11]

---

[9] S. John Byington, "Perspectives in product safety," *Professional Safety*, May, 1977, p. 20.

[10] Murray L. Weidenbaum, "The high cost of government regulation," *Business Horizons*, August, 1975.

[11] "Consumer protection: What's at issue," *Nation's Business*, June, 1977, p. 19.

Such a bill was vetoed by President Gerald Ford in 1976, but would be signed, if passed by both houses of Congress, by President Jimmy Carter. Most business firms oppose the legislation for reasons very close to those articulated by Weidenbaum; existing federal agencies can do the job and this new one would simply add costly new procedures and paperwork.

RESPONSES OF BUSINESS TO CONSUMERISM

Most business people assert that they prefer self regulation, and the standard theme of most business publications and conferences is that firms ought to self-regulate and clear their own houses before the government does step in and regulate. Other writers are urging that business should respond because it is just the right thing to do. For example, two writers give the following guidelines to companies responding to consumerism.

1. Establish a strong and powerful and separate corporate division for consumer affairs, with that unit having participation in all consumer-related activities such as "research and design, advertising, credit, pricing, quality assurance and other similar decisions."
2. Change corporate practices that are perceived as deceptive.
3. Educate channel members to the need for a consumerism effort throughout the channel system.
4. Incorporate the increased costs of consumerism efforts into the corporate operating budget.[12]

Other standard responses by business include improved complaint procedures, furnishing maximum usable information in readily understandable form, improved product safety and testing, retailers taking consumers' cases to suppliers, consumer education, review of advertising, improving product service, training of salespersons, and upgrading of merchandise.

Most of these recommendations fall into what is called the "marketing concept." Simply stated, the marketing concept means that the reason for a firm existing is to satisfy the customer, and that the firm's efforts should be directed to ascertaining what the consumer needs and wants, adapting products to those needs, delivering those products, and constantly adapting the company's response to consumer needs. The fact that consumerism arose during the period when the marketing concept was being refined and developed, however, may be an indictment that many firms simply do not practice what they preach, or that the marketing concept simply isn't enough.

More than likely, there are firms that reject consumerism and the true sense of the marketing concept. For example, after the Warranty Act was enacted into law, many firms, rather than refine the legalistic language in their warranties, simply eliminated them.

But just as likely, consumerism would have arisen despite the best efforts of marketers and business people. The time was probably right; increasing prices,

---

[12] Buskirk and Rothe, *op. cit.*, p. 65.

protest over Vietnam, and decreased confidence in all institutions, including business (and even religious institutions), such that business firms had to take their share of the discontent, not only on the other social issues, but in the very reason for their existence—the provision of goods and services. Marketing can continue to develop responses to consumerism, but it may not be a function restricted to marketers alone; the response will involve a real injection of the marketing concept throughout the entire firm.

SELECTED READINGS

Our first selection, entitled, "Consumers Complain—Does Business Respond?" by Alan R. Andreasen and Arthur Best, is based on "Data on consumer satisfaction with 28,574 purchases in 26 product and 8 service categories . . . collected in the spring of 1975 in a telephone-interview study of 2,419 households in 34 major metropolitan areas in the continental United States." Generally, based on their findings, the authors are pessimistic about the quality of business response to consumer complaints. They offer a number of guidelines for improving performance.

The second article, "Manufacturers' Malpractice" by E. Patrick McGuire, traces the rise in product-liability suits and the resultant increase in premiums for product-liability insurance.

Consumers Complain—Does Business Respond?

A survey discloses much dissatisfaction among purchasers of goods and services and mediocre work by business in handling their complaints

Alan R. Andreasen and Arthur Best*

A telephone interview survey of some 2,400 metropolitan households reveals that (a) one in five purchases of products and services resulted in consumers' dissatisfaction with something other than price, (b) less than half of these perceived problems elicited complaints from the apathetic public to the producers and purveyors involved, and (c) about one in three of the complaints ended with an unsatisfactory resolution of the problem. This article lays out

Author's note: We thank David Caplovitz, Seymour Sudman, and Ellen S. Strauss for assistance in the design and implementation of this study. The work of the Center for Study of Responsive Law on this study received support by a grant from the Carnegie Corporation of New York.

the findings of the survey of attitudes toward 26 product and 8 service categories, ranging from air conditioners to mail order merchandise to medical and dental care. The findings are not very encouraging to the authors, who have some suggestions for improving the treatment of customers' complaints as a marketing tool.

Since consumerism reared its critical head in the 1960's, companies, trade groups, and local Better Business Bureaus have substantially increased their complaint-handling capabilities. Companies such as American Motors have effectively used consumer concerns as a central element in their marketing strategy. The appliance industry has substantially improved its market credibility through its Major Appliance Consumer Action Panel.

Nevertheless, government agencies and consumer organizations continue to claim that business is not doing enough, and they have increased their pressure on business to improve its responsiveness to consumer complaints. These forces have also urged the establishment of more and better nonbusiness mechanisms to handle such complaints which contribute to the renewed interest in a federal consumer protection agency.

Considering the energy expended on both sides of this issue in recent years, it is surprising that the debate has been conducted in the absence of any basic data on consumer complaint behavior and business's response. We have not had answers to such questions as:

- How often do consumers have problems with the products and services they buy?

- How often do consumers express their discontent with these products and services to business?

- Do businesses receive a representative number of consumer complaints? Are some problems voiced more often than others?

- Who utters these protests? Are they a small vocal minority or do they represent a spectrum of the entire public?

- How good are complaint-handling processes? Are consumers generally satisfied with business's handling of their complaints?

- From the consumer's standpoint, which industries are doing a good job and which a poor job?

This article reports the findings of a national urban study designed to answer these questions. The data provide a base of comparison for managers to assess their present performance in dealing with complaints and a bench mark against which to track future successes and failures. The article also offers suggestions to help ensure more successes.

Data on consumer satisfaction with 28,574 purchases in 26 product and 8 service categories were collected in the spring of 1975 in a telephone interview study of 2,419 households in 34 major metropolitan areas in the continental United States. The products and services chosen reflected the major categories in the consumer price index and categories like mail order goods, where customer dissatisfaction has been reported to be serious. Call For Action, a media-based consumer action organization, and the Center for Study of Responsive Law jointly sponsored the study. The former organization conducted the field interviews under the supervision of one of the coauthors.

SATISFIED & UNSATISFIED

The study began with this question: "How often do consumers feel dissatisfied with the products and services they buy?" The answer to this question depends in part on the definition one uses and whether one is describing a product or a service. If we had merely asked consumers to rate a purchase made within the last year or so as "satisfactory" or "unsatisfactory" on a four-point scale, about 11% of products and 13% of service purchases included in this study would have been described as unsatisfactory.

Because the question is highly subjective, this kind of global measure poses problems. What one consumer means by "somewhat satisfied" may be different from what another means by the same phrase. Satisfaction, furthermore, is related to expectation. Indeed, as a businessman improves his product performance and as consumers' expectations increase, perceived satisfaction with products and services may actually, and perversely, decline.*

For these reasons, we sought a more objective measure of satisfaction by focusing on specific problems. This we did in two ways: by asking the dissatisfied what the problem was and by asking the satisfied whether the product could have been improved in any way.

The latter question often elicited criticism of the product or service that had not surfaced initially. The data presented in this article distinguish between "unsatisfactory" responses (for which there was no subsequent probe) and "satisfactory" responses (which were accompanied by a probe). The probe elicited either a reiteration of satisfaction or a complaint based on price or some other problem.

This procedure yielded the data shown in Exhibit I. About 7% of all problems involved complaints about price. The spring of 1975 was a period of rapid inflation and many of our respondents said something to the effect that "It should have cost less" (particularly when we asked, "How could it have been better?").

Since these complaints are much more likely to reflect changes in economic conditions than managerial action, we eliminated such problems from our "objective" measure of consumer satisfaction. So the incidence of nonprice problems became our measure of industry performance. By this criterion, about 20% of all purchases resulted in some dissatisfaction, about one-half being mentioned before our probe and one-half after.

While the use of a probe may have introduced some upward bias in these figures, the *types* of problems mentioned after the probe were virtually identical

---

*For a fuller discussion of measurement problems, see Alan R. Andreasen, "A Taxonomy of Consumer Satisfaction/Dissatisfaction Measures," to be published in *Journal of Consumer Affairs,* Winter 1977.

Exhibit I
Satisfaction and perceived problems by purchase category

	Satisfactory			Unsatisfactory			Number of purchases
	No problem	Price problem only	Nonprice problem	Price problem only	Nonprice problem	Otherwise or no answer	
Infrequently purchased products							
Dentures, hearing aids	73.2%	2.8%	7.7%	0.7%	14.8%	0.7%	142
Cars	63.5	3.0	18.5	0.5	13.8	0.7	827
Vacuum cleaners	70.4	2.5	14.4	—	12.4	0.3	355
Eyeglasses	74.3	3.2	8.6	0.7	12.2	0.9	834
Tape recorders, stereos	77.5	1.2	9.9	0.2	11.0	0.2	564
Washers, driers	75.6	0.8	12.2	—	10.6	0.8	254
Cameras	81.8	1.4	6.5	0.3	10.5	0.3	354
Bicycles	72.6	1.6	14.9	—	10.0	0.9	430
Television sets	77.2	1.6	11.1	0.2	9.7	0.2	495
Calculators	80.4	2.0	7.9	0.2	9.1	0.4	494
Floor coverings	78.7	2.3	10.7	—	7.8	0.4	522
Air conditioners	78.3	1.1	12.0	—	7.4	1.2	175
Tires	82.6	4.7	6.2	0.5	5.8	0.2	1,041
Radios	84.1	2.2	8.0	—	5.1	0.7	414
Lamps	90.3	1.2	5.9	—	2.6	—	340
Averages	76.9	2.5	10.4	0.3	9.5	0.5	7,241*

Exhibit I (continued)

	Satisfactory			Unsatisfactory			Number of purchases
	No problem	Price problem only	Nonprice problem	Price problem only	Nonprice problem	Otherwise or no answer	
Frequently purchased products							
Mail order goods	66.1	0.9	11.7	0.2	19.4	1.7	537
Toys	66.3	1.9	14.8	0.1	15.9	1.1	1,049
Clothing	64.4	5.5	14.9	0.6	13.2	1.4	2,135
Jewelry, wristwatches	77.1	0.9	7.8	0.4	12.7	1.1	803
Furniture	72.6	3.5	12.2	—	11.2	0.6	690
Groceries	35.5	28.1	15.2	8.1	10.6	2.7	2,402
Pots, pans, utensils	81.4	2.1	7.0	—	9.4	—	710
Books, records	83.7	2.5	6.9	0.1	5.8	1.0	1,566
Blankets, sheets	84.6	3.5	6.3	0.1	5.3	0.3	1,069
Tools	86.2	2.2	6.8	0.3	4.2	0.5	650
Cosmetics, toiletries	85.2	4.7	5.7	0.4	3.5	0.5	1,939
Averages	69.4	7.7	10.5	1.6	9.6	1.2	13,550*
Averages, all products	72.0	5.9	10.5	1.2	9.5	0.9	20,791*

Services

Car repair	55.8	5.8	13.5	1.4	21.5	2.2	1,277
Appliance repair	60.9	5.2	9.6	2.3	19.9	2.1	563
Home repair	65.6	4.4	9.8	0.4	18.6	1.2	537
Car parking	57.0	10.3	8.2	6.0	15.2	3.1	683
Film developing	75.9	3.8	9.4	0.7	9.1	1.2	1,250
Legal services	76.8	3.6	7.2	3.1	8.2	1.0	388
Medical or dental care	75.9	6.4	8.3	1.5	6.6	1.2	1,910
Credit	80.4	5.5	4.6	2.0	6.0	1.6	1,191
Averages, all services	69.9	5.7	8.9	1.9	12.0	1.6	7,783*
Averages all products and services	71.4	5.8	10.0	1.4	10.2	1.1	28,574*

*Total

to those mentioned before. A more important source of upward bias, however, is the occasional faulty perception of consumers; not always are the problems valid. They may simply be the result of misunderstanding about proper product use or of unreasonable expectations for product performance.

At a recent American Management Association conference on handling consumer complaints, representatives of both consumer and industrial markets estimated that the proportion of valid complaints they receive ranges anywhere from 20% to 80%. This upward bias may, however, be partly or even completely offset to the extent that purchasers remain unaware of defects in products.

Furthermore, while we asked each respondent to tell us only about his or her last purchase, it is possible that many of them scanned a history of purchases in a particular category and reported whether they had had problems with any recent purchase of the product or service. But the fact that the "problem rates" for the two sets of product data are similar makes us confident that this difficulty does not unduly bias our findings.

As the exhibit indicates, the worst offender from the consumer's standpoint is the automobile repair industry. More than one out of three of these purchases yielded protests such as "poor workmanship" and "wasn't done right in the first place." Close behind came appliance and home repairs and mail order purchases, toys, automobiles, vacuum cleaners, and clothing.

The categories showing the best performance were lamps, tires, cosmetics, tools, blankets, sheets, and credit purchases—all having nonprice problems in 12% or fewer cases. This figure may support the argument of Donald Hughes, manager of the Consumer Research Division of Sears, Roebuck & Company. His experience leads him to believe that a 10% or a 12% problem rate may be the lowest figure one could expect to achieve in any survey of consumers.

VOX POPULI

In response to their dissatisfactions, the consumers we queried mainly did nothing; well over half of all nonprice purchase difficulties precipitated no action.

The actions that they did take were distributed as follows:

Contacted manufacturer or retailer	79.1%
Contacted nonbusiness complaint-handling organization	2.4
Switched products or sellers	12.3
Took some other action	6.2

The infrequent use of third parties surprised us for two reasons:

1. Business executives have complained in the media of late that outsiders meddle too much in the relations between buyers and sellers. Our data suggest that "meddling" is very rare. In only 1 out of 27 cases where customers were motivated to take any action about a problem did they ultimately talk with official third parties. And in more than 1 in 4 of these cases, they dealt with a business-sponsored agent like the Better Business Bureau or a professional association. Clearly, the complaint adversary system begins with business and only rarely moves to the public forum.

2. Much government policy making in this area is based on submitted protests. As our data show, the government is seeing only the tip of the iceberg—and our analysis suggests that this tip may not be fully representative of the types of complaints consumers actually perceive. This is obviously a very weak base for effective government regulation.

Whether or not they talk to the government, do consumers talk back to business? The answer, as indicated in Exhibit II, is that consumers complain to sellers or formal complaint-handling organizations (which presumably in turn contact business) in about four out of ten cases where there are nonprice problems. In other words, for every four cases business hears about, there are six in the marketplace still unvoiced.

The likelihood that a consumer will speak up ranges from 62.5% for nonprice problems mentioned without a probe for infrequently purchased products to 26.9% for problems with frequently purchased products mentioned after a probe. This pattern is to be expected since (a) problems that occur to respondents only after a probe are probably less serious and (b) infrequently purchased products are usually much more expensive than those that are purchased often.

Consumers seem least reluctant to complain about problems with their dentures or hearing aids or with home repairs—categories in which, as noted in *Exhibit I,* problems appear very frequently. On the other hand, although vacuum cleaners and toys are major sources of dissatisfaction, only 29% and 22% of complaints in these categories ever reach management's ears. In general, while there is little relationship between the dollars involved in a purchase and the likelihood that a problem will occur, there is a relationship between expense and the likelihood that a complaint will be expressed to management.

Moreover (as one might expect), the more serious the problem, the more often it is voiced. For example, when a consumer told us, "My partial denture always breaks" or "The furniture was broken, took a year to replace, then got lost," he was very likely to make known his dissatisfaction. This did not always occur, however, when we expected it; one respondent, for example, who touchingly spoke of dentures that "should have been smaller" apparently did nothing about it.

Many important problems were reported to us that were not called to the attention of business. A case in point is the design of products or of ways of providing a service. After product breakage, this was the most frequently mentioned problem, representing 11.6% of all difficulties cited. Yet it accounted for only 6.4% of all the problems mentioned to sellers and manufacturers. Obviously, the manufacturer needs to know if customers are dissatisfied with a product's design. But consumers presumably think that nothing can be done, so instead of taking action they can remain silent or simply change brands the next time they buy.

Consumers speak out on problems that are important to them and/or that have a high probability of resolution. This portrait of a responsible, careful consumer runs contrary to the views of some executives, who view them as wild-eyed crazies who delight in vexing business. Indeed, Exhibit III indicates that the respondents represent a rather broad sample of the buying public. Although

Exhibit II
Voicing rates for, and number of complaints about, nonprice problems by purchase category

	After probe		Before probe		All problems	
	Percent	Complaints	Percent	Complaints	Percent	Complaints
Infrequently purchased products						
Dentures, hearing aids	54.5%	11	81.0%	21	71.9%	32
Air conditioners	50.0	20	76.9	13	60.6	33
Tape recorders, stereos	47.3	55	70.5	61	59.5	116
Television sets	44.4	54	72.9	48	57.8	102
Cars	50.0	151	67.6	108	57.1	259
Eyeglasses	45.1	71	63.7	102	56.1	173
Bicycles	44.4	63	61.9	42	51.4	105
Cameras	43.5	23	54.1	37	50.0	60
Washers, driers	41.9	31	53.8	26	47.4	57
Calculators	21.1	38	68.9	45	47.0	83
Tires	31.3	64	62.7	59	46.3	123
Floor coverings	23.2	56	52.5	40	35.4	96
Vacuum cleaners	12.0	50	47.8	46	29.2	96
Radios	24.2	33	23.8	21	24.1	54
Lamps	0.0	20	55.6	9	17.2	29
Averages	37.6	740	62.5	678	49.5	1,418

Frequently purchased products

Mail order goods	34.9	63	74.5	102	59.4	165
Furniture	40.5	84	77.6	76	58.1	160
Books, records	42.9	105	61.1	90	51.3	195
Jewelry, wristwatches	34.9	63	53.0	100	46.0	163
Groceries	32.5	360	41.6	250	36.2	610
Tools	15.9	44	63.0	27	33.8	71
Clothing	26.2	312	40.4	280	32.9	592
Toys	16.1	155	28.3	166	22.4	321
Blankets, sheets	12.5	64	31.6	57	21.5	121
Pots, pans, utensils	10.0	50	23.9	67	17.9	117
Cosmetics, toiletries	11.0	109	19.7	66	14.3	175
Averages	26.9	1,409	44.6	1,281	35.3	2,690
Averages, all products	30.6	2,149	50.8	1,959	40.2	4,108

(Continued)

Exhibit II (continued)

	After probe		Before probe		All problems	
	Percent	Complaints	Percent	Complaints	Percent	Complaints
Services						
Appliance repair	45.3	53	75.0	112	65.5	165
Home repair	51.0	51	72.3	94	64.8	145
Car repair	55.2	172	63.0	273	60.0	445
Credit	48.1	54	58.0	69	53.7	123
Film developing	29.3	116	43.4	113	36.2	229
Medical or dental care	28.3	152	38.3	120	32.7	272
Legal services	25.0	28	32.3	31	28.8	59
Car parking	14.3	56	29.0	100	23.7	156
Averages, all services	38.6	682	54.6	912	47.7	1,594
Averages all products and services	32.5	2,831	52.0	2,871	42.3	5,702

Note: This exhibit includes only instances in which the presence or absence of a probe was ascertained.

Exhibit III
Frequency of complaints

Voiced Complaints	Percent of All Respondents	Percent of Complainers	Percent of Complaints
0	46.8%	—	—
1	25.5	47.9%	23.8
2	13.0	24.4	23.8
3	8.2	15.4	22.6
4	3.3	6.3	12.3
5	1.5 } 6.5	2.9 } 12.4	7.0 } 30.0
6 or more	1.7	3.2	10.7
	100.0%	100.0%	100%
Base	2,419	1,288	1,288

there is a "heavy half" of complainers who generated three-fourths of the objections, this does not appear to be an excessive concentration when compared with other aspects of consumer behavior.

Across households, the inclination to make a complaint about a perceived problem with a particular product or service varied surprisingly little. While an analysis of characteristics leading to expression of dissatisfaction is still in process, our early research suggests that socioeconomic status is not a good predictor of behavior. This conclusion runs counter to the findings of some researchers who say that persons in high-status households are the most active in this respect. Their studies, however, did not consider the type of purchase and the type of problem. It appears to us that whether a consumer talks back to business depends not so much on who he or she is as on what the purchase or the problem is.

Corporate record

How often do consumers feel that their efforts to tell business about their problems yield satisfactory outcomes? For all product and service categories in the survey, 56.5% of voiced complaints were resolved to customers' complete satisfaction, and a further 9.5% resulted in at least some satisfaction (see Exhibit IV). Low-cost, frequently purchased products received the highest satisfaction rates, presumably because business was more likely to resolve problems in order to maintain goodwill if the effort involved little or no outlay of money. Services yielded the lowest levels of satisfaction, appliance repairs and medical-dental care producing only one in three happy outcomes.

Exhibit IV

Consumers' characterizations of business responses to nonprice complaints

	Satisfactory	Unsatisfactory	Mixed Results	Other	Number
Infrequently purchased products					
Washers, driers	80.8%	15.4%	3.8%	—	26
Cameras	71.4	21.4	7.1	—	28
Television sets	61.1	13.0	22.0	3.7%	54
Tires	59.3	25.9	14.8	—	54
Calculators	57.9	18.4	15.8	7.9	38
Tape recorders, stereos	57.4	19.7	16.4	6.6	61
Cars	56.4	30.5	8.3	4.5	133
Bicycles	56.4	27.3	14.5	1.8	55
Eyeglasses	54.3	19.6	20.7	5.4	92
Vacuum cleaners	48.0	36.0	12.0	4.0	25
Floor coverings	46.7	36.7	6.7	10.0	30
Averages	57.5	24.3	14.5	3.7	649*
Frequently purchased products					
Clothing	75.3	18.7	4.0	2.0	198
Books, records	75.2	17.1	2.9	4.8	105
Toys	69.4	14.3	9.7	5.6	72
Cosmetics	69.2	26.9	3.8	—	26

Mail order goods	67.5	18.8	2.5	11.3	80
Groceries	60.1	32.3	4.4	3.2	248
Furniture	59.2	14.5	15.8	10.5	76
Tools	58.3	25.0	16.7	—	24
Jewelry, wristwatches	57.7	22.5	14.1	5.6	71
Blankets, sheets	56.0	40.0	4.0	—	25
Averages	65.8	23.1	6.5	4.7	944*
Averages, all products	62.4	23.6	9.7	4.3	1,593*
Services					
Home repair	52.6	29.5	12.8	5.1	78
Car repair	49.8	36.0	9.2	5.0	261
Credit	49.3	29.0	2.9	18.8	69
Film developing	45.2	38.1	8.3	8.3	84
Appliance repair	35.5	43.9	15.9	4.7	107
Medical or dental care	34.5	46.4	8.3	10.7	84
Car parking	29.8	63.8	4.3	2.1	47
Averages	43.9	39.7	9.2	7.2	746*
Averages, all products and services	56.5	28.7	9.5	5.3	2,339*

*Total

Note: Pending cases excluded, six categories, each with fewer than 13 resolved complaints, are not listed in the table but are included in the totals. They are radios; air conditioners; lamps; pots, pans, and utensils; hearing aids and dentures; and legal services.

In the marketplace there is a good deal of unresolved dissatisfaction, as Exhibit V shows. Only one in four of all nonprice problems consumers perceived in their purchases were completely resolved—whether or not they complained about them. This figure ranges from a high of one in three for problems mentioned before a probe for the more expensive, frequently purchased products (problems which one can assume were relatively serious) to a low of one in five for problems mentioned after the probe for infrequently purchased products.

Substantial unremedied nonprice problems showed up in several purchase categories. Consider the following figures giving the proportions of all purchases in which a problem mentioned without prompting was not remedied:

Car repair	14.8%
Appliance repair	14.6
Car parking	13.9
Toys	12.8
Mail order goods	9.8
Clothing	9.2

It is not surprising that the state and federal government are hearing more about these cases. According to HEW's Office of Consumer Affairs, automobiles, appliances, and mail order goods represent three of the four most frequently criticized categories in correspondence that this office receives from consumers.

GROUNDS FOR PESSIMISM

The data from this study permit both an optimistic and pessimistic view of business's performance in respect to complaints. The optimist might offer these views:

Hasn't business done well! In only 10 of every 100 purchases did people mention a nonprice problem before being pushed by interviewers. Half of these problems had been voiced to business by consumers, and probably many of those that hadn't were either invalid or of the type that management couldn't really be expected to fix. Finally, almost 60% of the complaints made were completely resolved, and a further 10% resulted in at least partial satisfaction. Certainly, this performance is hard to improve.

On the other hand, the business critic might say, "Business has a long way to go!" In only 7 purchases out of 10 were consumers completely mollified. More than half the sample had had at least one nonprice purchase problem. And when they did have problems, in 6 out of 10 cases customers were not encouraged to express their dissatisfaction to management. When they did, only in a little more than half the cases were they fully satisfied. The business community, which often proclaims "satisfaction guaranteed," resolved only 25% of all nonprice problems. In some categories like car and appliance repair and mail order goods, as many as 1 in 7 purchases resulted in a serious unresolved consumer problem.

The last two figures and the pattern of responses sway us toward the pessimistic view of business performance. While we cannot claim that our figures have no upward or downward bias, business should be alarmed at the amount of

Exhibit V
Proportions of all perceived problems that were satisfactorily resolved

	Infrequently Purchased Products		Frequently Purchased Products		Services		Average	
Before probe	32.8%	(678)	29.1%	(1,281)	21.3%	(912)	27.6%	(2,871)
After probe	25.5	(740)	19.6	(1,409)	23.3	(682)	22.0	(2,831)
All problems	29.1	(1,418)	29.1	(2,690)	22.3	(1,594)	24.9	(5,702)

Note: This exhibit includes only instances in which the presence or absence of a probe was ascertained.

unresolved dissatisfaction that apparently exists in the marketplace. Those who voice complaints are activists who challenge the system head on. If their complaints remain unsatisfied, presumably they will lead the chorus of criticism about the business system and its unresponsiveness to consumers' needs.

Those who don't bother to complain at all may represent an even more potentially explosive group. People who are upset but who take no action, say three researchers, are "a frustrated and even possibly an alienated group of consumers. . . . In frustration, they direct their anger toward the system, viewing both business and government in very negative terms."*

What can business do? First, companies should make consumers' satisfaction data of the type reported here an integral part of their information systems. Such data can pay off (particularly after repeated measures that permit plots of trends) in keeping management aware of otherwise undiscovered attitudes toward the company's products and services.

Whether a consumer perceives a problem depends in part on his or her expectations. Many managers who handle complaints find that a significant source of them is salesmen who promise too much for the product or service. Complaint managers, however, are often poorly situated organizationally or lack adequate organizational clout to be able to curb such practices.

The reduction of consumers' complaints is sufficiently important to continued market success to warrant the formation of a top-level complaint review committee, including senior marketing, production, accounting, and service personnel made responsible (and given the authority) for improving performance. This committee, we believe, could significantly improve coordination while lodging responsibility with those whose word carries the most weight.

Inasmuch as half the serious complaints are never mentioned to business, the obvious solution is to *market* the complaint-handling system to customers. Business should encourage customers to speak out when things go wrong—and make it more convenient for them to do so. Through advertising, point-of-sale promotion, and product inserts, business can tell customers that it wants to know when things go wrong. Toll-free telephone numbers help facilitate responses. This recommendation, of course, flies in the face of conventional business thinking: don't encourage complaints; take care of them if they appear, but more complaints mean more costs.

Another avenue for improving complaint performance is in dealing with the complaints received. Careful, speedy procedures to handle letters, telephone calls, and even visits can improve consumers' satisfaction. Many complaint managers believe that the faster a communication is handled, the more satisfied the customer is, whatever the problem or the outcome. Many of these managers are substituting telephone response systems for elaborate, written follow-up systems. A telephone-based procedure is not only more effective but also cheaper.

---

*Rex H. Warland, Robert O. Herrmann, and Jane Willits, "Dissatisfied Consumers: Who Gets Upset and Who Takes Action," *Journal of Consumer Affairs,* Winter 1975, p. 161.

Our last recommendation concerns company attitude. Unfortunately, complaining consumers are often looked on by business as being "the enemy." This in part explains why management may not encourage complaints; encouragement invites the enemy to your doorstep. Those who deal with complaints may technically take care of the particular problem but still leave the customer angry: the "enemy" mentality begins with the assumption that the customer is wrong.

But as we have tried to show here, the customer with a problem is not part of a coterie of chronic gripers: if he or she remains unsatisfied, the cost to business in sales, directly and through word of mouth, could be substantial. To gain full value from the voice of the consumer, the company must want to hear from him and must believe that he is right until proved otherwise.

This positive attitude must first be adopted at the top because the staff will act only when it believes that top management is fully committed. It is a commitment we believe management must adopt if it is to maximize its success in the increasingly "consumerist" business environment of the 1970's and 1980's.

Manufacturers' Malpractice

In this litigious society, more and more injured parties are suing manufacturers and collecting large settlements, sometimes with the help of technical "hired guns." The result has been soaring premiums for product liability insurance.

E. Patrick McGuire

Despite exhortations on billboards, bumper stickers, and company bulletin boards to live and work safely, most Americans remain only dimly aware of the toll that accidents exact of our society. To take the extreme case, accidents are *the* leading cause of death among all Americans ages one through 38, and the fourth leading cause of all deaths. And the true economic cost of accident-caused injuries and deaths is impossible to calculate.

Many accidents are caused not by an individual's carelessness or stupidity (like lighting a match to look into an auto gas tank), but by a product. Defectively designed or produced products are estimated to kill 30,000 Americans each year. If a manufactured product—either a consumer product or a tool in a factory—is judged to be the culprit in an accident, its manufacturer faces the specter of being held financially responsible for the resulting damages.

From *Across the Board,* Vol. XIII, No. 11, November, 1976. Reprinted by Special Permission of The Conference Board.

Product liability is the manufacturer's counterpart of the physician's liability for "medical malpractice." But unlike the latter issue, which has generated considerable public attention and debate, product liability considerations remain less well known. Ironically, the potential economic impact of product liability costs on the American economy far out-shadows that of costs relating to medical malpractice.

Responding to mounting complaints from the business sector that rising premiums for product liability insurance were threatening even the survival of some firms, the Office of the President earlier this year directed the Bureau of Domestic Commerce to conduct a quick survey. Among other things, it concluded:

"1. Exposure to product liability claims is extensive and increasing for many manufacturers and distributors.

"2. Insurance coverage is not available for a number of significant industry sectors or available only at large premium increments.

"3. For some industries, with extensive product liability exposure, the increase in insurance premium rates for product liability is more than *tenfold* [emphasis added] over the past year or two."*

These observations held few surprises. The cost of liability insurance for coverage other than auto-related accidents has been climbing steeply for a long time. It reached the $1 billion mark in 1961, rose to $2 billion by 1970, jumped to $3 billion by 1974 and, according to some estimates, could reach $30 billion by 1980.†

No overall statistic, however, gives much hint of the serious consequences within individual companies and industries—especially those most susceptible to product liability claims (i.e., those most likely to be sued by product users—either workers or consumers—regardless of their safety or accident-prevention efforts). At the very least, such firms are already paying much more for their product liability insurance, as well as for associated claims, settlements and awards arising out of product-related accidents.

Some firms are finding it increasingly difficult or even impossible to obtain insurance coverage. For example, the Safeguard Manufacturing Company of Woodbury, Connecticut, lost its product liability coverage even though it had been paying the equivalent of more than 10% of its gross sales for such coverage. Apparently, in appraising Safeguard's product line (industrial safety devices attached to machines) and potential liability risks associated with similar product lines, insurers had decided that the company was no longer insurable. In a few extreme cases, firms like the Harvir Manufacturing Company of St. Paul (a producer of power press equipment), unable to assure customers that they had product liability insurance, have been forced to liquidate.

---

*Special report on product liability prepared by the Bureau of Domestic Commerce, U.S. Dept. of Commerce, March 1976, p. 50.

†Special Insurance Report–1975," *Forbes*, Sept. 1, 1975, p. 63.

The more typical consequences for manufacturing companies, however, have been increased outlays for product liability claims and insurance coverage, and the need then to pass these costs on to their customers in higher prices. Often, a company must run faster just to stay in place. Orville R. Mertz, chief executive officer for Koehring Company, maker of construction machinery, pointed this out last fall. "For Koehring," he said, "product liability insurance premiums have jumped nearly 200 times what they were just 12 years ago! To put it another way, this year it may well take $30 million of our sales merely to earn a profit sufficient to pay the premiums for our product liability and property damage insurance."*

Koehring's experience is not unique. The Department of Commerce survey found numerous capital equipment manufacturers similarly reporting substantial increases in their product liability insurance premiums. Among the makers of woodworking machinery surveyed, for example, such premiums were said to have risen from an average of $2,100 in 1970, to $10,500 in 1975 and to $29,000 in 1976. One packaging machinery company, with annual sales of $10 million, reputedly paid $110,000 in premiums in 1974; $268,000 in 1975; and $385,000 in 1976. In yet another case, premiums paid by a producer of printing machinery with annual sales of $170 million had risen by 1975 to $700,000 per year — or $1.40 per $1,000 of sales.

In the cases of the industrial products manufacturers cited above, the rise in their product liability insurance rates was caused by claims for on-the-job accidents.

Such claims are rapidly on the rise — and that is ironic, for the rise comes at a time when U.S. industry has been providing a safer work environment. According to the U.S. Department of Health, Education and Welfare, workplace accidents actually declined by 19% in the period 1963 through 1973. And a recent McGraw-Hill survey found industry planning to invest about $3.2 billion this year in employee safety and health measures, a 17% jump over such investments last year. Projections for the years immediately ahead indicate that manufacturing companies will probably be allocating about 3.3% of all their planned capital investments in responding to employee safety and health requirements.

But why the rapid rise in product liability costs? First, more Americans than ever before are resorting to the courts to obtain redress for their grievances. Furthermore, consumers' expectations for the products they buy, and their ideas about the responsibilities of manufacturers for making products safe, have shifted dramatically. At the same time have come changes in the judicial climate, encompassing principally the doctrine of strict liability in tort, which is said to be abetting individuals' efforts to gain recompense for product-related injuries incurred at home or work.

Under the now-prevailing doctrine, an individual seeking damages for product injuries need not prove either that the product's manufacturer had been

---

*"Social and Legal Changes in Product Liability and Property Damage Claims," *Koehring News,* autumn, 1975.

negligent or had violated an expressed or implied warranty. The producer can be held liable simply by reason of having produced an inherently dangerous or defective product. As one analyst has pointed out, "The liability of the manufacturer does not stem from either contractual or promissory understanding; instead liability and tort arises from the fact that the courts are imposing a social responsibility on manufacturers and sellers."

The size of the awards won by plaintiffs in injury cases is increasing —another factor influencing the filing of product liability suits. Since the 1960's the $1 million award level was exceeded at least fifty times. Some of the major examples include:

- A jury awarded $1.2 million to a 12-year-old boy with brain damage suffered on a school field trip. The boy had caught his foot on a tree root, tripped, and struck his head.

- A 16-year-old boy was awarded $1.8 million for sustaining permanent paralysis while attempting to score in a baseball game by diving headfirst into the opposing catcher. The school board was found guilty for having failed to warn the player against the hazard.

- A Maryland youth was given $7 million for injuries received after diving into a swimming pool from an allegedly defective diving board. And a 19-year-old California boy, diving off a railroad trestle and sustaining paraplegia, received $3 million from the railroad that failed to post a "no diving" warning.

In the industrial sector, workers lose limbs and sight from improperly maintained machines, or even machines that—because of improper use—topple over on them. They sue the producers of the machines. Their employers' contributory negligence is not a defense that has proved effective for the equipment producers.

And it should be remembered that the consumer's negligent use of the product is also not an effective defense against product liability actions. For example, one man lifted his rotary mower to waist height and attempted to use it as a hedge trimmer before severely injuring himself. A housewife reputedly immersed an electric fry pan in a basin of water in an attempt to heat the water. In both instances the product manufacturer was sued. He collected, she didn't. The literature of product liability litigation is replete with instances of product abuse or misuse.

Aiding plaintiffs in winning larger settlements is a growing army of "hired guns"—technical specialists, such as physicians, engineers, economists, retained by attorneys to support their clients' claims in court. The use of such experts is a source of some controversy. It has been argued that at least some expert witnesses are capable of "prostituting" themselves in exchange for their testimony fees. The general counsel of one manufacturing company, for example, asserts that "these witnesses will swear to both sides of a technical question, depending on who's paying them."

A significant portion of product liability cases, as mentioned earlier, arises from product injuries sustained at work. (Accidents at work cause one death every 37 minutes and one injury every 13 seconds, according to the National Safety Council.)

Jeffrey O'Connell, professor of law at the University of Illinois and an architect of no-fault insurance legislation, estimates that 30% or more of the product liability cases currently in the courts involve industrial accidents.* In theory, the cost of such accidents might be expected to be borne by workmen's compensation systems. In recent years, many injured parties have come to regard workmen's compensation awards as only partial payment.

It was back around the turn of the century that social pressures to reimburse workers for job-related accidents first became intense. In time, every state in the union adopted workmen's compensation laws. Thereafter, employers were obligated to pay employees injured on the job for their medical expenses and a portion of their lost wages, regardless of how an accident may have been caused or who was at fault. These laws, embodying the first "no-fault" provisions for liability, also protected an employer from civil suit, the theory being that an injured employee should be willing to give up the right to sue in exchange for the compensation assured for on-the-job losses. But even though employees may be proscribed by law from suing their own employers, they are in no way inhibited from suing for damages the manufacturer of any equipment involved in job injuries.

In the years immediately ahead, the issues of product liability are likely to become even more worrisome. Experts expect the costs of product liability insurance to continue to rise at a rate of nearly 50% per year. Nevertheless, insurers say their premium income is insufficient to pay claims against their policies and to establish the reserves required to deal with future product liability suits which are certain to be filed. Indeed, they assert, there is a great deal of uncertainty as to the amount of reserves they will need. As T. Lawrence Jones, president of the American Insurance Association, has said, "Experience—the hallmark of insurance operations—is no guide. Most companies are facing unparalleled financial pressures. Different kinds of pressures are being exerted by legislatures, regulators, and the purchasers of our products, in both commercial and personal lines."

It also appears likely that, given projections of present cost trends, the insurers themselves could be in real trouble. According to the Department of Commerce survey, property and casualty insurance underwriters experienced losses of all kinds amounting to $4.2 billion in 1975, following losses in the previous year of $2.6 billion which had been coupled with a $6 billion capital loss in the bear market. And the same study went on to explain that capital and surplus accounts, the reserves used to underwrite product liability protection, have been so severely depleted as a result of losses as to seriously impair the industry's capacity to provide such protection to both new and existing customers.

While it is clear that the casualty insurance industry is experiencing substantial losses, it is not equally clear that rises in insurance premium rates have been based on a particular company's—or even an industry's—claims-and-loss experience. For example, in the recreational vehicles sector, the counsel for this industry's trade association told the Senate hearing that a survey of their membership

---

*"Bypassing the Lawyers," *Wall Street Journal,* 4/8/76.

had shown no appreciable rise in either the number of claims or damage payments, yet premium costs had soared by several hundred percent in two years.* In other cases, manufacturers report that although they have never had a product liability claim, let alone a damages payment, they have lost their insurance or faced staggering increases in premium costs.

High insurance rates could mean that more and more manufacturers will have to operate without insurance protection. In turn, this could mean that, in some instances, major product liability claims of plaintiffs—and even court awards to them—might exceed the capital asset value of the company they were suing. This suggests that more than a few companies might be forced to liquidate in order to pay off. If there were a large number of uninsured companies, this would also hold out the prospect of less money going to individuals injured by defective products. As it is, Professor O'Connell estimates that only 37.5% of every product liability premium dollar ever finds its way into the pockets of injured parties. The remaining 62.5%, he says, goes for insurance overhead and legal fees incurred by both the manufacturers and the insurance carriers.

The burden of the product liability crisis may be most heavily felt by small business. In recent testimony before the Senate Select Committee on Small Business (September 7, 1976), witness after witness recounted the difficulties of even obtaining product liability insurance, let alone paying the soaring cost of such protection. Increasingly, smaller companies are "going self-insured." But self-insured is, in a majority of instances, a synonym for uninsured. Self-insurance involves the establishment of contingency funds that can be drawn on to pay injury claims. But such funds are not being established. Indeed, current tax law, which requires that such funds be established with after-tax dollars, makes the setting up of such reserves a financial impossibility for most small firms.

The inability to obtain product liability insurance has, according to the Senate testimony, been responsible for the failure of several small manufacturers and the pace of such involuntary closures is likely to accelerate this year and next as many insurance policies run out and cannot be renewed. In the consumer goods sector, inability to provide major retailers with assurance that a producer has product liability coverage results in lost sales and cancelled purchase orders. Lack of such insurance can put some manufacturers out of business within months.

There are still other consequences, less obvious but no less serious. Traditional producers of certain kinds of products that automatically carry above-average product liability risks may, in some cases, decide to abandon such elements of their business. There are already instances of this in the sporting goods and toy industries (see box on page 312). One worry is that such abdications from a market lessen competition and could leave the field to producers less concerned about product safety, and possibly uninsured as well.

---

*Testimony of David J. Humphreys, general counsel, Recreational Vehicle Industry Association, to Senate Select Committee on Small Business, Washington, D.C., September 7, 1976.

The recent flap over the preparation of swine-flu vaccine underscores manufacturers' concerns. In a telegram to President Ford, chairman E. Burke Giblin of Parke-Davis & Company, one of the vaccine manufacturers, stated: "Our company is more than willing to produce the [swine-flu] vaccine for the government [inoculation] program. However, we are placed in an untenable position when we are requested to supply influenza vaccine to be used in a mass immunization program without any insurance coverage or other liability protection." Finally, under mounting time pressure, the government agreed to become the insurer of last resort.

Whether the Administration's Product Liability Task Force will quickly turn up promising possibilities for government action at the Federal level remains to be seen. Actually, the only thing on which nearly all observers agree is that there can be no single solution to the nation's product liability dilemma. No proposed legislative remedy, including provision for no-fault product liability coverage, is likely to remove it. Further, it is at the state level that many laws and potential laws affecting product liability are to be found.

As for legislative action to reduce the manufacturer's burden of product liability expense, there are conceivable instances where the Federal government might step in as an underwriter or reinsurer of last resort (as in the swine-flu vaccine). But serious doubts have been raised that Congress would or could underwrite product liability insurance for most manufacturers.

Some observers say that both insurers and manufacturers must act together to educate the public and lawmakers about the costs of product liability, and also to press for the elimination of what they regard as some of the "most unreasonable" aspects of current laws pertaining to product liability. Among the steps suggested: binding arbitration of product liability claims, which proponents say would reduce litigation and probably result in a higher percentage of claims dollars being recovered by injured parties.

Business interests are being advised as well to press for some restriction on the open-ended statute of limitations which prevails in many states and allows plaintiffs to sue for injuries resulting from the use of machinery that could be decades old. Such changes, however, would probably be opposed by labor and consumer groups on the grounds that the result would be to discriminate against employees working in plants using older equipment. Also, it could be argued that shortening the statute of limitations would run contrary to a philosophy which holds liability to exist essentially in tort rather than in some contractual relationship.

There have been suggestions, too, that it would help if workers' compensation laws in the various states were to be amended to increase the maximum benefits for accidents arising from workers' use of equipment or materials. Part of the rationale is that this might remove some of the need for litigation in jurisdictions where workmen's compensation payments have been inadequate to cover full damages resulting from injury. To some extent, action in this direction is already taking place. Thirty-two states have increased workers' compensation benefits during 1975. And the proposed Williams-Javits bill would tend to increase and standardize benefits throughout the states. The bill would also provide protection for the 12 million American workers (principally farm and domestic workers) out of a total of 85 million who are not now covered by workers' compensation laws.

In the long run, efforts to make products and factories safer could, of course, have the most beneficial impact of all on the product liability picture. The results won't come overnight, but dramatic gains in time could reduce the feedstock for product liability costs.

There are reports of some promising beginnings in this direction. Within the chemical industry, for example, the Dow Chemical Company is said to have tripled its safety program budget and mobilized over 600 employees in what it called a "monumental effort" that included preparing of complete safety profiles on 1,100 company products. Union Carbide reportedly lowered its industrial accident frequency rates 60% between 1969 and 1974. DuPont has been sharing its expertise in work safety techniques with other firms through a safety management consulting service. (See *Business Week*, 4/21/73, p. 82.)

A great deal hinges perhaps on the attitude of management in individual companies toward product safety issues. To protect the company and the public in general, personnel in all key functions—marketing, product design, production, etc.—must be made continually aware, and in more specific ways, of the need to make the company's products as nearly "idiot proof" as they can reasonably be expected to be.

The Case of the Football Helmet

In a perverse way the product liability issue may turn out to be one of the most anti-consumer forces yet encountered within our economy. There are several contributing factors behind this, but the most important center about the impact that the crisis is having, and is likely to have, on consumers' choices in the marketplace and in the quality of products they are able to obtain. Recently, a jury awarded $5.3 million to an injured high school football player. The culprit was supposedly a poorly designed football helmet, although it was not clearly established that the injured party had even been wearing the helmet in question. The helmet producer, who supplies most of the NFL teams, is likely to either go out of business or drop this line of sporting goods. And faced with the possibility of loss of that magnitude, it is doubtful that too many other companies will wish to produce football helmets. This same effect is being noted in several product categories.

As reputable, insured producers of consumer goods drop certain lines, consumers will have less buying choice, prices will rise, and certain product lines will be dominated by only a few producers—those able to absorb the losses and pass the resultant costs on to the consumer.

QUESTIONS FOR DISCUSSION

1. "There are several definitions of consumerism in the literature. This generally reflects the looseness of the movement in terms of direction. Perhaps the most appropriate are those that recognize the disproportionate distribution of power between consumer and marketer." Explain and discuss.

2. The rise of consumerism has been attributed to many reasons. Some of those revolve about changes in the law, some are related to increasing education, some to changing social and economic standards. Discuss and evaluate the various contributing factors.

3. Discuss some of the ways in which the growing consumerism movements are manifesting themselves in the marketplace.

4. Define and discuss the substance and actual or potential effects of the various pieces of consumer legislation passed since the early 1960's. Are there any unintended effects?

5. Evaluate Weidenbaum's argument that higher prices caused by regulation "represent a 'hidden tax' which is shifted from the taxpayer to the consumer."

6. Review and discuss some of the recommended business responses to the consumerist movements. How far should a firm go in responding to the call for consumer protection?

7. What is the nature of the findings that made Andreasen and Best pessimistic about the quality of business response to consumer complaints? Do you agree with their interpretations of the data?

SELECTED READINGS

Aaker, D. A., and G. S. Day, "Corporate responses to consumerism pressures," *Harvard Business Review,* November–December, 1972.

Byington, S. J., "Perspectives in product safety," *Professional Safety,* May, 1977.

"Consumer Protection: What's at issue," *Nation's Business,* June, 1977.

Day, G. S., and D. A. Aaker, "A guide to consumerism," *Journal of Marketing,* July, 1970.

Herrmann, R. O., "Consumerism: Its goals, organization, and future," *Journal of Marketing,* October, 1970.

Jones, M. G., "The consumer interest: The role of public policy," *California Management Review,* Fall, 1973.

Kotler, P., "What consumerism means for marketers," *Harvard Business Review,* May–June, 1972.

Lambert, Z. V., and F. W. Kniffin, "Consumer discontent: A social perspective," *California Management Review,* Fall, 1975.

McGuire, E. P., "What's ahead in product safety?", *The Conference Board Record,* August, 1976.

Mechling, "Is the consumer movement waning?" *Public Relations Journal,* November, 1976.

Olander, F., and H. Lindhoff, "Consumer action research: A review of the consumerism literature and suggestions for new directions in research," *Social Science Information,* 1975.

"Product liability — The search for solutions," *Nation's Business,* June, 1977.

Rosenberg, L. J., "Retailers' responses to consumerism," *Business Horizons,* October, 1975.

Weaver, P. H., "The hazards of trying to make consumer products safer," *Fortune,* July, 1975.

Webster, F., "Does business misunderstand consumerism?" *Harvard Business Review,* September–October, 1973.

Weidenbaum, M. L., "The high cost of government regulation," *Business Horizons,* August, 1975.

Case

HASBRO INDUSTRIES, INC.*

Hasbro Industries, Inc., is a consumer products manufacturer and one of the ten largest toy manufacturers in the United States. In the fall of 1972 it faced certain consumer pressures, many of which have been strongly felt by Hasbro and other toy companies in the past. The Federal Trade Commission, Food and Drug Administration, Federal Communications Commission, Consumers' Union, and parents groups were continuing to pose challenges to the toy industry, particularly in the area of product safety and promotional techniques.

Company Background

Hasbro Industries, Inc., began in Rhode Island in 1926. Originally the firm was engaged in the textile business, and in the early 1930's the company wrapped school pencil-boxes in cloth. In the 1940's the company entered both the pencil-manufacturing and toy-making industries.

Hasbro has grown substantially over the years. The company now employs a permanent labor force in its toy operations of approximately 2750 persons, about 78 percent of whom are engaged in production, and about 600 in its school-supplies and pencil-manufacturing operations.

The tremendous growth of Hasbro is largely a result of changes in the company's management and marketing approaches. These included assigning responsibility for all day-to-day operations of the

---

*This case was modified from the original form by Dr. David Loudon and Dr. Albert Della Bitta, both of the University of Rhode Island.

firm to Stephen Hassenfeld—Hasbro's 30-year-old executive vice president and the third generation of the founding family—and his introduction into the company of a new, young group of executives. Most of the new executives were drawn from outside the toy industry and outside Rhode Island.

According to Steve Hassenfeld, who recruited the new management team, "Five years ago we were what Wall Street would call a small family business. We've worked hardest lately in getting the kind of management team a small family business doesn't have."

One major result was that Hasbro diversified into new fields: children's television (Romper Room), day-care centers, and housewares. Together with its toy and pencil business, these operations have made Hasbro a small conglomerate. Recent financial performance for the company is given in Exhibit 1.

Hasbro's Toys

The company designs, manufactures, and markets a broad line of toys, dolls, games and accessories, designed for children of different age groups. Over 90 percent of the company's toy sales result from the sale of items retailing at prices from $1 to $10.

Because the company's toy business is seasonal, shipments during the second half of each calendar year are much greater than shipments during the first half. During the first half, Hasbro produces toys for inventory, largely to satisfy orders calling for later delivery and, to a lesser extent, in anticipation of future orders.

Hasbro seeks to avoid large amounts of unsold toys, after Christmas and after fads; therefore the company pursues the "promotional staple," that is, a toy that requires only moderate advertising to sell well all year round, year after year.

Hasbro stresses the marketing of product groups bearing recognizable names rather than individual toy items, since advertising costs are not substantially greater for a whole line than for one toy.

The company's toy line now consists of approximately 450 items, the principal categories of which are the following:

Preschool toys, including the ROMPER ROOM line, introduced in 1970, CAPTAIN KANGAROO'S WOODEN TOYS, introduced in 1972, and YOUR BABY line of infant playthings, introduced in 1972;

Action toys, including the G. I. JOE ADVENTURE TEAM and accessories, introduced in 1964, and SCREAM'N' DEMONS motorcycles, introduced in 1971;

Dolls, including the WORLD OF LOVE dolls and accessories, introduced in 1971; and

Craft sets, including the ARTS AND CRAFTS TODAY line, introduced in 1971.

EXHIBIT 1
Sales and earnings for Hasbro, 1967–1971

	Net Sales (In Thousands of Dollars)				
Line of Business	*1967*	*1968*	*1969*	*1970*	*1971*
Toys	$27,156 73%	$30,234 74%	$32,252 72%	$32,053 71%	$53,570 79%
School Supplies	9,863 27	10,727 26	11,954 27	12,309 27	13,228 20
Nursery Schools	—	—	—	61 0	163 0
Other	—	—	593 1	713 2	787 1
Totals	$37,019	$40,961	$44,799	$45,136	$67,748

	Earnings before Income Taxes (In Thousands of Dollars)				
Line of Business	*1967*	*1968*	*1969*	*1970*	*1971*
Toys	$ 504 74%	$ 1,483 99%	$(2,012) (105)%	$ 878 133%	$ 2,925 123%
School Supplies	177 26	15 1	63 3	(48) (7)	93 4
Nursery Schools	—	—	—	(189) (29)	(473) (20)
Other	—	—	36 2	19 3	(174) (7)
Totals	$ 681	$ 1,498	$(1,913)	$ 660	$ 2,371

Hasbro also produces a substantial volume of staple items, including chess and checker sets, doctor's and nurse's kits, banks, and other items such as its Mr. Potato Head and Lite-Brite toys.

In 1969 Hasbro effected a "repositioning" of G. I. Joe, a toy which accounts for a significant share of the company's volume. The toy became more adventure-oriented and less a military figure. The reason for the image change was the apparent waning interest in military toys. At the peak of its popularity in 1965, G. I. Joe had sales of $23 million, but by 1968 the category was producing only $4.8 million in sales. After the repositioning in 1969, the G. I. Joe Adventure Team and related accessories reassumed its importance within the industry, and in 1971 accounted for approximately $12.5 million in toy sales.

In 1970, Hasbro introduced the Romper Room preschool line, in an attempt, as Steve Hassenfeld puts it, "to upgrade the quality level of the products that we were then manufacturing." This line, which presently consists of over 65 items, accounted for approximately 22 percent of net toy sales in 1971.

Manufacturing and importing

Hasbro manufactures most of its toy products from basic raw materials such as plastic and wood and has elaborate injection-molding, blow-molding, heat-sealing, box-making, and printing equipment. In addition, the company manufactures most of its own dies, jigs, and fixtures, but purchases molds from independent sources. Independent contractors are used from time to time to supplement the firm's own molding capacity. Certain items are purchased in finished form from other manufacturers in the United States; and Hasbro also purchases partially and totally finished items from manufacturers in Hong Kong, Taiwan, and Japan.

Hasbro's quality-assurance department has grown faster than any other department in the company; and it, along with the marketing department, has been given control over product quality. Both have the authority to shut down any production line which either of them feels is not turning out significantly high-quality products.

Product testing and test marketing

One problem for the toy industry has been the conflict between the desire to maintain competitive secrecy and the need for test marketing of new products.

Hasbro began several years ago to test market its new products. At the time this decision was made Steve Hassenfeld stated, "We're tired of having made mistakes because of not going into test markets. We're not worried about knock-offs. We have a six-month tooling lead. The big companies won't copy a $2 or $3 item."

Product quality and "playability" is an important concern for Hasbro. The company utilizes laboratory tests of its products and also observes children at play with the items—the latter serves as much to determine how well the children like a certain toy as it does to test the product quality and durability. The company also interviews parents to obtain their viewpoints.

Promotion

Hasbro advertises its toy products extensively on children's network television programs. The company also utilizes commercials on local television stations in the more important consumer markets. In 1971, Hasbro spent approximately $5,700,000 in its toy advertising and sales-promotion program, nearly all of which was used for television advertising. The amount spent is expected to increase significantly in 1972. Hasbro advertises a few specifically selected items in its product groups. Last year, product groups which the firm advertised accounted for approximately 80 percent of the company's net toy sales. The remainder of 1971 toy sales included staple items which sell from year to year, and items promoted in prior years.

In utilizing television advertising to promote its toys and games to final consumers, Hasbro has advertised in the past on such varied shows as the "Tonight" show and "H. R. Pufnstuf." The company has also considered using CATV—cable television—as one possible solution to the commercial clutter on network television. In addition, Hasbro uses color inserts in Sunday newspaper comics sections in its major markets.

The company's products are frequently utilized in premium programs. For example, Borden's has offered G.I. Joe to promote sales of its Dutch Chocolate mix, instant coffee, and malted milk.

Hasbro inaugurated the industry's first incentive program involving trips and merchandise prizes for jobbers and jobber salesmen.

Industry Background and Competitive Situation

Sales by U.S. toy manufacturers increased to over $2.3 billion in 1971, from about $800 million in 1960. Shipments rose only 4.7 percent in 1971, however, compared to an annual growth rate of almost 10 percent in the late 1960's. (See Exhibits 2 and 3.)

Success in the toy industry largely reflects a particular company's ability to respond to changing shifts in buying preferences through development of new products. The toy industry is rather volatile because most manufacturers change a large segment of their product lines each year in an attempt to find a big-selling item. Moreover, the sales pattern is highly seasonal, with the Christmas selling season accounting for over 50 percent of retail toy volume. In attempts to provide greater earnings stability and new growth opportunities, while smoothing out the seasonal aspects of the toy business, most of the leading manufacturers have diversified into other areas. Meanwhile, large food companies have moved into the toy market.

EXHIBIT 2

Toy industry sales 1965–1971 (in millions of dollars)

Year	Manufacturers' Sales	Retail Sales*
1971	$2,351	$3,600
1970	2,259	3,400
1969	2,041	3,000
1968	1,824	2,700
1967	1,560	2,600
1966	1,420	2,400
1965	1,304	2,200

*Estimated

SOURCE: Toy Manufacturers of America, Inc.

EXHIBIT 3

Sales of selected toy manufacturers (in millions of dollars)

Company	Year				
	1967	1968	1969	1970	1971
Mattel	154.2	210.9	288.6	357.9	272.2
General Mills	n.a.	n.a.	91.7	104.1	148.7
Milton Bradley	43.0	69.4	72.9	90.1	109.7
Ideal	49.3	52.2	61.7	75.1	70.9
Quaker Oats	n.a.	n.a.	n.a.	34.7	69.0
Aurora	n.a.	n.a.	n.a.	n.a.	30–40
Kenner	n.a.	n.a.	n.a.	n.a.	18–20

SOURCE: Moody's and Standard & Poor's

The toy industry will probably remain a highly competitive field. The large publicly held companies which are financially strong should continue to secure an increasing share of the consumer dollar spent for toys. These firms have the capital and management expertise necessary to develop and then aggressively advertise a broad and constantly changing product line. However, the changing social-economic patterns developing in the U.S., particularly consumer demands for safer toys and low-key approach to television advertising, are presenting major challenges to the industry.

Thus, an uninterrupted growth rate for toy manufacturers may be difficult to sustain, particularly for promotional toy producers. The future merchandising outlook for promotional toys in the U.S. is clouded by the consumer pressure to tone down television advertising and to ban unsafe toys. In addition, a decline is projected in the television-oriented 5-to-14 age group. Approximately 40.21 million children were in the age group in 1971, but a decline to 37.37 million in 1975 is projected by the Department of Commerce, with a decrease to

36.48 million in 1980. However, with the number of children under five years of age expected to rise from 17.30 million in 1971 to approximately 20.51 million in 1980, the preschool age group should continue to be one of the fastest-growing market segments over the balance of the 1970's.

The trend toward smaller families, along with the projected rise in upper-income families, is expected to produce steady increases in the average yearly expenditure for toys per child. In 1971, the average annual expenditure on toys for children under 15 years old was $62.50, in contrast to $60.55 in 1970, $55.00 in 1969, and $49.50 in 1968.

An important structural transformation has taken place within the industry in the past few years. There has been a trend toward larger companies, with about 40 percent of industry sales now accounted for by the ten largest manufacturers.

Consumerism

Various facets of toy marketing have come under increasing criticism over the past few years. The areas of major concern to toy producers are those relating to product safety and advertising.

Product safety

The U.S. Public Health Service has estimated that there are about 700,000 injuries involving toys every year. Because of congressional reaction to dangerous toys, toy products are now subject to the provisions of the Federal Child Protection and Toy Safety Act of 1969. Under this legislation, the Secretary of Health, Education, and Welfare may prohibit the marketing of items intended for use by children, which, after appropriate proceedings, have been determined to be hazardous. In addition, the marketing of items which are deemed imminently hazardous to the public health and safety may be barred by the Secretary for limited periods without a hearing. Furthermore, manufacturers may be required to repurchase hazardous items and reimburse certain expenses, even if such items were manufactured and sold prior to the adoption of the Act. From time to time the government has issued regulations which affect the manufacture of toys, specifically with respect to such aspects as the lead content of paint and the classification of electrically operated toys. Regulations have been proposed affecting other aspects of toy manufacture. However, Hasbro is uncertain as to what effect such regulations, if finally adopted, will have on its business or on the entire toy industry.

Hasbro did not anticipate that some of its products would draw government and consumer criticism. For example, the company's Javelin Darts (one of a number of lawn dart games then on the market) would come under government fire as a hazardous toy. Another product, Super-Dough, drew a warning to toy buyers from *Consumer*

Reports. The product contained an elaborate instruction sheet, along with warnings that the product was not for internal consumption and that children with allergies could undergo serious reactions. Hasbro removed both of these toys from the market.

In responding to the issue of dangerous products, Toy Manufacturers of America, the industry association, has officially approved a set of safety guidelines. However, because of the huge number of products involved, the organization will not undertake the testing of each separate product in order to issue a seal of compliance.

In order to maintain and improve the safety of its toy products, Hasbro has instituted more extensive screening and quality-control procedures. Nevertheless, there can be no assurance that the firm's products will not be investigated by the government or recalled from the market.

Violent toys

The marketing of war toys has elicited opposition from some consumer groups. The American Toy Fair has been picketed by various anti-war-toy groups in the past few years. For example, a group of mothers concerned about the psychological development of their children has picketed the fair demanding that war toys be taken off the market. Concern over such toys is expressed by these groups because of the potentially harmful influence which they feel such toys may have on the child's development.

The toy industry's position has been that war toys don't cause war—they only reflect it. In other words, the industry association feels that violence is learned from human example, not from things.

Nevertheless, in deference to the antiwar sentiment, Hasbro's G. I. Joe, which used to be outfitted in military dress, has taken on an adventure theme. However, the company does maintain, in its G. I. Joe line, a replica of an Army jeep with a recoilless rifle mounted on it.

Although not classified as a violent toy, a water gun which Hasbro marketed—called "Hypo Squirt"—was fashioned like a giant hypodermic needle. Even though the product had been on the market for seven years, when the drug issue developed the toy was suddenly dubbed "play junior junkie" in the press, and drew considerable criticism from the public. Hasbro withdrew the toy from the market.

Packaging

The Federal Trade Commission has spot-checked the packaging of Hasbro's toy products as part of an apparent investigation of "slack-filled" packaging practices within the toy industry. Although no action was taken by the F.T.C. against Hasbro, the company has no assurance that the packaging of some of its products does not violate F.T.C. regulations.

Advertising

Children's television advertising has come under increasing scrutiny by government and mounting criticism from retailers, parents, and consumer groups. The focal point for such concern centers around the use (or, as consumer groups term it, the misuse) of advertising on television shows aimed at children, particularly within Saturday and Sunday morning programming.

In 1970, marketers spent $75 million on network television programs. Eight companies—primarily cereal and toy manufacturers—accounted for about half of this total.

Even toy retailers have criticized the magnitude of such advertising. According to a survey conducted among 5200 toy and hobby retailers by Pepperdine College of Los Angeles and directed by Consultants to Management, Inc., toy-store operators dislike national television advertising despite the fact that such advertising of toys by manufacturers has increased the retailer's business.

According to the report, the reason for the toy retailers' dislike of television is their suspicion that the cost of television advertising is so high that manufacturers are forced to put exorbitant prices on toys, counting on the appeal of television to children to force the sale, to the ultimate disappointment of child and parent and the resentment of the latter against the retail store which sold him the overrated merchandise. Of those surveyed, seventy-seven percent of the toy store retailers and 81 percent of the discount department store and chain drug store managers felt that television advertising increased prices.

The survey reports that toy-store managers resent the fact that discount houses take advantage of the heavy television advertising of some toys to cut prices far below a reasonable retail profit (that is, from 35–45% down to 1–5%) and/or to use the items as loss leaders.

Protests have been made by parents and consumer groups concerning the nature of advertising on children's shows, as well as the extent of such promotion. One rather vocal organization in the forefront of the criticism has been ACT (Action for Children's Television), a Boston-based citizen's group that claims 2500 members and supporters.

ACT is fundamentally opposed to commercialization of television aimed at children and has argued for the elimination of advertising during such programming. The Federal Communications Commission (FCC) has instituted an Inquiry and Proposed Rule-Making Procedure in response to a petition from ACT, which requested that the FCC prohibit sponsorship and commercials on children's programs and prohibit the inclusion, use, or mention of products, services, or stores during such programs. The petition cited the Romper Room television program produced by Hasbro's subsidiary, among other programs, as being commercially oriented.

ACT argued that children were being unfairly influenced in the program's advertising through the use of Romper Room teachers who were doing the commercials. In addition, the group criticized the fact that the toys used on the program were those advertised on Romper Room.

Slightly before the ACT charges surfaced, Hasbro was taking steps to counter such criticism. The company decided that no Romper Room teacher could do a commercial for any toy product. In addition, the company stopped advertising any Romper Room toy used on the program.

At the time this action was taken, however, it did not appear to satisfy ACT. For example, early in 1971 one of ACT's directors and a mother of two stated, "I don't think Hasbro has reached the heart of the problem, which is selling to unsophisticated preschool children." By using Hasbro products on the program, she added, "they still have their commercial by having the children play with the toys on the program."

The ACT group has criticized not only Hasbro's advertising but also that of many other companies which heavily promote their products to children.

Particularly distressing to such critics are the number of advertisements typically run within children's programs shown between 7:00 A.M. and 2:00 P.M. on Saturdays and Sundays. Commercials and non-program material may amount to no more than 12 minutes per hour (down from 16 minutes), according to the Television Code Review Board of the National Association of Broadcasters. Critics have also advocated that commercials during the children's programs be clustered.

The FTC has brought action against several toy manufacturers (although not against Hasbro) for deceptive advertising practices. Hasbro attempts to comply with the principles established in these actions, as well as with the rules promulgated by the FTC and with the regulations prescribed by the National Association of Broadcasters.

The NAB standards for toy commercials are quite specific. Before a toy commercial can be shown on television, it must be approved by the NAB.

The FTC is expected to hold public hearings to study the impact of advertising on children and consumers. Rules or regulations, if any, which may result from the FCC or FTC investigations are likely to affect the advertising practices of Hasbro and the rest of the toy industry.

Some firms within the industry have made moves to reduce the criticism of advertising practices affecting children. For example, Ideal Toy Company, which advertised directly to children via network television, has dropped sponsorship of Saturday morning television (where the major controversy is) and now buys early weekday evening prime time.

Nielsen data indicate that 2- to 5-year-olds watch an average of 3.2 hours of television on fall Saturday mornings (8:00 A.M.–1:00 P.M.) and 6- to 11-year-olds watch 2.6 hours. However, both groups watch approximately 3.5 hours per week between 5:00–7:00 P.M. on weekdays.

Other toy marketers, such as Fisher-Price, have for some time been pursuing a strategy of targeting their message almost exclusively at parents, particularly mothers.

Hasbro had decided to continue its present policy of weekend television advertising.

One Prognosis

Although a leader can sometimes turn into a follower in a season, Steve Hassenfeld declares, with regard to Hasbro, "We believe we have the momentum that will carry us to leadership in the industry." As far as the consumer movement and its effects upon the toy industry and Hasbro are concerned, Hassenfeld remarked that, "The worst seems to be over."

8. Doing Business Abroad: Southern Africa

Southern Africa is in a turmoil. Mozambique and Angola have, within the past five years, won their independence from Portugal, but both societies are far from settled. Indeed a guerilla war is still being waged by a dissident faction within Angola. A war between blacks and whites is raging in Rhodesia, where 270,000 whites hold power over six million blacks. Namibia, the former Southwest Africa, is due to become independent within two years from its trust-territory status administered by South Africa. The question of who will govern the territory, once independence is achieved, however, is still not clear.

But the biggest problem for American business centers about the Republic of South Africa, the most prosperous and heavily industrialized country in Africa. A little over one percent of total United States overseas investment is in the Republic of South Africa—about $1.5 billion. Yet that relatively small stake in another country has created an accelerating issue for some American managers as to the appropriateness of American investment in a society with policies distasteful to most Americans.

The problem raised by South African investment revolves about the official racial policy of the South African government: *apartheid*. Apartheid (literally, separation (of the races)) encompasses a broad spectrum of laws and regulations designed to prevent whites and blacks from integrating. Officially, the policy is said to encourage separate development of the races with eventual independence in terms of a number of separate states for the black-populated areas. In fact, two black states have already been granted "independence"; but there are serious questions as to whether all the states will ever be created. Some tribes have turned down the offers of independence and most blacks who live near the major cities—and have never even visited their tribal homelands—are not happy over receiving citizenship in a state they have never seen, simply because they are members of the particular tribe of that state.

Critics of apartheid contend that the policy, which involves petty harassment as well as more serious racial restrictions, and is resulting in quite uneven development of whites and blacks, is discrimination, pure and simple, and is designed to maintain white supremacy. In fact, some of the data seems to support the critics. Whereas South African blacks are the highest paid blacks in all of Africa, they still are paid in some cases as low as one-fifth of the wage of whites for comparable work. And the independent-states project will assign only approximately 13 percent of the land to the blacks, who constitute 70 percent of the total population. Finally, even the independence plan makes no provision for the Asians and coloreds (people of mixed race).

SOUTH AFRICA: THE COUNTRY AND ITS HISTORY

South Africa is a relatively large country situated at the lower tip of Africa. The country is one of the world's leading producers of diamonds and the world's largest exporter of gold, major sources of its wealth. South Africa sits on the crossroads for the major markets of Europe and Asia, and its geographic position is strategic. Even with the Suez Canal open, major ships, which cannot navigate the Canal, must round the Cape of Good Hope at the tip of Africa.

The total population of South Africa is about 22 million, of which 4 million are white, 15 million black and 3 million Asian and colored (mixed race). The white population is divided between Afrikaaners (the descendants of the Dutch, German and Huguenot settlers (the Boers)) and English-speaking peoples.

South Africa has an interesting history. The Dutch East India Company settled the original colony in 1652 and administered the land until the British occupied the territory in 1795. Independent Boer republics, the Orange Free State and the Transvaal, were established in the 1850's; and a confederation of the Boer republics and the British colonies was attempted in the 1870's. But the British and the Boers had several irreconcilable differences, not the least among them the less liberal policy of the Boers toward the native population. In 1899, the Boer War broke out; it ended in 1902 with British occupation of the two Boer republics. In 1910, the various states (Orange Free State, Transvaal, and the former British colonies, Natal and the Cape of Good Hope) were merged into the Union of South Africa, until 1961 a self-governing dominion of the British Empire. In 1961, South Africa, under the administration of the Afrikaan Nationalist Party, withdrew from the British Commonwealth of Nations and declared itself a republic.

South Africa used to have a geographical position that isolated it from the ferment against racism and colonialism present in the rest of the African continent. Rhodesia, Mozambique, and Angola (the latter two formerly controlled by Portugal) and its own loss of control of Namibia no longer provide this isolation, so that the independence movements creep southward.

AMERICAN FIRMS IN SOUTH AFRICA

Today over 400 United States firms are involved in the South African economy (including many of the giants of American industry). One group of critics contends that this involvement bolsters an essentially racist regime, and it is demanding that U.S. firms pull out of South Africa as a means of weakening apartheid. Many corporations remain silent on the issue, hoping that the clamor will dissipate. But others respond that their presence actually benefits the black population, a position supported by another group of critics, who nevertheless, would like to see American firms take steps, beyond mere presence, to combat apartheid. Indeed, many leaders of the South African blacks take the position that the presence of the American firms is beneficial.

As in most such situations, there is probably some substance to the positions of both those who say that the presence of American firms bolsters apartheid and those who say that it benefits the black and other nonwhite populations. There is little doubt that industrial development strengthens the economic system of South Africa, nourishes self-sufficiency, and increases the state's ability to withstand external pressures. But with a limited white population, there is also no doubt that economic development means greater employment opportunities for blacks, since fewer whites are available to fill jobs.

This does not mean that, in the short run, blacks will necessarily move up to positions of social and economic power. Given South African values, however, without industrialization and commercial development, *all* jobs would be reserved for whites. In essence, the growing economy, with a limited white population, essentially forces the society to bend its racist posture when the economic growth rate is threatened by a lack of workers. Some evidence suggests that this is already occurring. To that extent, the presence of outside investment is an effective limitation to apartheid.

But the mere passive activity of presence is not sufficient to calm the protests of groups seeking to change South African policy. Critics contend that, in many cases, the personnel of foreign firms are as racist as the South Africans, and that American corporations—if they stay—should be taking positive steps to speed change in the South African society. Some firms are moving beyond mere presence and becoming actively involved. There is also some evidence to suggest that the reluctance of American banks and firms to invest further in South Africa is also having an effect. South Africa is, in the late 1970's, undergoing a prolonged recession; sustained racial violence is also undermining the economy and exacerbating the recession. Businessmen, whether through real concern for the black population or through a concern with self-interest, no longer look upon South African investments uncritically. A number of large investments have been canceled or decreased in scale.

A CASE STUDY: POLAROID IN SOUTH AFRICA

An interesting case concerning the activities of an American corporation in South Africa involved the Polaroid Corporation, the well-known manufacturer of cameras, films, sunglasses, and identification photo systems. Polaroid had no direct investment in South Africa, no plants or sales offices. The company's products were distributed by a locally owned company. Polaroid's sales through its South African subsidiary were relatively modest: $1.5 million out of a total of $500 million worldwide. But it was alleged (although it is often denied) that Polaroid film and equipment was being used for the identification photos in the passbooks carried by all nonwhites.

In the United States, Polaroid was considered a model company by social-responsibility proponents. Its work force was 10 percent black and its organizational and personnel policies were based on affirmative action long before that process became fashionable or before the United States government began requiring it from government contractors. Quite early, an all-black Volunteer Committee was established to expedite the grievances of black employees against top and middle management.

In October of 1970, a group called the Polaroid Workers' Revolutionary Movement, led by a Polaroid design photographer, staged a protest demanding that the company completely sever its ties with South Africa. Edwin Land, inventor of the original Land camera and chief executive officer of Polaroid, first banned the direct sales of film and cameras designed for identification photos to the South African government. But, rather than accede completely to the demands of the PWRM, Land dispatched an employee committee, including black employees, to South Africa to study the effects of apartheid and the role that Polaroid products played there. In late 1970, Land announced that Polaroid would continue to sell consumer film, cameras, and sunglasses to its South African affiliate, but would embark on a program to improve the lives of blacks living in South Africa. Polaroid encouraged its distributor to give equal pay for equal work and to promote blacks into supervisory positions. In addition, funds were granted to organizations to underwrite the education of South African black children.*

Other groups of Americans who have visited South Africa have come back endorsing the approach that Land took. Obviously, Polaroid's action alone is not going to have major impact, but it does offer some evidence of response by American firms to the growing expression of concerns.

The Polaroid case also offers some interesting insights into the related protest tactics and their possible effects that are no less important to managerial decision-making than the South African situation itself. Polaroid's decision cut short a threatened boycott of its products in the United States and a potential strike situation in its plants. Boycotts and strike action have become increasingly utilized weapons of activists concerned about American corporate behavior overseas. The effects of such boycotts on corporate profits as well as reputations then become important variables in decision-making. There can be little doubt that managerial responses in terms of policy changes in another country are made as much to forestall domestic challenges as they are to mitigate the conditions in the foreign country.

THE FUTURE OF U.S. INVOLVEMENT IN SOUTH AFRICA

American investment in South Africa is decreasing, relatively, and projects are either being postponed, canceled, or re-examined. The reasons for these re-examinations of investment decisions in what was formerly considered a stable and secure country which assured a very high rate of return, are many, as we have seen. First, the buffer between South Africa and the rest of Africa no longer exists; and despite the fact that the South African military is rated as the best in Africa, the possibility of continued military action exists. Second, race riots in Soweto and other black areas have injected a note of pessimism regarding the tranquil-

---

*In late 1977, Polaroid announced that it was ceasing sales to its South African affiliate after discovering that the affiliate was continuing sales of film to the South African government.

lity of South African society. Third, South Africa is in the midst of a long and painful recession, and although its trade relationships with its neighbors are intact, the dream of constant success is over. Finally, and one should not underrate this, corporations and banks may be becoming more responsive to the protests of United States race-relations organizations and church groups who are protesting the role of U.S. corporations in South Africa. It is significant that, when a group of oil companies terminated their exploration in Namibia, they cited, as reasons for pulling out, not finding any oil and the instability of the possible future government there. However, all of the companies took pains to notify the church groups who had protested the activity; that notification took place before the decisions were made public.

Few are expecting U.S. businesses to pull out of South Africa entirely, although the contemplated possibility of reducing U.S. tax credits for taxes paid there could be a significant step toward accelerating withdrawal. Further, the reduction of continued investment is distinctly possible, although the reasons for such a reduction may be entirely self-interest ones rather than the moral reasons offered by various protesting groups.

THE READINGS

Our first selection, "Doing Business with a Blacker Africa" (from *Business Week*) focuses more on the trouble spots in Southern Africa and the prospects for both accommodation and business development in that part of the continent.

The second article, "The Proper Role of U.S. Corporations in South Africa" by John Blashill (from *Fortune*) reports on some of the activities being undertaken by subsidiaries of U.S. firms to upgrade the status of South African blacks. Blashill also cites the lagging of U.S. firms even in areas where South African law allows companies wide latitude in pay and job assignments irrespective of race.

Doing Business with a Blacker Africa
At stake are billions in U.S. investments and one of the world's great storehouses of oil and vital minerals

Like a thunderstorm over the veld, profound changes are sweeping the vast subcontinent of southern Africa. The demand for racial justice—one of the great political and moral imperatives of the 20th century— is powering a drive by blacks for equality with whites in the last remaining enclaves of white minority rule in the African continent. The result, almost inevitably, will be black-dominated governments in Rhodesia and South-West Africa within the next two years and an expanding political role for blacks over a somewhat longer period in South Africa's complex society.

Reprinted from the February 14, 1977 issue of *Business Week* by special permission. © 1977 by McGraw-Hill, Inc.

For 5 million whites and 26 million nonwhites in those countries, the prospects for future prosperity and racial harmony will depend on whether the transfer of power is peaceful or violent. For the U.S., the changing politics of southern Africa creates new dangers, and new opportunities for constructive influence in the area. For U.S. companies, there will be new rules of doing business.

South-West Africa, administered as a colony by South Africa for nearly 60 years, may move toward independence soon under a formula currently being negotiated by a constitutional conference. But Rhodesia is poised on the brink of civil war following the breakdown of talks between the white minority regime of Prime Minister Ian Smith and black nationalist groups. If the guerrilla fighting in Rhodesia's borderlands continues, racial animosities will be inflamed and political extremists will attract followers throughout the region.

The strategy. U.S. Ambassador to the U.N. Andrew Young, a former black congressman from Georgia and outspoken supporter of African liberation movements, was scheduled to visit Africa this week for talks with African leaders in hopes of heading off such an outcome. The U.S. has a great deal at stake. Southern Africa is one of the world's great storehouses of vital minerals, and U.S. companies have more than $1.5 billion invested in South Africa alone. The endless string of oil tankers that rounds the Cape, carrying oil from the Persian Gulf to Europe and the U.S., underlines the area's strategic importance.

The way to assure continued access to the raw materials and the sea lanes, the Ford Administration concluded last year, is to support demands for racial equality in hopes that black governments that come to power will be friendly to the U.S. Such a policy should also pay dividends in improved relations with the rest of black Africa, a potential market of 200 million persons and an important source of basic commodities. In pursuit of this goal, former Secretary of State Henry Kissinger nudged Smith into the negotiations on a transition to majority rule in Rhodesia.

Kissinger's policy shift followed years of tacit U.S. acceptance of the status quo in southern Africa. The Carter Administration clearly intends to promote majority rule in southern Africa even more actively. Young told the Senate Foreign Relations Committee last week that he favors the use of economic sanctions as a political lever in Africa. Secretary of State Cyrus Vance followed up this week by announcing a push by the Administration to repeal the Byrd amendment, which exempts U.S. chrome importers from the U.N.-sponsored economic boycott of Rhodesia. Congress is expected to repeal the amendment. Such action will improve U.S. credibility among black Africans and will end any illusions on Smith's part that the U.S. will ultimately support him in a showdown against black nationalists.

Slim chance. Such U.S. pressures, if they bring Smith back to the conference table to negotiate a peaceful transfer of power, should benefit white Rhodesians as well as blacks. Few observers give the Smith regime any chance of surviving in a prolonged civil war against the guerrillas from the surrounding black countries.

Young also suggested ending U.S. multinational corporations' credits against U.S. income taxes for taxes paid by their subsidiaries to the South African government. Congressional sources say such a measure, designed to prod South Africa to ease its apartheid restrictions, is under consideration within the Administration. Loss of the tax credit would discourage U.S. investment that South Africa badly needs to shore up its sagging economy.

Both President Carter and Ambassador Young believe, though, that U.S. business has a constructive role to play in southern African's evolution toward racial equality. American companies, Young told BUSINESS WEEK, "should educate every person working for them so that Africans could eventually run the businesses." He added: "It is a sort of transfer of technology."

American managers, no strangers to the problems of achieving racial justice at home, are already taking practical steps in southern Africa to improve opportunities for blacks within their own businesses (page 334). At issue, basically, is the legitimacy of their presence in South Africa. A. A. Cunningham, General Motors Corp. vice-president and general manager for overseas operations, recognized this in describing GM's South African activities to a Senate subcommittee. "We certainly realize," he said, "that far more is at stake than simply the status of a business investment in South Africa."

SOUTHERN AFRICA:
Trade feeds on interdependence

Despite bitter political divisions and racial resentments, southern Africa, more than any other part of the continent, forms a natural economic unit. The nine countries of the region are joined by many economic ties: flows of migrant labor, technical aid, joint river developments, transport networks, electric power grids, and — most important — trade.

Border closings, guerrilla warfare, and the U.N.'s economic sanctions against Rhodesia have torn the fabric of interdependence. Normal trade flows have been distorted, to the cost of both sides in the black-white confrontation. But in the long run, mutual economic needs seem bound to spur a growing exchange of goods and services throughout the region.

Right now, although Zambia has formally closed its frontier with Rhodesia, the two countries continue to share electric power from the jointly owned Kariba dam on the Zambesi River. Zambia also continues to buy coal from Rhodesia's Wankie mines, while both Zambia and neighboring Zaire import Rhodesian corn and beef. Copper from Zaire moves 1,500 mi. by rail across Zambia, Rhodesia, and South Africa to loading docks of East London.

South Africa, for its part, is propping up the tottering Mozambican economy despite the profound political cleavage between the two countries. The South African government is purchasing electric power from Mozambique's new Cabora Bassa dam, helping run Mozambican railroads, and encouraging industries in the Transvaal to export through the Mozambican port of Maputo. And it is paying the Mozambican government in gold for the labor of 60,000 Mozambican migrant workers who are employed in South African mines.

In doing so, South Africa is buying peace with its militant neighbor. "The more prosperous our neighbors are, the better off we are," says Piet Riekert, economic adviser to South Africa's Prime Minister John Vorster.

The foreign exchange earnings from South Africa, in turn, help Mozambique to offset its loss of revenues from Rhodesian traffic. Rhodesia now routes most of its exports through South Africa. But part of the traffic continues to move through Botswana, even though Botswana is one of the five "front-line" countries that support Rhodesian black nationalists.

Legacy of colonial days

In part, such interdependence is a heritage of the region's colonial past. The railroad network that spurred the development of the southern African heartland was started by the British, originally as part of empire builder Cecil Rhodes' scheme for a rail route from Cairo to the Cape. "In the days when malaria and the tsetse fly were killers, the railways were built up in the central, relatively healthy plateau," says Michael O'Dowd, manager of special projects for Anglo American Corp. of South Africa Ltd., the mining and industrial combine.

East-west links were completed later, including a line from the Zambia-Zaire copper belt to Benguela and Lobito in Angola. But traffic on the line is still disrupted by attacks by UNITA, an antigovernment guerrilla movement. Zambia now ships most of its copper over the new Chinese-built Tazara railroad through Tanzania.

Much of the economic linkage in the region focuses on South Africa, the subcontinent's industrial powerhouse. Botswana, Lesotho, and Swaziland belong to a South African-led customs union and tie their currencies to the South African rand. South Africa exports its products throughout the region, and South African companies such as Anglo American have investments all over southern Africa.

Gerhard de Kock, senior deputy governor of the South African Reserve Bank, sees great scope for future economic cooperation with black African countries. "We are making offers all the time which they cannot refuse," he says.

SOUTH AFRICA:
Wary investing policy — until reform

South Africa, which despite racial tension seemed for years to be a haven of stability and lush profits to U.S. corporate investors, no longer looks so secure. Fluor Corp., the Los Angeles engineers and builders, was reminded of that last year when the Export-Import Bank of the U.S. turned down its request for a 15-year, $375 million loan guarantee to help finance an oil-from-coal plant that Fluor is building for the South African government. Ex-Im was unable to find "reasonable assurance of repayment" of the loan, Stephen M. Minikes, the bank's senior vice-president, told a congressional committee.

More recently, Citibank and four other U.S. and German banks took a hard look at South Africa's request for a loan of more than $300 million. They scaled it down to a more modest $110 million for five years. And the University of Delaware downgraded South Africa to 19th place, behind Iran and just ahead of Venezuela and Brazil in its latest worldwide Business Environment Risk Index, compiled by an international panel of businessmen.

What worries businessmen is a faltering South African economy and, more disturbing still, the potential for continuing racial conflict in a country where 4 million whites wield political and economic control over 18 million nonwhites. Rioting last year in Soweto—the segregated city of 1 million blacks near Johannesburg—and other urban areas may be only the beginning of a prolonged period of racial tensions. The outburst virtually halted new investments by U.S. companies, which already have a $1.5 billion stake in 300 corporate affiliates in South Africa.

The result has been to deepen and prolong South Africa's first real recession in 30 years. Gross national product, which increased at an average 6.4% annually from 1959 through 1973, grew less than 2% last year as the government of Prime Minister John Vorster squeezed the economy to get inflation and a $2 billion balance-of-payments deficit under control. Among the casualties of the slump, which slashed auto sales, is Chrysler Corp., which merged its ailing South African operation last fall with a subsidiary of Anglo American Corp. of South Africa.

Criticism from businessmen

The riots and the recession have pushed many of the country's leading business-men into the unaccustomed role of reformers rather than defenders of the status quo. They are challenging the government to make far-reaching economic, politi-cal, and social changes.

"You can't divorce economics from politics, particularly in a place like this," says Ted J. Smale, executive director of AECI Ltd., South Africa's biggest chem-ical company, and president of the Johannesburg Chamber of Commerce. Norman H. Herber, chairman of Greaterman's, a 250-store retail chain, calls for "a crash program . . . aimed at raising the status of blacks in South Africa to one of dignity, self respect, and opportunity."

Business groups are also calling for removal of curbs on black businessmen, who are now limited to ownership of a single store. Continuation of the restric-tions, businessmen fear, will only increase the appeal of leftist ideologies among blacks. "They deliberately make it impossible for a black or brown in South Africa to enjoy any of the benefits of private enterprise," says Gordon W. Waddell, a director and executive committee member of Anglo American.

Prime Minister Vorster's reaction to such prodding was to warn businessmen in a speech last October to stick to business and let him take care of government. But the troubles that worry businessmen are deep-seated. Stellenbosch University's economic research bureau estimates, for example, that the country will need to attract more than $1.3 billion in capital in 1977.

Why investors are wary

Very little of that is likely to come from foreign corporate investors. "If I were a foreigner looking clinically at South Africa," says Zac de Beer, an executive director of Anglo American, "I would refrain from investing here until South Africa looked safe for private investment—which means until the obviously essential political reforms are carried out."

Currently, the only major U.S. investments in the works are refinery expan-sions by Mobil Corp. and Caltex Petroleum Corp. that have been under way for some time, and a 40% interest in a $290 million titanium sands mining venture with the South African government by Quebec Iron & Titanium Corp., jointly owned by Kennecott Copper Corp. and Gulf & Western Industries.

Not only is direct foreign investment falling but uncertainties about South Africa's future also are pushing up the costs of borrowing abroad. "New Zealand loans and bonds are rated two full points better than South Africa's," laments Max Borkum, a partner in the brokerage firm of Davis, Borkum, Hare & Co. and a

---

U.S. Companies Feel Pressure for Change

U.S. companies have often dramatically changed the economy and society of regions where they operate, but only as a byproduct of their activities. In South Africa, U.S. corporate managements are being called upon for the first time to act consciously as agents of wide social and political reform. Critics and friends, at home and in South Africa, are pressing them to help break down the system of racial apartheid that has been the cornerstone of white government policies in South Africa for nearly 30 years.

Among the prodders is President Jimmy Carter. In a pre-election interview with Johannesburg's *Financial Mail*, he said: "American businessmen can be a constructive force, achieving racial justice within South Africa." He added: "Economic development, investment commitment, and the use of economic leverage against what is, after all, a government system of repression within South Africa seems to me the only way to achieve racial justice there."

Companies that try to promote racial reform could stir resentment among white South Africans and come into conflict with labor unions, customs, and laws. But, at least for the big multinationals that live in the public limelight, the role as catalysts of change seems unavoidable.

Response to criticism. At a stormy shareholders' meeting a few weeks ago, Chairman Charles G. Bluhdorn of Gulf & Western Industries had to defend the company's South African titanium mining project from criticism by church groups that charged G & W with supporting apartheid. Many similar resolutions have been submitted by church groups for discussion at the coming annual meetings of such companies as Mobil, General Electric Co., Ford Motor Co., and Citibank.

Corporate managements, increasingly sensitive to charges that their investments strengthen apartheid, are beginning to respond. Chase Manhattan recently decided not to lend to black homelands or to areas bordering on them. It also ruled out loans to gold and diamond mines because of the poor wages and bad working conditions in those industries. Wells Fargo and some other banks earlier decided not to lend to South Africa at all.

Equally important, U.S. subsidiaries in South Africa are initiating steps to improve the status of their nonwhite workers. "We've done our damnedest to do away with petty apartheid around the plant," says William Mott, managing director of General Motors South African Ltd., in Port Elizabeth. One U.S. subsidiary has stepped across an undefined

former president of the Johannesburg stock exchange. "That's a butter-and-eggs economy; ours is gold, diamonds, coal, and a superabundance of other resources."

The slump also brought home to businessmen the economic costs of the apartheid system, which results in companies paying white clerks up to 5 times as much as blacks for doing the same job. One result is that the affluent but numeri-

---

racial barrier by putting two black and two Asian supervisors in charge of whites. On another tack, abrasives manufacturer Norton Co. is providing loans and management advice to black-owned small businesses.

Independent action. Local managers, anxious to avoid charges of foreign corporate interference in South African affairs, deny that such policies are dictated by the American head office. "Multinationals should not act in terms of the political goals of the parents," warns William F. de la H. Beck, an Afrikaner who is chairman of Mobil Oil South Africa Ltd. "It also would be completely wrong for the American government to try to enforce policy through companies." But Beck is promoting blacks to jobs as depot managers, computer programmers, and staff executives. "It is simply enlightened self-interest to give all people equal opportunity," he says.

Not all the 300-odd U. S. companies in South Africa are known to be "enlightened" in this respect. For example, a stockholder resolution filed with Goodyear Tire & Rubber Co. charges that the company pays "virtual starvation wages" to its black South African workers. Nonetheless, "American business is in the van of change" in South Africa, according to Stephen Pryke, Chase Manhattan's man in Johannesburg and chairman of a forum of top U.S. companies in the country. He adds: "That is different from five years ago."

The whip hand. U.S. companies are in a better position than South African companies to promote racial equality, says Colin Eglin, a partner in a construction management firm and a member of Parliament who heads the opposition Progressive Reform Party. "South African companies don't have the option of disinvesting. The government very much wants American companies to stay, and American managers can point to the pressures on them from home."

GM Chairman Thomas A. Murphy and other top executives of the company have met with Prime Minister John Vorster to stress the need for equal-opportunity legislation. And in Senate hearings last fall, Norton Co.'s Vice-President Thomas S. Green Jr. declared that if South Africa pursues racial policies of "heavy suppression, many including Norton Co. might reconsider the advisability of continuing their presence in South Africa."

Still, managers of American subsidiaries feel they are on uncertain ground. The company that put blacks and Asians in charge of whites is worried about reprisals by labor inspectors if the move becomes widely known. "We don't think there is a law against it," says a spokesman. "But it is dicey."

cally small white market has become saturated, many businessmen believe, while the country's 19 million nonwhites lack both the skills to produce and the money with which to buy.

"We had been accustomed to thinking that there was a huge black reservoir that we could bring into the labor force and make into consumers any time we waved the magic wand of government noninterference," says Merton Dagat, chief economist for Nedbank Ltd., the biggest South African-owned bank. "The great black pool wasn't there, and now we have to face the cost of having fed, paid, educated, and housed blacks less well than whites. We realize whites are, relatively speaking, getting economically smaller and contributing less. It's in our own interest to get blacks a bigger share."

AECI had planned to do this by wiping out all racial wage differentials among workers doing the same job by 1977. But now, says a company spokesman, "the economic recession has rendered this unattainable by several years."

The black 'homelands'

Such easing of the effects of apartheid, in any case, would not affect the "separate development" plan by which Vorster hopes to maintain white supremacy in South Africa. The aim, eventually, is to carve off nine "homelands" or tribal enclaves as nominally independent nations in which blacks would hold citizenship rather than in South Africa itself. The proclamation of independence last October for Transkei, homeland of 4 million members of the Xhosa tribe, was the first step in this scheme.

Theoretically, the scheme gives blacks equal status with whites as citizens of self-governing sovereign states. But in terms of territory it is inequitable because it would assign just 13% of South Africa's land to 70% of its population. And leaders of other tribes, including Gatsha Buthelezi, chief minister of the 5 million Zulus, have rejected independence for their homelands.

The plan has defenders, though, among leading white South African businessmen, including William F. de la H. Beck, chairman of Mobil Oil South Africa Ltd. and an outspoken opponent of racial discrimination. "The homelands policy is absolutely correct," Beck says. "It is a good development concept." Adds Ernest Nicholas, managing director of Citibank Ltd.: "In Africa there are so many tribal and different groups that don't get along, to Westernize them doesn't make sense."

The South African government has managed to attract a few foreign investors to the homelands by offering cheap financing and other incentives. But Seagram Co. Ltd. backed out of a $10 million distillery venture with South Africa's Stellenbosch Wines in Kwazulu when Canadian church groups charged that it would strengthen South African racial policies.

What may finally wreck the homelands plan is the explosive potential of the urban townships where 8 million blacks, the best educated and politically most aware half of South Africa's black population, now live. The anomaly of the urban blacks' status is cited by Greaterman's Herber, who was unable to find a Zulu within his organization who was willing to take a job as manager of a new

department store in Kwazulu. City-bred black executives turned down the opportunity, he said, because they feared the government would not allow them to
return to Johannesburg from their "homeland."

"Separate development is a fraud and a fiction," says Anglo American's
Waddell. "If we can reach a settlement with the urban blacks, all the rest will fall
in place. But you can't reach a settlement unless they have a real political voice."
Waddell is a member of Parliament for the Progressive Reform Party, an opposition group that favors abolition of racial discrimination and greater local self-
government within a federal system.

So far, the Vorster government's response is to defend its course of separate
development. "We will just have to sweat it out," says adviser Riekert. Adds Citibank's Nicholas: "We are preparing for war in order to have peace."

Whatever their political views, though, many businessmen seem almost
relieved that South Africa is finally facing up to the crisis that has been
developing for decades. "A lot of whites are asking themselves whether to clear
out," says Dagat of Nedbank. "My wife and I have decided to stay." He adds:
"We have been buried inside the logjam so long that, now that it seems to be
breaking, we welcome it."

RHODESIA:
Bracing for a larger state role

James Rankin carries a pistol and automatic rifle on his 2,400-acre farm near Mt.
Darwin in northern Rhodesia, for he is on the front line of a war that is spreading
through the nation's borderlands. Rankin himself has been ambushed by guerrillas infiltrated into Rhodesia by the Patriotic Front, a black nationalist group,
and his farm has been attacked twice. He and his wife intend to stay, but they are
not all that confident. "Maybe you'll see me in the U.S. or Canada one of these
days," he says wryly.

Rankin and other farmers in border areas face the prospect of more fighting
as the result of Prime Minister Ian D. Smith's decision last week to call off talks in
Geneva with black nationalist leaders on a peaceful transition to black majority
rule in Rhodesia. In reply, black countries that border Rhodesia reiterated their
support for the Patriotic Front, led by Joshua Nkomo.

The U.S., which launched the talks last year, hopes to get them restarted
again. Meanwhile, the Rhodesian economy is hurting. Economic sanctions
imposed by the United Nations in 1966, cutting the country off from direct access
to international markets, are still in effect. The guerrilla fighting has discouraged
foreign tourists, an important source of hard-currency earnings. Closing of the
Mozambique border has raised shipping costs an estimated 3% to 5% in trade
with the rest of the world, which must now be routed through South Africa. Labor
costs are rising because employers must give workers time off to serve as military
reservists. Businessmen are holding off on investments, and whites in increasing
numbers are simply packing up and leaving.

Even a peaceful shift of power in Zimbabwe, as the country will be called,
would raise new business uncertainties. The reversal of political roles between

the white minority of 270,000 and black majority of 6 million is bound to create serious social strains and is likely to bring with it basic changes in the structure of the economy as well. Whites, with a per capita income of $7,100 that is among the world's highest, will be expected to share their affluence with blacks, whose per capita slice of the national income is only $565.

"There has to be a redistribution of wealth so all can benefit," says Gordon C. Chavunduka, secretary general of the United African National Council, a major black political organization. Spreading the wealth will require stepped-up government programs in housing, education, welfare, and other social services, financed by higher taxes on businesses and personal incomes. It will probably also mean a bigger government role in business. "We need a mixed-capital, modified state socialism," says Chavunduka, who lectures on sociology at the University of Rhodesia. He says the government should take shares in mining, forestry, and other industries.

Such an expanded government role in business would follow the pattern in most other black African countries. Although UANC is only one of several contending political groups, any future government of Zimbabwe will come under intense pressure to extend black control over the economy as well as government. And future regimes will certainly prod employers to advance black employees rapidly, even though few have been trained by white managements up to now for jobs as skilled workers or managers.

Wary investors

For many companies, the transition to the new business climate will be a rocky one. "Efficiencies will suffer," warns Gerald Carey-Smith, chairman of Anglo-American Rhodesia Ltd., the biggest foreign investor in Rhodesia, with operations that range from mining to sugar plantations. He adds: "The biggest task for any industrialist is to convince his European staff, who now have to be teachers and should have been all along, not to distrust the Africans."

In such a business climate, investors will be wary of putting money into Rhodesia even if sanctions are lifted. The result, as in other black African countries that have won independence from European colonial powers in the past quarter century, is likely to be an initial slump in economic activity. Real growth of the gross national product has already fallen off, to 0.5% in 1975 and around zero last year, as a result of the worldwide economic recession, the closing by Mozambique of Rhodesia's traditional trade outlets through the ports of Beira and Maputo, and rising guerrilla activity.

Despite these problems, there are optimists among Rhodesian businessmen. One such is Michael Daffy, president of the Associated Chambers of Commerce and owner of a Salisbury advertising agency. "With majority rule and removal of the sanctions, the stage is set for explosive growth," Daffy says.

Besides giving Rhodesia direct access to world markets, an end to the boycott would reopen neighboring black African countries to Rhodesian products. While many countries in Africa are having trouble feeding themselves, Rhodesia's big white-owned farms are efficient producers of everything from wheat and cotton to tropical fruits for local consumption and for export.

But the prospect of up to $2 billion worth of financial aid, offered by the Ford Administration as part of former Secretary of State Henry Kissinger's proposals for a negotiated transfer of power, has begun to fade. Kissinger suggested that the assets of whites in Rhodesia should be guaranteed, in part, to head off a flight of white businessmen, skilled workers, and farmers that would cripple the economy. But the Carter Administration is wary of the proposal, according to congressional sources, because black nationalist groups view it as mainly benefitting the whites of Rhodesia.

Despite the uncertainties, one foreign company that is betting on the future in Zimbabwe is Anglo-American. It announced plans for a $16 million expansion of its chrome-refining facilities last fall on the strength of Prime Minister Smith's offer to negotiate a shift to majority rule.

Lonrho Ltd., a London-based conglomerate with a flock of investments in Rhodesia, should benefit if the pipeline that it built from Rhodesia to the Mozambican port of Beira is reopened. "We in industry always felt we should get this thing settled," says John G. Hills, chairman of David Whitehead & Sons (Rhod) Fabrics Ltd., another Lonrho subsidiary.

A U.S. company that could gain by a settlement is Union Carbide Corp., the biggest American investor in Rhodesia. It has two chrome mines and a smelter that were taken over by the Rhodesian government in 1967, and UC has not been able to bring out any profits since then. Nor does it get any preference over other customers in purchases of Rhodesian chrome, authorized for U.S. companies by Congress as an exception to the sanctions. But UC still owns the properties, and meantime the Rhodesian management has been plowing profits back into expansion and modernization.

Whether Union Carbide will ever get the operations back is problematic, however. Callistus P. Ndlovu, who is observer at the United Nations for the African National Council of Zimbabwe, a part of the Patriotic Front, said this week he doubted that a new government would return the properties. "If we believe it will be in the interest of the country to permit Union Carbide to continue managing the company, they will probably be able to do so," he said. But he added: "They will probably have to negotiate completely new arrangements."

SOUTH-WEST AFRICA:

Building on a base of rich resources

South-West Africa has the best chance of any country in the turbulent subcontinent of achieving a peaceful transition to a multiracial society under black majority rule. By the end of 1978, South Africa proposes to relinquish control of the mineral-rich territory where diamonds are scooped from the beaches along the Namib desert coast. A constitutional convention in Windhoek, the tidy capital city, is currently drafting a charter for Namibia, as the country will be known, that calls for an interim government of blacks and whites to take over within the next few months.

Even before independence, executives of Britain's Rio Tinto-Zinc Corp. are meeting with representatives of the South-West African Peoples' Organization, a militant black political party, to discuss working conditions at Rossing, where the company has just opened the world's biggest open-pit uranium mine.

Whatever the shape of the Namibian government that emerges, and despite bitterness by blacks over the apartheid imposed by South Africans, the close economic links between the two countries should remain. "I have been fighting for independence for 30 years," says Clemens Kapuuo, chief of the Herero tribe and a delegate to the convention. "But it would be difficult not to have economic ties with South Africa."

Even SWAPO's military wing, which sends guerrillas across the border into South-West Africa from Angola, says it wants foreign investors to stay. "Of course we will accept foreign investments," says Sam Nujoma, leader of SWAPO. "We need them and they are beneficial for the country." Right now, more than one-third of South-West Africa's gross domestic product, half of its exports, and more than half of its tax revenues are contributed by two foreign-owned mining companies: Consolidated Diamond Mines of South-West Africa Ltd., controlled by Anglo American Corp. of South Africa, and Tsumeb Corp., a copper, lead, and

---

The Shattering Effect of Tribal Allegiances

"Racism, regionalism, and tribalism are enemies to be fought against, just like colonialism," President Samora Machel warned fellow Mozambicans in his inaugural address.

The inclusion of tribal ties in Machel's catalog of foes reflects the problems encountered by his Front for the Liberation of Mozambique (FRELIMO) in its war against the Portuguese colonial regime. At the outset, FRELIMO forces were made up mainly of Makonde tribesmen from northern Mozambique who ran into opposition from the Makua tribe farther south. So fierce was the Makua's tribal resistance that FRELIMO guerrillas eventually had to march hundreds of miles through Malawi and Zambia to infiltrate Mozambican territory from another direction. Now Machel, himself a member of the Thonga tribe, no longer relies exclusively on the Makonde. His cabinet consists mainly of people from southern tribes — itself a source of discontent in the rest of the country.

Throughout southern Africa and across the continent, such tribal rivalries are a crucial factor in the struggles for power. Tribalism is a force to be feared by national movements, for it lies behind the bitterest conflicts in Africa — among them, the rebellions by the Balubas of Katanga, the Ibos of Biafra, and the Amharas in Eritrea. A rising generation of political leaders sees traditional ethnic ties as a major obstacle to political movements based on ideologies, programs, and national loyalties.

Factionalism in action. In Rhodesia, for example, Joshua Nkomo, a leader of the nationalist Patriotic Front, is backed by black "front-line" governments, but he is handicapped because most of his support comes

zinc producer that is managed by the U.S.'s Newmont Mining Corp. and partly owned by AMAX Inc.

The biggest stumbling block to a peaceful shift of power, nevertheless, is SWAPO, recognized by black African countries and the United Nations as the sole "legitimate representative" of the Namibian people. SWAPO boycotts the Turnhalle conference, which it calls an assemblage of South African puppets, and demands direct talks on independence between itself and South Africa.

Aims and compromises

Chances seem good for an eventual settlement of rival claims for political power because none of the contenders can impose a solution. SWAPO's internal political wing, which operates legally within the country, has a following among workers in Windhoek and other towns, but draws its main support from the Ovambo tribesmen. They account for nearly half of the territory's 950,000 population, but they are concentrated along the border with Angola. SWAPO guerrillas have had little success in infiltrating beyond the border area into the

---

from the minority Matabele tribe around the industrial city of Bulawayo. Rival political leader Bishop Abel Muzorewa enjoys the support of the more numerous Shona tribesmen concentrated around the capital of Salisbury.

In Angola, Agostinho Neto's Popular Movement for the Liberation of Angola won a civil war among tribal factions with the support of Mbundu tribesmen and of detribalized followers among racially mixed *mesticos* in the shanty-towns around Luanda, backed by Cuban soldiers and Soviet arms. But Neto still has not won the loyalty of 2 million Ovimbundu tribesmen. The Ovimbundu remain the ethnic base of support for guerrilla leader Jonas Savimbi's continuing antigovernment operations on the central plateau.

In Namibia, the appeal of the South-West African People's Organization (SWAPO) is limited by its tribal origins among the Ovambo, who live on both sides of the Namibian-Angolan border. There are 11 ethnic groups in Namibia, including the nomadic Bushmen. Particularly hostile to SWAPO are the Herero tribesmen, whose chief, Clemens Kapuuo, was the target of a SWAPO assassination plot.

In attempting to transcend tribalism, many of the new breed of nationalists are turning to militant ideologies. For leaders such as Samora and Neto, Marxism has provided a ready doctrine. Some tribal chiefs, such as Gatsha Buthelezi of South Africa's Zulu, have turned themselves into modern politicians. But in most of Africa, tribal leaders have lost out to military men whose tribal ties have been diluted by careers in the officer corps. Nineteen African countries are now ruled by generals. The most entrenched among them have cloaked their power by establishing one-party socialist states.

vast, sparsely settled interior. Black delegates to the Turnhalle conference propose that an interim government negotiate with SWAPO on its future political role.

If a political settlement is worked out, Namibians will inherit a potentially rich endowment of natural resources scattered across an area bigger than France and Britain combined. "This could be a viable country, which many Third World nations are not," says G. A. MacMillan, chief executive of the Rio Tinto-Zinc subsidiary that operates the Rossing mine. Much of the country is arid, but farmers graze cattle and sheep on the central highlands. Along the coast, in a 300-mi. restricted zone patrolled by armed company helicopters, Consolidated Diamond Mines dredges gems from beach sands. Offshore, the cold Benguela current nourishes prolific fishing waters similar to Peru's.

Right now, the wealth is in the hands of whites who own the big farms and ranches and manage the country's mines and other businesses. Their control is buttressed by apartheid, although some cracks have begun to appear in the system. "In 1977 we'll see the end of all this apartheid," predicts Desmond O'N. Mathews, a mining company representative and secretary of the South-West African Mining Assn.

Africa's Oil Nations Tempt Investors

Oil from the fields of West Africa is helping to finance the liberation movements in southern Africa. Oil-rich Nigeria, which with an output of more than 2 million bbl. per day last year was the continent's biggest producer, has given $32 million to Angola's revolutionary government and $3 million to Mozambique, and it is supplying funds to the Rhodesian guerrillas. For Angola, the $500 million of annual revenue from Gulf Oil Corp.'s fields in the Cabinda enclave, in effect, keeps the regime afloat.

The oil-producing countries, including Gabon, also offer a sampling of the varied climate for doing business in Africa. Angola is working out its own brand of Marxist socialism. French-speaking Gabon encourages private enterprise and offers incentives to foreign investors. Nigeria has a mixed economy with a sizable government role, a tradition of private entrepreneurship in trade, and an "indigenization" policy that requires foreign investors to sell at least a 40% stockholding to Nigerian partners. To comply with the rule, foreign companies, such as Cadbury Ltd., the British confectioner, are selling public issues that are snapped up by small investors, from doctors to bank clerks.

A $7 billion market.   Nigeria's population of nearly 80 million and gross national product of $25 billion—roughly equal to the rest of black Africa combined—make it the continent's prime market. And Nigerians are sophisticated buyers. "A chap without much money will pay $16 for a good British shirt because it will last," says a British banker.

Such market characteristics make Nigeria a major target for Euro-

With independence, whites will also face demands for more equal sharing of the wealth. Kapuuo of the Hereros aims to recover some of the tribal lands that the South African government sold to white farmers a half century ago. "It should be the duty of the government that sold those lands to compensate the white farmers," he says. Despite this, "we whites will not need any special protection," says Jack Levinson, a real estate developer and deputy mayor of Windhoek. "The white people are quite willing to tighten belts, cooperate, and share."

SWAPO'S program calls for the government to take a 51% share in mining ventures, but the group's internal wing, at least, appears to have been sobered by the economic debacle in neighboring Angola. "We are not prepared to inherit chaos," says Daniel Tjongarero, SWAPO'S spokesman in Windhoek. He adds: "We are looking for ideological solutions from another country."

There are other uncertainties, particularly for new investors, about the impact of a 1974 decree issued by the U.N. Council for Namibia requiring companies to get permission from the council for natural resource ventures. Companies that fail to comply, according to the decree, may be liable for payment of damages to a future independent government. Nujoma hints that SWAPO, if it

---

peans, Japanese, and U.S. exporters, and for investors as well. The British, aided by their former colonial ties, are among the most active.

Relations between Nigeria and the U.S. have been cool, particularly since the Angolan civil war when the two countries backed opposing Angolan factions. But U.S. companies are picking up Nigerian business. International Telephone & Telegraph Corp. sold $120 million worth of communications equipment, and Telcom Inc., of McLean, Va., will be consultant to the Transport Ministry on 16 new airports. But Citibank decided to pull out rather than "indigenize" its operation.

Heavy taxes. Another U.S. company that left Nigeria was Occidental Petroleum Corp., which turned in its concessions even though it had struck oil. The finds were not worth developing because the Nigerian government's big tax bite leaves little margin for profit on oil. Right now, the government owns a 55% share in oil-producing operations. Eventually, oilmen say, Nigeria will take full ownership, leaving foreign oil companies to produce oil for a fee as contractors.

Gabon, by contrast, takes the lowest revenue bite per barrel of any country in OPEC. That encourages a brisk rate of exploration by ELF, the French oil company, Royal Dutch/Shell, and U.S. independents.

Besides oil, Gabon has a rich trove of other resources — manganese, uranium, gold, iron ore, timber. They yield a gross domestic product, for the country's population of less than a million, of more than $2,600 per capita, compared with only $357 for Nigeria. In a sumptuous display of the country's growing wealth, President Albert B. Bongo is building a palace at Libreville that will cost an estimated $80 million.

gains power, could demand compensation for taxes and royalties equal to the amounts paid to the South African government.

Another worry is the potential for friction between Namibia and the Cuban-supported Marxist regime in Angola. A joint project to harness the hydroelectric and irrigation potential of the Cunene River along the Namibian-Angolan border, launched before the Portuguese pullout, was slowed recently when the Luanda government sent troops to stop work by South African contractors on the Angolan side of the border.

Such potential troubles do not daunt RTZ's MacMillan. "Where the hell can you go in the world today and establish a mine without problems?" he says. "You learn to live with them."

FIVE BLACK NATIONS
Living with more activist government

The five black countries that form the "front line" of opposition to Rhodesia's white-dominated regime span the political spectrum from multiparty democracy in Botswana to revolutionary Marxism in Angola and Mozambique. But economically, most are moving toward a strong government role in ownership and management of the economy. Zambian President Kenneth D. Kaunda has put most of Zambia's industry under government control with his policy of "New Economic Humanism," while Tanzanian President Julius K. Nyerere is trying to build a socialist society based on cooperative rural villages. The exception is Botswana, a Texas-sized country of desert and grazing land, where President Sir Seretse Khama encourages private enterprise and foreign investment.

These three leaders, along with Prime Minister Agostinho Neto of Angola and President Samora M. Machel of Mozambique, are coordinating strategies to force a change in the Rhodesian regime. If the guerrilla war against Rhodesia from bases in Zambia, Mozambique, and Botswana is prolonged, it will radicalize the political climate throughout the entire region. By contrast, a peaceful settlement would allow greater scope for the pragmatism in politics and economics that even Angola and Mozambique have displayed.

Zambia in confrontation

One key to the outcome is Zambia, economically the most advanced country among the five. Kaunda, a political moderate, is a leading advocate of a negotiated settlement—the more so because Zambia has been hard-hit economically by the confrontation with Rhodesia. Zambia's closing of its border with Rhodesia in 1973 has so far cost the country an estimated $360 million in increased transport costs and the disruption of normal supply patterns. Prior to the closure, 55% of all Zambian trade went through Rhodesia.

The border closing aggravated the impact of a slump in the price of copper, which accounts for half of Zambia's gross national product. The country's troubles were compounded by the civil war in Angola, which stranded 750 Zambian railroad cars between blown bridges on the Benguela rail line. "Some of our copper is on the Benguela," says John Harper, technical director of the government-controlled Roan Consolidated Mines. "We've written it off, and if it comes back it's just a bonus."

Part of Zambia's troubles though, is the result of inefficiency in the government-controlled copper mines, which are operating at very low profit margins. In 1974 Zambia took over management from minority shareholders AMAX Inc. and Anglo American Corp., which had been running the mines under contract. "We have little or no function except to be an enforced investor," says Ian MacGregor, AMAX chairman.

The cost of such "Zambianization" of the mines, according to one industry observer, is the gap between capacity and current production, a difference of 120,000 tons per year. One problem is a shortfall of 5,000 skilled foreign workers needed to help run the mines. Kaunda does not believe in expelling whites, and there still are 20,000 expatriates in Zambia. But many have left, partly because, in the country's current financial straits, they are having difficulty in converting any of their earnings to hard currency.

In Botswana, there are no such problems. Its foreign exchange needs, as a member of the rand bloc, are supplied by South Africa's central bank. In economic approach, in fact, President Khama has more in common with the white-dominated regimes that he opposes than with the other black front-liners. AMAX and Anglo American are the principal shareholders in Botswana RST Ltd., a $300 million nickel-copper mine and refinery. But in contrast with the situation in Zambia, AMAX manages the operation. "It is a very easy country to do business in," says MacGregor.

Where they talk Marxism

At opposite geographical ends of the front line, Angola's Neto and Mozambique's Machel talk the language of orthodox Marxism. But their actions to date leave some uncertainties as to how far or fast they will go.

In Angola, where the civil war wiped out four-fifths of the country's coffee crop and disrupted other activities such as diamond mining, Gulf Oil's offshore field now accounts for 80% of government revenues. So far, Neto has not interfered with Gulf's operations, nor has he taken over the Benguela railroad, owned and operated by London-based Tanganyika Concessions Ltd. Britain's Imperial Chemical Industries is trying to reopen for business with $1.5 million in agrichemicals that it left in storage.

"Definitely, Angola will allow foreign investments to continue, but under new contracts," says Elisio de Figueredo, Angola's new ambassador to the United Nations. He adds: "We do intend to be pragmatic."

Mozambique, equally hard-hit by civil war and equally pragmatic, earned around $230 million last year from cooperative deals with South Africa and a number of foreign companies continue to operate there, despite confusion about the government's aims. Nicholas Labuschagne, a director of John Orrs Holdings Ltd., a South African retailer with operations in Mozambique, believes the government will eventually take controlling shares in businesses but allow minority private partners to manage them.

Amid such doubts, what seems certain is that the front-line countries, supported by the rest of black Africa, will keep up the pressure for black majority rule in Rhodesia and Namibia. When that is achieved, the line of confrontation will move south to the borders of South Africa—and the number of front-line countries will increase to seven.

The Proper Role of U.S. Corporations in South Africa

John Blashill

The Republic of South Africa has always been regarded by foreign investors as a gold mine, one of those rare and refreshing places where profits are great and problems small. Capital is not threatened by political instability or nationalization. Labor is cheap, the market booming, the currency hard and convertible. Such are the market's attractions that 292 American corporations have established subsidiaries or affiliates there. Their combined direct investment is close to $900 million, and their returns on that investment have been romping home at something like 19 percent a year, after taxes.

And yet South Africa is also the home of apartheid, where 4,000,000 whites rule some 15,000,000 "Bantu" (blacks), 2,000,000 "coloreds" (mulattoes), and 600,000 "Asiatics" (mostly Indians). The intense moral fervor aroused in its critics by apartheid has made South Africa an international pariah. The United Nations has passed more than thirty-five resolutions aimed at South Africa, including an arms embargo. South African trade unions have been forced to withdraw from the International Labor Organization. South African athletes have been banned from the Olympics. It has become a highly attackable place, one that stirs up explosive emotions. In the U.S. those emotions are beginning to explode at stockholders' meetings—and even in the boardrooms—of corporations doing business in South Africa.

Many of these companies are now being forced to face the question that Polaroid Corp., under pressure from some of its black employees in the U.S., asked itself in a series of advertisements a year and a half ago: "Is it right or wrong to do business in South Africa?" It was a fairly uncomplicated question for Polaroid, since the company sells its products through a local distributor and has none of its own money invested in the country. The answer Polaroid came up with cost the company itself little or nothing, and proved to be a triumph of good public relations. Polaroid decided to continue its South African sales on condi-

Reprinted from the July, 1972 issue of *Fortune* magazine by special permission. © 1972, Time, Inc.

tion that its distributor "improve dramatically the salaries and other benefits" of its nonwhite employees (which has been done).

The issue of American corporate involvement in South Africa has been taken up by civil-rights leaders, labor unions, churches, stockholders groups, the Ford Foundation, the State Department, and Congress, with varying bias and varying answers. Some, including Representative Charles Diggs, a black Congressman from Detroit, have decided that American corporations can stay—if they mend their ways. A number of critics, however, are demanding that they get out. "American firms in South Africa are partners in apartheid," asserts George M. Houser, executive director of the American Committee on Africa, a privately funded organization in New York that promotes freedom for Africans. Representatives of six Protestant denominations returned from a three-week tour this winter to report that "most of us believe that American corporations should totally disengage from South Africa."

The issue profoundly affects the lives of all of South Africa's nonwhites, as well as many of its white citizens. But those who cry "Abandon ship" have not consulted the passengers. Many of South Africa's blacks, on whose behalf the issue is supposedly being fought, want U.S. business to stay. "I feel if the Americans withdraw it will lower the general standard of living here, and the Africans will be the first to suffer," says Lucy Mvubelo, general secretary of the National Union of Clothing Workers and one of the nation's few African labor leaders. Aside from whatever moral cleansing might be gained by refusing to dine with the devil, it would serve no useful purpose at all for American corporations to get out. Indeed, the closing of U.S. subsidiaries would throw at least 100,000 Africans out of work immediately, and could eventually cost the jobs of 150,000 more. "Foreign investment can help us," says Julius Moikangoa, a white-collar worker in Johannesburg, "by working for us from within." That is the crux of the South African challenge for U.S. corporations.

FACING AN OBVIOUS TRUTH

The withdrawal of American investment would not bring down the apartheid system. More likely, the system would be worsened, for an enforced U.S. retreat would almost certainly cause a violent reaction among South Africa's whites. In fact, American withdrawal might be the only thing that could save apartheid in the long run.

For perhaps the first time, most South African whites are becoming aware that there is something wrong with their elaborate structure of apartheid laws. Not only does it not work justly, it just doesn't work. The society is beginning to move—slowly, perhaps, but fundamentally. Some of South Africa's leading industrialists have long opposed restrictive labor practices, under which the whites get all the best jobs and the blacks only the worst. "It is just a plain, obvious truth," says Harry Oppenheimer, chairman of the giant Anglo American Corp., "that a country that refuses to allow something like 80 percent of its labor force to do the best work of which they are capable cannot hope to progress as it should or hold its place in the world."

The ferment is beginning to permeate South Africa's political life. Apartheid was invented by another generation, and reflects the views of the old Boer pioneer, who could claim as much land as he could cover on horseback in a day. The system was, in many ways, the legal application of the Boer's ancient tactic of self-defense: when attacked, he "went into *laager*," barricading himself inside a circle of covered wagons. Stringent apartheid laws are still very much on the books, but such tactics don't fit an industrialized society, and South Africa's younger voters—those now forty or below—do not live in fear of the Africans to the extent that their elders did. They are increasingly concerned with torments that are more universal: taxation, traffic jams, inflation, and keeping up payments on the house. And since these younger voters will be in the majority by the next election, their attitudes are an important fact of life in South African politics today.

The climate is ripe for change. What strikes an observer forcibly, however, is that few American subsidiaries in South Africa seem to know it—or want it. With some notable exceptions, they are behind the times, even for South Africa. They should not be compelled to leave the country, but for their own good they should reform their ways. "We should be in the forefront of the social changes that are happening here," says Bill Marshall Smith, fifty-nine, a South African who is managing director of Caltex, which is jointly owned by Texaco and Standard of California. "It just makes bloody business sense," declares Peter Loveday, forty-two, another progressive South African. He is managing director of Standard Telephones & Cables (S.A.) Ltd., the principal I.T.T. subsidiary in the country.

But most executives who run U.S. subsidiaries in South Africa like the system as it is. In 1969 a market-research organization conducted a poll of 106 American and Canadian businessmen living in the country. More than three-quarters of them approved of apartheid as "an approach that is, under the circumstances at least, an attempt to develop a solution." Only 20 percent opposed it. Less than one in ten felt it was "altogether incorrect." In 1970, Jim Hatos, the managing director of the International Harvester subsidiary, told a visitor from New York's Council for Christian Social Action: "I am sympathetic to what the South African Government is trying to do. I don't want hundreds of Africans running around in front of my house."

The truly extraordinary thing about that statement was its frankness. A good many of Hatos' colleagues might agree with the views he expressed, but they would no longer dare say so in public. Most of them, in fact, have become afraid of saying anything about anything. "We are justifiably proud of our record, but it would serve no useful purpose to talk about it," said the manager of a factory where African workers with ten years of service earn less than 50 cents an hour. "My home office doesn't want to give any publicity to the fact that we have a South African operation," pleaded another man, whose company has one of the world's best-known trademarks.

The nervousness among these executives bears its own message. American companies are finding their records in South Africa suddenly very embarrassing, for the very good reason that they don't live by the same rules they practice at home. "American firms aren't really any better than the Boer firms," says Dabula-manzi Tantsi, a lawyer in Johannesburg's sprawling African township of Soweto.

There are exceptions — including Caltex, I.T.T., General Motors, Ford, Mobil, Gillette, and, most notably, I.B.M. These companies and a few others pay their nonwhite workers considerably more than the usual wage rates. For example, even though its union keeps the top ranks of jobs for whites only, I.T.T.'s non-white workers — mostly colored and Asian — get an average of $135 a month. Loveday raised their wages 19 percent last year and plans to keep moving toward what he calls "wage parity."

DOUBLE NAUGHT IS STILL NAUGHT

Could Americans alone, by paying top wages, have any meaningful effect on the living standards of South Africa's nonwhite population, particularly the blacks? An African teacher in Soweto supplies an answer: "I, personally, would derive no immediate benefit if the Americans decided to pay fair wages. Not many of us would. But this would spread. It would have to. If Factory A increases wages, Factory B will be forced to increase wages too, and before you know it, every-body's wages go up, even mine."

All companies in South Africa do give occasional raises to their African em-ployees, and the management of most firms can pull out seemingly impressive figures on how much they have raised the salaries of their Africans over a term of years. But the figures are apt to be flawed. "You double naught and it's still naught," explains Fred van Wyk, director of the South African Institute of Race Relations, a private foundation that has been fighting against apartheid for years. Besides, white wages have gone up more than those of the Africans. Because they have replaced white workers with black, moreover, some companies actually find themselves spending less on their payrolls than they did ten years ago.

Another claim often made by American companies is that "we pay the rate for the job, regardless of race." In the U.S. that would mean equal pay for equal work. In South African jargon, however, the statement has a special meaning. "There is no such thing as equal pay for equal work," says F. P. Sauls, national secretary of the colored National Union of Motor Assembly and Rubber Workers Union of South Africa. Most companies that say they pay "the rate for the job" operate under union agreements in which all jobs are categorized and assigned minimum rates. But the rates are pegged artificially low, and invariably all whites are paid considerably more than the minimum.

Moreover, blacks and coloreds are often employed at jobs for which they are not "rated." A colored shop foreman, for example, will be rated as a group leader (sometimes called a "team leader" or "charge hand") and paid 50 cents to $1 an hour less than if he were a white doing the same job. In the electrical in-dustry there is a union rule forbidding black electricians to be called electricians or to work from blueprints. They can, however, be called electrical assistants and are allowed to work from pictures, even if the pictures happen to be photographs of blueprints. But their pay is less than half that of white electricians.

Only at the middle grades of the factory pay scales do blacks and whites work at the same wages. The blacks start at the bottom and can rise no higher than the middle. The whites start no lower than the middle and can go to the top. It's a pyramid, all black at the base, all white at the top, with a few Zebra stripes in a thin line at the center. Or, as Ford's industrial-relations manager Fred H. Ferreira explains it, "There is an upward movement of the whites as they make way for the progression of nonwhites."

SCRAPING THE LABOR BARREL

Ferreira's comment is an accurate summary of the pattern in South Africa. Black workers are being allowed to rise, but in most cases only to fill jobs vacated by upward-moving whites. It's a process of massive readjustment, all of it motivated by the same fundamental cause. South Africa, whose economy was largely based on mining and farming until World War II, is rapidly transforming itself into an industrial power, and the accompanying demand for labor has far outstripped the traditional labor supply. One survey showed 6 percent of all "white" jobs to be vacant because there was no one to fill them. Unless these jobs can be filled, the Federated Chamber of Industries (South Africa's equivalent of the National Association of Manufacturers) has warned, the projected growth of the economy will be curtailed by 20 percent.

But filled by whom? Not, certainly, by whites, for there are no more left to employ. The white unemployment rate is officially calculated at less than 0.2 percent—a total of some 3,000 workers, including assorted drunks and misfits, who are unemployed only because they are absolutely unemployable. An additional 50,000 whites, perhaps, would be classified as unemployables in any other country, even though they hold jobs. "You can imagine," says Ian Hetherington, the British-born managing director of the Norton Co. plant near Johannesburg, "how deep into the barrel we've scraped."

Faced with the prospect of empty assembly lines, industry has had no choice but to turn to African workers. "If I had to depend on white labor to run my plant, I'd have to close down tomorrow," says a typical American manager. Another tells this story: "When we came here at government request ten years ago, we were told that we could hire only white workers. Well, we couldn't get them. Five years ago a government labor inspector came around and found the place full of nonwhites. So we told him, either we employ them or you don't get your equipment. And that was the end of it."

Given their choice, many employers would rather hire blacks than whites. The whites, pampered and protected by tradition, tend to be unreliable and shoddy workers. They often wander from job to job, quitting on the slightest pretext. Sometimes they refuse to work at all unless management provides them with African "assistants," who do everything for them—brew their tea, hand them their tools, and even fill in for them when they play hooky. In one American heavy-equipment plant, where welding jobs are reserved for members of the white union, the managing director reports that the welders seldom come to work more than two days a week, and go fishing—without pay—the other three. When they're absent, the welding is done by their supposedly untrained African assistants—who work twice as fast at one-third the pay. "I get six times the production per dollar out of my Bantu," the manager says.

I.T.T.'s Peter Loveday calls this indefensible exploitation. "In practically every situation where you've got whites and nonwhites doing the same job," he says, "you're dealing with the cream of the coloreds and blacks, and the dregs of the whites." Yet the blacks cannot afford to be prima donnas, for there is a vast pool of unemployed African labor. Once an African lands a job, he does his best to keep it. If he quits or gets fired, he runs the very serious risk of being shipped back to his "homeland," or reservation. In most American subsidiaries the only employees with twenty years' service are Africans.

Under the circumstances, industry in South Africa might be expected to make better use of black and colored workers. Yet there are some important barriers. Some white unions enforce closed-shop rules on the skilled jobs and forbid their members to train nonwhites; this is the case at I.T.T., among others. White artisans usually refuse to accept nonwhite apprentices. There is an unwritten rule against putting blacks in charge of whites. In most industrial areas management must obtain government permission to increase the number of African workers.

But as the manager of a major American industrial plant puts it, "If you're smart enough to recognize an impediment, you're smart enough to find a way around it." Unions can be cajoled, artisans can be trained elsewhere, and permission to hire more Africans usually can be obtained: 72 percent of all such applications have been approved, according to Prime Minister Balthazar Vorster. The trouble is that most American companies don't appear to try to overcome the impediments.

LOOKING AFTER THE GARBAGE DRIVERS

Among the abused and misunderstood bars to the advancement of African workers are South Africa's so-called "job-reservation laws," which reserve for whites a variety of jobs in specified industries and areas. Job reservation is cited by countless American managers as the principal reason why they cannot promote their blacks. But so far only twenty-seven specific job-reservation "determinations" have been issued by the government, and they affect only 2,080 individual workers. Most of the determinations are either riddled with exemptions or apply to only a handful of jobs. Determination No. 9, for example, concerns only the twelve white garbage drivers in the town of Springs, near Johannesburg. With all the exemptions taken into account, it appears that the only American company subject to a specific determination under the job-reservation laws is Chrysler.

One of management's responsibilities is to know the laws that affect its operations, but in too many cases in South Africa the top men in U.S. subsidiaries seem not to bother. "They believe the myths," says a senior American diplomat with long service in South Africa. "They think everything is illegal, and they don't care." Ignorance of the law is especially prevalent in subsidiaries headed by

Americans. South Africa may be just another step in their corporate careers, and their stay is likely to be a short one. Their success is measured in the short-run terms of this year's profits, and many of them are simply not interested in anything else. They come and they go, and what happens after they leave South Africa does not concern them. "They're semiskilled barbarians," concludes the American diplomat. "They have little minds." Adds Loveday of I.T.T.: "It's bad management."

In the past, of course, South Africa has not been regarded as a corporate problem area, and so it has been assigned a fairly low rung in the overseas promotion ladders of many American corporations. Too many of the managers sent to South Africa are like the man who runs an American subsidiary's factory in the state of Natal, southeast of Johannesburg. Accountable only to his home office in New York, he likes to get his picture in the paper from time to time with African community leaders because "it's good for P.R." He directs a work force of more than 400, of whom 150 are nonwhite. His starting wage for Africans is $13.17 a week, which is far below the poverty datum line for the area.

There is one rather bold innovation in his factory. He employs both white women and African men on his assembly line. This could be an explosive combination, he says, "except I let those Bantu know that the first sign of trouble, they're out." The white women earn 3 cents to 6 cents an hour more than the black men—even though the blacks have proved more productive and more reliable. The managing director doesn't know how much it would cost him to pay equal wages, because he has no intention of doing so. "If New York orders me to pay the rate for the job, I'll pay it," he says. "But if I don't have to, I won't. I'm here to make profits. If the Bantus don't like it, they can work somewheres else."

This manager would like to convert his assembly line to only black workers, thereby reducing his total payroll somewhat. But he says he cannot do so because "it would be against the law. I have to maintain a quota of white workers." In point of fact, there is no specific law setting race quotas on his industry in Natal. He could fire all his white workers tomorrow, if he wanted to.

GETTING AWAY WITH HERESY

Even some companies that are serious about change in South Africa have made only token gestures, such as not having separate water coolers and not putting signs on restroom doors to indicate whether the facilities are for whites, coloreds, or Africans. But other actions are more substantive, such as putting the desks of black stenographers next to those of white ones.

Now and again there are calculated frontal attacks against the underlying structure of the apartheid system. A heavy-equipment manufacturer in the Capetown area has installed an interracial cafeteria for its white and colored workers; that is plainly illegal. The manager of a plant near Johannesburg says that "whenever we can safely employ a black to do a job, we'll discriminate against a white to do it." He has installed a black supervisor over a partly white assembly line; this, although not strictly illegal, is at least heretical. He has also hired black security officers who have the authority, though they rarely use it, to search the persons of white workers coming off shift—and this is not only heretical in South Africa, but absolutely unthinkable.

The miraculous thing is that the managers who have ventured into heresy have [gotten] away with it. Their white workers have not complained, because great pains have been taken to prepare the ground. Where blacks have been put in sensitive positions, they have been chosen with care and know their jobs.

Of the companies willing to talk about what they're doing, the two most impressive are Gillette and I.B.M. Like the majority of progressive U.S. subsidiaries, both are managed by South Africans. Gillette's wage scales are not as good as I.B.M.'s—"We still have some warts," concedes Denis Sanan, forty, managing director of Gillette. But his company is moving aggressively to wipe out its warts. Says Sanan: "We can't wait for opportunities to appear for the blacks. We have to create areas of opportunity."

A colored chemist is chief of Gillette's research and development department, two black quality-control inspectors work on its production lines, and there are nine black salesmen and a black field supervisor on the sales staff. The chemist, Sanan reports, is so capable that he is being sought out by white department heads for advice on production problems. The quality-control inspectors enjoy "excellent relations" with the whites whose work they inspect. The black salesmen "are my most effective sales force, at least in the amount of territory they can cover. They average twenty-seven calls a day, versus eleven a day for white salesmen." As for the field supervisor: "He's tops. He could eventually become this company's general sales manager."

BLACK AND WHITE AT THE COMPUTER BANK

I.B.M. is unbelievable—in the sense that Africans outside the company cannot believe what it manages to do for its workers. The company's starting wages for Africans are above $200 a month, which is by far the highest minimum rate in the country, and more than the maximum in most companies. I.B.M. still has few black workers, but is aggressively seeking more. Once it hires a talented individual it keeps moving him up, regardless of race. Frank Molobi, for example, is a twenty-four-year-old black. He joined the company five years ago as a junior clerk and is now a trainee programmer—a title that means he has completed his programming courses but has less than a year's experience.

I.B.M. is entirely open about its color-blind corporate policies. In its show windows on Johannesburg's Rissik Street, a computer bank is in constant operation, and the operators are both black and white. The mixture is more than a window display; it is a symbol of deep-seated company philosophy. "What the companies here should ask themselves is whether they have a basic philosophy of human dignity that they apply," says Morris Cowley, forty-six, I.B.M.'s managing director for South Africa.

Among other companies that do apply such a philosophy are Caltex and Mobil. Their subsidiaries are both based in Capetown, and both are headed by enlightened South Africans. "We give equal pay and equal conditions and are proud of it," says Caltex' Bill Marshall Smith, a squirish and sometimes eloquent man who grew up in the interior of Natal and learned Zulu along with English. "We try to stay about ten yards ahead of the troops," says Mobil's William de la Harpe Beck, forty-nine, a former rugby player from the Orange Free State who is fluent in Sotho. "If you get much further ahead than that," he adds, "you start running into fire."

Both Marshall Smith and Beck have turned to Africans and Capetown's large colored population to find the skilled workers they need. Mobil uses colored computer operators and key punchers, for example, and Beck says that approximately one-fifth of his 750 nonwhite workers are employed at skilled jobs, earning salaries comparable to whites. For laborers, Mobil's starting wage, including a Christmas bonus that amounts to an extra month's pay each year, is $123 a month; the total is well above the poverty line and almost unrivaled in South Africa.

Caltex starts lower—$112 a month—but the wages it pays go up rapidly. Most of the company's 700 nonwhites are doing skilled or semiskilled work, and "we're looking for areas to employ more nonwhites." One remarkable accomplishment—remarkable for South Africa, at least—is that Caltex now has Africans driving its oil tanker trucks in the Johannesburg area. Their starting wage, as trainees, is $207 a month, and they can eventually earn $500 once they have been on the job long enough (none earn that much as yet). Most remarkable of all, these drivers make deliveries to Afrikaner gas-station operators in Johannesburg. This means they must cross traditional color bars. "They're more than drivers," says Marshall Smith. "They have to discuss how much the client wants, make out the bills, and collect his money. It was touchy, at first. The whites didn't like it. They'd never had to explain to a black man why they couldn't pay until next time. It was losing face before an inferior, as they saw it. But they got over it."

CHAPS WHO ARE GIVEN AUTHORITY

The biggest American companies in South Africa are the three major auto makers, each of which has a plant measurable in the hundreds of acres—Ford and General Motors in the Indian Ocean city of Port Elizabeth, Chrysler near Pretoria in the north. Among them, they employ nearly 13,000 workers, and account for nearly 40 percent of all new-car sales in the country. All three companies are now beginning to give more attention to the welfare of their nonwhite workers.

Ford, with a labor force totaling 5,576, is the largest American employer in South Africa. Its lowest rate is 53 cents an hour, which is a livable wage. Ford has more colored workers than blacks and offers them opportunities for advancement that are considerably above average. Twelve colored employees are now ranked as group leaders, according to Sauls, the national secretary of the colored auto workers' union, "and these chaps are really given authority."

Until recently, Ford's medical plan made a sharp distinction between white and nonwhite employees: the families of white workers were covered after three months' employment, the families of nonwhites only after ten years. Last January all employees, regardless of race, were given coverage for their families after three months. Ford still has no coloreds or blacks in the top two of its eleven labor grades, and Sauls does not credit the company's claim that it gives equal pay for equal work. "A colored with fifteen years' experience gets the same pay as a white starting out," he says.

General Motors, which is smaller than Ford in South Africa, has roughly 5,000 workers (70 percent of them nonwhite), and treats them well. Its wage scales and fringe benefits are approximately the same as Ford's. Even more important, says van Wyk of the South African Institute of Race Relations, "General Motors is very aware." One sign of G.M.'s awareness is the practically constant flow of company officers from Detroit to inspect the plant in Port Elizabeth. One such visitor was Chairman of the Board Richard C. Gerstenberg, who flew to South Africa in April "to assure myself that General Motors is doing everything it can to hasten the day of equality there."

Much has happened at G.M. in the past six months alone. The number of workers enrolled in in-plant technical programs has been doubled. G.M.'s African workers, forbidden by law from belonging to registered unions, were encouraged to form a "Works Committee," which can take up grievances with management. The company also announced it would pay full tuition for any employee who wished to continue his education after hours.

Potentially more important in the long run is a program, similar to one started by Gillette, to help black children go to school. (In South Africa, education is free and compulsory only for whites; for blacks, with their low incomes, going to school can be a prohibitively expensive proposition.) Under its program, G.M. will pay tuition and the cost of books for the children of its African workers; that amounts to $7.53 a year for each child, which could take care of about one-third of the total cost in the lower grades. Since January, when G.M.'s education subsidy was announced, 475 black children have started to school with company support. In addition, G.M. has provided 125 scholarships of $33.25 a year for high-school students; small as it is, the sum is enough to take care of a large part of their total costs.

As with Ford, there are still areas where G.M. falls short in the view of its nonwhite workers. Sauls, the union secretary, complains that "the communication between employer and employee is not very good," and criticizes the technical training courses as having no visible results. "They train the chaps," says Sauls, "but once they graduate they don't give them the jobs. It's a dead end." G.M., however, insists that this is being changed. Several colored group leaders, it says, have been trained to become foremen, the first of them will be installed—title, salary, and all—in his new post by the end of the year. Because of pressures from the white union, however, those new foremen will be given supervision only over nonwhite workers.

In the past, Chrysler has lagged behind both Ford and G.M. in its treatment of nonwhite workers, but that is now changing. Since 1968 the average wage paid

African workers by Chrysler has nearly tripled. This occurred even though the company has moved its main plant from Capetown, a high-wage area, to a location near Pretoria, where the going rates are lower. The new plant is not far from an African township, which provides a considerable pool of potential labor. About 1,000 of the plant's 2,038 workers are black, and another 111 are coloreds. Under a job-reservation determination issued in 1970, Chrysler is required to keep 30 percent of the assembly-line jobs at this new plant for whites, but it has undertaken an active training program to upgrade the skills—and pay—of its African employees.

SOOT IN THE CAFETERIA

Not all American companies involved with the auto industry get high marks for their treatment of nonwhites. Firestone, for example, recently built a new factory near an African homeland in a location that has been designated as a "border area"; the designation means that the normal minimum-pay scales do not apply there. This factory—at Brits, a town near Pretoria—has 140 workers, almost all African (there are twenty whites). Firestone put some of the blacks through a five-month training course to equip them for better jobs, but it has not been paying them as skilled labor. The going rate for skilled blacks in Brits industries is 45 cents an hour.

At the main Firestone plant in Port Elizabeth, where there are almost 1,400 workers (380 whites, 450 coloreds, and 525 blacks), minimum rates do apply, and the average wage of nonwhites is higher than at Brits. But the company's wages at Port Elizabeth are low for the area. For example, Firestone starts its colored workers at 40 cents an hour, or considerably less than Ford or General Motors, its two largest competitors for labor. The result, according to Sauls, is that Firestone has to take "the dregs, the people Ford and G.M. don't want." Firestone recently installed a cafeteria for its colored workers, but Sauls says: "It is so bad that our people won't eat there. The tables are covered with soot. The food is covered with soot."

And what of Polaroid, the company that started all the fuss? Having no direct subsidiary in South Africa, Polaroid has no employees of its own there. Since the "Polaroid experiment" began, however, the company has persuaded Frank & Hirsch, the local (but independent) distributing company for its products, to give black employees wage increases of 22 percent. Frank & Hirsch now pays its 151 Africans an average of $121 a month; the increases cost the distributor $39,500 a year in additional wages. Polaroid itself has provided grants totaling $75,000 to promote education of Africans. That may not be a great deal, but it is considerably more than most American companies have done.

"STOP HIDING BEHIND THE LAWS"

All together, there are probably not more than twenty-five subsidiaries of American corporations that can be considered to be reacting responsibly to the growing pressures for change. In addition to those already mentioned, they include companies such as Norton Co., PepsiCo, Coca-Cola, and General

Electric.* The others—and there are more than 250 of them—either oppose change or are dragging their feet. The O'okiep Copper Co., for example, 57.5 percent owned by Newmont Mining Corp., still maintains a feudalistic labor system that has long been standard in South African mines. O'okiep has 2,000 black workers. It recruits them from poverty-ridden tribal areas, signs them to one-year contracts at wages averaging about $40 a month (plus bed and board in the company compound), then ships them back home when their year is up.

Even in the manufacturing industries, American employers as a whole are falling short—and not just in their pay scales. "They have no communication with their Africans," say Dudley Horner, of the South African Institute of Race Relations. "It's just hire and fire. How can you run a plant if you don't even talk to your workers?"

What most American subsidiaries need is thorough, fundamental, and genuine reform. The first thing they must do, says Morris Cowley of I.B.M., is to "stop hiding behind the laws." They should pay a living wage, which means roughly $50 a month above the local poverty datum line, even to common laborers. They should train Africans for skilled and responsible jobs, then put them into those jobs and pay them for performing them. They should encourage their Africans to form a Works Committee that can serve both as a union and a channel of communication with management. Whenever possible, they should put blacks and whites at the same job in the same room. Finally, they should prepare the ground for putting black supervisors in charge of whites.

Daring as some of these measures may seem, they have all been put into effect in today's South Africa by one or more companies. Such changes have to be made quietly of course, and with discretion. "Any employer who goes whole hog, publicly, can expect retribution from the government," concedes Robert Kraft, assistant general secretary and economist of the Trade Union Council of South Africa. On the other hand, there is a widespread belief that the government would like to see a general liberalization of labor practices, though it cannot afford to admit it openly because of pressures from rigid Afrikaners. "Vorster is happy to see the laws bent and broken," says Loveday, "but he cannot openly condone it." The strongest position for an enterprising employer, according to Kraft, is to "present the public and government with a *fait accompli*, a situation that has been working for a year or two. There's nothing anyone can do about it then."

Many of the actions open to employers are subject to no pressures at all. Any manager can insist that his African workers be treated with the same basic human dignity as his whites. He can give financial support to such worthwhile

---

*Time Inc., the publisher of Fortune, maintains a business office for Time magazine in Johannesburg with six employees, including an African messenger-chauffeur who is paid $144 a month. In addition, Keartland Press of Johannesburg prints 55,000 copies of Time each week on a contract basis. About half of Keartland Press's 407 workers are Africans. The minimum wage for these black workers is $79.80 a month, their average wage is $159.60 a month.

South African institutions as the National Development and Management Foundation, which has recently started a series of courses designed to train Africans for management positions. He can also, and at a minimal cost, follow the lead of Gillette and G.M. and subsidize the education of African children. Along with higher wages, what most African workers want most is education for their children.

DIRECTION FROM THE TOP

Only top management in U.S. headquarters can take the steps necessary to improve the lot of their nonwhite employees in South Africa. "The direction for change must come from the boardrooms back home," says Bill Marshall Smith of Caltex. "And let's face it, we could all be moving faster." Too often, however, home-office decisions must be made on the basis of faulty or misleading information from the field. An auto-company executive, resident in South Africa, explains the danger: "Corporate decisions are made from tiny slips of paper with maybe just the figures written on them. The slips are the distillations of reports from the field. But no subsidiary tells its home office the truth. We all lie as much as we think we can get away with. We even lie about figures, so you can imagine how much we lie about everything else. If anybody back there really knows what we're doing, it's certainly not our fault."

Top managements that want to protect the future of their companies in a changing South Africa will face a difficult, and perhaps painful, task. One important step would be to quit judging local managers solely by the size of their current profit margins. Instead, they should be encouraged to act in the longer-term interest of the company, with power to increase wages and improve the benefits of African workers. In most cases, the profits from South African operations are so substantial that the increased labor costs would not be overly burdensome—especially since productivity would be likely to improve.

The challenge U.S. corporations face in South Africa was capsulized last year by a fast-growing black group called South African Students Organization. Its manifesto declared: "The white man must be made aware that one is either part of the solution or part of the problem." The words are hardly original, but the implicit challenge to U.S. business is all too real.

QUESTIONS FOR DISCUSSION

1. What are the fundamental arguments both for and against continuation of U.S.-based business involvement in South Africa? On balance, with which position do you agree?

2. Why are the U.S.-based firms interested in doing business in Southern Africa? For each of the many reasons, who are the primary and secondary beneficiaries?

3. What are the fundamental provisions and value differences exhibited between race relations in the Union of South Africa and the U.S. legislative posture on civil rights?

4. Summarize at least five major socioeconomic and/or sociopolitical events that have been of major importance to firms operating in Southern Africa.

5. What are the "cracks" that are appearing in apartheid in the Republic of South Africa? How many have resulted from U.S. multinational "heresy"? Are the "cracks" significant enough to indicate that the end of apartheid is near?

6. At the time, Polaroid employed a unique strategy to deal with U.S. domestic concern over its involvement in South Africa. Suggest alternative strategies that you feel would have been equally effective.

7. Why is it that the cliché "When in Rome, do as the Romans do" is no longer of universal value to the multinational business manager? What major evolutionary changes have brought this about?

8. U.S. businesses are now being called upon by some groups to be progenitors of major social reform around the globe. What specifically is being demanded in regard to the social structure in Southern Africa?

9. Our study of U.S. business in South Africa is primarily for expository purposes — to demonstrate how the far-reaching arms of multinational companies can create significant socioeconomic and political problems for management. What other areas of the world might just as graphically provide issues of concern to multinational managers? How are these issues now being handled?

SELECTED READINGS

"A black and white issue faces polaroid," Business Week, November 14, 1970.

"Churches mount first joint campaign against U.S. firms in Southern Africa," Wall Street Journal, February 15, 1972.

Gaither, W., "Apartheid: The earth trembles," The Nation, December 11, 1976.

Leger, R. R., "U. S. firms' operations in South Africa cope with varied pressures," The Wall Street Journal, March 16, 1972, p. 1.

"Namibia: Foreign companies are running scared," Business Week, May 5, 1975.

Pelissier, R. F., "American private enterprise in South Africa," California Management Review, Summer, 1972.

South Africa — A National Profile, Ernst and Ernst International Business Series, May, 1971.

"The Transkei Puppet Show," Time, October 25, 1976, p. 39.

Vicker, R., "Some U.S. firms ignore urgings to leave, instead seek to upgrade status of blacks," Wall Street Journal, September 22, 1971.

Case

SAPPHIRE MANUFACTURING INVESTS IN SOUTH AFRICA

Sapphire Manufacturing Company is a medium-size tool company with total sales in the neighborhood of $225 million annually. The company makes precision hand tools of a general nature, but its bread-and-butter products are specialized tools designed for the servicing of industrial equipment, heavy trucks, construction equipment, military weapons, railway rolling stock, and aircraft. In its sales brochure, the company claims it is prepared to design and manufacture tools for servicing any engine, transmission, electrical or mechanical system in the world.

Sapphire's first overseas investment is being planned for South Africa, a joint venture with Capetown Machine Works, Limited. Sapphire and Capetown would form a new corporation called Cape Sapphire Tool Company, Limited, with each of the partners owning 50 percent of the venture. Under the agreement, Sapphire would supply design and technical expertise and Capetown the local management, production, and sales efforts. A new plant would be built and equipped outside Capetown. Maximum employment has been estimated at 350 persons, and the companies figure that 220 now unskilled persons would be trained to be skilled toolmakers.

Sapphire's management in the United States views the prospect of the joint venture with enthusiasm. Even though South Africa is in the midst of a recession and investment in that economy is low at present, that country is still the most developed on the continent. Most of the specialized tools used to service the already existing capital stock of the country are now imported; Sapphire figures that, with its expertise and the country's drive to conserve foreign exchange, it should become an instant factor in the tool market. Also, if originating countries ever embargo heavy-equipment sales to South Africa, the need for repair tools should increase, as the country tries to maintain and stretch the life of the existing capital stock.

Several of Sapphire's shareholders, however, have notified the company that they view the new venture with displeasure. Included in this group were several church groups with a long history of opposition to apartheid, the official racial policy of the South African government. George Stratton, Chairman of the Board of Sapphire, and Thomas Polomak, President, were both of the opinion that the South African joint venture was important to the company's continued success. They thought that Sapphire, being a small company, should be immune from the swirl of protests engulfing General Motors, Polaroid, Gulf Oil, and other business giants, since Sapphire's impact would be relatively minor; and smaller companies, fighting for their lives, must be allowed concessions that larger firms could be called to task for. Although Stratton and Polomak both "earned their business spurs" in the growing days of the tool industry, they were thought to be model contemporary businessmen. Sapphire hired without regard to race or religion and was a strong supporter of local and regional civic and social activities.

Three church groups, holding *in toto* 324 shares of Sapphire stock (one-fiftieth of one percent of the total shares outstanding), have announced that they are combining to raise the issue of the South African venture at the annual meeting. They also announced that, if Sapphire management would not agree to put the issue on the meeting's agenda, they would petition the Securities and Exchange Commission. Sapphire Manufacturing was incorporated in the State of Delaware, under whose laws a company can dispense with its annual meeting for proxy matters if shareholders so indicate. Stratton and Polomak, along with their families, own six percent of the shares outstanding.

Stratton and Polomak called in Jim Jenkins, a corporate staff public-relations officer who recently joined the company after a three-year stint as public relations officer at Crampton Oil, where he handled an incident involving Crampton's investment in Namibia. They wanted to discuss the strategy and substance of responding to the church groups. The two men lectured Jenkins for over an hour on the importance of the South African operation, on the role that Sapphire could play in the South African economy, and on their opinions of the groups seeking to raise the issue. Then they gave Jenkins the assignment of devising the corporate strategy and drafting the corporate response to be presented at the annual meeting.

Jenkins, who is a member of one of the church denominations involved in this issue, had been through something like this before at Crampton, but then the issue was not apartheid directly, but Namibia. He returned to his office and slumped into his chair. "Out of the frying pan and into the fire," he muttered. "Will it ever cease?"

9. *Business and Government*

The commonly held needs and values of a society's members or of the influential groups in a society are reinforced by all sorts of social mechanisms and conventions, not the least of which is government. When new needs or new values coalesce into some form of unity (or older values become more widely held), that unity is expressed very often through some action by the government in terms of legislation. This is not meant to imply that government always responds with knee-jerk reaction. The transformation of social values to law is a slow and evolutionary process subject to cultural lags, competing values, and varying degrees of political power.

Relative to business, if the social body comes to view a business practice with enough alarm, then that alarm may be manifested in some action by government. Put another way, when the noninternalized external costs of a business practice become onerous, legislation may be enacted to force business firms to absorb those costs. All sorts of laws and regulations come to mind in this regard—child-labor laws, pollution-control laws, equal-opportunity acts, occupational safety and health acts, noise requirements, zoning and billboard restrictions, and hazardous-substance regulations, for examples. Thus, business–government relationships—both legislative and enforcement—are increasingly crucial elements in the managerial decision process.

Business relationships with government can be classified for our purposes into four fairly distinct categories: the seller–customer relationship, government as the keeper of competition, government as the regulator of price and entry, and government as the promoter of citizen well-being.

GOVERNMENT AS THE CUSTOMER

We do not intend to cover this seller–buyer relationship in great depth; the topic, for the most part, properly falls under marketing. Our purpose in looking at this relationship is to mention a few of the social and political issues that are unique to this market relationship.

With the increasing governmental share of the national product, governments at all levels become valued, but fickle, customers. These relationships raise some serious ethical and social-power issues. One has to do with firms hiring former high-level military officers and governmental officials in sales or administrative posts. The practice is widespread, particularly among defense-related firms, leading some to question the potential for conflict of interest and cooperative processes. Many commentators, viewing noncompetitive bidding practices as well as staffing crossovers in the defense business, argue that, for all intents and purposes, the industries involved are close to being nationalized. Some have suggested that the arrangement be formalized.

Another important issue concerns the power of government to force firms and other contracting institutions to comply with side regulations in order to obtain or retain government contracts. For example, all government contractors must now abide by affirmative-action regulations promulgated by Executive Order 11246. Firms with government contracts are now required to set guidelines or goals on minority, female, and handicapped hiring, and file written reports on compliance. Side regulations pose few operational problems for the new bidder or the bidder with a small portion of its business in government contracts; the firm can simply opt out of the bidding process, or adjust its practices to conform to government requirements. But for the contractor locked into a long-term government contractual relationship, or for one with a substantial part of its business geared to government work, the value of the relationship may be decreased markedly with side conditions imposed.

One shouldn't look on the previous paragraph as a criticism of affirmative action; we are not passing judgment on that issue. We are more concerned with pointing out the power of government to impose side conditions on contracts. The power of government looms as the crucial issue, not the substance of the requirement.

GOVERNMENT, THE KEEPER OF COMPETITION

The federal government (as well as the states) has antitrust legislation on the books whose objectives are to maintain competition, preclude economic conspiracy, forestall monopoly, and prevent unfair competitive practices. While it is not possible here to cover very much of this exciting field, we should like to highlight some of the more important points and examine some of the issues.

Antitrust is an old doctrine, much older than the Sherman Act, which was passed in 1890 as the first federal antitrust law in the United States. The roots of antitrust go far back into common law, where practices such as monopoly and restraint of trade were held illegal. The Sherman Act was enacted because of the growth of the trusts and the activity of the so-called "robber barons." The states were unable or unwilling to control that growth.

It should be noted, however, that both the enactment and enforcement of antitrust laws are just as much politically inspired as they are necessitated by economic conditions. The Sherman Act was enacted in a period of populist unrest, along with a number of other laws to control business. The enforcement or nonenforcement of antitrust laws is related to political expediency, political and economic outlooks of the party controlling the White House, international relations, the state of business conditions at the time, and other political processes; sometimes these factors have a greater effect on antitrust action than do economic or concentration criteria.

At a minimum, all managers ought to know the rudiments of antitrust and be aware that the field is a complex one necessitating competent legal counsel. The

Sherman Act generally covers monopolization and conspiracy to fix prices, allocation of markets and restriction of competition. For monopolization, the "rule of reason" prevails; the process involves the action of a single firm and the question to be decided by the courts is: "Were the actions of the firm reasonable business practices, or was the intent of the firm clearly to create or sustain monopoly?" For example, in the famous 1911 case involving Standard Oil Company of New Jersey, the court found that the company did engage in several predatory practices designed to force other firms out of business. These practices were found to be unreasonable competitive acts calculated to enable Standard Oil to monopolize the oil business. Note that monopoly is not necessarily illegal under the Sherman Act; there are several cases in which the court has declared having a monopoly not to be illegal. The key question is whether the firm acted *unreasonably* in trying to achieve a monopoly — e.g., monopolization.

With a conspiracy (involving more than one party), the *per se* doctrine generally is applied. Price fixing, market allocation, and similar anticompetitive practices are *per se* illegal; no defense based on the reasonableness of the results of the conspiracy is allowed. Thus, in the celebrated 1960 electrical manufacturers' price-fixing case, once the managers admitted meeting to fix prices, the case was closed except for sentencing. Some companies attempted to mollify shareholders by stating, in their annual reports, that no customers were harmed by the actions of the managers who conspired. These statements may have been good public relations, but they were bad law. Such pleas are inadmissible for the court.

The Clayton Act covers chiefly price discrimination, tying contracts, and mergers, "where the effect . . . may be substantially to lessen competition or tend to create a monopoly . . ." Unlike the Sherman Act, the cases under the Clayton Act need not require the establishment of intent, or proof of predatory practices. The Act's key words are "may be"; and a potential merger, for example, may be disallowed if the government is able to establish its case that the merger *would tend* to diminish competition.

Antitrust is also covered in Section 5 of the Federal Trade Commission Act, which declares unlawful "unfair methods of competition in commerce, and unfair or deceptive acts or practices in commerce . . ." While the two major statutes in antitrust remain the Sherman and Clayton Acts, the Federal Trade Commission does have concurrent jurisdiction with the Justice Department in enforcing the Clayton Act.

For managers, the key questions concern their behavior and the possible penalties for running afoul of the laws. Civil penalties concern the firm as an entity and are aimed at restoring conditions to those that obtained prior to the case at hand, preventing new conditions from developing, or paying for inconveniences. A merger may be disallowed, a cease-and-desist order or an injunction issued, or a divestiture may be ordered. Criminal penalties — or punishment for wrongdoings — can directly affect the manager. The Sherman Act, as amended, provides for penalties of up to $100,000 in fines for individuals and $1 million in fines for corporations, per offense. In addition, the law provides for possible jail sentences of up to one year per offense. Monetary sentences are most common, but the 90-day jail sentences meted out in 1960 dispelled any notion that penalties of incarceration were *not* being applied. Even more important to the managers than penalties, however, may be the effect that a conviction has on his or her reputation and chances for advancement.

Antitrust is a complex and confusing area. Many business people complain that they do not know what is expected of them. Others cite the contention that the administration in power, or the social or economic tenor of the times, has more to do with the enforcement of antitrust than do the economic issues involved in any one particular case. At least one economist has commented that, in merger cases, antitrust is grossly unfair. While the large firms are generally immune from prosecution for monopolization under the Sherman Act by the Rule of Reason, the merger of two smaller firms would tend to reduce competition under the Clayton Act and hence would be subject to challenge. Finally, some writers have complained about the lack of expertise of the courts in adjudicating economic cases. Judges have little training or expertise in economics, and get little assistance in the area. As an administrative agency, the Federal Trade Commission is supposed to apply this expertise, but the fact remains that major antitrust cases end up in the courts.

GOVERNMENT AS A REGULATOR OF PRICE AND ENTRY

Many firms are vested with what is called the public interest—their services are indispensable, and they must be encouraged to provide those services; yet, if they were left to operate freely, they could cause harm to the public welfare. Hence, the business practices and the scope of operations of these firms come under government scrutiny.

Here we deal with such natural monopolies as electric power, telephone services, and water provision. These natural monopolies are regulated because it is inconvenient to have several sets of utility lines or pipes serving a community, because the services are deemed essential to the public welfare, and primarily because the industry incurs large capital costs in relation to the market; in essence, the size of the market relative to the technology *requires* a monopoly. No electric company, for example, adds the relatively small kilowatt-hour capacity to service one new home; the company would add millions of kilowatt-hours at one time, because power plants of that size are the minimum necessary to yield economically optimum output.

Thus, utilities are generally regulated in terms of price. Their prices are set to allow all costs to be recovered, along with a reasonable return on investment; the price, however, is supposedly set below a monopoly rate of return. The public, in theory at least, is guaranteed prices below those of an unregulated monopolistic seller, while the utility is guaranteed sufficient income to pay all operating costs and sustain its necessary capital base.

Questions are continually raised about the efficiency and effectiveness of regulation in protecting the public. Calculating costs and valuing the rate base continue to consume the time of economists and accountants, and recent controversies over the fuel-factor charge (in some states, utilities are allowed to adjust electric charges based on the cost of fuel, without going to the utility regulatory commission) have stirred legislative study of utility pricing.

Also, the question has been raised as to whether it is really in the public interest to totally protect the monopoly status of a utility. For example, telephone companies usually retain control of the equipment that can be installed on their lines; yet competitive manufacturers can make equipment of equal or better quality that can be installed by the customer. Should the customer be precluded from using that equipment? Should the company be given the authority to charge the customer a fee for connecting his equipment to company lines? Can the telephone company be treated similarly to the electric company, where the customer buys and installs the appliances and merely buys the *current* from the utility? Since the Carterphone decision, telephone companies must allow privately owned equipment, but can require the user to buy an interconnect device, supposedly to prevent the telephone system from being damaged by electrical surges. There is, however, urging that the interlock be done away with and that the installation of privately owned equipment be allowed without it. The Federal Communications Commission has indeed ruled that way, provided the equipment is approved by the FCC.

Government also regulates the prices and/or entry of many professions, trades, and industries beyond those classified as natural monopolies. Liquor stores, funeral parlors, airlines, taxicabs, doctors, lawyers, plumbers, electricians, truckers, are all examples. Indirectly, some local communities, through the use of zoning regulations, limit the entry of many types of firms even though the areas for commercial and industrial use exist. Many communities, for example, bar the operation of fast-food restaurants. Entry regulations are usually rationalized in terms of guaranteeing expertise, or because of some moral or ethical positions of the community. In the case of liquor stores, for example, limiting consumption of alcoholic beverages both in total and to specified age groups are primary objectives.

The question raised by many economists is whether all of this regulation is really in the public interest. Some commentators have expressed the opinion that businesses might prefer to be regulated. Regulation can limit competition and free the industries being regulated of the uncertainties of market mechanisms. Others perceive that regulatory commissions go through a life cycle, the last phase of that cycle being virtual captivity by the very industry they were supposed to regulate. The practice of limiting entry is also subject to question. Does limiting the number of liquor stores benefit the public or the fortunate few liquor-store licensees? Does the passage of requirements for funerals benefit the public or the funeral directors? Does the regulation of passenger fares benefit the public or the airlines? These are all questions being asked these days as the topic of deregulation becomes very fashionable in economic and political circles.

PROMOTION OF CITIZEN WELL-BEING

Finally, government regulates all businesses in many social areas related to the well-being of the citizenry. In some cases, the regulation is strictly convenience-related, such as when the business firm may act as a tax collector for government (withholding Social Security and income taxes, collecting sales taxes, etc.). In others, the laws simply extend government's role as a protector of the public welfare into the workplace, where much of the public's time is spent. Occupational Safety and Health Acts, child-labor laws, and equal-opportunity acts are illustrative here. In still other instances, government may act to force business to be more open to the public; unit-pricing regulations, for example. Under the social well-being category, we can also include our pollution laws, plant-beautification regulations, flammable-product restrictions, and many others.

The essence of many of these laws (although this is not articulated when the law is passed) is that government is taking action to mitigate effects on the public and to force business to absorb social or external costs. Those side-effects for which business does not pay (lung damage, foul odors, polluted water, unsafe or unsanitary conditions) are now forced back on the firm in terms of real rather than external—and not absorbed—costs.

Obviously, the area of business–government relations is a huge one, and we can sample but a few of the relationships in this book. But the student is encouraged to think critically in this area. One might consider, for example, just what government really is. Most people refer to government as some monolithic body when, in fact, it is a multisided institution in which one hand often moves in different directions from the other. It is not unusual to find the Pentagon awarding a contract to a firm which is under investigation by the Internal Revenue Service or the object of an antitrust case by the Justice Department or the Federal Trade Commission. Nor is it unusual for a state or a municipality to be at loggerheads with the Federal government over pollution or desegregation. Thus, the locus of power within our governmental system is a key consideration.

Students are also encouraged to think critically about regulation: Is a particular regulation good for society? Or is it good for business? Or perhaps it might only be good for government, where often regulatory agencies refuse to depart the scene even when no longer relevent.

Government is a powerful social tool, and its wise use accomplishes many valued social ends, but as with any institution, its virtues usually are accompanied by problems.

THE READINGS

The first article, by former Secretary of Labor, John T. Dunlop, is entitled "The Limits of Legal Compulsion." Dunlop examines the problem of regulation, which he views as mostly process-oriented in the area of social regulation. He writes, "Regulation to achieve a public purpose continues, but the central concern is the methods, approaches, and mutual attitudes of the regulators and the regulatees." He reserves the question of deregulation to "economic regulation of prices, rates, or fees, and related conditions of entry to a market." Following his listing of problems, he offers a set of suggestions toward improving the regulatory process.

The *Business Week* selection provides us with insight into some of the controversy surrounding proposals for change in the antitrust laws, new tactics of the Justice Department and the Federal Trade Commission, the concerns of business people and economists, and a consideration of the structural efficacy of U.S. industry.

Finally, again from *Business Week*, we have included a compendium of federal regulatory agencies, their functions, characteristics, and other data concerning their operations.

The Limits of Legal Compulsion*

John T. Dunlop

In recent years a rapid expansion of government controls has been associated at the same time with a growing dissatisfaction with the effects of regulation. Scholarly books and journals have offered detailed criticisms of specific regulatory policies, but these analyses have neither slowed the growth of formal regulation nor encouraged the development of alternative approaches to problems.

The issue confronts those involved in public policy generally. The Department of Labor, however, is an unusual vantage point from which to survey different types of regulatory programs and the arguments about their usefulness. In recent years the Department has been assigned one of the most extensive sets of regulatory programs in the Federal government. In 1940 the Department administered 18 regulatory programs; by 1960 the number had expanded to 40; in 1975 the number stands at 134. At present the Department has responsibility for promulgating and administering complex regulations under the Occupational Safety and Health Act, the Urban Mass Transportation Act, the Consumer Credit Protection Act, the Davis–Bacon Act, the Civil Rights Act of 1964, the Equal Pay Act, the Employee Retirement Income Security Act, and many others. All of these regulatory programs establish substantive—and in many cases quantitative—definitions of acceptable conduct for employers, employees, and third parties

The Department thus provides examples for a broader comparison between essentially private methods for rule-making within a broad and general governmental context—exemplified by collective bargaining—and the more intensive approach of governmental promulgation of mandatory regulations.

A distinction also needs to be drawn between economic regulation of prices, rates or fees and related conditions of entry to a market, on the one hand, and social regulation, on the other, affecting conditions of work such as discrimination, health and safety and the like. In the case of economic regulation it may often be appropriate to raise the question of whether the interests of a sector and

From *The Conference Board Record*, March, 1976. Reprinted by Special Permission of The Conference Board.

*This article is drawn from remarks prepared for the White House staff in December 1977 by the author in his capacity as U.S. Secretary of Labor.

the public may not better be served by deregulation. In the field of social regulation, while some deregulation may be appropriate, the major areas of review are likely practically to be concerned with methods of regulation, involvement of those affected, enforcement, compliance approaches and communication to those affected. Regulation to achieve a public purpose continues, but the central concern is the methods, approaches and mutual attitudes of the regulators and the regulatees.

Over the years regulation has proved to be a practical and effective approach to some social and economic problems. The inspection of meat and poultry is an obvious example and suggests the sort of concerns that prompted the development of regulation in the late 18th century. In the words of a foremost student of administrative law, Kenneth Culp Davis, "Practical men were seeking practical answers to immediate problems. . . . What was needed was a governmental authority having power not merely to adjudicate, but to initiate proceedings, to investigate, to prosecute, to issue regulation having force of law, to supervise." From these perceived needs developed the structure of modern regulation, an approach which is now used, without significant modification, as our principal policy tool for dealing with occupational disease, discrimination, dangerous toys and pollution.

THE REGULATORY PROBLEM

A major reason for the attraction of regulation over the years has been the belief that it is a speedy, simple and cheap procedure. It should be apparent that the administrative procedure is by no means fast or inexpensive, but the prevailing belief is that it is. This misconception, in large part, is due to the fact that the constraints on the rule-making and adjudicating activities of regulatory agencies are not widely perceived or appreciated. Perhaps, too, because the majority of Congressmen are lawyers, and not business executives, labor leaders, economists or labor mediators, they are apt to think of social and economic problems in legal terms. For these and other reasons, when a problem acquires national attention—as pollution, inflation and occupational disease have in recent years—the natural reaction has been to create a new regulatory agency to deal with it. There are a variety of problems with this approach.

1. The first problem with regulation is that it encourages simplistic thinking about complicated issues. To get regulatory legislation passed in a pluralistic society often requires the evocation of horror stories and the mobilization of broad political support. To quote Professor Wilson: "Political inertia is not easily overcome, and when it is overcome, it is often at the price of exaggerating the virtue of those who are to benefit (a defrauded debtor, a sick industry) or the wickedness of those who are to bear the burden (a smog-belching car, a polluting factory, a grasping creditor)."

2. Second, designing and administering a regulatory program is an incredibly complicated task. How successfully and efficiently occupational disease or discrimination in hiring practices will be reduced depends not just on the kind of goals set by Congress or a few key decisions by civil servants in Wash-

ington but upon tens of thousands of individual actions taken by business firms and private citizens across the country. Ensuring compliance with a regulation is far more difficult than promulgating it, though that too can be a complicated and lengthy process. There are, for example, 5 million workplaces and 1,200 OSHA inspectors. All affected parties can never be notified of a new rule's existence, and thus reasonably be expected to comply — and the means of informing regulatees of new rules (mainly through publication in the *Federal Register*) is severely inadequate.

3. Third, oftentimes policies that appear straightforward will have unintended consequences which can create problems as severe as those with which the regulations were intended to deal. For example, the Wagner Act meant to encourage the development of unions and collective bargaining, but its concept of "exclusive representation" — where the employees in a unit decide which union, if any, they want to represent them in bargaining with management — contradicted the traditional union principle of "exclusive jurisdiction" — in which all workers in a particular craft or industry are legitimately represented by one union. The Wagner Act had the effect of encouraging competition between unions for members, hence disputes between unions and changing the internal governance of organized labor — an entirely unintended effect. Article XX of the AFL-CIO Constitution was later adopted to provide a method for mitigating these disputes through limited arbitration; competitive elections, rational bargaining structures and union jurisdiction are not entirely compatible. It is very hard for affected groups to perceive the longer-term and often unintended consequences of regulation.

4. Fourth, the rule-making and adjudicatory procedures of regulatory agencies tend to be very slow, creating conflicts between the different groups involved, and leading to weak and ineffective remedies for the people the programs aim to help. Early experience demonstrated the need for the regulatory agencies' procedures to include the same sort of safeguards to ensure fairness that were present in the judicial and legislative processes. The result eventually was the Administrative Procedure Act of 1946, which established formal procedures for the promulgation of rules and the adjudication of cases. The purpose was to ensure that each party affected by a proposed rule would have an opportunity to present its views, thereby limiting the possibility that regulations or decisions would be arbitrary, unworkable, or unfair.

Common sense recognizes the importance of these procedures, but while they are designed to make regulation fair, they can also make it rigid. When a regulatory program is imposed immediately upon passage and the administrative agency lacks authority to adjust the law to fit the realities of business practices — as is the case with some requirements of the new pension law (ERISA) — the result is often based on abstractions which are fair and effective in some settings and pointless and burdensome in others. In the case of one ERISA provision, for example, the Department of Labor received over 220,000 individual requests for exemption, some taking more than 12 months to process. The procedure is lengthy and complicated: if an exemption is proposed, it is then published in the *Federal Register* and comments are solicited; a public hearing can be requested and if, as a result, the exemption is modified, then the procedure may be repeated. The process is often prolonged by different groups taking advantage of procedure to advance their interests; thus, a legitimate exemption may take months to obtain.

5. Fifth, the rule-making and adjudicatory procedures do not include a mechanism for the development of mutual accommodation among the conflicting interests. Opposing interests argue their case to the government, and not at each other. Direct discussions and negotiations among opposing points of view, where mutual accommodation is mutually desirable — as in collective bargaining — forces the parties to set priorities among their demands, trading off one for another — creating an incentive for them to find common ground. The values, perceptions, and needs of each become apparent. And some measure of mutual understanding is a by-product. As compulsory arbitration undermines the willingness of the parties to bargain conscientiously over the differences, so regulation lessens incentives for private accommodations of conflicting viewpoints. Public hearings encourage dramatic presentations and exorbitant demands and the government's disclosure rules and the Advisory Committee Act inhibit private meetings between the affected parties and the agency.

The regulatory agency is thus ignorant of the parties' true positions, and is forced to guess each interest's priorities and needs from the formal and often extreme public statements the parties have presented at public hearings. The regulatory process encourages conflict, rather than acting to reconcile opposing interests. Moreover, there is a sense that it is wrong for the regulatory agency to try to bring parties together and develop consensus. Relying on public and highly formal proceedings makes the development of consensus extremely difficult, if not impossible. And unless this consensus can be developed, neither party has any stake in the promulgated rule, thus is free to complain that it is biased, stupid or misguided. Moreover, each side is free to continue the controversy in the form of endless petitions for review, clarification and litigation before the agency and the courts. Nothing is ever settled because true settlement can come only through agreement, consent or acquiescence.

6. A sixth problem is that regulatory efforts are rarely abandoned even after their purpose has been served. As James Q. Wilson has pointed out: "Both business firms and regulatory agencies operate on the basis of a common principle: Maintain the organization . . . for the public agency that means creating and managing services (or a public image of services) that please key Congressmen, organized clients, and the news media."

A parallel problem affects the agency's body of regulations: repealing or modifying those rules is a lengthly and complicated process and is rarely done. Thus the code becomes bloated with anachronistic and rarely enforced regulations that nonetheless have the force of law and could be applied at the convenience of a compliance officer. Trivial and important regulations are mixed; to the regulatee the program appears irrational and arbitrary. Also, as the body of rules expands, it becomes increasingly more difficult and expensive for the regulatees to figure out what is required of them. In this way, the agency and its rules remain in place long after their usefulness has been served.

7. A seventh problem involves the legal gameplaying between the regulatees and the regulators; the tax law is the classic example, but it is typical of regulatory programs in general. The regulatory agency promulgates a regulation; the regulatees challenge it in court; if they lose, their lawyers may seek or find another ground for administrative or judicial challenge. Congressional amendments may be developed. Between a challenge to the regulation's basic legality, pressure on the agency for an amended regulation, and administrative and judicial enforcement proceedings, there is ample opportunity for tactical strategies, allegations of ambiguity, pleas of special circumstances and the like.

It should be a first principle that no set of men is smart enough to write words around which others cannot find holes when the stakes are high.

8. An eighth problem with regulation concerns the difficulty encountered by small and medium size firms in complying with the regulations of the various agencies, and the problems the government has in trying to enforce compliance. Many regulations do not well fit the circumstances of small enterprises. It is often difficult if not impossible for small to medium size firms to keep track of the large number of regulations issued by various agencies. And there is little reason to do so; the chances of a small or medium-size firm being inspected are minute, and if it is inspected and found to be in violation fines for a first offense are usually small. Thus, it may make practical business sense for a firm to put off the expenses required to achieve compliance until after an inspection has specified those changes which have to be made. Compliance cannot be compelled through a police effort in every workplace, given any practicable levels of funds and personnel.

To a degree "public examples"—where a company found in violation is given harsh and visible treatment— encourages other companies to come into compliance. But this tactic is generally unsuccessful for several reasons: nearly every company—particularly small ones—has a good or plausible excuse for not being in compliance (e.g., they were not aware of the regulations), thus, a large fine tends to get whittled down to a small one through the successive stages of administrative review; also, such tactics are perceived to be unfair and generate strong resentment in public opinion and the press and create hostility to the program and attempts to change it in the political arena.

9. Ninth, over time as the rule-making and compliance activities of regulatory agencies become routine, it grows increasingly difficult for the President and the agency to attract highly qualified and effective administrators into leadership positions. As the quality of leadership declines, problems often receive increasingly less imaginative treatment or no attention at all.

10. Tenth, uniform national regulations are inherently unworkable in many situations because the society is not uniform. There are significant differences among industries and sectors and regions of the country. Consequently, a regulation may be unrealistically harsh in one industry or sector or part of the country and too lenient in another.

11. An eleventh problem is what is called "regulatory overlap," where a number of different regulatory agencies share some of the same responsibilities. Although the creation of a new specialized agency probably heightens effectiveness in one field, the danger is that a series of uncoordinated steps, each quite sensible in themselves, can set up a feedback of unanticipated consequences that is overwhelmingly negative. No one regulatory program is ever able to see the problems through the eyes of those subject to regulation, and the total consequences of regulatory programs on the firm or industry are never perceived. There is no mechanism in government to add up these consequences. Moreover, jurisdictional conflict among agencies, even with the best of good will, consumes vast amounts of time and energy and stimulates general disrespect for governmental agencies.

TOWARD IMPROVEMENT

It is not realistic to expect any significant reduction in the number of Federal regulatory programs in the immediate future; in fact, it is likely that the political processes and the Congress will seek to add new ones. Regardless of the theoretical merits of regulation, it is important, as a practical matter, that more attention be given towards improving the quality of regulation. In a sense, accommodation with practical reality has always occurred. While some inspectors in the field enforce the letter of the law, others develop an array of informal operating rules of thumb which drafters of the regulations never thought of, or indeed rejected. Sometimes these rules of thumb call for nonenforcement in trivial cases or where application of a rigid rule would be unreasonable. "Policy-makers" would do well to address explicitly that which lower level implementers will do anyway —though unevenly—through the application of common sense or prejudice. The following suggestions are designed to make the regulatory process more responsive to the problems cited above.

First, *the parties who will be affected by a set of regulations should be involved to a greater extent in developing those regulations.*

The way regulations are currently developed is inherently contentious and acts to maximize antagonism between the parties. The result is poorly framed rules, law suits, evasion and dissatisfaction with the program by all parties. In our society, a rule that is developed with the involvement of the parties who are affected is more likely to be accepted and to be effective in accomplishing its intended purposes.

There is no single way by which the parties can be involved in the rule-making process, but a method is suggested by the Department of Labor's recent experience with section 13(c) of the Urban Mass Transportation Act. UMTA gives grants to cities to take over failing private transit systems. Section 13(c) requires that funds not be granted until the Secretary of Labor has certified that employees would not be adversely affected by the Federally funded activities. This requirement has caused substantial delays and confusion as unions and private managers or city officials haggled over what constituted equitable compensation. Rather than prepare regulations, the Department brought together union and transit representatives and got them to prepare a three-year agreement as to what protection employees should receive as a consequence of the Federally funded activities. The Department mediated and provided technical assistance helping to create the standards to apply to individual cases presented to it. Processing time will be very noticeably reduced.

This approach is not necessarily applicable without modification to, say, OSHA or ERISA, but it represents a useful spirit of reliance on private mechanisms which sometimes can achieve a program objective most efficiently.

Second, *anachronistic and unnecessary regulations should be repealed and, in the future, rules should be promulgated with greater reluctance.* It is an open question as to how many regulations a business, particularly one of small or medium size, can absorb. Not only is it difficult for the regulatee to figure out what is required but it is equally hard for compliance officers to determine violations. Often they rely on a small percentage of the rules with which they are familiar; thus the trivial rules are enforced as often as the important ones. This causes annoyance with the program without producing substantial benefits.

Third, *greater emphasis should be placed on helping regulatees achieve compliance, especially through consultation.* Trying to force compliance primarily through threats of inspections and stiff fines has not proved successful. It has worked against acceptance of the programs by isolating the regulators (and their expertise) from the regulatees and creating antagonism and distrust between the two. As pointed out earlier, the chances of a small or medium-size business ever being inspected are minute and the cost of coming into compliance is often high. If the business executive asks the agency for technical assistance, in effect the person is asking to be inspected; at least this is the common perception. The regulatory agencies have the expertise to deal with complicated, technical problems such as pollution and occupational disease. But because the programs appear punitive, there is little constructive interplay between the regulators and the regulatees.

Fourth, *the activities of the various regulatory agencies need to be coordinated better.* As it is now, a single firm may be under the purview of OFCC, OSHA, the Wage and Hour Administration and a variety of other programs. Simply the number of forms required poses a substantial burden, again, encouraging antagonism for the programs. More significantly, the jurisdictions may overlap. As a long-range goal, perhaps some consolidation and more coordination and sensitivity can occur.

Fifth, *regulations must be made to reflect differences between industries, sectors, and geographic regions.* A rule that is fair and workable in New York may be excessively severe or unnecessary in Utah. Similar problems exist between industries and types of enterprises and labor organizations. Uniform, national rules may assure equity but they do not reflect the reality of the workplace.

Sixth, *the actions of the various regulatory agencies need to be brought into greater harmony with collective bargaining.* Many of these programs undermine relations between organized labor and management, as when issues of safety and health, apprenticeship and training, and pensions are placed under government regulation. Without limiting its responsibility to administer the law, and recognizing that some laws are designed explicitly to change the results produced by private collective bargaining, there are ways to involve the parties better to achieve practical and acceptable solutions.

THE CENTRAL ISSUE

The country needs to acquire a more realistic understanding of the limits to the degree to which social change can be brought about through legal compulsion. A great deal of government needs to be devoted to improving understanding, persuasion, accommodation, mutual problem-solving and informal mediation. Legislation, litigation and regulations are useful means for some social and economic problems, but today government has more regulation on its plate than it can handle. In many areas the growth of regulations and law has far outstripped our capacity to develop consensus and mutual accommodation, to our common detriment.

It has well been said that the recreation and development of trust is the central problem of government in our times. The development of new attitudes on the part of public employees and new relationships and procedures with those who are required to live under regulations is a central challenge of democratic society. Trust cannot grow in an atmosphere dominated by bureaucratic fiat and litigious controversy; it emerges through persuasion, mutual accommodation and problem-solving.

Is John Sherman's Antitrust Obsolete?

Business Week

The head of the major U.S. corporation spoke feelingly: "I would be very glad if we knew exactly where we stand, if we could be free from danger, trouble, and criticism." His plea could have been made yesterday, by executives at IBM, Xerox, GTE, General Motors, AT&T, Exxon, Standard Brands, Chrysler, or dozens of other large companies that have recently stood in the dock, accused of violating the nation's antitrust laws.

It was, in fact, said back in 1912 by Elbert H. Gary, chairman of U.S. Steel Corp. He was giving a Congressional committee his views on the need for updating the country's first antitrust law, the Sherman Act, to which Ohio Senator John Sherman gave his name in 1890. Echoing the sentiments of many executives, Gary complained bitterly of the restraints imposed by the antitrust law on his company's ability to compete in world markets. Business had grown too big and complex, Gary maintained, to be shoehorned into laws drawn from Adam Smith's economic model of many small companies competing in local markets.

Two years later Congress gave Gary an unwelcome answer to his plea. It passed an even more restrictive antitrust measure, the Clayton Act, and set up the Federal Trade Commission to police business practices and methods of competition even more closely.

Today business faces much the same danger, trouble, and criticism that disturbed Gary, and is raising much the same complaints against antitrust. The International Telephone & Telegraph Corp. scandal and corporate participation in Watergate has stirred up deep public distrust of national institutions, including business. In response, as in Gary's day, the antitrust wind is rising, blown up currently by the oil crisis and fanned by consumerists, such as Ralph Nader, who argue that antitrust weapons have been used like peashooters against dinosaurs. Business almost certainly faces even tougher antitrust enforcement and possibly even a new antitrust law aimed at breaking up the corporate giants in the country's basic industries.

This prospect points up the underlying question businessmen ask about antitrust: Are laws framed more than three-quarters of a century ago appropriate legal weapons in a market system grown increasingly large, complex, and multinational? In raising this basic issue, businessmen can point to a far-reaching, intricate web of laws and rules that has made the government the regulator, watchdog, and even partner of business. Wage and price controls, health and safety regulations, and disclosure laws, are all a far cry from the economy of Sherman's or Gary's day.

Businessmen complain of the unsettling vagueness of the antitrust laws, which permits antitrusters to attack many long-standing business practices in their effort to root out restraints of trade and monopoly. The FTC, for example, is now suing Kellogg, General Foods, General Mills, and Quaker Oats, alleging that such procedures as having route men arrange their breakfast cereals on supermarkets shelves are anticompetitive. The Justice Dept. has a similar suit against tire makers Goodyear and Firestone.

Executives of International Business Machines Corp., caught by both government and private antitrust suits attacking pricing and promotion policies, privately declare that they are baffled over what they can legally do. Bertram C. Dedman, vice-president and general counsel for INA Corp., echoes a widely held view: "We never really know precisely what antitrust means. It's frequently strictly a matter of opinion."

Enormous economic stakes are involved in antitrust enforcement. Such current cases as those against IBM, Xerox Corp., and other giants involve billions of dollars' worth of capital investment and stockholder interests. Executives fear that such suits give broad power to courts not schooled in business, economics, or industrial technology. This power was dramatically illustrated last fall when U.S. District Judge A. Sherman Christensen announced a $352-million judgment against IBM and then confessed error, sending IBM's stock into wild gyrations.

Many businessmen wonder whether their companies are often targets of antitrust prosecution simply because they are big and successful. Philadelphia lawyer Edward D. Slevin sums up this attitude: "If the free market is pushed to its fullest extent, somebody wins. But the Justice Dept. seems to say: 'Now that you've won, you've cornered the market. We're going to break you up and start over.'"

All this, say many executives, makes it increasingly difficult for American business to compete internationally. Douglas Grymes, president of Koppers Co., argues that "big corporations are the only ones that can compete with big corporations in world markets." He says that the antitrust laws seem to equate bigness itself with monopoly and thus hinder American corporations from reaching the size necessary for world competition.

TOUGHER ENFORCEMENT LIKELY

Despite all these deeply felt concerns, the antitrust laws are likely to become even tougher and more restrictive. Starting with the Sherman Act, antitrust has been a product more of politics than of economics. Today's rising populist sentiment has led to demands for tighter antitrust enforcement. Only a decade ago historian Richard Hofstadter wrote, "The antitrust movement is one of the faded passions of American reform." Today it is the darling of reform. As James T. Halverson, director of the FTC's Bureau of Competition, sums up: "The political atmosphere is very favorable to antitrust right now."

The many signs of stepped-up antitrust activity in the last one or two years make an impressively lengthy list. They include:

New investigations

Last week three federal agencies—Justice, the FTC, and the SEC—as well as some congressmen, revealed that they are turning to a little-used section of the Clayton Act to investigate the complex of interlocking directorships among major oil companies.

New legislation

The industrial reorganization bill that Senator Philip A. Hart (D-Mich.) introduced in Congress last year would provide a new legal basis for breaking up leading companies in the nation's most basic industries: autos, iron and steel, nonferrous metals, chemicals and drugs, electrical machinery and equipment, electronic computing and communications equipment, and energy. It is given no immediate chance to pass, but its ideas could find their way into future legislation. Another bill introduced by Senator John V. Tunney (D-Calif.), already approved by the Senate and taking a back seat to impeachment considerations in the House, would increase the current maximum criminal antitrust fine from $50,000 to $500,000 for corporations and $100,000 for executives. It would also require the Justice Dept. to explain publicly its reasons for accepting a consent decree instead of preparing a case and actually going to trial.

Bigger enforcement budgets

The Administration is seeking large increases, by usually puny antitrust standards, in the fiscal 1975 budgets of both the Justice Dept. and the FTC for their antitrust departments. If Congress approves, Justice's Antitrust Div. will pick up 83 additional staff slots, more than half lawyers and economists. At the last big increase, fiscal 1970, the division got only 20. The FTC is due for an additional $3 million, or a 20% increase in its present antitrust budget.

Growing muscle at FTC

After a long hibernation, the FTC is stepping out as a feisty agency with a new esprit, a highly professional staff, and a taste for going after bigness. It filed the monopoly suits against Xerox Corp. and the four biggest cereal makers. It has a special unit with an extra $1-million appropriation to litigate its case to break up the eight leading oil companies. And it got important new powers from Congress last year, including the right to demand otherwise unavailable product-line sales and profit figures from companies without first clearing with the Office of Management & Budget.

How Justice and the FTC Compete

The antitrust laws exist to preserve the values of competition, so it may be entirely logical that two agencies compete to administer them. On paper, the Antitrust Div. of the Justice Dept. and the Federal Trade Commission are different kinds of agencies. Justice is the law enforcement branch of the Executive Branch, the FTC is an independent regulatory commission. But in their antitrust responsibilities they are quite similar.

The Antitrust Div., headed by Thomas E. Kauper, is responsible for enforcing the Sherman and Clayton Acts. It has the exclusive power to bring criminal prosecutions. It also tries to enjoin anticompetitive mergers and a variety of collusive practices. The FTC's power springs from the Federal Trade Commission Act of 1914. Over the years, the courts have interpreted Section 5 of that Act to include all offenses proscribed by the other antitrust laws, giving the FTC equal civil jurisdiction with Justice. In fact, it has a broader civil authority, since it is required to proceed against "unfair methods of competition" and, as added by the Wheeler–Lea Act of 1938, against "unfair or deceptive acts or practices in commerce." These phrases permit the FTC to go after business conduct that is not necessarily collusive. The FTC, for example, has premised the cases against four big cereal makers on a variety of practices that it charges are unfair methods of competition, allegations that are not open to the Justice Dept. to make.

Resources The Antitrust Div. has an annual budget of some $14 million, the FTC $15 million for antitrust purposes. Both together represent tiny sums contrasted with the resources private business is able to draw on. International Business Machines Corp., for example, reimbursed Control Data Corp. $15 million in legal fees and expenses in settling the private suit CDC filed against IBM.

Reorganizing justice

If the Justice Dept.'s monopoly case against IBM, filed more than five years ago, is successful, it would give new spirit to the Antitrust Div., which at least until recently has been demoralized by the successive shocks of ITT and Watergate. Even so, the division reorganized and beefed up its economics staff last fall to enable it to undertake investigations and prosecutions with a sharper eye to the economic impact of its actions.

More and tougher antitrust enforcement is foreshadowed by more subtle changes in mood and belief as well as by these specific developments. One such change is a growing recognition that the government itself creates monopoly power. Several weeks ago Columbia Law School called together many of the nation's leading industrial economists and antitrust lawyers for a conference on industrial concentration. The participants examined what business concentration means both for the economy and for the antitrust policy. About the only thing

---

Occasionally the agencies take potshots at each other. The FTC last year finally got the power, formerly reserved to the Justice Dept., to go into court on its own to enforce its own decrees. The FTC complained that Justice sat on requests for action. Justice countered that the requests were poorly framed.

But the agencies usually work reasonably well together. Now, when good politics dictates making headlines as tough antitrusters, the brass at each shop says the rivalry between the two to bring and win significant cases serves as a spur to both. The rivalry, says Justice's Kauper, is a "friendly" one. "Each has kept the other at it," he says. The FTC's Halverson concurs, citing "good practical results" from the existence of two agencies.

Neither agency launches an investigation without first clearing it with the other. The first agency to propose a particular investigation gets it, provided there is no conflict with the other's on-going work. Disagreements are settled at weekly liaison meetings. When a conflict cannot be settled at meetings, the assistant attorney general and the chairman of the FTC, Lewis A. Engman, deal with it.

The home for a particular kind of case is partly a matter of historical accident and partly the predilection of staff lawyers. Price discrimination cases under the Robinson–Patman act are traditionally prosecuted by the FTC, which also generally probes problems in food and textile industries. Justice almost always gets steel cases. While Justice must proceed on a case-by-case basis, the FTC has the power also to issue rules with the force of law, in effect to promulgate codes of commercial conduct. Until recently, Justice alone had specific authority to try to block an unconsummated merger. But the FTC just gained similar powers in the law authorizing the Alaska pipeline.

generally agreed on was that governmental attempts to regulate an industry often result in preserving the monopoly power of those being regulated. In line with this belief, insiders say that the Antitrust Div. will step up its policy of intervening in other government proceedings to shape regulatory policy consistent with antitrust principles. Last January, for example, the division formally intervened in FCC proceedings in an attempt to deny renewal of the broadcasting license of Cowles Communications, Inc., in Des Moines, and those of Pulitzer Publishing Co. and Newhouse Broadcasting Corp. in St. Louis. All these companies also own newspapers.

Another change has been the dramatic multiplication of private antitrust suits—those brought by one company against another. These include the 40-odd private business suits against IBM, ITT's suit to split up General Telephone & Electronics Corp., and the large class actions against plumbing and wallboard manufacturers. In fiscal 1973 the government filed 45 antitrust suits. By comparison, businessmen and other private parties filed 1,152, making the business community itself a significant factor in antitrust enforcement.

All this is leading to an antitrust Congress. Victor H. Kramer, director of Washington's Institute for Public Interest Representation and a leading antitrust lawyer, expects that "more supporters of an effective antimonopoly program are going to be elected to the 94th Congress than to any previous Congress in many years."

THE ALTERNATIVES

But as antitrust action steps up, so do the conflicts over the direction antitrust policy should take. The populists contend that antitrust enforcement in the past has been spineless. Businessmen complain that current policy paralyzes corporations because they are uncertain what practices are lawful and that they are being punished for being successfully competitive. Who is right?

The conflicts lead many businessmen to push for an updating of the antitrust laws. Richard L. Kattel, president of Atlanta's Citizens & Southern National Bank, which has been sparring with the Justice Dept. over the bank's expansion plans, feels that the antitrust laws "need complete revamping."

Major revamping, though, will not come because there is no general agreement on what form it should take. Most of the Columbia conference participants believe that the economic evidence for a change in policy is scanty and inconclusive. Suggestions ranged from doing nothing to pushing the tough Hart bill through Congress.

In approaching antitrust policy, there are alternatives:

1. Abolish the laws altogether.

A very few economists, such as Yale Brozen of the University of Chicago, talk as though antitrust laws are largely unnecessary. But as Robert L. Werner, executive vice-president and general counsel of RCA Corp., told a Conference Board antitrust seminar earlier this month: "There should be little disagreement by industry over the basic validity of the doctrine of antitrust. Certainly no businessmen would seriously suggest that we scuttle that doctrine and return to a pre-Shermanite jungle." The courts have ruled that such practices as fixing prices, dividing markets, boycotting, some mergers, and predatory pricing designed to destroy competitors unlawfully impose restraints on the market.

2. Clarify the laws by specifying precisely what business practices are unlawful.

If various practices can be identified and prohibited through case-by-case litigation, why not draft a detailed code of conduct?

But the very difficulty of identifying such practices when business conditions are constantly changing led to the broad wording of the Sherman Act originally. No one has ever produced an all-inclusive list of anticompetitive conduct. No one can possibly delineate all the circumstances that amount to price fixing and other illegal practices. If publication of future prices by members of a trade association is unlawful, as the Supreme Court held in 1921, is dissemination of past inventory figures and prices equally unlawful? (No, said the Court in 1925. For other such cases, see box.) Moreover, as Thomas M. Scanlon, chairman of the American Bar Assn.'s 8,500-member antitrust section points out: "There's uncertainty in any kind of litigation. Laws intended to bring more certainty often bring less."

3. Replace antitrust laws with direct regulation.

U.S. Steel's Gary favored and Koppers' Grymes favors a business–government partnership with this approval. Its advocates agree with John Kenneth Galbraith that antitrust is a "charade," that it has not and cannot produce a competitive economy in the face of the technological imperatives of large corporations. University of Chicago's George J. Stigler concludes that antitrust has not been "a major force" on the economy to date. "The government has won most of its 1,800 cases," he points out, "and there has been no important secular decline in concentration." On the other hand, many economists and lawyers would argue that Stigler has drawn the wrong conclusion. As Almarin Phillips, professor of economics and law at the Wharton School of Finance & Commerce, puts it: "The success of antitrust can only be measured by the hundreds of mergers and price-fixing situations that never happened."

Moreover, in the view of an increasing number of observers, regulation that is designed to mitigate the effects of "natural" monopolies, such as telephone service, often winds up fostering them instead. Civil Aeronautics Board regulations, for example, have compelled higher airline rates than prevail on federally nonregulated intra-state flights. Wesley James Liebler, recently named director of policy planning at the FTC, says: "What the airline industry needs is a little competition. In the long run we should get rid of the CAB and let in some free competition." Liebler also wants to abolish fixed commission rates for stockbrokers.

Much of the energy of regulatory commissions seems to be devoted to anticompetitive ends. The Federal Communications Commission promulgated rules several years ago designed to stifle the growth of pay-cable television. Sports events, for example, may not be broadcast on pay-cable TV if similar events have been shown on commercial television any time during the previous five years.

Walter Adams, a Michigan State University economist, notes that regulatory commissions can exclude competitors through licensing power, maintain price

---

The High Court's Tougher Stance

Although there have been hundreds of antitrust decisions, the following Supreme Court cases would be on any list as landmarks on the road to tougher antitrust:

Standard Oil Co. of N.J. v. U.S. (1911)
Only "unreasonable" restraints of trade are prohibited. To be guilty of monopolization, a company must have "purpose or intent" to exercise monopoly power.

American Column & Lumber Co. v. U.S. (1921)
Control of competition through a trade association that distributes current price and inventory information and company-by-company forecasts is unlawful.

Maple Flooring Manufacturers Assn. v. U.S. (1925)
Mere dissemination of cost and past price and inventory statistics through a trade association is not unlawful.

U.S. v. Trenton Potteries Co. (1927)
Price-fixing is inherently unreasonable, and any such agreement is a *per se* violation of the Sherman Act.

Interstate Circuit, Inc., v. U.S. (1939)
Consciously parallel behavior, where each competitor knew, even without direct communication with the others, how to act in order to control the market, is unlawful.

U.S. v. Socony Vacuum Oil Co. (1940)
Program by a group of oil companies to purchase surplus gasoline on spot market from independent refiners in order to stabilize price violates the Sherman Act.

Fashion Originators Guild v. FTC (1941)
Group boycotts are *per se* unlawful.

U.S. v. Aluminum Co. (1945)
It is not a defense to a charge of monopolization that the company was not morally derelict or predatory in its abuse of monopoly power. Even though monopoly may have been "thrust upon" the company because of its superior foresight, actions designed to prevent competition from arising constitute unlawful monopolization.

International Salt Co. v. U.S. (1947)
Tying agreements are unlawful *per se.*

supports by regulating rates, create concentration through merger surveillance, and harass the weak by supervising practices that the strong do not like. To combat this kind of government behavior, the Antitrust Div. itself has, for the past several years, been intervening or attempting to intervene in such agencies as the ICC, CAB, and SEC to force decisions that spur competition in industry.

Theatre Enterprises v. Paramount Film Distributing Corp. (1954)
Parallel behavior in the absence of any collusive activity is not unlawful per se.

U.S. v. United Shoe Machinery Corp. (1954)
Business practices that "further the dominance of a particular firm" are unlawful where the company has monopoly power.

Du Pont–GM Case (1956)
The government may move to undo a merger not only immediately after stock is acquired but whenever the requisite lessening of competition is likely to occur, even if that is decades after the merger.

Brown Shoe Co. v. U.S. (1962)
For purposes of determining a merger's effects on competition, there may be broad markets "determined by the reasonable interchangeability" of products and also "well-defined submarkets," whose boundaries may be determined by examining industrial customs and practices.

U.S. v. Philadelphia National Bank (1963)
"A merger which produces a firm controlling an undue percentage share of the relevant market and results in a significant increase in the concentration of firms in that market is so inherently likely to lessen competition substantially that it must be enjoined in the absence of evidence clearly showing that the merger is not likely to have such anticompetitive effects."

El Paso Natural Gas Co. v. U.S. (1964)
A merger that eliminates substantial potential competition violates the Clayton Act.

U.S. v. Penn-Olin Chemical Co. (1964)
A joint venture by two competitors may violate the Clayton Act.

U.S. v. Pabst Brewing Co. (1966)
A merger with "substantial anticompetitive effect somewhere in the U.S." is unlawful.

U.S. v. Arnold, Schwinn & Co. (1967)
It is unlawful per se for a manufacturer to limit its wholesalers' rights to sell goods purchased from the manufacturer.

U.S. v. Topco Associates (1972)
All territorial allocations among distributors are unlawful, even if they might foster competition against others.

In support of their position, reformers make a further point: Large corporations have the political muscle to force the government to support their anticompetitive goals. Adams charges that the government has established an industry-wide cartel for the oil companies through publishing monthly estimates of demand; through establishing quotas for each state pursuant to the Interstate Oil Compact, which Congress approved at behest of the oil companies; and through "prorationing devices" that dictate how much each well can produce. It is illegal to ship excess production in interstate commerce. Tariffs and import quotas protect only the producers, Adam says.

What this all amounts to is maintenance of shared monopoly power with the active cooperation of government. Only when the power of large companies is reduced, argue the populists, will the government be able to guide a competitive economy rather than serve as a prop for large interests. This was one of the original arguments for the Sherman Act in the 1880s.

4. Move toward tougher enforcement.

Populist critics of antitrust, such as Nader and Senator Hart, agree with Galbraith that antitrust has been all too ineffectual, but they move in the opposite policy direction. Since they believe that government regulation usually entrenches the power of big firms and concentrated industries, they favor a get-tough antitrust approach. They argue for two related tactics: extending existing law through the courts to curtail many practices of large firms in concentrated industries and getting Congressional legislation such as the Hart bill to attack the structure of these industries.

The Hart bill would permit the prosecution of companies because of their size alone. The history of antitrust has largely been to define and prosecute practices that courts would rule were restraints of trade, such as price fixing by agreement among competitors. But with increasing fervor "structuralists" argue that size itself can be harmful.

HISTORICAL DEFICIENCIES

Before the Civil War, Americans felt uncomfortable with corporate bigness. The image of the yeoman farmer and the small, fiercely competitive businessman largely reflected economic reality. But the growth of railroads, with their "pools" carving up markets, changed all that. By 1871, Charles Francis Adams, grandson and great-grandson of presidents, was writing that corporations "have declared war, negotiated peace, reduced courts, legislatures, and sovereign states to an unqualified obedience to their will."

Populist politics, such as the formation of the Grange movement, picked up steam, but at the same time, in 1882, the first big trust, Standard Oil of Ohio, was born, followed by the Whiskey Trust, the Sugar Trust, the Lead Trust, and the Cotton Oil Trust. Senator Sherman warned that without federal action the country would confront "a trust for every production and a master to fix the price for every necessity of life." The upshot was his Sherman Act.

But federal prosecutions were limited, aimed mostly at fledgling labor unions, and the Sherman Act failed to curb bigness. Corporate mergers speeded up. U.S. Steel, Standard Oil (New Jersey), American Tobacco, American Can, International Harvester, and United Shoe Machinery were all put together at this time. As a result, antitrusters increased pressure for even tougher laws and an independent agency, which could develop industrial expertise, to enforce them.

These efforts came to fruition in 1914, with the passage of the Clayton and Federal Trade Commission Acts. The Clayton Act specifically banned anticompetitive mergers, while the FTC Act set up an agency to police "unfair competition" in the marketplace but not to regulate prices and output.

Like the Sherman Act, the Clayton Act proved ineffectual for many years, largely because of the way courts interpreted the law. As recently as 1948 the Court permitted U.S. Steel to acquire one of its own customers.

Partly in response to this decision, Congress passed the Celler–Kefauver Act in 1950, amending the Clayton Act to prohibit mergers through acquisition of assets or stock as well as those that would tend to foreclose competition in any market in the country. This effectively closed the door on many mergers. But the merger wave of the late 1960s comprised so-called conglomerate get-togethers of companies in different, often unrelated, industries. The case intended to settle this issue—ITT—never got to the Supreme Court because it was settled by a consent decree.

Mergers became the target of antitrusters because they mean the disappearance of independent competitors and lead to concentrations of industrial power. And, argue antitrusters, a few large companies may "share" monopoly power simply by dominating a given market. But unless collusion among competitors can be proved, there is no way under conventional enforcement to prosecute them.

CONFLICTING VIEWS

To remedy this supposed defect, Senator Hart's new law would create a presumption of monopoly power whenever:

> • A company's average rate of return is greater than 15% of its net worth for each of five consecutive years.

> • There has been no substantial price competition for three consecutive years among two or more corporations within an industry.

> • Four or fewer companies account for half or more of an industry's sales in a single year.

Clearly, these criteria create a net that would sweep up hundreds of large corporations. Hart's staff estimates, for example, that a quarter to a third of all U.S. manufacturing concerns meet the third condition.

A company that met any of these criteria would not automatically have to divest. Its defense before the special agency and court the bill would create could be either that its position rests on legally acquired patents or that divesting would deprive it of "substantial economies." (At present economies are not a defense.)

Howard O'Leary, chief counsel to Hart's antitrust subcommittee, argues that without "some mandate" from Congress, the Justice Dept. would be unlikely to embark "on an antitrust crusade." The bill would provide that mandate.

Senator Hart asserts that statistics can be misleading. He cites concentration ratios which according to economists show competition in the oil industry. But, says Hart, "Look at the evidence of joint ventures, banking interlocks, vertical integration, joint ownership of facilities, joint production, absence of real price competition, and lockstep decision-making, and one must wonder."

Economist Walter Adams agrees. He points out that between 1956 and 1968, 20 major oil companies were involved in 226 mergers and thereby gained control over a variety of substitute fuels, such as coal and atomic energy. The oil companies also moved into allied businesses, such as fertilizers, plastics, and chemicals, through vertical integration. Adams believes that a new law is necessary to fragment the power of the companies in the oil and other industries.

The only businessmen to come forward so far in support of at least the thrust of what Senator Hart is trying to do, says O'Leary, are some in communications and data processing. Through a series of hearings the subcommittee hopes, says O'Leary, "to persuade politicians and to some extent the public that it is feasible to come up with more firms than now exist, that the market won't crash, and that jobs won't be lost."

Most other businessmen see little good in the Hart bill. Carl H. Madden, chief economist for the U.S. Chamber of Commerce, brands its basic thrust as "faulty." He told Senate hearings last spring that the bill would thwart competition, not aid it, "by changing the legally permitted goal and cutting back the prizes."

Legal experts have many other objections. Richard Posner, of the University of Chicago Law School, feels that the Hart bill is symptomatic of "antitrust off on a tangent." Antitrust chief Thomas E. Kauper is not "satisfied with the economic evidence favoring broad deconcentration statutes." Kellogg Co. vice-president and corporate counsel J. Robert O'Brien says: "There is no reason whatever to assume that a 'concentrated' industry will necessarily be any less competitive than a fractionated industry. A course of antitrust enforcement that seeks to break up companies and restructure industries by looking at little more than concentration levels is misguided, to say the least."

Many have pointed out that among the defects in Hart's approach is the difficulty of measuring and the ease of manipulating rates of return. Further, even Ralph Nader, a supporter of the bill, says that deconcentrating an industry "is a 15-year job, at least."

OTHER TACTICS

Antitrusters are not holding their breath waiting for legislation. In a series of cases initiated during the past five years, they are using existing laws prohibiting monopolization and unfair methods of competition to check alleged anticompetitive conditions in concentrated industries.

The FTC's suit against Xerox and the Justice Dept.'s against IBM represent marked change from the past. The government has brought very few cases against single companies for alleged monopoly, partly because of limited prosecution budgets, partly because of political pressure from business, and partly because officials thought them unnecessary. These two recent suits single out a variety of practices—pricing policies, for example, and such things as announcing products embodying new technology far in advance of actual availability—that are alleged ways the two companies exercise monopoly power. The antitrust subcommittee's O'Leary says, "The IBM case is potentially very significant, if it is won and a remedy can be found. It is the first such case in 25 years."

The Justice Dept. also brought suit last August against Goodyear and Firestone, charging them with monopolizing the replacement tire market through a combination of practices, including acquisitions, periods of uneconomically low prices designed to drive out competitive products, service station tie-ins, and reciprocity deals. The two companies are charged with acting independently to maintain their dominant positions; they are not charged with collusion.

Perhaps the most innovative case is the FTC's suit against the four leading breakfast food makers, charging them with a variety of unfair methods of competition. The Commission is not claiming any conspiracy among the companies. It is trying to prove, instead, that a lengthy list of long-standing industry practices are anticompetitive and permit the companies, whose market shares have gone from 68% in 1940 to 90% today, to "share" monopoly power in their respective industries. If successful, this suit would strengthen the commission's ability to use its statute to go after many heavily concentrated industries.

The FTC's current prosecution against the eight major oil companies also attempts to break new ground. The key allegation is that the majors have been "pursuing a common course" in using control of crude oil and shipping facilities to stall the development of independent refineries. This includes eliminating retail competition by keeping prices low at the refinery and marketing end and high at the production end of the business. The FTC also charges the companies with such practices as using barter and exchange agreements to keep crude oil in their own hands and reluctance to sell to independent marketers. Unlike the cereal suits, the FTC charges that some of the oil practices are collusive.

CAN WE COMPETE?

In the face of government attack, some businessmen wonder whether such antitrust action aimed at cutting down corporate size might not handicap U.S. companies in keeping pace with the growing number of multinational corporations around the world. Koppers Co.'s Grymes, who argues for permitting mergers, would prefer to see the government "adopt a whole new philosophy of life." He would like to see 26 steel companies, for example, merged into five or six. "Let them get together, produce together, sell together," he says. He concedes that to make up for the absence of competition, the government would have to levy an excess-profits tax or put limitations on investments. He vigorously opposes the Hart bill.

So does J. Fred Weston, a professor at the University of California at Los Angeles' Graduate School of Management, and for similar reasons. "The world market requires increasingly large firms," he argues. "If we hold onto the 18th Century idea of a nation of small shopkeepers and small farms, we will become a small nation." Unlike Grymes, Weston would not encourage mergers. Rather, he is against "fighting a rear-guard battle to prevent deconcentration based on invalid premises." Corporate size, he insists, should be judged in relation to the world market. "If there are firms of increasing size abroad and there are economies of scale, U.S. firms have to be able to compete."

When Companies Sue Each Other

Professor George J. Stigler of the University of Chicago, chairman of President Nixon's Task Force on Antitrust, finds the whole subject of antitrust " a dull field with few sensations." He makes an exception of the rise of the private antitrust case, which he calls "fascinating."

In recent years private companies have been suing each other furiously under the antitrust laws, far outpacing the government. In the past two fiscal years the government filed 108 antitrust suits against private business. But in the same period companies filed 2,451 suits against other companies. In fiscal 1960 there were only a paltry 228 private suits.

Dr. Irwin M. Stelzer, president of National Economic Research Associates, Inc., a large antitrust-oriented consulting firm, explains that private suits began to increase markedly following the electrical equipment price-fixing conspiracy cases in the early 1960s. State public utility commissions said, in effect, that if utilities had a remedy for overcharges as a result of antitrust violations but failed to bring suit to recover, the commission would not approve rate increases to cover the losses. The same principle applied to all corporations: Failure to pursue antitrust remedies could subject them to stockholder derivative suits. So, according to Stelzer, what had seemed to the big names in the antitrust bar as seamy litigation far beneath their notice, like chasing ambulances, suddenly became necessary and glamorous.

Maxwell Blecher, antitrust attorney in Los Angeles, sees the rise of private antitrust suits in the past 10 years as a transfer of power. "The government has failed to act and the private sector has filled the vacuum," he says. He attributes the change in part to different business atitudes. "Management is now result-oriented rather than concerned about being accepted at the club." He expects the number of private suits to continue to increase.

Supporters of deconcentration policy do not quarrel with the premise that U.S. companies must be able to compete, but they do argue that existing levels of concentration in many industries are more than adequate. They believe that size alone is not a guarantee of economies of scales or of efficiencies. And they point to industrial studies indicating that economies of scale relate primarily to plant size but not necessarily to the numbers of plants that any one manufacturer controls.

Frederic M. Scherer, the FTC's incoming economics bureau chief, believes that economic studies show that many industries are more concentrated than efficiency requires. Nader argues that the best evidence is "clinical, not statistical." He says that studies of industries that have become less concentrated would show consumer gains without loss of efficiency. The arrival of a new supermarket

---

Anyone can sue.

Stigler strongly supports private use of the antitrust laws, a concept introduced into the Clayton Act in 1914. Anyone injured by a violation of the laws can sue as a "private attorney general." To sweeten the burden, courtroom success is rewarded with triple money damages plus attorney's fees. "Anybody should be able to enforce the antitrust laws," says Stigler. "There is no way for bureaucrats to know what is happening. The only way the government finds out is through letters of complaint."

In 1966 the Supreme Court approved changes in the procedural rules governing class actions, making it easier for large classes of people or groups to pool common claims and seek relief through coordinated efforts of their attorneys. The number of private antitrust suits soared.

Businessmen began to see the specter of numerous nuisance suits. Victor H. Kramer of the Institute for Public Interest Representation agrees that there may be some but believes that "this is a fair price" for the meritorious suits. Thomas E. Kauper, Justice Dept. antitrust chief, says there is some basis for the businessman's concern, but he thinks that the courts will become increasingly experienced in using the class action rules to strike a fair balance. George R. Kucik, an antitrust attorney with Arent, Fox, Kintner, Plotkin & Kahn in Washington, suggests that consideration be given to changing the law with respect to the large class action sponsored by municipal or state governments in order to permit ordinary, not treble, damages. "If the pool is big enough to begin with," he says, "there is no need for the trebling." This idea is embodied in the Uniform State Antitrust Act, a new law being pushed by the National Conference of Commissioners on Uniform State Laws. It permits individuals and businesses to seek treble damages but holds governmental units to actual damages plus attorneys' fees.

chain in the Washington metropolitan area several years ago, he says, forced prices down, and he cites the aluminum industry after Aluminum Co. of America had to face competition. It was still able to compete.

Moreover, the fact that a company can be efficient does not mean that it will be. On the contrary, absence of competition may make the company fat and lazy—capable of efficiency but acting inefficiently because it is not spurred by the need to compete.

In the 1950 Congressional hearings on monopoly power, Benjamin Fairless, president of U.S. Steel, admitted that his company had less efficient production processes than its competitors, including much smaller foreign companies. Studies have demonstrated that American steel producers lagged woefully in innovation. Between 1940 and 1955, 13 major inventions came from abroad, yet American steel boasted the largest companies in the world.

The basic oxygen process, which Avery C. Adams, chairman and president of Jones & Laughlin Steel Corp., described in 1959 as "the only major technological breakthrough at the ingot level in the steel industry since before the turn of the century," was perfected by a tiny Austrian steel company in 1950. It was introduced into the U.S. in 1954 by McLouth Steel Corp., which then had less than 1% of American ingot capacity. Jones & Laughlin waited until 1957, and U.S. Steel and Bethlehem Steel Corp. waited until 1963 to adopt the process, resulting in lost profits to the steel industry, according to one study, of some $216 million after taxes by 1960 alone.

As for ability to compete abroad, there is practically no evidence that the Justice Dept. has impaired the competitive posture of U.S. companies in world markets. In the past few years the Justice, Commerce, and Treasury Depts., as well as Congressional committees, have practically pleaded for businessmen to come forward with examples of how Americans have been hurt, with minimal results. The Antitrust Div.'s recent release of business review letters from 1968 through 1972 indicates not a single turndown of joint export ventures.

David H. Baker, director of the Commerce Dept.'s Office of Export Development, made an intense search for examples of antitrust harm. A large food company wanted to enter a joint venture with another big U.S. outfit to bid on a plant an Eastern European government planned to build. The Justice Dept. indicated it might refuse to approve the deal, and the food company pulled out. A small U.S. company then bid for the contract on its own and won.

A NEW APPROACH

Some experts believe that the government cannot deal with business complaints adequately unless it develops a comprehensive approach to competition generally. Victor Kramer suggests the creation of an "office of antimonopoly affairs" within the Executive Office of the President. The function of this office, Kramer says, would be to implement a new executive order he would like to see promulgated, directing all federal agencies to act to promote a "free competitive enterprise system." It would require the federal departments and bureaus to prepare antitrust impact statements whenever they suggest action that would "significantly affect competition in the private sector."

Professor Neil H. Jacoby, of UCLA's Graduate School of Management, agrees with the general thrust of Kramer's suggestion. Jacoby, who believes that oligopoly is here to stay, proposes the creation of a Federal Competition Agency, either as an independent commission or within the White House. He would have it submit a "competition impact report" for "all proposed federal legislation."

Kramer concludes that his policy would have compelled the State Dept. to evaluate publicly the competitive impact of the voluntary steel import agreements with Japan and European nations. The Pentagon would have been called on to explain how the public benefits from the awarding of nonbid contracts. The Internal Revenue Service and the White House, he believes, would have to consider the competitive effects of proposed changes in tax laws.

This broadened approach to competition could come closer to resolving the conflicts between the tendency of companies to exert control over their markets and the public requirement that monopoly be held in check. Short of this, the evidence suggests that antitrust is the best we have.

The Grand Scale of Federal Intervention
Hundreds of federal departments, agencies, divisions, and bureaus regulate to one degree or another the nation's commerce. Below is a list of the most powerful and pervasive of the U.S. government's economic and social regulators.

Reprinted from the April 4, 1977 issue of *Business Week* by special permission. © 1977 by McGraw-Hill, Inc.

Agency	Vital Statistics	Major Functions	Special Characteristics
BANKING AND FINANCE			
Commodity Futures Trading Commission	**The newest of the independent agencies, it has 400 employees, five field offices, and a budget of $14 million**	**Regulates futures trading on 10 commodity exchanges whose total transactions this year will be valued at $1 trillion**	**With very few resources, the commission has had little impact so far on an industry with no regulatory tradition**
Comptroller of the Currency	The office was created in 1863, and now employs 2,800, maintains 14 regional offices, and has a budget of $89 million financed by the regulated industry	Charters and regulates national banks	The most permissive regulator. It opened the door to the go-go banking era of the 1960s. The Comptroller has belatedly developed a top-notch system for early warning on bank problems
Federal Deposit Insurance Corp.	**Created in 1933, it employs 3,500, has 14 regional offices and a budget of $83 million derived from fees and premiums from regulated institutions**	**The New Deal's response to bank failures, the agency shares regulatory powers with the states over state-chartered banks not in the Federal Reserve System, and over mutual savings banks**	**As a regulator of smaller banks, it is subject to less criticism than other bank regulators. But its procedures lag behind the industry's problems**
Federal Home Loan Bank Board	Created in 1932, it has 2,900 employees and 12 regional home loan banks. Its budget of $105 million is financed by the regulated industry	Charters and regulates federal savings and loan institutions, and insures S&L deposits through a subsidiary	The bank board quietly drifted for most of 40 years, and is very chummy with its industry. But new demands on S&Ls as a primary source of mortgage financing may wake up the board

Agency		
Federal Reserve Board	**Regulates state-chartered banks that are members of the Federal Reserve System and has jurisdiction over bank holding companies. Also sets money and credit policy**	**At the Fed, bank regulation has always been secondary to making monetary policy. Now that big banks are having problems, the regulatory staff is considered not quite adequate to meet the challenge**
Created in 1913, it fields 26,000 people in a network of 35 offices—plus the 12 regional reserve banks, which have substantial autonomy. Its $700 million budget is paid by the banks that it regulates		
Securities & Exchange Commission	Regulates all publicly traded securities and the markets on which they are traded. Administers public disclosure laws and polices securities fraud	Most prestigious of the independent agencies, the commission has a reputation—occasionally unmerited—for aggressive policework and zealous protection of investors. Current preoccupations: foreign bribes and creation of a national securities market
Created in 1934, it has 2,000 employees, 16 field offices, and a budget of $56 million		

COMPETITION AND TRADE

Antitrust Division (1)	**Regulates all activity that could affect interstate commerce, from trade restraints and illegal agreements to mergers**	**Enormously influential because of the criminal and financial sanctions it can obtain through the courts, the division is a factor in every company's strategic planning. But it has not managed to stem industry concentration**
Since 1890 the office has grown to 900 employees, eight field offices, and a budget of $27 million		

(1) Justice Dept.
(2) Labor Dept.
(3) Defense Dept.
(4) Transportation Dept.
(5) Health, Education & Welfare Dept.
(6) Interior Dept.

Agency	Vital Statistics	Major Functions	Special Characteristics
Civil Aeronautics Board	Created in 1938, it has 800 employees, eight field offices, and a $22 million budget. It also administers $80 million in subsidies to airlines	Regulates airline fares and routes	Its enforcement of laws that limit competition in the airline industry has built substantial pressure for reform that would ease restrictions on fare and route decisions. A reform bill is in Congress
Federal Communications Commission	**Created in 1934, it has 2,100 employees, 24 field offices, and a budget of $60 million**	**Regulates broadcasting and other communications through licensing and frequency allocation, and interstate telephone and telegraph rates and levels of service**	**One of the most heavily 'judicialized' of the independent commissions, it takes forever to reach decisions. It is bogged down in new radio station license applications, and is considered to lack the resources to deal effectively with AT&T's far larger bureaucracy**
Federal Maritime Commission	Created in 1936, it has only 300 employees, five field offices, and a budget of $9 million	Regulates foreign and domestic ocean commerce, mainly by overseeing agreements reached by a variety of ratemaking conferences of ship carriers	Concentrates on maintaining stability in ocean shipping and policing discrimination in ratemaking. Known as a rubber stamp for the shipping conferences, the commission has recently shown its teeth on rate kickback cases
Federal Trade Commission	**Created in 1914, it has 1,700 employees, 11 field offices, and a budget of $55 million**	**Has very broad discretion to curb unfair trade practices, protect consumers, and maintain competition**	**Once so absorbed in trivia that there were serious plans to disband it, the commission is now both aggressive and innovative in fulfilling its mandate. But it still stumbles on really complex procedures**

| Interstate Commerce Commission | Regulates rates and routes of railroads, most truckers, and some waterway carriers | Created in 1887, it has 2,100 employees, 79 field offices, and a $57 million budget | The oldest and most hidebound independent regulator, it spends most of its time adjudicating motor-carrier tariffs and operating rights, is deeply committed to keeping competition among carriers in delicate balance |

EMPLOYMENT AND DISCRIMINATION

| Equal Employment Opportunity Commission | **Investigates and conciliates complaints of employment discrimination based on race, religion, and sex** | **Created in 1964, it employs 2,500, maintains 39 field offices, and will spend $70 million this year** | **Although it has filed—and won— some big court cases involving millions of dollars in back-pay awards, the commission is essentially without powers or real authority. It may be folded into a unified antidiscrimination agency** |
| National Labor Relations Board | Regulates labor practices of unions and companies and conducts representation elections | Created in 1935, the board has 2,700 employees in Washington and in 48 field offices, and a budget of $83 million | Basically a judicial agency, the board conciliates or decides thousands of cases brought each year by individuals, unions, and companies complaining of unfair or illegal labor practices. The board is considered one of the slowest agencies in Washington |

(1) Justice Dept.
(2) Labor Dept.
(3) Defense Dept.
(4) Transportation Dept.
(5) Health, Education & Welfare Dept.
(6) Interior Dept.

Agency	Vital Statistics	Major Functions	Special Characteristics
Pension & Benefit Welfare Programs (2)	One of the newest agencies, the office has 521 employees and a budget of $21 million	Oversees pension plans under the Employee Retirement Income Security Act	The full force of the act has yet to be felt, so the agency is something of an unknown quantity. But of the 1.8 million pension plans in the U.S., the agency has exempted 1.2 million from filing
Office of Federal Contract Compliance Programs (2)	Created in 1962, it has a staff of 107 and a budget of $15 million	Administers prohibitions against discrimination by race or sex on the part of employers holding federal contracts	The office oversees enforcement activities of about 1,800 people in contract compliance sections in other federal agencies involved in federal contracting. It is generally considered a weak agency with limited powers

ENERGY AND ENVIRONMENT

Agency	Vital Statistics	Major Functions	Special Characteristics
Corps of Engineers (3)	Founded in 1824, it employs 700 regulatory personnel in 38 offices. It will spend $35 million on regulatory activities in the current fiscal year	A new judicial interpretation of an old law a few years ago—plus amendments to the Water Pollution Control Act—gives the Corps a say in construction along waterways and marshlands and in dredging operations and mine dumping	A river dredger and dam builder, it was long viewed as the enemy by environmentalists. But sensitive to political winds, it has turned zealous environmental champion, and may get more powers from Congress this year

Agency	Facts	Function	Commentary
Environmental Protection Agency	Founded in 1970, it employs 10,000, maintains 10 regional offices, and operates more than 20 laboratories, spending $865 million. In addition, it administers more than $4 billion in sewage treatment construction grants	Develops and enforces standards for clean air and water, controls pollution from pesticides, toxic substances, and noise. Approves state pollution abatement plans and rules on environmental impact statements	Preoccupied with developing standards and writing broad rules, it prefers negotiating compliance to twisting arms. But under an active new administrator, it is likely to be a tougher enforcer in the future
Federal Energy Administration	Launched in 1973, it has 4,000 employees, nine field offices, and a budget this fiscal year of $156 million. Administers $840 million for strategic petroleum storage	Controls the price of most domestic crude oil and some refined products, principally gasoline. Charged with developing a national energy policy	Created in the crisis of the Arab oil embargo, it has been anything but an enthusiastic regulator. The agency may disappear into a new Cabinet-level Energy Dept.
Federal Power Commission	**Established in 1930, it has 1,450 employees and maintains five field offices on a budget of $42 million**	**Regulates interstate transmission and wholesale price of electric power, rates and routes of natural gas pipelines, and, under a court ruling in the 1950s, the wellhead price of gas for interstate shipment**	**The archetype of the reluctant regulator, it is unremitting in its efforts to escape regulating the prices charged by thousands of natural gas producers. Smack in the middle of the great gas shortage flap, it passively waits for Congress to deregulate the prices of gas—and perhaps legislate the agency out of existence**

(1) Justice Dept.
(2) Labor Dept.
(3) Defense Dept.
(4) Transportation Dept.
(5) Health, Education & Welfare Dept.
(6) Interior Dept.

Agency	Vital Statistics	Major Functions	Special Characteristics
Nuclear Regulatory Commission	Spun off from the Atomic Energy Commission in 1973, it has a staff of 2,500 in six offices and a budget of $256 million	Regulates civilian nuclear safety, which basically involves licensing atomic power plants	It has a record of fast approval of plant construction. Some critics say it is too fast. The commission's weaknesses: inconsistent national standards and a jurisdiction that overlaps the EPA's—a problem now being ironed out

SAFETY AND HEALTH

Agency	Vital Statistics	Major Functions	Special Characteristics
Consumer Product Safety Commission	**Established 1972, it employs 890 on a budget of $39 million and maintains 13 field offices**	**Mission is to reduce product-related injuries to consumers by mandating better design, labeling, and instruction sheets**	**Notorious for concentrating on trivia, it has been reorganized to stress rational priorities. But its administrators' effort to reach into too many new areas means poor follow-up**
Federal Aviation Administration (4)	Created in 1958, its 5,000 regulatory employees operate on a budget of $228 million. The bulk of its money—$1.3 billion—goes to operate the nation's air traffic control system	Regulates aircraft manufacturing through certification of airplane airworthiness. Also licenses pilots	A tough enforcer. But officials tend to be chummy with top aircraft industry executives. Result: some big flaps, such as the DC-10 cargo-door controversy
Food & Drug Administration (5)	**Founded in 1931, it fields a staff of 7,000 with a budget of $240 million**	**Responsible for the safety and efficacy of drugs and medical devices and the safety and purity of food. It also regulates labeling. It oversees about $200 billion worth of industrial output**	**An entrenched bureaucracy notorious for caution and close identification with the industries it regulates. Bold actions can usually be traced to legislative mandates that give the FDA no leeway to stall**

Agency			
Occupational Safety & Health Administration (2)	Created in 1971, it employs 2,400 people, runs 125 field offices, and spends $128 million	Responsible for regulating safety and health conditions in all workplaces—except those run by governments	Few regulators have been the target of as much vituperation and antagonism. Both labor and business have accused it of everything from triviality to harassment. Major administrative reforms are expected
Mining Enforcement & Safety Administration (6)	**Created in 1973 to remove mine safety from the industry-dominated Bureau of Mines, it fields 2,000 employees in Washington and in 10 district offices. Budget: $95 million**	**Enforces all mine safety regulations, including air quality and equipment standards**	**Caught between management and labor and subservient to the Interior Secretary, the agency now has a vigorous, pro-enforcement administrator**
National Highway Traffic Safety Administration (4)	Created in 1970, it has 800 employees, 10 field offices, and a $100 million budget. It also administers $129 million in grants to states	Regulates manufacturers of autos, trucks, buses, motorcycles, trailers, and tires in an effort to reduce the number and severity of traffic accidents	An aggressive young regulator, it has promulgated hundreds of regulations on everything from auto bumpers to mandatory seat belt installation. Its new administrator comes from Ralph Nader's organization

(1) Justice Dept.
(2) Labor Dept.
(3) Defense Dept.
(4) Transportation Dept.
(5) Health, Education & Welfare Dept.
(6) Interior Dept.

QUESTIONS FOR DISCUSSION

1. Carl Kaysen, a prominent writer on the relationships between business and government, once entitled an article he wrote, "Business and Government: Do Good Fences Make Good Neighbors?" How would you answer the question, and what support can you give for your answer?

2. As federal intervention expands its grand scale, is free enterprise becoming less "free," or does it appear that governmental efforts are necessary to make it more "free"? Essentially, to what does the "free" in free enterprise refer?

3. Why might the government have difficulty in passing legislation that would ultimately lead to the "break-up" of the highly concentrated automobile industry? How much of this difficulty do you expect would emanate from the industry and how much from the general public?

4. Suggest specific methods that might be used to overcome the problems with government regulation that are outlined by John Dunlop.

5. Why have the federal antitrust laws come under such severe attack recently? How might the laws and their enforcement be changed in a way that would lessen criticism?

6. Under the auspices of administrative law, we often find that regulatory agencies have the power to promulgate regulations, police compliance, and sit as judge and jury in litigation. Occasionally, one individual (typically a commissioner) has the power to perform all these functions. What advantages and disadvantages exist with a legal system of this form? What fundamental Constitutional provisions might form a basis for challenging this structure?

7. In many cases, the chief administrator of a regulatory agency is chosen from a firm in the industry which the agency regulates. Further, the tenure of an administrator is often cut short by the administrator's return to an executive post in the industry. What advantages and disadvantages exist with the acquisition of regulatory talent in this fashion? How might the disadvantages be alleviated?

8. When the government becomes a major customer of a business firm, what unique powers might accrue to government that might not otherwise exist?

9. Do you feel that business executives should play an active role in government? Why or why not?

SELECTED READINGS

Baker, D. F., "Price-fixers, beware!" *Across the Board,* February, 1977.

"The escalating struggle between the FTC and business." *Business Week,* December 13, 1976.

"Government intervention," Special Issue. *Business Week,* April 4, 1977.

Green, M. J., *The Closed Enterprise System,* Ralph Nader's Study-Group Report on Antitrust Enforcement. (New York: Grossman Publishers, 1972.)

Guzzardi, W., Jr., "What the Supreme Court is really telling business," *Fortune,* January, 1977.

Kaysen, C., "Business and government: Do good fences make good neighbors?" *American Bankers' Symposium on Business and Government Relations,* 1966.

Liebhafsky, H. H., *American Business and Government.* (New York: John Wiley & Sons, 1971.)

Monsen, R. J., and M. W. Cannon, *The Makers of Public Policy.* (New York: McGraw-Hill Book Co., 1965.)

Preston, L. E., and J. E. Post, *Private Management and Public Policy.* (Englewood Cliffs, N.J.: Prentice-Hall, 1975.)

Reid, S. R., *The New Industrial Order.* (New York: McGraw-Hill, 1976.)

Schultze, C. L., "The public use of private interest," *Harper's,* May, 1977.

Select Committee on Small Business, House of Representatives, *Congress and the Monopoly Problem.* (Washington: U.S. Government Printing Office, 1966.)

Stigler, G. J., "The theory of economic regulation," *Bell Journal of Economics and Management Science,* Spring 1971.

Wilcox, C., and Shepherd, W. G., *Public Policies toward Business,* 5th edition. (Homewood, Ill.: Richard D. Irwin, 1975.)

Wilson, R. A., "The verdict on antitrust: Hiding the corporate rip-off from the nice folks back in Peoria," *Antitrust Law and Economics Review,* **8**, No. 1, 1976.

Case

BERKELEY SAVINGS AND LOAN ASSOCIATION*

On September 1, 1971, the Berkeley Savings and Loan Association, in compliance with the New Jersey Savings and Loan Act of 1963, filed an application with the Commissioner of Banking of the State of New Jersey requesting permission to relocate its Chancellor Avenue, Newark, branch office to the Five Point Shopping Center in Union, New Jersey. Pursuant to the provisions of the Act, the New Jersey Department of Banking, which administers the law, held hearings on the relocation application and opposing arguments. On September 12, 1972, the hearing officer, Mr. Clifford F. Blaze, submitted a report to the Acting Commissioner of Banking, Mr. Richard F. Schaub, recommending approval of the application. Upon review of the case, however, Commissioner Schaub found that such a relocation would adversely affect the economic climate of Newark and therefore would not be in the public interest. Consequently the application was denied on January 24, 1973.

---

*Copyright© 1973 by Gordon K. C. Chen and Arthur Elkins.

Since the case involves the issues of private versus public interests, business social responsibility, freedom of choice and movement in a free enterprise system, and the regulatory process and its attendant standards, it is fruitful to review the background and developments of the events leading to the commissioner's decision.

Company Background

Berkeley Savings and Loan Association is a mutual savings institution (that is, it serves the interests of depositors only) chartered and regulated by the State of New Jersey. The Association maintains its principal office at 421 Millburn Avenue, Township of Millburn, County of Essex, and operates two branch offices in Newark—one at 88 Lyons Avenue and another at 434 Chancellor Avenue, the one for which the Association has applied for relocation. Berkeley also has another branch office in East Hanover Township.

Berkeley's main office was originally located in Newark and had been relocated to Millburn only recently. All of Berkeley's facilities are currently located within the "first savings and loan district" of New Jersey, as defined by statute.

Berkeley was established in 1941 with assets of over $1 million and a reserve of a little over $61,000. The Association enjoyed a rapid growth and expansion during post-World-War-II years. By June 30, 1973, the end of the current fiscal year, its total assets amounted to more than $125 million, with reserves and deferred income totaling over $8.6 million. The bank offers a complete thrift and home financing service, having some 19,300 savings accounts and about 6300 mortgage accounts in 1971. The Association had 42 officers and employees in 1971. Berkeley's Chancellor Avenue Branch was opened for business in November, 1954. Because of the convenient location for its customers and the lack of competing institutions in the vicinity, the branch's deposits grew from a modest beginning of $400,000 in the first two months to $19.2 million in 1963.

Following the period of rapid growth, an increasing number of the branch's customers, starting in the early 1960's, were moving from the area into the suburbs of Essex and Union Counties. By 1971, 87 percent of its new savings customers came from the suburban communities.

Concurrently, a number of large thrift and banking institutions moved into the vicinity during the latter part of the 1960's. This combination of increased competition plus the out-migration of its older customers caused the branch, beginning in 1968, to experience a decline in deposits. In 1970, the branch suffered its highest annual savings loss of more than $2 million, while aggregate savings in New Jersey rose by $600 million in that year. Similar declines were felt in other types of thrift accounts, such as the Christmas Club.

Berkeley attributed the decline in business to a number of significant factors.

1. The suburban exodus of the residents.
2. The substantial increase in the number of competitive institutions.
3. The Newark riots in the summer of 1967.
4. The sharp increase in crimes of violence, particularly muggings.
5. The destruction of property for Route 178 displacing 1900 families and 7000 people.
6. The overcrowding of schools and the deterioration of the educational system.
7. The closing of most of the religious institutions, mostly of the Jewish faith as their members left the area.
8. The disappearance of most social and civic organizations.
9. Fear of safety.
10. Exodus of almost all of the Chancellor Avenue merchants.
11. Immigration of low income, financially burdened families into the Chancellor Avenue Area.*

The Application

In view of the decline in business and the fear of further deterioration of its neighborhood (the condition of which was characterized as a "day-to-day stage of siege"†) the management of Berkeley decided it was time to move the branch from the area. On September 1, 1971 Berkeley filed an application with the New Jersey Commissioner of Banking requesting permission to move the Chancellor Avenue office to a new site located in the Five Point Shopping Center, Union, New Jersey.

The 27-page application provided background information on Berkeley's history and operations, as well as analyses and reasoning for the proposed relocation. It also included attachments giving detailed facts and figures and exhibits in support of the application.

The proposed new branch site is located within the boundary of the so-called "second savings and loan district of New Jersey." Under the provisions of the New Jersey Savings and Loan Act (N.J.S.A. 17: 12B–26), three savings and loan districts were established. The first district consists of Bergen, Essex, Hudson, Morris, Passaic, Sussex, and Warren Counties of northern New Jersey. The second district includes Hunterdon, Mercer, Middlesex, Monmouth, Somerset, and Union Counties in the central part of New Jersey. The third district consists of the remaining eight counties in the southern part of the state.

---

*Berkeley Savings and Loan Association, *Brochure,* p. 16, August 1971.

†*New York Times,* p. c 39, January 1, 1973.

The New Jersey Savings and Loan Act requires that a state-chartered Savings and Loan Association may establish a *de novo* branch only in the *same* savings and loan district of its principal office, but makes no mention about the relocation of any branches.

In compliance with Section 17: 12B–27. 1 (2) of the New Jersey State Acts, which requires that: "If the proposed new location is in another municipality, the state association shall comply with the notice requirements set forth in subsection 2 of section 26 of the Act," Berkeley served notice of its application to other associations having offices located in Union Townships or within two miles of the proposed site. The New Jersey Department of Banking also notified the New Jersey Savings League, the New Jersey Bankers' Association, and the Savings Banks' Association of New Jersey of the pending application. In September 1971, a notice of the application was published in the bulletins of the aforementioned associations.

The Hearings and the Reactions

Following the announcement and notifications of Berkeley's intention to relocate its Chancellor Avenue branch, objections to the application and requests for hearings began to pour into the office of the Department of Banking. Among the objectors were the Colonial Savings and Loan Association, the First New Jersey Bank, the Investors Savings and Loan Association, the Union Central National Bank, and the Stonewall Savings and Loan Association of Linden. The Greater Newark Chamber of Commerce also objected to the move and requested a hearing, but subsequently withdrew the request.

Upon receipt of the requests, the Department held a series of hearings conducted by hearing officer Mr. Clifford F. Blaze, on February 14, March 6, March 17, and March 20, 1972. The Department, in accordance with its usual procedures, placed all relevant materials in evidence as exhibits. Included in the exhibits were the brochures prepared by Berkeley in support of its application, and some feasibility studies prepared by Berkeley's consultants. Some objectors also submitted documents and exhibits as evidence. Several people testified on behalf of the applicant and some on behalf of the objectors. Among those who testified against the application was Mr. William Cohen, Liaison Officer of the Office of Economic Development of the City of Newark, who appeared as a representative of Deputy Mayor Frisina.

At the conclusion of the hearings, the parties involved filed written summations and legal briefs in support of their respective positions. At about the same time, the Department of Banking received a letter dated June 5, 1972 from Mayor Kenneth A. Gibson of Newark. Gibson stated in part that:

I do not believe that the proposed move of Berkeley Savings and Loan Association Chancellor Avenue Office to Union is in the public interest of the citizens of Newark. I would, therefore, strongly recommend that your Department refuse to grant this application.*

The Hearing Officer's Findings

Subsequent to the hearings and upon review of the arguments and legal briefs submitted by both sides, hearing officer Blaze prepared and submitted a 26-page report and recommendations to Acting Commissioner of Banking, Richard F. Schaub. The hearing officer recommended approval of the application.

Blaze based his conclusions and recommendations primarily on the statutory criteria provided in N.J.S.A. 17:12B–27(2), which reads:

If the proposed new location is in another municipality than that in which the existing branch is located, the State Association shall comply with the notice requirement set forth in subsection 2 of section 26 of this act, and the Commissioner, before approving the application, shall determine (1) that the establishment and operation of such proposed branch office is in the public interest, (2) will be of benefit to the area served by such branch office, (3) that such branch office may be established without undue injury to any other association in the area in which it is proposed to locate such branch office, and (4) that the conditions in the area to be served afford a reasonable promise of successful operation.†

In interpreting these provisions, the hearing officer found that the applicant had satisfied each and every procedural requirement set forth in subsection 2 of N.J.S.A. 17:12B–26. The critical issue that the hearing officer addressed himself to with greater deliberation was the question of the relocation of a branch office across district lines, as was contemplated by the applicant. On this issue, the Hearing Officer noted that the major positions given in the objectors' arguments centered around the following points:

1. It was the intent of the Legislature, in enacting the legislation pertaining to the three savings and loan districts, to make the Savings and Loan Act consistent with the Banking Act, but that in the instance at bar, banks would not be allowed to relocate branch offices across district lines, so the savings and loan associations should also be prohibited.

---

*Hearing Officer's Report and Recommendation, p. 54, Division of Savings and Loan Associations, Department of Banking, State of New Jersey, September 12, 1972.

†Ibid., p. 5.

2. The applicable rules of statutory construction require that the savings and loan districts set forth in Section 26 of the Act be "read into" the provisions of 27.1 of the Act.

3. The applicant is attempting to accomplish by indirection what it cannot do by direction, i.e. to establish a *de novo* branch in a "foreign" district.

4. If the statute is read and interpreted as it has been by the applicant, results inconsistent with the purpose of the Savings and Loan Act would be reached.

5. The Savings and Loan Act, read as a whole, sets forth a consistent pattern of regulation and control, the obvious intent of which is to keep financial institutions from exercising statewide or semistatewide influence.*

It was the Hearing Officer's finding, after a careful search for legislative evidence, "that the recent legislative history with respect to the provision in question does not give us a specific indication of the Legislature's intent with respect to district and/or county lines when considering branch-office relocations for savings and loan associations."†

In his view, "as the statute in question presently stands, there is absolutely no direct reference to any district limitations."‡ He flatly rejected "the notion that the Legislature of the State of New Jersey intended that each and every branch-office relocation of a savings and loan association must be constrained by district lines."§ and concluded "that there is not, and should not be, any complete prohibition contained within the wording and/or intent of N.J.S.A. 17:12B–27.1 which would prohibit the relocation, in all instances, of a branch office from one district to another."#

Concerning the objectors' charge that the applicant attempted to accomplish (i.e., to establish a *de novo* branch in a "foreign" district) by indirection what it could not do by direction, the hearing officer found no legislative restrictions in recent cases involving the movement of certain New Jersey banks and bank holding companies. The fact that there has been a general liberalization of New Jersey banking legislation since 1948 is indicative of the desire of the state to achieve

---

Ibid., p. 8.

†*Ibid.,* p. 9.

‡*Ibid.,* p. 10.

§*Ibid.,* p. 11.

#*Ibid.,* p. 13.

and maintain some degree of competitive parity between the state-chartered and the federally-chartered financial institutions, according to the examiner. He cited some recent cases in which the federal savings and loan authorities gave permission to several savings and loan associations to establish de novo branches across district lines. "If my reasoning and conclusions are sustained," he argued, "substantial parity between state and federal associations will exist. If my reasoning and conclusions are rejected, state associations would be left in a severely debilitated competitive position.*

Turning to the question of whether the relocation offered a reasonable promise of successful operation for the applicant, one of the statutory criteria to be met before approval of an application, the hearing officer heard and examined testimony and presentations of expert witnesses on behalf of the applicant and the objectors. The testimony centered around the issues of trade areas and projected clientele and sales of the proposed branch. It was the hearing officer's opinion that the estimates and projections made by the experts, in terms of relative influence of competing financial institutions within and between the trade areas, the rate of penetration, and the potential dollar deposits of the new branch in the first few years, could not be credited with any great degree of precision and are likely subject to errors. However, even giving allowance to those errors and reducing the experts' estimates by a wide margin, he concurred with the applicant that the branch could operate on a profitable basis with average deposits of $6.5 million or less. Thus, he concluded that he had reason to believe that conditions in the area to be served offer a reasonable promise of successful operation.

In deliberating the possibility of the proposed branch causing "undue injury" to other associations in the area, the hearing officer found that there were no mutual thrift institutions located at or near the shopping center, or within the trade area. In fact, there are no savings and loan associations located within a half-mile of the extremes of the trade area. Therefore, it was difficult for him to conceive that the establishment of the branch would inflict undue injury to others, in a statutory sense.

On the issue of whether the proposed branch was in the public interest, Mr. Blaze found that, inasmuch as the Five Points Shopping Center and its surrounding trade areas lacked any mutual thrift institution to serve their large numbers of local residents, the establishment and operation of the branch office was in the public interest and would be of benefit to the area residents. Whether or not the relocation was in the public interest of the Newark area seemed to be an irrelevant question. Mr. Blaze found that the New Jersey Savings and Loan Law

---

*Ibid., p. 16.

provided no reference or guideline other than the requirements that notice of the application be made to the associations located within two miles of the proposed site or within the community in which the relocated office is to be placed, and that the *proposed branch* be in the public interest. It was his interpretation that the Legislature has not delegated the judgment of the public interest beyond that which pertains to the proposed branch. For this reason he felt he was not in a position to discuss this matter in a statutory sense even though he might personally think it a pertinent or relevant consideration.

However, in order to provide background information on this issue for the commission to reach a final decision, he summarized the arguments from both sides. The opponents' arguments are generally represented by those submitted by Mr. Manahan, on behalf of Investors Savings and Loan Association.

1. That a savings and loan association is quasi-public and therefore apparently owes a duty (undefined) to the persons residing in the area it serves.
2. That the "public interest" considers the public and not an advantage or benefit to a financial institution.
3. That the applicant's two expert witnesses ignored the issue.
4. That the Lyons Avenue office of the applicant could be the "next to go."
5. That an unhealthy precedent would be established.
6. That the situation in the Chancellor Avenue branch's area is not as bad as represented by the applicant.
7. That the old site has a better potential for the applicant than the new site.
8. That the denial of the application would help solve the problems in Newark to which the applicant has referred.*

Countering the preceding arguments, Mr. Blaze observed that "the record demonstrates that, for social, demographic and physical reasons, the applicant's Chancellor Avenue office has experienced a decline in deposits and influence in the community in recent years. It might well be concluded that the residents of Newark left the Berkeley before the Berkeley decided to leave Chancellor Avenue. Furthermore, the record demonstrates that, after the removal, there will remain in the Chancellor Avenue area, offices of savings and loan associations and mutual savings banks which are more than adequately located and equipped to handle the savings needs of the residents therein.

*Ibid., p. 24.

"No unhealthy precedent will be established here. The decision must of necessity rest on the facts of the case. No consideration can be given to a *possible* relocation application of the Lyons Avenue branch. Finally, even if the Newark site had a better potential than the Union site, such a fact could not be used to deny the application. As Mr. Manahan stated in his brief . . . the 'advantage to any banking institution, be it an *applicant* or an established objector' is not dispositive of the public interest."*

The Commissioner's Decision and Order

Having concluded his hearings and deliberations, Mr. Blaze submitted his report and recommendation to Acting Commissioner Richard F. Schaub for final decision. Upon careful review of the complete file of the case, including all records and reports of the hearings and comments, the Commissioner made an independent evaluation and arrived at the following findings and conclusions.

The Commissioner agreed with the hearing officer that the applicant had satisfied the procedural requirements set forth by statute. He also concurred with Mr. Blaze that the trade area, as delineated by the applicant, was reasonable. On the issues of a promise of successful operation, of the potential of causing undue injury to other financial institutions, and of the likelihood of benefiting the area to be served by the branch, the Commissioner was again in agreement with the hearing officer.

However, on the concept of the public interest, the Commissioner departed from the hearing examiner's findings and opinions. It was his opinion "that in the applicable statute, N.J.S.A. 17:12B-27.1 (2), a specific distinction is made between the Commissioner's determining first, 'that the establishment and operation of such proposed branch is in the public interest,' and second, 'will be of benefit to the area served by such branch.' " He asserted: "If the fact that a branch would benefit a particular area does not in itself guarantee a serving of the public interest, then I am obliged to examine other criteria in considering this latter issue."† He cited a 1959 New Jersey court ruling in which the concept of "public interest" was broadly interpreted to mean the legislative objectives of achieving "(1) a sound banking structure, (2) healthily competitive, and (3) fully adequate for the needs of the community."‡ He believed, therefore, that his decision should be based on his evaluation of the alternatives — to relocate the subject branch or to

---

Ibid., p. 25.

†*Commissioner's Decision and Order*, p. 7, Department of Banking, State of New Jersey, January 24, 1973.

‡*Ibid.*, p. 7.

retain it at the present site — and to select that alternative that best meets the objectives of the public interest.

On the question of healthy competition, he noted that, although the relocation may tend to introduce more competition in the proposed location, it also, in the meantime, would diminish to a similar extent competition in the existing trade area. Considering the issue of providing adequate service for the needs of the community by weighing the relative merit of improving service outside a central city against that of decreasing service within it, the Commissioner was of the opinion that "the continued presence of the applicant's branch office at the Chancellor Avenue location would convey both an actual and symbolic measure of economic stability (in the city)."* Although he recognized the physical and economic deterioration over the years in central-city communities which lack the means to reverse the trend of decline, he nonetheless felt "it is an acknowledged role of government at all levels to attempt to arrest such trends."† Thus, in his judgment, ". . . the detriment to the public interest which would result from the closing of the Chancellor Avenue office more than outweighs the favorable aspects relating to its relocation at the proposed site and . . . the subject application should therefore be denied."‡ This decision, he believed, would also contribute to the soundness of the New Jersey banking structure, also meeting the objective of public interest.

Having denied the application, the Commissioner conceded that, while finding it in the public interest to maintain this facility, it was beyond his power "to require an association to remain within an area where its employees and customers face a real threat of physical harm."§ And he warned that "officials of the City of Newark who deem it important to retain the Berkeley at its present site have a responsibility to ensure the safety of its customers and the residents of the neighborhood."# Finally, having decided to deny the application based on the criterion of public interest, the Commissioner found it unnecessary to address the question of relocation across district lines.

---

*Ibid., p. 8.

†Ibid., p. 8.

‡Ibid., p. 8.

§Ibid., p. 10.

#Ibid., p. 10.

10. *Ethical Issues*

Merchant One: "Ethics? What's that?"
Merchant Two: "Well, it's like this: A customer comes in and he buys a brass sconce, $5. He gives me a five-dollar bill. Just as he's leaving, I notice another five-dollar bill attached to it. 'Ethics' is, shall I tell my partner?"*

Bishop James Pike's tongue-in-cheek anecdote above probably reveals more about the ethical crisis in business than it does about what ethics is (or are)—and for good reason. As many would disagree with the abstract principle underlying Merchant Two's definition, they may also disagree with his gross oversimplification. Obviously, there is more to the business of ethics than simply a stray five-dollar bill and a business partner.

But what is it about? Essentially, business ethics, as a field of study, deals with questions of right and wrong (and the foggy abyss between) in business decision-making and practice. It deals with the nature of morals in business. Ethics themselves are rules or standards, whether verbalized, written, or not, that govern the conduct of a group.

Unfortunately, we cannot simply list these rules or standards so that they may be memorized like the basic elements in chemistry. And herein lie the truly difficult managerial problems that contribute in part to the present "ethical crisis." Aside from strictly *illegal* corporate malfeasance, managers and the general public have often agreed to disagree between and among themselves as to what constitutes proper and moral conduct in business. We, therefore, treat ethical issues in business as phenomena, rather than pontificate on what is right and wrong in the manager's world.

DIRTY LAUNDRY

If we were to confine an investigation of business ethics to an examination of recent news releases, the prognosis would be "in critical condition," at best. It would appear that business firms (many highly revered in the ranks of the *Fortune* 500) have somehow gone astray . . . somehow failed to remain a part of the flock of upright corporate citizenry. Headlines read, "Five Former Aides of Stirling Homex Accused of Fraud,". . . "Equity Funding Fraud is Far from Resolved," "The Big Payoff," "The Biggest Payoff" (are we sure?), "How a Floating Corpse Led to a Fraud Inquiry and Ousters by GM . . . A Warranty Racket Alleged," and even,

---

*Bishop James A. Pike, "The Claim of Situational Ethics," *Papers of the 1967 A.A.A.A. Meeting.* (New York: American Association of Advertising Agencies, 1967.)

"Study Shows Colleges Skimp on Business Ethics." A complete bibliography would fill a volume.

Without doubt, the public is being deluged with the dirty laundry of business, though we might wonder whether they've yet gotten the best (or worst) part of it. The point is, the ethical dimension of business practice is now in the forefront. *Business Week* recently referred to our brethren, including lawyers and accountants, as "The Troubled Professions." Surely, general managers and their corporate siblings must be in the fold.

WHAT'S THE TROUBLE?

A cynic might be inclined to say that the growing concern over business ethics is simply a "business" matter. That is, when business is tried in the press or in a courtroom, there is often some form of financial repercussion that results. It may come through the form of a fine, demand of retribution, declining stock prices, marketing difficulties, lost contracts, and/or some combination of legal, public-relations, and administrative expenses. For that reason, business managers are becoming particularly concerned about the propriety of their conduct.

Surely, the cynic would be only partially on target. It is not simply the impact of disclosure of corporate misdeeds that is troubling the manager. Possibly much more important is the fact that the increasing complexity of business is generating increasing moral complexity—what Blumberg refers to as "ideological disorder."* The gray area between right and wrong is expanding, leaving greater responsibility on the manager to make moral judgments, something for which he or she may feel unprepared or ill equipped.

THE ROLE OF LAW

To the extent that the law clearly expresses society's moral imperatives, ethical dilemmas in business are resolved. Corporate contributions to federal political campaigns are clearly prohibited in the U.S., for example. The relevant statutes, therefore, form the basis for determining right from wrong on this issue. Similarly, truth-in-advertising statutes prohibit falsifying performance claims on products. But can the law clearly address each and every issue that the business manager faces where questions of right and wrong are involved? Can we even expect the law to be everywhere consistent? Surely not.

Laws and regulations change over time and differ across cultures, often drastically. At one time, for example, the Christian world adhered to the doctrine that money is "barren," without inherent worth. Charging interest for its use was considered immoral and was therefore prohibited. Obviously, morals changed around the globe to the point where the antithesis of the earlier doctrine has formed a cornerstone of business activity. While the impact of changes in law are rarely of this magnitude in business, legal alterations are of considerable concern in the manager's solution to ethical problems.

---

*Philip I. Blumberg, "Corporate Morality and the Crisis of Confidence in American Business," Invited Essay (St. Louis: Beta Gamma Sigma, January, 1977), p. 2.

It is not so much what the law *does* cover that is of primary interest in studying the morality of business behavior, but what it does *not*, or does ambiguously or inconsistently. The "gray" areas of ethical decision-making are created by the conspicuous absence of consistent and clear expression of society's moral imperatives.

Is it proper, for example, for an employer to fire a 39-year-old, white, Anglo-Saxon Protestant male, primarily on the basis that, once the employee reaches 40, he will be protected by the Age Discrimination in Employment Act and will, therefore, be more difficult to dismiss, even for cause? Is it proper to favor an employee/friend over a less close, but more productive, candidate in a promotion decision? Is it proper to advertise a product as "the best money can buy," when one knows full well that higher-quality products are available on the market? For the most part, the law, in a prohibitive sense, stands mute on these questions. Does that mean, then, that a manager should answer affirmatively to all?

Or should the manager resort to judicial decisions for guidance on social expectations? Many would argue not, citing a curious decision by a New York Supreme Court judge a few years ago. "Reluctantly" finding the co-chairman of the nation's largest beef company guilty of bribing union officials and supermarket executives, the judge said he realized that, to do business in New York, "the company had to join the corrupt system . . ."* The co-chairman was set free without personal fine or penalty. Certainly, many business people would feel uncomfortable relying on this kind of legal endorsement of otherwise illegal (and immoral) activity.

A major point here is that the law, in all its nobility, is a frail, incomplete reflection of society's moral standards. It is not intended to, nor can it, establish fundamental ethics.

THE "SPECIAL CASE" OF MULTINATIONALS

The legal and sociocultural gap also creates peculiar ethical problems for business people, particularly those engaged in multinational enterprise. Much of the recent popular press on the morality of business conduct deals with this issue. Illegal and questionable political payoffs, bribes, and "grease payments" abroad by U.S.-based multinationals have unfolded as matters of grave concern. As of this writing, over 250 firms have disclosed such payments, totalling in excess of $300 million.† Such corporate stalwarts (heretofore) as Gulf Oil, Lockheed, 3M, United Brands (Chiquita Bananas), Phillips Petroleum, Goodyear, and Exxon have joined the flock, disclosing payments under decree by the Securities and Exchange Commission. Exxon alone, for example, has admitted to more than $46 million in illicit and questionable payments made between 1963 and 1972. United Brands' activity ultimately led to the suicide of its chairman. And the S.E.C. is pressuring for still further disclosure by these and other multinationals.

---

*"Iowa Beef and Its Co-chairman Convicted for Plotting to Bribe Union and Retailers," *Wall Street Journal,* October 8, 1974, p. 4.

†Blumberg, *op. cit.,* p. 3.

From an ethical perspective, these revelations are particularly interesting for what appear to be moral inconsistencies in the "character" of the major players. Many of these firms have been highly acclaimed for progressive programs in E.E.O., pollution abatement, charities, and other socially advantageous endeavors. How, then, can their managements so ruefully mix what is right with wrong in the eyes of the law and the morals of U.S. society?

Surely much of the wrongdoing can be attributed to overzealous managers consciously violating the law in the interest of improved corporate and, therefore, personal performance. U.S. law clearly prohibits political campaign contributions in foreign countries where such is considered illegal. Nevertheless, the major oil companies engaged in that activity on a broad scale, in Italy, among other countries. Purportedly, this led to financial returns higher than would otherwise be realized.

It appears, however, that much of the legal violation in international payments arises not so much from the payments themselves, but from failure to properly disclose them in financial statements. What, then, about many of the payments themselves? An ethical question! Essentially, is it proper for U.S.-based multinationals to "do as the Romans do, when in Rome"? Specifically, is it proper to make payments to government officials in foreign countries where, although the practice may be prohibited by law, it is nonetheless a common and recognized part of business life? By whose ethical standards should a multinational firm abide? Is there such a thing as "honest graft"?

While it may appear blatantly unfair to pose such questions to the student of business ethics, such dilemmas are precisely those that face the manager. There are no universal answers that will satisfy the moral standards of all. Nevertheless, these decisions must be made now, often without the aid of moral imperatives expressed through law. The legal and moral propriety of the answers will be judged in the future.

ETHICAL CONFLICTS AND PERSONAL BENEFIT

Certainly not all the ethical dilemmas facing management are of the magnitude thus discussed. On the surface, at least, many would appear trivial, almost victimless. Nonetheless, "minor" infractions of accepted social standards can be every bit as troublesome to the business person as grand schemes to buy political favors abroad. Indeed, when the business person as an individual is to benefit directly from a questionable decision or action, strain on his or her conscience may far exceed that when "the company" is the primary beneficiary.

Think, for example, about the business person deciding whether or not to use company secretarial staff to type personal business—or to make long-distance personal phone calls at company expense, or to "pad" an expense account, claiming expenses for reimbursements that were not really incurred. Or to sell, for personal gain, sample items received free from vendors. Or to take office supplies home to the kids. An outsider, not experiencing the whole moral climate of a given business person, may easily respond that there really are no decisions here. All of these practices are clearly unethical. But what if these are common practices in the company? What if they can be rationalized as part of the benefits of working for the company? What if the boss knows about these practices and does nothing? What if they really don't amount to much in dollars and cents? Are the ethical norms still as clear?

The answers to these and other questions often lie unstated in the manager's "ethos"—in the mores and morals formed in a complex trellis of values that form personal interpretations of right and wrong. These values arise out of inputs from religion, family, friends, and acquaintances, business superiors, subordinates, and peers, experience, professional groups, the greater society, and often to a much lesser degree, from law and company policy.

Occasionally, these values are based on adherence to articulated religious and philosophical doctrine, the Ten Commandments and the Golden Rule (which some think is becoming more bronze than golden), for example. Occasionally, professional codes dictate proper behavior. Taken with law and company policy, however, interpretation of the principles and the specific situation to which they are to be applied becomes a major element in making an ethical decision. Where conflicts or trade-offs exist, possibly as in the examples above, ethical decision-making becomes particularly troublesome. To the degree that articulated guidelines to behavior are inexact (and they are), personally formed value sets must dominate. As one prominent writer poignantly stated, "In the end, the problem comes down to individuals and their personal sense of morality."*

PROFESSIONAL CODES OF CONDUCT

As an aid to shaping personal senses of morality, a number of professions have attempted to establish codes of conduct for members of their fold. The intent, in most cases, is to provide a set of propositions that will result in continuity, predictability, and hopefully, consistency of members' behavior with accepted social norms. These standards are purportedly in addition to, and in consonance with, the law that governs society.

The American Medical Association, American Bar Association, and the American Institute of Certified Public Accountants are among those groups whose codes of ethics are often held as standardbearers in the institutionalization of professional ethics. Their codes address such issues as responsibilities to clients, responsibilities to colleagues, technical standards, solicitation and advertising, disciplinary action, and even determination of fees. As with law, the codes are only intended to be incomplete representations of the moral expectations set forth for the membership. For example, all three codes prohibit solicitation of patronage and advertising, but do not clearly establish what constitutes solicitation and advertising. They do, however, set general tones that many feel are valuable guides to right and wrong in the respective professions. Indeed, many other professional and trade organizations have adopted such codes, tailored to their particular lines of business.

Then why not a code for all business managers? Are not managers professional people? Is there no need for a code? These questions and more have led to a variety of attempts at establishing codes of conduct for the general business

---

*Blumberg, op. cit., p. 7.

person. For instance, the Commerce Department charged a specially formed ethics advisory council with such a task shortly after the great electrical price-fixing scandal of the early 1960's. The end result was not so much a code as a series of thought-provoking questions. Interest in the code waned rapidly, since it had a severely limited value as a guide to behavior.

One of the more recent attempts at a broad business code was undertaken upon the initiative of W. Michael Blumenthal. In late 1975, then active chairman and president of Bendix Corporation, Mr. Blumenthal enjoined a group of business executives to establish a professional monitoring group to devise and police a code applicable to all U.S. business people. Within approximately one year of initiation, Mr. Blumenthal admitted defeat.

What are the problems associated with establishing such a code? First is the difficulty of forming a consensus on what a code should state. If it is to be specific, what business practices should be addressed? If it is to be general, how are vague, pious platitudes that might make little or no contribution to be avoided? If it is to be specific, where does the code stop, short of a never-ending, incomprehensible list? Who is to be covered by the code? How are the weaknesses of existing professional codes to be overcome (particularly the charge that professional groups promulgate principles under the guise of serving society, when often the result is to form a highly protected, closed group)? And finally, how is a code to be enforced? These and other difficulties have left the U.S. business person without a universal codification of the principles by which he or she should behave.

COMPANIES' INTERNAL CODES

Partially in response to this problem, a number of business firms have drafted their own internal standards—forming policy in regard to selected moral expectations for employees. In some cases, these statements are revisions of long-standing policy, updated to address current ethical questions of critical importance (payoffs abroad for example). Other firms, like Heublein and Pitney-Bowes, have recently drafted codes for the first time. Some codes are short and terse, as in Gulf Oil's one-page "Statement of Business Principles," while others attempt to be more complete as in Caterpillar's model ten-page "Code of Worldwide Business Conduct." To lend credence to a firm's commitment to a code, some have even demanded that all managers sign annual pledges that the rules set forth have been obeyed.

While some critics might argue that much of this code drafting is simply a public-relations ploy, others will argue that on an individual basis, business is making a noble attempt in response to the increasing ethical complexities of managerial decision-making.

TAKING THE PULSE OF ETHICAL
CONCERNS THROUGH RESEARCH

A number of interesting studies have been conducted which, among other things, attempt to assess the perceived status of business morality in the U.S. In a 1975 survey of 238 managers, Archie Carroll found that 47 percent disagreed with the statement that "Business ethics today are far superior to ethics of earlier periods."* Carroll also noted that 54 percent *agreed* with the statement that "The illegal business campaign contributions of the last year or so are realistic examples of the ethics of business today."†

In a classic study of business ethics conducted in 1961, the Reverend Raymond Baumhart reported that nearly 70 percent of his 1,459 manager–respondents replied affirmatively when asked if there were any "generally accepted practices," in their industries which they felt were unethical.‡ Replicating Baumhart's work in 1976, Brenner and Molander reported that a majority of their 1,227 respondents answered affirmatively to the same question.§ These researchers also concluded that business executives generally see their profession as less ethical than the professions of doctors and professors (though more ethical than some others). Indeed, four out of seven of their respondents reported conflict between the "profit-conscious expectations" facing business managers and ethical expectations.# (These findings and others are given in the Brenner and Molander reading which follows.)

With international bribes, payoffs, and "questionable" payments in the news each day, a number of studies have been directed at the public's and business leader's perception of the problem. In a 1975 Conference Board survey of 73 business leaders, three-fourths of the respondents reported having encountered demands from foreign officials or others for unusual payments, and half said that companies *should* make payoffs in countries where such practices are accepted.¶ This latter point was addressed in a complementary study by Opinion Research Corporation in the same year, with similar results. Interestingly, a survey of "heads of households" by *U.S. News and World Report* found that only 25 percent of these people agreed that business should be permitted to make such pay-

---

*Archie B. Carroll, "Managerial Ethics: A Post-Watergate View," *Business Horizons,* April, 1975, p. 78.

†*Ibid.,* p. 78.

‡Raymond Baumhart, S. J., *Ethics in Business.* (New York: Holt, Rinehart and Winston, 1968); p. 27.

§Steven N. Brenner and Earl A. Molander, "Is the Ethics of Business Changing?" *Harvard Business Review,* Jan.–Feb., 1977, p. 61.

#Brenner and Molander, *Ibid.,* p. 59. Similarly, Carroll found that more than 64% of his respondents agreed with the statement that "Managers today feel under pressure to compromise personal standards to achieve company goals." Carroll, *op. cit.,* p. 77.

¶James R. Basche, Jr., *Unusual Foreign Payments: A Survey of the Policies and Practices of U.S. Companies.* (New York: The Conference Board, 1976), cited in Jack G. Kaikati, "The Phenomenon of International Bribery," *Business Horizons,* February, 1977, p. 27.

ments.* These findings point to the atmosphere for the significant debate we are witnessing in the press, on the streets, and in executive suites, over the "special case" of multinationals mentioned earlier.

ANY CONCLUSIONS?

If any conclusion can be drawn from the ethics-related research conducted to date, it is that the ethical dimension of business decision-making is not a matter reducible to any known scientific calculus. Instead, it is a human matter, fraught with inconsistencies and subject to human frailties. Because of that, resolutions of ethical questions may be the most creatively challenging tasks facing today's and tomorrow's business manager.

THE READINGS

Given that ethical issues in business are not only worthy of, but *demand* discussion, we include for reading three articles that touch base on topics and findings that should stimulate significant moral interchange, if not heated debate.

In the first article, Joel Seligman graphically portrays his perception of the contemporary problem of business payoffs abroad. As an attorney for the Ralph Nader-affiliated Corporate Accountability Research Group, he reports on the disclosures of corporate "bribes" and foreign payments that have bombarded the public. While somewhat dated, his graphic portrayal should give the reader at least a hint of the immensity of the problem and the impact that what many consider an ethical issue can have on corporate enterprise — now and in the future.

Albert Carr's classic article, "Is Business Bluffing Ethical?" follows. This controversial piece suggests that the ethics of business are special — that is, that the rules of the game business plays are quite different from those governing the greater society. Thus, for example, untruths in business are often to be expected and tolerated — they are often simply a part of a game strategy. Surely not all will agree with Carr.

Finally, the Brenner and Molander article, referenced earlier, is presented. Their survey of 1,200 *Harvard Business Review* readers attempts to assess what change, if any, has taken place in business ethics since the early 1960's, the role of codes of conduct, and the relationship between ethics and the social responsibility of business. Their study references baseline data from the earlier work of the Reverend Baumhart, who surveyed a similar sample of the readership in 1961.

---

*Cited in Blumberg, *op. cit.,* p. 6.

Crime in the Suites

Joel Seligman

Since the earliest "Watergate" disclosures of company payments to politicians and political campaigns, corporate bribery has played a crescendo in the business press. And now reports of payments to government officials abroad and politicians at home are bombarding the public with numbing regularity. To some U.S. businessmen the public uproar over payoffs is naive. These people consider bribes a necessary component of doing business in a pragmatic world. To others, however, bribery constitutes a challenge to the right of corporate management to conduct its affairs independent of stricter government regulation. While no one can say precisely what legislative action may ensue, one thing is certain: our perception of how companies are managed has been unmistakably altered.

This spring there has been a steady stream of bribery disclosures. On Wednesday, March 3 [1976], Securities and Exchange Commission Chairman Roderick M. Hills made some startling revelations to the Senate Banking Committee. Civil actions had been filed by the SEC against nine major corporations for improper and illegal payoffs. Some 80 publicly held companies—with total assets of almost $219 billion—were under agency investigation. Fifty had already admitted to such practices.

On that same day, March 3, Goodyear Tire & Rubber, the nation's 23rd largest industrial, revealed $845,000 in questionable payments to foreign officials, and Rollins, Inc., acknowledged $127,000 in payments to local officials in Mexico. Before the week was out Boeing disclosed that the SEC was investigating $70 million in overseas commissions, all of which the aircraft firm insisted were legal; American Cyanamid admitted $1.2 million in "irregular" payments abroad; Honeywell, $1.8 million; and the Mercantile Trust Company, Missouri's largest bank, found that it had "lost" $232,000 in bond deals and trust funds with J. V. Conran, a late Democratic party boss.

In the following weeks, the steady stream of bribery disclosures became a flood. On March 11, Carnation, Johnson & Johnson, and Sterling Drug each disclosed foreign payoffs. On the 15th, seven companies including Tenneco and Fairchild Industries did so; an eighth company, Ingersoll-Rand, stated it had begun its own internal inquiry into questionable payments that may have been made by its domestic and international operations. On the 23rd, General Telephone & Electronics revealed $2.6 million of payments made by "elements of the GTE organization" in the Philippines; Northrop named six more Pentagon officials it had unlawfully benefited; and Braniff agreed to pay a $300,000 civil fine to settle charges brought by the Civil Aeronautics Board arising from its distribution of more than 3,000 airline tickets to generate "off-the-books" cash to make an illegal campaign contribution to President Nixon.

Four days later, Upjohn estimated that it had paid $2.7 million to employees of 22 foreign governments. On the 28th, Colgate-Palmolive, Southern Bell, and Cook United revealed their "sensitive payments." On the 30th, they were joined by Control Data and American Standard; on April 7, by AMF; on April 10, by United Technologies, Amerada Hess, and Norlin, the nation's leading maker and distributor of musical instruments. On the 12th, by Koppers, Inc.; and then, on the 13th, in the largest settled case to that date, Lockheed admitted making secret payments to foreign officials "totaling at least $25 million between 1968 and 1975."

By the date of the Lockheed settlement the framework of the debate had fundamentally altered. SEC staff attorneys were speculating that as many as 200 U.S. corporations would disclose that they had violated the securities laws by failing to disclose foreign payoffs that have a "material" effect on stock prices.

But the basic issue was no longer this somewhat technical sin. Increasingly the issue was perceived as one of tax fraud. It had long been suspected that U.S. corporations were violating the Internal Revenue Code by unlawfully claiming foreign bribes as "necessary and proper" business deductions. On April 7, the Internal Revenue Service substantially confirmed this suspicion by announcing that, after months of case by case investigations, it would question the nation's 1,200 largest corporations as to whether they had made any bribes, kickbacks, or payoffs in any "open tax year," and, if so, who in the company was responsible.

And increasingly the issue was perceived as one of domestic bribery. On March 15, Herbert Robinson, a New York lawyer who specializes in fraud cases, estimated that the amount of money secretly pocketed by American businessmen through commercial bribery and kickbacks may be as high as $15 billion a year. Jules Kroll, a former New York assistant district attorney, asserted that for every domestic kickback case reported by the media or taken to court an "infinite" number are handled without publicity or prosecution. A New York *Times* article summarized recent cases of domestic bribes and kickbacks implicating officials or employees of major firms such as Sears, Grumman, International Harvester, and Zenith.

Until Lockheed's disclosure of $25 million in foreign payments, much of the public debate concerning corporate bribery had centered on a series of pragmatic questions: Should U.S. corporations be barred from making payoffs when such payoffs are allegedly common in certain foreign countries? Should U.S. corporations be required to disclose the names of recipients of overseas bribes when this might jeopardize their ability to do business abroad and hand valuable markets over to foreign competitors? Should U.S. corporations be required to disclose small commissions at all when such disclosures were hardly likely to affect stock prices? The confidence with which businessmen and the business press phrased these tough "real world" questions withered in the ensuing months as the disclosures of successive corporations shattered many convenient exculpatory myths: the when-in-Rome myth (many corporations may pay off local customs officials but only behemoths like Gulf and United Brands apparently bribed heads of state); the technical-nature-of-the-sin myth (tax fraud, embezzlement, bribery of U.S. politicians are less defensible than overseas payoffs; indeed they are indefensible); and the de minimis-exception-myth (lots of small illegal contributions to members of the United States Congress pose a greater threat to U.S. political processes than million dollar payoffs to foreign middlemen).

Yet the bribery scandals raise one basic issue that, until the last few weeks, had been ignored: what the hundreds of foreign and domestic payoffs show about the way giant U.S. corporations are governed. Historically, state corporation law has given shareholders the power to elect directors "to manage the business and affairs of the corporation." Federal law, as interpreted by the SEC, has required corporations to make detailed disclosures about their finances. The SEC also requires the outside financial auditor and general counsel to further assure that senior operating executives stay within the bounds of law and loyalty to company's shareholders.

The corporate bribery cases show that these legal controls often do not work. In many firms, a moderately determined chief executive officer can circumvent the law at will.

The classic illustration of this breakdown of corporate governance was presented in a 298-page report on the Gulf Oil Corporation, prepared for the board of directors by a special committee headed by John J. McCloy, a prominent New York attorney. After ten months of investigation by 32 attorneys and accountants, the committee found that Gulf had allegedly made $12.6 million in foreign and domestic payments over a 15-year period. Among the payments were more than $4 million in illegal campaign contributions to U.S. politicians, including President Richard Nixon, Senator Henry Jackson, Senator Hugh Scott, Senator Hubert Humphrey, Congressman Wilbur Mills, and more than a dozen other members of Congress as well as state political officials in Texas, Kansas, Louisiana, and Pennsylvania.

Gulf's illicit course of action apparently began in 1959, when William K. Whiteford, chairman and chief executive officer, concluded he would get no effective support from the State Department in connection with Gulf's overseas expansion unless he could develop a "more conducive political atmosphere." Whiteford dispatched an assistant comptroller to Nassau to launder funds, which were then returned to Gulf's Pittsburgh headquarters and later sent to Washington or abroad for pay-out. Ultimately Whiteford and his two successors as chairman directly or through Gulf's Washington lobbyist, Claude G. Wild, supervised payments delivered by 19 Gulf executives. They also supervised fraudulent accounting by another 20 or so executives, the creation or employment of three phony corporations in the Bahamas to launder funds, and the banishment of at least one squeamish vice president — all without the knowledge of outside directors on the board or senior executives reputed to be "boy scouts," and without effective challenge by the company's general counsel, Royce Savage, a former federal district court judge, who allegedly knew of some of the payoffs.

The Mellon family, holder of approximately 20 percent of Gulf's stock, was apparently outraged by the deception. Soon after the McCloy committee report was published, Mellon representatives led a revolt of outside directors that culminated in the ouster of Robert R. Dorsey, chairman of Gulf.

The expulsion of a chief executive officer is extraordinary—only a few other corporations such as Lockheed and American Airlines have done so after bribery revelations. What is not extraordinary is the unfettered power Gulf chief executives wielded for so long. Other SEC-instigated reports have found similar situations in other companies. The complex program of disguised corporate contributions at American Ship Building was organized by its chief executive officer, George Steinbrenner, who persuaded several senior executives to accept "bonuses" that they passed on as political contributions; Steinbrenner also persuaded other executives to falsely record the "bonuses" in the company's books. At Northrop, Chairman Thomas V. Jones and Vice President James Allen administered a slush fund to stimulate jet sales in Europe without the knowledge of the board. At Minnesota Mining and Manufacturing, the chairman and financial vice president ordered the insurance department to pay out $509,000 for imaginary insurance—the money was actually used for political contributions. This transaction was later "verified" by the outside auditor, Haskins and Sells. Similarly, journalist Anthony Sampson concluded a meticulous examination of Senate testimony regarding Lockheed's foreign bribes with the assertion that to most of the firm's executives, "Lockheed *was* (Chairman Daniel) Haughton. It was Haughton who inspired the Lockheed men to go abroad to sell their planes with singleminded determination. And it was his drive and impatience that pressed them to use whatever hardselling methods they could employ, including bribery."

The bribery cases seem likely to precipitate a summer-long debate on corporate power in Congress. For the first time since the 1930s, Congress seems determined to investigate how giant corporations are managed. The image of management revealed by the bribery reports will be the immediate focus of the debate: company after company where the senior executives have violated federal laws time and time again, doing so unchecked by board, auditors, counsel, or SEC disclosure rules.

Already the battle lines are forming. By late April it was apparent that the Ford administration was engaged in an administration-wide policy of publicly deploring the bribery scandals and privately opposing strong legislative action. SEC Chairman Roderick Hills has called for the reformation of SEC and N.Y. Stock Exchange rules. The White House and State Department are moving on at least three other highly publicized fronts.

On March 31, President Ford established a Cabinet-level task force chaired by Commerce Secretary Elliot L. Richardson "to conduct a sweeping policy review of this matter" by December of this year. Although the staff of the task force and methods of investigations were not publicly identified, its existence and prestigious membership (the secretary of state, the secretary of the treasury, the attorney general, and others) offered Republicans in Congress the opportunity to oppose congressional actions before the November election as "premature."

True, the December report may propose "sweeping" reforms, but two State Department initiatives are patently intended to prevent them. In April, State Department negotiators, reversing an earlier stand, moved to adopt an antibribery provision in a voluntary code of conduct for multinational companies sponsored by the 24 industrial nations that belong to the Organization for Economic Cooperation and Development. These State Department officials have emphasized that they assume multinationals would prefer a nonenforceable international accord to an enforceable one that the Congress might enact. A voluntary code would give U.S. executives a "shield" to employ against Congress. They could argue, as Under Secretary of State Charles W. Robinson, himself a former corporate executive, had argued to the Senate Banking Committee on April 8, "First and foremost, unilateral action cannot be an adequate solution to an international problem. Effective international cooperation is the only real answer." On April 15, the State Department moved to develop a second shield by urging the United Nations Economic and Social Council to consider an international agreement dealing with corrupt practices. It was widely reported that such an agreement could not be ratified in less than two years.

Many Democrats in Congress were clearly unwilling to wait. On March 11, Senator William Proxmire introduced a bill to outlaw all payoffs designed to influence foreign political officials. Five days later, Senator Frank Church introduced his "Multinational Business Enterprise Information Act of 1976," designed among other things to require multinationals to disclose the "dollar amount of all expenditures made in the United States or in foreign countries, by foreign country, directly or indirectly through any agent or pursuant to any contractual agreement."

The Senate Commerce Committee and the House Government Operations Committee scheduled extensive hearings on a much broader approach: A Ralph Nader proposal for federal chartering of all corporations with $250 million or more in annual sales. Nader's proposal would restructure internal corporate management by removing all operating executives from the board and by requiring full-time independent directors, aided by their own staff, to act as internal auditors to prevent violations of law or disloyalty to shareholders. Although it is unlikely such a law can be enacted unless a Democrat is elected president this November, its serious consideration at this time indicates how angered many in Congress are by the myriad of payoff disclosures. If the exposé of corporate payoffs continues, Congress may be finally persuaded to turn its anger into legislative action.

After "Bananagate" the Deluge

The flood had begun as a trickle. Ultimately the corporate bribery cases would involve the Watergate special prosecutor, the Securities and Exchange Commission, the Internal Revenue Service, the Defense Department, the State Department, the White House, four Congressional committees, and numerous private citizens, who sued companies in which they owned stock. But the current rash of disclosures began with a Common Cause lawsuit against the Finance Committee to Re-elect the President, which was initiated during Nixon's successful 1972 campaign.

Prior to April 7, 1972, when the Federal Election Campaign Act of 1971 went into effect, individual contributions to political candidates to finance primary campaigns did not have to be disclosed. Common Cause, aware that Nixon's finance committee had raised over $22 million by that date, brought suit in a federal district court to require disclosure of the contributors, arguing that most of that money would actually be used to finance Nixon's general election bid and therefore did have to be disclosed under the law in effect. Five days before the 1972 election, Nixon's committee agreed to make available the origins of $6 million in contributions it had received before March 10, 1972. Then, in September 1973, as part of a final settlement of the Common Cause lawsuit, the committee made public information about another $11.4 million in contributions it had received between March 10 and April 7, 1972. Among the latter disclosures was a list of 29 favored contributors, kept by Nixon's personal secretary, Rosemary Woods. Two of the contributors listed were firms that had generated their contributions illegally from corporate funds.

Soon after receiving this list, Special Prosecutor Archibald Cox announced that, if a corporation or its executives voluntarily admitted guilt, he would prosecute them only for misdemeanors. Cox thought that the fear of harsher penalties would move many executives to come forward whom he otherwise would not catch.

At first, his reasoning seemed to work. American Airlines and its chief executive officers, George Spater, confessed in October 1973. In the next two months, Minnesota Mining and Manufacturing, Goodyear, Braniff, Gulf, Ashland, Phillips Petroleum, and Carnation came forward and accepted $3,000–5,000 fines. But the pace of admissions then slowed. Diamond International, Northrop, Greyhound, and Time Oil only confessed when the special prosecutor confronted them with incriminating evidence. Northrop and its chairman, Thomas V. Jones, were charged with felonies for actions including lying to government investigators and attempting to cover up the political gift. After that, the special prosecutor's voluntary program collapsed. Only one additional major corporation was cited, American Ship Building, for a particularly clumsy cover-up engineered by George Steinbrenner, its chief executive officer. Although a handful of other prosecutions were brought, no prison sentences were imposed on corporate executives, and the individual $500, $1,000, and $2,000 fines assessed seemed mere wrist slaps for the corporate officers involved.

By 1974, both Cox and his successor as special prosecutor, Leon Jaworski, were being harshly criticized for their handling of the corporate contribution cases. "The one lesson the corporations learned is that the next time they're going to stonewall it," one lawyer was reported to have remarked. "If they think they can get away with it—and a lot of them do—then they'll go right back to paying off the bag man." In retrospect, this type of criticism of the special prosecutor's office seems unfair. The real villain in the crippling of the U.S. campaign contribution cases was Congress. In 1974, when the focus of investigation shifted from Nixon's White House to Capitol Hill, Congress abruptly shortened the statute of limitations from five to three years. "Almost two-thirds of our cases had to be dropped because time ran out," one former prosecutor stated in April 1976. Still, the special prosecutor's office did convict one Congressman, James R. Jones (D.–Okla.) for illegally receiving a corporate contribution, brought related charges against Nixon's Finance Chief, Maurice Stans, and former Montana Governor Tim Babcock, and late in 1975 began a new action against Gulf's Washington lobbyist, Claude G. Wild.

Enter the Securities and Exchange Commission and its hardnosed enforcement chief, Stanley Sporkin. When Sporkin learned that several corporations subject to the SEC's jurisdiction had made illegal campaign contributions, he initiated investigations to determine whether those firms had disclosed to shareholders all the information that was required under the Securities acts. In six early cases—American Ship Building, Ashland Oil, Gulf, Minnesota Mining and Manufacturing, Northrop, and Phillips Petroleum, Sporkin and his staff soon uncovered substantial undisclosed payments and brought suit. Each case was settled at or shortly after the time of filing with a no contest plea. In settling, each corporation agreed to hire a special independent agent or committee to prepare a detailed report on all illegal campaign contributions or questionable foreign payments the company may have made. The SEC reserved the right to reopen the proceedings if it was dissatisfied with the actions the companies themselves took pursuant to these undertakings.

The special committee procedure was Sporkin's masterstroke, the single action most responsible for the flood of foreign bribery disclosures that would eventually follow. Sporkin knew that if he went to trial to prove all of a firm's illegal payoffs in even a single major case, it would drain the resources of his division, perhaps making it impossible to bring other major cases. But he also knew how much a guilty corporate executive would prefer a single special committee report to a protracted trial, and a summary voluntary disclosure of their firms' illegal payoffs to a special committee report. Recognizing his advantage, Sporkin encouraged the first special committee reports to be painstaking, creating the likelihood of subsequent shareholder suits against the responsible executives.

The long string of foreign bribery cases began in February 1975, when United Brands chief executive Eli Black swung his briefcase through the window of his 44th floor office and jumped to his death. The next morning, Sporkin directed an assistant to summon United Brands officials to Washington, and a few weeks later the company disclosed that Black had paid General Oswaldo Lopez, the president of Honduras, $1.25 million to reduce an export tax on bananas.

Soon after "Bananagate," Gulf Oil admitted payments of $4 million to President Park Chung Hee of Korea and $350,000 to the political party of General Rene Barrientos, who was campaigning for the presidency of Bolivia. Ashland Oil acknowledged making payments to government officials in Gabon, Libya, and the Dominican Republic. Northrop admitted it paid $450,000 to Saudi Arabian businessman Adnan Khasshoggi to bribe two Saudi generals.

It became known that the Commission would not require detailed disclosures of questionable overseas payments if the companies volunteered the amounts involved in their detailed 10K annual reports or 8K quarterly reports filed with the SEC. Corporations were soon approaching the commission as to how to phrase these reports, and most of the bribery disclosures eventually came as confessions in 8K or 10K reports.

Meanwhile new prosecutors were joining the hunt. In February 1975, the Internal Revenue Service brought criminal charges against Minnesota Mining and Manufacturing, alleging it had made phony tax deductions to cover up money that was going into a political slush fund. The Civil Aeronautics Board initiated investigations of American Airlines and Braniff for misusing blank tickets to generate funds for illegal political contributions. The Defense Department began investigating legal and illegal agents' fees paid by U.S. defense contractors to facilitate sales abroad. The amounts involved were staggering. Raytheon, for example, paid $4.8 million to grease missile system sales in Kuwait; Grumman paid $28 million to sell fighters in Iran; Northrop may have paid as much as $30 million worldwide; Lockheed's legal and illegal "questionable" commissions totaled over $200 million.

There were also private suits by shareholders demanding, among other things, that the money misappropriated from corporate treasuries be returned by the responsible corporate officers. In the most important private suit to date, Northrop accepted a landmark settlement requiring four independent directors named by a federal judge to be added to the board. A similar settlement tentatively accepted by Phillips Petroleum is being challenged by a shareholder for not going far enough to prevent future violations of law.

Yet by early 1976 the very frequency of these disclosures had become numbing. The stunning February 13 disclosure that General Tire & Rubber may have paid $200,000 to Moroccan government officials to keep a major American competitor out of that country went largely unnoticed by the press. The steady stream of 8K disclosures was relegated to the back pages.

Then, late in February 1976, Senator Frank Church's Subcommittee on Multinational Corporations revealed that Lockheed had spent some $22–$24 million allegedly to bribe Netherlands Prince Bernhard, husband of Queen Juliana; Japanese political leaders; and high-ranking officials in West Germany, Italy, Colombia, and other countries. The bribery scandals became cover stories the week of February 23, governments in half a dozen foreign countries trembled, and for the first time, the Ford administration realized that corporate bribery was an election year issue that could not be ignored.

Is Business Bluffing Ethical?

Albert Z. Carr

A respected businessman with whom I discussed the theme of this article remarked with some heat, "You mean to say you're going to encourage men to bluff? Why, bluffing is nothing more than a form of lying! You're advising them to lie!"

I agreed that the basis of private morality is a respect for truth and that the closer a businessman comes to the truth, the more he deserves respect. At the same time, I suggested that most bluffing in business might be regarded simply as game strategy—much like bluffing in poker, which does not reflect on the morality of the bluffer.

I quoted Henry Taylor, the British statesman who pointed out that "falsehood ceases to be falsehood when it is understood on all sides that the truth is not expected to be spoken"—an exact description of bluffing in poker, diplomacy, and business. I cited the analogy of the criminal court, where the criminal is not expected to tell the truth when he pleads "not guilty." Everyone from the judge down takes it for granted that the job of the defendant's attorney is to get his client off, not to reveal the truth; and this is considered ethical practice. I mentioned Representative Omar Burleson, the Democrat from Texas, who was quoted as saying, in regard to the ethics of Congress, "Ethics is a barrel of worms"—a pungent summing up of the problem of deciding who is ethical in politics.

I reminded my friend that millions of businessmen feel constrained every day to say *yes* to their bosses when they secretly believe *no* and that this is generally accepted as permissible strategy when the alternative might be the loss of a job. The essential point, I said, is that the ethics of business are game ethics, different from the ethics of religion.

He remained unconvinced. Referring to the company of which he is president, he declared: "Maybe that's good enough for some businessmen, but I can tell you that we pride ourselves on our ethics. In 30 years not one customer has ever questioned my word or asked to check our figures. We're loyal to our customers and fair to our suppliers. I regard my handshake on a deal as a contract. I've never entered into price-fixing schemes with my competitors. I've never allowed my salesmen to spread injurious rumors about other companies. Our union contract is the best in our industry. And, if I do say so myself, our ethical standards are of the highest!"

He really was saying, without realizing it, that he was living up to the ethical standards of the business game—which are a far cry from those of private life. Like a gentlemanly poker player, he did not play in cahoots with others at the table, try to smear their reputations, or hold back chips he owed them.

Reprinted by permission of the publisher from the *Harvard Business Review*, Vol. 46, No. 1, January–February, 1968. © 1968 by the President and Fellows of Harvard College; all rights reserved.

But this same fine man, at that very time, was allowing one of his products to be advertised in a way that made it sound a great deal better than it actually was. Another item in his product line was notorious among dealers for its "built-in obsolescence." He was holding back from the market a much-improved product because he did not want it to interfere with sales of the inferior item it would have replaced. He had joined with certain of his competitors in hiring a lobbyist to push a state legislature, by methods that he preferred not to know too much about, into amending a bill then being enacted.

In his view these things had nothing to do with ethics; they were merely normal business practice. He himself undoubtedly avoided outright falsehoods —never lied in so many words. But the entire organization that he ruled was deeply involved in numerous strategies of deception.

PRESSURE TO DECEIVE

Most executives from time to time are almost compelled, in the interests of their companies or themselves, to practice some form of deception when negotiating with customers, dealers, labor unions, government officials, or even other departments of their companies. By conscious misstatements, concealment of pertinent facts, or exaggeration—in short, by bluffing—they seek to persuade others to agree with them. I think it is fair to say that if the individual executive refuses to bluff from time to time—if he feels obligated to tell the truth, the whole truth, and nothing but the truth—he is ignoring opportunities permitted under the rules and is at a heavy disadvantage in his business dealings.

But here and there a businessman is unable to reconcile himself to the bluff in which he plays a part. His conscience, perhaps spurred by religious idealism, troubles him. He feels guilty; he may develop an ulcer or a nervous tic. Before any executive can make profitable use of the strategy of the bluff, he needs to make sure that in bluffing he will not lose self-respect or become emotionally disturbed. If he is to reconcile personal integrity and high standards of honesty with the practical requirements of business, he must feel that his bluffs are ethically justified. The justification rests on the fact that business, as practiced by individuals as well as by corporations, has the impersonal character of a game—a game that demands both special strategy and an understanding of its special ethics.

The game is played at all levels of corporate life, from the highest to the lowest. At the very instant that a man decides to enter business, he may be forced into a game situation, as is shown by the recent experience of a Cornell honor graduate who applied for a job with a large company:

> This applicant was given a psychological test which included the statement, "Of the following magazines, check any that you have read either regularly or from time to time, and double-check those which interest you most. Reader's Digest, Time, Fortune, Saturday Evening Post, The New Republic, Life, Look, Ramparts, Newsweek, Business Week, U.S. News & World Report, The Nation, Playboy, Esquire, Harper's, Sports Illustrated."
>
> His tastes in reading were broad, and at one time or another he had read almost all of these magazines. He was a subscriber to The New Republic, an

enthusiast for *Ramparts,* and an avid student of the pictures in *Playboy.* He was not sure whether his interest in *Playboy* would be held against him, but he had a shrewd suspicion that if he confessed to an interest in *Ramparts* and *The New Republic,* he would be thought a liberal, a radical, or at least an intellectual, and his chances of getting the job, which he needed, would greatly diminish. He therefore checked five of the more conservative magazines. Apparently it was a sound decision, for he got the job.

He had made a game player's decision, consistent with business ethics.

A similar case is that of a magazine space salesman who, owing to a merger, suddenly found himself out of a job:

> This man was 58, and, in spite of a good record, his chance of getting a job elsewhere in a business where youth is favored in hiring practice was not good. He was a vigorous, healthy man, and only a considerable amount of gray in his hair suggested his age. Before beginning his job search he touched up his hair with a black dye to confine the gray to his temples. He knew that the truth about his age might well come out in time, but he calculated that he could deal with that situation when it arose. He and his wife decided that he could easily pass for 45, and he so stated his age on his resume.

This was a lie; yet within the accepted rules of the business game, no moral culpability attaches to it.

THE POKER ANALOGY

We can learn a good deal about the nature of business by comparing it with poker. While both have a large element of chance, in the long run the winner is the man who plays with steady skill. In both games ultimate victory requires intimate knowledge of the rules, insight into the psychology of the other players, a bold front, a considerable amount of self-discipline, and the ability to respond swiftly and effectively to opportunities provided by chance.

No one expects poker to be played on the ethical principles preached in churches. In poker it is right and proper to bluff a friend out of the rewards of being dealt a good hand. A player feels no more than a slight twinge of sympathy, if that, when—with nothing better than a single ace in his hand—he strips a heavy loser, who holds a pair, of the rest of his chips. It was up to the other fellow to protect himself. In the words of an excellent poker player, former President Harry Truman, "If you can't stand the heat, stay out of the kitchen." If one shows mercy to a loser in poker, it is a personal gesture, divorced from the rules of the game.

Poker has its special ethics, and here I am not referring to rules against cheating. The man who keeps an ace up his sleeve or who marks the cards is more than unethical; he is a crook, and can be punished as such—kicked out of the game, or, in the Old West, shot.

In contrast to the cheat, the unethical poker player is one who, while abiding by the letter of the rules, finds ways to put the other players at an unfair disadvantage. Perhaps he unnerves them with loud talk. Or he tries to get them drunk. Or he plays in cahoots with someone else at the table. Ethical poker players frown on such tactics.

Poker's own brand of ethics is different from the ethical ideals of civilized human relationships. The game calls for distrust of the other fellow. It ignores the claim of friendship. Cunning deception and concealment of one's strength and intentions, not kindness and openheartedness, are vital in poker. No one thinks any the worse of poker on that account. And no one should think any the worse of the game of business because its standards of right and wrong differ from the prevailing traditions of morality in our society.

DISCARD THE GOLDEN RULE

This view of business is especially worrisome to people without much business experience. A minister of my acquaintance once protested that business cannot possibly function in our society unless it is based on the Judeo-Christian system of ethics. He told me:

> I know some businessmen have supplied call girls to customers, but there are always a few rotten apples in every barrel. That doesn't mean the rest of the fruit isn't sound. Surely the vast majority of businessmen are ethical. I myself am acquainted with many who adhere to strict codes of ethics based fundamentally on religious teachings. They contribute to good causes. They participate in community activities. They cooperate with other companies to improve working conditions in their industries. Certainly they are not indifferent to ethics.

That most businessmen are not indifferent to ethics in their private lives, everyone will agree. My point is that in their office lives they cease to be private citizens; they become game players who must be guided by a somewhat different set of ethical standards.

The point was forcefully made to me by a Midwestern executive who has given a good deal of thought to the question:

> So long as a businessman complies with the laws of the land and avoids telling malicious lies, he's ethical. If the law as written gives a man a wide-open chance to make a killing, he'd been a fool not to take advantage of it. If he doesn't, somebody else will. There's no obligation on him to stop and consider who is going to get hurt. If the law says he can do it, that's all the justification he needs. There's nothing unethical about that. It's just plain business sense.

This executive (call him Robbins) took the stand that even industrial espionage, which is frowned on by some businessmen, ought not to be considered unethical. He recalled a recent meeting of the National Industrial Conference Board where an authority on marketing made a speech in which he deplored the employment of spies by business organizations. More and more companies, he pointed out, find it cheaper to penetrate the secrets of competitors with concealed cameras and microphones or by bribing employees than to set up costly research and design departments of their own. A whole branch of the electronics industry has grown up with this trend, he continued, providing equipment to make industrial espionage easier.

Disturbing? The marketing expert found it so. But when it came to a remedy, he could only appeal to "respect for the golden rule." Robbins thought this a confession of defeat, believing that the golden rule, for all its value as an ideal for society, is simply not feasible as a guide for business. A good part of the time the businessman is trying to do unto others as he hopes others will *not* do unto him. Robbins continued:

> Espionage of one kind or another has became so common in business that it's like taking a drink during Prohibition — it's not considered sinful. And we don't even have Prohibition where espionage is concerned; the law is very tolerant in this area. There's no more shame for a business that uses secret agents than there is for a nation. Bear in mind that there already is at least one large corporation — you can buy its stock over the counter — that makes millions by providing counterespionage service to industrial firms. Espionage in business is not an ethical problem; it's an established technique of business competition.

"We don't make the laws"

Wherever we turn in business, we can perceive the sharp distinction between its ethical standards and those of the churches. Newspapers abound with sensational stories growing out of this distinction:

> We read one day that Senator Philip A. Hart of Michigan has attacked food processors for deceptive packaging of numerous products.
>
> The next day there is a Congressional to-do over Ralph Nader's book, *Unsafe At Any Speed,* which demonstrates that automobile companies for years have neglected the safety of car-owning families.
>
> Then another Senator, Lee Metcalf of Montana, and journalist Vic Reinemer show in their book, *Overcharge,* the methods by which utility companies elude regulating government bodies to extract unduly large payments from users of electricity.

These are merely dramatic instances of a prevailing condition; there is hardly a major industry at which a similar attack could not be aimed. Critics of business regard such behavior as unethical, but the companies concerned know that they are merely playing the business game.

Among the most respected of our business institutions are the insurance companies. A group of insurance executives meeting recently in New England was startled when their guest speaker, social critic Daniel Patrick Moynihan, roundly berated them for "unethical" practices. They had been guilty, Moynihan alleged, of using outdated actuarial tables to obtain unfairly high premiums. They habitually delayed the hearings of lawsuits against them in order to tire out the plaintiffs and win cheap settlements. In their employment policies they used ingenious devices to discriminate against certain minority groups.

It was difficult for the audience to deny the validity of these charges. But these men were business game players. Their reaction to Moynihan's attack was much the same as that of the automobile manufacturers to Nader, of the utilities to Senator Metcalf, and of the food processors to Senator Hart. If the laws governing their businesses change, or if public opinion becomes clamorous, they will make the necessary adjustments. But morally they have in their view done nothing wrong. As long as they comply with the letter of the law, they are within their rights to operate their businesses as they see fit.

The small business is in the same position as the great corporation in this respect. For example:

> In 1967 a key manufacturer was accused of providing master keys for automobiles to mail-order customers, although it was obvious that some of the purchasers might be automobile thieves. His defense was plain and straightforward. If there was nothing in the law to prevent him from selling his keys to anyone who ordered them, it was not up to him to inquire as to his customers' motives. Why was it any worse, he insisted, for him to sell car keys by mail, than for mail-order houses to sell guns that might be used for murder? Until the law was changed, the key manufacturer could regard himself as being just as ethical as any other businessman by the rules of the business game.

Violations of the ethical ideals of society are common in business, but they are not necessarily violations of business principles. Each year the Federal Trade Commission orders hundreds of companies, many of them of the first magnitude, to "cease and desist" from practices which, judged by ordinary standards, are of questionable morality but which are stoutly defended by the companies concerned.

In one case, a firm manufacturing a well-known mouthwash was accused of using a cheap form of alcohol possibly deleterious to health. The company's chief executive, after testifying in Washington, made this comment privately:

> We broke no law. We're in a highly competitive industry. If we're going to stay in business, we have to look for profit wherever the law permits. We don't make the laws. We obey them. Then why do we have to put up with this "holier than thou" talk about ethics? It's sheer hypocrisy. We're not in business to promote ethics. Look at the cigarette companies, for God's sake! If the ethics aren't embodied in the laws by the men who made them, you can't expect businessmen to fill the lack. Why, a sudden submission to Christian ethics by businessmen would bring about the greatest economic upheaval in history!

It may be noted that the government failed to prove its case against him.

Cast illusions aside

Talk about ethics by businessmen is often a thin decorative coating over the hard realities of the game:

> Once I listened to a speech by a young executive who pointed to a new industry code as proof that his company and its competitors were deeply aware of their responsibilities to society. It was a code of ethics, he said. The industry was going to police itself, to dissuade constituent companies from wrongdoing. His eyes shone with conviction and enthusiasm.
>
> The same day there was a meeting in a hotel room where the industry's top executives met with the "czar" who was to administer the new code, a man of

high repute. No one who was present could doubt their common attitude. In their eyes the code was designed primarily to forestall a move by the federal government to impose stern restrictions on the industry. They felt that the code would hamper them a good deal less than new federal laws would. It was, in other words, conceived as a protection for the industry, not for the public.

The young executive accepted the surface explanation of the code; these leaders, all experienced game players, did not deceive themselves for a moment about its purpose.

The illusion that business can afford to be guided by ethics as conceived in private life is often fostered by speeches and articles containing such phrases as, "It pays to be ethical," or, "Sound ethics is good business." Actually this is not an ethical position at all; it is a self-serving calculation in disguise. The speaker is really saying that in the long run a company can make more money if it does not antagonize competitors, suppliers, employees, and customers by squeezing them too hard. He is saying that oversharp policies reduce ultimate gains. That is true, but it has nothing to do with ethics. The underlying attitude is much like that in the familiar story of the shopkeeper who finds an extra $20 bill in the cash register, debates with himself the ethical problem—should he tell his partner?—and finally decides to share the money because the gesture will give him an edge over the s.o.b. the next time they quarrel.

I think it is fair to sum up the prevailing attitude of businessmen on ethics as follows:

We live in what is probably the most competitive of the world's civilized societies. Our customs encourage a high degree of aggression in the individual's striving for success. Business is our main area of competition, and it has been ritualized into a game of strategy. The basic rules of the game have been set by the government, which attempts to detect and punish business frauds. But as long as a company does not transgress the rules of the game set by law, it has the legal right to shape its strategy without reference to anything but its profits. If it takes a long-term view of its profits, it will preserve amicable relations, so far as possible, with those with whom it deals. A wise businessman will not seek advantage to the point where he generates dangerous hostility among employees, competitors, customers, government, or the public at large. But decisions in this area are, in the final test, decisions of strategy, not of ethics.

THE INDIVIDUAL AND THE GAME

An individual within a company often finds it difficult to adjust to the requirements of the business game. He tries to preserve his private ethical standards in situations that call for game strategy. When he is obliged to carry out company policies that challenge his conception of himself as an ethical man, he suffers.

It disturbs him when he is ordered, for instance, to deny a raise to a man who deserves it, to fire an employee of long standing, to prepare advertising that he believes to be misleading, to conceal facts that he feels customers are entitled to know, to cheapen the quality of materials used in the manufacture of an established product, to sell as new a product that he knows to be rebuilt, to exaggerate the curative powers of a medicinal preparation, or to coerce dealers.

There are some fortunate executives who, by the nature of their work and circumstances, never have to face problems of this kind. But in one form or another the ethical dilemma is felt sooner or later by most businessmen. Possibly the dilemma is most painful not when the company forces the action on the executive but when he originates it himself — that is, when he has taken or is contemplating a step which is in his own interest but which runs counter to his early moral conditioning. To illustrate:

> The manager of an export department, eager to show rising sales, is pressed by a big customer to provide invoices which, while containing no overt falsehood that would violate a U.S. law, are so worded that the customer may be able to evade certain taxes in his homeland.
>
> A company president finds that an aging executive, within a few years of retirement and his pension, is not as productive as formerly. Should he be kept on?
>
> The produce manager of a supermarket debates with himself whether to get rid of a lot of half-rotten tomatoes by including one, with its good side exposed, in every tomato six-pack.
>
> An accountant discovers that he has taken an improper deduction on his company's tax return and fears the consequences if he calls the matter to the president's attention, though he himself has done nothing illegal. Perhaps if he says nothing, no one will notice the error.
>
> A chief executive officer is asked by his directors to comment on a rumor that he owns stock in another company with which he has placed large orders. He could deny it, for the stock is in the name of his son-in-law and he has earlier formally instructed his son-in-law to sell the holding.

Temptations of this kind constantly arise in business. If an executive allows himself to be torn between a decision based on business considerations and one based on his private ethical code, he exposes himself to a grave psychological strain.

This is not to say that sound business strategy necessarily runs counter to ethical ideals. They may frequently coincide; and when they do, everyone is gratified. But the major tests of every move in business, as in all games of strategy, are legality and profit. A man who intends to be a winner in the business game must have a game player's attitude.

The business strategist's decision must be as impersonal as those of a surgeon performing an operation — concentrating on objective and technique, and subordinating personal feelings. If the chief executive admits that his son-in-law owns the stock, it is because he stands to lose more if the fact comes out later than if he states it boldly and at once. If the supermarket manager orders the rotten tomatoes to be discarded, he does so to avoid an increase in consumer complaints and a loss of good will. The company president decides not to fire the elderly executive in the belief that the negative reaction of other employees would in the long run cost the company more than it would lose in keeping him and paying his pension.

All sensible businessmen prefer to be truthful, but they seldom feel inclined to tell the *whole* truth. In the business game truth-telling usually has to be kept within narrow limits if trouble is to be avoided. The point was neatly made a long time ago (in 1888) by one of John D. Rockefeller's associates, Paul Babcock, to Standard Oil Company executives who were about to testify before a government investigating committee: "Parry every question with answers which, while perfectly truthful, are evasive of *bottom* facts." This was, is, and probably always will be regarded as wise and permissable business strategy.

For office use only

An executive's family life can easily be dislocated if he fails to make a sharp distinction between the ethical systems of the home and the office—or if his wife does not grasp that distinction. Many a businessman who has remarked to his wife, "I had to let Jones go today" or "I had to admit to the boss that Jim has been goofing off lately," has been met with an indignant protest. "How could you do a thing like that? You know Jones is over 50 and will have a lot of trouble getting another job." Or, "You did that to Jim? With his wife ill and all the worry she's been having with the kids?"

If the executive insists that he had no choice because the profits of the company and his own security were involved, he may see a certain cool and ominous reappraisal in his wife's eyes. Many wives are not prepared to accept the fact that business operates with a special code of ethics. An illuminating illustration of this comes from a Southern sales executive who related a conversation he had had with his wife at a time when a hotly contested political campaign was being waged in their state:

> I made the mistake of telling her that I had had lunch with Colby, who gives me about half my business. Colby mentioned that his company had a stake in the election. Then he said, "By the way, I'm treasurer of the citizens' committee for Lang. I'm collecting contributions. Can I count on you for a hundred dollars?"
>
> Well, there I was. I was opposed to Lang, but I knew Colby. If he withdrew his business I could be in a bad spot. So I just smiled and wrote out a check then and there. He thanked me, and we started to talk about his next order. Maybe he thought I shared his political views. If so, I wasn't going to lose any sleep over it.
>
> I should have had sense enough not to tell Mary about it. She hit the ceiling. She said she was disappointed in me. She said I hadn't acted like a man, that I should have stood up to Colby.
>
> I said, "Look, it was an either-or situation. I had to do it or risk losing the business."
>
> She came back at me with, "I don't believe it. You could have been honest with him. You could have said you didn't feel you ought to contribute to a campaign for a man you weren't going to vote for. I'm sure he would have understood."
>
> I said, "Mary, you're a wonderful woman, but you're way off the track. Do you know what would have happened if I had said that? Colby would have

smiled and said, 'Oh, I didn't realize. Forget it.' But in his eyes from that moment I would be an oddball, maybe a bit of a radical. He would have listened to me talk about his order and would have promised to give it consideration. After that I wouldn't hear from him for a week. Then I would telephone and learn from his secretary that he wasn't yet ready to place the order. And in about a month I would hear through the grapevine that he was giving his business to another company. A month after that I'd be out of a job."

She was silent for a while. Then she said, "Tom, something is wrong with business when a man is forced to choose between his family's security and his moral obligation to himself. It's easy for me to say you should have stood up to him—but if you had, you might have felt you were betraying me and the kids. I'm sorry that you did it, Tom, but I can't blame you. Something is wrong with business!"

This wife saw the problem in terms of moral obligation as conceived in private life; her husband saw it as a matter of game strategy. As a player in a weak position, he felt that he could not afford to indulge an ethical sentiment that might have cost him his seat at the table.

Playing to win

Some men might challenge the Colbys of business—might accept serious setbacks to their business careers rather than risk a feeling of moral cowardice. They merit our respect—but as private individuals, not businessmen. When the skillful player of the business game is compelled to submit to unfair pressure, he does not castigate himself for moral weakness. Instead, he strives to put himself into a strong position where he can defend himself against such pressures in the future without loss.

If a man plans to take a seat in the business game, he owes it to himself to master the principles by which the game is played, including its special ethical outlook. He can then hardly fail to recognize that an occasional bluff may well be justified in terms of the game's ethics and warranted in terms of economic necessity. Once he clears his mind on this point, he is in a good position to match his strategy against that of the other players. He can then determine objectively whether a bluff in a given situation has a good chance of succeeding and can decide when and how to bluff, without a feeling of ethical transgression.

To be a winner, a man must play to win. This does not mean that he must be ruthless, cruel, harsh, or treacherous. On the contrary, the better his reputation for integrity, honesty, and decency, the better his chances of victory will be in the long run. But from time to time every businessman, like every poker player, is offered a choice between certain loss or bluffing within the legal rules of the game. If he is not resigned to losing, if he wants to rise in his company and industry, then in such a crisis he will bluff—and bluff hard.

Every now and then one meets a successful businessman who has conveniently forgotten the small or large deceptions that he practiced on his way to fortune. "God gave me my money," old John D. Rockefeller once piously told a Sunday school class. It would be a rare tycoon in our time who would risk the horse laugh with which such a remark would be greeted.

In the last third of the twentieth century even children are aware that if a man has become prosperous in business, he has sometimes departed from the strict truth in order to overcome obstacles or has practiced the more subtle deceptions of the half-truth or the misleading omission. Whatever the form of the bluff, it is an integral part of the game, and the executive who does not master its techniques is not likely to accumulate much money or power.

Is the Ethics of Business Changing?

Here is what some 1,200 of our U.S. readers today think compared with what their counterparts fifteen years ago thought

Steven N. Brenner and Earl A. Molander

Concern over the ethics of U.S. business executives was at a high point in 1961 when the Reverend Raymond C. Baumhart, S.J. asked HBR readers for their opinions on the matter. Prompted by a decade of writings on the subject and the revelation of collusion and price fixing by electrical equipment manufacturers, they expressed their feelings on professional conduct and standards and ethical dilemmas and codes. Yet public awareness and concern over business ethics is probably even higher today than it was then, as is the concern among those in business over their own values, norms, and conduct. Thus the authors' update of that study provides a timely snapshot of the feelings of current readers against a backdrop of how their predecessors felt. The authors also explore how executives feel about the issue of corporate social responsibility and how it affects their thinking on business ethics.

What would you do if . . .

- the minister of a foreign nation where extraordinary payments to lubricate the decision-making machinery are common asks you for a $200,000 consulting fee? In return, he promises special assistance in obtaining a $100-million contract which would produce at least a $5-million profit for your company. The contract would probably go to a foreign competitor if your company did not win it.

- as the president of a company in a highly competitive industry, you learn that a competitor has made an important scientific discovery that will substantially reduce, but not eliminate, your profit for about a

Reprinted by permission of the publisher from the *Harvard Business Review*, Vol. 55, No. 1, January–February, 1977. © 1973 by the President and Fellows of Harvard College; all rights reserved.

year? There is a possibility of hiring one of the competitor's employees who knows the details of the discovery.

- you learn that an executive earning $30,000 a year has been padding his expense account by about $1,500 a year?

These questions were posed as part of a lengthy questionnaire on business ethics and social responsibility completed by 1,227 *Harvard Business Review* readers—25% of the cross section of 5,000 U.S. readers polled (see Exhibit I).

Our study was prompted by the same concern that Raymond C. Baumhart had in 1961 when he conducted a similar study for HBR: the numerous comments on business ethics in the media contained little empirical evidence to indicate whether large numbers of business executives shared the attitudes, behavior, and experience of those whose supposedly unethical and illegal conduct was being represented (or denied) as typical of the business profession.*

In updating and expanding his study, we designed our survey around three main questions: Has business ethics changed since the early 1960s, and if so, how and why? Are codes the answer to the ethical challenges business people currently face? What is the relationship between ethical dilemmas and the dilemma of corporate social responsibility?

Here are some of the highlights of our study:

1. There is substantial disagreement among respondents as to whether ethical standards in business today have changed from what they were.
2. Respondents are somewhat more cynical about the ethical conduct of their peers than they were.
3. Most respondents favor ethical codes, although they strongly prefer general precept codes to specific practice codes.
4. The dilemmas respondents experience and the factors they feel have the greatest impact on business ethics suggest that ethical codes alone will not substantially improve business conduct.
5. Most respondents have overcome the traditional ideological barriers to the concept of social responsibility and have embraced its practice as a legitimate and achievable goal for business.
6. Most respondents rank their customers well ahead of shareholders and employees as the client group to whom they feel the greatest responsibility.

TODAY VS. 15 YEARS AGO

Like other professions, business is continually scrutinizing its behavior relative to its own standards and those of the society around it.

What do business executives see when they look at themselves? One thing we found was that they see their profession as less ethical than the professions of professors and doctors, but more ethical than those of government agency officials, lawyers, elected politicians, and union officials, in that order.

---

*Raymond C. Baumhart, "How Ethical Are Businessmen?" *HBR* July–August 1961, p. 6.

Exhibit I
Profile of respondents

	1961 percentage	1976 percentage
Management position		
Top management—chairman of the board; board member; owner; partner; president; managing director		17%
Other top management—division or executive vice president; treasurer; secretary-treasurer; controller; secretary (to the corporation); general manager; general superintendent; editor; administrative director; dean and assistants thereto	45%	25
(Total in 1961 is for first two categories.)		
Upper middle management—functional department head (e.g., advertising, sales, promotion, production, purchasing, personnel, engineering, public relations, brand manager, and the like)	27	13
Lower middle management—assistant to functional department head; district manager; branch manager; section manager; and the like	12	21
Staff and nonmanagement personnel —all others employed in business	9	13
Professional—doctor; practicing lawyer; CPA; professor; consultant; military officer; government official; union official; clergy; and the like	7	8
Other or didn't answer	0	3

Note: Percentages calculated from 1,531 respondents in 1961 study and 1,227 respondents in 1976 study. Categories may not add up to 100 due to rounding errors.

Exhibit I (continued)

	1961 percentage	1976 percentage
Income group		
Under $20,000	57%	15%
$20,000–29,999	23	28
$30,000–39,999	8	24
$40,000–49,999	4	10
$50,000–74,999	4	13
$75,000–99,999	2	5
$100,000 and over	2	4
Didn't answer	0	2
Company size by number of employees		
1–99	22%	19%
100–999	29	25
1,000–9,999	26	23
10,000 and over	23	25
Didn't answer	0	7

	1961 percentage	1976 percentage
Formal education		
High school or less	5%	1%
Some college	19	8
Bachelor's degree	36	30
Graduate school	40	60
Didn't answer	0	1
Functional area of most experience		
Accounting	*	9%
Engineering	*	10
Finance	*	15
Marketing	*	24
Personnel or labor relations	*	9
Production	*	9
Public relations	*	3
Other	*	18
Didn't answer	*	4

Age

29 or under	6%	13%
30–39	28	37
40–49	35	26
50–59	23	19
60 and over	8	5
Didn't answer	0	1

Sex

Male	*	94%
Female	*	5
Didn't answer	*	1

Industry

Manufacturing consumer goods	16%	13%
Manufacturing industrial goods	25	22
Engineering; research and development	6	3
Management consulting and business services	6	8
Banking; investment; insurance	10	12
Construction	2	2
Mining or extraction; oil	2	3
Retail or wholesale trade	7	7
Transportation; public utilities	5	6
Advertising; media; publishing	4	3
Consumer services	3	4
Other	14	17
Didn't answer	0	2

*Not reported in 1961 study.
Note: Percentages calculated from 1,531 respondents in 1961 study and 1,227 respondents in 1976 study. Categories may not add up to 100 due to rounding errors.

Common dilemmas

Of course, the ethics of business includes not only the moral values and duties of the profession itself, but also the existing values and expectations of the larger society. Because ethical systems are created by fallible people, they generally have some inherent contradictions. Further, the values and ethics of various organizations differ from those of other sectors of society in which business people participate (such as the family, church, and political parties). For these reasons executives inevitably face some ethical dilemmas in their daily work.

To learn how chronic a problem such ethical dilemmas are in the contemporary business environment, we asked our respondents if they had ever experienced a conflict between what was expected of them as efficient, profit-conscious managers and what was expected of them as ethical persons. Four of every seven of those who responded (399 of 698) say they have experienced such conflicts, compared with three of four respondents in 1961 (603 of 796)—a substantial decrease of 19%.

One possible explanation for this decrease is that the internal pressures for profit and efficiency are not as great as they once were. Since we can find no evidence of such a change, two other possible explanations must be considered: ethical standards have declined from what they were or situations that once caused ethical discomfort have become accepted practice.

As Exhibit II shows, we did find that the *nature* of compromising circumstances has changed. Honesty in communication is a significantly greater problem in 1976 than it was in 1961. This includes honesty in advertising and in providing information to top management, clients, and government agencies. We found number manipulation to have become a particularly acute problem.

Dilemmas associated with firings and layoffs are significantly less of a problem in 1976. Either terminations and their related problems are becoming accepted as routine in today's business world, or they are being handled more equitably when they occur. Undoubtedly because of government prosecutions, price collusion is also far less of a problem.

We feel it particularly noteworthy that relations with superiors are the primary category of ethical conflict. Respondents frequently complained of superiors' pressure to support incorrect viewpoints, sign false documents, overlook superiors' wrongdoing, and do business with superiors' friends. Either superiors are expecting more than subordinates in 1976 or subordinates are less willing to do their bosses' bidding without questions, at least to themselves. Both possibilities suggest a weakening in the corporate authority structure and an attendant impact on ethical business conduct that deserves future study. The following examples demonstrate ethical dilemmas being faced in business today:

- The vice president of a California industrial manufacturer "being forced as an officer to sign corporate documents which I knew were not in the best interest of minority stockholders."

- A Missouri manager of manpower planning "employing marginally qualified minorities in order to meet Affirmative Action quotas."

• A manager of product development from a computer company in Massachusetts "trying to act as though the product (computer software) would correspond to what the customer had been led by sales to expect, when, in fact, I knew it wouldn't."

• A manager of corporate planning from California "acquiring a non-U.S. company with two sets of books used to evade income

Exhibit II
Conflicts between company interests and personal ethics

	1961 percentage	1976 percentage
In relations with:		
Superiors	*	12.8%
Customers	*	12.0
Employees	*	11.5
Agents and customers	*	9.5
Competitors	*	4.8
Law; government; and society	*	4.8
Suppliers	*	2.5
Potential investors	*	0.5
Other and unspecified	*	41.6
With regard to:		
Honesty in communication	13.5%	22.3%
Gifts; entertainment; and kickbacks	8.9	12.3
Fairness and discrimination	*	7.0
Miscellaneous law breaking	*	5.8
Honesty in executing contracts and agreements	*	5.5
Firings and layoffs	16.2	4.8
Price collusion and pricing practices	12.5	2.3
Other and unspecified	48.8	40.1

*Not reported in 1961 study.

taxes—standard practice for that country. Do we (1) declare income and pay taxes, (2) take the "black money" out of the country (illegally), or (3) continue tax evasion?"

• The president of a real estate property management firm in Washington "projecting cash flow without substantial evidence in order to obtain a higher loan than the project can realistically amortize."

• A young Texas insurance manager "being asked to make policy changes that produced more premium for the company and commission for an agent but did not appear to be of advantage to the policyholder."

Accepted practices

Clearly, that ethical dilemmas do exist and are too often resolved in ways which leave executives dissatisfied seems to be a matter of substantial concern for today's business people. And too often unethical practices become a routine part of doing business. To determine just how routine, we asked:

> In every industry there are some generally accepted business practices. In your industry, are there practices which you regard as unethical?

If we eliminate those who say they "don't know," we see from Exhibit III that two-thirds of the responding executives in 1976 indicate that such practices exist, compared with nearly four-fifths who so responded in 1961.

Could this decrease be a sign of improvement in ethical *practices?* Perhaps, but it is also possible that such practices are now less visible than they once were. Even more disturbing is the possibility which we raised earlier—that ethical *standards* have, in fact, fallen in business so that practices once considered unethical are now not viewed as such. Further, these figures say nothing about the conduct that all agree is both unacceptable and unethical.

Nearly half (540) of all respondents and 84% of those indicating the existence of such practices were willing to tell us which practice or practices they would most like to see eliminated (see Exhibit IV). Both the changes and similarities in these "most unwanted" practices in the past 15 years are interesting.

As in 1961, the practice that most executives want to eliminate involves "gifts, gratuities, bribes, and 'call girls.' " Typical examples given by the 144 respondents in this category are:

• "Payoffs to a foreign government to secure contracts." [The vice president of an Oklahoma oil exploration company]

• "Egg carton contracts with grocery chains can only be obtained by kickbacks—the egg packers do not have the freedom of choice in buying, thus stifling competition." [A young Southern consumer goods executive vice president]

• "Loans granted as favors to loan officers." [An Indiana bank vice president]

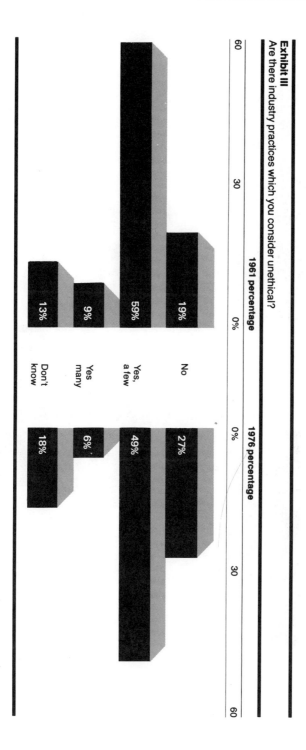

Exhibit III
Are there industry practices which you consider unethical?

Exhibit IV
Unethical practices executives want to eliminate

	1961 percentage		1976 percentage	
30	15	0%	0%	15	30

1961		1976
23%	Gifts; gratuities; bribes; "call girls"	26%
18%	Price discrimination; unfair pricing	8%
14%	Dishonest advertising	5%
10%	Miscellaneous unfair competitive practices	14%
9%	Cheating customers; unfair credit practices; overselling	14%
8%	Price collusion by competitors	3%
7%	Dishonesty in making or keeping a contract	1%
6%	Unfairness to employees; prejudice in hiring	9%
5%	Others	20%

- "Dealings with travel agencies that involve kickbacks, rebates, or other pseudonyms for 'bribes.' " [A Florida transportation industry executive]

Of the 80 respondents who mentioned practices which included cheating customers, unfair credit practices, or overselling, typical comments are:

- "Substitution of materials without customer knowledge after the job has been awarded." [A young New York salesman]

- "Misrepresenting the contents of products." [A Texas vice president of engineering]

- "Scheduled delivery dates that are known to be inaccurate to get a contract." [A California director of engineering]

Both the sharp drop from 1961 to 1976 shown in Exhibit IV in concern over "price discrimination and unfair pricing" and "dishonest advertising" and the increase in concern over "unfairness to employees and prejudice in hiring" and "creating customers" are probably attributable to government enforcement and higher legal standards.

Economic pressures

We have confirmed the continued existence both of ethical dilemmas inherent in everyday business and of generally accepted practices which individual managers feel are unethical. To observe the impact of such an environment on our respondents' ethical beliefs, we turned our attention to a number of issues of general ethical concern.

Simply returning our questionnaire reflected, we think, a general concern about business ethics among our respondents. Nevertheless, 65% of them feel that "society, not business, has the *chief* responsibility for inculcating its ethical standards into the educational and legal systems, and thus into business decision making."

Another important aspect of the debate over ethics focuses on whether any absolutes exist to strive for or whether ethics should be purely "situational" or "relative." Four out of five respondents agree that "business people should try to live up to an absolute moral standard rather than to the moral standard of their peer group."

Not only do executives believe in ethical absolutes; they also believe that "in the long run, sound ethics is good business." As in 1961, fewer than 2% of the respondents disagreed with this statement. Yet, in practice, many of these same executives see their associates losing sight of this standard. Again, as in 1961, close to half of our respondents agree that "the American business executive tends not to apply the great ethical laws immediately to work. He is preoccupied chiefly with gain."*

---

*Rabbi Louis Finkelstein, "The Businessman's Moral Failure," *Fortune*, September 1958, p. 116.

Our results suggest two explanations for this failure. First, despite its long-run value, ethical conduct apparently is not necessarily rewarded. Within the business organization, 50% of our respondents feel that one's superiors often do not want to know how results are obtained, as long as one achieves the desired outcome.

Second, competitive pressures from outside the organization push ethical consideration into the background. Of our executives, 43% feel that "competition today is stiffer than ever. As a result, many in business find themselves forced to resort to practices which are considered shady, but which appear necessary for survival."

Societal forces

In the period since Baumhart's study, American business has seen some significant changes. A sustained period of economic euphoria which began in 1961 has been replaced by recession, inflation, and resource scarcity. Charges of corporate irresponsibility relative to critical issues of the 1960s and 1970s (minority relations, consumerism, and the environment) combined with the recent disclosures of corporate wrongdoing at home and abroad have raised serious questions about the trend in business's ethical standards.

To determine if any such trend existed, we asked our HBR respondents:

> How do you feel ethical standards in business today compare with ethical standards 15 years ago?

The old French proverb, "The more things change, the more they stay the same," seems appropriate in describing the responses. Rather than reporting a clear-cut shift in either direction, our respondents split fairly evenly; 32% (388) feel standards are lower today, 41% (492) that they are about the same, and 27% (325) that they are higher.

But among those respondents who sense a more extreme change, a trend is identifiable with the 12% who believe ethical standards to be *considerably* lower outnumbering the 5% who believe them to be *considerably* higher by a 2.4-to-1 ratio.

We asked our respondents to describe "the single factor which has most influenced (or caused) the shift (you) observe in ethical standards." By splitting responses into two groups, those who see today's ethical standards as lower and those who see them as higher, it is possible to isolate which factors our respondents feel have influenced ethical standards in business.

The fact that 95% of the 713 respondents who see some shift in ethical standards provided further explanatory factors in brief sentences confirms our earlier assertion that ethics is an important personal concern to executives. The factors are listed in Exhibit V.

It is noteworthy that of the six major factors seen as causing *higher* standards, only two are subject to any significant measure of direct business influence and control—the education and professionalism of management and business's greater sense of awareness and responsiveness.

Exhibit V
Factors influencing ethical standards

Factors causing higher standards	Percentage of Respondents Listing Factor
Public disclosure; publicity; media coverage; better communication	31%
Increased public concern; public awareness, consciousness, and scrutiny; better informed public; societal pressures	20
Government regulation, legislation, and intervention; federal courts	10
Education of business managers; increase in manager professionalism and education	9
New social expectations for the role business is to play in society; young adults' attitudes; consumerism	5
Business's greater sense of social responsibility and greater awareness of the implications of its acts; business responsiveness; corporate policy changes; top management emphasis on ethical action	5
Other	20

Factors causing lower standards

Society's standards are lower; social decay; more permissive society; materialism and hedonism have grown; loss of church and home influence; less quality, more quantity desires	34%
Competition; pace of life; stress to succeed; current economic conditions; costs of doing business; more businesses compete for less	13
Political corruption; loss of confidence in government; Watergate; politics; political ethics and climate	9
People more aware of unethical acts; constant media coverage; TV; communications create atmosphere for crime	9
Greed; desire for gain; worship the dollar as measure of success; selfishness of the individual; lack of personal integrity and moral fiber	8
Pressure for profit from within the organization from superiors or from stockholders; corporate influences on managers; corporate policies	7
Other	21

Note: Some respondents listed more than one factor, so there were 353 factors in all listed as causing higher standards and 411 in all listed as causing lower ones. Categories may not add up to 100 due to rounding errors.

Exhibit VI
I'm more ethical than the average executive

Case 1 An executive earning $30,000 a year has been padding his expense
account by about $1,500 a year.

	What I think		What the average executive thinks		
	45	0%	0%	45	90
Acceptable if other executives in the company do the same thing	6%		27%		1961
	4%		28%		1976
Acceptable if the executive's superior knows about it and says nothing	11%		28%		1961
	9%		33%		1976
Unacceptable, regardless of the circumstances	86%		60%		1961
	89%		53%		1976

Case 2 Imagine that you are the president of a company in a highly competitive industry. You learn that a competitor has made an important scientific discovery which will give him an advantage that will substantially reduce, but not eliminate, the profits of your company for about a year. If there were some hope of hiring one of the competitor's employees who knew the details of the discovery, would you try to hire him?

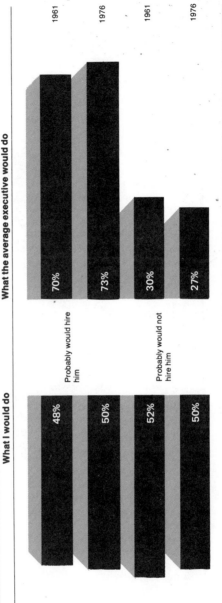

Exhibit VI

Case 3 The minister of a foreign nation where extraordinary payments to lubricate the decision-making machinery are common asks you as a company marketing director for a $200,000 consulting fee. In return, he promises special assistance in obtaining a $100 million contract which should produce at least $5 million profit for your company. What would you do?

What I would do		What the average executive would do	
90	45	0%	0%	45	90

Pay the fee, feeling it was ethical in the moral climate of the foreign nation — What I would do: 36% — What the average executive would do: 45%

Pay the fee, feeling it was unethical but necessary to help ensure the sale — What I would do: 22% — What the average executive would do: 46%

Refuse to pay, even if the sale is thereby lost — What I would do: 42% — What the average executive would do: 9%

Case 4* At a board meeting of High Fly Insurance Co. (HFI), a new board member learns that HFI is the "officially approved" insurer of the Private Pilots Benevolent Association (PPBA), which contains 200,000 members. On joining PPBA, members automatically subscribe to HFI's accident insurance for a premium included in the standard dues assessment. In return, HFI pays PPBA a fee tied to the volume of business PPBA members generate and gets use of the PPBA mailing list, which it uses to sell aircraft liability policies (its major source of revenues). PPBA's president sits on HFI's board of directors and the two companies are both located in the same office building.

What the average new director **who is a recently promoted HFI employee** would do in this situation

Would do nothing — 55%

Would privately and delicately raise the issue with the chairman of the board — 29%

Would express opposition in a director's meeting, but would go along with whatever position the board chose to take — 13%

Would express vigorous opposition and resign if corrective action is not undertaken — 3%

What the average new **outside** director would do in this situation

36%

34%

19%

11%

*Not asked in 1961 study.

And of the six major factors seen as causing *lower* standards, only one is subject to such influence and control by business—pressure for profits in the organization.

Our respondents seem to be sending us three clear-cut messages:

1. Public disclosure and concern over unethical business behavior are the most potent forces for improvement in ethical standards.
2. Hedonism, individual greed, and the general decay of social standards are the factors which most influence a decline in ethical standards.
3. The elements which influence shifts in ethical standards are ones over which they have little direct control.

Growing cynicism

The situation, then, is that today's executive often faces ethical dilemmas and observes generally accepted practices which he or she feels are unethical. At the same time he is more likely to attribute questionable conduct to his business colleagues than he is to himself.

In 1961, Baumhart found his respondents to be quite cynical when comparing their own ethical decisions with what they expected the "average" executive to do in the same circumstances. To measure cynicism, we presented four case situations in two different ways. We asked one half of our sample, "What would *you* do?" and the other half, "What would the *average* executive do?" (See Exhibit VI.)

The two groups' answers differ more than Baumhart's respondents'. In Case 1, current respondents report themselves as less willing to pad their own expense accounts and report others as more willing to do so than did respondents in 1961. This perception spread (between "I feel it is unacceptable" and "the average executive feels it is unacceptable") grew from 26% in 1961 to 36% in 1976.

In Case 2, while the spread is nearly the same (22% in 1961 versus 23% in 1976), the respondents indicate that both they and the average executive would be more inclined than 1961 respondents to hire a competitor's employee to get a technological secret.

The real magnitude of such cynicism is shown in Case 3's international situation where facilitative payments could help land a large contract: 42% of the respondents said they would refuse to pay a bribe no matter what the consequences, while only 9% felt that the average executive in the same situation would refuse to pay. Even more disturbing, seven-eighths of the respondents who report that the average executive would see such payments as unethical also feel that he would go ahead and pay them anyway! And more than one-third of the respondents who themselves see such payments as unethical admit a willingness to pay them to help cement the contract award. Apparently, economic values override ethical values.

Case 4 illustrates another aspect of cynicism. Here we presented a potential conflict of interest and asked half of our respondents what an inside director would do and half what an outside director would do. The results suggest that executives expect outside directors to be more likely than inside directors to find fault in this situation (64% versus 45%) and to be more overt in their opposition when they do (30% versus 16%).

Our respondents apparently are cynical not only when they compare their own motives and actions to those of others, but also when they consider how business people with different organizational perspectives handle identical situations. This makes sense; organizational loyalty tends to inhibit an employee's perception of an ethical dilemma and to constrain his actions when ethical dilemmas are recognized.

Could our results be simply a flaw in our sampling method or in our analysis? This possibility is unlikely. We split our sample at random into two equal groups. Demographically, our groups were virtually identical. So, too, were their responses to the other questions we asked. So the differences must indicate that while executives see themselves as being faced with ethical dilemmas and as handling them correctly, they are not so confident about their peers' reactions.

GUIDEPOSTS & CODES

What can be done to restore this confidence? And what can help reduce unethical acts?

We asked our respondents what factors they feel influence executives to make unethical decisions. As Exhibit VII shows, they believe that the behavior of one's superiors is the primary guidepost, with formal company policy a somewhat distant secondary influence.

In other words, when faced with ethical dilemmas, people first refer to their immediate organizational framework for guidance. If the unethical acts of others and the lack of formal company policy provide a rationale for unethical behavior, would a formal policy, that is, an ethical code, be beneficial? The current popularity of ethical codes would seem to suggest as much.

Exhibit VII
Factors influencing unethical decisions

	Rank	
	1961	1976
Behavior of superiors	1.9	2.15
Formal policy or lack thereof	3.3	3.27
Industry ethical climate	2.6	3.34
Behavior of one's equals in the company	3.1	3.37
Society's moral climate	*	4.22
One's personal financial needs	4.1	4.46

*"Society's moral climate" was not asked in the 1961 study, which means that the rank cannot be compared numerically since 6 factors were used in 1976 and only 5 in 1961.
Note: The ranking is calculated on a scale of 1 (most influential) to 6 (least influential).

When we asked our respondents for their feelings about ethical codes for their industry, 25% said they favor no code at all. Of those who favor a code, 58% prefer one dealing with general precepts while only 17% prefer one delineating specific practices. Despite this lack of enthusiasm for specific codes, Exhibit VIII shows that the majority of respondents expect that such a code would help executives to (a) raise the ethical level of their industry, (b) define the limits of acceptable conduct, and (c) refuse unethical requests.

While respondents in 1976 are less certain of a code's efficacy than were their counterparts in 1961, these expectations support an argument many observers have made: the mere existence of a code, specific or general, can raise the ethical level of business behavior because it clarifies what is meant by ethical conduct. However, to an even greater extent than those in 1961, our respondents think a code is limited in its ability to change human conduct: 61% feel people would violate the code whenever they thought they could avoid detection and only 41% feel the code would reduce underhanded practices.

Appropriate enforcement

The single most negative response to our questions about a specific practice code concerns its enforceability: 89% of our respondents feel a specific practices code would *not* be easy to enforce. Anticipating this result since Baumhart's 1961 study had produced a similar response, we asked our respondents to identify an appropriate body for enforcing a code and the problems they foresaw in its enforcement.

In their choice of enforcement bodies, our respondents follow essentially the same pattern as Baumhart's did. Slightly more than a third favor self-enforcement at the company level, a third favor enforcement by a combined group of industry executives and members of the community, and slightly less than a third prefer enforcement at the industry level—either a trade association or a group of industry executives. Only 2.5% favor enforcement by a government agency.

Respondents foresee two major problems confronting all of these enforcement groups—getting information about violations and uniform and impartial enforcement. They feel that a third problem—lack of power and authority for enforcement—would be common to all groups except self-enforcement, which, understandably, they see as less of a problem. One young manager from Iowa hit on all three problems when he said, "You'll have problems with access to records, exceptions to the rules (and some may be legitimate), and punishment enforcement."

Our respondents feel that self-enforcement at the company level, the form of enforcement currently in widest use, has both substantial advantages and disadvantages compared with external enforcement.

Among the advantages they mentioned are:

1. Greater power and authority for those responsible for enforcement.
2. Easier access to information and detection of violations committed.
3. Easier interpretation when rules have been violated.
4. More natural definition of and execution of penalties to fit violations.

Exhibit VIII
Consequences expected from industry specific practice codes

	1961 percentage					1976 percentage				
	Agree	Partly Agree	Neutral	Partly Disagree	Disagree	Agree	Partly Agree	Neutral	Partly Disagree	Disagree
Would raise the ethical level of the industry	36%	35%	12%	7%	10%	19%	37%	15%	9%	18%
Would help executives by defining clearly the limits of acceptable conduct	48	33	7	5	7	29	38	11	9	12
Managers would welcome as a useful aid when they wanted to refuse an unethical request impersonally	59	28	5	4	4	45	34	8	6	6
People would violate whenever they thought they could avoid detection	13	44	8	20	15	22	39	11	19	9
In situations of severe competition, would reduce the use of underhanded practices	13	38	9	19	21	9	32	10	21	26
Would be easy to enforce	2	7	4	23	64	2	5	5	19	70

Note: Categories may not add up to 100 due to rounding errors.

At the same time certain disadvantages exist:

1. Uniform and impartial enforcement.
2. Difficulty of securing the full-fledged commitment of the enforcers (top management).
3. Greater tendency to ignore or wink at the rules.
4. Greater difficulty in resolving profits-versus-ethics conflicts.
5. Continuous worry over actions of companies not covered by a code.

As a systems sales representative from California rather curtly put it, "Self-enforcement won't always work, because those who make 'em, break 'em."

The enforcement problems inherent in ethical codes led us to question their potential effectiveness. We reexamined the data concerning (1) the dilemmas our respondents have encountered (Exhibit II), (2) the practices they would most like to eliminate (Exhibit IV), and (3) the factors causing shifts in standards (Exhibit V), and we asked, "In which of these areas could ethical codes have an impact?"

In general, the responses suggest that codes can be most helpful in those areas where there is general agreement that certain unethical practices are widespread and undesirable. Ethical codes do not, however, offer executives much hope for either controlling outside influences on business ethics or resolving fundamental ethical dilemmas. This is not to minimize the potential for codes to have an impact in narrow areas of concern. It is to emphasize that regardless of form they are no panacea for unethical business conduct.

Comment on Study

My interpretation of Professors Brenner's and Molander's data and the signs of the times indicate that business behavior is more ethical than it was 15 years ago, but that the expectations of a better educated and ethically sensitized public have risen more rapidly than the behavior.

This is the sixth, and most creative and extensive, replication of the series of questions I first asked in 1961. Each time the results have been remarkably similar, especially in the respondents' attitude that: I am more ethical than the average manager, and my department and company are more ethical than their counterparts; and a written code of ethics would help to improve business practices in my industry.

It is good to see the evidence that business managers accept the corporation as a social, as well as an economic, entity.

To me the most surprising finding of this study is that the 1,227 respondents rank responsibility to customers ahead of responsibility to stockholders and employees. What has happened to *caveat emptor?* Now it is the government and suppliers who should beware.

      Raymond C. Baumhart, S.J.,
      President of Loyola University

NEW VIEW OF SOCIAL RESPONSIBILITY

The current revival of interest in business ethics coincides with a renewed focus on corporate social responsibility. To provide some insight into how our respondents see the relationship between "social responsibility" and "business ethics," we asked:

Is social responsibility an *ethical* issue for the *individual business person,* or is it an issue that concerns the *role* the *corporation* should play in society? The overwhelming response we got is that it is *both*—65% agree with the former statement and 83% with the latter.

But can it be both? The answer is, of course, yes. Whereas responsibility, for both the individual and the corporation, tends to be defined in the social arrangements and obligations which make up the structure of the society, ethics concerns the rules by which these responsibilities are carried out. As in numerous other settings, it is often difficult to separate the rules of the game from the game itself.

Erroneous caricature

One important finding of our study is the rejection of the traditional ideology that says business is a profit-bound institution. Only 28% of our respondents endorse the traditional dictum that "the social responsibility of business is to 'stick to business,'" most often associated with the writings of Milton Friedman.*

Further, only 23% agree that "social responsibility is good business only if it is also good public relations and/or preempts government interference." And 38% agree that "the social responsibility debate is the result of the attempt of liberal intellectuals to make a moral issue of business behavior."†

By contrast, 69% agree with George Lodge's observation that "'profit' is really a somewhat ineffective measure of business's social effectiveness."‡

Not only do those in our sample reject the traditional ideological barriers to corporate involvement in social responsibility, but they also reject the practical ones. Of our respondents, 77% disagree with the idea that "every business is in effect 'trapped' in the business system it helped create, and can do remarkably little about the social problems of our time."§

Have business executives abandoned their traditional profit orientation? Not necessarily. We still found strong support for long-term profit maximization

---

*Milton Friedman, *Capitalism and Freedom* (Chicago: University of Chicago Press, 1962), Ch. 8.

†Henry G. Manne, in Henry G. Manne and Henry C. Wallich, *The Modern Corporation and Social Responsibility* (Washington, D.C.: American Institute for Public Policy Research, 1972), p. 10.

‡George Cabot Lodge, "Top Priority: Renovating Our Ideology," HBR September–October 1970, p. 50.

§Neil V. Chamberlain, *The Limits of Corporate Responsibility* (New York: Boise Books, 1973), p. 4.

among our executives. But these findings do indicate that the American business executive has incorporated a new view of his role and potential, and those of his company, into his profit concerns.

Those critics who continue to characterize the American business executive as a power-hungry, profit-bound individualist, indifferent to the needs of society, should be put on notice that they are now dealing with a straw man of their own making.

Before we go as far as to predict a revolution in corporate behavior, however, a word of caution is in order. First, the corporate organization still resists specific measures when trying to put social responsibility into practice. Of our respondents, 75% feel the rhetoric of social responsibility exceeds the reality in most corporations. And 58% agree that "the socially aware executive must show convincingly a net short-term or long-term economic advantage to the corporation in order to gain acceptance for any socially responsible measure he might propose."*

A second major barrier is uncertainty—uncertainty as to what "social responsibility" means. Almost half (46%) of our respondents agree with the assertion that "the meaning of social responsibility is so vague as to render it essentially unworkable as a guide to corporate policy and decisions."

This uncertainty as to meaning is further amplified by an uncertainty as to consequences. Our respondents were almost evenly split on two statements:

1. Social responsibility invariably will mean *lower* corporate profits in the *short run*—41% agree, 16% are neutral, and 43% disagree.

2. Social responsibility invariably will mean *higher* corporate profits in the *long run*—43% agree, 22% are neutral, and 36% disagree.

The nearly even split and the high number of neutral responses on these statements, together with the feeling of vagueness about the meaning of social responsibility, suggest that bringing social responsibility to the operating level is an objective which its advocates have yet to realize.

Customer's servant

To further clarify our respondents' concept of social responsibility, we asked them to rank the various groups whose relations to the corporation define the corporation's place in the social system.

As Exhibit IX shows, the group to whom executives feel the greatest responsibility comes through clearly and unmistakably: *the customers.* Stockholders and employees are a clear second and third, and the interest of society at large and its elected governments—the "public interest"—appears to receive the least consideration.

This rather surprising result—the primacy of customer interest—suggests that we need to reexamine the thesis that the guiding principle of American

*Albert Z. Carr, "Can an Executive Afford a Conscience?" HBR July–August 1970, p. 58.

Exhibit IX
Responsibility of your company to various groups

	Rank
Customers	1.83
Stockholders	2.52
Employees	2.86
Local community where company operates	4.44
Society in general	4.97
Suppliers	5.10
Government	5.72

Note: The ranking is calculated on a scale of 1 (most responsibility) to 7 (least responsibility).

business and the justification for its power is service to stockholders. We may be observing a return to the original capitalist doctrine of the customer as the client whom production is intended to serve and the replacement of the doctrine of "long-run profit maximization" with the "long-run customer satisfaction" doctrine.

The primacy of customer interests also raises some serious questions about any unethical conduct at the expense of customers which is rationalized on grounds of profit maximization. If the assertion of customer primacy is valid, it follows that business should also make ethical conduct in dealing with customers a first priority, a condition which our data suggest does not currently exist.

Societal obligations

How do these attitudes affect policy and decision making on specific issues? We asked HBR readers to express the degree of responsibility they felt in each of nine areas along a scale of 1 (absolutely voluntary) to 5 (absolutely obligatory). The third-place standing of "maximizing long-run profits," shown in Exhibit X, confirms our observation that it is no longer perceived as the primary responsibility of today's executives.

But we were surprised to find two areas of general responsibility to *society* —"being an efficient user of energy and natural resources" and "assessing the potential environmental effects flowing from the company's technological advances"—are first and second. The strong feeling of obligation toward these areas, together with "using every means possible to maximize job content and satisfaction for the hourly worker," demonstrates the desire of the business person to define his responsibility in those areas which involve externalities directly associated with his operation, areas where he can see clearly the internalized

Exhibit X
Areas of responsibility

	Degree
Being an efficient user of energy and natural resources	4.00
Assessing the potential environmental effects flowing from the company's technological advances	3.96
Maximizing long-run profits	3.78
Using every means possible to maximize job content and satisfaction for the hourly worker	3.35
Having your company's subsidiary in another country use the same occupational safety standards as your company does in the United States	3.05
Acquiescing to State Department requests that the company not establish operations in a certain country	3.01
Making implementation of corporate Affirmative Action plans a significant determinant of line officer promotion and salary improvement	2.91
Instituting a program for hiring the hard-core unemployed	2.28
Contributing to the local United Fund	2.17

Note: The ranking is calculated on a scale of 1 (absolutely voluntary) to 5 (absolutely obligatory).

benefits of his "socially responsible" actions, either in reduced costs or preempted government regulation.

By contrast, the strong voluntary rankings for the United Fund and hardcore hiring indicate that executives do not feel a significant obligation concerning social problems of a remedial or welfare nature whose benefits to the company are not readily apparent.

Voluntary measures

Perhaps not surprisingly, our respondents favor those measures for improving corporate social conduct that are both general in nature and leave room for voluntarism over those that involve compulsion and outside interference in corporate affairs. This result could be expected given our respondents' uncertainties about what social responsibility means and about its consequences, as well as their natural reluctance to accept any further constraints on the traditional freedom of the business decision maker.

We have already seen that respondents feel the media have had a powerful impact on business ethics simply by virtue of publicizing unethical conduct. They also feel that "endorsement of 'social responsibility' by the business media" would have the greatest positive influence on corporate social behavior. Altogether, 72% feel that such an endorsement would have a "positive impact," 55% believe that there would be "some positive impact," and 17% believe that the impact would be "very positive." Only 4% think it would have a "negative impact," while 24% think it would have "zero impact." Clearly executives look to the business media, not only for information and education, but for guidance in areas of uncertainty as well.*

About 62% of our respondents also agree that "the equalization of managerial rewards and punishments for social performance with those for financial performance" would have a positive effect in making corporations more socially responsible. This view is corroborated by our earlier observation that most executives support the view that proposals for corporate social action must convincingly show a net economic advantage to the company.

Polling stockholder opinions on sensitive social issues (part of "shareholder democracy"), public interest representation on boards of directors, educating the average citizen to the realities of corporate operations, and corporate social audits have all been advanced, and debated, in business and academic circles. Our respondents' generally positive view toward these measures—no more than a fourth think any of them would have a negative impact—suggests that, if properly conceived and advanced, these measures might also be acceptable to most executives.

This willingness to accept outside inputs does not include input from government, however. Less than one-sixth of our respondents see anything positive in federal chartering of corporations, strongly endorsed by Ralph Nader among others, while 39% feel that such a measure would be deleterious. And our respondents are least sanguine about increased governmental regulation: 64% fear it would have a negative impact and 14% say it would have none, while only 21% feel it might be beneficial.

FREEDOM & CRITICISM

At the outset we posed three basic questions for our study. The generous response of HBR readers has allowed us to answer them in this article. Now a fourth question is in order: "What do the results mean for managers and students of business ethics?"

Our results suggest changes are necessary in two primary areas: managerial outlook and managerial actions.

The four aspects of change in managerial outlook indicated are:

- You will face ethical dilemmas, created by value conflicts, for which there may be no totally satisfactory resolution. But don't use this condition to rationalize unethical behavior on your part.

---

*The susceptibility of business people to the ideology of the business media has often been noted; see, for example, Norton Long, "The Corporation, Its Satellites, and the Local Community," in *The Corporation in Modern Society*, edited by Edward S. Mason (Cambridge, Massachusetts: Harvard University Press, 1959), p. 210.

- Don't expect ethical codes to help solve all problems. Codes can create a false sense of security and lead to the encouragement of violations.

- If you wish to avoid external enforcement of someone else's ethical code, make self-enforcement work.

- Don't deceive yourself into thinking you can hide unethical actions.

The five aspects of managerial action suggested are:

- Fair dealing with customers and employees is the most direct way to restore confidence in business morality.

- Corporate steps taken to improve ethical behavior clearly must come from the top and be part of the reward and punishment system.

- If an ethical code is developed and implemented, have an accompanying information system to detect violations. Then treat violators equitably.

- Test decisions against what you think is right rather than against what is expedient.

- Don't force others into unethical conduct.

It seems to us our respondents are saying that managers facing ethical dilemmas should refer to the familiar maxim, "Would I want my family, friends, and employers to see this decision and its consequences on television?" If the answer is yes, then go ahead. If the answer is no, then additional thought should be given to finding a more satisfactory solution.

Business executives and the companies they serve have a personal and vested interest in the resolution of ethical and social responsibility dilemmas. Our respondents recognize these dilemmas and to some extent appear willing to accept generalized guidance for their resolution in the form of general precept codes and statements from the business media. Although such measures will help in this regard, they are obviously no panacea for the continued strain arising from challenges to business ethics and responsibility. They also are not as action oriented as specific practice codes or government regulation.

The manager appears to prefer uncertainty and tension to the loss of freedom and complications that would accompany these more rigorous measures. In making this choice, he has to realize that he must continue to bear the criticism of the larger society in both the business ethics and corporate social responsibility areas.

QUESTIONS FOR DISCUSSION

1. Why is it that "the ethical dimension of business decision-making is not a matter reducible to any known scientific calculus"?

2. Why is the role of law limited in resolving ethical dilemmas? Should law play a more important role in overcoming the "ethical crisis" in business?

3. Do you agree or disagree with Albert Carr's contention that the rules of the game which business plays are and should be quite different from those that govern the greater society? Why? Are there fundamental economic rationales to support your position? Are there other rationales?

4. Why do you suppose 47 percent of the respondents in Carroll's 1975 survey of business ethics disagreed with the statement, "Business ethics today are far superior to ethics of earlier periods"? Cite specific examples that support their contention.

5. In what ways have the ethics of business changed over the past fifteen years, according to the *Harvard Business Review* surveys? Do you feel that these changes are healthy or unhealthy for the business community? For the greater society?

6. What are the primary difficulties associated with establishing a universal code of ethics for the business person? Suggest mechanisms for resolution of these difficulties.

7. Do you feel that requiring corporate disclosure of "questionable" payments abroad is necessary? Do you feel that other measures are necessary? Why?

8. Do you feel that U.S.-based multinational companies are deserving of special standards in evaluating the moral propriety of their activities abroad? If so, on what should the standards be based? If not, why not?

SELECTED READINGS

Austin, R. W., "Code of conduct for executives," *Harvard Business Review,* Sept.–Oct., 1961, pp. 53–61.

Baumhart, R., S. J., *Ethics in Business.* (New York: Holt, Rinehart and Winston, 1968.)

Blumberg, P. I., "Corporate morality and the crisis of confidence in American business," Invited essay (St. Louis: Beta Gamma Sigma, January, 1977).

Blumenthal, W. M., "Business morality has not deteriorated—Society has changed," *Advanced Management Journal,* January 17, 1977.

Bowman, J. S., "Managerial ethics in business and government," *Business Horizons,* October, 1976, pp. 48–54.

Burgen, C., "How companies react to the ethics crisis," *Business Week*, February 9, 1976, pp. 78–79.

Business and Professional Ethics, A Quarterly Newsletter/Report. (Troy, New York: Center for the Study of the Human Dimension of Science and Technology, Rensselaer Polytechnic Institute.)

Carroll, A. B., "Managerial ethics: A post-Watergate view," *Business Horizons,* April, 1975, pp. 75–80.

Dorfman, D., "Another black mark for corporate ethics," *New York,* March 21, 1977, p. 11.

Faber, E., "How I lost our great debate about corporate ethics," *Fortune,* November, 1976, pp. 180–182.

Guzzardi, W., Jr., "An unscandalized view of those bribes abroad," *Fortune,* July, 1976, pp. 118–121.

Jurgen, R. J., "The business of business ethics," *Intellect,* December, 1976, pp. 177–178.

Kaikati, J. G., "The phenomenon of international bribery," *Business Horizons,* February, 1977, pp. 25–37.

Kristol, Irving. "Ethics and the corporation," *Wall Street Journal,* April 16, 1975, p. 18.

Mechling, T. B., "The mythical ethics of law, PR, and accounting," *Business and Society Review,* Winter 1976–77, pp. 6–10.

Morgan, L. L., "Business ethics start with the individual," *Management Accounting,* March, 1977, pp. 11–14.

Nehemkis, P., "Business payoffs abroad: Rhetoric and reality," *California Management Review,* Winter, 1975, pp. 5–20.

Pike, J. A., "The claim of situational ethics," *Papers from the 1967 A.A.A.A. Annual Meeting* (New York: American Association of Advertising Agencies, 1967).

Proceedings of the First Annual Conference on Business Ethics. (Waltham, Mass: Bentley College, 1977.)

Purcell, T., "A practical guide to ethics in business," *Business and Society Review,* Spring, 1975, pp. 43–50.

Schollhammer, H., "Ethics in an international business context," *MSU Business Topics,* Spring, 1977, pp. 55–63.

Silk, L. and D. Vogel, *Ethics and Profits: The Crisis of Confidence in American Business.* (New York: Simon and Schuster, 1976.)

Walton, C., (ed.), *The Ethics of Corporate Conduct.* (Englewood Cliffs, N.J.: Prentice Hall, 1977.)

Cases

TO THE BOARD

Jake Brazen returned to his office looking as if he had just run the Boston Marathon in his Brooks Brothers suit. He nervously sat at his desk trying to piece together the logic the board of directors had just used to question his international venture proposal. He knew he had built a convincing case for international expansion and he was totally convinced that the venture was sound. If properly handled, American Printing Chips could double its book value and profits within three years. "The mushy minds of the self-righteous board," he thought.

Three hours earlier, the young Financial Vice President had enthusiastically addressed the board on a proposal for a joint venture and licensing agreement with the Ducose de Braway. As APC had done years earlier, Ducose was beginning to ride the tide of explosive expansion in specialized high-speed printing equipment, but Ducose was doing it in the prospering Brawanian economy. APC had done it at home, orchestrated from its Chicago office.

The business is simple enough. Under contract, APC designs and manufactures printing chips used in computer-controlled impact printers. Essentially, the chips provide the typeface for printing high-volume publications, primarily paperback books. From a modest start in 1963, APC's sales had expanded to $40 million by 1977. The Company was, however, beginning to feel the impact of increased competition in U.S. markets; thus its growth in sales was beginning to taper off.

Looking to foreign markets, the Board of Directors had earlier instructed Jake Brazen to investigate the possibility of expansion into South America. After 15 months of near full-time effort, Jake prepared a report with detailed recommendations for expansion into Braway. His report focused primarily on a joint-venture arrangement with Ducose, wherein APC would hold a near majority, but noncontrolling interest in the joint company. Furthermore, if the deal went through, the joint company would license from APC the right to manufacture the printing chips and would, for a few years at least, buy finished chips directly from APC for resale. Financially, it appeared to be a "Golden Goose." Ducose was prepared to sign as soon as the APC board approved the proposal.

Jake's Presentation

Jake had been before the board on a number of occasions, none of which he found particularly enjoyable. APC's six-person board was made up entirely of Ribenthal family members, only two of whom took an active part in the day-to-day management of the company. While Abe Ribenthal usually dominated the board's meetings as chairman and chief executive officer, other family members always had something to say and always voted their minds.

When Jake began his proposal on the Ducose deal, he was more confident than he had ever been before this austere group. He had the figures and volumes of background material. He even had drafts of contracts prepared in discussions with Ducose people. He was like a sprinter on his mark waiting for the gun—except that what he had to win in this race, he thought, was appointment to the board. If the deal went through and performed as forecasted, he felt he *had* to become a director. The Ribenthals couldn't leave him out any longer.

Discussions of Jake's prepared material began without a hitch. He skillfully answered all of the questions posed to him about the venture, including some challenging ones dealing with international monetary exchange and customs provisions. He had done his homework, he thought.

Into the third hour of generally favorable discussion, Julia Ribenthal took the opportunity to get her "two cents worth" in. The 68-year-old woman was nearly totally naive in the complexities of corporate finance, not to mention those conducted on an international basis. But what Julia spotted in Jake's pro-forma cash-flow statements set all the board members back. She asked Jake about the $200,000 per year that had been projected for "agents' fees." She recalled that she had never seen an expense category like that on any of APC's previous statements.

Very confidently, Jake explained that that sum was projected for the joint company as an expense of doing business in Braway. Certain Brawanian government officials would have to be paid to ensure, for example, that customs clearances and plant inspections were conducted properly and conducted rapidly. "It is simply a means of ensuring that Brawanian officials do their jobs—Ducose has been paying these 'fees' since they started five years ago. It's really only illegal on the books in Braway; it's not really illegal in practice. The only reason we plan to carry it as agents' fees is so we don't openly offend the Brawanian legal system. Besides, we won't control the joint company; Ducose will. We'll only hold stock in it, sell to it, and receive licensing royalties. We've got to let a Brawanian company do as Brawanians do."

With that, Julia demanded that any further discussion of the matter proceed without her, and without her vote of approval. She also forewarned the other members "to do as a Ribenthal would do." She left the board room.

Abe anxiously drew the meeting to a close, postponing any further discussion of the matter until the next board meeting, scheduled in three months. His only remark to Jake was, "Thank you, Mr. Brazen." He had never referred to Jake as anything but J. B. until that moment.

CASELETS FOR COMMENT

Mike Reardon

At 3 P.M. on Tuesday, July 31, the Teamsters' Union declares a strike against Progressive Foods Company. Everyone in the company expects the strike to last at least two weeks. At 5 P.M., Progressive's Sales Manager, Mike Reardon, signs a contract to deliver fifty cases of Foremost Olive Oil to a major grocer by Friday. Progressive is an exclusive distributor of the product. Sales commissions are posted and paid monthly.

Bill Schwartz

Bill Schwartz, manager of the Dockside Restaurant, declines to raise the hourly wage of the restaurants' waitresses, but agrees to have "kindly pay tips in cash, not by credit card" imprinted on all guest checks.

Delores Peabody

Heading out for a driving vacation, Delores Peabody stops at her local gas station and instructs the attendant to "fill it up and put it on the charge account, as usual." Delores always buys gas at this station when she fills up the company car.

Henry Smith

Henry Smith, a young test engineer, notices that the test results on a braking system for a new Navy aircraft have been altered. He decides to ignore what he has seen since he knows that if the brakes his company designed don't meet specifications by the week's end, the company will lose its million-dollar contract with the government.

John Young

John Young, a recent accounting graduate, is offered an interview trip to a company in southern California. Just this morning, John accepted a position with a company in his home state of New Jersey. John has never visited southern California, and it has been a blustery December in New Jersey. John wants to keep his career options open.

Betty Allen

Betty Allen, a diligent file clerk, reports to her boss, Ted White, one morning and asks to have the next day off to visit her ailing father. Ted grants the request and asks her whether she'd like to take the day as sick leave or vacation time.

Duke McLean

Duke McLean finds his friend and fellow warehouseman, Wally, loading a case of the company's fresh vegetables into the trunk of his car. Wally asks Duke if he'd like to come to the house for a "super-salad."

Carl Ellis

Wishing to start a small furniture-manufacturing company, Carl Ellis calls all the nearby companies that are presently in the business. Posing as a potentially large customer, Carl asks each what their production capacity is. Most answer, and Carl concludes that there is room for him in the market.

Cynthia Carson

Cynthia Carson, a real-estate agent, has decided that the best way to tell right from wrong is by the "Watergate TV Test." Whenever she faces a morally perplexing issue, she asks herself "If I do such and such, would I be willing to report and explain my action on TV?" Since ascribing to the test, Cynthia finds that the number of morally perplexing issues she faces seems to increase each day.

11. *Business and Its Critics*

Corporations and the very institution of business are coming under increased criticism from many quarters. Survey after survey seems to show that the public has less confidence in the performance of American business; and special interest groups are being formed weekly to take issue with corporate performance or nonperformance. While the impact of these groups is not great in terms of victories at shareholders' meetings and suits won in courts, the subtle impacts of their existence are gaining in significance.

It is probably safe to say that few firms would have initially responded to societal or environmental issues had not some activists or critic groups raised those issues. Practically all of the substantive problems that form the basis for today's corporate concern with its environment were (and continue to be) brought into focus by critics of business.

This external generation of corporate substantive issues is unusual, in that the corporation and managers must deal not only with the issue, but often with the strategies and tactics of the critics as well—groups beyond the control of management hierarchy, policy, and internal procedure. No longer is it sufficient to deal with issues internally, with quiet contemplation and long-range staff studies, and make decisions on the substance of the issues only. Critics and activists cannot be filed away to be forever forgotten; they reappear often with new ways of badgering managers and with new issues to raise. Thus, it seems appropriate that we close this section on operational problems with a discussion of social criticism of business and the tactics of critical activists.

INSTITUTIONAL CRITICS: AN AMERICAN TRADITION

Dissent, protest, criticism, and even disobedience are not new phenomena in the United States, despite what the members of contemporary groups might suppose. Activism preceded the American Revolution, and the populists, muckrakers, and pamphleteers of the turn of the last century take no back seat to today's critics and activists, including the most dedicated radicals. Neither does the generation of the 1930's, which spawned many of our leading social commentators of the present day. What might be new is the use of the campus as a base for criticism, although astute commentators like Joseph Schumpeter, writing in the late 1930's, predicted that might happen. Unlike Europe, or perhaps Latin America, however, the United States has little tradition of student activism or politically charged campuses. But to some extent in the 1930's, and very definitely in the 1960's, student activism peaked, and produced strong forces for social change, innovation, and experimentation. If any one group was responsible for bringing the Vietnam War to the forefront of the nation's conscience, that one group had to be the student population of the country.

Many commentators think we are now living in an activist or at least an iconoclastic age, albeit some perceive it as a fading phenomenon. Few really know why criticism, protest, activism, and dissent are so particularly pronounced at this time. The Vietnam War was certainly one catalyst, and the Watergate episode was certainly another. The successes of the various critical groups during those two episodes, along with the accomplishments of the various civil-rights groups and environmentalist organizations, certainly encouraged them and other groups to push toward further confrontations. Today, the issues of racism, sexism, and the environment continue to be important, and they form core issues for critical cohesion.

Some have suggested that the affluence and security of today's youth, including the ability to sustain oneself through public benefit programs, allow them to be "involved" with comparatively little risk; this may be accurate, for a cooling off on the campuses seems to have accompanied the decline in job availability. But the military draft and the Vietnam War ended also, so the link between affluence and activism may be a weak one.

However we explain critical activism, today's critic and activist finds a primary and very convenient target in the corporation and in business in general. As we noted above, surveys show less and less confidence in the corporation in terms of its role in society. Critics are not prepared to accept corporations only as providers of goods and services, and they question the efficacy of corporations in those roles as well.

The surveys also show increasing numbers of people prone to change. As the Watergate revelations unfolded and the news about the participation of some of the nation's leading corporations in election contributions, political payoffs, and overseas bribes became better known, the numbers of change-prone individuals increased. Business simply has not presented a good public image in recent years, and the confidence of many people in the business system is ebbing. For the manager, consequently, criticism and activism are not trifling issues.

CRITICS AND THEIR TACTICS

Like Heinz products, critics and activists and their tactics come in many varieties. The most troublesome, dangerous, and serious varieties for the immediate short run are the terrorists, with their practices of violence, destruction of property, and physical abuse. From the celebrated "Fox" who dumped Lake Superior sludge sewage on the carpets at corporate offices of U.S. Steel Corporation (to protest, obviously, the company's dumping of waste into the lake), to the extremist groups who deposit bombs or ignite fires in corporate offices and banks; from the protestors who carry magnets into corporate computer centers (and thus destroy records stored on magnetic tapes), to those who dump sand in the lubricating fittings of expensive machinery—these actions pose both physical danger and expense to the business organization. Managers must now fear for their own safety and that of others, as well as for the security of corporate records and assets.

Violent actions have given corporations the task of developing elaborate alarm systems, adding security personnel, and taking extra care in the handling of corporate records (in many cases ensuring that *multiple copies of everything* exist). These actions, of course, have the side effects of adding to costs and making corporate offices less inviting and more restrictive places to work, in some ways further negating an already sagging business image. Fortunately, terrorists and activists who are prone to physical violence are few in number; generally they are criticized not only by leaders of the "establishment" social institutions, but by nonviolent critics and activists as well.

The corporation has long faced the traditional gadfly at annual shareholder meetings. Wilma Soss, Lewis Gilbert, and other lesser-known but equally sharp-tongued shareholder activists, have been more or less permanent fixtures at the annual meetings of many of the major United States corporations. And while they have often provided comic relief to what was normally a rather dull affair (box lunches notwithstanding), they rarely had much impact or success in altering particular corporate policy; the proxy machinery, firmly in the hands of management, typically stacks any vote in management's favor. Such critics may be reaping some of the fruits of their long labors, however, as government agencies such as the Securities and Exchange Commission and the Federal Trade Commission demand greater disclosure of corporate records and activities—demands that the shareholder activists made for years, but which went unheeded.

A new critical activist is of much the same pattern—seeking to use the shareholder's meeting to effect change—but the issues are less oriented to traditional shareholder concerns. Instead of stressing dividends, sales, profit, executive compensation, and other similar dollars-and-cents issues, the newer activist is more concerned with raising public and social responsibility issues: pollution, auto safety, minority hiring, political connections, compliance with the Arab boycott of Israel, consumer safety, and the like. Ralph Nader groups, church organizations, and some colleges and universities are trying to use the corporate annual meeting to effect broad corporate and social change.

For example, Campaign GM, a Nader-launched attempt to force General Motors Corporation to deal with social issues, included focus on minority employment, South Africa, auto safety, pollution, product warrantees, mass transit, and wide representation on the company's board of directors. Even though the three-year Campaign GM may be classified as a failure from the activists' and critics' points of view (fewer than 2 percent of the shares of General Motors were ever voted with the Nader groups), for the first time some of the larger holders of shares did not automatically assign their proxies to management. A number of university endowment funds, as well as some pension, mutual, and trust funds, either withheld their votes or voted for some of the proposals submitted by the Nader-inspired campaign. This voting of shares with the corporate antagonists represented a complete change of philosophy for many of the funds or trusts. Typically, they espoused no interference with management. If the fund managers did not care for the way a corporation was being run (and this dissatisfaction usually related only to profits), they might have sold out the fund's holdings in the firm, but rarely would they use their votes to take issue with management. Now, however, many of the large brokerage houses and underwriters are even setting up funds consisting of securities of companies whose actions are considered socially responsible. Most likely, the managers of these funds would have less reluctance to vote the shares contrary to management's view if they felt that the corporation was engaging in socially irresponsible behavior.

As we have seen, activists also attempt to influence the corporation through an impact in the marketplace. Consumer boycotts are quite commonplace; many of the issues covered in earlier sections of this book were raised and emphasized through the use of the boycott. Saranwrap, grapes, lettuce, Farah Slacks, Gulf Oil products, J. P. Stevens products, and the products of Standard Oil of California have all been faced with boycotts (which had varying degrees of success) in order to force changes in corporate policy. Saranwrap and Dowguard were boycotted to force Dow Chemical Company, their manufacturer, to cease producing Napalm, a jellied gasoline used in bombs and flamethrowers (this boycott accompanied picketlines set up around college placement offices to prevent Dow recruiters from interviewing prospective applicants). Grapes, lettuce, and some California wines were boycotted, to force growers to recognize and bargain with Cesar Chavez's United Farmworkers Union. Gulf Oil Corporation was hit with a boycott undertaken to force a change in the company's exploration intentions in Angola, which at that time was controlled by Portugal (Gulf was also a target on college campuses, as activists attempted to force university administrators to remove Gulf stock from endowment portfolios). Standard Oil of California products were boycotted by Jews who were angered by a letter sent out by the Corporation's Chairman of the Board, O. N. Miller, to shareholders and employees urging sympathy with the Arab cause in the Middle East. Finally, Stevens textile products are being boycotted to support the unionization of the company's textile workers in its Southern plants. On a limited scale, a group of University of Massachusetts professors tried to eliminate Honeywell as a contender for a new computer installation because of Honeywell's defense contracting, in particular the manufacture of Claymore mines. Finally, recent boycotts have been called against Japanese and Russian products to protest the whaling carried on by those two nations.

Most companies have attempted to ride out boycotts. Others, of course, have varied product lines, or have consciously sold their products to several classes of customers, so that a consumer boycott becomes virtually impossible. But, for the single-product firm (marketers of grapes, for example) or the firm whose product is readily identifiable (e.g., Farah, J. P. Stevens, Dow, or Gulf), a successful boycott can be particularly debilitating. Although consumer boycotts are extremely difficult to get started and then sustain, recent successes should be testimony enough to alert the manager to their potential effects.

MANAGERIAL TACTICS IN DEALING WITH CRITICS

In the earliest confrontations between managers and activists, either the activists were superb tacticians or the managers were not. College and university administrators, for example, were caught flat-footed by activists in the 1960's. Few could respond; those who did respond often later regretted their actions. Many demands were met automatically with little consideration of their impacts or ramifications. Corporations often acted with no better effectiveness. Many credit General Motors Corporation with "creating" Ralph Nader; without the Corporation's hiring of a detective to trail Nader, he might now be just one more of the great body of social critics who faded into oblivion.

Since that time, many managers and administrators have learned to deal more effectively with activists and critics. They don't always win, of course, but they are no longer outfoxed at every turn by agile critics. Too many organizations were encrusted with procedures and ponderous organizational processes; critics' organizations are much more loosely organized, have little to lose through a mistake, and can move very swiftly. Since the early 1970's, business organizations have established organizational and policy mechanisms to respond more effectively and more swiftly. In addition, elaborate security measures have been installed in many companies for protection against terrorists, and those prone to physical violence.

Strategies have been devised against activists and critics, but each has its place and its costs. For example, some situations may call for ignoring critics in the hope that they will go away. Often they do go away, but the possibility still exists that they will not, and managers who use that strategy may find themselves bending after a while or coming under even more extreme criticism. On the other hand, a manager may accede to the demands and ideas of critics. This may succeed, but it also carries the risk of whetting the appetites of the critics for more confrontations. Critics may interpret a manager's cooperation as a sign of weakness, and bore in for more concessions.

Some companies are moving onto the offensive in their confrontations with critics. Perhaps the most notable example is the Mobil Oil Company effort. Mobil maintains a high-level public information group headed by a vice-president. Advertisements conveying the Mobil side of an issue are periodically purchased in the leading newspapers of the country. The topics range from energy, pollution, and government regulation, to divestiture and other pertinent economic and political subjects. The company even asks for equal time on radio and television to rebut critical programs which they perceive as anti-oil company, or misleading. In one confrontation with the networks, they even offered to buy the time necessary to get their message across. In sum, Mobil views it necessary to get their message across to the public; not just to react to criticism that happens to come its way. Other companies, such as Dresser Industries, are also starting to use similar offensive strategies.

Confrontations between critics and the corporation demand that executives apply all the skill at their command, tempering any accommodation with discretion and toughness. Any accession should be based on the soundness of the issue, and its value to management, the corporation, or society, rather than on the tactics of the critics or the activists. If managers must refuse accommodation, they should be prepared to support decisions with reason, not, as so often happens, with utterances that fuel the passions of the critics.

THE READINGS

The first article in this section traces the activities of the growing number of lobbying and special-interest groups and assesses their impacts. "As for knowing what the world is all about, the most important groups are dominated by savvy political pros and sophisticated lawyers with ready access to the corridors of power." And the organizations are not all radical; several of the most powerful groups have moderate and conservative aims.

Ralph Nader, the best-known corporate critic, is the subject of Richard Armstrong's *Fortune* article. Armstrong discusses Nader's philosophies, the work of the various Nader groups, and some of the effects that Nader's activities have had on business and the Washington bureaucracy. Ralph Nader emerges as a deeply dedicated, driving, and complex individual. Armstrong comments, "Nobody has been able to explain the deep personal anger that erupts when Nader begins to speak about corporations. He himself simply denies that he is anti-business . . . But anger of some kind is unmistakably there."

The final selection focuses on the emergence of a new critic or activist group, the elderly. In Betsy Gelb's article, "Gray Power: Next Challenge to Business?", she suggests that, "early warning signs . . . give evidence that 'seniors' . . . will be the next group to make demands on the business system." Ms. Gelb reviews the evidence to support her thesis, and offers some guidelines to business for meeting the challenge of "gray power."

The Growing Clout of 'Do Good' Lobbies

Public-interest groups have enormous influence at the White House and in Congress. They play a major role in pushing legislation and getting lawmakers elected.

Gerald R. Rosen

Not a day goes by that one public-interest group or another doesn't testify before Congress, petition City Hall or picket some corporation in the interest of energy, the environment or causes that may range anywhere from Congressional ethics to Pentagon waste. Indeed, the anti-Establishment movement seems to be everywhere, and it sometimes even appears to be bigger than the Establishment itself.

The members of these organizations are generally perceived as being young, woolly-headed idealists, ranging from liberal to radical, with little knowledge of the real world and the practical problems involved in getting things done.

The reality is far different. Certainly, public-interest organizations contain their share—more than their share—of naive youngsters. But the movement includes much, much more. There are literally thousands of groups. Exactly how many is impossible to say, but the Committee for the Advancement of Public Interest Organizations has published a directory that runs to 999 pages and includes groups such as Public Interest Accountants Inc., The Council on Southern Mountains and Get Oil Out, Inc. While most of the organizations appear to be liberal, there are a great many devoted to conservative causes such as tax reduction, greater military efforts and bans on abortion and busing. As for knowing what the world is all about, the most important groups are dominated by savvy political pros and sophisticated lawyers with ready access to the corridors of power.

Right now, the public-interest movement seems to be wielding more clout than ever. Ralph Nader has ready access to President Jimmy Carter, and longtime Nader aide Joan Claybrook has been named head of the National Highway Safety Administration. Carter has also appointed consumer lobbyist Carol Tucker Foreman Assistant Agriculture Secretary and James Speth, cofounder of the Natural Resources Defense Council, as a member of the White House Council on Environmental Quality, among others. Environmental groups have successfully lobbied the White House to raise the budget of the Environmental Protection Agency, while Congress has responded to pressure from Common Cause for many procedural changes. In California, Governor Jerry Brown has appointed many public-interest lobbyists to state commissions.

But what, exactly, is a public-interest group? And why has their power to influence the Establishment grown so much?

Admitting that the public interest is "an elusive concept," John Gardner, who steps down this month as head of the 250,000-member "citizens' lobby" Common Cause, defines such a group as one organized around ideas that aren't based on their members' economic interest. A special-interest group, in marked contrast, stems from its members' economic (business, labor), occupational (doctors, lawyers) or institutional (schools, hospitals) self-interest.

Some public-interest groups directly lobby Congress, and contributions to them are not tax-deductible. The non-lobbying organizations enjoy tax deductible status as educational groups. The 1976 Tax Reform Act eased things a bit for the educational groups by allowing them to use as much as 20% of their budgets for lobbying without altering their tax-exempt status—a change that is itself evidence of the growing clout of the movement.

These groups have a Constitutional right to press their views on the government. It is enshrined in the First Amendment right to petition, and it has been used by individuals and organizations since the Republic was founded. One of the first periods of growth in public-interest groups came in the 1830s, when antislavery societies sprang up. But their golden age didn't arrive until the mid-1960s, when the civil rights and peace movements sparked a great deal of citizen activism. After seeing that their efforts could move society, many activists turned to other causes like consumerism, tax reform and the environment. Starting with enthusiastic indignation, many of the groups became professional, well-organized lobbies.

GREATER AFFLUENCE

Increasing affluence is another reason the citizens' movements grew. Their membership is largely college-educated and in the middle- and upper-income brackets, and their idea-oriented causes are the logical outgrowth of a society in which the majority is no longer struggling simply to obtain the necessities of life.

Probably the most important reason for the burgeoning of these groups, according to John Gardner, is the enormous growth of government and the plethora of issues in which government is assuming a role. Sheer indignation is not enough to make the government more responsive. Only organized pressure will do the job, says Gardner. At the same time, both business and labor have reached gargantuan size and their lobbies have grown and proliferated. As in an arms race, when one group adds more weapons, the other steps up its efforts to meet it. Public-interest groups have now inevitably become an integral part of this byplay—and a permanent power broker on the Washington scene.

Of the untold number of public-interest groups that try to pressure the federal government, the most influential—the anti-Establishment Establishment, if you will—are Common Cause, the Consumer Federation of America and the various groups associated with Ralph Nader. The first two derive power from their ability to seize popular issues and then create grass-roots pressure for their positions on legislators in their home districts. The Naderites get their influence from the ability of Nader himself to dramatize an issue, and the sheer tenacity of the 100 or so bright young people who work for his causes at admittedly substandard wages.

Here is a rundown on some of the more powerful and interesting groups and what they have accomplished:

The brainchild of former Health, Education and Welfare Secretary John Gardner, Common Cause was founded in 1970 when the well-connected Gardner persuaded about 100 wealthy individuals and corporations to put up seed money with which Gardner mounted a massive advertising and direct-mail campaign. Among the contributors were John D. Rockefeller, III ($50,000), IBM's Thomas J. Watson, Jr. ($10,000) and Lazard Frères Andre Meyer ($10,000). Most of the $5.3 million-a-year Common Cause budget now comes from the dues ($15 a year) of its 250,000 members. In sharp contrast to its sister public-interest groups, which are largely concerned with very specific issues, Common Cause concentrates on the political process itself. "We want to make the system responsive and accountable," says David Cohen, a onetime AFL-CIO lobbyist who is Gardner's hand-picked successor.

When it wants to put pressure on Congress, Common Cause Washington staffers call ten members in a Congressional district, each of whom calls ten other CC members. Almost overnight, the network produces 100 letters or tele-grams to the legislator whom the citizens' lobby wishes to pressure. But the system doesn't always work. While Common Cause played a major role last January in persuading the House to oust Florida's Robert L. F. Sikes as Chairman of the Military Construction Subcommittee for alleged conflicts-of-interest, it was unable to put the pressure on Sikes in his Florida panhandle district. "The few members we have in Sikes' district wouldn't help because they knew how important his chairmanship was to the district's economy," admits Cohen.

Other successful Common Cause fights include the public financing of Presi-dential elections, opening Congressional bill-drafting sessions to the public and the breaking of the House seniority system in 1975. The demise of this time-honored system ousted three veteran chairmen—Armed Services' F. Edward Hebert, Agriculture's W. R. ("Bob") Poage and Banking's Wright Patman —because of their "autocratic" ways. Common Cause broke with the Naderites over Patman. Nader tried to save Patman because he agreed with the Texan's lib-eral views. "We were fighting against autocratic rule of these committees, and Patman was one of the worst in this regard. You can't make an exception just because you agree with his views," says Gardner.

Common Cause's emphasis on government structure and processes has re-sulted in a constantly shifting series of friends and enemies. The AFL-CIO supported CC in seeking more disclosure of spending by lobbies, but fought hard against Common Cause's successful effort to abolish the Senate Post Office Committee. CC's unsuccessful drive to restructure the House committee system, which included putting all energy issues under one committee, ran into tough opposition from environmental groups. They felt that environmental consider-ations would be subordinated to energy if the committees were combined. The U.S. Chamber of Commerce and the AFL-CIO also fought House reorganization because they felt more comfortable with the status quo. At the same time, CC expects that the Chamber will support its drive for "sunset" laws, which require a termination date for every federal program enacted.

Common Cause played a major role in last month's House vote tying a tough ethics code to the Congressional pay raise. Its current goals include public fi-nancing of the 1978 Congressional elections and the enactment of a very strict lobbying disclosure bill. That last effort is being fought by both the Naderites and the Consumer Federation, which contend that the paperwork involved in strict disclosure would discourage grass-roots organization that want to be heard in Washington. "It would choke the efforts of small groups," insists Kathleen O'Reilly, a tough-minded young lawyer who recently became CFA director.

Founded in 1967 to give the myriad consumer groups a national voice, CFA is an amalgam of 220 organizations, including local consumer groups, coopera-tives, labor unions and senior citizen's groups. With a budget of $165,000 and thirteen employees, CFA lobbied hard last year for such measures as the Toxic Substances Act, which regulates the introduction of new chemicals, the tough new Omnibus Antitrust law and no-fault insurance. It was successful with the first two measures, but lost out on no-fault, where it faced the opposition of the

Naderites. "I don't think the lawyer in Nader can accept the idea of no-fault," says one consumer lobbyist.

Unlike Common Cause, which never endorses candidates, CFA labels legislators either pro- or anti-consumer and then goes to work to elect its friends and defeat its enemies. Ms. O'Reilly claims that CFA played a key role in last year's defeat of Tennessee Senator William Brock and Marvin Esch, the GOP Senatorial candidate in Michigan. She also says that her organization was an important factor in the elections of Ohio Senator Howard Metzenbaum and Illinois Congressman Abner Mikva, both of whom won tight races. The CFA did some tough soul-searching on whether to endorse California Senator John Tunney, who invariably supported its positions when he was present. But, says Ms. O'Reilly: "Tunney missed too many key votes when we needed him, so we decided not to endorse an absent advocate." Tunney was defeated by S. I. Hayakawa.

Ralph Nader has become the conglomerateur of the public-interest groups since he achieved national fame in the mid-1960s as the auto industry's chief critic. Under the umbrella of Public Citizen, which has a budget of $1.1 million raised from public donations and Ralph Nader's pocket (he gives six or seven speeches a month for fees as high as $4,000), there are nine different Nader organizations. They include Critical Mass, an antinuclear group; the Tax Research Group, which pushes tax reform; and Congress Watch, which does most of the hard lobbying. This year's legislative goals include an Agency for Consumer Protection, a government financed cooperative bank and a measure to make class-action suits easier to file.

The Tax Research Group, which does lobbying as well as research, is continually pressing its views on the members of the tax-writing House Ways and Means and Senate Finance Committees. In February, the group lined up behind Ways and Means' Chairman Al Ullman's successful effort to substitute a corporate tax credit for hiring new employees for a hike in the investment credit. The Nader tax group has fought to abolish all tax shelters and such corporate benefits as the foreign tax credit, deferral of taxes on unrepatriated profits and DISC. Robert Brandon, director of the group, says that his basic goal is to wipe out all deductions and have a straight progressive system with a maximum rate of 50%. "Taxes should be used to raise revenue, not for social purposes like encouraging home ownership," says Brandon.

A pragmatic lobbyist who operates out of a row house just behind the Cannon House Office Building, Brandon takes credit for the defeat of Ways and Means members Joel Broyhill and Donald Brotzman in 1974. The Tax Research Group blanketed Broyhill's suburban Virginia district with flyers purporting to show how the Congressman's campaign contributions were linked to his committee votes. Similarly, Brandon gave a story to a Boulder, Colorado, newspaper that connected local Congressman Brotzman's votes in the same manner. Brandon is pleased that Laurence Woodworth, formerly Congress' top tax staffman, was named Assistant Treasury Secretary for tax policy because Woodworth knows how the system works. Tax reformer Brandon was afraid that Carter might appoint a "way-out reformer" who would not present a package that could be passed. If Carter proposes "real" tax reform next year, Brandon wonders how much support it will receive from Common Cause, whose high-bracket membership benefits from the present complex system.

The election of Jimmy Carter has had a major impact on Nader's Raiders. After Ralph Nader spent the night at candidate Carter's home in Plains last August, he and his followers became convinced that the Georgian was receptive to their point of view. While Carter rejected the Nader call for the federal chartering of corporations, he backed the Agency for Consumer Protection. The President subsequently rejected a Nader choice for membership on the Council of Economic Advisers—Gar Alperovitz, an advocate of worker participation in economic planning. But he then tapped Joan Claybrook to head highway safety. How long the Nader-Carter honeymoon will last is an open question, but it is clear that long-time pariah Nader is enjoying his access to the top and the possibility of achieving some of his goals. At the same time, he must worry that if he loses his franchise as a rebel, his underpaid foot soldiers might desert en masse.

No issue has caused such a proliferation of public-interest groups as the environment. The California-based Sierra Club and Friends of the Earth are most influential in the West. The New York-based Environmental Defense Fund and Natural Resources Defense Council have carried the brunt of the legal battle against pollution. The EDF, headed by former Time-Life staffer Arlie Schardt, has 45,000 members and a budget of $1.7 million. The NRDC, led by former Wall Street lawyer John Adams, has 35,000 members and a $2 million budget. Both groups have received substantial grants from the Ford Foundation and the Rockefeller Brothers Fund. They have also received large contributions from actor Robert Redford. EDF was started by scientists and has specialized in the toxic substances area, while lawyer-led NRDC has pushed hard on the nuclear front.

Schardt insists that his organization is not anti-growth and he argues that the enironmental movement has given birth to new industries and created many jobs. "Businessmen should stop characterizing us as no-growth people. That's wrong," says Schardt. Contributions to both the EDF and the NRDC are tax-deductible, and the groups have left the lobbying to the Washington-based Environmental Policy Center.

Founded in 1972, the EPC is headed by Joseph Browder, a onetime staffer for both Friends of the Earth and the National Audubon Society. EPC got $30,000 in seed money from Arthur Godfrey and additional funds from Laurence Rockefeller, Paul Newman and Robert Redford. Operating out of a run-down building three blocks from the Capitol, EPC has a $213,000 budget, raised from large contributors, and fourteen employees. Its young staffers consider themselves experts on all the energy-related environmental questions. EPC has lobbied hard for a strip-mining bill and tighter tanker safety standards and against both granting eminent domain to coal-slurry pipelines and giving subsidies for synthetic-fuels projects like coal gasification and liquefaction. "Such subsidies discourage conservation by subsidizing production costs and hiding the true cost of energy," says Browder.

THE EPC STANCE

EPC is unalterably opposed to any measure that brings the government and the energy industry into partnership—in large part because, as Browder sees it, the government would not be any more "environmentally responsible" than industry. Besides, Browder is basically a free-enterprise conservative who strongly opposes Ralph Nader's proposal for a federal oil and gas corporation to compete with the private companies. Browder was a Carter environmental adviser until late in the campaign, when he resigned for reasons he refuses to discuss. Some say he was made a sacrificial lamb when Carter was wooing Southwestern energy interests; others insist that it was simply a personality clash with the Carter inner circle.

The environmentalists' influence with the Carter Administration was demonstrated in late February. After learning that Carter's budget would continue the cuts in the Environmental Protection Agency instituted by Ford, the environmentalists demanded an audience with Office of Management and Budget Director Bert Lance. Within a week, the environmental leaders received a call to be in Lance's office at 10:30 A.M. on a Friday. Lance completely disarmed the six representatives when he opened the meeting with an announcement that 600 slots were being added to the EPA. "We never had this kind of communication with the Ford Administration. Its attitude was one of complete hostility," says Arlie Schardt, who attended the session. Perhaps because of his falling out with the Carter campaign, the EPC's Joe Browder was not invited. Other pro-environmental moves in the Carter budget include the slashing of $200 million from the breeder-reactor program and of $268 million from "environmentally unsound" dam projects.

While the public-interest movement is often equated with liberal and left-leaning groups, there are many conservative ones as well. Among the most active on the Washington scene is the Liberty Lobby. Founded in 1956 to fight the "left-ward drift" in the United States, the Lobby has a $1.2 million budget and 35 employees supported by its 25,000 members. The lobby is headed by eighty-year-old former Wall Streeter Curtis Dall, a onetime son-in-law of President Franklin D. Roosevelt, who says that the group is "anti-Establishment and pro-American." It lobbied against the confirmation of Theodore Sorensen as Central Intelligence Agency Director and Paul Warnke as U.S. arms negotiator.

The Liberty Lobby also opposes deficit spending, the United Nations, the Rockefeller interests that "foster corporate socialism" and doing business with communist countries. "We are against the internationalists who would tear this country down," says Dall.

At the other extreme is the People's Business Commission, which contends that "capitalism cannot be patched up" and that it must be replaced with cooperatives. "We are against nationalization, because that would only concentrate power in government hands," says PBC head Jeremy Rifkin. Successor to the People's Bicentennial Commission, which used the nation's 200th birthday to promote its radical ideas, PBC is financed by its 23,000 members, royalties from books and the lecture fees (up to $850) of Rifkin and other staffers. PBC's eight employees receive "the lowest salaries in town," boasts Rifkin. Everybody, including Rifkin, gets $85 a week.

A native of Chicago who was president of the class of 1967 at the University of Pennsylvania's Wharton School, Rifkin received an MA from the Fletcher School of Diplomacy. He emphasizes that both he and most of his staffers come from working-class backgrounds compared to the largely middle-class origins of the Nader people. PBC zeros in on two or three issues each year. This year, one PBC concern is the pharmaceutical industry's experiments with DNA, the basic ingredient of human genes. Rifkin claims that there must be public control over "the new forms of life" that might be produced. PBC's other prime issue is pension funds. Rifkin believes that pension funds already run the economy, and that they must be brought to some kind of public accountability.

PBC propagates its ideas through books, pamphlets and through materials it provides schools. About 5,000 schools use PBC materials, according to Rifkin. PBC eschews lobbying. "The people on Capitol Hill only listen to clout, and we don't have it. So sitting around over lunch with a staff aide won't accomplish very much," says Rifkin.

An anti-Establishment group that takes the opposite tack is the Energy Action Committee, headed by James Flug, a former top aide to Senator Edward Kennedy. Founded last year with the avowed purpose of taking on the oil and gas lobby on Capitol Hill, EAC's $250,000 budget and seven employees is funded by four wealthy Californians, including Paul Newman. EAC provides a great deal of data that challenges the statistics provided by the industry.

The EAC wants to break up the oil companies, both horizontally and vertically; it also opposes the deregulation of natural gas. Still another EAC concern is tight regulation of the development of energy on federal land. "We have a basic choice in this country. The price of energy must either be set by Schlesinger and Dunham or Yamani and Garvin. I prefer the former," says Flug. (James Schlesinger is White House energy adviser and Richard Dunham is Chairman of the Federal Power Commission. Sheik Yamani is Saudi oil minister and C. C. Garvin is Exxon chairman.)

A CONSERVATIVE GROUP

An anomaly among the public-interest groups, since it is hard to pigeonhole ideologically, is the National Taxpayers Union. It could be called a conservative group because of its opposition to big government and its determination to achieve a balanced federal budget. At the same time, in sharp contrast to the Liberty Lobby and other right-wing groups, it is strongly anti-Pentagon. A. Ernest Fitzgerald, who was fired as a Pentagon cost analyst because of his exposure of military waste (and then subsequently reinstated), is on the NTU executive committee. The organization worked with environmentalists to block federal money for the SST and additional funds for nuclear development, because it is basically opposed to more spending.

NTU was founded in 1969 by a group of businessmen worried about the growth of government, and is headed by 28-year-old William Bonner, who left his small construction company to take up the cudgels for less spending. Its $425,000 budget and ten employees are supported by 35,000 members who pay $15 dues each. Right now, NTU is fighting for a Constitutional amendment to force the government to balance the budget. The amendment has passed sixteen states and has been introduced in the House by Indiana Democrat Andrew Jacobs.

The latest public-interest group to hit the Washington scene is New Directions, which describes itself as the international counterpart of Common Cause. It is headed by former Delaware Governor Russell Peterson, who chaired the Federal Council on Environmental Quality during the Ford Administration. ND has just launched a direct mail campaign for members, using free lists supplied by Common Cause and the United World Federalists. The brainchild of World Bank President Robert McNamara, anthropologist Margaret Mead and *Saturday Review* Editor Norman Cousins, ND plans to zero in on such issues as the arms race, population growth and the law of the sea. "Remember, our leaders got us into Vietnam and the people got us out. Maybe if we had a lobby like New Directions, we would not have gotten in so deep," says Peterson.

Among the other public-interest groups that are making their presence felt in Washington are the Center for Defense Information, a group of retired military men who campaign against Pentagon waste; the Center for Science in the Public Interest, which describes itself as a consumer-environmentalist organization; and Zero Population Growth, which fights for more federal funds for family planning as well as monies to cut down illegal immigration.

As this rundown suggests, public-interest groups come into being in numerous ways—by being bankrolled by wealthy individuals, by capitalizing on a hot public issue, by raising funds from the public or from foundations. Once in business, they also use different approaches when it comes to deciding on what specific issues to pursue—and ironically, for organizations that purport to speak for the public, some of the techniques are quite autocratic.

Common Cause is probably the most democratic. It polls its members on issues and does not take a position unless the rank-and-file favor it overwhelmingly. CC refused to speak out last year on California's Proposition Fifteen, which would have sharply limited nuclear development, because only 60% of its members favored it. At the other end of the spectrum is the Nader empire. The issues are pretty much set by one man, and a telephone call from Nader can start one of his groups moving full steam on an issue. The Consumer Federation has a system of weighted voting that represents the relative strength of its 220 constituent organizations. Energy Action Committee policy is decided among Flug and his four angels, while New Directions plans to emulate Common Cause.

It is the big three—Common Cause, the Consumer Federation and the Nader groups—plus the environmentalists, that seem to have the most clout in Washington, and the appointments of Joan Claybrook and Carol Foreman to key Administration posts for the first time puts the nose of the public interest groups under the White House tent. While Nader aide Andrew Feinstein insists that the difference between the Carter and Ford Administrations is "earth-shattering," it is really too early to tell what Carter's long-term relationships with these groups will be. In the meantime, both business and government now realize that a professionalized public-interest movement has become a permanent part of the tugging and hauling process through which national policy is hammered out.

California: The State Takes on the Public Interest

Several weeks ago, Dow Chemical Co. stunned many Californians when it abandoned a $500 million petrochemical complex it planned to build forty miles northeast of San Francisco. Dow decided to throw in the towel because it had been unable to clear a series of environmental hurdles.

At first glance, the company's action appeared to be another victory for the state's powerful public-interest groups. And, indeed, Executive Director Michael McCloskey of the Sierra Club, which had sued Dow over potential ecological damage by the proposed plant, greeted the announcement with a pleased: "We consider it an achievement of our immediate goal there."

But it wasn't the Sierra Club, or any of the state's other vaunted public-interest groups, that was fundamentally responsible for Dow's decision. The credit—or blame—goes to a combination of state and local government agencies whose tangled environmental regulations had completely frustrated Dow's efforts. After nearly three years of trying, Dow had received only four of the 65 permits needed to go ahead with its project, and decided to cancel it now rather than waste more funds. The cost to the company: $10 million.

The episode was only the latest in a series that underscores a significant trend in the Golden State: a rising tide of activism among governmental bodies—particularly the state government—that is virtually preempting the role of many public-interest groups. Partly because of this, businessmen now complain that the state administration headed by Governor Edmund G. Brown Jr. has created an anti-business climate that is damaging the state's economy.

For one thing, they charge that the Governor is stocking top administrative posts with personnel inimical to business. By way of example, they cite the appointments of Claire Dedrick, former vice president of the Sierra Club, as Secretary of the Resources Agency, Gerald Merail, former scientist with the Environmental Defense Fund, as Deputy Director of Water Resources; and J. Anthony Kline, formerly with Public Advocates, Inc., as legal affairs secretary to the Governor. And Brown recently appointed about thirty nonprofessionals, many from activist groups, to a number of state bodies that oversee and license people engaged in various professions and other occupations.

In addition, businessmen are increasingly irate over specific actions taken by government agencies recently. Henry F. Lippit, executive secretary of the California Gas Producers Association, notes with considerable displeasure that the director of the State's Natural Resources Department filed a detailed memorandum opposing the Dow plant. He also points out that newly appointed members of the California Public

Utilities Commission, citing environmental problems, insisted on cancel-ing contracts that utilities had negotiated for Alaskan natural gas they needed; further, he says that the staff of the newly constituted Califor-nia Energy Commission suggested that transshipments of Alaska oil be made through Canada rather than southern California, which would de-prive the state of political income. In still another grievance, President Ronald Zumbrun of the Pacific Legal Foundation, a public-interest group supporting many business interests, complains that the head of the California Water Resources Department testified in a recent lawsuit against the construction of the San Felipe water project, a development considered essential to the survival of drought-stricken areas of the state.

An Affirmation

To be sure, the public-interest groups themselves claim they feel no threat from government activity in their areas. As a matter of fact, says McCloskey, the Sierra Club welcomes state action as an affirmation of its own goals. Moreover, the public-interest groups show no sign of slow-ing their own efforts.

For example, the Sierra Club, the biggest and most influential of all the California-based organizations, with a full-time staff of 125 paid employees and 170,000 members, is spending more than $7 million this year on a broad variety of environmental-protection projects all over the country. It will be lobbying in the U.S. Congress to strengthen water-pollution-control laws and strip-mining regulations, for substantial addi-tions to national parks and wilderness areas and for greater control over offshore-oil production. It will also continue to use its legal arm to press lawsuits against various organizations—in government and business —that it believes threaten the environment.

McCloskey insists that the club is not anti-business. Less than 10% of its activities, whether in the legal or legislative arena, are directed against business interests, he claims. But the fact is that business is affected more heavily than that because of the indirect results of Sierra Club legal actions. The club's success in spearheading lawsuits and leg-islation has stopped dams, slowed strip-mining and timber-clearing on federal lands and curtailed offshore oil production and nuclear-power plant construction—all of which add up to a material, if undefined, impact on business all over the U.S.

Other California groups are also making themselves felt. Friends of the Earth, a San Francisco-based organization with a $1 million annual budget, 55 full-time staff employees and 25,000 members around the country, concentrates on energy. It claims major credit for preventing the construction of a huge coal-powered generating plant at Kaiparo-wits, Utah, last year, as well as for an anti-nuclear-power initiative in California.

In California, as in several other Western states, public-interest groups wield a weapon alien to most of the country. Citizens can take a particular proposition directly to the electorate to turn it into law. To place such a proposition on a statewide referendum in California, sponsors need only secure valid signatures from 5% of those who voted in the latest gubernatorial election, do it within 150 days of the forthcoming election, and have the signatures validated by the California Secretary of State.

Last year, Friends of the Earth and several other organizations joined with a new group called Californians for Nuclear Safeguards to put a proposition on the ballot that would, in effect, have halted all future nuclear-power-plant construction and operations in the state. After throwing a huge scare into the utility industry with their early success and skill at promoting their cause, the groups saw the initiative go down to defeat. But they still pursue their anti-nuclear concerns actively.

In the meantime, other groups are picking up new issues to battle over. The most recent is taxation—and specifically, real-estate taxes. Following a wave of sharp increases in real-estate levies throughout the state last year, there was a groundswell of homeowner opposition. At first, it was confined to small groups of individuals in various towns and cities taking their complaints to county and state agencies. But now, the People's Lobby, a Los Angeles-based group that had previously accented environmental concerns, is attempting to organize tax-payer leagues in each county.

Eventually, the organization hopes to lobby for tax reform in the state legislature. Among other things, taxpayers have long complained that certain industries, such as insurance, do not pay their fair share of taxes, thus overburdening individuals. "The issue of tax reform and relief is of paramount concern to the people in this state," says Carol Hamcke, assistant director of the People's Lobby.

Control of Corporations

One time-worn issue—"the oppression and exploitation of the public by giant corporations"—has recently been resurrected by a new group called the California Conference on Alternative Public Policy. The group is a coalition of mostly liberal democrats, left-wing progressives and socialists guided by such well-known personalities as Tom Hayden, who lost a bid for the U.S. Senate last year, Cesar Chavez and Congressman Ronald Dellums. It aims at stronger control of corporations by such methods as public representatives on corporate boards, wider corporate disclosure of decisions affecting the public and enactment of a law requiring a firm to earmark some of its income for such community requirements as cleaning up the environment.

Somewhat surprisingly, there are no longer any major public-interest groups primarily concerned with consumer complaints about products and services. This is mainly because the state government has vigorously taken the lead in this area. In addition, consumer advocates on many television and radio stations around the state are popular and influential, answering the complaints of thousands of Californians.

But in the broad area of environmental concerns, there is not likely to be any slackening in the activities of the major groups. With their sizable budgets and apparently growing memberships, organizations such as the Sierra Club and Friends of the Earth promise to be around a long time.

At the same time, however, the public-interest organizations have begun to feel the sting of a counter-movement. Using one of the public-interest groups' principal tools, the lawsuit, various land developers and business groups have taken to countersuing the environmentalists. The Pacific Legal Foundation has handled much of this litigation. Since it was founded in 1973, it has won more than 25 cases; among other things, it has kept environmentalists from halting construction of the Auburn Dam in northern California and from preventing the building of an atomic-submarine base in Bangor, Washington.

Some environmentalists, such as McCloskey, insist this activity isn't seriously impeding their own work. But others are equally insistent that the threat is hurting. According to Joseph T. Edmiston, a Sierra Club legal officer, many smaller public-interest organizations have been harassed by the lawsuits and fear their limited operating funds may be consumed in defending themselves in court. At this stage, no one is able to predict how far the counterattack may go or what its impact on the entire public-interest movement may be.

The Passion That Rules Ralph Nader

Richard Armstrong

On a recent visit to Marymount College in Arlington, Virginia, Ralph Nader arrived at the school gymnasium an hour late. But he then proceeded to pacify an overflowing crowd of restless students — and earn a lecture fee of $2,500 — by denouncing America's big corporations in venomous language. Afterward one question from the audience brought a rousing and spontaneous burst of applause. When, the questioner asked, did he plan to run for President?

A slightly more measured assessment of the Nader phenomenon came from Bess Myerson, New York City's commissioner of consumer affairs, when she introduced him as star witness at a recent hearing on deceptive advertising. "Mr. Nader," she said, "is a remarkable man who, in the last six years, has done more as a private citizen for our country and its people than most public officials do in a lifetime."

The remarkable thing about this tribute is that it is literally true. In the seven years since he moved to Washington from Winsted, Connecticut — without funds

Reprinted from the May, 1971 issue of *Fortune* magazine by special permission. © 1971, Time, Inc.

and with a narrow base of expert knowledge in a single subject, automobile safety—Nader has created a flourishing nationwide movement, known as consumerism. He is chiefly responsible for the passage of at least six major laws, imposing new federal safety standards on automobiles, meat and poultry products, gas pipelines, coal mining, and radiation emissions from electronic devices. His investigations have led to a strenuous renovation at both the Federal Trade Commission and the Food and Drug Administration. And if the quality and convenience of American life do not seem dramatically improved after all that furious crusading, Nader can point to at least one quite tangible result. Last year, for the first time in nine years, traffic fatalities in the U.S. declined, to 55,300 from 56,400 in 1969. Unless the decline was a fluke (and officals at the Highway Traffic Safety Administration do not think it was), then for those 1,100 living Americans, whoever they may be, Nader can be said to have performed the ultimate public service.

MORE THAN TEN KREMLINS

And yet, despite all this, it is easy to conclude after a conversation with Nader that he is not primarily interested in protecting consumers. The passion that rules in him—and he is a passionate man—is aimed at smashing utterly the target of his hatred, which is corporate power. He thinks, and says quite bluntly, that a great many corporate executives belong in prison—for defrauding the consumer with shoddy merchandise, poisoning the food supply with chemical additives, and willfully manufacturing unsafe products that will maim or kill the buyer. In his words, the law should "pierce the corporate veil" so that individual executives could be jailed when their companies misbehaved. He emphasizes that he is talking not just about "fly-by-night hucksters" but the top management of "blue-chip business firms."

The lawyers who provide legal cover for all these criminal acts are, to Nader, nothing but "high-priced prostitutes." As for the advertising profession, Nader recently served up the following indictment: "Madison Avenue is engaged in an epidemic campaign of marketing fraud. It has done more to subvert and destroy the market system in this country than ten Kremlins ever dreamed of." With the certainty of the visionary, Nader would sweep away that shattered market system and replace it by various eccentric devices of his own, such as a government rating system for every consumer product.

If, on the one hand, Nader has advanced the cause of consumer protection by his skillful marshaling of facts in support of specific reforms, he has, on the other hand, made reform more difficult through his habit of coating his facts with invective and assigning the worst possible motives to almost everybody but himself. By some peculiar logic of his own, he has cast the consumer and the corporation as bitter enemies, and he seems to think that no reform is worth its salt unless business greets it with a maximum of suspicion, hostility, and fear.

Nader is a strange apparition in the well-tailored world of the Washington lawyer. His suits hang awkwardly off his lanky frame, all of them apparently gray and cut about a half size too large. His big brown eyes in their deep sockets have a permanent expression of hurt defiance, and before a crowd he blinks them nervously. The eyes, the bony face, and a small, set chin give him, at thiry-seven, the look of an underfed waif.

Nobody has been able to explain the deep personal anger that erupts when Nader begins to speak about corporations. He himself simply denies that he is anti-business. "People who make that charge are escalating the abstraction," he told an interviewer recently, his long hands clasped together, his brown eyes flashing. "They don't dare face the issues." But anger of some kind is unmistakably there. It seems to spring out of some profound alienation from the comfortable world he sees around him, and perhaps dates back to his early days in the conservative little town of Winsted, where he was something of an oddball, the son of a Lebanese immigrant, the boy who read the Congressional Record. He recalls proudly that his father, who kept a restaurant and assailed customers with his political views, "forecast the corporate take-over of the regulatory agencies back in the 1930's." Princeton and Harvard Law School trained Nader's brilliant mind, but their social graces never touched his inner core. There seems something of the desert in him still, the ghost of some harsh prophet from his ancestral Lebanon. .

According to one old friend, Nader has always had a conspiratorial view of the world, and when General Motors put private detectives on his trail in 1965 just before the publication of *Unsafe at Any Speed* that view was strongly reinforced. "He thought somebody was following him around," says the friend, "and then, by gosh, somebody *was* following him around." Apparently, at the time, Nader was convinced that G.M. planned to have him bumped off. He still moves about Washington in great secrecy from one rendezvous to the next.

THE FIFTH BRANCH OF GOVERNMENT

In his role as scourge of the regulatory agencies, Nader is aggressive and ill-mannered as a matter of calculated policy. "Rattle off a few facts so they will know you can't be bluffed," he tells his teams of young investigators setting out to interview government officials. "Get on the offensive and stay there." Says Lowell Dodge, who runs Nader's Auto Safety Center: "If somebody is messing up Ralph wants to embarrass them."

But Nader can be an engaging fellow when he chooses. He takes care to maintain good relations with Washington journalists—parceling out news tips with an even hand—and many of them pay him the ultimate tribute of calling him the best reporter they know. To these men he seems to serve as a sort of ghost of conscience past, a reminder of investigations not pursued and stables left uncleansed. Both reporters and professional politicians find him extremely useful. "Nader has become the fifth branch of government, if you count the press as fourth," says a Senate aide who has worked with Nader often in drafting legislation. "He knows all the newspaper deadlines and how to get in touch with anybody any time. By his own hard work he has developed a network of sources in every arm of government. And believe me, no Senator turns down those calls from Ralph. He will say he's got some stuff and it's good, and the Senator can take the credit. Any afternoon he's in town you still see him trudging along the corridors here with a stack of documents under his arm, keeping up his contacts."

What Nader gets out of the intercourse is power—not the trappings but the substance—more of it by now than most of the Senators and Congressmen on whom he calls. When an important bill is pending he is quite capable of playing rough, threatening to denounce a Representative to the press unless he goes along on a key amendment. "Does Ralph like power?" The Senate aide laughed at such a naive question. "Good gracious, yes. He loves it." Compared to other powerful men in Washington, Nader enjoys a rare freedom of action, flourishing as a sort of freebooter who is able to pick his targets at will, unconstrained by an electorate or any judgment but his own. "You will find sensitive people around town who are saying it's time to take a second look at this guy," says the Senate aide. "There are people who wonder whether he ought to be the final arbiter of safety in autos or in the food supply. Nader has something the companies don't have—credibility—especially with the press. There is a danger that people will be afraid to go up against him for that reason alone."

Notches on Nader's Gun

The Automobile
An auto-safety enthusiast while at Princeton and Harvard Law School, Nader went to Washington in 1964 to work on his pet subject as an aide to Daniel Patrick Moynihan, then Assistant Secretary of Labor, who happened to be interested in a field far removed from his assigned duties. Bored with office routine, Nader quit the following year and wrote *Unsafe at Any Speed* in ten weeks. During the Senate hearings on auto safety, he came out a clear winner in a much-publicized confrontation with James Roche, president (now chairman) of General Motors. The publicity assured passage of the Motor Vehicle Safety Act of 1966, establishing a government agency to set mandatory vehicle-safety standards, of which there are now thirty-four.

Unsanitary Meat
For his second campaign, Nader found ready-made evidence in a study done by the Department of Agriculture of state-regulated packing plants, considered to be in intrastate commerce and so not covered by federal law. Many of the plants were filthy and rodent infested, but apparently nobody of any consequence had ever bothered to read the study's report. Nader did. The result was the Wholesome Meat Act of 1967, giving states the option of bringing their inspection programs up to federal standards or having them supplanted by federal inspection. In 1968 the provisions of the act were applied to poultry products.

Federal Trade Commission
A team of student raiders assigned by Nader to the FTC in 1968 found one official at the agency literally asleep on the job, others frequenting nearby saloons during working hours, and still others who seldom both-

REGRETS TO DAVID SUSSKIND

By any measure, Nader's power is still growing. He remains absolute master of his own movement, but he is no longer alone. "When I think of all the lean years Ralph spent knocking on doors—" says Theodore Jacobs, who was Nader's classmate at both Princeton and Harvard Law School and now serves as a sort of chief of staff. Jacobs had just concluded a telephone call that, from his end, had consisted only of various expressions of reget. "That was Susskind. He's got a new show, he wants Ralph, and I had to turn him down. Ralph hates New York—all that traffic and pollution—and I can't get him up there unless it's imperative. I spend a lot of my time saying no. Among other problems, he's got two people on his tail right now who are writing full-length biographies. He has to husband his time. He's down for the *Today* show next Tuesday, but that's right here in town. If there is an important bill pending in committee and they need some input, he'll be there. He'll duck anything else for that."

Jacobs presides, loosely, over a modern suite of offices in downtown Washington housing the Center for the Study of Responsive Law. This is home base for

---

ered to come to work at all. President Nixon commissioned a study of the FTC by an American Bar Association panel, which confirmed the major findings of the Nader report: low morale, lack of planning, preoccupation with trivial cases and timidity in pursuing important ones. Outcome: new faces and new vigor at the FTC.

Food and Drug Administration
Student raiders studying the FDA in the summer of 1969 compiled evidence on two important regulatory blunders: approval of cyclamates and monosodium glutamate for ·unrestricted use in the food supply. Alerted by the raiders, the news media covered both stories with unrestrained enthusiasm until the FDA banned cyclamates from soft drinks and manufacturers voluntarily stopped putting monosodium glutamate in baby food. In December, President Nixon fired the three top officals at the FDA.

Other Doings
Legislation inspired by Nader: Natural Gas Pipeline Safety Act (1968), Radiation Control for Health and Safety Act (1968), Coal Mine Health and Safety Act (1969), Comprehensive Occupational Safety and Health Act (1970). Published reports: *The Chemical Feast* (on the FDA); *The Interstate Commerce Omission* (it recommends abolishing the ICC); *Vanishing Air* (a critical look at air-pollution-control laws and industry compliance); *What To Do With Your Bad Car* ("an action manual for lemon owners"); *One Life—One Physician* (on the medical profession). Reports in progress on: the Department of Agriculture, nursing homes, water pollution, Du Pont, First National City Bank of New York, the Washington law firm of Covington & Burling, land-use policies in California, supermarkets, and "brown lung" disease in the textile industry.

the seven most senior of Nader's "raiders" and is one of the three organizations through which Nader now operates. The other two are located a few blocks away: the five-man Auto Safety Center and the Public Interest Research Group, staffed by twelve bright young graduates of top law schools, three of them women. In addition, there are the summertime student raiders, who this year will number about fifty, only one-quarter as many as last year. The program is being cut back, Jacobs explains, because the students are a mixed blessing, requiring a good deal of nursemaiding by the full-time staff. "But we still think it's useful for the regulatory agencies to see a fresh batch of faces wafting through."

One of the center's main functions is to handle a flood of crank calls. "No, I'm afraid Mr. Nader isn't here," says the young girl at the switchboard. "Can you tell me what it's about?" After a protracted conversation, she explains with a grin: "He said it was something so big he didn't dare put a word on paper. No name either, but still he wants to speak to Ralph." Nader drops by for a few minutes every day or so, and the other raiders emulate his casual example; by the switchboard, message boxes improvised out of brown paper are filled to overflowing with notices of calls never returned.

The Center for the Study of Responsive Law is tax-exempt, supported by well-known foundations, such as Field, Carnegie, and Stern, and by wealthy benefactors such as Midas muffler heir Gordon Sherman and Robert Townsend, author of *Up the Organization*. (Townsend gave $150,000.) On a budget of $300,000 a year, the center is able to pay its raiders a stipend of up to $15,000 each. "A far cry from five years ago," says one of the veteran raiders, Harrison Wellford, thirty-one, "when Ralph was being trailed by G.M. gumshoes and we would meet at night at the Crystal City hamburger joint on Connecticut Avenue to compare notes. We'd work our heads off and then get gunned down by someone from Covington & Burling [a large Washington law firm] who had been on an issue for a corporate client for ten years."

Consumers Union is the biggest single donor to the Auto Safety Center, which operates on a slender budget of $30,000 a year. The Public Interest Research Group, or PIRG as it is called, is Nader's own nonprofit law firm, and he pays all the bills out of his own pocket, including the stipends of $4,500 a year to the twelve young lawyers. It is an irony that must warm Nader's heart that the money comes out of the $270,000 he netted in the settlement of his lawsuit against G.M. for invasion of privacy. Since PIRG's budget is $170,000 a year, Nader is obviously going through his windfall at an unsustainable clip.

CONSCIOUSNESS III DOESN'T GIVE A DAMN

Nader calls his own organization "a big joke really, a drop in the bucket compared to the size of the problem." It is in his nature to conceive of the enemy as being enormous, pervasive, and exceedingly powerful. "How many public-interest lawyers would it take to oversee the Pentagon? A hundred? Multiply that by the number of departments and agencies. This country needs 50,000 full-time citizens, including 10,000 public-interest lawyers. And I could get that many applicants if I had the money." Last month Nader began a campaign to raise

$750,000 from students in two states, Connecticut and Ohio, where the money would be used to set up Nader-like centers for investigating state and local government. Students in two other states, Oregon and Minnesota, have voted to donate $3 each from their college activities funds to finance similar organizations. Nader hopes that one plan or another will spread across the country.

To the young, Nader is a hero of great stature. Thousands of students in law, medicine, engineering, and every other field want to "conform their careers and their ideals," as he puts it, by going to work for him. They are the mass base of his movement, and he is able to pick and choose among them for his staff. (They say on campus that getting a job with Nader is "tougher than getting into Yale Law School.") And yet this appeal is in many ways hard to fathom. Nader has no use at all for the "counterculture," and he abhors drugs. "There's a conflict between living life on a level of feeling on the one hand and Ralph's product ethic on the other," admits Lowell Dodge. "To produce, to have an impact—that's what Ralph admires. Consciousness III doesn't give a damn about the FTC. Ralph does." Dodge thinks Nader is growing ever stronger on campus as revolutionary ideas begin to fade. "There's more interest in change *within* the system, and Ralph is the most effective example of an agent for change."

Nader hectors students mercilessly about their public duties, about their "anemic imaginations," about their "thousands of hours on the beach or playing cards." And they seem to love it. "Suppose students would engage in one of history's greatest acts of sacrifice and go without Coke and tobacco and alcohol, on which they spend $250 each a year?" he asked a student audience at Town Hall in New York. "They could develop the most powerful lobby in the country. Write to us! We'll tell you how to do it." Hands dived for pens as he called out his address in Washington.

It is possible to question, nevertheless, whether this enthusiasm would survive a close association with Nader. Although most of the members of his full-time staff plan to stay in public-interest legal work, many of them talk with enthusiasm about the day when they will be leaving Nader. One reason, of course, is money. "On $4,500 a year, it's tough," says Christopher White, one of the young lawyers at the Public Interest Research Group. And then these young people are blither spirits than Nader and have a spontaneity and graciousness he lacks. Although they refrain from criticizing him directly, the picture that emerges is of a boss at least as dictatorial as any they would find in a private law firm. "The emphasis is on production," one of them says. "Ralph thinks that if a brief is 90 percent right, it's a waste of time to polish it." Nader tells them that a work week of 100 hours is "about right." He lectures them about smoking, refuses to ride in their Volkswagens, and never has time to waste socializing. Lowell Dodge got a call from Nader last Christmas Eve, but only because Nader had a question to ask about work in progress.

The warmth and empathy so important to the young are not to be found in any relationship with Nader. Robert Townsend's daughter Claire, a pretty blonde student at Princeton, says with unblushing candor that she became a raider last summer partly because "I had a terrible crush on Ralph. All the girls have crushes on Ralph." But Nader apparently never has crushes on them. He still lives monk-like in a rented room. His most pronounced concession to cravings of the flesh comes in appeasing a voracious although picky appetite. He is leery of most meats but often tops off a meal with two desserts. It is somehow typical of the man that when the soon-to-be-famous blonde detective tried to pick him up, back during his fight with G.M., she found him in a supermarket buying a package of cookies.

TRYING TO FIND FREE ENTERPRISE

What young people admire in Nader is a dark and uncompromising idealism, coupled with a system of New Left economics that he is able to shore up with all sorts of impressive-sounding facts. They think he has got the goods on "the system." And he is completely free of any humdrum sense of proportion. A conversation with Nader makes the consumer society sound as gory as a battlefield: motorists "skewered like shish kebab on non-collapsible steering wheels"; babies burned to death by flammable fabrics improperly labeled; a little girl decapitated because a glove-compartment door popped open in a low-speed collision; "thousands of people poisoned and killed every year through the irresponsible use of pesticides and chemicals."

The corporate criminals responsible for this slaughter always go unpunished. "If we were as lenient toward individual crime as we are toward big-business crime we would empty the prisons, dissolve the police forces, and subsidize the criminals." The regulatory agencies are "chatteled to business and indifferent to the public," and Congress is "an anachronism, although a good investment for corporations." As for the market economy, it is rapidly being destroyed by the same corporate executives who are always "extolling it at stockholder meetings."

"Where is the free-enterprise system?" Nader asks, a sly smile lighting up his face. "I'm trying to find it. Is it the oil oligopoly, protected by import quotas? The shared monopolies in consumer products? The securities market, that bastion of capitalism operating on fixed commissions and now provided with socialized insurance? They call me a radical for trying to restore power to the consumer, but businessmen are the true radicals in this country. They are taking us deeper and deeper into corporate socialism—corporate power using government power to protect it from competition."

DOWN TO ZERO PROFITS

Nader is not exactly the first social critic to be astonished at the functions—and malfunctions—of a market economy, and to render them in overtones of darkest evil. But sinister tales of this sort, while they go down well enough with college crowds, throw no light at all on the issues Nader claims to want to face. It is true enough that unless consumers themselves are concerned about product safety, corporations have no particular bias in its favor. This is due, however, not to corporate depravity but rather to the economics of the case: an extra margin of safety is an invisible benefit that usually increases costs. When products, automobiles for example, are too complicated for consumers to make independent judgments as to safety, government must usually set standards if there are to be any—and it is a measure not just of business power but also of consumer indifference that safety standards for autos came so late.

Government must also counter the ceaseless efforts of corporations to escape from the rigors of competition through the acquisition of monopoly power, through tariff protection, import quotas, and the like. Granted that government hasn't done a very good job of this. All the same, most corporate executives, obliged to immerse themselves daily in what feels very much like competition, would be surprised to learn from Nader how free of it they are supposed to have become.

Given Nader's own diagnosis, it might be thought that he has been spending his time battling restraints on trade, but this is far from the case. He has instead been devoting his considerable ingenuity to devising new schemes for regulating and "popularizing" business, by such means as a federal charter for all corporations, "which would be like a constitution for a country," publication of corporate tax returns, and the election of public members to corporate boards. He would require an attack on pollution "with maximum use of known technology and down to zero profits."

Nader denies any desire to take the country into socialism, and in this he is apparently sincere. One of his raiders, Mark Green, told the New York *Times* recently that when Nader thinks of socialism "he doesn't think of Lenin but of Paul Rand Dixon," former Chairman of the FTC and, in Nader's mind, the quintessential bureaucrat. Yet Nader seems never to have grasped that when he talks about operating on "zero profits" he is talking not about a market economy but about a confiscatory, state-imposed system that would inevitably bring in train a host of other controls.

In his "consumer democracy" of the future, as he outlines it, everybody could order business around. Tightly controlled from above by the federal government, business would be policed at the local level by what would amount to consumer soviets. Nader thinks it will be easy to organize them, by handing out application forms in the parking lots of shopping centers. "Then collectively you can bargain with the owners of the center. You can say, 'Here are 18,000 families. We want a one-room office where we can have our staff within the center that will serve as a liaison between us and you. And we're going to develop certain conditions of our continuing patronage on a mass basis.' It might take the form of banning detergents with phosphates, improving service under a warranty, or holding down prices." Nader's product-rating system, including a telephone data bank for easy reference, would force manufacturers, he says, to abandon their present policy of "severe protective imitation" for one of "competition on price and quality." (Nobody has been able to explain just how such a system would make the millions of decisions the market makes now, many of them involving subjective judgments as to quality or value.)

While otherwise holding business in low esteem, Nader seems to have a blind faith in instant technology, insisting that if corporations are given tough enough deadlines, on antipollution devices or on proving the safety of food additives, they will somehow manage to comply. While it is true that some corporations plead ignorance as a convenient alibi for doing nothing about pollution, it is also true that feasible systems have not yet been developed to control a number of crucial pollutants, including sulphur dioxide. On the question of food additives, James Grant, deputy commissioner of the Food and Drug Administration, says, "Scientific advances solve problems but also raise new questions. We can prove that certain chemicals are unsafe, but we can never prove, once and for all, that *anything* in the food supply is safe. We frequently are obliged to make absolute decisions on the basis of partial knowledge. If I have one criticism to level at the consumer advocates, it's that they're unwilling to take scientific uncertainty into account."

DOES SEARS, ROEBUCK CHEAT?

Economics, clearly, is not Nader's strong suit. He seems to think of figures as weapons, to be tossed around for maximum effect. To cite one of his current favorite examples of business fraud, he says that the orange-juice industry is watering its product by 10 percent, and thus bilking the public out of $150 million a year. And he adds: "You may wish to compare that with what bank robbers took last year in their second most successful performance to date: $8 million." Nader says he arrived at the 10 percent figure on the basis of "insider information." He applied it to total sales of the citrus industry and, lo, another "statistic" on business fraud. Even if the industry were watering, which it strenuously denies, it does not follow that the public is being gypped out of $150 million. On a watering job of that scale, the price would reflect the water content, and if water were eliminated the price would have to go up.

Another of Nader's current favorite targets is Sears, Roebuck & Co. "Nobody thinks Sears, Roebuck cheats people. But they charge interest from the date the sales contract is signed rather than from the date of delivery—a few pennies, millions of times a year." But Sears no longer has ownership or use of the merchandise once the contract is signed, and could not, for example, apply any price increase that might subsequently be decided upon. The contract is perfectly open and aboveboard and should be considered in the context of the total transaction, price versus values received.

Nader quotes and endorses an estimate by Senator Philip Hart of Michigan that the whole gamut of business fraud and gouging, from shoddy merchandise to monopoly pricing, costs the consumer over $200 billion a year, "or 25 percent of all personal income." That utterly fantastic figure is also more than four times as large as all corporate profits in 1970. For a clipping of that magnitude to be possible, even theoretically, it would have to run as a sort of inflationary factor through the whole economy—wages as well as prices—and thus the argument becomes something of a wash, but a grossly misleading one all the same.

Like reformers before him, Nader is extremely reluctant to admit that any progress at all has been made in any area of consumer protection, even where he has helped write new legislation. "Very little progress, really," he sums it up. "It's a push-and-shove situation." He still refers to the nation's meat supply as "often diseased or putrescent, contaminated by rodent hairs and other assorted debris, its true condition disguised by chemical additives." This is the identical language he used three years ago to arouse Congress and propel passage of the Wholesale Meat Act. Since then the Department of Agriculture has declared 289 packing plants "potentially hazardous to human health," and has told state authorities to clean them up or shut them down. The department says "much remains to be done" to eliminate unsanitary conditions—but perhaps not as much as Nader seems to think. Similarly, despite the thirty-four automobile safety standards enforced by law and 701 recall campaigns, Nader says that "the changes are purely cosmetic."

SHOCK WAVES AT THE AGENCIES

The most impressive documents to come out of the Nader movement are the reports on the regulatory agencies. In most respects they are detailed and thoughtful, written with surprising skill by various groups of amateurs working under Nader's direction. And they have sent shock waves through Washington's bureaucracy. Since their publication, agency awareness of the public interest has greatly increased, and a certain distance has crept into the previously cozy relations between the regulators and the regulated. That distance, however, is still not nearly great enough to please Nader, who wants industry policed with eternal suspicion. "Sharpness" is one word he uses to describe the proper attitude. Jail terms for executives, he says, would be far more effective than the voluntary compliance on which the agencies now mostly rely. "Jail is a great stigma to a businessman, and even a short sentence is a real deterrent," explains James Turner, who wrote the FDA report. "You would get maximum compliance with a minimum of prosecutions."

That may well be so. But in the atmosphere of hostility that would result, regulation might actually be less effective than at present. The agencies can now make sweeping judgments—that a rate is "discriminatory" or a trade practice "deceptive"—on the basis of a simple hearing. "If criminal penalties were involved, our statutes would be interpreted in a much less flexible way," says Robert Pitofsky, the new head of FTC's Bureau of Consumer Protection. Most regulatory matters are exceedingly complex, and the agencies have trusted the industries concerned to furnish the data. If this system were replaced by a program of independent government research on countless topics, the sums expended could be huge enough to dent the federal budget. "It has to be a cooperative effort," argues Administrator Douglas Toms of the National Highway Traffic Safety Administration, which sets auto safety standards. "We're not going to get anywhere with an ugly, persistent confrontation, where the two sides try to outshout each other. We'd be pitting a tiny government agency against the worldwide auto industry."

At the FDA, a new leadership is attempting to stay on cordial terms with the $125-billion food industry while attacking the two key problems documented in great detail in the Nader report, *The Chemical Feast*. First, the FDA is undertaking a comprehensive review of the hundreds of chemicals added to the food supply as preservatives, colorings, or flavorings. "None of these chemicals, perhaps, has been put to the most rigorous testing that present-day science could muster," admits Deputy Commissioner Grant, one of the new men at the agency. Second, the FDA has also acted on mounting evidence that many prepared foods are deficient in nutritional values, and is now setting guidelines for their fortification with vitamins and minerals. "In many ways the FDA was a bar to progress," says Grant, "and we are attempting to turn that around."

CONFESSIONAL FOR SINNERS

Among the agencies Nader has investigated, the FTC comes closest to the tough, pro-consumer point of view that he is pushing for. Under its new leadership the FTC has filed a flurry of complaints on deceptive advertising, and in a number of these cases it has gone far beyond the traditional cease-and-desist order (known around the FTC as "go and sin no more"). To the dismay of the advertising profession, the FTC now seeks what it calls "affirmative disclosure"—that is, an admission in future advertising, for a specific period, that previous ads were deceptive. Howard Bell, president of the American Advertising Federation, says this amounts to "public flogging."

"Somebody is going to take us to court on affirmative disclosure, and they should," Pitofsky cheerfully admits. "It is a substantial expansion of FTC power." The FTC is also insisting that claims be based on evidence. "We're not after something that 'tastes better,'" Pitofsky says. "That's just puffery. But if you say it's twice as fast or 50 percent stronger, we will take that to mean faster or stronger than your competitor's product, and it better be so."

By swinging to "a fairly stiff enforcement of the law," as Pitofsky puts it, the FTC hopes to encourage self-regulation by industry. "Voluntary compliance comes when companies see that they are better off cleaning house themselves than letting government do it for them." And that is what seems to be happening. Warning of "the regulatory tidal wave which threatens to envelop us," the American Advertising Federation is trying to establish a National Advertising Review Board, which would set standards for ads, seek voluntary compliance with the standards, and refer ads it finds deceptive to the FTC for action.

In all this unaccustomed bustle, the agencies are, of course, just doing what they were supposed to be doing all along. To say only that, however, is to ignore the extraordinary difficulty of the regulatory function when there is no counterpressure to the steady, case-by-case intervention of skilled lawyers with specific and valuable corporate interests to protect. Congress, like the agencies, responds to the pressures applied—it's a case of "who's banging on the door," in Nader's words. Yet the pressures applied by individual corporations in individual cases can work to subvert the larger interests of the business community as a whole. "Intriguingly enough," says the FDA's Grant, "the overwhelming majority of the food industry believes that it is better off with a strong FDA, because all get balanced treatment." It is Nader's accomplishment, and no small one, that he has given the agencies the other constituency they need, the public. "Until we came along," says Nader, "the people at the agencies had forgotten what citizens looked like."

Nader will bend all of his lobbying skill this year to persuade Congress to pass a bill that would give the consumer permanent representation before regulatory bodies. The consumer agency to be established by the bill would, in fact, attempt to do just the sort of thing that Nader is doing now, but with the help of government funds and powers. A number of other consumer bills have broad support this year, including regulation of warranties and power for the FTC to seek preliminary injunctions against deceptive advertising. But Nader says, "I'd trade them all for the consumer agency."

THE PROBLEM OF MAINTAINING CLOUT

But can a movement like consumerism, powerful and yet amorphous, really be institutionalized? Certainly the passion and craft of a Nader cannot be. Nor would the director of a consumer agency enjoy Nader's complete freedom of action. A Senate aide who helped draft the bill predicts that the new office might "have its time in the sun, like the Peace Corps or OEO. Then it will carve out a rather cautious domain of its own and become part of the bureaucracy."

That being so, there will be opportunities for Nader, always provided that he can stay in the sun himself. His support is volatile, a matter of vague tides of public opinion. "His problem is maintaining clout," says Douglas Toms, the Traffic Safety Administrator. "He has a strange kind of constituency, people with a burr under their saddle for one reason or another. He has to constantly find vehicles to keep him in the public eye." Financing will continue to be a problem. Nader himself is well aware of all these difficulties. He says that a basic error of reform movement is expecting to succeed. "You will never succeed. All you're trying to do is reduce problems to the level of tolerability."

Nader's answer to that question about the presidency is this: "I find that I am less and less interested in who is going to become President. A far more interesting question is, who's going to be the next president of General Motors?" Despite any such disclaimers, it is easy to imagine the movement going political and Nader running in some future year as, say, a candidate for the U.S. Senate from Connecticut. Nader might do well in politics, as a sort of latter-day Estes Kefauver. A recent Harris survey revealed that 69 percent of the people think "it's good to have critics like Nader to keep industry on its toes," while only 5 percent think he is "a troublemaker who is against the free enterprise system." This is the sort of public response that most politicians, including Presidents, yearn for in vain.

Judging Nader on the basis of the specific reforms he has brought about, it would be hard to disagree with this public verdict. There has been some cost, however, and this cannot be measured. He has visited his own suspicions and fears upon a whole society, and in the end his hyperbole may prove to be a dangerous weapon. But this year at least, the public apparently expects its crusaders to be twice as fast and 50 percent stronger.

Gray Power: Next Challenge to Business?

**Will retirement-age consumers be the next group
to increase demands on business? Social scientists
disagree on the future of "gray power," but
early warning signs of its emergence do exist.**

Betsy D. Gelb

The need for the organization to heed early warning signs of social change has become the message of the 1970s. Joseph Nolan, a former senior vice-president of the Chase Manhattan Bank, has told business leaders: "The recent past is littered with examples of business's inability to perceive social and political trends before they become issues of great public concern." His solution? A systematic effort to detect relevant clues.*

This article will examine the early warning signs which give evidence that "seniors" (as the sixty-five-and-over group is now called by professionals in the social services) will be the next group to make demands on the business system. If the specter of white-haired pickets outside his store or factory does not pique the interest of a manager, perhaps the possibility of nationwide retirement clubs spreading the word about a boycott of his products will. Fantasy? Lunatic fringe? Or future reality? The following review of material from diverse sources may shed some light on the issue of the retirement-age consumer versus business.

"SENIOR LIB": PRO AND CON

If the history of social movements in this country holds true for the elderly, managers may be forced to make hasty reevaluations of hiring practices and advertising, as the group consciousness of an additional market segment grows. For guidance, they have analyses by social scientists who are by no means in agreement on the future of "gray power." A brief look at the arguments on both sides may be helpful to managers. Furthermore, this overview can offer clues as to which changing conditions may dramatically affect the likelihood that seniors will follow blacks, Chicanos and women, figuratively or literally, into the corporate boardroom with megaphones in hand.

Assessments of those who foresee no gray power movement can be summarized as follows:

Because the elderly are of little value as labor, they will remain powerless.

The elderly will remain powerless because every culture protects itself by giving little importance to those it is likely to lose through death.

---

*Joseph Nolan, "Protect Your Public Image with Performance," *Harvard Business Review* (April 1975), pp. 138–139.

One precondition for a social movement is identification with the group (blacks, women, or whomever), and the elderly do not define themselves by age.

Another precondition is membership in age-specific groups, and the elderly are not joiners.

Even if the group membership picture is changing, seniors are not a population segment that engages in political action.

Even when they have engaged in political action, their successes have been the exception rather than the rule.

Those expecting a senior challenge to business offer the following ideas:

The elderly are potentially of value as consumers; therefore, they can improve their relative power position.

Today's elderly are more experienced in participation in social movements than seniors of ten years ago, and in another ten years, even more will have that experience.

They are becoming more physically clustered in retirement villages and the like, which points to increases in membership in age-specific groups.

They will increasingly be a more homogeneous population segment, compared to the elderly of ten years ago who were in many cases foreign born and had limited education.

They need "enemies" to thrive as a social movement, and business offers that potential.

They are becoming more militant, joining, for example, the Gray Panthers.

Their activities to force change in the business world have brought some success, which is likely to attract adherents to their causes.

SKEPTICAL VIEWS

Social scientists who are skeptical of gray power see several differences between the sixty-five-and-over population and other corporate constituencies such as ethnic/racial groups and women. One difference is their potential economic benefit in the labor force. With retirement moving toward younger age brackets, it would appear that the perceived value of seniors in the labor force is decreasing. Thus, if economic contribution is what leads to enough public attention to make a social movement feasible, then the elderly cannot be expected to develop such a movement in the near future.

A second argument reaching the same negative conclusion says, in effect, the society cannot afford psychologically to give the elderly much influence—they are too likely to die. One author draws a parallel to the high mortality rate of infants in France many years ago.* Newborn children were "devalued," he says; a family would not display a picture or speak of a very young child. This is typical of the way any culture protects itself from disruption by assigning no significant roles to those who are statistically likeliest to disappear.

---

*Robert Blauner, "Death and Social Structure," in *Life Cycle and Achievement in America,* ed. Rose Laub Coser (New York: Harper and Row, 1969), pp. 223–263.

Thus, according to this line of reasoning, only when "retirement age" and "likely to die" are separated in the public mind can the elderly be influential.

The third basis for discounting the possibility of gray power rests on the idea that identification with and pride in a group is a necessary prerequisite for a social movement. Sociologists holding this view doubt that the sixty-five-and-over individual really defines himself or herself by age group. Says one, "Age simply does not appear to be a variable that unites people regardless of their differences.* Ethnicity or race, sex, part of the country, and occupation or former occupation all are seen as more relevant to an individual's view of himself. Therefore, these observers declare that there will never be any profit in "Buy Old," as there is in "Buy Black."

Pride-in-group is a critical factor, according to some observers. They see association with other older people as a prerequisite to development of a subculture. However, they see among the elderly in this country a reluctance, particularly among middle-class seniors, to join age-related groups. The elderly may in fact downgrade their age category even while belonging to it: A 1967 study found that 83% of retirement-age respondents felt personally "useful," but only 37% felt that elderly in general were "useful."†

Another study from the mid-1960s reported that older persons are more likely than those under sixty-five to drop out of groups, let alone join them.‡ Whether this tendency to downgrade aging and to withdraw from organizations is increasing or decreasing in this decade clearly offers a useful indicator for assessing the likelihood of "senior lib."

However, joining together in groups, while perhaps necessary for social action, is hardly sufficient. To assess the probability of an age-related posture toward the business community, it appears useful to look at approaches to political action. Such a parallel suggests bases for doubting the emergence of "senior clout" for two reasons:

> First, while seniors vote in numbers higher than the adult population as a whole, their total political activity level traditionally has been lower. Campaigning, circulating petitions, and attending meetings all were found in the 1960s to decline in the sixty-five-and-over population.
>
> In addition, where seniors have been politically effective in the past, either that effectiveness has sprung from groups cutting across age lines (such as labor unions) or from one leader of a group of elderly. Says a skeptic: "Despite the 86% increase in Social Security benefits in the past decade, a dispropor-

---

*Robert C. Atchley, "Politics and Government," in *The Social Forces in Later Life,* eds. Irene Elmer and Levin Gleason (Belmont, California: Wadsworth Publishing Co., 1972), p. 247.

†Irving Rosow, *Social Integration of the Aged* (New York: The Free Press, 1967), p. 261.

‡Joel Smith, "The Narrowing Social World of the Aging," in *Social Aspects of Aging,* eds. Ida H. Simpson and John C. McKinney (Durham, N.C.: Duke University Press, 1966), pp. 226–242.

tionate number of the elderly are still found among the low-income population. . . . Back in the 1930s Francis Everett Townsend mounted a crusade of the elderly with his platform calling for a $200-a-month payment to every American over sixty. The average retired worker today gets $188 a month out of Social Security.*

SUPPORTING VIEWS

Countering these arguments are ideas supporting the likely emergence of gray power. Turning the economic argument around, for example, managers might see the improving financial status of the elderly as an indicator that they will be heard by the business community. Factors here are the growth of pension plans and the view that the financial strength of seniors should be measured by assets, not just income. Both factors increase the likelihood of this population being viewed as a lucrative market for many products, and their improving financial position is seen as an indicator of increased demands on business in the future.

Furthermore, say other observers, the seniors of the next ten years will include veterans of earlier social movements—black, Chicano, but principally the woman's movement. The majority of the sixty-five-and-over population is female, and women who have forcefully demanded new rights and recognition in middle age will hardly put such demands on the shelf at sixty-five; they will shift demands from feminism to a pro-age stance.

Experience in other movements has at least two significant components, it is believed. First, such experience offers individuals some expertise in managing organizations, shaping issues with popular appeal, and bringing a cause to the attention of the mass media. Second, it means that today's seniors have reared a generation of children now in their forties who have been socialized to participate in social movements and who, two decades from now, will in a sense be seeking a new cause.

A third factor affirming an active stance by seniors is their increasing physical clustering. Retirement villages, as a replacement for multi-generation households, are a significant development, since they increase the likelihood of age-specific groups, a prerequisite of activism. According to one writer:

> While such associations may have no ideology prescribing attitudes and beliefs that should be held in common, immersion in a social environment exclusive of other generations may cause a narrowing of political expectations and provide the organizational preconditions which foster involvement in political affairs from the perspective of aging. For members of groups of age peers, participation in a political organization of the aged is defined as appropriate and, in some cases, necessary activity, while for members of mixed generation groups, political participation on the basis of age may be perceived as illegitimate.†

*William Chapman, "The Aged: Pitiable and Powerful," *Houston Chronicle* (March 21, 1975).

†James E. Trela, "Some Political Consequences of Senior Center and Other Old Age Group Memberships," *The Gerontologist* (Summer 1971), pp. 118–123.

To another writer, the key to expectations of concerted action by seniors lies in their increasing homogeneity. In the future, according to this argument, the aged will have more similar educational backgrounds than they do today, and language barriers will slowly disappear. Viewing this homogeneity as a "most important qualification for effective interest group political action" suggests the emergence of a "subculture of aging, with old-age interest groups forming around various issues and problems."*

One final argument is that the success of a value-oriented movement depends on a hierarchy of goals, some immediately attainable, some practically unattainable, and that while these goals must not conflict with those of society, the movement "needs enemies." This framework reads like a prescription for one symbol of "senior power"—Maggie Kuhn of the Gray Panthers.

Kuhn founded the national pro-age organization in 1971, when she was sixty-six. Its goals include better housing, medical care and employment opportunities for the aged. However, other goals are more global, looking toward the market system as a whole. In a 1975 issue of *Gray Panther Network,* a militant tabloid, was a front-page picture of Kuhn holding aloft a banner which read "Gray Panthers Say: Roll Back Profits."

SENIOR LOBBY EFFORTS

The Gray Panthers are by no means an isolated instance of a successful pro-age lobby. The National Council of Senior Citizens represents a coalition of more than 3,000 local organizations of the elderly. Many are chapters of the American Association of Retired Persons (AARP) and the National Retired Teachers Association, with a combined membership of about 2.5 million persons. Results of the efforts of groups like these in confronting business have included the following:

Some banks now waive activity charges for the elderly, offer free checks, and have revised loan policies, which had in the past led to rejection of the elderly as "unemployed."

The National Association of Broadcasters amended its code to include a prohibition of "agism in programming."

Several companies have revised their policies toward retired employees, moving beyond pension planning to inclusion of the retirees in company activities on a personal basis. In one case, retired employees were hurting new employee recruitment by their criticisms of the way their former employer was now ignoring them. In a second instance, a utility found a rate increase delayed when a committee of the utility's own retired employee organization opposed the increase, reporting that they as retirees felt "discarded."

Miami Beach developers, who had profitable uses in mind for a tract of beachfront land, found that the land would instead be used for low-cost public housing, thanks to the political pressure of that city's seniors.

Some drug stores have decided to stay open longer hours and offer discounts to seniors. Furthermore, the advertising of prescription drug prices, a

---

*Michael Kaye Carlie, "The Politics of Age: Interest Group or Social Movement?" *The Gerontologist* (1969), pp. 259–263.

crusade of senior groups, is permitted by a growing number of state legislatures. A group of Houston seniors obtained half-price bus fares for riders over sixty-five, then announced through their seventy-four-year-old spokesman, "Next comes the gas, telephone and lighting companies, and then the stores. We will take one group at a time and get them to give special rates for senior citizens."*

Several lawsuits are now pending to challenge the legality of compulsory retirement at sixty-five, or at any specific age.

These achievements can be viewed as likely to attract publicity and, therefore, more adherents seeking more confrontations. Furthermore, group action may inspire some individual action. An AARP study of its own members showed their reaction to "a consumer problem." According to the study, only one-fourth reacted to a problem by "doing nothing." The others contacted the dealer or manufacturer, an attorney, the Better Business Bureau, or a federal agency or consumer office.†

HOUSTON RESEARCH PROJECT

To test the applicability of these two opposing views on the likelihood of a senior challenge to business, a study was undertaken in Houston in 1975. The purpose of this research was to shed light on several of the areas seen as relevant by social scientists whose views have already been quoted.

Subjects for the study were 403 seniors, all of whom were attending a meeting of some retirement-age group. This sample was selected in the belief that if these individuals showed no inclination toward action, then in all likelihood none could be expected from seniors at large. It was recognized, however, that any gray power propensity among these respondents could not be projected to the sixty-five-and-over population as a whole. These subjects simply constituted a convenience sample of those who could be assumed to be the vanguard of any possible social movement; therefore, their attitudes and behavior were of greatest interest as early warning signs of approaching change.

Respondents were from four groups: AARP, International Brotherhood of Electrical Workers Retired Members, Service Core of Retired Executives, and Retired Senior Volunteer Program. Exceptionally large type was used for the questionnaire, and assistance was available from University of Houston personnel. At least part of the form was filled out by more than 99% of those present. Respondents were not asked to sign the forms, and were assured anonymity on that basis.

Possible senior challenges

The survey dealt with four areas relevant to a possible senior challenge to business.

---

*Doris and David Jones, *Young Till We Die* (New York: Coward, McCann & Geoghegan, 1973), p. 295.

†Fred E. Waddell, "Consumer Research and Programs for the Elderly—The Forgotten Dimension," mimeographed, Virginia Polytechnic Institute and State University, pp. 11–12.

Identification with the senior age segment
Perception of business as an "enemy"
Sympathy with militancy by seniors
Personal history of action after a perceived consumer problem.

The first area of interest, the extent to which seniors identify themselves by age, was approached by questions on degree of activity in retirement-age groups; degree to which neighbors are retirement-age people; like/dislike of being called a "senior citizen"; and belief that someone "speaks up for" the senior age segment. For the last two areas, it was assumed that strength of reaction was more relevant than direction—that strong agreement or strong disagreement would indicate age-segment identification, but indifference would indicate the opposite.

The second area, possible perception of business as "the enemy," was approached by a question on the degree to which respondents agreed or disagreed that "stores try to cheat me." The other two areas—approval of senior militancy and their own behavior after a consumer problem—were probed by questions on the :

Likelihood of switching away from a store that retirement-age people were boycotting
Degree of support for the instigation of such a boycott
Degree of approval of picketing
Degree of belief that older people accept "new ways of doing things"
Hypothetical reaction if a purchased item "did not work the way it was supposed to"
Actual course of action chosen by those who reported getting angry with a store or with someone working there.

Responses on perceptions of business were compared to indicators of identification as a senior and also to demographic data. Chi-square tests were used to see whether indicators of militancy were disproportionately associated with, for example, certain income categories.

Survey responses

The data showed the sample of respondents to be similar to the U.S. retirement-age population on several demographic dimensions. Half were under seventy, and half seventy or older. Two-thirds were female. Blacks made up 11% of the sample and Mexican Americans 2%. One-tenth were single; the remainder was divided evenly between the married and widowed categories. Median monthly household income fell between $401 and $500, and one-fifth reported that they were employed. Education, however, was disproportionately high; nearly half said they had at least some college.

Simple frequency counts on issues related to group identification showed that roughly one-third of the sample selected answers associated with age-segment awareness. This one-third agreed or disagreed strongly with the statement "I don't like being called a senior citizen." (Gray Panther Maggie Kuhn has been quoted as strongly agreeing; she considers "old" a better term.) Respondents agreed strongly that they attend more than one meeting per month of a retirement-age group. They agreed at least somewhat that most of their neighbors are retirement-age people, and they agreed or disagreed strongly with the statement "Nobody speaks up for people my age on TV or in the newspapers." Relating either demographic characteristics or these indicators of age-group identification to an antibusiness stance did not bring out significant associations, however.

In the area of specific reactions to business, only 10% of the respondents agreed even somewhat that "stores try to cheat me." However, Table 1 shows a higher degree of agreement with statements related to senior militancy. Table 2 shows somewhat lower figures than Table 1 for any stronger reaction to a defective purchase than simply returning it.

TABLE 1.
Reactions of respondents sixty-five or older to issues of senior militancy (percentages)

	Agree Strongly	Agree Somewhat	Neither Agree Nor Disagree	Disagree Somewhat	Disagree Strongly
Would change stores if seniors boycotted mine	38	20	23	9	10
Favor boycott of stores uninterested in seniors	39	23	15	8	15
Approve of picketing	20	12	16	14	38
Would expect seniors to accept "new ways" of doing things	28	22	13	23	14

TABLE 2.   Reaction of respondents sixty-five or older if a purchase did not work properly

	Percent Who Would Take Each Action*
Would keep item and do nothing	5
Would return item	85
Would have someone else return item	4
Would tell others not to buy item	28
Would write letter of complaint	21
Would call or see someone to complain	43
Would never go back to store	14
Would never buy other products of manufacturer	18
Would sign a petition against manufacturer	10

*Multiple responses possible.

TABLE 3.
Behavior reported by seniors who became angry with a store or with an employee

	Percent of Respondents Taking Each Action*
Did nothing; continued to shop	24
Left store immediately	35
Told others not to shop at store	23
Wrote a letter to complain	12
Called or saw someone to complain	49
Never returned to that store	32

*Multiple responses possible.

Finally, the seniors were asked whether they had, in the past year, gotten angry with a store or someone working there. A "yes" response was checked by 38%, and Table 3 shows that a relatively high percentage of these respondents said they took some action.

Managers reviewing the arguments on both sides of the gray power issue might well infer that problems for business lie more in the future than in the present. However, studies which minimized the likelihood and impact of senior activism largely date from the 1960s or earlier. Then, the seniors studied included many foreign-born, and those of limited education. Current observers believe these seniors will be replaced in the next decade or two by alumnae of other social movements.

The Houston research, to the limited extent that it can be generalized beyond the sample, appears to substantiate the unlikelihood of near-term activism by the elderly. However, managers looking at these findings might reasonably ponder two thoughts relating to the future. First, today's seniors, simply because they are not oriented toward protest, may be more unhappy with business in general or with specific businesses than many managers realize. Lack of complaints should not be taken as an indicator of belief by seniors that their age segment is well treated. Rather, businesses simply may be benefitting from seniors' reluctance to protest forcefully, and this reluctance may disappear in a decade.

Second, businesses need to keep abreast of senior attitudes. Studies repeated at three- or five-year intervals can help isolate two possible explanations for those attitudes. One possibility is the "cohort effect"—the influence of growing up during a certain period. Today's seniors could be expected to differ from future retirement-age generations because of their Depression-World War II history. The other possibility is, of course, age-related attitudes/behavior. Possibly, seniors in 1987 will show similarities to seniors of 1977, but will differ from today's fifty-five-year-olds. In that case, business could be more confident in the stability of seniors' behavior.

What role does business have in such research? Granted, businesses are not, by and large, sponsors of social science investigations per se. However, managers do influence marketing research by their firms or industry groups, and can specify—and examine—more specific age data. Too often, age brackets are set to include a fifty-five-or-over category, depriving management of the opportunity to separate the retirement-age buyers from those considerably younger.

Furthermore, any management attention to this age segment can help to preclude a gray power confrontation which might lurk in a company's future. Today, most individuals in this age segment are not marching on the business community or voting for candidates who seek to restructure the system under which businesses operate. Tomorrow, however, may be a different story.

QUESTIONS FOR DISCUSSION

1. As an alternative to direct confrontation with business, activist groups often bring pressure to bear on government, which in turn forces alteration of business behavior. Cite at least three major business-related issues where activists have used this strategy. Were the activists successful? How did business ultimately respond?

2. Nader-affiliated organizations have occasionally been accused of serving their own interests rather than the interests of the greater public. Are there any issues on which these organizations have taken a stand with which you disagree? What do you feel would be the most effective route for getting your voice heard?

3. A liquor store in a small college town was once picketed by students sympathetic to attempts by a farm worker's union to organize a major California vineyard. The students demanded that the store owner remove the vineyard's brand of wine from his shelves. At the same time, a major trucker's union was attempting to organize the same vineyard. The truckers union threatened to make no more deliveries to the liquor store unless the challenged wine remained on the shelves. How might the store owner effectively respond to these conflicting demands?

4. We note in the readings one writer's forecast that senior citizens will be the next group to make major demands on business. Can you think of any other latent groups that might form and bring pressures on the business system? What do you think the major thrust of their demands will be? How should business respond?

5. One strategy for dealing with activist groups is to appoint representatives of some of the most powerful to a company's board of directors. What general advantages are offered by such a strategy? What pitfalls might be encountered?

6. The Polaroid Workers' Revolutionary Movement (challenging Polaroid's involvement in South Africa, among other things) consisted primarily of employees of Polaroid. What peculiar problems arise when challenges to a

company's behavior come from within? What suggestions can you make for dealing with internal dissent that is highly visible to the public?

7. Ralph Nader comments, "They (businessmen) call me a radical for trying to restore power to the consumer, but businessmen are the true radicals in this country. They are taking us deeper and deeper into corporate social-ism—corporate power using government power to protect it from competi-tion." Comment upon and evaluate this statement from the country's fore-most activist.

8. Your corporation, a large retail chain with 350 stores, has just received a threat of violence from a group protesting your company's unwillingness to grant credit to welfare clients. As a staff specialist, what recommendations would you give to your company's officers in this case?

SELECTED READINGS

Bloom, P. N., and L. W. Stern, "Emergence of anti-industrialism," *Business Horizons,* October, 1976.

Braznell, W., Jr., "Radicals are coming; are you ready?" *Public Relations Journal,* October, 1976.

Burton, J., "De-activated activist," *Forbes,* September 15, 1976.

Cathey, P., "Business—the easily reached prime target for terrorists," *Iron Age,* April 4, 1977.

"Corporate Performance and Private Criticism—Campaign G. M., Rounds I and II," in G. A. Smith, C. R. Christensen, N. A. Berg, and M. S. Salter, *Policy Formulation and Adminis-tration,* 6th Ed. (Homewood: Richard D. Irwin, 1972.)

Costello, J., "What shareholders may ask at your annual meeting," *Nations Business,* April, 1977.

Gross, S., "The Nader network," *Business and Society Review,* Spring, 1975.

Leone, R. C., "Public-interest advocacy and the regulatory process," *Annals of the American Academy of Political and Social Science,* March, 1972.

McGuire, E. P., "The terrorist and the corporation," *Across the Board,* May, 1977.

"Nader vs. G. M.," *Time,* August 24, 1970.

Nash, J. M., "The Fox: He stalks the wild polluters," *Business and Society Review,* Autumn, 1973.

"Nibbling at the Nader myth," *Time,* September 6, 1976.

Perham, J., "Dissidents gear up for annual meetings," *DUN's Review,* April, 1977.

Perrow, C., *The Radical Attack on Business: A Critical Analysis.* (New York: Harcourt Brace Jovanovich, 1972.)

"Radical confrontation and its challenge to management," *Financial Executive,* Decem-ber, 1970.

Sanders, M. K., *Professional Radical: Conversations with Saul Alinsky*. (New York: Harper & Row, 1970.)

Vogel, D., "The political and economic impact of current criticisms of business," *California Management Review*, Winter, 1975.

"A Who's Who of corporate-responsibility action groups," *Business and Society Review*, Winter, 1972–73.

Zeigler, H., *Interest Groups in American Society*. (Englewood Cliffs, N.J.: Prentice–Hall, 1964.)

Case 1

McDONALD'S*

McDonald's, the nationwide chain of hamburger restaurants, has a policy that the American flag will fly in front of each of the company's outlets. The policy was personally promulgated by Ray Kroc, Chairman of the Board.

On Monday, May 4, 1970, four students at Kent State University were killed by National Guardsmen. The Guard was ordered to Kent State after students, like students all around the country, struck and rioted in protest to the Vietnam war and the invasion of Cambodia. At Kent State, the students had burned the ROTC building a few nights earlier.

On Tuesday, May 5, students about the country were in a state of shock and confusion because of the Kent State killings. At the Carbondale campus of Southern Illinois University, students were asking that all flags be lowered to half mast in memory of the Kent State students. When they confronted the manager of the local McDonald's, he complied and lowered the flag.

A neighbor who witnessed the confrontation reported it to McDonald's chairman, who in turn called the manager and ordered the flag hoisted to full mast. The manager complied with the chairman's directive.

A few hours later, the students returned, disturbed that the manager hadn't kept his word. They threatened in no uncertain terms to burn the shop down.

The manager, perplexed, called McDonald's headquarters for guidance. The manager's call was put through to the president of the corporation.

*The substance of this incident was reported in J. Anthony Lukas, "As American as a McDonald's Hamburger on the Fourth of July," *The New York Times Magazine*, July 4, 1971, p. 26.

Case 2

NEW ENGLAND RETAIL CREDIT CORPORATION*

On June 17, 1974, a small article appeared in the business section of the *Boston Chronicle* describing a computer order placed by New England Retail Credit Corporation (NERCC). The brief article quoted an announcement by John P. Daunt, president of NERCC, in which he stated that the firm, the largest credit-reporting agency in New England, had signed a 7.2-million-dollar contract with one of the country's largest computer manufacturers to install a computer system in their Waltham, Massachusetts, office. Included in the system will be input/output devices for NERCC's eight regional offices, three banks, and a local franchised credit agency.

The new system is scheduled to be in operation by January 1, 1976. By 1979 it is expected that the firm will have input/output devices in 90 percent of the banks in New England and will have franchise operations in nearly all of the more than two hundred local credit bureaus in the six state area. NERCC will then (for all practical purposes) become the custodian of *all of the credit information* on New England residents.

After reading the *Chronicle* story, Philip Kleinglass, a Boston attorney who had worked on several cases with the Boston chapter of the Civil Liberties Protective Society, became concerned about the effect that this new system would have on the privacy of the citizens living in the area. After much thought, he contacted James Kohanek, executive director of the Boston chapter of the CLPS, and asked that they meet to discuss the implications of such a system.

On June 22, 1974, Kleinglass and Kohanek met and discussed the issue over lunch. From their discussions it became apparent that the executive board of the CLPS should look into the issue further. Kleinglass agreed that he would contact Daunt to find out more about the system and then would make a report to the executive board.

When Kleinglass contacted Daunt about meeting with him, Daunt appeared to be delighted to talk about his proposed system. At that meeting Daunt explained the background of NERCC, why the system was needed, and how it would benefit the individuals living in the area. Kleinglass was shown the final report from Long and Retz Associates (Exhibit A), which was commissioned by NERCC to investigate the credit-reporting business in New England and NERCC's role in that business.

Daunt pointed out that the volume of their business was increasing at an average annual rate of 22 percent, but that was still approxi-

---

*This case was prepared by Leslie D. Ball, copyright 1974.

mately 4 to 5 percent less than the growth rate of credit volume in the New England area. While they were experiencing this growth, they were also experiencing increasing errors in their reports and an increase in the amount of response time required to fill a credit-report request. Because of these problems, NERCC's profitability was decreasing at an alarming rate. The Long and Retz report clearly shows that a continuation of NERCC operations employing current practices would lead to eventual bankruptcy.

"The system now being planned will accomplish many goals," said Daunt. He pointed out that it will offer improved service to a person applying for installment credit, reduced expenses for the credit grantor, and centralized credit information in New England.

The current functions of NERCC are to answer inquiries about credit, make credit reports, and attempt to collect uncollectable accounts. An *inquiry,* Daunt pointed out, results in only the information in their files being reported, while a *credit report* requires that NERCC update all information in its file and *then* make a report to the client. Daunt gave Kleinglass a sample credit report (Exhibit B). When the new system is installed, the cost of inquiries will be immediately reduced to $0.75 per inquiry from the current $1.50 charge; the cost of credit reports will be reduced to $2.00 from $3.00; and the number of collections done by the firm will be reduced substantially. Because of the reduced costs and the added accuracy of the computer system, it is expected that the local credit agencies will begin using NERCC's services more frequently through franchised operations.

Daunt also noted that the computer system was a modular system. Because of the modularity, the storage capacity for the system could be increased, as need be, to an almost infinite size. In addition, eventually it might be possible for the system to tie into planned systems in other areas of the country.

When Kleinglass asked Daunt to explain how the firm was going to ensure (1) that the system contained only accurate information, (2) that access to that information would be made only by authorized users and for authorized purposes, and (3) that an individual could correct erroneous information, Daunt explained that the rights of the individual would be amply protected and that the system was "errorproof." He further stated that the system complied with the Fair Credit Reporting Act of April, 1971. In addition, the data base will contain a credit history of the individual containing both positive and negative items of objective information, and will *not* contain any *subjective* information, as most traditional credit reporting agencies usually include.

Following this meeting, Kleinglass reported to the CLPS. He first distributed copies of a summary of the Fair Credit Reporting Act (Exhibit

C) and remarked that, if complied with, this act would protect the rights of privacy of the individual. In his report he stated that the need for credit information was, indeed, required for the effective operation of business and industry in the country. However, the past history of NERCC with respect to errors in their files raised a number of questions about the possible effect on the privacy of the citizens of New England. It was suggested that the CLPS work with NERCC to ensure that they complied with the Fair Credit Reporting Act. One board member recommended that the CLPS supply a computer programmer to NERCC to work with their staff in the development of the computer system and its related computer programs. Finally, it was decided that Kleinglass should approach Daunt with the offer of the computer programmer.

During the next two weeks, Kleinglass attempted to contact Daunt on several occasions. Daunt did not respond to over a dozen telephone calls and two letters. Kohanek and another member of the board received similar results when they attempted to contact Daunt.

On July 26, 1974, the CLPS petitioned Judge Warren Perry of Boston's Federal District Court to issue an injunction against the further development of the computer system by NERCC. In their petition, they stated that the central ingredient in a credit-reporting system was that the information about the individual be complete and accurate. The CLPS petition argued that the history of NERCC's activities showed a lack of concern for maintaining any standards of completeness or accuracy. Furthermore, the CLPS continued, it appears that the proposed system does not comply with the intent of the Fair Credit Reporting Act. A number of questions were raised: What personal information will the NERCC system include in credit reports? How accurate is the information reported by them? How complete are the derogatory entries in the file? What procedures are available for handling items of information which involve disputes between businesses and the consumer? And what precautions have been taken to prevent unauthorized access to NERCC's files?

The petition also pointed out that the system would have the capability of continuously monitoring various consumers with the intent of notifying all creditors when the consumer became late in any of the accounts that he owed. The petition stated that this would cause creditors to demand more rapid payments and would force individual bankruptcy upon many individuals unnecessarily. Further abuses of the system could also be possible.

CLPS asked the court to enjoin the system development until such time as these issues were cleared up to the satisfaction of the court, and appoint a panel to inspect the development of the system when, and if, it were given the go-ahead. Judge Perry then gave NERCC 48 hours to respond.

EXHIBIT A

Long and Retz Associates, Inc.
Consultants to Business and Industry
1272 Avenue of the Americas
New York, New York 10012

January 15, 1974

John P. Daunt, President
New England Retail Credit Corporation
Waltham, Massachusetts 01789

Dear Mr. Daunt:

Enclosed is the final report of a study conducted by Long and Retz. As the study is quite lengthy, I have decided to summarize a few of the major points made in the report.

Our study involved a review of your current operating practices, trends in retail credit in New England, your position within the industry, and different operating practices that you might follow. The results presented in our report are for each year from your inception in 1945 through December 31, 1973, with the time from 1974 to 1990 estimated. These estimates were based on currently available statistics and an evaluation of current trends. We believe that these estimates have a high degree of accuracy.

It is quite obvious that your firm is not operating as effectively as it once did. Net income as a percentage of sales has continually been declining, with the largest declines in recent years. In addition, net income itself declined in 1972 for the first time in the company's operating history and continued declining in 1973.

There are two principal reasons for the decline. First, the volume of your business is growing so rapidly that your current manual operating procedures have become ineffective. This large increase has caused an increased percentage of errors in reporting and caused an increase in the amount of time that it takes to respond to an inquiry or to make a credit report. For the period through 1960, less than 5 percent of your records contained errors in some form or another. Yet, in a sample taken during 1973, 37.6 percent of the records were in error. In 1960 inquiries were processed in an average of 7 minutes and it now takes approximately 18 minutes. Credit reporting has seen a similar increase. A report in 24 hours was nearly always possible in 1960, but it seldom is now. Most often reports are turned out within 48 hours but some have been as long as 96 hours.

Secondly, NERCC is facing a tremendous cost squeeze. The cost of labor has pushed your costs up rapidly but income has been unable to expand. You cannot increase the costs of your service as you are competing with many local credit bureaus and a rapidly increasing number of banks that provide the same service.

After World War II, installment loans became part of virtually every American's liabilities. Increased home buying also produced many more home mortgages. Thus, the ratio of private debt to GNP has grown from 69.4

TABLE I.   Ratio of private debt to GNP (in billions of dollars)

Year	Private Debt	GNP	% of GNP
1945	147	212	69.4
1950	221	284	77.7
1955	372	398	93.5
1960	597	503	118.5
1965	883	681	129.4
1970	1299	974	133.2
1975(e)	1787	1286	138.8
1980(e)	2261	1607	140.4
1985(e)	2790	1946	143.1
1990(e)	3321	2391	144.9

percent in 1945 to over 135 percent today (Table I). While this growth should continue, it is expected to only reach 145 percent by 1990. However, due to the large increases in the GNP, private debt will increase by almost three-fold from 1970 to 1990. Conditions within the New England area are parallel to those of the nation. The large increases in your early years of operation are a direct result of this increase in installment loans and home buying and NERCC should put itself in a position to profit from future growth in these two areas.

Since you started operations, NERCC has been the largest credit-reporting agency in New England. A summary of your business activity appears in Table II. While NERCC remains number one, your business activity as a per-centage of the total New England business is declining (Table III). This is largely attributed to an increase in local credit bureaus and the increase in credit information supplied by banks.

After reviewing your firm and the credit-reporting practices in New England, we find only two avenues open to NERCC. In what we call "Option A," you could continue operations as they currently exist. This, however, will lead to smaller profits in 1974 and substantial losses beginning in 1975 (Table IV). Option A is the "Bankruptcy" option.

Option B provides an exciting approach to credit information reporting, as well as satisfying the needs of businesses and individuals in the area and making NERCC a profitable firm once again. From our discussions with banks and local credit bureaus, it has been determined that a need exists for a central depository of credit information and a quick procedure for accessing it. No organization now exists that can fill this need and NERCC is the only firm that has the potential.

Initially, a computer system will be put in your home office. All currently available data would be converted to machine readable form. Once that phase is completed, video display tubes will be put in your branch offices and a few selected banks and local credit bureaus. These tubes will allow the user to request information from the computer. They will then receive the most up-to-date credit information that NERCC has on the individual.

By typing a special code, a complete credit report will be generated on the computer in your home office and then be sent to the requester. Additions and deletions to the information will be transmitted from the various remote locations via the terminals, verified by your staff, and then entered into the computer system.

While this computer system introduces more opportunity for control than the hazards of the old procedures, it also provides a number of other benefits. Among them are:

1. Credit information will be at the grantor's fingertips which, of course, will save him time and the time of the individual applying for credit.

2. Fewer loans will be granted to high-risk individuals as a result of more up-to-date information.

3. Charges for this service can be reduced substantially due to, first, a reduction in the number of employees required to handle requests by approximately one-half and, secondly, the increased effectiveness of the system.

TABLE II. Business activity (options A & B included)

Year	Inquiries	Credit Reports	Collections Number	Collections Dollars
1950	38,146	11,441	156	$ 15,674
1955	78,443	22,373	469	$ 52,646
1960	131,396	30,490	1276	$ 171,592
1965	259,482	59,387	2819	$ 421,937
1970	612,561	151,076	2746	$ 549,114
1971	758,792	197,145	2611	$ 548,792
1972	912,356	226,780	2697	$ 593,345
1973	1,125,000	281,000	2500	$ 527,000
Option A				
1974(e)	1,337,000	343,000	2425	511,675
1975(e)	1,601,000	397,000	2350	498,200
1976(e)	1,937,000	482,000	2300	507,400
1977(e)	2,216,000	573,000	2250	518,600
1980(e)	3,236,000	806,000	2000	600,000
1985(e)	6,841,000	1,732,000	2500	875,000
1990(e)	15,896,000	4,001,000	3000	1,200,000
Option B				
1974(e)	1,400,000	360,000	2450	513,000
1975(e)	3,225,000	795,000	2800	735,000
1976(e)	4,149,000	1,035,000	3200	780,000
1977(e)	5,456,000	1,362,000	3600	825,000
1980(e)	8,891,000	2,345,000	6200	1,112,000
1985(e)	17,675,000	4,880,000	12,300	2,775,000
1990(e)	46,900,000	11,375,000	18,550	4,995,000

TABLE III.   NERCC's business activity as a percent of New England activity (options A & B included)

Year	Inquiries	Credit Reports	Collections
1950	7.1	7.4	6.2
1955	12.9	12.6	13.7
1960	26.4	26.1	31.4
1965	30.7	31.2	37.8
1970	31.4	30.7	32.6
1971	30.3	30.8	30.2
1972	30.2	29.7	28.9
1973	29.7	30.2	26.4
Option A			
1974(e)	29.4	29.1	24.6
1975(e)	29.0	29.6	21.7
1980(e)	26.0	25.4	12.0
1985(e)	24.7	25.1	8.1
1990(e)	23.2	22.8	6.0
Option B			
1974(e)	29.5	29.2	24.1
1975(e)	57.0	56.8	23.1
1980(e)	74.1	73.7	35.7
1985(e)	74.6	74.2	39.2
1990(e)	71.8	72.3	36.3

4. As costs come down, more requests will come in and more local credit bureaus and banks will become more interested in becoming a part of the system.

In conjunction with the establishment of the computer system, we urge that NERCC substantially cut back the collection segment of the business. This segment of the business has become a haven for illegal activities in other firms. Therefore, NERCC's collection business is also looked upon by some as illegal. It is suggested that, as a courtesy to clients, collection accounts be telephoned twice and then, if not collected, labeled as a "difficult" account and turned over to an agency specializing in difficult account collection.

While the above is very brief, the complete report gives details of our study and the resulting suggestions. If there should be any questions, please feel free to contact me. As always, Long and Retz Associates, Inc. is ready and able to serve you.

Sincerely,

Robert T. Long
President

TABLE IV. Income projections (000's omitted)

Year	Inquiries	Reports	Collections	Total	Expenses	Net Income
1950	57	33	5	95	71	24
1955	117	66	18	201	148	53
1960	196	91	57	344	263	81
1965	390	180	141	711	569	142
1970	918	450	183	1551	1344	207
1971	1137	600	182	1919	1707	212
1972	1368	775	191	2334	2148	186
1973	1687	840	176	2703	2562	141
Option A						
1974(e)	2005	1012	170	3187	3161	26
1975(e)	2402	1200	166	3768	3871	(103)
1976(e)	2905	1446	169	4520	4848	(328)
1977(e)	3324	1719	172	5215	6058	(843)
1980(e)	4848	2412	200	7460	8880	(1420)
1985(e)	10261	5196	291	15748	19958	(4210)
1990(e)	23844	12003	400	36247	43747	(7500)
Option B						
1974(e)	1250	720	171	2141	3850	(1709)
1975(e)	2419	1590	245	4254	4120	134
1976(e)	3086	2070	260	5416	5019	397
1977(e)	4101	2724	275	7100	6246	854
1980(e)	6668	4690	371	11729	8620	3109
1985(e)	13256	9760	925	23941	17165	6776
1990(e)	35200	27750	1665	59615	37430	22185

EXHIBIT B

New England Retail Credit Corporation
Credit Report

NAME_Sharpe, John J._____   DATE_6/13/74_____
ADDRESS_365 Maple Street_____   AGE___40_____
_____Brandon, MA 01356_____   S.S.N._15-056-0609_____
WIFE__Martha_____   DEPENDENTS_5_____
TELEPHONE_413-762-9873_____

PREVIOUS_63 Fredrick Street_____
ADDRESS_Rumney, N. H. 02273_____

EMPLOYER_Atlas Sand & Gravel Co.   POSITION_Foreman_____
_____Brandon, MA 01356_____   SALARY__$245/week (a/o 2/1/74)
SINCE_____January 12, 1961_____

MORTGAGE OR_Federal Savings Bank   ORIGINAL_$21,500_____
RENT FROM____Brandon, MA 01356____   CURRENT_$16,757 (a/o 2/1/74)__
PAYMENT_____$252 pit_____

WIFE'S_Brandon Gift Shop_____   POSITION_Clerk_____
EMPLOYER_167 Main Street_____   SALARY_$1.95/hr. (a/o 2/1/74)_
_____Brandon, MA 01356_____

CHECKING_First National Bank____   AMOUNT_$35.89 (a/o 6/13/74)__
_____Brandon, MA 01356_____

SAVINGS____Federal Savings Bank____   AMOUNT_$842.13 (a/o 6/13/74)_
_____Brandon, MA 01356_____

IN FILE SINCE:_1966_____   LAST CHECKED:__2/1/74_____
INQUIRIES:_Sears 2/66; 7/69; 11/73; FSB 1/66; IRS 6/69; Davis Ford
_____8/66; 10/68; 3/71; 2/74_____

CREDITORS	OPEN	HIGH	BALANCE	TERMS	RATINGS
Fed. Sav. Bk	21500	21500	16757	360@185	R-1
Sears	156	482	266	36@21	R-2
BankAm.		652	114		R-2
B&B Fuel		382	214	12@62	R-1
Mobil		112	54		R-1
Exxon		23			R-1
Singer	457	457	186	24@21	R-2
Ford M.C.	2600	3150	2213	24@116	R-2

PUBLIC RECORDS:_Small Claims 2/69 Acme TV $385.00 Pd. 4/69
_____Speeding Ticket 8/71 Fined $25.00 9/71_____

REMARKS:__Consistent low bal. in checking and savings_____
_____Youngest child is a mongoloid_____
_____Dentist refuses to report_____
_____Family reported to be nudists._____

EXHIBIT C

SUMMARY OF FAIR CREDIT REPORTING ACT*

Purpose

To insure that consumer reporting agencies exercise their grave responsibilities with fairness, impartiality, and a respect for the consumer's right to privacy.

Requirements

1. *Accuracy of Information* — reasonable procedures must be followed to insure maximum possible accuracy of the individual's information.

2. *Obsolete Information* — certain terms of adverse information may not be included after they have reached specified "ages" (i.e., 7 years old for paid tax liens).

3. *Limited Uses of Information* — a report about an individual can only be used for the following purposes:

   a) in response to a court order;
   b) from written instruction of the individual;
   c) to determine the individual's eligibility for (i) credit or insurance, (ii) employment, including promotion, or (iii) a license or other benefit for which the law requires a consideration of the individual's financial status;
   d) to meet a legitimate business need for a business transaction involving the individual.

4. *Notices to Individuals* — whenever credit, insurance, or employment is denied, information is reported that might adversely affect his employment, or an investigation report (including interviews with neighbors, friends, etc.) is prepared, he must be so notified in advance.

5. *Individual's Right of Access to Information* — the individual has the right to be informed of the nature and substance, the sources, and recipients of information about him whether or not adverse action has been taken.

6. *Individual's Right to Contest Information* — when a dispute arises concerning the accuracy or completeness of information, the agency must reinvestigate and record the current status. If this does not resolve the dispute, the individual has the right to file a brief statement explaining the dispute.

---

*Portions extracted from: *Records, Computers, and the Rights of Citizens,* Report of the Secretary's Advisory Committee on Automated Personal Data Systems, U.S. Department of Health, Education, and Welfare, July, 1973, p. 66–69.

PART 3
SOCIAL DECISION-
MAKING AND
MEASUREMENT

12. *Social Policy and Decision-Making*

Despite the wealth of material in the area of social responsibility, social involvement, and the exhortation to corporations to behave in a socially responsible manner, surprisingly little research is available that shows how corporations or managers have responded, in terms of a systematic organizational or policy sense, either to social responsibility in general or to specific social issues in particular. And there is very little that prescribes planning, policy, or decision processes that executives might use—such literature being derived from either experimental studies, trial-and-error analysis, or just plain armchair moralizing.

Some studies have been done that have attempted to trace the policy-making process in corporate social involvement and the development of organizational procedures and relationships for handling social issues. Callaghan, for example, undertook to study the donative activity of six insurance companies, ranging from the major ones in the industry to some of the smaller firms. His findings included that the policy process and organizational relationships and controls varied widely and were typically not up to the calibre of more traditional managerial functions.* In another study, Edwin A. Murray used the social-response process, as described in an article by Robert Ackerman (Ackerman's article is included in the readings of this section), to research minority loans in two large New York commercial banks.† Murray, using Ackerman's framework as

---

*Callaghan, D. W., *Management of the Corporate Gift-Giving Function: An Empirical Study in the Life Insurance Industry.* Doctoral dissertation (University of Massachusetts at Amherst, 1975).

†Murray, E. A., Jr., "The social-response process in commercial banks: An empirical investigation," *Academy of Management Review,* July, 1976.

a guide, described the policy-institutionalization phases as follows: *Policy Phase* — The Chief Executive Officer takes an interest in the issue and spans the boundary between environment and organization; *Learning Phase* — Senior management designates a specialist to head a separate staff unit to institute social activity; *Administrative Learning* — Newly developed procedures are promulgated, and the staff units offer line units technical assistance; *Institutionalization Phase* — Chief Executive Officer instills a sustained organizational commitment to a specific social issue by adopting (or adapting organizational *performance measures* to activity.

In another study presently being conducted, six firms in six different industries are being analyzed to determine how a social issue was first injected into a company — at what level and under what circumstances — and, if it became an ongoing program, the process by which a one-time situation became institutionalized and standardized as company policy.

The most important aspects of social decision-making, however, concern the effects that social parameters have when they are injected into the traditional types of decisions that business managers have always been making. Occupational safety and health regulations affect and redirect plant construction, equipment purchases, and maintenance policy; zoning and planning on the local level affect not only the location of plants and facilities, but their design and beautification as well; equal-opportunity and affirmative action are often not separate social programs *per se,* but are instead integrated into the more traditional hiring and personnel policies and procedures of a business organization. The same can be said for most of the other issues we have covered in this book. With the exception of singular programs such as donations, voluntary allocations of organizational resources to nonbusiness or nonprofit-related activities, and similar types of organizational responses, most of the social factors have effects throughout the total organization and on most of the regular business decisions that the managers within that organization will make.

THE RATIONAL APPROACH TO SOCIAL ISSUES

Suffice it to say that business managers are *not* the omniscient, ever-present figures of classical economic doctrine, as discussed in Section I of this book. Nonetheless, managers are expected to make logical, calculated decisions, even in the context of the uncertainties that are characteristic of the firm's social environment. Whether pro-acting or reacting to environmental forces, the manager is entrusted with the task of making decisions such that, in the long run, benefits derived from the decisions outweigh the costs.

In the ideal, managerial processes are dictated by the "rational" model. Essentially, the model prescribes a sequence of steps to be followed that form a logical chain. Figure 1 presents a simplified schematic of this chain.

To cover all, or even many, of the implications of the model for socioeconomic decision-making, would be a formidable task, and is not to be undertaken here. But brief examination of its major elements may serve to provide some insight into the value of its use in the social arena.

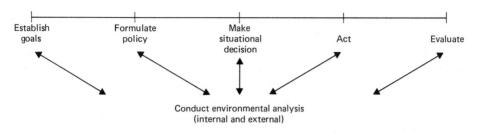

Fig. 1   The rational model.

ESTABLISH GOALS

First of all, the rational model adheres to the notion of goal-directed behavior; that is, that behavior of the firm and the individuals within it is and should be purposeful, directed toward the accomplishment of goals or objectives. To the extent that those goals are made explicit, the process followed is more rational.

Goals themselves are generally hierarchical, with lower-order goals dictated in part by higher-order goals. Thus, for example, the firm that establishes employment quotas (goals) for minority hiring may do so as a *means* of meeting affirmative-action guidelines (higher-order goals). In turn, the latter may simply be a means to achieve yet higher-order goals, be they retention of a government contract, improvement of regional minority employment, or any others.

Establishing goals may, at first glance, appear simple enough. But in the context of corporate social action, it is often extremely difficult. Witness the great debate over the general purpose of the firm, as discussed in Section I. Often the vagaries of abstraction force confusion of the means–end relationship of goals, so that much of their value is lost, if indeed they can be stated at all. For example, what higher-order goal or goals are being served by the establishment of a corporate charitable contribution program? Are they simply profit-oriented? Are they nonprofit-oriented? If the latter, then what are they?

While the rational model would dictate that these higher-order goals be made explicit (indeed, *prior* to the establishment of lower-order objectives), they often are not, in practice. Instead, managerial decision-makers often establish lower-order objectives, assuming or speculating that they are indeed purposeful, according to some unspecified greater purpose. Actually, that is all that is necessary if the criteria of rationality are to be applied only at the level of an individual decision. Thus, for example, once a firm establishes a pollution-emission level and a target date, the purpose behind that emission level *may* be irrelevant when it comes down to purchasing abatement equipment. The emission level itself establishes that which is to be served by acquiring the equipment.

FORMULATE POLICY

Policy-making itself is a decision process that involves the establishment of standing guides for decision-making and action. Policies are designed to ensure that behavior is goal-directed, and relatively consistent and predictable. Policies may be formal, written statements or informal, implied mandates. In either case, they are essential to the rational model.

Following the rational construct, we find firms often establishing policies in regard to the conduct of employment interviews, prohibiting the gathering of information that is either questionable or clearly unacceptable in the eyes of the law. This policy may serve a number of goals simultaneously, not the least of which may be the minimization of litigation and legal penalties. Other policies may be of a nonrestrictive, positive nature, such as requiring that all middle-management employees directly serve their local communities in some fashion each year. Whether restrictive or positive, those policies are designed to provide guidelines for situational decisions.

Of course, in practice, the formulation of policies to guide decision-making in all situations is impossible. Witness, for example, the difficulties in establishing a code of conduct (a formal policy statement) for business managers, as described in an earlier chapter. Or think about the difficulty in establishing all-encompassing policies just in regard to product labeling. Obviously, if carried to rational extremes these would be never-ending, yet essential, tasks.

MAKE SITUATIONAL DECISIONS

Given goals and guiding policies, the rational model calls for the situational decision, in that sequence. Here, for example, we find the process of deciding upon an employment candidate, a plant location, a product package, a response to a protest group, a lobbying scheme, and so on.

In a fully rational sense, this step is to be carried out by (1) identifying the problem and constraints; (2) identifying all alternative courses of action; (3) determining the outcome of each alternative; and (4) selecting the most appropriate action — all within the context of goals and policies.

Obviously, making decisions in this fashion is impossible in a strict sense. Given the manager's lack of omniscience, steps 2 and 3 are a realistic absurdity. Nonetheless, the more information available in a decision situation, the more rational the process. If, by this juncture, you have studied the dilemma of U.S. business in South Africa, think, for example, about the mass of social, political, and economic information needed to make a decision regarding locating a plant there. Or think about the many parameters and factors involved in designing work on an assembly line.

ACT, EVALUATE, AND REFORMULATE

Once a decision is made, action (or inaction, as the decision dictates) must follow. This, in turn, is followed by evaluation of the action itself, its results, and the implications those results have on goals, policies, and later decisions.

At the evaluation stage, goals and policies established earlier form the criteria for evaluating the decision. If, for example, a particular stack-scrubber was chosen and installed to meet a specified particulate-emission level, was consistent with company policy to buy from U.S. manufacturers, and was in fact effective in both regards, then, from the standpoint of those two simplistic criteria, the decision and action were rational.

But evaluation must extend further than just the most immediate decision. Evaluation of goals and policies also must be undertaken continuously to ensure continuity and complementarity. One would wish to avoid conflicting policies such as those where existing seniority-based layoff policies conflict with those of affirmative action. Or where energy-conservation procedures smack head on with pollution-abatement procedures. This, then, becomes a never-ending task which is essential to the rational process. The next chapter discusses social accounting and social audit as general techniques for evaluation and control of the sort required by the rational model.

CONDUCT ENVIRONMENTAL ANALYSIS

While last in our discussion here, environmental analysis is a critical part of the entire process set forth in the ideal model, and forms a basis for carrying out all the other steps. Essentially, environmental analysis involves scanning, forecasting, general information-gathering, and deciphering, for the purpose of identifying both internal and external *threats* and *opportunities*. In large part, this book has been directed at developing, through exercise, the skills involved in such analysis.

We examine South Africa, for example, in the context of the opportunities available for U.S. business firms there, and the threats to those firms as a result of racial and political strife. We examine not only the threats associated with energy shortages, but the opportunities that lie in the solution to those shortages, and so on.

It should be clear by now that *information* is essential to analyzing the business environment. If anything, lack of knowledge poses the most serious deterrent to compliance with the rational model. And proper information gathering obviously cannot be confined to a weekly news magazine or textbooks. It is a life-long proposition for the operating manager on whom rests the responsibility for the quality of proaction and reaction to environmental forces.

IN SUM

Since this is not a business-policy textbook, nor a discourse on management principles, we have confined our discussion to a very simple, albeit valuable, model for social decision-making and policy formulation. Indeed, the rational model serves as the ideal for *all* managerial decision-related activity and, as such, is not confined to the socioeconomic arena. While its value lies in its relative simplicity and prescriptive nature, it is, in fact, an ideal rarely exercised in pure fashion in executive suites. But we'll not pontificate on alternatives. After having examined many of the issues addressed in the text cases and elsewhere, any student should be well aware how nonrational (not necessarily irrational) decisions are made.

THE READINGS

The first selection, "How Companies Respond to Social Demands," by Robert Ackerman, uses a model to describe how social issues become effectively handled within a business firm. Ackerman's findings indicate a pattern of response that includes the issue becoming a policy matter through Chief Executive

Officer interest, the hiring and charging of a staff specialist in the area of social concern, and then finally, organizational involvement. Ackerman then includes some guidelines for strategy for injecting social issues into policy.

The second article, Ramon Aldag and Donald Jackson's "A Managerial Framework for Social Decision-Making," offers a decision-flow chart for making social decisions, along with a series of challenging questions to be answered in the decision-making process.

How Companies Respond to Social Demands

Edicts from on high and staff activity don't effect change; it has to be 'institutionalized' in the operating units

Robert W. Ackerman

As concerns of society like clean air, fair employment, and honesty in packaging are thrust on U.S. business with growing intensity and frequency, corporations are finding it very difficult to integrate responses to these demands into their regular operating procedures. This is especially true of the large, decentralized companies, whose profit-center managers are reluctant to change their procedures as long as they are judged on their bottom-line performance. This article is based on a year of intensive study of a number of large companies that are wrestling with this problem. The author analyzes the painful response process that starts with futile attempts from the top to accomplish change and ends (if the organization is adaptive) with the institutionalization of the new corporate policy at the operating level.

The president of a consumer goods company and the manager of one of its divisions were confronted recently with different but equally uncomfortable problems.

The former had been an early supporter of fair employment, especially in respect to minority hiring and training. He devoted much time to federal and state commissions locating job opportunities for minorities in the business community. The company from time to time had assisted minority enterprises in various ways and, on his initiative, had accepted a government contract to operate a job training center.

The president had communicated in strong terms his commitment to a policy of equal employment at all levels in his organization, and he had received general support for it. Despite these efforts, he felt that the company's record in

Reprinted by permission of the publisher from the *Harvard Business Review,* Vol. 51, No. 4, July–August, 1973. © 1973 by the President and Fellows of Harvard College; all rights reserved.

hiring blacks and other minority group members and advancing them into management positions left much to be desired.

He pondered how to close the gap between his public statements and the indications he received of actual performance. He also worried about the impact—tangible and intangible—of stricter government enforcement.

The division manager's problem was in some respects more difficult. He managed one of seven operating units in the company and was responsible for six plants, several dozen sales offices, and 2,200 employees. Each year, he and his management group assembled a plan that included a financial projection supported by an environmental analysis and a strategy for achieving the goals. After negotiations, top management and division management agreed on somewhat revised figures as the division's performance commitment for the coming year. Although the division manager took pains to keep the president and others on the corporate staff alerted to major strategic developments or changes in the forecasts, he was expected to take responsibility for managing the business.

The division manager understood and agreed with the president's position on equal employment. In view of the diversity of attitudes and values in his organization, he became convinced that the only way of implementing the president's policy was to agree on minority hiring and advancement targets with each of his manufacturing, sales, and administrative managers, and to hold them accountable for the results.

He had not, however, taken this step. He rationalized that the plants operated against very tight budgets; as long as a plant performed well on this measure, the plant manager knew he would win praise, earn pay raises, and preserve his relative autonomy. For several reasons the division manager was unwilling to disturb this arrangement by appearing to put limits on the plant managers' autonomy in choosing their subordinates. He was equally reluctant to insist on the hiring of minority salesmen, thus risking damage to the sales managers' commitment to meeting volume targets. At least for the time being, the task of establishing standards and getting action was left to government enforcement agencies.

This familiar illustration is not unique to this company or issue. By rearranging the situation, I could present comparable cases for other organizations struggling with pollution control, occupational health and safety, consumerism, and so forth.

The U.S. corporation is faced with a twofold dilemma:

- The organizational innovations enabling it to manage growing product diversity and to adopt to technological, economic, and competitive change may inhibit effective responses to societal concerns.

- The need or desire to absorb a growing array of societal demands into its operations—affecting product design and marketing policy, to name just two—may reduce its effectiveness as a producer of goods and services.

When a company falls victim to either of these dangers, the cause, in my view, lies in the difficulty of the management tasks involved, rather than moral or ideological intransigence. In the long run, the more successful corporations will be those that can achieve both social responsiveness and good economic performance.

In the remainder of this article, I shall first sharpen the issue by providing a framework for thinking about the managerial problems created by social responsiveness. Then I shall describe the response patterns I observed during a year of field research in corporations attempting to implement programs covering a variety of social concerns. Finally, I shall offer suggestions for improving the management of this difficult process.

My primary concern will be with the large U.S. corporation. This is not because small enterprises are lacking in social or economic impact, but because the concentration of resources in large companies and the prominence of their chief executives often endow them with positions of leadership and make them inviting targets for critics. Moreover, for larger companies the internal dilemmas are the most acute.

A POOR FIT

Periodically in our history, the scope of corporate accountability has been extended. The rapid expansion of the labor movement in the 1930's is one obvious example among many manifestations of social change that businessmen had to assimilate during the Depression years. So, if the responsive corporation managed to adapt to them without serious damage, is not our problem today merely one of relearning the solutions to old problems? I think the answer is *no* — not so much because of the intensity of public expectations as because of the radically changed configuration of today's large corporation.

According to recent studies, the divisionalized organization has rapidly replaced the functionalized organization as the dominant formal structure among the largest U.S. industrial corporations.* Exhibit I shows the dramatic shift.

The adoption of the divisionalized structure, a result of the sharp swing toward diversification, has been accompanied by important modifications in the internal dynamics of the corporation and in the assignment of responsibilities for responding to environmental change.†

But the results have not always been satisfactory. A prime reason is the poor fit of social responsiveness into the modus operandi of the decentralized company. In its attempt to fashion flexible and creative responses to changing social demands, top management faces three main problems. I have summarized these in Exhibit II and shall explain them in some detail:

1. *The separation of corporate and division responsibilities is threatened.* In the illustration cited at the beginning of this article, the barriers between corporate and division offices had been built on mutual consent. The division manager, in exchange for the opportunity to run his own show and the promise of rewards if

---

*Richard P. Rumelt, *Strategy, Structure, and Economic Performance* (unpublished DBA dissertation, Harvard Business School, Boston, 1972).

†For a discussion of this transition, see Bruce R. Scott, "The Industrial State: Old Myths and New Realities," HBR March–April 1973, p. 133.

Exhibit I
Structure of the Fortune "500" companies in three time periods

Organization	Estimated percentage of companies		
Structure	1949	1959	1969
Functional	62.7%	36.3%	11.2%
Functional with subsidiaries	13.4	12.6	9.4
Product division	19.8	47.6	75.5
Geographic division	.4	2.1	1.5
Holding company	3.7	1.4	2.4
Total	100.0%	100.0%	100.0%

Exhibit II
Critical aspects of managing corporate responses to social demands in a decentralized company

Existing management patterns	Problems in responding to social issues

Allocation of responsibilities

Corporate level: secures division performance commitments and monitors the results, while fostering operating autonomy.

Divisional level: formulates strategy for the division's business and accepts responsibility for achieving the results.

A corporatewide responsibility is implied, with the demand or desire for a corporatewide response. But that response involves operations, and implementation is possible only at divisional levels.

Management through systems

Division performance is monitored by financial reporting systems that are:

related to division commitments

amenable to corporatewide aggregation

reasonably simple to communicate and understand.

Social costs and benefits are often not amenable to financial measures or planing:

Current expenditures are real; long-run benefits are uncertain.

Benefits may be general and not related to the spending unit.

Executive performance evaluation

Performance of assigned responsibilities—often measured through the financial reporting system—is reinforced by incentive compensation and is the determinant of career paths in the organization.

Benefits of social responsiveness may appear in time frames longer than the manager's tenure in his job.

Current expenditures of time and money may penalize the financial performance to which the organization is committed.

Trade-offs are required which involve values and judgments on which managers may reasonably differ.

he did it well, had shouldered the responsibility for achieving agreed-on results. The president was then relieved of the task of formulating and implementing strategy in a number of (possibly unfamiliar) businesses and devoted his attention to matters of companywide interest.

However, as a result of the president's public statements and actions concerning equal employment, the world assumed he was responsible for seeing that it was accomplished in his organization. Successes or failures anywhere in the corporation reflected on him. Yet performance in employment opportunity—as in most areas of social concern—was closely related to operating decisions that had been delegated to managers down the line.

How can any president ensure an effective corporatewide response without interfering with his division managers? Should he choose to use the influence of his office, what effect would it have on the commitments he could expect for the achievement of corporate financial goals? Sharing the responsibility for social responsiveness may entail making traditional responsibilities more ambiguous. That is a result which most managers naturally want to avoid.

2. *The financial reporting system is inadequate.* Divisionalized companies rely heavily on sophisticated financial reporting systems to monitor the performance of operating units. Indeed, the flow of plans, budgets, and accounting reports often constitutes the primary dialogue between corporate and division offices.

However reliable the reporting system may be in measuring operating unit performance against financial goals, not only is it ineffective in measuring social responsiveness, but by and large it is irrelevant. Analysis of a division's financial statements provides little indication of its effectiveness (however that may be judged) in controlling waste emissions, providing safe working conditions, or manufacturing safe products.

Aggregation of the direct costs of programs related to social commitments is getting increased attention. For instance, one large packaging company isolates the projected expenditures for pollution control equipment in the capital budget (though the associated operating costs are not reflected in the projected income statement). A bank keeps track of expenses associated with its community relations program. The results, however, are at best incomplete, even on the cost side, and little progress has been made in the measurement of social benefits. Nor are substantial breakthroughs to be expected in the near future.*

The obvious alternative is to create new measures of social responsiveness for each area of concern. Aside from whatever methodological problems such an attempt might pose, the result would be an enormous increase in the complexity of managing the organization—assuming that each reporting system was taken seriously. That, again, is a result most managers would prefer to avoid.

3. *The executive performance, evaluation, and reward process is challenged.* This dilemma is in part an outgrowth of the first two and is perhaps the most difficult to resolve.

---

*See Raymond A. Bauer and Dan H. Fenn, Jr., "What *Is* a Corporate Social Audit?" HBR January–February 1973, p. 37.

In the case of the company whose situation was described at the beginning of this article, the division manager participated in setting the standards to be used in evaluating the performance of his unit, and he secured commitments of support from his subordinates. He was not assuming that their behavior was predicated solely on the desire to meet the budget; their needs and satisfactions were defined in much broader and subtler ways. So he did not evaluate their performance solely in terms of the bottom line. Yet financial appraisal was an important tool for securing the subordinates' support in the pursuit of the division's strategy. The division manager was reluctant to insist on minority hiring and advancement quotas which he felt would introduce new restrictions, ambiguities, and, possibly, discord into the process of evaluating his managers.

How can an organization obtain its middle managers' support for social responsiveness if their careers do not in some explicit way depend on it? A division manager in a large electronics company made the point to me very clearly: "Look, let's start with the idea that I don't need pollution control equipment or minorities to run my business. If the company wants me to do these things, they'll have to make it worth my while."

PATTERN OF RESPONSE

There is an argument that appears to justify ignoring the administrative implications of managing corporate responsiveness. It holds that social expectations for business's behavior become legitimate only when the government requires compliance, and to the extent that governmental regulations exact penalties, a social issue is converted into an economic one and so can be managed just like any other business problem. The fallacy in this reasoning lies in the premise that corporate *action* on social issues is either voluntary or required. In fact, during the period when responsiveness is most important, it is neither.

For every issue there is a time period before it becomes a matter of social concern, and espousing the issue may even arouse economic and social sanctions. There is also a time when its acceptance is so widespread that adherence is an unquestioned part of doing business. (Child labor laws create little anxiety in 1973.)

Between those two points there is a period of uncertainty as to the strength and durability of public support for the issue, standards of socially acceptable behavior, timing of desired confirmity, and the technologies or resources available for complying. This period might be called a zone of discretion, in which the signals the company receives from the environment are unclear. It cannot avoid responding in some way, but it still has discretion in the timing and strength of the response.

The history of federal air pollution control legislation is one current example. The first national standards and enforcement provisions appeared in the 1963 Clean Air Act; it was another four years before the Air Quality Act strengthened them; and three more before nationwide ambient air standards were established, to be fully effective in 1975. Regulations have also been imposed at the state and local levels, frequently permitting variances for those facilities with the "latest available technology"—itself a changing standard. So for many years, while the federal legislation was evolving, corporations were engaged in activities affecting air quality and had choices whether to alter them.

A number of social issues have progressed so far through the zone of discretion that their final dimensions are beginning to take shape. Equal employment and ecology are two examples, although even in these instances great uncertainty remains as to the intensity of enforcement and the ultimate standards to be applied. Other issues are much less well defined.

Based on intensive observations in several companies that have been recognized as leaders in managing those social issues of particular relevance to their businesses, I think a common response pattern is developing. (The nature of these particular issues creates differences, but the similarities are far more noticeable.) There are three phases to this response process, spanning a period of at least six to eight years. The first two phases are necessary but insufficient in themselves for an effective response. I shall discuss each in turn.

1. A policy matter

First, the chief executive recognizes the issue to be important. He may rationalize his interest as a matter of corporate responsibility or as farsighted self-interest. Either way, it coincides with his recent experience, often outside his business milieu. One chief executive I know became concerned about minority opportunities during the widespread urban disturbances in the mid-1960's, when a riot took place near the company's headquarters. Several years earlier, some personnel managers had tried to generate his interest in the issue, but they had got nowhere.

The chief executive's involvement is marked by several activities. Initially, he begins to speak out on the issue at meetings of industry associations, stockholders, and civic groups. He becomes active in organizations and committees involved in studying the issue or influencing opinion on it. He may also commit corporate resources to special projects, such as ghetto businesses, waste recovery plants, and training centers.

Soon he perceives the need for an up-to-date company policy, which he takes pains to communicate to all managers in the organization. Responsibility for implementing the policy is assigned as a matter of course to the operating units as part of the customary tasks performed in running the business.

The directives from top management, couched in terms of appeals to longterm benefits and corporate responsibility, fail to provoke acceptable action or achievement. Heads nod in agreement, but the chief executive's wishes are largely ignored. Managers in the operating units lack evidence of the corporation's commitment to the cause; responsibilities are unclear, scorecards are lacking, and rewards for successes or penalties for failures are absent. The managers view as foolhardy any attempt to implement the policy at the risk of sacrificing financial and operating performance.

2. Onus on the specialist

The first phase may last for months or even years. The key event heralding the beginning of a new phase is the president's appointment of a staff executive reporting to him or one of his senior staff to coordinate the corporation's activities in the area of concern, help the chief executive perform his public duties, and, in general, "make it happen." The new manager, often a specialist in his field, carries one of a variety of titles that have recently appeared on organization charts: vice president or director of urban affairs, environmental affairs, minority relations, consumer affairs, and so on.

The vice president of urban affairs views the problem as essentially a technical one that can be attacked by isolating it and applying specialized skills and knowledge to it. He begins to gather more systematic information on the company's activities in the area and matches these data with his assessment of environmental demands. If his responsibility includes minority relations, he gets personnel statistics from the operating divisions and attempts to pinpoint where problems exist in minority representation. During the audit process, he also develops methods for systematically collecting information, which he plans to use as a control device in the future. Finally, he mediates between operating divisions and external organizations, including government agencies, that are pressing for action.

But these efforts, while not without impact or merit, do not elicit the response envisaged in the corporate policy. The staff manager's attempts to force action are so alien to the decentralized mode of decision making that he becomes overburdened with conflict and crisis-by-crisis involvement. The only arrows in his quiver, aside from his own powers of persuasion, are the corporate policy and the demands of outsiders. But line managers may consider neither one credible. One environmental control director commented to me:

> We find ourselves in a "damned if you do, damned if you don't" situation a lot of the time. We get accused by the regulators of backsliding when we argue that the company is doing the best it can. Then when we argue for a program inside the company, we get accused of giving money away. The operating managers fail to see that if they don't take steps now, the cost in the long run could be a lot greater. They hear the wolves howling out there, but they only notice the ones that get in and not the ones we're keeping outside.

Consequently, if staff proposals interfere with its operations, middle management stands aside and lets the staff take responsibility (or blame) for the results. Faced with a choice between supporting his senior line executives (who have major operating responsibilities and probably a long history of sound judgments) and his new urban affairs vice president, the chief executive usually backs up the former.

Nevertheless, the job done by the corporate specialist is essential for the eventual implementation of the policy. He crystallizes the issue for top management. He also unearths and collects a great deal of information that serves to clarify what will be expected of the corporation in the future and the techniques or technologies that will be available to fulfill those expectations.

3. Organizational involvement

The chief executive recognizes at this juncture that responsiveness entails a willingness to choose among multiple objectives and uses of resources. Fundamentally, such judgments are a general management responsibility. Top management sees the organizational rigidities to be more serious than previously acknowledged; they cannot be waved away with a policy statement nor can they be flanked by a specialist.

Instead, the whole organizational apparatus has to become involved. In this third phase, the chief executive attempts to make the achievement of policy a problem for all his managers. That is accomplished by institutionalizing policy, which I take up next.

INSTITUTIONALIZED PURPOSE

In the cases I have observed, the chief executive's problem was not winning acceptance of the new company policy; in numerous instances, managers down the line were found who, from a personal standpoint, wished the policy had been stronger. Rather, the problem was in the institutionalization of the policy—that is, working it into the process through which resources were allocated and ultimately careers decided.

A well-known characteristic of large organizations is that, unless somehow provoked to do otherwise, they tend to approach today's problems in the same way that worked yesterday, even though the context in which the new problems arise may be different. A study of the Cuban missile crisis ascribed this phenomenon to "standard operating procedures" that are enormously useful in simplifying complex problems and organizational interaction.*

To illustrate, companies with strong unions and a long history of successful labor-management relationships develop routines for processing employee grievances that grow out of the union experience. If a complaint arises alleging plant-wide discrimination, both union and management try to rephrase it in traditional terms; then they can handle it in their usual fashion.

However, the minority employees may feel that their situation will not receive the special attention they believe it warrants if they rely on a decision-making process that has failed to satisfy their needs in the past. Consequently, they avoid the union and attempt to communicate directly with executives many levels above those managers normally responsible for employee grievances. The normal reaction in such instances is to rule the employees' tactic inadmissible and insist that they "play by the rules."

This phenomenon helps to explain the stability (stated negatively, the unresponsiveness) of most large organizations. For the chief executive of the decentralized corporation, the problem of securing responsiveness to social issues is compounded by the rules governing the interrelationships between corporate and division levels. The rules state that while the chief executive is obtaining and evaluating divisional results, he is not to meddle in the divisions' standard operating procedures. If he wants to change those procedures to coincide with the spirit of the new corporate policy, he presumably must attempt it indirectly by changing the standards for judging performance.

---

*Graham Allison, *The Essence of Decision: Explaining the Cuban Missile Crisis* (Boston, Little Brown, 1972).

The chief executive does indeed try to play by the rules. This letter, written by one president to his subordinates, is a graphic illustration:

> The most significant change this year — the one that is basic to all others — is to place responsibility for achieving equal opportunity objectives where it rightfully belongs: with operating management, with each of us. Achieving these objectives is as important as meeting *any other* traditional business responsibility.
>
> It follows, of course, that a key element in each manager's overall performance appraisal will be his progress in this important area. No manager should expect a satisfactory appraisal if he meets other objectives, but fails here.

If one talks with operating managers shortly after such an announcement has been made, one finds interest in the policy but considerable skepticism about the corporation's will to enforce it. They detect gaps between pronouncement and performance:

- Since reporting on implementation of, say, a minority hiring quota cannot be integrated directly into the financial control system, it must be communicated separately. Consequently, it must compete for attention with the regular reporting system. In view of the technical problems likely to be encountered with the new procedure and the central position and historic importance of the old one, the competition may be very one-sided.

- It is doubtful that a manager who has met his economic targets will be criticized, let alone severely punished, for failure to perform adequately in the area of social concern. The president may be uttering strong words on appraisal, but it is the manager's immediate boss several layers down, not the president, who appraises him.

Creative function of trauma

In due course, a test case is encountered, though at the time it may not appear to be particularly significant. The institutionalization of purpose may hinge on the creative use of trauma. The trauma results not from the problem posed in the test case, but from the organizational dynamics through which the problem is resolved. Top-level executives suspend the rules governing their relationship with the operating divisions. For a brief period, division executives lose control of their operations: their decisions are countermanded and staff managers reporting to their superiors exercise inordinate influence in directing the outcome.

The whole affair is very unsettling for the divisions. Worst of all, questions are raised in the operating executives' minds about who really is responsible for managing the divisions' response and what the consequences may be if it is not them.

For instance, shortly after the letter quoted earlier had been sent, a smoldering controversy about minority relations erupted in a small service unit four levels down in a division. Eventually, no fewer than seven levels of line management, from the first-line supervisor to the president, were involved with their associated staffs in attempting to settle it. For a two-week period, the normal chain of command was tenuously observed. Then, the president intervened directly by issuing a decision that overturned the one announced by his subordinates. By his own forceful action, he dramatically illustrated the quality of management he expected in response to employee problems.

Intervention from the top level may not have been executed effectively in the test case, but that is not the issue. The experience has had two very beneficial results:

1. The managers in the division realized that to prevent such a fracas from recurring, they must be responsive to the issue in the future. That may mean incorporating action programs related to the issue into the division's strategy and modifying the process of evaluating the managers who are positioned to influence responsiveness directly.

2. The company has provided clues to the new standard operating procedures that it wants adopted to establish the policy in the operating units. The policy has been tested and a precedent established that can serve as a guide for its implementation throughout the corporation.

The response patterns I have described may appear to be chaotic, and, in fact, they were often characterized as such by the managers involved. Yet there is underlying order and logic to the process.

Exhibit III illustrates how a policy problem is converted into a managerial problem through the process of institutionalization. During these three phases of involvement of the organization, concern for responding to the social issue spreads from the chief executive to middle-level managers. The awareness of a social need that produced the policy is enriched by the infusion of new skills and finally matures into a willingness on the part of middle-level managers to commit resources and reputations to responsible action.

The process receives strong impetus from the changing and increasingly demanding environmental conditions that often parallel the response pattern in this manner:

- *Phase 1* — social concerns exist but are not specifically directed at the corporation.

- *Phase 2* — broad implications for the corporation become clear but enforcement is weak or even nonexistent.

- *Phase 3* — expectations for corporate action become more specific and sanctions (governmental or otherwise) become plausible threats.

UNDESIRABLE CONSEQUENCES

While the particular response pattern may eventually produce acceptable results, it is often inefficient and entails some undesirable side effects:

1. If the six- to eight-year cycle that I have observed in relatively successful instances is typical, the elapsed time required may be excessive. Unless social issues can be processed with reasonable speed, they may pile up and ultimately

Exhibit III

Conversion of social responsiveness from policy to action.

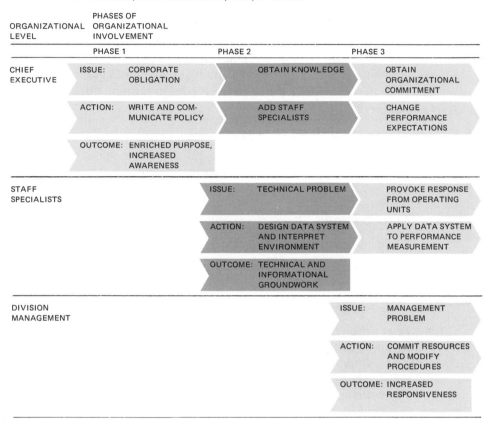

ORGANIZATIONAL LEVEL	PHASES OF ORGANIZATIONAL INVOLVEMENT		PHASE 1	PHASE 2	PHASE 3
CHIEF EXECUTIVE		ISSUE:	CORPORATE OBLIGATION	OBTAIN KNOWLEDGE	OBTAIN ORGANIZATIONAL COMMITMENT
		ACTION:	WRITE AND COMMUNICATE POLICY	ADD STAFF SPECIALISTS	CHANGE PERFORMANCE EXPECTATIONS
		OUTCOME:	ENRICHED PURPOSE, INCREASED AWARENESS		
STAFF SPECIALISTS				ISSUE: TECHNICAL PROBLEM	PROVOKE RESPONSE FROM OPERATING UNITS
				ACTION: DESIGN DATA SYSTEM AND INTERPRET ENVIRONMENT	APPLY DATA SYSTEM TO PERFORMANCE MEASUREMENT
				OUTCOME: TECHNICAL AND INFORMATIONAL GROUNDWORK	
DIVISION MANAGEMENT					ISSUE: MANAGEMENT PROBLEM
					ACTION: COMMIT RESOURCES AND MODIFY PROCEDURES
					OUTCOME: INCREASED RESPONSIVENESS

put the company in a position where it cannot function effectively in its traditional role as a producer of goods and services.

2. Until the final phase, operating managers are not intimately concerned with the issue; specialists direct the responses. The legal staff and the environmental control director work out compliance schedules for pollution control, the minority relations specialist communicates with factory personnel managers about affirmative action programs, and so forth.

But without middle-level management commitment, it is likely that the specialists will interfere with operating activities, misapply resources, or be ineffective in securing results. That is, in the two examples I just cited, compliance schedules do not mesh with planned capital spending programs, and minority relations seminars are taken lightly. Deservedly or not, the specialist often shoulders the blame.

3. Performance evaluation is usually skewed to distributing penalties for failures rather than rewards for successes. Moreover, the process is very unsystematic; it relates not so much to consistent performance against objectives as it

does to poor handling of particular conspicuous situations. The manager cited for polluting a stream or charged with discrimination may find his career badly tarnished. His counterpart, who fails to construct and implement an effective environmental program or meet his hiring and advancement goals—but is not guilty of an overt action—may escape sanctions.

The excuse normally given is, "We needed an example for the rest of the organization." Perhaps so, but it is unfortunate that such sacrifices must be made when the entire organization is trying to learn how to respond effectively to a new set of problems.

NEEDED: RESPONSE PROCESS

Issues of social concern are generally recognized as certain unrelated environmental phenomena demanding substantive corporate responses of some kind. Product safety, equal employment, ecology, and work safety each require a particular set of activities that change over time and are dealt with separately. A more sophisticated concept calls for a systems approach to the environment through which the interrelationships among issues are explored and the likely trends and impacts predicted.*

A third way of viewing corporate responsiveness focuses on organizational requirements. Social issues arise not as discrete events but as a flow of events which may or may not be closely related, but which share a call on corporate attention.

They are at different stages in the zone of discretion. The outlines of some, such as air pollution control, have been well described; while the shape of others, such as "the new work force," is still murky. For example, referring to the evolving regulations covering noise levels, an experienced engineer charged with applying federal environmental standards in his company commented to me. "If the company gave me $10 million to spend on getting noise levels down to 90 decibels, I wouldn't know how to spend it." He had neither the technology nor the directions for using it.

Guidelines for strategy

From an organizational standpoint, the need is for a response process through which issues can be recognized and formed into policy, implications and possible solutions explored, and, finally, plans generated to govern action. The challenge for management is to facilitate a means of organizational learning and adaptation that will permit flexible and creative responses to social issues as they arise. In the divisionalized organization, that assignment will not be easy; some preliminary suggestions on the nature of such a process follow.

Do not overload the response process. The process for responding to social demands described in this article is a reasonable way of approaching a difficult managerial problem. There is, however, a real danger of overloading the process.

*Herman Kahn and B. Bruce Biggs, *Things to Come: Thinking about the 70's and 80's* (New York, Macmillan, 1972), Chapter I.

The time and energy of the chief executive are limited. So are the tolerance and capacity of the organization for wrestling with the environmental uncertainties that accrue to the ones who take forceful action. Top management should balance the numerous social demands pressing on the organization and the social goals it seeks. It should give priority to those areas that are most likely to have an impact on the company's business and should try to maintain a low profile on the others.

To ease the problems of implementation, top management must anticipate the transition from one phase to the next and clearly communicate to middle-level management the ground rules for managing the new phase.

Use specialists effectively. New skills and knowledge are particularly necessary in the formative stages of the company's response. It must scan an unfamiliar environment, master new technologies, and collect and analyze a vast amount of information, both internally and externally. The staff specialist has the difficult task of developing approaches to this environment and designing systems to permit the planning and evaluation of programs for adapting to its needs. Although the specialist's role as an agent of change is vital, there are two dangers to be considered:

> • Operating managers often resist or even ignore the specialist's advice. This is predictable; after all, he is usually a purveyor of bad tidings. Furthermore, since his is a new field, he may be new to the organization and therefore lack the mutual trust built up over time with the operating executives. Worse, he is both highly visible and largely void of influence other than having the proverbial "boss's ear," which can be seldom used and then only with caution. Clearly, the specialist is vulnerable and needs support from the top if he is to be successful.

> • The specialist may keep his hand in the issue too long. His vantage point at the corporate level and his inclination to tackle the job himself may impede the assumption of responsibility and commitment by operating managers. Independent responses at the middle levels are essential for effective action.

The staff specialist's role in implementation of new policy should be temporary. Top management support during the critical second phase is necessary, but as soon as responsibility and accountability have been lodged with operating managers, the staff specialist's involvement should be limited to providing technical advice as requested.

But he has a crucial, broader role in the organization. If he has managed his relationships in the organization well, he will be immensely useful in equipping it to respond to the next social issue. For instance, the specialist who has been concerned with air and water pollution has skills in engineering, environmental analysis, and government relations that may prove to be very useful in working with, say, the occupational health and safety issue. He can become a multipurpose corporate change agent.

Formulate response strategies. To plan a rational sequence of activities in support of goals in areas of social concern, a response strategy is necessary. Placing the responsibility for formulating these strategies with middle-level managers who also set operating strategy exploits, rather than subverts, the organizational strengths of the decentralized company. The procedure of goal setting and strategy evaluation is second nature for both corporate-level and operating managers.

Insisting on a direct parallel between social response strategies and the more familiar business strategy yields three benefits:

1. The response becomes anticipatory and not merely reactive.

2. The response demands a level of analysis that is too often lacking when resources are allocated to social problems. It may not be possible, or in the long run even worthwhile, to measure social costs and benefits in economic terms; however, requiring rigorous justification for the action to be taken makes the best use of the information and analytical tools available.

3. The articulation of a strategy provides the basis for subsequent measurement and evaluation.

Complicate the evaluation process. This final suggestion is, in my judgment, the most important but the least likely to happen of the four. It is commonplace to hear managers describe their jobs as being more complicated now than in the past. One division vice president summed it up this way: "Business used to be fun. But now there are so damn many people around demanding this and that, I just don't enjoy it any more."

Ironically, while the job of the manager—especially those in the middle levels—has been growing more complex, the basis on which his performance is evaluated has often become simpler. The reason, of course, lies in the need for a lowest common denominator that can be used for allocating resources and making comparisons among units operating in different businesses and geographical environments. The financial plan serves these purposes admirably.

If the corporation is to be socially responsive, however, this divergence may have to be arrested. Top management may have to tolerate a greater degree of complexity in the measures it uses to evaluate the performance of middle-level executives. The path need not lead to more subjective or less results-oriented evaluations. Indeed, if attention has been paid to setting strategy in areas of social concern, the power of the results orientation may actually increase over a procedure that does not subject social programs to planning and analysis. Economic performance no doubt will always remain the dominant yardstick (and with good reason), but it should be augmented to reflect the greater complexity and scope of middle management's responsibilities.

IN CONCLUSION

There are hopeful signs that large corporations in this country are developing processes for converting the rhetoric of corporate responsibility into meaningful action. The burden for implementing corporate policy on social issues is ultimately placed on middle-level managers, the same managers who are primarily responsible for planning and directing the operations of the business. Through the creative and persistent leadership of top management, the barriers to incorporating social change in the decentralized company can be overcome.

The response to social demands is not without human cost. Managers' careers have been tarnished by the bad luck of getting caught up in conspicuous incidents that may be learning experiences for the organization, but at their expense. Does somebody have to get hurt? Unfortunately, the answer all too often is *yes*. An urgent challenge for the top managements of large corporations is to make their organizations more understanding of the human costs of change as well as the demands of society.

A Managerial Framework for Social Decision Making

Arguments on this subject are due more to failure to consider certain points than to differences of opinion over issues.

Ramon J. Aldag
Donald W. Jackson, Jr.

Should the firm devote more funds to the financing of education? Why were certain "public service" television programs funded? How can the corporation in good conscience fail to establish programs in ghetto areas? The social implications of questions such as these place the practicing manager in the uncomfortable position of trying to justify action or inaction taken on the basis of an extremely complex set of opposing and, often, apparently irreconcilable factors. Yet, despite mounting interest in the broad question of social responsibility, the resulting debate has been largely vague, value laden, and of little practical use.

Coupled with this unsatisfactory, confusing situation are clear signs of rapidly mounting managerial concern over the societal role of business. Evidences of that concern include voluntary installation of costly pollution abatement equipment, increased activity in ghetto areas, and such structural changes as formation of high-level offices dealing exclusively with consumerism. Increased sensitivity to public and private concern has also been shown by the high response rates firms have made to social surveys and by the tremendous advertising budgets many firms employ to show their corporate good citizenship.

Ramon J. Aldag and Donald W. Jackson, Jr., "A Managerial Framework for Social Decision Making," pp. 33–40, *MSU Business Topics,* Spring, 1975. Reprinted by permission of the publisher, Division of Research, Graduate School of Business Administration, Michigan State University.

To properly approach the question of whether a particular action of a supposedly socially responsible nature should be undertaken requires both a systematic means of determining the elements of the tradeoffs involved and a decision
criterion with which to weigh those elements.

The framework presented in this article is intended to serve a dual purpose.
First, it tries to clarify the various questions subsumed under the broader topic of
social responsibility. Second, and more specifically, it should prove useful to
those practicing managers faced with the concrete problem of proper actions to
be taken in view of apparent responsibility.

STEPS IN THE DECISION PROCESS

A simple flow chart is provided (see Fig. 1) in order to highlight a few key steps.
The model should help classify and analyze argument of certain recent writers.
Although it will not remove all subjectivity, the chart will at least help place
bounds on that subjectivity. That is, although value judgments will remain, the
framework is intended to differentiate between areas necessarily subject to such
judgments and those where objective analysis is possible. The chart expresses in
concrete form the need to answer a whole series of questions before undertaking
actions of a "socially responsible" nature. It is the contention of the writers that
arguments over corporate social responsibility are due more to failure to consider certain points than to true differences of opinion over issues. Perhaps the
most important key step is that the chart indicates that socially responsible
action cannot be properly examined if viewpoints are restricted. Such simplistic
solutions to complex problems are presented by: the consumer crusader who
argues that businesses should act because they must be responsible citizens, the
economist who advocates strict reliance on profit maximization in order to prevent weakening of the market mechanisms, and the advocate of massive business
programs in ghetto areas who uses the sole rationale that such actions will improve the environment of business.

A brief listing of the flow chart steps follows. The order of such a listing is
less important, of course, than is inclusion of relevant steps. These steps can be
viewed as a set of questions the corporate executive might profitably ask prior to
his decision concerning appropriate action:

1. Does a social responsibility really exist in this case?
2. Does the firm have a right to undertake this action?
3. Does an assessment of all interests indicate that the act is desirable?
4. Do benefits outweigh costs?
5. Could the action be better handled by other willing parties?
6. Can we bear the cost of this action?
7. Do we possess the managerial competence to do the job?

An examination of these questions and consideration of certain alternatives
available at each stage follows. It should be stressed that such an analysis is not

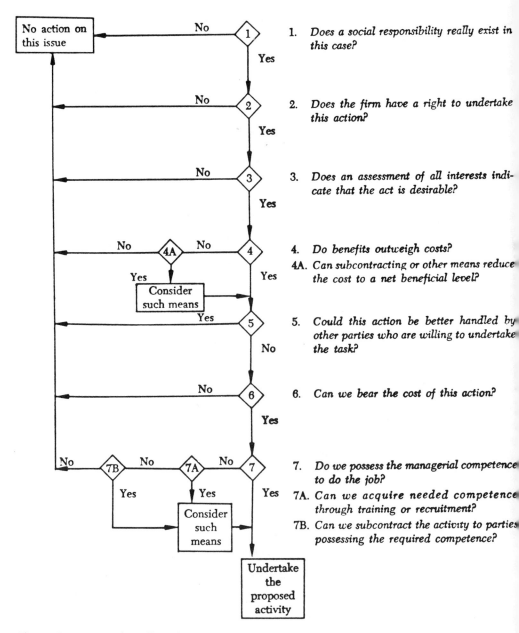

Fig. 1   Decision-making flow chart.

intended in any way to reduce corporate responsibility. Rather, it is meant to encourage direction of energies to projects where the firm possesses a unique capability and enjoys stockholder and societal support.

DOES SOCIAL RESPONSIBILITY REALLY EXIST IN THIS CASE?

This question perhaps can best be approached by categorizing the adversaries. On one side of the issue are those, such as Milton Friedman, Eugene V. Rostow, and Theodore Levitt, who argue that the responsibility of business is to pursue profit.* In that way, barring severe violations of market efficiency, societal benefits will, they say, be maximized. Similarly, Reavis Cox says of the businessman:

> If we think of social responsibility in the sociological sense of being the role he plays in society, the nature of that responsibility is clear—he is supposed to keep operating efficiently the intricate mechanism by which man's material needs are met.†

By engaging in "corporate philanthropy," it is claimed, the firm will misallocate resources and impose what amounts to a mandatory tax upon its customers. Some, such as Paul T. Heyne, go so far as to state that, "The notion of corporations having social responsibilities is a snare and delusion." The doctrine of social responsibility is composed, he adds, of "ambiguities, misconceptions, wishful thinking, and elitism."‡ It should be noted, however, that these authors do not view the corporation as operating within a vacuum; rather, they see the social conditions as environmental constraints that have to be accounted for when trying to effectively carry out the corporation's mission. Thus, in attempting to operate his business, an executive would recognize that discrimination and other clear violations of social sanctions are contrary to his ascribed role, often illegal, and not necessarily sound business.

Arrayed against this view are at least three general groups. These might be classed as foreboders, demanders, and constrainers. Foreboders are those who warn of the consequences of corporate emphasis solely on short-run benefits to the firm. They point to such factors as potential governmental intervention and long-run deterioration of profits that may accompany societal illness. Elisha Gray II says, for instance, that if corporations fail to invest in social projects, they will ultimately find themselves forced to do so.§ Admiral Ben Moreell, former chair-

---

*Milton Friedman, "The Social Responsibility of Business is to Increase Its Profits," *New York Times Magazine,* 13 September 1970, pp. 32–33; Theodore Levitt, "The Dangers of Social Responsibility," *Harvard Business Review,* September–October 1958, pp. 44–50; Eugene V. Rostow in Edward S. Mason (ed.), *The Corporation in Modern Society* (Cambridge: Harvard University Press, 1959), p. 63.

†Reavis Cox, "The Business of Business is . . .?" *Wall Street Journal,* 15 October 1969, p. 18.

‡Paul T. Heyne, "The Free-Market System Is the Best Guide for Corporate Decisions," *Financial Analysts Journal,* September–October 1971, pp. 26–27, 72–73.

§Elisha Gray II, "Changing Values in the Business Society," *Business Horizons,* August 1968, p. 26.

man of the board of Jones and Laughlin Steel Corporation, has taken a similar view:

> I am convinced that unless we do [accept social responsibilities], the vacuum created by our unwillingness will be filled by those who would take us down the road to complete statism and inevitable moral and social collapse.*

It seems clear that such arguments say nothing about social responsibility. Rather, if sincere, they are concerned with the consequences of failure to meet alleged responsibilities. As such, corporate adherence to such a view could be seen as largely a reflection of self-interest and is thus extraneous to the central question of the existence of social responsibility.

The second group, demanders, believes that the corporation, because of its superior resources, has an active role to play in societal betterment, regardless of whether it has contributed to societal ills. Since the firm does not fit the model of powerless perfect competition, it should assume, the demanders believe, responsibility in proportion to its power. This, they say, is the "iron law of responsibility."† There is little ground for objective debate in this area. It is hard to argue that a wealthy firm (or an individual living comfortably above the subsistence level) should ignore starvation, poverty, or other social ills. What must be recognized, however, is that by acting in ways contrary to the best interests and wishes of its owners, the corporation may be forcing a redistribution of income. It may seem that the stockholder's ultimate ownership and theoretical control of the firm would prevent continued redistribution which he does not approve. There is much evidence, however, that corporate ownership is so broadly based that any real stockholder control is ruled out. Widespread indications are that large numbers of corporate managers practice satisficing—that is, seeking a safe, satisfactory solution rather than trying to maximize returns. Such actions could be cited as concrete evidence of slackened stockholder control, as could the scarcity of effective shareholder suits. Thus, forced redistribution of income is quite possible without effective stockholder redress. Although the justifiability of such redistribution is basically a question of values, it is nevertheless an issue that the manager must seriously weigh.

The final group, constrainers, argues that the corporation is no longer effectively constrained by competition. Therefore, it should be subjected to various constraints aimed at eliminating the arbitrary power it may exercise. They also argue that constraints should be imposed to remedy the causes or effects of market imperfections. Legal codification, they say, is resorted to only in cases of prolonged abuse of social sanction or when such abuse would cause great poten-

---

*Admiral Ben Moreell, "The Role of American Business in Social Progress" (Indianapolis: Indiana State Chamber of Commerce, 1956), p. 20.

†Keith Davis, "Understanding the Social Responsibility Puzzle: What Does the Businessman Owe to Society?" Business Horizons, Winter 1967, pp. 45–50. Many of the arguments of Davis, it should be noted, also neatly fit the "foreboder" category.

tial harm. Consequently, the contention that the firm is acting in a socially responsible manner by strictly obeying written codes is spurious—exploitable imperfections remain and must be removed.

At least three classes of abuse would seem to be justifiably cited by these constrainers as springing from failures of the market mechanisms. The first set of cases are those in which costs to the firm do not equal true social costs (that is, "externalities" exist). A second set of cases relate to the needless endangering of consumers by products of the firm. Finally, cases are cited in which actions of the firm prevent proper functioning of the market. Among these latter cases would be actions to prevent competition either by restricting entry or creating monopoly. Faulty information such as deceptive advertising or misleading warranties would be additional examples.

Although other considerations may serve to counterbalance the harmful effects evident in certain of these examples, it is clear that some issues (for instance, consumer safety) may be so important that they would preclude counterbalancing. Government curtailment of cyclamate sales to provide for the public's safety may be such an example.

When the corporate manager is faced with a question of whether he does have a social responsibility to perform a given action, he must weigh the arguments of each of these viewpoints in relation to his particular situation. He must ask himself such questions as, "Do stockholders of the firm have an effective voice in assessing corporate goals and actions?" and "Are consumers needlessly endangered by the product?" At this point, it should be remembered, only corporate *responsibility* is being considered. Other issues, such as economic consequences, will be weighed subsequently.

DOES THE FIRM HAVE A RIGHT TO UNDERTAKE THIS ACTION?

Assuming that the manager does believe that a social responsibility exists, he faces a second question, closely related to the first, which asks if there might in fact exist obligations of the firm to refrain from action.

Some individuals would argue that such obligations for restraint do exist. Allowing firms to undertake actions beyond those dictated by their primary role of providing goods and services, these individuals argue, could lead to misallocation of resources and have detrimental effects upon stockholders and other segments of society. They feel such dangers are especially acute because of the businessman's alleged lack of training in social areas. Thus, there are those who question whether businessmen should be allowed to take relatively unconstrained actions that may create net costs for society or for segments of society. Although these doubts are based to an extent on considerations of inefficiency, even more fundamental is the question of whether business should be allowed to determine societal priorities. Some writers argue that businessmen should not be allowed to dictate, no matter how benevolently, to a relatively powerless public. Ben Lewis, for instance, writes:

> Economic decisions must be right as society measures right rather than good as benevolent individuals construe goodness. An economy is a mechanism designed to pick up and discharge the wishes of society in the management of its

resources; it is not an instrument for the rendering of gracious music by kindly disposed improvisers.*

Similarly, in a recent ruling Federal Judge Edward Tamm alluded to management's "patently illegitimate claim of power to treat modern corporations, with their vast resources, as personal satrapies implementing personal political or moral predilections."†

A serious corollary question thus becomes readily apparent: "Does society really want the firm to undertake this action?" Regardless of whether a right to undertake social action exists, the businessman must ask himself whether he would be performing a net service to society by following such pursuits. It is clear from this discussion that there are at least two factors involved in answering this question.

On an economic basis, the public's net gain must be assessed by weighing the benefits of such actions against a pair of costs—the direct cost to consumers of increased prices and the more indirect costs of possible weakening of market mechanisms.

On a less tangible level, it must be remembered that when society allows corporations to initiate social action, it diverts power from society in general to those corporations. There are some who would argue that such a channeling of power removes many vital questions from the reach of the ballot box, thereby eliminating a major democratic check on the ordering of social priorities. The danger here, if such arguments are valid, is that since businessmen are often faced with conflicting interests and obligations, the forfeiture of such checks is potentially costly.‡

In some areas, such as minority hiring, there is evidence of societal sanction of corporate actions having social impact. However, in other cases businessmen have been legally constrained from taking "socially responsible" action. For instance, a firm economically incapable of acting alone on "socially desirable" problems often is currently constrained by antitrust laws from acting in concert with competitors. As an example, competitive joint ventures in ghetto areas or to combat pollution have often not been allowed. Thus, in some cases societal preferences have been codified and present no problem of interpretation to the corporate decision maker. Because there is a lag between changes in society's desires and the reflection of those changes in altered legal structures, however, businessmen must attempt to gauge these fluid preferences. Such an assessment may prove to be a useful leading indicator of future areas where corporate freedom may be challenged. Affirmative response at this step leads to the next question:

---

*Ben Lewis, "Economics by Admonition," *American Economic Review,* Papers and Proceedings of the Seventy-First Annual Meeting of the American Economic Association, May 1959, p. 395. Hazel Henderson has also forcefully argued this point in "Should Business Tackle Society's Problems?" *Harvard Business Review,* July–August 1968, pp. 77–85.

†Quoted by Heyne, "Free Market System," p. 26.

‡Henderson, *op. cit.*

DOES ASSESSMENT OF ALL INTERESTS
INDICATE THAT THE ACT IS DESIRABLE?

The firm obviously is responsible to a variety of claimants, all of whom should be considered. Employees of the corporation, members of the community in which the firm is located, and numerous others have a legitimate interest in actions of the firm. Primary emphasis for the purpose of this discussion will be directed at the shareholders.

The following listing is intended to stress certain key factors of interest to stockholders. The relevance of individual items, of course, must be examined in the light of the specific situation.

"Socially responsible" actions may have several positive effects upon the stockholders. For example:

- Improvement of managerial morale may increase efficiency.

- Improvement of the quality of society may be considered a kind of return on investment to the firm.

- Failure to act may lead to governmental intervention.

- Attention to certain social questions, although a constraint, may lead to greater efficiency. (For example, consumerism, by forcing greater consideration of consumer needs and wants, may in certain instances improve corporate returns. Similarly, greater social awareness and action may lead to better understanding of market needs.)

- Such actions may promote long-run profitability through consumer recognition and appreciation of corporate efforts.

- To the extent that investors are more willing to back issues of "socially responsible" firms than of others, such actions may be reflected in heightened price/earnings ratios.*

However, socially responsible actions may also have such adverse effects as the following on the stockholders:

- If profit maximization is not rigidly followed, shareholders will have no objective criterion on which to judge the efficiency of management.

- If businessmen too readily agree to perform social tasks, eventually they may find themselves guided by or absorbed by political agencies.

- If a firm undertakes unilateral action, in the absence of corresponding action by competitors, it may seriously weaken its competitive position.

---

*On the other hand, it may be possible that investors are primarily concerned with investment aspects of corporate social action. See, for example, the following articles: J. Parker Hall III, "The Professional Investor's View of Social Responsibility," *Financial Analysts Journal,* September–October 1971, pp. 32–34; Burton G. Malkiel and Richard E. Quandt, "Moral Issues in Investment Policy," *Harvard Business Review,* March–April 1971, pp. 37–47.

Balancing these pros and cons requires consideration of specific cases. The outcome of that balancing is a function of such factors as the likelihood of government response if corporate action is not taken, the visibility of the act to consumers, the current level of corporate efficiency, the probability that competitors will follow the action, and the degree of precision with which costs and benefits can be gauged. If the manager then feels that the act is desirable, he must next ask himself:

DO BENEFITS OUTWEIGH COSTS?

Although this question was in a sense subsumed within the previous step, it is considered separately here to stress the need to attempt quantification of costs and benefits. Thus, while the previous question focused essentially on qualitative factors, it seems clearly unwise to take action on a proposal without attempting to attach concrete figures to possible consequences. In spite of this, numerous instances of failure to quantify superficially desirable actions are documented.

Arrival at this step in the flow chart presupposes affirmative responses to preceding steps. Thus, a negative response at this stage implies no lessening of corporate responsibility. What may be required, as the flow chart indicates, is alternate or supplementary action. A pair of possibilities, not meant to be exhaustive, is indicated by 4A on the chart. As one option, the firm may attempt to subcontract the necessary action to a specialized firm capable of achieving economies of scale. In the event that such subcontracting is infeasible, it may be desirable for the firm to attempt socially responsible action in an alternative way that is more amenable to corporate capabilities and resources. For example, economies of scale may suggest the handling of certain tasks by governmental units capable of achieving those economies. In such a case, the firm could seek alternate action of equivalent social worth but more in line with its unique capabilities. The important point here is that total denial of responsibility on economic grounds cannot be justified without full consideration of alternatives.

Even though certain costs and benefits may not immediately be apparent, they are implicitly considered in any managerial decision. Thus, decision makers must attempt to enumerate and objectively quantify such factors. If benefits appear to outweigh costs, the manager can ask the following question.

COULD THIS ACTION BE BETTER
HANDLED BY OTHER WILLING PARTIES?

This question again forces the manager to focus upon the central issue of optimal allocation of corporate resources and energies. Thus, attempts to implement an apparently desirable action should await consideration of whether such a pursuit could be better accomplished by others. In that event, redirection of efforts may be advisable. Barring such evidence, a relevant question to be examined is whether the firm can bear the cost of the action.

CAN WE BEAR THE COST OF THIS ACTION?

This determination is to a degree dependent on the current profit position of the firm. If that position is favorable, the corporation may be able to absorb a large portion, or the entirety, of costs incurred in undertaking this action. On the other hand, if the cost structure and competitive conditions are such that absorption is infeasible, increased costs perhaps can be passed on to consumers or covered by governmental subsidy. As was pointed out earlier, antitrust laws may preclude investment and rule out even a desirable action if the competitive structure is such that unilateral action is not possible. On the other hand, governmental sanction of certain actions may be reflected in incentives such as: tax credits on capital investments, accelerated depreciation on investments, construction grants, and training or other grants to help defray costs. If costs of the proposed action can be covered, the manager must ask the next question.

DO WE POSSESS THE MANAGERIAL COMPETENCE TO DO THE JOB?

Given that all preceding stages have been passed, the question of managerial competence remains. A common argument is that since the training of corporate managers is primarily in business matters, they cannot be expected to expertly handle delicate social and ethical issues. While such a view may reflect a degree of bias and seems essentially to ignore increased business emphasis on sociological and psychological factors, it does seem advisable to appraise managerial capabilities and interests. Determination of deficiencies may lead (step 7A) to managerial training or to revised recruitment and selection procedures. If even those routes seem infeasible, subcontracting may be considered.

CONCLUSION

This article, while necessarily brief, has attempted to present a framework for systematic examination of the complex sequence of decisions implicit in any action on social issues. If bounds of subjectivity have been narrowed, or at least clarified, and if simplistic answers now seem less satisfactory, the writers will have considered their major purposes fulfilled. Use of the approach outlined should simplify decision making by highlighting important questions. However, because it offers for consideration factors which may have been overlooked before, these simplifying effects may be somewhat offset. Nevertheless, the resulting decision, while perhaps no easier to reach, should be both better and more readily justifiable than would otherwise be the case. As noted previously, it must be recognized that analysis of a situation in this manner is not meant as a means of avoiding responsibility. Rather, it is intended to aid in the proper channeling of energies toward activities that will best utilize corporate strengths and produce results that will be supported by stockholders and society.

It is recognized, of course, that the framework presented is largely skeletal and merely suggestive of relevant issues at each stage. Nevertheless, we feel that to analyze the desirability of certain acts within this framework will prove beneficial to the manager in several ways. It should clarify issues, point out relevant areas of necessary consideration, and provide a more solid basis for explanation of corporate actions to interested parties. As such, it should serve both as a useful tool and as the nucleus for further clarification and consideration of process steps.

QUESTIONS FOR DISCUSSION

1. What constraints exist on the application of the rational model in social decision-making? How might the constraints be overcome?

2. The use of a staff specialist to deal with specific social issues is becoming ever more common in corporate structures. What are the advantages and disadvantages of this organizational approach?

3. Overreaction and underreaction are common pitfalls in business response to external pressures. How can corporate policy aid in preventing those pitfalls? Give examples.

4. What are the limits on the use of cost–benefit analysis in social decision-making? In the absence of clear trade-offs, what alternative methodologies might be used?

5. What general categories of policies do you feel would be essential to the formal conduct of a company's charitable contribution program? To what degree would a company's line of business dictate the content of these policies?

6. Some practitioners contend that policies and planning can often prohibit much-needed creativity in a company's response to social pressures. Do these practitioners misunderstand the role of policy and planning, or is there substance to their contentions.?

7. In earlier chapters we have studied examples of specific corporate responses to a variety of social issues. Using the Aldag–Jackson decision framework, critique any of those responses. In what ways has the model aided in your analysis? What problems were encountered in applying the model?

8. To what degree do human frailties impinge on the continuity and consistency of social decision-making in business? (Reference, for example, the earlier Monsen, Saxberg, and Sutermeister article.)

SELECTED READINGS

Anshen, M., ed., *Managing the Socially Responsible Corporation.* (New York: Arkville Press, 1973.)

Baker, H. G., "Identity and social-responsibility policies," *Business Horizons,* April, 1973.

Bowman, E. H., and M. Haire, "A strategic posture toward corporate social involvement," *California Management Review,* Winter, 1975.

Bradt, W. R., *Organizing for Effective Public Affairs.* (New York: The Conference Board, 1969.)

Callaghan, D. W., *Management of the Corporate Gift-Giving Function: An Empirical Study in the Life Insurance Industry.* (Unpublished dissertation, University of Massachusetts, 1975.)

The Conference Board, *Corporate Organization for Pollution Control.* (New York: The Conference Board, 1970.)

Keller, I. W., "Planning corporate social performance," *Management Accounting,* June, 1975.

Lund, L., *Corporate Organization for Environmental Policy-making.* (New York: The Conference Board, 1974.)

McAdam, T., "How to put corporate responsibility into practice," *Business and Society Review,* Summer, 1973.

Moyer, R. C., "Efficiency and corporate social investment," *Business and Society Review,* Spring, 1974.

Murray, E. A., Jr., "The social-response process in commercial banks: An empirical investigation," *Academy of Management Review,* July, 1976.

Novick, D., "Cost–benefit analysis and social responsibility," *Business Horizons,* October, 1973.

Paluszek, J. L., "How three companies organize for social responsibility," *Business and Society Review,* Summer, 1974.

Steiner, G. A., "Institutionalizing corporate social decisions," *Business Horizons,* December, 1975.

Steiner, G., "Social policies for business," *California Management Review,* Winter, 1972.

Steiner, J. F., "The business response to public distrust," *Business Horizons,* April, 1977.

Case

SOCIETY LIFE INSURANCE COMPANY (A)

In June of 1977, the Society Life Insurance Company was considering the matter of a corporate commitment, of both funds and human resources, to the fund-raising drive of the Essex Hospital Center, located in Salem, Massachusetts, which is also the location of Society's home office. This subject came up at a propitious time, since Society Life had already formally reviewed the topic of corporate citizenship or social responsibility.

Company Background

The Society Life Insurance Company is a mutual life insurance company; that is, its profits are returned to its policyholders through the declaration of dividends. Each policyholder, as a proportionate owner in the firm, has a vested interest in the firm's operations. Although the company has a favorable asset structure (over $300 million) and in-force policies representing over $1.3 billion of insurance, the Company is small by industry comparison, employing about 270 home-office personnel and ranking, in 1977, 200th in insurance volume

This case was prepared by Nicholas Speranzo and Arthur Elkins as a basis for class discussion. While based on a true corporate situation, names, dates, places, and selected facts and figures have been changed.

© Copyright 1977 Nicholas Speranzo and Arthur Elkins.

among over 1,500 insurance companies. Exhibit A summarizes the Company's asset and liability structure, and Exhibit B is a composite of its operating summary, both as of September 30, 1977.

Established in 1874, it has been only during the past decade and a half that the Company has enjoyed a rapid sales growth (an 8.2% in-force volume amount gain in 1976); its sales goal for the future is $2 billion of in-force insurance by 1985.

Such rapid sales growth has been achieved through an aggressive re-cruitment process for new salesmen in all of its forty-three agency offices in twenty-six states. Additionally, the Company offers a wide product line (Society deals in life, health, and mutual funds and is a recognized leader in noncancellable health coverages), competitive rates for its products, and a reputation as a small "blue-chip" firm. Be-cause Society is small by industry comparison, the need to recruit and retain new agents is vital to its growth. (Currently, Society employs over 300 agents who sell exclusively for Society, and about 2,000 brok-ers who sell Society's as well as other insurers' products.)

An aggressive attitude has permeated the Company's outlook on corporate citizenship as well. Many of Society's executives serve as chairmen or committeemen on various fund-raising drives. Society has been an active supporter of the United Way campaign drives, and its executives have served as officers on Cerebral Palsy fund-raising drives, the Association of Business and Commerce, and various civic associations and campaign drives. Currently, the Company's President, Mr. Frank Seward, is the chairman of the Essex Hospital Center's fund-raising drive.

EXHIBIT A

Society Life Insurance Company
Balance Sheet
September 30, 1977
(All amounts rounded to nearest thousand)

Assets		Liabilities	
Cash	$ 2,707	Reserves	$254,238
Bonds	129,041	Accrued dividends and	
Stocks		proceeds	30,435
Preferred	1,481	Premiums in advance	2,045
Common	7,905	Unpaid claims	1,343
Mortgages and real estate	125,951	Premium taxes	220
Policy loans	44,083	Securities valuation reserve	1,474
Accrued income	9,876	Dividend liability	6,026
Other assets	4,427	Reserve for prior years'	
		Federal income tax	450
		Other liabilities	7,092
		Total Liabilities	$303,323
		Surplus	22,148
Total Assets	$325,471	Total Liabilities and Capital	$325,471

EXHIBIT B

Society Life Insurance Company
Summary of Operations
For the Year Ending
September 30, 1977
(Nearest Thousand)

Receipts

Cash premiums (adjusted for unpaid and in-advance premiums)	$29,366	
Reinsurance premiums paid	−663	
Earned premium income		$28,703
Gross investment income		13,888
Miscellaneous income		61
Total income		$42,652

Disbursements

Death benefits, surrenders, endowments, other paid benefits	$18,876	
Home office expenses	3,693	
Commissions	3,547	
Field expenses	2,149	
Insurance, real estate taxes and fees, depreciation	2,481	
		$30,746
Gain from Operations		$11,906
Less: Reserve liability	$ 5,963	
Dividends	4,310	
F.I.T.	1,052	
Surplus adjustment	491	
		$11,816
New Surplus		$ 90
Beginning surplus	$22,058	
New surplus	90	
Total Surplus	$22,148	

General Factors Influencing the Company's Social Responsibility Position

Society Life, in an effort to determine how much of its resources should be expended toward fulfilling its social responsibilities, had recently spent $15,000 to participate in a research study involving several other insurance companies, as well as a variety of other firms. The results of the study, prepared by the Institute for Social Research located in Hartford, Connecticut, indicated:

a) Society Life spent, relative to the other firms surveyed, about the median percentage of its income and per capita employee time on activities falling under the category of corporate citizenship.

b) Based on other insurance companies of comparable size either participating in the study or about whom data was available, Society Life was in the top five percentiles for corporate giving and executive or employee time spent on "socially responsible" activities.

While the results of the study were interesting from a statistical perspective, Society's top management felt they were inconclusive, and that no concrete decision could be made, based on this study, as to the appropriateness of Society's pledge to the areas of social responsibility. Far more concrete, however, were several political and financial factors that loomed on the horizon:

1. Society Life, as one of several Massachusetts-based insurers, has been engaged in an intensive lobbying effort to change the state tax structure for home-based insurance companies. Essentially, in 1976, the State had increased the tax rate for domestic insurance companies, while leaving unchanged its tax structure for out-of-state insurers writing business in Massachusetts. Society and other insurance companies felt this resulted in an unfair competitive burden on domestic companies. In 1976, Society's state tax liability increased from its 1975 figure of $140,000 to $300,000.

2. The aggressive recruitment process Society had initiated for prospective salesmen continued to be a financial drain on current profits. New agents, whose income is subsidized by the Company for a period of 36 to 48 months, have a failure rate of 60%; often, in such cases, repayment of the subsidized portion of their income is impossible. In 1977 (see also Exhibit B), the dollar amount invested in the field sales staff increased $266,530, from $1,882,830 in 1976 to $2,149,360.

3. To continue its growth pace and achieve its 1985 goal of $2 billion of in-force insurance, Society Life has begun the laborious procedure of being licensed in all fifty states. (Currently, Society is licensed to write business in only twenty-six states.) It is hoped that this move, coupled with continued recruitment of quality salesmen, will bring further sales impetus as new sales territories, especially California, are explored.

4. The Company's entrance into the mutual-fund business, considered at the time to be a natural outgrowth of its insurance and financial interests, was ill-timed. Through its subsidiary, Society Equity Sales, the Company began its mutual-fund venture in 1972, and the disastrous results have kept mutual-fund sales low and profits in this area almost nonexistent.

5. While a recognized leader in health insurance, the Company, as of July 1, 1977, stopped writing hospital and major-medical coverages due to an unfavorable premium/claims loss ratio, an occurrence that has been industrywide and that has prompted similar action by many

companies. The effect of this decision will eventually reduce the amount of the Company's claim payments as these policies lapse or terminate; however, in the short run, adverse claims experience will still be present for this small but expensive line of business.

6. Society Life has also been subject to another industry trend—a significant increase in the number and amount of policy loans. This is due to policy provisions providing a stated interest rate on such loans of 5 or 6 percent, well below bank-loan rates. In 1977, there has been an outflow of over $4,000,000 to policy-owners for such loans, causing a continuous drain on the Company's cash position. (It might also be noted that with an interest rate of 5 or 6 percent there is little if any incentive to repay such loans.)

Essex Hospital Center

The Essex Hospital Center is the largest of the two hospitals serving Salem, Massachusetts, and the surrounding communities. It is the only area hospital with maternity facilities and cobalt and X-ray treatment centers. In 1966, Essex Hospital merged with the now nonexistent Fairview Hospital to provide better and more economical service to the area communities, and to increase its patient capacity.

Presently, the Essex Hospital Center can accommodate over 300 patients on an in-patient basis. Room rates vary from $65 per day for wards to $190 per day for intensive care. While Essex Hospital has repeatedly offered to merge with the Clinic Hospital, also in Salem, on the basis of economy, better total service through a single cooperating staff and further expanded patient facilities and accommodations, Clinic has just as adamantly refused the offer.

Clinic Hospital

Clinic Hospital, the city's other hospital, is small in comparison to the Essex Hospital Center. Clinic has facilities for 144 patients; it offers no maternity facilities or sophisticated cobalt and X-ray clinics. Clinic Hospital has maintained, throughout the merger controversy, that the total community can well afford two hospitals.

Clinic contends that a merger would result in a larger hospital bureaucracy with more "red tape" and, with no competition for hospital services, even higher hospital costs. Clinic's room rates are $65 per day for semiprivate rooms (it has no ward facilities) and $100 per day for intensive care. Clinic has also indicated that the only benefits to be gained from a merger would be a standardization of medical facilities and uniform doctor and nurse care quality, subjects which Clinic contends each hospital can just as well administer separately as together.

Both the Clinic Hospital and the Essex Hospital Center are engaged in fund-raising drives at the present time. Essex Hospital's fund-raising goal is $5 million over a three-year period; Clinic's fund-raising goal, though unannounced, is known to be more modest.

The Hospital Fund Decision

In June of 1977, Mr. Seward met with the Board of Directors and the senior officers of the Company to decide on the Company's posture on the Essex Hospital Center's fund-raising drive. As Chairman of the drive, Mr. Seward noted: "Society Life has long recognized its responsibility, as a public citizen, to the community in which it resides. This commitment to the community can best be expressed in a corporate gift to Essex Hospital Center's fund-raising drive."

In addition, Seward cited the following three factors as important considerations for support of the Essex Hospital Center.

1. The insurance industry has a vested, albeit principally financial, interest in the health-care industry. Rising hospital costs have engendered ever-higher insurance premiums for health coverages. As noted earlier, Society, as well as many other insurance companies, abandoned the health-insurance field as a result of poor claims experience. Such adverse premium/claims ratios are, in great part, a reflection of both higher claims costs and the reluctance of state insurance commissioners in general to grant premium increases on such coverages when needed.

2. Inasmuch as the premiums for the Company's group employee health coverage (underwritten by Blue Cross/Blue Shield) are based on individual company experience, for which Society absorbs 55% of the cost as an employee benefit, the gift to the Essex Hospital Center would be an expedient one. It would, in the long run, both reduce the cost of such coverage and increase the quality of health care for its employees and the community in general.

3. An urban medical facility, as envisioned by the Essex Hospital Center, would enhance the area's attractiveness to other firms interested in new plant location sites. The further development of the area would result in lower taxes due to a larger and more diversified tax base, increased employment and a higher standard of living for the community.

Seward proposed that a "soft-sell" in-house solicitation be conducted. This, he felt, should best be spearheaded by an officer of the Company.

The Senior Vice President of the Investment Division, Mr. Berrigan, and the Vice President of Personnel, Mr. House, both expressed concern for this proposal in the following areas:

a) The subtlety of the in-house solicitation

Both Mr. Berrigan and Mr. House felt that, if improperly handled, an in-house fund-raising compaign might alienate some employees. This possibility was further enhanced by Mr. Seward's position as Chairman of the drive.

b) The Clinic fund-raising drive

Mr. House noted: "If we give to your drive, are we compelled to give to Clinic's drive? Any controversy about this gift could cause adverse publicity at a time when we need public support the most." Mr. House was referring directly to the proposed legislative change on the home-based tax-structure issue, an effort in which Society had asked for public support.

c) Financial considerations

Both Berrigan and House expressed concern over the size of the gift to either or both drives, especially in view of the Company's growth plans and its increasing expenditures to achieve these goals.

SOCIETY LIFE INSURANCE COMPANY (B)

In June of 1977, Society Life allowed an in-house solicitation for the Essex Hospital Center's fund-raising drive. This solicitation was aimed at three levels: the officers of the company, the management staff, and the clerical staff. This solicitation was handled on a very low-key level, as follows:

1. Mr. Ames, a soft-spoken man who is also the Claims Director, was chosen to be chairman of the in-house solicitation. He held several short meetings with small groups of the Company's officers, at which he outlined the goals of the drive and the communities' needs. Each group was encouraged to contribute and given a brochure containing literature on the services the Essex Hospital Center provides, as well as a pledge form.

2. A general one-hour meeting of the management staff was held on a variety of subjects. At this meeting, Mr. Ames made a ten-minute presentation on the in-house drive, stressing that the contribution was purely a matter of personal choice. As he had done with the officers, he distributed brochures and pledges and stressed salary deduction as the preferable contribution route. Mr. Ames made no attempt to contact any employees beyond this initial presentation.

3. A general all-staff memorandum was distributed to the clerical and management staff, encouraging a contribution to the Essex Hospital Center's drive. The letter was signed by Mr. Ames and attached were pledge cards for any employees desiring to make a contribution.

Three weeks later, in early July of 1977, it was announced at a management meeting that the Company had donated $125,000 to the Essex Hospital Center's fund-raising drive. It was also announced that the Company's employees had contributed an additional $26,000 in pledges over a three-year period. It was also announced that Clinic Hospital would be allowed to solicit contributions for their fund drive at the Company's exits and entrances later that week.

13. Social Accounting and Reporting

With all the writing on social responsibility or the role of the corporation in solving social problems (as well as the criticism on the softness of the whole topic), it should not be surprising that, in time, some forms of measurement or accounting for corporate social activity would be attempted. There isn't much to show yet in the area; for a topic so liberally strewn about the literature, the techniques are surprisingly nonstandard, underdeveloped, and often unaccepted.

Yet the area of social audit or social accounting is becoming standard fare at corporate and business meetings; it has absorbed the time of some reputable scholars, and is finding increased interest among practitioners.

Managers have all sorts of reasons to undertake or advocate social audits. Some simply seek to forestall activist protests. If these managers can present some form of data, they hope they can at least fend off accusations and condemnations. Other executives want to know how much they are really spending. After all, corporations have been lending executive time, operative time, facilities, and equipment for years to all sorts of civic and charitable causes; few ever bothered to calculate the real costs of these contributions. Still other managers firmly believe in the social responsibility doctrine and want to develop social audits for planning, control and reward purposes. In some companies, official policy, publically announced at least, is that lower-level managers will be rewarded according to social performance as well as profit performance. Finally, in the ultimate, some managers would like to find that nebulous net benefit figure.

The problem, of course, is that there is little agreement on what to measure and how to do it. As the concept has evolved, there seems to be at least two schools of thought on the approach an audit should take; one advocates starting now to find a measure of corporate net social benefit, the other centers on a more traditional determination of costs incurred. These two approaches are illustrated in our readings by the Linowes article and the piece by Bauer and Fenn.

Linowes proposes that firms develop what he calls a "socio-economic operating statement" (SEOS). Briefly, the Linowes approach sets onto paper voluntary expenditures made by the firm for public or employee welfare. Set off against the expenditures would be what he calls "detriments," the costs of projects which have been brought to management's attention, but which were not undertaken. The bottom line of a SEOS statement would be "total socio-economic contribution or deficit for the year."

Bauer and Fenn are much more cautious. They propose that firms must first get on the learning curve by initially designing the audit for internal purposes only and by first focusing on programs and not on social impact. In essence, Bauer and Fenn advise companies to start by listing items resulting from an "explicit corporate policy involving a meaningful level of resource commitment." Then management can proceed to include costs as well as measures to determine the effectiveness of programs. For programs with no adequate performance measures, Bauer and Fenn recommend the "process audit," which is a description of origins, goals, rationale, and actual operations of the programs.

Since the area of social audit is so new, there are a number of critiques of the early attempts at measurement. This is especially true of the Linowes approach. We should like therefore to offer a summary of the critiques after the readings.

What Is a Corporate Social Audit?

Raymond A. Bauer and Dan H. Fenn, Jr.

Once the murky notion of the social responsibility of business began to take on popular appeal and specific shape, it was inevitable that public pressure would begin to build for some sort of business accountability in the social sphere. After all, if society really believes that corporations should broaden their concept of their own function to include social responsibility, articulate members of society are going to demonstrate and implement that belief by demanding some kind of accounting of corporate performance in noneconomic areas.

This demand that corporations be socially accountable has been augmented by a growing realization among businessmen that corporate social programs have been haphazard in their growth, poorly aimed and weakly coordinated, and little known or understood—even within a given corporation. Further, if specific programs are hazy and obscure, the notion of "total social impact" has proved almost completely opaque, not just to businessmen, but to society as a whole. Thus it should surprise no one that the pressure for and talk about a formal "social audit," in some way analogous to a financial audit, have increased measurably in recent months, both within and outside companies.

The social audit is indeed a relatively new development; it has only a thin history prior to the 1970's. It first appeared on the scene when the accepted definition of "corporate social responsibility" was no longer being formulated primarily by businessmen, but rather by social activists who had reason to capitalize on a general suspicion of all "establishment" institutions, including business. What the term means is commensurately vague, and there is precious little agreement on how such an audit ought to be conducted.

In the pages that follow, we present a description and analysis of some of the problems encountered by those who are attempting to perform social audits and outline an approach that appears to us to be viable. We term this approach the "first-step audit." It is designed to provide data that are immediately useful for corporate executives; it is also designed to put the whole effort toward social accounting on an upward learning curve by combining descriptive information with quantitative measures in a meaningful way. Hopefully, the first-step audit will be helpful to businessmen who are trying to resolve such questions as: "What activities should I be auditing? What measures should I use? And what standards of performance should I use to calibrate my record?"

Some readers will say what we are proposing is not an *audit* at all, but rather a form of social *report*. So be it; but we cannot see that the question of terminology has much significance at this point. The loose usage of the word "audit" has characterized discussions of corporate social audits and is sanctioned neither by dictionaries nor the accounting profession. An audit means the independent attestation of facts by some outside party, but it is clear to us that independent attestation is a step that still lies far down the road. The first-step audit we shall describe will prove, we believe, a useful way station.

For the purpose of this discussion, we shall take "social audit" to mean: a *commitment to systematic assessment of and reporting on some meaningful, definable domain of a company's activities that have social impact.* This definition is a fairly disciplined one, and one that will allow the activities now carried on under the social-audit banner to be included in a more embracing form, with independent attestation, at a later date.

SOURCES OF PRESSURE

As we have said, there are powerful forces loose in the land that are demanding some kind of social audit:

1. Executives generally desire to acquire both an individual and a corporate image of social responsibility, one that harmonizes with a public concern which they (and we) do not believe is going to subside.

2. Businessmen, like everyone else, are caught up in the changing mores and priorities of the society and are concerned today about matters which only a few years ago did not worry them. The level of the concern should not be underestimated. Pollution, the disadvantaged and minorities, clarity and directness in advertising—issues like these have moved rapidly onto (and higher and higher on) the agendas of corporate executives.

3. Another influence is commercial. A number of consultants, sensing the possibility of a new source of business and inherently curious about the whole complex area, are trying to develop ways of performing social audits.

4. Then there is the stimulus of the outside "auditors"—the Naders, the Council on Economic Priorities, the new mutual funds, the recently established journal called *Business and Society Review,* minority groups, ecologists, and so forth, all of whom have a stake in making public almost anything that a company

may want to hide. Obviously, such stimuli encourage managements to present their cases in ways they think accurate and proper; but, perhaps even more important, managements want to know what is in store for their companies if they are attacked. This second motivation has obtained in some of the companies with which we are acquainted, where managements actually do not (or did not) know what or how well they were doing, although they may have had some suspicions.

5. Nonprofit organizations such as churches and educational institutions have spurred the idea of social auditing. Urged by their constituents to establish a "social portfolio," to sanitize their holding of paper from companies adjudged irresponsible, or to influence the policies of those in which they have investments, these organizations have been seeking (usually with painful unsuccess) to establish some way of determining if Company X is or is not socially responsible.

6. Investment houses which, for a variety of reasons, are establishing funds specializing in "clean" securities are also generating interest. These houses face the problem of identifying companies that both act responsibly and promise to be good long-term gainers. This is not a simple matter: it begs a gaggle of questions turning on what is "good social performance."

7. The social activists themselves have an obvious stake in some kind of measurements. If they expect to have significant impact on corporate behavior, they need some yardsticks to use in advising the general public of the social health of this or that company.

CONFUSION OF METHODS

It is precisely this broad spectrum of pressures for social auditing that causes much of the confusion. Everybody is talking about the social audit, but scarcely anyone agrees with anyone else as to exactly what it is, and no two organizations are doing it quite the same way. To illustrate:

> • In one company, the chief executive assigned the task of designing a social audit procedure to his public affairs group. This group, naturally enough, was primarily interested in increasing the company's role in community affairs and consequently designed an audit that would demonstrate a close linkage between social programs and long-range profitability.

> • Another CEO wanted to satisfy his own conscience that his company was, indeed, behaving responsibly. Inevitably, the issues and norms selected for the audit were those which were important to him personally, and the nature and precision of the data generated were determined by how much he needed to know to sleep at night.

> • One president wanted to make sure that his corporation's social programs were producing the maximum benefit to society for the investment being made. He focused the auditing effort on making an inventory of what the company was doing and evaluating the usefulness

of each program vis-à-vis others in which the company might engage. Hence his audit was designed to answer such questions as this: "Should we be working with the public schools in town instead of sponsoring low-income housing?"

• The relevant question for a church or an educational institution is this: "Which companies are doing well in ways that are of particular concern to our constituency?" If a constituency is upset about apartheid, or antipersonnel weapons, or pollution, the only questions the audit must answer—within the bounds of financial prudence—are whether or not any companies represented in the institution's portfolio are viewed by the constituency as socially responsible on this particular range of points; and, correspondingly, the audit will be designed to provide just the data that show whether the criteria are in fact being met.

• Consider the social activist who seeks to force corporations to halt activities that have (as he thinks) antisocial effects, and who also seeks to enlist them in the effort to improve the world around them. Here, again, the task is different, and the audit will be different. The activist will select the issues that strike him as being especially significant and collect enough data to convince himself and the general public, which is the ultimate source of his influence, that improper things are being done.

• The consulting firm interested in helping clients with the auditing problem obviously wants to develop a version of the social audit which is financially and professionally feasible and applicable for as wide a variety of clients as possible. Its nonindividualistic approach is bound to conflict and contrast with those of other auditors.

• The company that is seeking either a good image or protection against attack will select those areas for investigation that, in its judgment, will satisfy the public it is trying to impress (which may, incidentally, include its own employees). Since the audit data must be made public, the company will probably need to make investigations and disclosures that are very extensive—extensive enough to convince an audience that is growing ever more skeptical of corporate pronouncements. Its audit is bound to be company-specific, by virtue of the nature and depth of the data required.

In short, many purposes and programs are currently crowding and jostling under the umbrella of the social audit. Nevertheless, the full vision continues to be that, in the future, companies shall report their social performance with the same regularity and the same appearance of precision with which they now report their financial performance.

The question to be asked is whether the audit can ever be developed to a state that will satisfy that austere vision.

THE VISION VS. EXPERIENCE

In the past few months, we have investigated a number of organizations that are engaged in one or another kind of social auditing. We have talked with consulting firms and looked at their efforts. We have met with and, in some cases, worked with companies in many different industries that are taking bites at the apple. We have been associated with several of the social action groups. We have studied some of the investment houses. And we have now reached the point, we feel, where we can define five significant difficulties imbedded in this auditing process.

1. How do we decide what to audit?

As the social auditor enters the thicket of implementation, the first bramble bush he will meet is the question of what to audit. What are the areas of social responsibility, anyway? As we have surveyed current practice, we have found almost as many answers as there are auditors.

Pollution and the hiring and promotion of minorities (including women) receive a roughly consistent priority, but after that things are fairly wide open. Some auditors virtually ignore corporate giving and community programs; others include them. Quite a few stress consumerist issues of various kinds; others go heavy on munitions manufacturing, or investments in South Africa or Portugal. Still others focus on employee well-being—fringe benefits, promotion opportunities, safety, and so forth.

The choice is not easy to make. When he comes to decide whether to include a specific factor, the auditor inevitably realizes the full complexity of some of these issues. For many, Polaroid's involvement in South Africa was a simple matter, but the company did not find it so. Finally, after a strenuous internal debate, the company came to the conclusion that it would better satisfy its social responsibility in the long run, even in the eyes of the groups pressing for withdrawal, by remaining in that unhappy land than by leaving it.

Equally, some of the components of social responsibility are as vague as they are complex. For example, how does the auditor grapple with a subject like "quality of work?" This term can—and does—mean everything from the adequacy of fringe benefits to the degree of employee participation in corporate decisions. Executives in one company found to their surprise that employees felt it was socially irresponsible for management to demand of them as much time and effort as the corporate mission required. Clearly, quality of work is too imprecise a quantity to be taken for granted.

Defining the *relevant parts* of social responsibility creates further difficulties. For some, a social audit is adequate if it simply examines the community activities in which a corporation is engaged. For others, this is ducking the issue: the relevant point, they feel, is the impact a company is having on society because of the business it is in or the way in which it is conducting that business. An insurance company might ask itself, for example, what good it does to audit its investment in low-income housing and minority enterprises but ignore its red-lining policies in the ghettos? Similarly, one might argue that a change in the traditional hiring practices of a company is going to have a far greater beneficial effect on a community than all the gifts it makes to the Community Fund.

Finally, the definitions of corporate social responsibility are still evolving. If one takes the recent past as a basis for prediction, he would have to guess that expectations will rise, that standards of performance will be hoisted, that new unforeseen issues will be introduced, and that some of today's causes will become less relevant. Thus, in 1973, good labor relations is no longer much of an issue; similarly, if pollution laws are strengthened and enforced, pollution control may not be worth auditing in the future. Social responsibility is a moving target, and this fact greatly complicates the choice of what to audit.

Roughly, the decision as to what to audit has to be determined in one of two ways. Either the top corporate executives, on the basis of their interests and their perceptions of the concerns of their constituents, must make the choices, or some kind of survey of the relevant constituencies must be conducted. A good case can be made for either approach; it is largely a question of what purpose a company has determined for the audit.

2.   What are the measures?

Once a company has defined the areas it wants to audit, it must decide how to measure its performance.

One obvious way is by cost—what it spends in each area. But even if a company selects only a narrow definition of social responsibility and focuses just on the costs of its so-called social programs (for example, English-language programs or housing rehabilitation), how does it determine what the true costs of such activities are? How does it measure the executive time that goes into them? How does it assign overhead to them? How does it assess the opportunity costs involved?

Furthermore, cost by itself is an inadequate measure, since the main question the company will want to answer about each activity is, "Was it a success?" The difficulty in answering this question is that such corporate activities can ordinarily be measured only in terms of such intermediate effects as the number of people who have received a given type of service—say, the number of community residents whose apartments have been rehabilitated. Few social programs can satisfactorily document what the delivery of these services did for the people who received them.

In addition, these activities are extremely expensive to evaluate, and it is doubtful whether any company would find it feasible to make frequent evaluations of its total contributions.

A compounding difficulty here is that the answer to the question, even if one gets it, may be valueless. If a company ascertains the number of high school students who use the computer it has donated, what has it really learned? Probably, not very much.

3. What constitutes success?

Thus we come to the problem of defining what constitutes success—that is, of defining the appropriate norms against which a company should measure. Even if a company can make a sound selection of items to audit and can develop some satisfactory measure for its performance on these items, how will it know when it has done a job right? How good is good?

Government standards (if they exist) may fill part of the need here, but most of us would feel that such standards are minimums for performance, not norms for judging success. Furthermore, in many areas such as pollution and minority hiring, there is so much variation of factors from industry to industry in the problems with which companies are confronted that one probably needs separate performance norms for each. Sometimes this is possible; more often it is not; but even when it is, it is rarely adequate. One would not expect Con Ed's records for hiring and promoting Puerto Ricans to look like those of PG&E. Specialized norms mean tougher comparisons in measurement.

In an effort to cut through such problems, some people have suggested that the effectiveness of a company's program in meeting a social issue is the norm that should be used. We have already referred to the difficulty of evaluating social programs and the even greater difficulty of comparing the ones selected with others which could have been undertaken.

There is also another difficulty with this approach. The success of a program for training the hard-core unemployed, for example, can be measured in terms of numbers completing the course, being hired, and being retained in the job. But if an observer tries to go the next step and judge whether a particular company's hard-core training program solved or even significantly contributed to the solution of a social problem, the verdict may well be dismal, simply because any one company's contribution is unlikely to solve a problem unless it is a very large company in a very small community.

4. Where are the data?

Next we should mention the difficulty of collecting data in this area. It is expensive and time consuming for a large, complex company to collect adequate data about its social programs, much less determine which of its activities have a social impact and thus should be studied. Quite frequently, outside auditors have difficulty getting at the kind of information they need. Even inside auditors may run into real problems. For example, one company with only minimal manufacturing operations but extensive retailing ones decided to hire a group of students to check on what it assumed were the few locations where it could be polluting. It very quickly became apparent that the job was truly immense, because the company was disposing of solid wastes in literally hundreds of company locations. The group could only sample, not study, the company's pollution programs.

Another reason for this difficulty is stubborn internal resistance. Even if the CEO wants a social audit, he is likely to encounter foot dragging, if not outright opposition, within his own family. In conglomerates in particular, division managers resent what they perceive as an intrusion into "their" private files.

Also, managers do not seem to care much for morale surveys to see what the people they supervise think of the company and its record in social performance. Others disagree philosophically with the whole social-responsibility idea; some even say that if the boss wants to fool around with it at his level and work with the Boy's Club somewhere, okay — but he had better keep his liberal do-goodism out of operations. This kind of controversy has forced more than one CEO to back off and scale down his internal audit from what he had intended.

In one company, the headquarters staff started to audit the condition of the employees because they thought it would be the easiest way to cut their teeth before they began to audit other matters. Believing that equal employment was well accepted in the company, both as the law of the land and the right thing to do, they sent people to check records in one of the divisions.

The division head, however, flatly refused to let them look at the files; and when he finally did consent to open the drawers as a result of a topside order, he continued to be as uncooperative as possible within the terms of the directive he had received. At this point, the company began to reconsider the whole social-audit idea.

5. How accurate can we be?

Unfortunately, there has been an inordinate amount of loose talk about the social audit, much of it in responsible journals or in responsible places. For example, Thomas Oliphant, writing in *The Boston Globe,* said: "Almost all of this data exists right now on some corporate executive's desk. What is lacking is the decision to put it all together and release it to the public in a manner modeled roughly after financial accounting standards to ensure a maximum of information and a bare minimum of public relations."* To that statement, and the many similar ones being made today, we reply, "Nonsense."

But, unfortunately, it is worse than nonsense. The twin myths that such a thing as a social audit exists and that financial audits are hard and precise have misled some businessmen into trying to create a report on their social performance which has the same precision and accuracy they attribute to the balance sheet.

The fact is that we are not yet at the point where such an audit is possible, and we may never get there — indeed, we may never have to. The social audit, even when we have learned how to do one that is credible internally and externally, may look nothing like a financial audit at all. We are only on the edge of the thicket, and what we really need is not a man with *the* answer, but a number of men with the courage to try to frame *an* answer — to experiment, to learn about how to measure and report on social performance, and to pass what they learn along to the rest of us.

---

*The New Accounting: Profit, Loss and Society," May 1971.

The Abt experiment: Only one of the companies we studied, Abt Associates, had completed anything that could meaningfully be called a social audit.

The Abt audit of its own activities is a public document included in the firm's annual report. It is an effort to represent, in purely dollar terms, the company's social assets and liabilities—in other words, its social impact. This represents a diligent and ingenious pioneering work, especially on the part of the president, Dr. Clark Abt, who spearheaded the effort. However, considering the novelty of this effort, it is no surprise that the firm's accountants did not give it their official sanction.

There are various reasons why we think that this format is *not* the one most likely to be adopted by large, complex companies:

- It does not appear to respond to the currently perceived needs of the executives of such organizations nor to the realities of their situations, as we understand them. For example, the Abt audit is organized around the total social impact of the company rather than around an assessment of its social programs. While this approach has great conceptual attractiveness, it is not particularly well adapted to the needs which are expressed by the executives with whom we are familiar, whose concerns, objectives, and aspirations for an audit are far more limited than Dr. Abt's.

- Abt Associates is a relatively small consulting firm. The total social impact of a large complex company is not nearly so amenable to this kind of financial summary.

- The goal of the Abt audit, once again, is to render social performance in dollar terms in balance sheet form. Thus it does not disclose (it may even hide) the firm's performance in social programs in which its executives are interested. For example, a company could be spending large amounts of money inefficiently, on pollution control or hard-core training, on giving substantial sums to irrelevant charities. And, indeed, in the course of conducting his audit, Abt found out some unwelcome facts about his organization and changed policy accordingly. But the actual rendering of his findings into balance sheet form was, in our view, a superfluous technical exercise. Our sense is that few companies are interested in supporting this last step of technical virtuosity *if the information can meaningfully be presented in other ways.*

- Abt's audit is designed for external reporting. However, most executives are interested at this time in internal reporting for internal assessment. The prospect of external reporting exacerbates the already considerable anxiety of such executives.

- Finally, the Abt form of a social audit is so abstract and complicated that we find few, if any, executives (never mind laymen) who claim to understand it as an overall entity—nor do we feel we can explain it as a totality.

We do, however, encourage the reader to consult the Abt annual report to form an independent judgment. We may well be too sharply critipal; and, indeed, we have a personal bias to which we must confess. We feel that the attempt to reduce social performance to dollar terms is perverse. While monetary measures are of great utility in many contexts, this utility is, finally, limited; we feel there is likely to be fatal error in employing the dollar measures as exhaustive representations of social phenomena.

Our judgment is not so negative with respect to proposals for auditing the dollar *costs* of social contributions, although we are respectful of both the difficulties and the tricky judgmental questions imbedded in such calculating. Mainly we are skeptical of the availability and possibility of rendering the social *consequences*—whether positive or negative—in dollar terms.

All in all, given the complexities and complications of doing a social audit, given the various forms which an audit might take, the varying uses to which it might be put, we judge it a mistake to specify at this time just what its final form should or will be. Instead, we believe that the task of management for the immediate future is to get on the learning curve.

This is best accomplished by tackling the auditing problem in a way that is sufficiently modest to be attainable, yet of sufficient scope to have both some utility and some value as a base for more ambitious versions of the social audit. The first steps toward a social audit should be defined with an eye toward the organizational conflicts that a social audit can bring about.

HINTS FOR GETTING STARTED

Thus our first suggestion is that the audit be initially designed for internal purposes only—that is, for aiding in the decision making process and for helping officers assess the company's social performance, both with a view to its vulnerabilities and to changes that management may want to make in its activities. Such a course offers dual benefits.

For one thing, it relieves the anxieties of those corporate officers who fear the embarrassment of disclosure, enabling the company to make corrections with a certain amount of privacy if it chooses to do so. Equally, it allows officers to take what guidance they can from data and judgments that may be too imprecise to present to the public, and it bypasses their natural fears that their professional and financial future may be adversely affected.

We make this suggestion—that the first effort to a social audit be aimed at internal decision making—in full recognition that the audit is likely to be reported to the public sooner or later. We only propose that there be no initial *commitment* to publication of the first-round audit, so that this learning experience can be entered into with a minimum of anxiety and a minimum of demand for technical elegance.

We also suggest that a company first focus on its programs rather than on its social impact. There are three strong practical reasons for this recommendation. Two of them are those we just cited for aiming the audit at internal decision making: the magnitude of the task and executive anxiety. The task of considering, measuring, and evaluating all the impacts of a large, complex company on society boggles the mind; it also seems very threatening to anxious executives, since the results of such an analysis may strike at the very core of the business. A deodorant manufacturer might become a stench in its own nostrils.

The third reason is the sheer difficulty of defining the limits of social impact, which is surely a conceptual haymaker, as terms go.

Again we recognize the limitations and counterarguments to what we are proposing. For many industries, one could argue that a company's social activities are merely cosmetics that conceal the impact of its regular business activities. There is little reason for crediting a drug company, say, with an excellent domestic employment policy without investigating its promotion policies and labeling practices in other countries. This counterargument concludes that the auditor's concern must be global. Nonetheless, we advise early simplification for the sake of avoiding endless debates that might well take on the color of theological disputes.

We also recognize that when a company is examining its social programs, it may also want to look at its regular business activities as a separate, parallel effort, especially if either its internal or external constituencies are demanding such an examination or are likely to do so.

For example, one bank is looking at the impact of its lending policies, realizing that these are related to the social audit it is undertaking; but the bank is not at this stage considering the policy investigation as part of the audit. Similarly, even where public pressure encourages or forces a company to look at one or more of its regular business activities—for example, munitions manufacturing, construction in Vietnam, or doing business in South Africa—such examinations ought to be handled separately from the initial audit.

If companies accept two suggestions—focusing only on internal use and social program evaluation—life will be much simpler, but still complicated enough to be interesting. The audit will have a "meaningful, definable domain," as our statement suggests it must, but the domain will still be virgin wilderness.

We must point out, however, that a compromise is available which some companies may prefer to adopt. A company may feel it imperative to define those constituencies to which its actions are most relevant—employees, customers, stockholders, "the community," and so on—and survey these constituencies to determine for which aspects of social performance they hold the company responsible and what their expectations are.

This procedure would establish a "definable domain" for social auditing in a quite different fashion from the path we have recommended; but it has one defensive advantage worth mentioning, namely, public attitudes. Its disadvantage may be that it probably does not provide as valuable a learning experience as our more orderly first step does for the company that plans to build toward a more complete audit. Hence, on balance, we believe that concentration on social programs as the "defined domain" is the preferable route.

Inventory + cost

Assuming a company decides to review its social programs first, its next step should be to compile an inventory of its explicitly social programs. For almost every company, this list will include the currently popular issues of pollution control, minority and female hiring, and promotion practices. Let us say that it will also include corporate giving. From there on, the nature of the list is likely to vary with the corporation in question, and it will not always be easy to decide what ought to be included and what ought to be excluded, or why.

A typical instance of such a difficulty is whether to include executive participation in community affairs when the executives contribute their own time. Our advice is to exclude any item from the list that is not the result of an explicit corporate policy involving a meaningful level of resource commitment. We also advise companies to exclude any item that causes substantial argument. (Of course, a company would do well to keep a list of rejected items, for future perspective.)

There will be other kinds of difficulty as well. In some instances, management may discover that there is no central source of information on everything the company is doing in the social area; hence compiling the list may take more effort than one would expect or accept.

Once the inventory has been reduced to those socially motivated activities to which the company has clearly made a commitment and which it accepts as "social programs," management can begin to assemble the costs and performance data associated with them, to get a picture of the extent of the company's commitment to each one and to social programs as a whole.

The first area is the matter of costs. Generally, there will be less difficulty in getting the direct costs of each activity than in ascertaining the true costs, which is quite a different matter, as we have already pointed out. These true costs should include allocated overhead and opportunity costs as well, wherever the resources might have been put to different use. A company's ability to get such true costs readily will depend on how the relevant items are represented in its accounting system, what system it is using to measure work, and the like. One should also realize that even if the basic data are available, special allocation conventions may be required.

Since considerable expense and effort are required, the auditors and management should make an explicit decision as to whether they deem it worthwhile to establish the true costs of social activities, whether they are willing to go with a rough estimate, or whether they will be content with knowing only the direct costs.

Our sense is that the public at large is not likely to be interested in the true costs of a company's social activities. Even though the true costs would represent a more accurate picture of the company's level of effort, they are likely to be perceived as padded figures.

However, for *management* decision making, true cost will be important. If it proves difficult to get true costs in the first audit attempt, and a decision is made to forgo this information, this circumstance should signal the need for establishing mechanisms for assessing true costs in the future. It is highly probable that there is no thoroughly satisfactory way to do this at present, although Professors Neil Churchhill and John Shank are currently researching this problem at the Harvard Business School.

The second area of quantitative measurement is performance data. The place to start is still readily available statistical data that show the level of effort expended and measure the output. For example, how many hard-core unemployed have been trained, or apartments renovated, or children served in a day-care center? It is true, as we have pointed out, that pulling together such material may be difficult. It is also true that this kind of material does not necessarily show, in and of itself, the *effectiveness* of the programs.

Perhaps the assistance extended to minority businesses has in fact done more harm than good in that the funds generated ultimately are spent outside the inner city, or the failures have served to discourage people from starting ventures instead of encouraging them to do so. But we shall return to this difficult matter of norms and social benefits in a moment. Suffice to say at this point that there are some figures that can be obtained, and that they do constitute legitimate data for a social audit.

Here again, we would opt for a kind of "creaming" approach. Rather than spending inordinate amounts of time either in determining what figures should be collected or which should be included, we would urge that the most obvious and easily ascertainable be the ones that are reported. It is too early in the state of the art to try to squeeze out the last, ultimate figure or to fight through the finest kind of judgments as to what should be in or out.

Ethics of public reporting. These first two steps of an audit will give a picture of the extent and nature of the company's social programs and of the resources committed thereto. The display of just these two sets of information will be of help to many managements in assessing their social performance. These sets of information could also be the basis for reporting to the public, should management choose to do so.

It may be argued that reporting data such as these is very little different than what is being done for public relations purposes by many companies in their annual reports or in special publications. We grant this. But we see nothing wrong in a company's communicating the extent and nature of its social activities and the magnitude of effort behind those activities, provided the coverage is complete and the reporting honest.

Such an audit would at least reveal the extent of the company's concern. One of us recently conducted a study of the reaction of Bostonians to the efforts Boston business was making to help the community, and we were struck by the fact that success or failure, or even quantity of effort, is outweighed in people's minds by evidence that companies or individuals actually are concerned and are doing something about it. Businessmen are not expected to solve the problems of the city, nor are they expected to be successful in every venture they undertake. However, they are expected to take the problems seriously.

Thus an honest and straightforward public reporting of what a company is doing, accompanied by the figures that are available, seems to us to be perfectly appropriate if public reporting is the name of the game.

Questions of measures and norms

We know a fair number of companies that have taken one or both of these first two steps—inventorying activities and assessing costs. Some have done it as part of a social audit activity; others, for the more straightforward reason that management wanted to know what the company was doing. None found that this was a trivial effort, and a number found that the mere assemblage of information as to what the company was doing was already of value to management.

However, we doubt that managers who take the concept of a social audit seriously will want to stop at this point. They will want to make an assessment of how well they are doing in their various social activities. Since this seems to us to be an inevitable direction for the social audit, we would encourage this step — but with moderation, because assessing performance is beset with grave difficulties. Assessment in the first audit should be limited to only several of the most important activities.

Here we must distinguish between cases where true measures of performance are available and cases where they are not (we shall discuss the second of these possibilities when we describe the process audit).

Now a true performance measure is a measure of the ultimate result that an activity is intended to accomplish. We have already identified the two types of program areas for which performance measures are most likely to be available — pollution and employment. Some of these performance measures may be the fallout of the "easily available" data which are noted at the inventory stage, but such data are bound to be incomplete; a company is very likely to have data available on emissions into the air and water, for example, but it is not equally likely to know about its contribution to solid waste. Personnel records, too, will vary with respect to the availability of information about the employment of minorities.

Norms, also, are required, and once again the picture is cloudy and uneven. These are laws of various kinds by which to judge one's levels of emissions into air and water, but not for emissions of solid waste. Nor are there likely to be industrywide norms of performance unless the industry in question has been studied by the Council for Economic Priorities or some similar organization.

Some commentators suggest that one should judge pollution performance by what is technologically feasible, and this may work out in some cases; however, cost/benefit trade-offs are only too likely to crop up. Again, companies can get industry norms for the employment status of minorities from the Equal Employment Opportunities Commission, but these industrywide norms may have to be adjusted to the idiosyncracies of the communities in which a company's installations are located.

However, while it may be possible to get adequate performance measures and norms for some of a company's social programs, for others it will be difficult to the point of virtual impossibility. The results of a community development program, for example, perhaps will not be clear until sometime in the future, and a particular company's contributions to these developments will be hard to isolate even then. Again, management might be satisfied with judging a program for training the hard-core unemployed by the number of candidates who graduate from the program and secure employment, but the management might also view these numbers as only intermediate measures of the long-term effects which it regards as crucial.

Whenever the auditing team and management feel that there are no adequate performance measures of a social program — and this is likely to be true of almost all service programs — we advocate a *process* audit, which we shall now describe. We have not yet seen a process audit completed. What we propose takes as its model such innovative efforts of the accounting profession as the management audit.*

THE PROCESS AUDIT

The first step in a process audit should be an assessment of the circumstances under which each social program being audited came into being. (We consciously avoid saying "the reason" for the program, since in many instances the circumstance is likely to be less rational than the term "reason" implies.) While this search into origins may at first glance look like navel gazing, it is likely to be crucial for informed future decision making. A company that does not know how it gets into things is likely to get into things it does not want to do.

The second step is to explicate the goals of the program — that is, to produce a statement of what it is intended to accomplish.

The third is to spell out the rationale behind the activity. A company should specify what it proposes to do to attain the goals, and why it thinks this set of actions will achieve them.

The final step in the process audit is to describe what is actually being done as opposed to what the rationale says ought to be done. We assume that this description will include any relevant quantitative measures, such as numbers and types of persons served, and any available intermediate measures of performance, such as proportions of defaults on loans.

The goal of such a process audit is to assemble the information that will make it possible for a person to intelligently assess the program, to decide whether he agrees with its goals, to decide whether the rationale is appropriate to the goals, and to judge whether the actual implementation promises to attain those goals satisfactorily.

Process audits are most likely to be appropriate for service programs, which are notoriously hard to evaluate but around which considerable amounts of expertise develop. Thus appropriate norms for process audits are likely to be standards of best practice. Where it seems in order, then, a process audit might be conducted in part by one or another expert in the area, especially since companies vary considerably in their relevant in-house capabilities.

Even where the purpose of the audit is just to clarify internal decision making, a company may want to bring in an outside expert to help define the relevant factors to assess and to make the final evaluation of a program. When such expertise is brought to bear, management can better judge whether it is satisfied with present activities, whether it wants one or another changed and improved, and whether it wants to shift its efforts among activities.

Once all the above information is assembled for management scrutiny, and possibly for presentation to the public (an option always open to management),

---

*See Olin C. Snellgrave, "The Management: Organizational Guidance System," *Management Review,* March 1972, pp. 41–45.

we would regard the first round of a social audit to be completed. It seems likely that the public will be uninterested in the first step of the process audit we have proposed—namely, the circumstances under which the company undertook the activity (though there may be instances where this is relevant). However, the remaining steps develop information that would be helpful and acceptable to the public in its evaluation of the company's performance.

There are many ways in which an initial process will be incomplete and imperfect, compared with what a company might aspire to later. It may be bulky and cumbersome. The format will be unstandardized. Only a portion of the company's social impact will be assessed. And of that which is assessed, only the most important activities will be given any treatment beyond bare identification, description, and specification of costs. Furthermore, such technical problems as assessment of true costs and performance measurement will be handled in a fairly rough and ready manner.

But the show will be on the road. Management will be in a considerably better position to make decisions and take actions. It will also know whether it wants to report to the public at this stage; and if it does, it will have a respectable report from which to work. Furthermore:

- The foundations for future auditing will have been laid.
- the nucleus of an auditing team will have been trained.
- The controller will have had his first taste of the problem of assessing the true costs of social programs.
- Management will have a realistic basis for estimating what an audit costs and is worth.
- Hopefully, the fears of corporate executives will be surfaced and assuaged.
- To the extent that management thinks it desirable, it can build expanded ambitions into future audits.
- The very fact that management has undertaken an honest, systematic effort will be a plus.

The reader will note that we have said nothing about the relationship between responsibility and profitability. This is intentional. We have specifically excluded from our version of a first audit any attempt to assess the contribution of social activities to the profitability of a company. We believe that this exercise is possible only in the case of a minority of such activities, and that the attempt to complete this exercise, while having a certain appeal to technical virtuosity, is likely to divert attention from the more straightforward objectives we have proposed—namely, management information and public reporting.

The future needs

We close on the question of whether a company can carry out such an audit on itself. As the reader would expect, there is not a yes-or-no answer to this question. It is better to rephrase the question and ask whether the company can benefit from outside help. In fact, at present, there is not much outside help to turn to. Only a few consultants have had any experience in social auditing, and the experience of even those few is limited.

Our conclusion is that a certain amount of outside help can be useful both as a source of discipline and direction, and as a spur to keep the audit moving. Most companies have had trouble on these scores. Outsiders can also supply technical help on such matters as assembling true costs, preparing information for distribution to management and the public, and the process audit

Eventually, we assume, if the social audit develops viably, the accounting profession will be centrally involved, both in setting up systems to gather data and in attesting to the truth of the data for the purpose of improving its credibility. This is already a matter of considerable interest in the accounting profession, but at this point everyone in the race is standing on the same starting line. The most important task now is to start running. Only in that way will we learn what the track is really like.

An Approach to Socio-Economic Accounting

David F. Linowes

"Social audits" will be required within the next decade for most business organizations, the author is convinced. Prepared by an internal interdisciplinary committee and audited by an external socio-economic audit committee, they will be demanded by consumer groups, special institutional investors, and an increasing number of regulatory governmental agencies. Before long business will be expected also to prepare Socio-Economic Operating Budgets to protect what the company expects to do in the social area during the succeeding year:

"Business managers must have available a meaningful measure of their long-range social and economic commitments for all the world to see and evaluate, along with the short-range measurement of profit-making operational activities which have always been given broad visibility through the profit and loss staements. The Socio-Economic Operating Statement fills this need."

Business management today is functioning in a new environment and is being forced to assume a share of society's problems. This is no longer news. But it is now also becoming apparent that the challenge to the role of business has become so widespread that executives can no longer look to dollar-profit measurement alone as an adequate reflection of their effectiveness. With the expanding exposure of business to the various facets of society, the traditional measure-

From *The Conference Board Record*, November, 1972. Reprinted by special permission of The Conference Board.

ment of profitability and growth reflected both in the profit-loss statement and balance sheet are no longer adequate.

Financial analysts have always been aware that those managements which neglect their machinery and equipment and do not make expenditures to train junior executives often show a higher earnings picture during the short term than is justified. In time, of course, this neglect of equipment and executive personnel training takes its toll in the operating effectiveness of the company, but for the present, the profits look better.

Those companies which undertake actions which may benefit society and incur costs for such activity are in effect being "penalized" on their profit and loss statements for such activity. Costs of hiring and training hardcore unemployables, making executives available to assist ghetto entrepreneurs, and incurring extra costs for environmental improvements presently serve to hurt the record of progressive management because they are charged as expenses against its operations. Obviously, business managements may show better operating profit results by not incurring these extra costs and by ignoring the harm caused by dumping production waste into streams or polluting the atmosphere.

In our present system of business reporting, however, we do not measure —or report in any statement of a management's stewardship—the damage done to that stream or to the air we breath. Nor do we, on the other hand, give proper reporting credit for the "good" that management does, either.

Admittedly, social programs are sometimes difficult to define. That does not mean we should not try to deal with them, for I am certain that society will no longer condone further avoiding the accountability. And I believe, clearly defined or not, we know a social action or nonaction when we see it. As Justice Potter Steward said of obscenity. "I can't define obscenity but I know it when I see it."

GIVING THAT GOES BEYOND THE LAW

Basically, the concept of what is included in a social action program is what a business has given to or held back from society. If this seems somewhat vague, the purpose is to permit management the widest latitude in the measurement of these activities and to encourage innovation. We must also make distinctions between the costs of actions voluntarily undertaken and those social programs required by law and/or contract, e.g., with the union or with local authorities, since these are arm's-length negotiated business deals and therefore a necessary cost of doing business. Thus a voluntary social action program *today* may be a necessary cost of doing business *tomorrow* by the passage of legislation or the decision of a court.

It may be years before we can invent and use social measurement with the confidence and relative precision with which we use economic and fiscal measurements in business and government, but we do have enough standards available now with which to begin. Indeed, considering the softness of much of the economic and fiscal data used (and often misused) today, I would think that the results of social measurements with all their present limitations can be just as effective as economic measurements.

What we might do at once, then, is to borrow from economics and apply the "system" of economic and fiscal measurement to social areas. It is this that I call Socio-Economic Measurement.

Dollars involving social costs incurred by business are usually determinable. However, the fact that a prepared statement of these costs may not be complete is not sufficient reason for us to delay further the preparation and use of such exhibits. Traditional financial statements have never themselves been able to reflect significant facets of business affairs fully—e.g., contingent assets such as the value of trained manpower, extent of provision for executive succession, potential profitability of new inventions and product development, or contingent liabilities which include potential adverse legal actions for faulty products.

MEASURING SOCIAL "DETRIMENTS" AND "IMPROVEMENTS"

There should be no reason to forbid us from developing a Socio-Economic Operating Statement (SEOS). It would be prepared periodically along with a business organization's profit and loss statement and balance sheet. The SEOS I visualize is a tabulation of those expenditures made voluntarily by a business aimed at the "improvement" of the welfare of the employees and public, safety of the product, and/or conditions of the environment. Such expenditures required by law or union contract would not be includable, inasmuch as these are mandatory and necessary costs of doing business.

An item is determined to be a "detriment" or negative charge for SEO Statement purposes when a responsible authority brings the need for social action to the attention of management, but management does not voluntarily take steps to satisfy such a need, even though it is of such a nature that a *reasonably prudent and socially aware business management* would have responded favorably. The fact that this determination is a subjective one should not discourage its implementation. In traditional business accounting, research and development items, work in process inventories, allowances for bad debts, depreciation charges, price–earnings ratios are also largely subjective determinations.

Several guidelines to help identify and classify socio-economic items can be offered:

> • If a socially beneficial action is required by law, but is ignored, the cost of such item is a "detriment" for the year. The same treatment is given an item if postponed, even with government approval. Similarly, if a socially beneficial action is required by law and is applied earlier than the law requires, it is an improvement. (In an inflationary period this might mean a saving of money for the company and could be categorized as a contingent asset.)

> • A pro-rata portion of salaries and related expenses of personnel who spent time in socially beneficial actions or with social organizations is included as an "improvement."

> • Cash and product contributions to social institutions are included as "improvements."

- Cost of setting up facilities for the general good of employees or the public — without union or government requirement — is an includable "improvement."

- Neglecting to install safety devices which are available at a reasonable cost is a "detriment."

- The cost of voluntarily building a playground or nursery school for employees and/or neighbors is a plus on the exhibit. Operating costs of the facility in each succeeding year are also includable.

- Costs of relandscaping strip mining sites, or other environmental eyesores, if not otherwise required by law, are listed as improvements on the SEOS exhibit.

- Extra costs in designing and building unusually attractive business facilities for beauty, health and safety are includable "improvements."

The results of an SEO Statement produce an amount of "Total Socio-Economic Contribution or Deficit for the Year." It can be effectively used by comparing such statements for various companies in the same industry. Also, analyzing SEO Statements for a particular company over several years helps establish the general directions of the social involvement of a company's management.

THE SOCIAL AUDIT AS AN OPERATING STATEMENT

The various positive and negative social actions and inactions mentioned are classified on the SEOS exhibit into three groups: *Relations with People, Relations with Environment* and *Relations with Product*. The Socio-Economic Operating Statement that I recommended be instituted would then have the appearance of the chart below.

XXXX CORPORATION
Socio-Economic Operating Statement for the Year Ending
December 31, 1971

I   *Relations with People:*
   A. *Improvements:*

1. Training program for handicapped workers	$ 10,000	
2. Contribution to educational institution	4,000	
3. Extra turnover costs because of minority hiring program	5,000	
4. Cost of nursery school for children of employees, voluntarily set up	11,000	
Total Improvements		$ 30,000
B. *Less: Detriments*		
1. Postponed installing new safety devices on cutting machines (cost of the devices)		14,000

C. Net Improvements in People Actions for the Year		$ 16,000*

II *Relations with Environment:*
  A. *Improvements:*

1. Cost of reclaiming and landscaping old dump on company property	$ 70,000	
2. Cost of installing pollution control devices on Plant A smokestacks	4,000	
3. Cost of detoxifying waste from finishing process this year	9,000	
Total Improvements		$ 83,000

B. *Less: Detriments*

1. Cost that would have been incurred to relandscape strip mining site used this year	$ 80,000	
2. Estimated costs to have installed purification process to neutralize poisonous liquid being dumped into stream	100,000	$180,000
C. Net Deficit in Environment Actions for the Year		($97,000)*

III *Relations with Product:*
  A. *Improvements:*

1. Salary of V.P. while serving on government Product Safety Commission	$ 25,000	
2. Cost of substituting lead-free paint for previously used poisonous lead paint	9,000	
Total Improvements		$ 34,000

B. *Less: Detriments*

1. Safety device recommended by Safety Council but not added to product		22,000
C. Net Improvements in Product Actions for the Year		$ 12,000*
Total Socio-Economic Deficit for the Year		($69,000)
Add: Net Cumulative Socio-Economic Improvements as at January 1, 1971		$249,000
Grand Total Net Socio-Economic Actions to December 21, 1971		$180,000

---

*The starred items are summed to obtain the Total Socio-Economic Deficit for the year 1971.

PREPARING THE SOCIO-ECONOMIC OPERATING STATEMENT

The SEOS exhibits themselves would be prepared by a small interdisciplinary team headed by an accountant. Other members of the team could include a seasoned business executive, sociologist, public health administrator, economist, or members of other disciplines whose specific expertise might apply to a particular industry or circumstance. Although SEO Statements would be prepared internally by an interdisciplinary group, they should be audited by an outside independent interdisciplinary team headed by a CPA.

Though determination of items to be included in the SEOS is to be based upon subjective judgments, a standard dollar value applied to these improvements or "detriments" would be a combination of what businessmen traditionally classify as capital expenditures and expense expenditures. For example, the full cost of a permanent installation of a pollution control device is included in the SEO Statement in the year the cost is voluntarily incurred, as is the annual operating cost of a hardcore minority group training program. For convenience of reference, the totals could be expressed in Socio-Economic Management Dollars (SEM$) so as to identify all expenditures made voluntarily of a socially beneficial nature.

Specific cost items which would be entered on a SEO Statement as "improvements" or positive actions would include:

1. Cost of training program for handicapped workers.
2. Contribution to educational institutions.
3. Extra turnover costs because of minority hiring policy. (The adverse of this item, the cost of not setting up adequate orientation programs, would be included as detrimental nonactions.)
4. Cost of nursery school for children of employees, voluntarily set up.
5. Cost of reclaiming and landscaping old dump on company property.
6. Cost of installing pollution control devices on smokestacks ahead of legal requirements.
7. Cost of detoxifying waste from finishing process this year, ahead of legal requirement.
8. Salary of vice president while serving on government Product Safety Commission.
9. Cost of substituting lead-free paint for previously used poisonous lead paint.

Contrariwise, these specific costs would be entered on the SEOS as negative or detrimental nonactions:

1. Postponed installing new safety devices on cutting machines (cost of the devices).
2. Cost that would have been incurred to relandscape strip mining site used this year.
3. Estimated cost to have installed a purification process to neutralize polluting liquid being dumped into stream.
4. Cost of safety devices recommended by Safety Council but not added to product.

I would emphasize that some of these examples may no longer be includable on a current Socio-Economic Operating Statement, but they serve to illustrate.

Notes on Critiques of Social Auditing

Any critique of the social audit must, of course, consider that the doctrine of social responsibility is itself a "muddy" concept. As one of our colleagues put it, "Trying to analyze social responsibility is like trying to cut smoke with a knife." There is little agreement on the logic of the concept, let alone on what should be included or whether the ingredients can be measured.

These inadequacies show up most in the Linowes proposal. Linowes' approach has been included in several journals and popular magazines. In one, his model was subjected to critique by six practitioners and scholars and found wanting in several respects.† Much of the criticism involves the subjectiveness of Linowes' work and the fact that his approach measures inputs only. For example, one critic bemoaned the subtraction of the undone from the completed projects as depreciating the value of the completed projects. He also asked who was to specify the "detriments." Others criticized Linowes' reliance on costs. A costly program could be impeding progress, yet look quite good on SEOS. Conversely, many lower-cost, but quite beneficial, programs would not show up well. Another critic thought that managers who were able to build social benefit into productive systems intrinsically would not appear as good as managers who had to add expensive gadgets to accomplish the same social purposes; in essence, the efficient manager might be penalized. Finally, another critic attacked Linowes' ground rules; because SEOS excludes the accomplishments of legally required activities, once legislation is passed, expenditures for a program initiated prior to the law would cease being counted, yet the firm may have been way ahead of others and receive little recognition in later years. And since SEOS is limited to one year's activities, debt service on a previously made expenditure would not be counted. In sum, Linowes' approach would severely penalize efficient firms, would open up firms to all sorts of subjective judgments on detriments, and would not really measure benefits.

The cautious approach of Bauer and Fenn also relies heavily on the reporting of cost information, although they suggest that, where possible, reliable impact measures can provide valuable control information. Listing and assigning "appropriate" cost values to social activities (as they suggest for the initial stages of implementation) is probably most appropriate as an internal expense-control device. Indeed, this initial approach is a logical extension of the popular "management audit" and reflects a broadening of the more traditional controllership activities of the firm.

Perhaps the key criticism of much of social auditing is that, *for societal purposes,* the techniques do not measure rigorously the real costs and benefits of externalities. They simply provide a list of good and evil compiled by management. Reporting the cost of a pollution-control device tells nothing but the out-of-pocket cost of the device. Reporting on the probable costs of a project that was not undertaken simply measures out-of-pocket costs that were *not* incurred. Re-

---

†Business and Society Review/Innovation, Winter 1972–1973

porting these data, of course, may have a cathartic effect for the manager. They may even be good public relations. From a societal point of view, however, the data are not so useful in measuring real social impacts. The social audit may simply provide the public with a corporate self-adulation sheet.

What is more useful (from a societal point of view) is a measure of external costs and benefits, and these can be determined best by those affected. And if those supposedly affected don't really suffer costs, then there are no external costs despite what managers may think. The same holds for social benefits. Perhaps, then, from a societal point of view, businessmen are not the ones to engage in social auditing; *society* is! And when society calculates those external costs and finds them unbearable, they might petition their government to pass legislation to force firms to absorb them. But that is nothing more than the traditional business-society relationship.

QUESTIONS FOR DISCUSSION

1. Cynics have contended that social accounting represents little more than attempting to measure the unmeasurable. Comment.

2. David Linowes has often been called the "Father of Social Accounting." Evaluate Linowes' work and present a critique of its applicability and practical use.

3. The focus of many challenges to social accounting is on errors of omission rather than commission. Is it valid to challenge social accounting on what it *cannot* do rather than what it *can* do for the business decision-maker? Has the literature in anyway contributed to critics' focus on errors of omission?

4. What arguments do Bauer and Fenn give for limiting the use of an initial social audit to internal purposes? Can you think of any others?

5. Why might a staff person responsible for a company's social accounting efforts have difficulty in securing the cooperation of line managers? How might the staff person go about securing cooperation?

6. What are the fundamental purposes behind developing a scheme for reporting on a company's social activities? Who could ultimately make use of such information? How might the users end up working at cross-purposes?

7. What is the "austere vision" of social accounting and reporting to which Bauer and Fenn refer? Does it serve any practical purpose or does it simply provide grounds for intellectual exercise?

8. Why are assessments of the "true costs" of a company's social activities so difficult? Are such assessments necessary?

SELECTED READINGS

Bauer, R. A., and D. H. Fenn, Jr., *The Corporate Social Audit.* (New York: The Russell Sage Foundation, 1972.)

Brandon, C. H., and J. P. Matoney, Jr., "Social-responsibility financial statement," *Management Accounting,* November, 1975.

Briloff, A. J., *Unaccountable Accounting: Games Accountants Play.* (New York: Harper and Row, 1972.)

Carroll, A. B., and G. W. Beiler, "Landmarks in the evolution of the social audit," *Academy of Management Journal,* September, 1975.

Dierkes, M., and R. A. Bauer, eds., *Corporate Social Accounting.* (New York: Praeger, 1973.)

"The first attempts at corporate 'Social Audit,' " *Business Week,* September 23, 1972.

Linowes, D. F., "Let's get on with the social audit: A specific proposal," *Business and Society Review,* Winter, 1972–73.

Mobley, S. C., "The challenges of socioeconomic accounting," *Accounting Review,* October, 1970.

Ross, G. H. B., "Social accounting: Measuring the unmeasurable," *Canadian Chartered Accountant,* July, 1971.

Sethi, S. P., "Getting a handle on the social audit," *Business and Society Review,* Winter, 1972–73.

Taylor, T. C., "Illusions of social accounting," *CPA Journal,* January, 1976.

Tipgos, M. A., "Reporting corporate performance in the social sphere," *Management Accounting,* August, 1976.

Tipgos, M. A., "The case against the social audit," *Management Accounting,* November, 1976.

Case

SPECIFIC MOTORS COMPANY*

Specific Motors Company (SMC) overhauls manufacturing equipment for resale. When the company started in 1938, Mr. George McClendon bought out the machines and equipment of depression-bankrupt manufacturers in the New York City area, and resold overhauled pieces to new and established businesses. In those days he relied upon inside information and the grapevine for tips on new businesses and for spreading the word about his wares. His father, with whom George had immigrated to New York from Ireland in 1906 when he was nine years old, worked with him as the business grew until his death in 1948. In those first ten years, the company grew from six employees, all of whom were cousins and uncles, operating out of a shed behind their tenement, to a small but adequate brick factory in Westford, Pennsylvania, with thirty-seven employees. Presently, the company operates five plants in the greater Westford area.

There were many business failures during the war, and many successes. In New Jersey, northern New York and New England, many of

---

*This case was prepared by Robert Comerford. All rights reserved.

the latter employed SMC machines. Early in the fifties, George added a sales force and began industrial advertising, both of which by 1959 had boosted sales significantly. In 1957 one of the salesmen, who had been in sales for a small plastic color manufacturer, convinced George that there was a whole industry developing in which the product was molded plastic parts, toys, and oddities. This mini-industry involved buying the appropriate machinery and going into business. SMC's strategy capitalized on the high turnover of these new businesses, the presence of many marginally operable machines floating through the market, and the high prices of new ones.

With the addition, in the late fifties, of the new line, and the formation of industrial marketing techniques, SMC grew and prospered. The strategy remained the same—in George's words, " . . . buy low, invest a little labor, and sell high, but not as high as new. But most importantly, service, advise, and befriend your customers." The main line had inadvertently become electric motors, and SMC's electric-motor group was its largest. Industrial electric motors can cost thousands of dollars new. Secondhand ones were easy to overhaul or repair for experienced people, but very difficult for the inexperienced.

By 1965, SMC had customers all over the country and several in Europe and Japan, but they were thinly spread. It had relatively few customers, but they were firmly entrenched. Suddenly, George retired in 1964, turning the business over to his State University-educated son, George, Jr.

Moving Plans

The company had incorporated years before, but it was closely held. George, Jr., wanted to expand because present facilities were quite dilapidated and operating near capacity. SMC was not heavily laden with debt, but George simply did not want to assume more. Almost ten percent of SMC's customers were located in the Albany–Troy, New York, area; and young George had in mind purchase of a large plant just south of Albany. It was in much better shape than the several Westford facilities, and he was thinking about moving his family to the upper New York state area. He said, "The people are friendlier up there, and it's more concentrated industrially."

The obvious solution to funding needs was to go public. Financially the company was quite healthy even though he wished to take on no more debt. George knew that the way to manage going public was to begin leaking information about it long before actually doing it. He planned to start locally with clients and suppliers and brag discreetly about sales and profits and growth for a year or two.

Community Reaction to SMC Plants

George was worried, however, about some bad publicity the company had received recently. Several editorials had appeared in a leading

Westford newspaper complaining about the ugly appearance of one of the Westford plants. In fact, it, and the others, were unkempt structures, which George, Sr., had saved from demolition years before when he purchased them. The consensus was that, while the McClendon family had become wealthy "buying junk, repainting it, and selling it to strangers," they had never done anything to improve the appearance of their facilities. There were piles of old, rusty machinery of all sorts piled in parking lots at the various plants. Those which were of wooden construction had not been painted or maintained externally since they were purchased by McClendon. Most of them had been bought from bankrupt companies and no capital had been "wasted" on cleaning them up. And they were eyesores!

The worst site, and the object of the public's interest, was the huge State Street shop. It was purchased for "a song" from a machine and tool manufacturer which had relocated in South Carolina. SMC occupied about one-fourth of its 275,000 square feet, the rest of which was empty and deteriorating. The building paralleled State Street, which was heavily traveled. Its windows were nearly all broken, clapboards were falling off, and it had not been painted in years. Across the street was a small park and a new high school. Since construction of both, the city had tried to force SMC to demolish the unused portion of the structure and upgrade the appearance of the remainder.

The issue had since degenerated into an emotional, highly unprofessional state of affairs. The city attorneys claimed that George, Sr., had made a verbal agreement with certain city officials to take care of the problem when the school and park were in the planning stages. George, Jr., flatly refused to do anything, stating that the company would need the space for warehousing and he would "shape it up when the time comes." Further, he said that he had the right to do nothing to the building if he wished, and no one could force him into it against his will. George, Sr., quite senile by now, did not remember any such agreement.

SMC Community Involvement

The elder McClendon had never encountered this kind of hostility. He was greatly respected for involvement in many community activities, charitable organizations, and a general propensity to share his modest wealth and his company's while he actively managed it. Many people felt that young George had swindled his way into the company and stories proliferated about his wrestling the company out of the old man's hands. None of this was true, but George, Jr.'s arrogance and aloofness and his "devil-may-care" activities while growing up all contributed to paint a hostile local image. Additionally, word had gotten around town that George was "tight" with donations and contributions to local organizations. In fact, the charitable activities of his father were continued by George, Jr., but with little fanfare. Further, young George directed the philanthropy of SMC more discriminately than had his father. That meant that some recipients were given less, and others more than they had received when George, Sr., ran the company. The bases for George, Sr.'s philanthropy had been mostly emotional. His son, who had majored in finance and marketing at State, saw philanthropy more as an investment. He felt that gifts by his company should be managed so as to maximize his perception of a sort of political, if not directly financial, return. Unfortunately, young George had taken no political science courses!

George and SMC's accountant and treasurer were afraid that this (heretofore not more than bothersome) set of problems would seriously interfere with the stock offering, or at least, keep the price down. At one meeting between the two, George launched into a tirade about the whole mess. He yelled, "What right have the people in this town to interfere with my operations? Last year we gave away ten thousand dollars to solve all of their problems and in return they do this to us!" The accountant, John Wettereid, self-taught, very calm, usually mild-natured, and above all, competent, recommended that they stop giving SMC's money away.

George responded, "Oh sure, they'll burn us to the ground!" He then asked John to go back to his office and start pulling together a list of all the company's charitable contributions. He felt that if the case ever got to court, such information had better be on the top of his head.

John said that he did not have "all that stuff around," and that "getting it would be one heck of a job."

With deliberately underscored finality, George made a statement about the size of John's paycheck and told him to begin immediately on the list.

The next three days saw John shuffling around the small offices, grumbling about "college kids," trying to track down all "the stuff." He was trying to find cancelled checks and receipts for the last year. George, Sr., had never recorded any of his charitable activities, and so none was accounted for when young George took over. Many of the earlier contributions were in cash; some of the company's employees were often loaned to public and charitable organizations, with no record, to work for a few hours or days. Almost every year for the last ten, for example, three or four men were sent over to the Boy's Club to paint. In 1959, a new swimming pool (and hockey rink) was donated to the city at a cost of $30,000. A fund was established which contributed $2,000 a year to the upkeep of the latter facility. There were memorials, other loans of employees, scholarship funds, free equipment, and donated services given by the company to the community.

Four days after their meeting, John notified George that he had accumulated all of the items he could identify. A meeting was called between the two men, in which John grumbled that if he was going to be held responsible for this information, maybe he should start keeping more detailed records of it. He also made it clear that George would have to notify him of any gifts he made.

The list presented to George at this meeting was as follows:

SMC Contributions, Donations, and Gifts for last year

	$ or Description
United Fund	$5,000
Westford High School Booster Club	200
Westford Public Library	300
American Cancer Society	400
Civil Air Patrol	50
Easter Seal Society	200
Kennedy Memorial	500
Audubon Society	100
McClendon Scholarship	500
Two ten-horsepower motors to Westford Vocational H.S.	220
Westford Jaycees	100
Westford City Hospital	1,200
NAACP	300
Red Cross	500
Salvation Army	200
Sickle Cell Anemia Fund	100
Christian College	200
State University	1,500
St. Ponts Church	1,000
Urban League	50
United Negro College Fund	200
Brothers Academy	500
Westford Lion's Club	75
Total	$9,395

George looked at the list and said, "This looks like just the things where we've written a check and given it to them!" John replied that it was precisely that.

George, irritated, replied, "There have been a lot more contributions than that!" He went on to say, "What about painting the Boys' Club—that was four two-hundred-dollar-a-week electricians for six days. And the pool—I sent two guys from Maintenance over there to fix the rest rooms. They worked for five hours. Those guys get a hundred and twenty bucks a week! And every wildlife conservation meeting has one of our secretaries taking shorthand. The Pollution Control Board—I'm vice chairman of that. I gave those old lawnmowers we got with the first Westford plant to the Boy Scouts so that they could raise some money mowing lawns. And you, John, you set up the bookkeeping system for that food co-op. I want all that stuff figured out! Do I have to hold you by the hand to get something done, John?!"

John responded that he had asked for a list of contributions and that was what he got! George counted to ten and calmed down a bit.

Then he said, "Ok, go back to your office and figure out everything we've done that has contributed to this town, this state, this country, poor people, sick people, rich people, and anything or anyone else! And John, don't make me wait four days this time!

"Oh, one more thing, I got a call from the State Street plant just before you came in here today—they haven't received their profit report for last month yet. Will you get on that—This whole operation is all of a sudden coming down around my ears!"

With that, John left the office and went to his own without saying a word